PAT WELSH'S
SOUTHERN CALIFORNIA
ORGANIC GARDENING

For Ray and
Linda ~
with love from
Pat Welsh
and happy organic
gardening!

PAT WELSH'S SOUTHERN CALIFORNIA ORGANIC GARDENING

MONTH BY MONTH

CHRONICLE BOOKS
SAN FRANCISCO

Library of Congress Cataloging-in-Publication Data available.

ISBN: 978-0-8118-6879-2

Manufactured in China

Designed by ANDREW SCHAPIRO
Typeset in Eldorado and BentonSans

10 9 8 7 6 5 4 3 2 1

Chronicle Books
680 Second Street
San Francisco, California 94107
www.chroniclebooks.com

In loving memory of my late husband, Lou,
who foresaw that this book would have a long
life in print, including many future editions.

Contents

Acknowledgments

Without the help of many people, this book never could have been written. To everyone who has helped with this revised edition, and with the original book upon which it was based, I thank you from the bottom of my heart. Among those who especially encouraged me during the last few months are my family, who cheered me on and were understanding of my deadlines. This includes my daughters and son-in-law, Francesca Filanc and Wendy and Larry Woolf, as well as my five grandchildren, their spouses, and my three great-grandchildren, Yvette, Ivan, and Anushka Urbietta; Erica and Jared Tanamachi; Rebecca, Hal, Archer, and Fable Isaacson; David Woolf; and Rachel Woolf. My brother, avid organic gardener John Fisher-Smith, gave me excellent input on soil and fertilizers. I am grateful also to my nephews, Jordan, Jeremy, and Jotham Fisher-Smith, and their wives and my cousin Harriet Bemus for their understanding.

Chief among my helpers has been Master Gardener Volunteer, the faithful, eagle-eyed, and ever-encouraging Denise Holcombe, who gave up every Wednesday plus countless hours at home to reread all copy, catch typos, and check every botanical name; many of them have changed since the first edition. Denise also prepared the list of sources, typed additions to the bibliography, helped sort photos, carried cameras, got me to scheduled talks and slide shows on time, and contributed many good ideas. Additionally, longtime friend, computer expert, and plant lover Lee Gardner Dewey came to my aid at the last minute unraveling problems with track changes, smoothing out computer glitches, and helping me meet a tight deadline. I'm also deeply grateful for the help of two organic gardening authorities, Connie Beck and Jack Shoultz. As soon as I finished the revision of each section or chapter, I sent the copy to both Connie and Jack, who read every bit of this book and were generous with their time and attention. Professional organic rosarian Jack Shoultz (www.organicrosecare.org) made many suggestions. The Rose-Pro Method mentioned throughout the book, and the rose chart in the back of the book, are based on Jack's system. Jack and his wife, Bonnie, visited my home, and we discussed in detail the practices and results of growing roses according to the organic system. Connie Beck, landscape designer and organic gardening instructor, for many years ran an organic garden and taught vocational landscape gardening at the San Diego County Women's Jail. Connie often sent her comments back to me the following day, with detailed suggestions based on her long experience. This quote from Connie tells all: "Compost is the answer to everything that ails your garden." If any errors remain in this book, they are mine, not those of Denise, Connie, Jack, or anyone else who helped me during its writing.

My sincere thanks also for the encouragement and help of many other friends, including graphic designer Natalie Yarnall and her sister, Rebecca Dembitsky. Natalie made the computer forms to fit my handwritten fertilizer and rose charts, and Becky typed in the information. Dwynn Robbie, organic rosarian, gave me helpful rose advice, introduced me to Jack and Bonnie Shoultz, and left bags and bottles of organic products in my potting shed for me to test. University of California Cooperative Extension, San Diego home gardening advisor Vince Lazaneo answered several questions and suggested additional UC experts for me to consult. David Diehl, product consultant with Gro-Power, spent a morning with me in my studio discussing organic sources of nitrogen and other nutrients. Avid gardener and Quail Gardens volunteer Mary Friestadt contributed a new and helpful tip about gophers. Aenne Carver made several good suggestions and helped free up my time to work. Danielle Earnest of Proven Winners checked a snippet of text and got back to me pronto with corrections. Richard Frost, of Plants That Produce, gave me input on soils and organic soil amendments. From the company Gardens Alive!, Karen in customer service came up with the tip on earwigs. Mike and Carol Brewer contributed the method of making large divisions of Matilija poppies after rain. Evelyn Weidner, owner of Weidner's Gardens in Leucadia, gave me input on new varieties and several new organic products.

Many people helped me unravel the complexities of lawn grasses and deal with recent changes in their management and nomenclature. James (Jim) H. Baird, Ph.D., turfgrass extension specialist at Botany and Plant Sciences, UC Riverside, fielded my endless questions and straightened me out on recent lawn varieties and other advances. Janet S. Hartin, Ph.D., environmental horticulture advisor and lawn expert at UC Davis and author of many books and publications on lawns, gave me input on mowing heights and additional information about characteristics of lawn grass varieties. Jeff Barber of Pacific Sod Farms explained the variously named mixes created by sod companies and the differences among them.

I also thank the following people who helped me with earlier editions of this book. The distillation of their years of knowledge and experience is still included in the current edition: Steve Gunther, for his photos; Vince Lazaneo, farm advisor, Home Horticulture; the late Chuck Kline, horticulturist emeritus and landscape advisor, Sea World; Jerry Stewart of New Leaf Geranium Nursery; Evelyn Weidner and Mary Weidner of Weidner's Begonia Gardens; Bob Smaus, garden editor emeritus of the *Los Angeles Times*; Bill Teague, agriculturist and flower grower; Virginia McKenzie, horticulturist, Hydroscape Products; Phil Lubars, sales manager, Drip-In Irrigation; Marnie Mahoney, founder of the Del Mar Garden Club; Becky Dembitsky, member of the Del Mar Garden Club; Linda Chisari, garden designer; Carol Carden, owner of Solo; Jack Engberg, sales representative, Grow More; Ed Rose, propagation manager, Ball Seeds; Sharon Drusch, rosarian, Sharon

Splane Drusch Design; Dick Streeper, rosarian and rose columnist of the *San Diego Union-Tribune;* Dr. Vic Gibeau, lawn scientist, UC Riverside; Hugh Wilkerson, ornamental grass gardener; John Greenlee, nurseryman and author of the *Encyclopedia of Ornamental Grasses;* Tim Galardi, owner, Rivera Gardens; Scott Daigre of Hortus Nursery, Pasadena; Janis Blackschleger, Perennial Productions; Tom Carruth of Weeks Roses; David Sakeroff, Hollywood art director; Loretta Foreman, plant lover and observant reader; Libby Doheny, avid gardener; Ruth Boron, avid gardener; Cathy Young, garden designer of "In the Garden," Calabasas; Judy M. Horton, garden designer; Patrick Anderson, horticulturist and Huntington Gardens volunteer; Shirley Kerrins, garden designer, Huntington Gardens; Chris Rosmini, garden designer; Agatha Youngblood, gardener extraordinaire, with a vast knowledge of perennials; and Judy Wiegand, owner of Judy's Perennials in San Marcos.

Many other people helped me with the first edition and were thanked in detail in that volume. Their contributions remain an integral part of this revised edition; to all these people, I say thank you once again for all the time, help, advice, and support you gave me: Betty Newton, Susan Locke Anderson, Stephanie Bise Shigematsu, Gilbert Voss, Bill Nelson, Tom Del Hotal, Victor Voss, Richard Streeper, Tom Cooper, Karen Kees, the late Ernie Chew, Michael MacCaskey, Bob Dale, Bill Teague, Linda Teague, Neil Cassidy, Jim Halda, Craig Miller, Karen O'Toole, Chuck Badger, the late Alice Menard, Dale Kolaczkowski, and Richard A. Haubrich.

Finally, I thank my agent, Sandra Dijkstra, whose help and advice I treasure; Elise Capron and Elisabeth James at the Dijkstra Agency; and all the good people at Chronicle Books, including editor Jodi Warshaw; editorial assistant Laura Lee Mattingly; copy editors Laura Harger and Mark Burstein; typist Karren Gulliam; designers Andrew Schapiro and Sarah O'Rourke; typesetter Janis Reed; managing editors Ann Spradlin, Doug Ogan, and Elissa Bassist; production coordinator Yolanda Accinelli; marketing manager Nancy Deane; and publicist Christina Loff.

Preface

In 1986, when I began to write the first edition of this book, I wanted it to fill a need. Local gardeners were brimming with questions, and my experience as a garden editor, speaker, TV host, and life-long hands-on gardener had provided me with many answers. I'd had a unique opportunity to meet and interview outstanding experts in every field of horticulture, and luckily I'd kept extensive notes and files. Many of those experts are now gardening in heaven, but their knowledge lives on in this book. I'd also learned that gardeners need to know how to deal with pests and diseases, poor soil, and alkaline water and how to select, prune, fertilize, and grow the best plants from among the vast number that thrive in our climate. Above all, it seemed to me that local gardeners wanted to know the right times of year to plant, feed, water, and prune specific plants in Southern California.

The first edition of this book was published in 1991 and soon became a classic. In the past eighteen years, gardeners have told me how much they love it and how often they refer to it. I've met a number of people who glued little tabs on the sides of its pages, like those in some dictionaries, in order to mark the months. I told

the editors at Chronicle Books about this, and they came up with the idea of putting thumb marks in the margin, which you will find in this new edition, too. I often meet people who show me their dog-eared copy of the first edition and say they keep it under their bed or in their potting shed. I'm still signing these old copies for owners who proffer them to me like well-worn, beloved teddy bears, but I tell them to please put their old copy in their bookshelf and get the new edition. There's so much more in it, and so many conditions have changed. Believe me, you can feel just as warm and cuddly about this new edition as you did about the first one. And here's a secret: A wide array of plants and subjects that are discussed in this edition never made it into the first one. It's high time to move on.

The first revised edition was published in 2000 with new photographs and a new cover, a vastly improved format, bigger type, new and up-to-date products, and coverage of many more plants, especially perennials. Perennial plants gained huge popularity during the 1990s and remain important today. No other book for California gardeners covers these plants in such detail or explains when and how to choose, plant, fertilize, divide, and prune them in our Mediterranean climate. The second edition's format gave me room to keep all the worthwhile facts of the first edition and to add a great deal of new information. All these improvements remain in the book you now hold in your hands.

Now yet another decade has passed, during which even more dramatic changes have taken place. This time, the changes are far more earth-shaking than simply the addition of new plants, products, and practices. Succulents and cacti have become more popular, while larger houses on smaller lots have increased the popularity of compact, disease-resistant plants. On a wider-ranging and more serious note, gardeners must now also deal with challenges to our climate and environment—indeed, to our very survival on this planet. During the last decade, Southern California, like much of the world, has been beset by the effects of global warming, increased population, and the expansion of communities into wildlands. The results have been devastating wildfires and the loss of homes and even of lives. We gardeners have been shaken to the core as some of the very plants we have nurtured in the past now threaten our sense of safety. In a new century that is projected to be far warmer and dryer than the past one, we must now plant for our Mediterranean climate while at the same time protecting our homes from fire. And to further complicate our task, we want to protect our environment from pollution. Gardeners still desire beautiful gardens, but now we must conserve water, reduce runoff, and protect our oceans and groundwater as well.

This new edition addresses all these concerns and more. As you read this book month by month throughout the year, you will find more emphasis on drought-tolerant and fire-resistant plants and more advice on how to plant for small spaces as well as large gardens.

Topics such as sun and shade, reduction of lawn areas, and choice of plants are discussed throughout with these factors in mind. At the same time, I haven't left out the many favorite plants, such as fuchsias, that may require more water but fill the needs of gardeners living in condos or whose only space is their patio or porch. Also, I have once again gone through this book word by word and taken out all plants and products that no longer are found in the trade. I've changed the names of plants and products as required and added new ones. Additionally, I've added more information on succulents and a new section on how to create a fire-resistant landscape. This edition also has a new cover and new photographs that I took myself, mostly of my own garden.

Most important, in this edition you will find a greater emphasis on organic gardening. Current economic conditions have made vegetable gardening the fastest-growing segment of the garden industry. I've always believed in the organic method of growing vegetables. It's the safe and nutritious way that I have followed in my own garden for years. Now I'm adopting organic fertilizers and pest controls for ornamental gardens as well. For example, the Rose-Pro Calendar on pages 418–421 is now fully organic and the monthly chapters now contain a detailed, practical organic system for growing roses. My reasoning is that our gardening practices should in no way endanger our health or the environment. Therefore, with few exceptions, I no longer discuss poisonous chemical sprays or synthetic fertilizers in this book, but instead focus only on organic nutrients and pest and disease controls. It's high time that home gardeners do all in their power to protect our oceans, watersheds, and groundwater. None of us want runoff from our gardens to add to pollution in the environment.

Recently a gardener introduced herself at a garden event and asked if I would include more on pest control—her main problem—in the next revision of my book. If this sounds like you, my response is that you're probably growing the wrong plants in the wrong places. More than ever, I want this book to help gardeners create healthy plants and gardens through proper cultural practices. Putting a plant in the wrong place leads to disease, which weakens the plant and makes it more susceptible to pests. For example, a gardenia growing on a patio may fall prey to whitefly or thrips. If so, too much shade and the wrong range of temperatures are what caused the problem; spraying won't help. (See page 242 for details.) Several elements produce a disease-and-pest-free garden, including good garden hygiene, healthy soil, the presence of beneficial creatures such as birds, exposure to or protection from wind, an appropriate degree of sun or shade, and finally the gardener's ability to resist the temptation to use chemical sprays. The way to create a healthy, pest-free garden is to grow plants the organic way and eschew chemical pesticides and synthetic fertilizers.

I know people with gardens in far from ideal locations. My own garden, for example, faces north instead of south, which would be a better exposure for most Mediterranean, subtropical, and sun-loving plants. But by careful choice of tough, easy plants, I (and many other local gardeners) have shown that it's possible to overcome problems and create a beautiful garden that is largely pest- and disease-free, and to accomplish all this without the help of poisonous sprays. If a plant gets sick in my garden, I cut it down or yank it out and replace it with something better. When you walk into a garden that's in harmony with nature, you find yourself surrounded by healthy, well-chosen plants that fit the space allotted to them. Such gardens usually contain a fountain or another water source other than the garden hose, and they are alive with bees, butterflies, and singing birds.

So now, as this book approaches twenty continuous years in print, and with thanks to Chronicle Books, I present it to you, the gardeners of Southern California, in a newly revised edition designed to address the problems and challenges of the second decade of the twenty-first century. My hope is that it will continue to help you and your garden to thrive, and that ten years from now—when I'm close to ninety—I'll be able to revise it yet again. As I've always said, "If I can do it, you can do it too!"

Pat Welsh
Del Mar, California

Introduction

WHAT THIS HANDBOOK INCLUDES

For the purposes of this book, the phrase "Southern California" means a large swath of the southernmost third of the state. The map shows that third to be a huge area, most of it sparsely populated. This book addresses the relatively narrow band of heavily populated coastal plains and adjacent inland valleys that begins at the Mexican border, on the south, and extends northward to Gaviota Pass, north of Santa Barbara. Throughout this region, where more than 80 percent of the state's population lives, approximately the same wide array of plants is grown.

The climate north of the Gaviota Pass differs from that in Southern California, and a somewhat different array of plants is grown, on a schedule that's not the same as ours. Mexico, too, has a different climate and differing conditions. Even so, many of the plants discussed in this book can also be grown in the central and northern areas of California and in Baja California. Mountains and desert areas are not themselves the subject here, but they are treated in discussions of plants and methods.

Though this book is written specifically for Southern California, parts of it may be of help to gardeners anywhere who have greenhouses. It can also help those who live in Mediterranean climates throughout the world, who can use it as an encyclopedia of Mediterranean gardening. (Gardeners in other parts of the world will need to vary the book's month-by-month schedule to fit their climates. Temperature requirements apply anywhere, but some specific recommendations, such as the ingredients of planting mixes and names of products, may be altered to fit what's locally available.) Many of the "Quick Tips" and step-by-step planting and growing directions are helpful to gardeners anywhere.

Our Unique Schedule for Garden Tasks. Gardening in Southern California offers endless surprises and challenges. It can be a delight, but in order to garden here successfully you have to understand the many problems and solutions that are unique to our region. If you don't have a certain amount of local know-how, you won't be able to avoid the pitfalls and reap the rich rewards of gardening in this area. Of all the conditions and problems that make gardening in Southern California quite different from gardening anywhere else, there's none more characteristic than our scheduling. Given our climate and our soil, when, what, and how should we plant, propagate, fertilize, and prune?

That's why this book is arranged month by month and why it is meant to be used as a handbook—it's really meant to hold your hand as you garden. You'll find step-by-step how-tos and special gardening techniques for the particular plants you grow. As you apply them, you'll develop the local savvy you need.

Special Aids in This Book. Each chapter begins with a brief table of contents and ends with a checklist detailing what to do in that month. The page number next to each item in the table of contents tells where that topic is discussed in detail, so you can refer to it easily no matter which month's chapter it's in. Use the checklists to check off jobs as they're completed. Remember as you consult the checklists that no gardener is likely to grow every plant mentioned, and please don't be overwhelmed by the number of jobs they recommend.

For topics of special interest to you, by all means consult other books—guides to native and drought-resistant plants, say, or to pruning. A number that I recommend are listed in the bibliography. Note too that this book wasn't designed to aid in plant identification. For that, see the *Smart Garden Regional Guide: Southwest,* which is listed under the publisher's name DK Publishing in the bibliography (see page 441), is a book I filled with plant lists and illustrated with many photographs from my garden to help local gardeners with plant choice and identification. If you don't know all the plants that are mentioned here, the best way to learn about them is to search them out at nurseries and botanical gardens, look them up in reference works, and search for photos on the Internet. Other good aids to plant identification are also included in the bibliography.

You'll also find many "Rules of Thumb" scattered throughout this book. They're designed to help you do things right the first time instead of learning through mistakes. Of course, you may think rules are meant for breaking, and there's some sense to that. No rule fits every occasion; an experienced gardener knows when and if a particular rule can safely be broken. But unless you're experienced, rules are helpful guideposts on the road to successful gardening.

While organizing the month-by-month chapters, I found that some topics could be covered in only one specific month—pruning roses in January, for example—but other topics could have been discussed in any of several months. For instance, planting and harvesting bananas is discussed in August because it's a hot month, but I could have covered that subject in June or July.

Many horticultural terms are defined briefly where first used in the text as well as more fully in the glossary at the back of the book. Because a number of these terms are commonly misunderstood or incompletely understood, just browsing through the glossary may answer many questions. Additionally, rose growers can consult the Rose-Pro Calendar chart on pages 418–421. It gives a quick summation of rose care throughout the year. This book also includes a list of seed and plant sources. The index will help you refer to any topic at any time of year.

What You Need to Know First

CLIMATE, PLANT CHOICE, SOILS, FERTILIZER, WATER, PLANTING,
PRUNING, PESTS, AND WEEDS

Gardening is different in Southern California. Anyone who's ever gardened elsewhere will tell you that. It's not like back East, where so many of us came from and where I once gardened. It's not like England, where I was born and began gardening at the age of three. It's not even like Florida, that other state that attracts retirees with year-round warm weather. Even people who've never gardened anywhere else soon realize how different Southern California gardening is; all you have to do is flip through any book on basic gardening to realize that much of its advice just doesn't apply here.

THE NATURE OF OUR CLIMATE

What It Means to Live in a Mediterranean Climate. Southern California is blessed with a Mediterranean climate, one of the most salubrious growing climates in the world. The main characteristics of a Mediterranean climate are mild winters with enough rain to support plant growth and warm, dry summers with virtually no rain. The factors that create our climate are much like those that create similar climates in other parts of the world: the Mediterranean Basin, South Africa, central Chile, and southwestern Australia. Our distance from the equator makes our temperatures subtropical, but our position on the southwest corner of a great land mass—in our case the North American continent—keeps our summers dry.

The Pacific Ocean, with its relatively even temperature, also keeps our climate mild. In general, the closer your garden is to the ocean, the cooler it will be in summer and the warmer in winter. The farther inland you live, the more extreme the temperatures your garden will undergo.

What's a Climate Zone? Within our overall Mediterranean climate, there are many geographical variations. These are called plant climates, or, more commonly, climate zones. Each of these is a geographical area in which the yearly temperature range, length of seasons, average precipitation, humidity, amount of sunshine, and other factors combine to make certain plants grow better than others. Climate zones are caused by masses of air moving over our varied topography of coastal plains, hills and valleys, central uplands, high mountains, and deserts.

Much study has been done on plant climates by the University of California Agriculture Extension and others. But because of the technical aspects of agricultural plant climates, many of which overlap, most California home gardeners rely on the zones and maps in the *Sunset Western Garden Book*. When I mention a specific zone by number or name, I'm referring to the zones found in this widely respected work. Usually, however, areas are described here in more general terms, such as "coastal" versus "inland," or, in some cases, a little more specifically, such as "gardens in inland valleys" in contrast to "right along the beach."

How to Recognize Microclimates in Your Garden.
In addition to major climate zones, there are minizones, called microclimates. Microclimates are small areas within a climate zone where conditions favor the growth of some plants and not others because of factors of climate particular to that spot. Every neighborhood, every yard has physical characteristics that produce slightly varying climates. Some plants may flourish on the east side of your home but die or do badly on the west. South-facing hillsides collect warmth and are especially good places for growing tropical plants; north-facing hillsides are cooler and thus good for camellias and azaleas.

Gaps on slopes let cold air drain off, while depressions, solid hedges, and walls catch or hold it. Garages, bushes, and walled patios can trap cold air in winter and warm air in summer, creating a more extreme climate than in the rest of the garden. Places that are open to the sky are more likely to be hit by frost than covered areas, because heat absorbed by the earth and by plants during the day radiates up to a clear, open sky and is absorbed by the atmosphere.

How Santa Ana Winds Affect Our Weather.
The so-called Santa Ana winds—a climate factor that cuts across several zones in Southern California—temporarily determine the condition of the weather. A Santa Ana is a dry wind, at its worst a gale-force one, that blows from the vast interior region to the sea, and it may strike several times a year, most often between October and March. Santa Anas usually last from one to three days. Though Santa Anas disrupt what we think of as "normal" weather patterns, they're as natural to our climate as winter rainstorms. Similar winds are not unknown in other Mediterranean climates.

Santa Ana winds damage plants by their force, drying out their leaves through excessive transpiration and sometimes killing new plantings. When these winds strike, gardeners should make sure plants are well watered. Hanging baskets and delicate container-grown plants should be misted and moved to areas protected from sun and wind.

PLANT CHOICE

The Varied Palette.
One of the things that makes gardening in Southern California so much fun—yet also a challenge—is the wide range of plants we can grow. Although we can't grow plants, such as viburnum and Bing cherries, that need a long period of winter chill in order to bloom, we are able to grow a great many plants, such as wisteria, lilac, peonies,

and privet, common to cold-winter climates. Among flowers and vegetables, most annuals and selected perennials flourish here. Native plants and those that hail from Mediterranean climates similar to ours broaden the palette still further. We can also grow many tropicals and subtropicals from all over the world, especially those from higher elevations. This mix of plants from many regions, with strong tropical and subtropical accents, is what gives our gardens their characteristically Southern California look. It's almost impossible to take a photograph of a local scene without a palm tree, an orange tree, a hibiscus, or some other exotic-looking plant in the background.

The Specialty Plants. Among the many species we grow are groups often called specialty plants because they require special attention and know-how. These plants and classes of plants include camellias, ferns, fuchsias, begonias, daylilies, hibiscus, pelargoniums (geraniums), irises, roses, orchids, epiphyllums (orchid cacti), cacti and succulents, bromeliads, palms, bonsai, vegetables, herbs, bamboo, rare and tropical fruits, and California native plants.

Specialty plants engender such enthusiasm among hobbyists that they have fan clubs—plant societies made up of beginners and old-timers alike—devoted to their culture. One of Southern California's most valuable botanical resources is its incredible number of active chapters of plant societies and the eminent experts among their members. One of the best ways to learn how to grow specialty plants is to join a plant society or simply attend one or two meetings.

Most of us grow specialty plants in our homes and gardens. You'll find advice on their care throughout this book.

SOIL PROBLEMS AND SOLUTIONS

How Plants Depend on Soil. Good gardening begins with good soil, the surface layer of earth that supports plant life. Soil is made up of particles of weathered rock, organic matter, air, water, and microorganisms. Plants anchor their roots in it and get most of their nourishment from it; thus the health of your plants is largely dependent on the condition of your soil. *Fertile soils* contain many elements and properties, such as minerals, organic matter, and good drainage, that make plants thrive, while *poor soils* are low in them. If you live in Southern California and have poor soil, you're not alone; that's what many of us have to start with.

How to Assess the General Condition of Your Soil. The first task of every gardener is to give plants good ground to grow in. Start out by assessing plant health and the general condition of your soil. If your plants are growing well and looking healthy, if water sinks into the ground readily instead of running off or puddling, and if the soil doesn't dry out too quickly, chances are your soil is in basically good condition. In this case, your concern should be to maintain it. But if your plants are in poor shape, if they look stressed and grow slowly or not at all, and if drainage is either very slow or so rapid that water runs right through the ground, your soil needs improvement.

Improvements Humus Makes in Soil. The best way to improve almost any soil is by working in organic soil amendments. As the organic matter decomposes in the ground, it becomes humus, largely decomposed animal and vegetable matter. The decomposition of organic matter, including the chemical properties of humus, improves soil's fertility and structure. Without

How to Deal with Bare Bulldozed Ground or Rock-Hard Subsoil

There are two ways to improve bulldozed ground so plants can grow in it. Either will work if done properly.

▸ **Add Topsoil.** But when adding topsoil, it's important to avoid creating a hard horizon between the topsoil and the subsoil. Don't just layer the topsoil on top; amend the subsoil first. Remove and haul away at least a foot of the existing soil. Create a proper marriage of soils by rototilling the subsurface and mixing into it soil amendments, gypsum if the soil is clayey (as explained on page 23), and some topsoil. Then replace the removed foot of soil with high-quality amended topsoil.

▸ **Amend the Soil You've Got.** This method is less expensive than the first and is used on most commercial and residential sites. First, have a soil sample tested (as discussed on page 20.) Next, unless you plan to fill depressions or mound the ground, haul away some of the native soil to make space for the amendments. Rototill 9 inches deep, or—better yet— use a backhoe or plow to loosen the ground a foot deep. Add minerals and fertilizers as indicated by your soil test, plus organic amendments measuring between 25 percent and 50 percent of the volume of soil you're amending. This means working a 4- to (preferably) 6-inch-deep layer of well-rotted organic amendment, such as homemade or commercial bulk or bagged compost and/or manure, into the top 8 to 12 inches of ground. Don't skimp on the organic amendments!

humus, minerals can be chemically locked up so plant roots can't use them. Humus helps sandy soils hold water, and it helps clay soil to drain.

In the West, where rainfall is sparse, our soils are generally very low in humus, while in the East, where rainfall is greater, most soils contain a high percentage of it. Humus doesn't stay in the ground forever; it gradually breaks down. So nature constantly replenishes its rich organic soils with fallen leaves, rotted twigs, grass, and animal matter. In your Southern California garden, it's up to you to do this job. In small areas you can use a spade to dig the amendments into the ground; in large areas you will need to rent a rototiller to incorporate the amendments into the soil.

When You Begin with Bare Ground. In many cases, owners of new homes start out with nothing but bare bulldozed ground. All topsoil—the uppermost and most fertile layer of soil—has been scraped away. This leaves nothing but bare subsoil, the lower layer that usually has lower fertility and a different texture and color than topsoil. In some cases what's left can hardly be called soil at all. But don't give up in dismay. By working in large amounts of organic soil amendments that will gradually break down in the soil, most subsoils can be eventually turned into topsoil. (See the box above for ways to cope with bulldozed ground.) Additionally, the cycles of wetting and drying of the soil that are a natural part of gardening can actually improve the soil's structure—the arrangement of the variously sized particles in the soil that determines how the particles work together. The very process of growing plants with fibrous roots that penetrate the ground can also help to break it apart, and so improve its structure.

Your Soil's pH Value. Another factor that determines how well plants grow in soil is its pH value, its degree of acidity or alkalinity. The pH scale is numbered from 0 to 14; 7.0 is neutral. As values decrease, soil is increasingly acid; as they rise above 7.0, the soil is increasingly alkaline. For most plants, a soil pH of 6.0 to 7.0 is ideal, because the elements that are essential for plant growth have their maximum availability in this range. However, a soil pH between 5.0 and 8.0 is usually satisfactory. Certain plants, such as azaleas and camellias, are called acid loving because they grow best at a soil pH of about 5.0.

In the eastern part of the United States, most soils are too acid for cultivated plants, so farmers and gardeners add lime to make them more alkaline; in other words, they raise the pH level. Many western soils are too alkaline, so when necessary we make them more acid by adding soil sulfur or such acidifying organic soil amendments as leaf mold, pine needles, peat moss, or wood shavings. To put it another way, we *lower* the pH level.

If you have an established garden and your plants appear to be in good health, it may never be necessary for you to determine the pH value of your soil. However, it's fun, easy, and informative to test pH. You can find an inexpensive kit at almost any nursery or garden-supply store. It takes only a few minutes to combine a dry soil sample with the solution provided, wait the required length of time, and check the results on the color chart that comes with the kit.

If you want to test your soil for plant nutrients, typically nitrogen, potassium, and phosphorus, you'll need to purchase a more complicated and expensive kit. Or you can have your soil professionally tested in a laboratory, a service that's available through many nurseries and some offices of the U.S. Department of Agriculture and the U.S. Bureau of Soil Conservation. Soil tests don't tell you anything about the structure of your soil or the percentage of humus in it, but they can sometimes pinpoint deficiencies or problems. It's wise to keep in mind, however, that the results of such tests can vary considerably among soil samples from a single garden. Don't depend on the results to indicate a simple cure-all, especially not for the whole garden.

How to Improve Drainage on a Bulldozed Lot Prior to Planting

▸ Grade the improved soil to a gentle slope; then dig trenches and install drains to carry excess water, by gravity, into the street or a drainage ditch. When properly installed, French and conventional drains can alleviate drainage problems in large areas. (Other kinds of drains, such as sleeve drains and chimney drains, are made for individual plants.)

▸ French drains allow excess and underground water to seep into perforated pipe that's laid in gravel. The perforated side of the pipe is laid face-down (or to the sides when there are two sets of perforations) so soil particles won't clog the openings, and the gravel is covered with a narrow sheet of plastic. Conventional drains remove excess surface water only. Flexible, unperforated pipe is used for these, and entrance grates are installed in low spots.

Your Soil's Texture. Before beginning any program of soil improvement, find out what type of soil you're dealing with so you can assess its strengths and weaknesses. Soil is usually classified according to its "texture," which means the size of the particles that are in it. The three basic particle sizes, from largest to smallest, are called sand, silt, and clay. Loam is a mixture of all three. All of these basic soil types can be found in Southern California; often more than one occurs in a single garden. Soils with particles larger than sand are often called gravelly soils. Decomposed granite is a gravelly soil with unique qualities and is found in many parts of Southern California. (Some decomposed granite soils might almost as well be called sand or loam; what distinguishes the granitic soils is that they contain some particles that are larger than sand.)

The box on page 23 will help you recognize which soil types you have in your garden. Once you know what type of soil you're dealing with, you'll be better able to choose appropriate amendments and techniques to improve its structure and fertility.

Why You Must Never Mix Sand into Clay. Because loam is a mixture of sand, silt, and clay, some gardeners think they can lighten clay soil by mixing sand into it. This is a drastic mistake.

It would be necessary to add an enormous volume of sand—well over 50 percent—to clay soil in order to improve it. Smaller quantities of sand would only fill up the spaces between the clay particles and turn good clay soil into something similar to cement. You'd make your soil denser and not improve drainage. The only safe way to improve soil structure is to increase its humus content by adding organic amendments.

When using soil amendments, be aware that organic matter that isn't rotted or naturally high in nitrogen or having adequate nitrogen mixed into it will rob nitrogen from the soil as it rots, thus killing plants by starvation. (Advice for maintaining adequate nitrogen is found on page 24.) Very wet vegetable matter, such as melon rind and papaya skins, can be put straight into a 12-inch-deep hole in garden soil. For guidelines, study the list on pages 28–30.

Finding and Solving Difficult Problems and Conditions. Regardless of which type, or types, of soil you have, you may have to overcome several frustrating problems and negative conditions before you can grow a good garden. The problems most often encountered in local gardens are hardpan, rock-filled soil, root-filled soil, and saline soil. Some of these problems may not be obvious at first glance, so it's important to know how to recognize them as well as how to deal with them if they appear.

The box on page 26 can help you recognize which, if any, of these problems you have in your garden and suggests ways to overcome them.

How Gypsum Helps Some Clay Soils Drain Better. Gypsum is a relatively inexpensive soil amendment. Adding it to clay soil often helps and never hurts. Organic gardeners prefer using mined gypsum (a natural granular form of calcium sulfate) instead of the soluble type that has been treated with sulfuric acid in order to make it soluble. Farmers have used mined gypsum as a soil amendment for more than two hundred years, but it needs to be worked into the soil in order to take effect, whereas the soluble type can be washed into soil.

Sodium pulls clay particles closer together. This makes the soil denser and less easily penetrated by water. In cases where clay particles in the soil have accumulated a high level of exchangeable sodium (alkali), gypsum

How Often to Add Organic Soil Amendments to Garden Soil

The **Rule of Thumb:** Every time you replant an annual bed or vegetable plot, dig in an inch or two (up to 4 inches) of organic soil amendment. Build the humus content of permanent beds and cool-season lawns by topping with organic mulch at least once a year.

or calcium sulfate ($CaSO_4$) can loosen the soil and help it drain. Gypsum added to soil releases soluble calcium, which replaces some of the sodium on the clay particles and thereby produces a more open soil structure. Gypsum will not correct poor soil drainage when it is caused by physical conditions, such as fine texture or compaction. Soils that have these problems can be improved by incorporating large quantities of organic matter.

In most cases, apply enough mined gypsum to make it look as though a light snow has fallen (between 2 and 5 pounds to 100 square feet), and then work it into the ground. As much as 10 pounds per 100 square feet can be used on clay soil prior to seeding or sodding lawns.

How Mulch Helps Soil. Mulch is a layer of organic matter, or such inorganic material as gravel or plastic sheeting, that's applied to the surface of the soil to reduce evaporation and heat or cool the soil. Mulches can also help control weeds, stop the surface of clay soils from cracking, improve water penetration, and increase the soil's biological activity. Organic mulch gradually rots and can then be worked in.

Many organic soil amendments, such as ground bark, wood or bark chips, stable litter, hay, straw, leaf mold, pine needles, dry grass clippings, and compost, can be used as mulch. Lightweight materials such as peat moss are less practical since they may blow away. Note that some organic materials that have a low nitrogen content—such as hulls, nutshells, and wood or bark chips—are suitable only as mulch and should not be dug into the soil until they are fully decomposed, or they'll rob nitrogen from the soil as they rot (rules of thumb for nitrogen use are included in the box on soil amendments on pages 28–30). Large-textured organic mulches may harbor pests—especially sow bugs, slugs, and snails.

Black, red, or clear plastic sheeting and some woven plastic fabrics are also used as mulches, but these inorganic mulches warm rather than cool the soil. Clear plastic makes the ground too hot for most crops in Southern California, other than strawberries planted in fall. Black or red plastic can increase yields of warm-weather crops such as corn and melons. However, unperforated plastic does not allow water penetration and thus requires the use of a drip system beneath it.

Why Plants in Containers Need Special Soil. When planting in containers, always use a bagged commercial potting soil mix recommended for planting in containers. You can also make your own potting mix, though it's easier and often cheaper to purchase a ready-made mix. Growing plants in containers is different from growing plants in the ground. With the possible exception of select decomposed-granite soils (such as those occurring in the city of Claremont in the San Gabriel Valley), garden soil packs down in containers and doesn't drain, killing plant roots.

How to Recognize and Deal with Five Basic Soil Types

▸ **Sandy Soil:** A loose earth mainly composed of tiny particles of rock between 0.05 and 2 millimeters in size. It feels scratchy or gritty to the touch. If you grip a damp handful, it won't hold together. Water and nutrients drain right out before plants can take a gulp. Sandy soils are often called light because they're easy to work.

Virtues: Ease of digging and good drainage.

Problems: Failure to hold water and nutrients. Apparently "hungry" since it eats up organic materials so rapidly. When completely dry, some sandy soils are difficult to get wet because the individual grains of sand have become coated with organic fats and waxes from decomposing organic matter, such as eucalyptus or acacia litter.

Solutions: Dig in copious organic amendments. Apply mulch and horse manure that does not contain salt from salt licks. Where necessary, use organic penetrants (surfactants) made from such plants as Mohave yucca (*Yucca schidigera*), a safe and highly efficient alternative to harsh chemical surfactants. Try not to let sandy soils dry out completely. Choose slow-releasing organic fertilizers instead of rapidly releasing types. (See the chart on pages 28–30.)

▸ **Silt:** A fine-grained earth composed mainly of particles that are rounder and more weathered than sand particles, and intermediate in size between sand and clay particles. If you rub it between your fingers when moist, it feels smooth, slippery, and soapy but not sticky. Silt holds more water than sand but less than clay. It's often found in river bottoms and on valley floors.

Virtues: Drains better than clay, yet holds more water than sand. Retains humus and nutrients longer than sand.

Problems: Compacts when walked on to a much greater degree than sand. When wet, it becomes almost like quicksand. Doesn't hold nutrients for long. Cultivating when too wet can make silt dense and restrict the free passage of air and water.

Solutions: Work in organic amendments at regular intervals. Apply organic mulch. Don't walk on vegetable rows and flowerbeds. Dig and cultivate only when soil is moist but not soggy.

▸ **Clay:** A firm, fine-grained earth containing a large amount of tiny mineral particles less than 0.002 millimeter in size that have negatively charged surfaces. The electrical charge helps clay retain positively charged minerals, such as ammonium, potassium, calcium, and magnesium. Clay feels slippery and sticky when wet. Grip a damp handful and it will hold together in a solid lump. Clay soils bake hard in hot weather and hold moisture when wet. Their color varies from white, gray, and greenish to dark brown (adobe) or red (terra-cotta). Clay soils are often called heavy because they're difficult to work.

Virtues: Mineral richness; water retention during drought.

Problems: Poor drainage. Hardness in dry weather. Heavy, sticky, and difficult to work when wet. Cultivating clay when wet can worsen drainage.

Solutions: Work in organic amendments. Apply gypsum. Install drains. Build raised beds.

continued . . .

How to Recognize and Deal with Five Basic Soil Types (continued)

▶ **Loam:** A combination of clay, silt, and sand. There are many types of loam, depending upon the percentages of the components. Clay loams (those containing more clay) are heavy soils. Sandy loams are light.

Virtues: Fertile. Holds water but also drains well.

Problems: Easily compacted when moist.

Solutions: Maintain with regular additions of organic soil amendment. Don't walk on moist garden soil.

▶ **Decomposed Granite:** A grayish or light brown, granular, and sometimes flaky soil composed mainly of variously sized particles of granite rock, some of which are larger in size than grains of sand. It feels loose, gritty, and abrasive to the touch. The unevenly sized particles are easily seen with the naked eye. On bulldozed ground and mesa tops, decomposed granite is often packed down as hard as rock, but when it's alluvial (deposited by water), as in canyons and valleys, it's often loose and friable.

Virtues: Excellent drainage, aeration, and mineral richness. Some alluvial types are easy to work.

Problems: Rocklike hardness when found in subsoils and on mesa tops makes the ground difficult to dig. Water and soluble nutrients leach out quickly.

Solutions: Rototill. Add large quantities of organic matter: homemade or commercial bulk or bagged compost, leached mushroom compost, green manures, or various animal manures (for example, poultry manure). Where ground is rock hard, plant in raised beds or plow up the surface of hard areas, mix in organic amendments and some topsoil, and then cover with a foot of topsoil.

FERTILIZER BASICS

Plants not only need humus; they also need fertilizer. A fertilizer is any material, either organic or inorganic, that supplies elements essential to plant growth. Our native Southern California soils contain only small quantities of nitrogen, which is probably the most important element plants need. Thus we must add it in some form or our plants will go hungry. (Specific recommendations for feeding particular plants are given throughout the month-by-month chapters. Also see the chart of generic organic fertilizers on pages 28–30.)

The Meaning of the Numbers on a Package of Fertilizer. Every package of fertilizer has a trio of numbers on its label. The first number is the percentage (by weight) of nitrogen in the product; the second is the percentage of phosphorus; the third is the percentage of potassium. These three elements, known simply as N, P, and K, their chemical symbols, are found singly or in combination in many fertilizers. For example, fertilizer labeled 16-8-4 contains 16 percent nitrogen, 8 percent phosphorus, and 4 percent potassium. The remaining 72 percent is made up of other chemicals, such as calcium, sulfur, and oxygen, and some filler, which is added to the product to make it less concentrated and more easily measured and spread.

A high first number (nitrogen) means the product will give plants a lot of top growth, green leaves, and fast growth. Formulas with a high second number or second and third numbers (phosphorus and potassium) give plants the elements essential for flowering and fruiting. Both phosphorus and potassium promote overall plant health and stimulate growth of strong, healthy roots, though in different ways.

If plants are starved for nitrogen, they won't be healthy or have a satisfactory rate of growth or enough vigor to produce ample flowers and fruit. On the other hand, too much nitrogen will damage roots; burn, twist, and deform leaves; or even kill the entire plant. Recommendations for fertilizing plants are often given in pounds of "actual nitrogen"—the true amount of nitrogen in a product. For example, a fertilizer labeled 21-0-0 (ammonium sulfate) contains 21 percent nitrogen, so a 10-pound bag of ammonium sulfate contains 2.1 pounds of actual nitrogen. Recommendations given in pounds of actual nitrogen are helpful because one can choose any formula and figure out how much of it to use.

Organic products are also labeled with NPK values, but in the example given above, ammonium sulfate is never applied to soil by true organic gardeners. (Synthetic fertilizers add salts to the ground, leach into ground water, and can burn plants. They also kill the natural biological activity in soil, including earthworms, so you end up with "dead" soil.) Also, the recommendations given in pounds of nitrogen, though mentioned occasionally in this book, have less application to organic gardening because the whole process of adding organic amendments to garden soil while avoiding the use of synthetic fertilizers allows natural microscopic organisms in soil to create nitrogen. As microorganisms break down partially rotted organic amendments

in soil into humus, nitrogen is released as a by-product. Plant roots absorb this nitrogen. You'll see the results in healthy growth, but there's no way a gardener could weigh or measure the amount of nitrogen released.

A number of terms are used to describe fertilizers. A "complete fertilizer" (sometimes called a balanced fertilizer) is one that contains nitrogen, phosphorus, and potassium, though the percentages can vary greatly among different

A Basic Soil-less Potting Mix for Containers

Dozens of potting mixes have been invented by nurserymen, researchers, and gardeners for different purposes. This formula is designed as an all-purpose mix for outdoor container-grown plants. (Some special formulas for specific plants are given in the month-by-month chapters.)

• 1 cubic foot premoistened peat moss, or coir, sometimes sold as "coco-peat," a renewable product made from coconut fiber

• 1 cubic foot nitrolized ground bark or nitrolized wood shavings

• 1 cubic foot sand or perlite (small, lightweight, air-filled granules made from volcanic rock expanded at high temperatures)

• ⅓ cup ground dolomitic limestone or agricultural lime (not quicklime)

• ½ cup 5-10-10 organic fertilizer containing trace elements

Mix all ingredients thoroughly, and use for immediate needs. If you want to store this mix for a month or two, omit the fertilizer and add a dry organic wetting agent according to package directions, and don't premoisten the peat moss.

How to Recognize and Solve the Four Most Common Soil Problems

The following soil problems have nothing to do with the fertility, pH, or type of your topsoil. Some are hidden from view and thus often go undetected, but any one of them, if not appropriately solved, could prevent you from growing a healthy garden.

▶ **Hardpan:** A layer of hard, compacted soil of any type cemented together by minerals and almost impenetrable by roots or water. Often buried beneath a layer of good soil; typical of housing developments where a layer of topsoil has been applied over bulldozed subsoil.

Virtues: None.

Problems: No drainage. Roots go down, hit bottom, and are stopped cold.

Solutions: Build French and conventional drains (see page 20). Plant in raised beds. In some localities, you can dig down and break through to a porous layer. When adding a layer of topsoil over hard subsoil, rototill and amend the bottom layer first.

▶ **Rock-Filled Soil:** Any type of soil that's largely filled with pebbles and rocks or shallowly based on rocky outcroppings.

Virtues: Rocks may have beauty, practical value, and design potential.

Problems: Difficult to dig; may have poor drainage; may not contain enough soil to support plant life. Tree roots may not be able to penetrate the rock substrate.

Solutions: In some areas, holes suitable for tree planting can be blasted with dynamite. Build raised beds and terraces and fill them with topsoil or organic materials such as nitrolized wood shavings and mushroom compost. Use hardscape (decks, paths, pergolas, and the like), container plants, and hanging baskets. Grow rock-garden plants and epiphytes. (Epiphytes are plants that grow on other plants but don't sap nourishment from them, as do parasites.)

▶ **Root-Filled Soil:** Any type of soil made hard, dry, and impenetrable by the roots of such invasive trees as eucalyptus, Monterey cypress (*Cupressus macrocarpa*), and melaleuca. Often encountered in old gardens.

Virtues: Shade from the trees is helpful for some plants. Old trees offer charm.

Problems: Water won't penetrate, the ground can't be dug, the roots invade planters from below, and new plants can't get started.

Solutions: Plant in raised beds. Cover bare ground with river rock and paving stone. Add hardscape; plant in containers. Place stepping stones under containers. Install commercial root barriers made of stainless steel, plastic, or fiberglass vertically in a trench; refill the trench so the barrier acts as a buried wall to stop the advance of roots. To prevent roots from invading raised beds from below, install a root barrier or heavy-gauge, plastic sheeting (visquine) horizontally beneath the boxes. (Allow for drainage by drilling drainage holes around the outside edges, or install stepping stones on top of the visquine or root barrier beneath the boxes so water can drain from drainage holes drilled in the bottom of the boxes.)

How to Recognize and Solve the Four Most Common Soil Problems (continued)

▸ **Saline Soil:** Soil of any type that contains enough salt to be injurious to plants. A frequent problem in desert areas, where salts accumulate in soil from salty irrigation water, fertilizers, and manures and where rainfall is insufficient to leach salts to low levels.

Virtues: None.

Problems: Salt injures roots and burns foliage; it may kill plants. Limits the types of plants that can be grown to those that are salt resistant. Evaporation can lift salts into the top layers of soil. Capillary action then pulls water to the surface, where it evaporates and deposits a white salt crust.

Solutions: No matter what type of irrigation is used, apply an adequate volume of water to wash salts out of the top levels of earth down into the ground. Use the furrow system for vegetables, but don't plant in the middle of the top of the mound because salts accumulate there; plant close to the edge of the mound. Construct watering basins for larger plants. Use mulches to reduce evaporation of water from the soil surface. An application of gypsum followed by heavy watering may leach away enough salts to reclaim some sodic (salty) soils.

---

products. An "incomplete fertilizer" contains only one or two of these elements. A product described as "high in growth ingredients" has a high first number and lower second and third numbers, while a "high bloom" formula refers to a product that has high second and third numbers. "Preplant" products have low first numbers and high second and third numbers.

In this book I often use such general terms and give examples of appropriate numerical formulations. This is because organic products with the formulas I mention are available in Southern California, and it may be helpful to gardeners to know the sort of formula that can fill a given purpose. It doesn't mean you should spend hours looking for a product with those exact numbers. The recommendations are meant only as basic guidelines and can help you find intelligent substitutions.

Some fertilizers also contain iron and trace minerals, which are necessary for overall plant health and for preventing chlorosis (an iron deficiency that causes yellow leaves and green veins). Whether trace elements are included is usually, but not always, noted on the package. Some fertilizers contain only one or two trace elements, and others contain many. Because fertilizers are made to do different jobs, there are great variations among their formulas—the combinations of ingredients and the amounts of each ingredient they contain.

Which Formula to Use. When you choose a fertilizer, consider the basic needs of the plant and the way nutrients act in soil. Nitrogen leaches out of soils quickly, but phosphorus and potassium are longer lasting. Thus, if you mix phosphorus and potassium into the soil prior to planting annual flowers or vegetables, there's no need to apply it again that season. Most permanent landscape plants need added phosphorus and potassium only once a year.

A Catalog of Organic Soil Amendments and How to Use Them

Soil amendments vary in cost and availability, as well as in the characteristics of use cited below.

▸ **Apple and Grape Pomace:** This by-product of wine and cider factories is excellent for working into soil—it's especially good in clay soil—and releases nitrogen slowly.

▸ **Bean Straw** (a by-product of field-grown California dried lima beans, available from farmers in some areas): Work it directly into soil. Bean straw decomposes rapidly in soil that's damp and is especially good for decomposed granite and clay soils.

▸ **Chipper Materials** (leftovers from tree trimming): Use as mulch or path cover. Coarse materials can be added to garden soil when fully decomposed, but watch plants for nitrogen deficiency (telltale signs are yellow leaves, which may drop off, and slow or stunted growth). Add extra nitrogen if necessary. Chipper materials may contain tree seeds. Pull up and destroy unwanted volunteers.

▸ **Coir:** The pith of the coconut husk located between the shell and the nut, used in ground form as a clean growing medium and soil amendment and substitute for peat moss. Unlike peat moss, coir has a nonacid, neutral pH. It is plentiful and renewable. It retains nutrients better than peat moss, is more easily wettable than peat moss, but retains water equally well.

▸ **Commercial Organic Soil Amendments** (many kinds): Work these into soil or use them as mulch, according to label directions.

▸ **Compost:** Make it yourself by the slow or fast method. (See pages 97–99.) Work it into garden soil.

▸ **Composted Wood Shavings:** Work into soil or use them as mulch.

▸ **Grass Clippings:** Work these into soil as "green manure" (see next item) or use them in compost. Either use works best when the clippings are dried first, and they must be dried first if used as mulch; otherwise the clippings form a smelly, sticky mat. They have a high nitrogen content.

▸ **Green Manure** (alfalfa, red clover, lupine, crown vetch, and others): Plant the seeds as a cover crop on bare ground in fall, then work the green plants into the ground in spring. They decompose rapidly in warm weather. A **Rule of Thumb:** *After turning green manure under the ground, wait one to two weeks before planting vegetables or flowers.*

▸ **Ground Carrot, Apple, and Vegetable Fibers** (from health-food stores or juice factories): Work apple into soil. Add other fibers to compost, or dig them into paths between vegetable rows to build soil and feed earthworms.

▸ **Kelp and Seaweed:** Hose these off and chop them with a spade before working them into soil or adding them to compost. They decompose rapidly and add trace minerals.

▸ **Leaf Mold:** Work this into soil or use it as mulch; reserve it for acid-loving plants. Leaf litter under native oaks can contain oak root fungus and shouldn't be used unless it's been sterilized.

▸ **Leaves, Unrotted:** Add leaves to the compost pile or use them as mulch. All leaves, including eucalyptus and ivy leaves, can be composted, but some take much longer to decompose than others.

A Catalog of Organic Soil Amendments and How to Use Them (continued)

▸ **Manure, Aged:** Work this into soil or use it as mulch. It sometimes has high salt content. Don't use it on carrots since it causes splitting. Both aged and raw manures contain nitrogen, phosphorus, and potassium in varying amounts.

▸ **Manure, Raw and Unaged:** Apply a layer on top of the ground in the furrows between vegetable rows or under trees or berry bushes. Raw manure will burn roots if it's applied too heavily or too soon before planting. Do not use manure chunks that contain salt from salt licks. A **Rule of Thumb:** *After digging or rototilling raw manure into soil, irrigate thoroughly; wait at least one month before planting.*

To turn raw manure into aged manure, pile it up in a shady place, cover it with plastic (to protect it from flies and reduce odors), and leave it to age. The **Rule of Thumb:** *Age horse manure three months; age cow, chicken, and rabbit manures one year or use them unaged to heat up the compost pile.* (Chicken and rabbit manures are more concentrated and hotter than horse and cow manures and should be used in smaller quantities.)

▸ **Peat Moss:** Work this into soil. It's highly acid, long-lasting, and holds moisture, but is difficult to get wet. Peat moss is not a renewable resource. The best substitute is ground coir. (*See* Coir, *facing page*.)

▸ **Pine Needles:** Use these as mulch under camellias and azaleas or as path cover in a vegetable garden.

▸ **Rotted Hay:** Work it into soil or use it as mulch. (No extra nitrogen is needed if the hay is completely broken down by composting.) Alfalfa is high in nitrogen and can be layered with horse manure to make a nutritious compost.

▸ **Sawdust:** Work it into soil or use as mulch. It robs nitrogen from the soil as it rots. In order to safely counteract this process, add nitrogen to the sawdust prior to digging it into the ground. One **Rule of Thumb:** *Add 1 to 1½ pounds actual nitrogen to every 100 pounds of raw shavings.* For a layer of sawdust you've spread 1 inch deep over 100 square feet, the nitrogen required would be that in approximately 1 pound of ammonium sulfate. (The specific recommended ratio by weight is 1.75 parts of nitrogen to 100 parts of unrotted organic matter.) As noted on page 25, ammonium sulfate is not an organic fertilizer, and thus is not an appropriate fertilizer to use in organic gardening. Blood meal can be used instead but is much more expensive. (Raw sawdust can also be used to slow down a hot or overly smelly compost pile.)

Besides the nitrogen that you supply when you first apply the sawdust, add nitrogen fertilizer regularly to feed plants. When using raw sawdust as mulch, you must compensate by feeding plants more often. The **Rule of Thumb:** *When using sawdust as mulch, increase the nitrogen fertilizer you would regularly give your plants by one-fourth and feed them at more frequent intervals.*

▸ **Sludge:** Work it into soil. Though it contains some nitrogen, it's not strong enough to burn roots, and it's good for sandy soils. Because it may, in some cases, contain heavy metals, don't add it to vegetable gardens.

continued . . .

A Catalog of Organic Soil Amendments and How to Use Them (continued)

▸ **Vegetable and Fruit Leavings from the Kitchen or Supermarket** (spoiled fruits and vegetables and green outer leaves of vegetables are available through produce managers): Add them to compost or bury them to feed earthworms. Or blend small quantities of fruit and vegetables waste with water in a blender, and pour the resulting liquid directly into garden soil.

▸ **Wheat and Oat Straw:** Use only as mulch. Don't work these into soil unless they've been composted and are largely decomposed. May contain weed seeds.

▸ **Wood and Bark Chips** (Available bagged or by truckload): Use as mulch. They're a useful amendment for heavy soils but dangerous to plants (like sawdust, above, but to a greater degree) unless sufficient nitrogen is frequently added. Before planting through woody mulches, rake mulch aside, so that it does not get mixed with soil.

Container plants are an exception. They need complete fertilizers at each feeding because most potting soils contain little or no phosphorus and potassium. (Instructions for fertilizing specialty plants—plants that require special treatment, as discussed on page 33—are given in the monthly chapters.)

Many fertilizers are sold under names, such as "rose food" or "citrus food," that specify their intended use. There's nothing wrong with using some of these products. High-quality products recommended for acid-loving plants—particularly camellias and azaleas—make it easy to supply the right amount of nutrients in an acid formula that's beneficial for these plants. A good lawn fertilizer also contains the proper balance of basic elements, including trace elements, for overall lawn health. But it's wise to read and compare labels because a particular fertilizer sometimes can be substituted for another. Often a product with a generic (use unspecified) label is a better buy than one with a specified purpose. You could use 1 pound of 5-10-5, for example, instead of 1/2 pound of 10-20-10.

What It Means to Be an Organic Gardener. Organic fertilizers are those derived from living organisms, whether animal or vegetable, such as manure, cottonseed meal, compost, blood meal, hoof and horn meal, bone meal, and wood ash. (Wood ash is often recommended in organic gardening publications as a source of potassium, but the University of California Extension advises against its use in Southern California because it's too alkaline for most local soils.) Organic gardeners, for either economic or philosophical reasons, feed all their plants with organic fertilizers and refrain from using chemical pesticides other than dormant sprays. Among the basic tenets of organic philosophy (and of this book) is the fact that chemical fertilizers and pesticides harm the soil and environment, kill natural and beneficial organisms, and negatively impact the flavor and health-giving properties of food plants, whereas naturally occurring materials have the opposite effects. (Chemical fertilizers and pesticides are "organic" too, in scientific terminology, but the word as it has come to be used in relationship to farming and gardening denotes live rather than synthetic origins.)

What the Numbers on a Package of Fertilizer Mean

Chemical	Nitrogen	Phosphorus	Potassium
Symbol	N	P	K
Sample formula (percentages)	16	8	4
Examples of chemical sources	Ammonium sulfate Ammonium nitrate Urea	Single superphosphate	Potassium sulfate
Examples of organic sources	Cottonseed meal Blood meal	Bone meal	Greensand Wood ash (too alkaline, saline for local use)
What each element does	Speeds vegetative growth; gives rich green color	Promotes growth of flowers and fruit plus good stems and roots; necessary for photosynthesis; good seed production	Promotes growth of flowers and fruit plus good stems and roots; gives flowers vibrant color; overall plant health
Evidence of severe deficiency*	Sickly yellow-green color, stunted growth	Purple or reddish leaf discoloration	Weak stems; browning and yellowing of leaf tips and edges

* Other factors can also cause these symptoms.

Organic fertilizers generally work slower and aren't as concentrated as chemical fertilizers, but knowledgeable gardeners can use them successfully. Some gardeners use the organic method only in the vegetable garden. Vegetables (plus many other garden plants) that grow in full sun can be kept healthy and productive using only the standard organic fertilizers—manure, compost, and other organic materials. Unfortunately, manure (particularly bagged cow manure), which is man's most ancient and inexpensive fertilizer, often contains large quantities of salt. Our water and soil are already too salty, and adding too much manure creates a buildup of salts that will retard growth. Chicken and rabbit manures usually, contain less salt in proportion to the amount of nutrients they supply. (Chicken manure contains more nitrogen and phosphorus than most other manures.) Horse manure that is picked up daily by the horse owner is largely free from salt and is safe to use.

Many commercial organic fertilizers, containing a variety of ingredients, are available in local nurseries. Always read the labels. (Some sludge products are unsafe for vegetable gardens.) Generic organic fertilizers are listed and explained in the chart on pages 28–30.

Organic versus Inorganic Farming and Gardening Practices. The word *organic* can be confusing. In the context of science, *organic* means any chemical compound containing carbon, but in the context of farming and gardening, *organic* means the process of growing plants without any poisonous pest controls and fertilizing them exclusively with animal or vegetable fertilizers, such as manure, bone meal, blood meal, or compost, together with naturally mined forms of minerals, as opposed to water-soluble salts. In this book I use the word *organic* as it applies to methods of farming and gardening.

Ancient Methods of Fertilizing. Prior to the development of commercial fertilizers, the feeding of plants was based on what people observed in nature. Rain fell, causing seeds to sprout; trees and other plants grew to maturity, fruited, and eventually died; leaves and dead plants and animals fell to the ground and rotted, creating humus in soil that in turn fed new plants. Through the centuries, farmers and gardeners learned from nature's example how to promote plant health by composting vegetable and animal wastes and by spreading manure, bones, and ash onto fields. Prior to the development of modern fertilizers, manure provided nitrogen and contributed to the humus content of soil. Bones provided phosphorus, and wood ash or greensand provided potassium for soils that didn't contain adequate amounts. (Unfortunately, wood ash is too alkaline for most western soils, but it can be used in small quantities on sandy soils. Consult the accompanying chart on pages 28–30 for more about generic organic fertilizers.)

Natural Sources of Nitrogen. During the eighteenth and nineteenth centuries, in addition to animal manures, human urine was used as a source of nitrogen, and is still commonly used today for feeding homegrown vegetables in Finland. Historically, it was used especially on roses, which were observed to benefit from generous applications as long as there was plenty of rainfall to dilute the urea contained in urine and to wash away its salts. On large estates, gardens were provided with a ready supply of nitrogen simply by dumping a pile of peat moss behind gardeners' sheds for the men to use as a latrine and then periodically spreading the moss around the gardens. (A noble lady in Galsworthy's *The Forsyte Saga* attributes the fine quality of her roses to the fact that she instructed her maids to empty the chamber pots over their roots.) Additionally, all plant wastes that couldn't be tilled straight into the soil were thrown onto a big rubbish heap in a hidden spot and allowed to rot. After a few years a farmer or gardener could dig into the bottom of his heap and mine barrowfuls of sweet-smelling black earth—the finest compost, made without fuss and perfect for spreading on the garden or forcing through a screen to fill pots and seed flats.

The Origin of Synthetic Fertilizers. For countless centuries farmers and gardeners had used largely unchanged methods of fertilizing. Then in the nineteeth century a series of scientific experiments proved, first, that plants need certain nutrients, mainly nitrogen, phosphorus, and potassium and second, that plant roots cannot tell the difference between *synthetic fertilizers* (man-made mixtures of nutrients) and those that occur naturally in the ground. Industrialists reading in their morning newspapers that plant roots will absorb what they need regardless of origin instantly saw the commercial possibilities and rushed to build factories for the manufacture of synthetic fertilizers. By the end of the nineteenth century, fertilizer companies had sprung up in Great Britain, Ireland, and Germany, and commercial fertilizers were being imported from Europe to America. The introduction of commercial lawn fertilizers to America coincided with the late-nineteenth-century enthusiasm for planting lawns as a way to clean up muddy New England towns. When people began feeding grass with synthetic fertilizers, cutting grass with mowing machines instead of cows and sheep, and passing laws requiring pigs to be fenced, the American front lawn came into being.

Eventually it was discovered that plants also need secondary nutrients—calcium, magnesium, and sulfur—as well as what we now call *trace nutrients*, or *trace elements*, manganese, iron, copper, boron, molybdenum, and chlorine. Advances in the manufacture of explosives during the First World War also affected fertilizers. After the war, companies used the new technology to produce plant nutrients in large quantities through chemical means. Thus the modern fertilizer industry was born, which revolutionized agriculture and to a lesser extent gardening.

Special Fertilizers for Specific Needs.

Manufacturers eventually realized that various plants need nutrients at differing rates, and that diseases can arise if a plant suffers a deficiency of a certain element necessary to its health, and so they began to create specialized fertilizers. For example, they designed specific fertilizers that fill the special needs of a tomato plant for magnesium and sulfur, while protecting it from blossom-end rot, which may occur if its roots fail to absorb adequate calcium. (For the facts on blossom-end rot, see page 250.) By the middle of the twentieth century, scientists had helped manufacturers develop formulas to provide exotic plants with all the elements for healthy growth that nature would have supplied in the wild. They made acid foods, for example, for acid-loving plants and a wide range of synthetic fertilizers to fill the specific needs of a host of other plants, including citrus, lawns, annual and perennial flowers, vegetables, roses, palms, houseplants, and African violets, to name only a few. Today these fertilizers can be purchased in many forms: granulated, powdered, liquid, and polymer-coated time-release pellets.

The Modern Revolution in Agriculture and Gardening.

The use of synthetic fertilizers simplified agriculture and often resulted in spurts of growth and larger harvests. Today many of the ingredients in fertilizers and pesticides are by-products of the petroleum industry. Companies combine these ingredients, including various forms of nitrogen, in carefully calculated proportions, mixing them with inert ingredients and other nutrients such as minerals mined from the earth.

The Birth of the Organic Movement.

As synthetic commercial fertilizers were coming into common use and spreading around the world, several voices arose in opposition. One was that of Sir Albert Howard (1873–1947), often considered the father of organic farming and gardening even though others preceded him. Howard's last and best-known book, *An Agricultural Testament*, promoted the idea of creating fertile, healthy soils by returning all agricultural waste to the ground, as he had observed being done in India. In 1942, Jerome Rodale, an American businessman influenced by Howard's ideas, began publishing *Organic Farming and Gardening* magazine. Rodale and his followers promoted the idea that unlike chemical fertilizers, organic materials do more than provide nutrients. They also improve soil structure and its ability to hold water and nutrients.

How Organic Soils Feed Plants.

The proponents of organic gardening observed that as microorganisms in soil break down organic materials into humus, they create a steady flow of nutrients that are long-lasting in the ground and don't wash into groundwater. Synthetic fertilizers, on the other hand, upset the natural organic chemistry of soil, kill earthworms and other beneficial organisms, and prevent the very microbial process that creates nitrogen in healthy soil. Among the people who eagerly supported these ideas were many farmers and gardeners who had never really changed from the older ways, including my parents, who considered compost and manure heaps an integral part of gardening. They immigrated to America and later brought us children. They bought a farm in Pennsylvania, and during the Second World War created a huge Victory garden in which we all worked. They ran farm and garden according to organic methods and fed everything with chicken manure. Like many others of my era, I grew up following the ideas of Sir Albert Howard and Jerome Rodale.

Environmental Threats. Though never completely abandoning the ideals of organic gardening, especially in regard to pesticides, I (along with many other gardeners of the past sixty years) have often used chemical fertilizers for reasons of convenience. But now we once again live in an era of dramatic change. The double-edged sword of global warming and environmental pollution threatens our health and indeed our very lives on this planet. We have learned that pesticides and chemicals found in chemically derived fertilizers leach into groundwater and eventually into the ocean. None of us wants to contribute to this problem. Further, studies have shown that vegetables and fruits grown organically, without artificial fertilizers, are healthier and contain more nutrients than those that are grown with commercial fertilizers. For this reason and to protect their families from cancer and other ills, home vegetable gardeners now want to raise vegetables without the use of synthetic fertilizers or pesticides, and they no longer wish to use fertilizers that are by-products of the petroleum industry. Today's gardeners realize that even the small choices we make in our home gardens might collectively help to reduce our society's dependence on foreign oil, as well as protect our own and our children's health. Seen in this light, the simple act of choosing to use an organic rather than a synthetic fertilizer has far-reaching consequences. Meanwhile, fertilizer companies are creating many new organic products that simplify our tasks.

The OMRI Label. As an ever-increasing number of gardeners adopts the organic method, organizations have sprung into being to make their work easier. The Organic Materials Review Institute (OMRI), for example, is a national nonprofit organization that decides which products fully comply with the standards necessary for them to be considered truly organic. Products that adhere to the standards set up by this organization can be awarded the OMRI label of approval, which indicates that they comply with the principles of organic farming and gardening. In most cases, you can use such products safely in an organic garden. (The monthly chapters in this book alert you to doubtful cases.) Farmers raising food products can use fertilizers and pesticides bearing the OMRI label while maintaining their right to advertise, label, and sell their products as fully organic.

Adopting the Organic Way. Whether to make the switch to organic fertilizers is between you and your conscience. There is no "organic sheriff" going door to door to check up on you, so you're free to tailor your choices to your abilities as a gardener. For example, until you develop your own system and find organic fertilizers suitable for your plants, garden, and budget, you might want to simply use one fertilizer for everything in the garden. One all-purpose, largely organic fertilizer is Gro-Power, a transitional product that can help people move away from synthetics. Gro-Power gradually builds organic soil, but it does contain a small amount of synthetic nitrogen and thus is not fully organic. Biosol Mix (7-2-3) is an all-organic fertilizer that you can use for feeding lawns, trees, and vegetables while adding to soil life. There are many others. For people who dwell in suburbs, simply replacing a commercial synthetic fertilizer with an organic one can be a big step toward a more environmentally friendly garden.

Choosing Organic Fertilizers. In order to choose the best organic fertilizers for use in your garden, refer to the chart on pages 28–30 or compare bagged and boxed organic fertilizers at your local nursery. Manufacturers are creating new, OMRI-labeled organic fertilizers with balanced or specific formulas. This simplifies the task of fertilizing, but they may cost more than using basic materials and devising your own formula. A systematized way to fertilize roses is recommended by the Rose-Pro Method, summarized in the charts on pages 418–421, but this method relies largely on named commercial organic products, some of which may be expensive. Fortunately, there are many free fertilizers, even strong nitrogen sources, and I will mention these as we go along. Some organic gardeners use a variety of products and materials rather than only one. Switching fertilizers may help you find a system to fit your specific needs and soil. In general, the most important step you can take is to build up the organic content of the soil by regularly adding homemade compost and other organic materials. (For simple composting methods, see pages 97–99.)

Controlling Animal Pests. One unfortunate characteristic of some organic fertilizers is that they attract animals. Some gardeners report that blood meal repels rabbits, but other gardeners find that blood meal, bone meal, feather meal, and alfalfa meal can *attract* such pests as rats,

voles, shrews, rabbits, ground squirrels, raccoons, and opossums. Dogs, cats, owls, and nonpoisonous king snakes are among the best controls for these pests, but they can't eradicate all of them. A dog or cat that is a good hunter is the best control, but many pets are themselves attracted to the organic fertilizers that attract wild animals. They may dig them up or eat, lick, or roll in them. Among organic animal controls are electric rat traps, including Victor Electronic Rat Trap, Rat Zapper, and others, which may help control rats, mice, voles, and shrews. But the best solution is to till organic fertilizers into the ground or cover them with a heavy layer of mulch and then water them thoroughly into the ground.

Manure as Fertilizer. Many gardeners find that manure, especially chicken, rabbit, or horse manure, provides almost all the nutrients their gardens need. Unaged manure may bring weed seeds to your garden, but manure does not attract animal pests. The main objection to manures is that some of them, especially cow manure, often contain salt. Salt can build up in clay and other poorly drained soils, sometimes to such an extent that it kills plants. People also worry that cow or steer manures may contain hormones.

Easy, High-Nitrogen Compost. For those who have access to horse manure, here is an easy compost recipe for all-around garden use: Build a pile by layering fresh horse manure with old, partially rotted, moldy, or otherwise unusable alfalfa hay. This combination creates a hot pile that needs no tossing and does not attract animals. Let the pile stand for three months, by which time it will have turned into dark brown, nitrogen-rich compost. Spread it around your garden, where it will continue to decompose and release nutrients into the soil. You can use this compost to feed and mulch everything, including shrubs, trees, roses, vegetable plots, flowerbeds, you name it. Supplies of horse manure and waste alfalfa hay can be obtained from horse ranches or private owners and may cost no more than the price of hauling. (When using manure in your garden, be sure to wash vegetables carefully, and make sure your tetanus shot is up to date.)

IRRIGATION AND WATER CONSERVATION

Our Dependence on Imported Water. In Southern California rainfall is seasonal, and the water we use for irrigation is imported, scarce, and expensive. During the last thirty or forty years, our population has exploded while our water supplies have dwindled until the inevitable has at last become a reality: There's not enough water to go around. In good years, when rains are adequate—and if we carefully conserve water—we can continue to keep our landscapes properly irrigated. But when there's a severe drought that lasts several years, such as the drought of the late 1980s and early 1990s, water prices escalate, cutbacks are common, and in some areas it's against the law to water for landscaping purposes. These problems are likely to persist unless the state of California changes its priorities.

But most Southern Californians deeply appreciate the value of plants and gardens and their importance to our quality of life. There's a growing awareness that landscape plants—especially trees—absorb carbon dioxide, give off oxygen, trap dust, muffle sounds, moisten and cool the atmosphere, and save power by reducing temperatures in buildings. Trees,

shrubs, and—yes—even lawns make our cities and suburbs pleasant places in which to live instead of cheerless concrete jungles. Under the right conditions, there's still a place for a few of the old favorites that need regular watering, including camellias, azaleas, roses, and hibiscus. However, when water supplies are cut back, painful choices must sometimes be made between plants that are worth saving and those that are expendable. In such times, use your precious water to save the larger plants, and let the smaller and younger plants go. Lawns, flower borders, vegetables, ground covers, and young shrubs can be quickly replaced. But mature and graceful trees, shrubs, and vines that add character to the landscape are irreplaceable.

When water supplies are cut back, many garden plants, even deep-rooted camellias and roses, can stay alive with much less irrigation than usual. (They'll just pull in their horns, produce no flowers, and stop growing; don't feed them.) But when water supplies are adequate, remember that all garden plants need to be watered in order to survive, at least during the summer months. (Some native plants are exceptions.) Most plants need irrigation from time to time during the winter, too, and all plants, even drought-resistant ones, need adequate water when they're first planted in order to get started.

Right and Wrong Ways to Irrigate. The methods and equipment used in irrigation are about as varied as the plants we grow, but—aside from an old-fashioned watering can—they fall into three basic categories. There are conventional underground irrigation systems, drip systems, and plain old garden hoses.

All automatic systems need to be regularly checked for leaks and malfunctioning parts. Also be sure your sprinklers are installed for proper overlap to keep all the plants evenly watered. A frequent problem with overhead sprinklers is that they can cause water to pour off slopes and dry ground and run into the street. Control clocks that pulse water, applying it in short bursts separated by time intervals, can help prevent this problem by allowing adequate time for the water to sink into parched soil.

Drip, mist, or trickle systems are among the best and newest ways to water plants. Most of these systems feed water at controlled low pressure into an approximately 1/2-inch-diameter hose, or header, which in turn feeds smaller spaghetti-sized hoses, or microtubing, leading to individual plants. At the plants, emitters release a measured amount of water to root zones or mist the foliage. Some systems emit water through hoses buried in the ground. These include hoses made from recycled auto tires, which weep water from pores—gardeners call this leaky hose— and perforated plastic drip tubing.

The worst way to water is to stand around, hose in hand, squirting water on bare ground. This only wets the surface, digs up the ground, and does more harm than good. If you must water with a hose, make watering basins around the root zones of shrubs and young trees and build dikes of earth or bender board (wooden or plastic lawn edging) around flowerbeds. Lay the hose on the ground inside these areas and flood them.

How Your Soil Type Affects Watering.

Some plants with shallow roots, including cool-season lawns, many annual flowers, and vegetables, need approximately an inch of rain weekly for optimum performance. Precise amounts and the intervals between watering can vary according to several factors—for example, when the weather is windy or hot, plants lose moisture from leaves and need more water. But on an

⚙ QUICK TIP

How to Measure Inches of Irrigation Water. *An inch of water from an overhead sprinkler can be measured by setting out empty juice cans here and there, both close to and far away from a sprinkler. Measure the time it takes to fill the can with an inch of water. (This technique can also be used to test a new irrigation system and locate dry spots in your sprinkler pattern.)*

everyday basis, soil type is the most important factor in how much to water.

Once clay soil has gotten thoroughly wet, it hangs on to water much longer than sandy soil, which soon dries out. If you have clay soil, you should water less frequently but for a longer time than a gardener in the same area who has sandy soil. The percentage of humus in the ground can also affect water penetration and retention. Organic soil amendments help water penetrate clay soils faster and drain more quickly. The amendments do the exact opposite for sandy soil, making water penetrate slightly more slowly and helping soil retain water longer.

In general, water penetrates sandy soil much faster than clay soil, so for sandy soil less is required to reach a given depth. The **Rule of Thumb:** *One inch of water will penetrate sandy soil about 12 inches, loam about 7 inches, and clay soil only 5 inches, perhaps less.* (Sandy soil that sheds water instead of absorbing it is an exception. See page 23 for an explanation and solutions.)

How to Determine the Depth of Water Penetration.
You can't tell whether plants have enough water by looking at the surface of the ground. Sometimes the ground can look like a swamp on top but be as dry as a desert

underneath. At other times the ground may look dusty dry on top but still be soggy wet below. How do you really know whether water reached those roots? The best way is to dig down with a trowel or spade and take a look: if the soil is saturated below the roots of plants, there's enough water.

Other ways to test soil moisture are with a soil probe (awl) or with a tensiometer. Though expensive, these instruments are a means to quantify moisture at specific depths of soil. A soil probe is a metal tube with handles on the top and a cut-out section on one side of the lower portion. Wind it manually into the ground a few inches at a time; then pull it up and remove the earth trapped in it. Keep repeating the process until you get a soil sample from the required depth. A tensiometer consists of a dial attached to a long metal probe, usually with handles at right angles so it can be thrust deeply into the ground.

How Shallow Watering Harms Plants.

Shallow watering makes roots grow close to the surface; deep watering encourages them to reach far down into the ground. Deep-rooted plants withstand winds and drought much better than shallow-rooted ones.

Always water deeply and infrequently rather than shallowly and often. For trees and shrubs, this means watering until moisture reaches 2 to 4 feet into the ground; for vegetables and perennials, 1 to 2 feet; for annuals, 6 to 12 inches; for cool-season lawns, also 6 to 12 inches; and for warm-season lawns, such as Bermuda, perhaps as much as 1 to 2 feet.

Why Overwatering Is as Bad as Underwatering.

When plants are underwatered, they show such signs of stress as wilting, browning, drying, and dropping of leaves, buds, and flowers—and eventually they die. But it's equally as bad to overwater them. Too much water deprives roots of the oxygen they need to function and grow. Overwatering causes root rot and crown rot, which in turn lead to softening, drooping, yellowing, and dropping of leaves. The plants become stunted and weakened, and often they die.

How Frequently Plants Need Irrigation.

Most cool-season lawns, vegetables, and annual flowers have shallow roots and need to be watered more frequently than deep-rooted plants—at least once a week in warm weather, more often in hot, dry weather and in sandy soils. Some shade plants, such as container-grown fuchsias and impatiens, may need water every day. Most shrubs are able to go longer between irrigations, perhaps as many as ten or fifteen days. Many mature trees growing in clay soil can go several weeks between irrigations. But when you do water them, water slowly for a long time, so the moisture sinks deeply into the ground. Some established drought-resistant plants may need only one or two irrigations in summer; some native plants must have no irrigation in summer, or they may die from root rot.

How to Conserve Water by Using the Local Evapotranspiration Rate.

Gardeners with lawns can conserve water by using an evapotranspiration (ET) rate chart. The ET rate is a number that indicates the inches of water that evaporate from soil plus the amount of water that transpires through blades of grass during a certain period of time. The philosophy behind ET is that if it's possible to figure out the amount of water that leaves the soil and evaporates from leaves, you can then determine how much must be replaced by annual rainfall combined with irrigation. ET rates are calculated by University of California scientists, and they vary by geographical area, from year to year, and even from day to day. Because of the variables involved, they aren't perfect, but they do help eliminate over- and underwatering. ET rates can't be used in their pure form without doing some fairly complicated mathematics. Fortunately, gardeners need not deal with these difficulties: ET charts for home gardeners are easy to understand and don't require you to do any figuring.

To obtain an ET chart, telephone your county's Cooperative Extension office or your local member agency of the Metropolitan Water District and ask for the current ET chart for the area in which you live. These charts tell you when and for how long you should water your lawn according to the time of year.

Also check the lawn for signs of dryness. If your lawn goes dry prior to the next suggested watering, you should water cool-season grasses slightly more frequently and warm-season grasses for a slightly longer time at each irrigation. Also water less when the weather is cool and cloudy and more when it's hot, dry, and windy. Water much less in winter than in summer.

How Plant Choice Can Save Water.

Choose drought-resistant plants for your basic landscape. Place plants that need more water in containers attached to a drip system, or grow them in the ground in small areas close to the house. Use drip systems for irrigating vegetables and annual flowers that need regular water. Grow these plants during years when rains are heavy and water supplies are adequate; cycle them out during drought years. If you need a lawn, plant a drought-resistant grass and keep the lawn area small. Most lawns, other than Bermuda and zoysia, use more water than many shrubs, trees, and flowers, and they're far more labor intensive.

When properly designed, small lawns can be just as pleasing as large ones.

◉ QUICK TIP

Make Softened Water Safe for House-plants. *To make artificially softened water safe for irrigating houseplants, mix in ½ teaspoon of gypsum per gallon of water. In most cases, this is enough gypsum to replace the calcium that was removed by the softening process.*

PLANTING

The act of planting is the most exciting and hopeful moment in gardening, but whether our hopes are realized depends on how well we do the job. Years ago they said a gardener should put a one-dollar plant into a ten-dollar hole. Today we know we should amend and improve all our soil (as described on page 18), not just the planting hole. The aim of proper planting is to encourage roots to get out into the surrounding soil as soon as possible. Except in the case of some specific plants, such as camellias, azaleas, and roses, filling the hole with soil amendments merely creates an underground plant pot; roots tend to stay inside it. In very sandy soil or hard decomposed granite, or when plants have small root systems, it's all right to amend the planting hole, but in general the **Rule of Thumb:** *When planting trees, large shrubs, and large vines, add no organic soil amendments except as mulch.* Sooner or later those roots will have to get out and live in the native soil, and it might as well be sooner. Specific instructions for planting specialty plants are given in the monthly chapters, but here are some basic guidelines.

How to Plant from Nursery Containers.

Most of the basic landscape consists of trees, shrubs, vines, and ground covers planted from nursery containers. When planting large areas, first prepare the ground as described on page 19. When planting in unknown conditions, first check the drainage (see the box, right). Plant when the soil is moist but not wet. If the soil is dry, water thoroughly; then wait for it to dry out enough that it can be easily worked. (Sandy soils can be worked sooner than clay soils but may be more difficult to moisten, as explained on page 23.) When planting from 5-, 10-, or 15-gallon containers, dig holes approximately twice as wide as the container and 1 to 2 inches shallower than the depth of the root ball. In hard or clay soils, roughen the sides of the hole with your spade, so it isn't like a smooth, hard wall and roots can more easily penetrate the surrounding soil. In heavy clay soils where drainage is slow, dig several handfuls of gypsum into the bottom of the hole and cover it with a shovelful of earth.

To remove the plant from the container, roll it on the ground or strike the sides to loosen them. With a small container, turn it upside down and strike the lip on a hard object, such as the edge of a wheelbarrow. Then slip the plant out—don't pull it out by the crown—and take a look at the roots. If the roots are like a mat on the outside of the root ball, cut the roots apart and loosen them by slicing through them with a knife in several places across the bottom and on the sides. Next place the plant into the hole. Make sure the top of the root ball is 1 to 2 inches higher than the surrounding ground. Backfill with native soil from the hole, unless it approximates pure beach sand. In that case, amend the soil from the hole with one-third organic amendment before backfilling. Press the soil down gently but firmly all around the

How to Check Drainage Prior to Planting

Fill the hole with water and let it drain out. Then fill the hole a second time. Place a yardstick on edge across the hole with its side touching the surface of the water all the way across the hole, and make a note of the time. Return several hours later and use a ruler to measure how far the water level has dropped below the yardstick. The **Rule of Thumb:** *If the water level in the planting hole drops ¼ inch or more per hour, drainage is adequate. If the water level drops less than 1/10 inch per hour, drainage is too poor for most cultivated plants.* In that case, install a drain, construct a raised bed, or choose another spot.

plant with your hands—never with your feet. Make a berm of earth around the hole to act as a watering basin, and cover the surface of the soil with 2 to 4 inches of mulch. Then irrigate thoroughly so that water reaches the bottom of the planting hole and drains out.

Water frequently for the first week or two to keep the root ball moist until the plant is established. Thereafter, manage irrigation according to each plant's individual needs. Just how often and how much you need to water each plant during its early stages depends on your soil and the weather conditions. But more new plants die from underwatering than from overwatering. If the surrounding soil is dry, it can act like a wick, pulling water out of the root ball and drying it out. You can tell for sure that this is happening when cracks appear between the root ball and the surrounding soil.

Most plants need good drainage, so after digging a planting hole and prior to planting,

✺ QUICK TIP

Help Vegetables Get a Good Start in Heavy Soils. *Instead of covering vegetable seeds with soil, cover them to the recommended depth with packaged soil mix designed for container planting. Rows are then easy to see, the ground doesn't crust, and sprouts break through easily.*

check the drainage using the method described in the accompanying box. If the hole doesn't drain well and you're planting on a slope, you can install a sleeve drain (a pipe covered by gravel that drains water from the bottom of a planting hole and releases it farther down on the slope). If hardpan is a problem, it's better not to dig a hole below the roots, as this only creates a basin that will fill with water. A better solution is to build a raised bed.

Raised beds need be only 8 or 12 inches high. This is enough to lift roots above the surrounding soil and keep them from rotting. Build the sides of the bed of rock, brick, concrete, or wood; loosen and amend the subsoil under the bed and fill with good amended topsoil. For large trees, dig the planting hole down through the raised bed into the lower level. Roots will reach down and out, and your tree will eventually get established in the native soil beneath the bed.

How to Plant Annual Flowers and Vegetables. When planting transplants of annual flowers and vegetables from color packs, pony packs, and 4-inch containers, prepare the whole bed in advance of planting. Dig deeply—at least a foot deep. Add a layer of organic soil amendment an inch or two thick—up to 4 inches in poor soil—and work it in. Add organic fertilizer recommended for the flowers or vegetables, according to package directions, and cultivate it into the top 6 inches of earth. Water the ground and let it settle overnight.

Once the soil has been dug up, amended, and cultivated, never step in a flowerbed or vegetable row. Standing on ground compacts it. The **Rule of Thumb:** *Make flowerbeds no more than 3 feet wide, or 6 feet wide with a path at the back. Make raised beds for vegetables no wider than 5 feet.* That way you can reach the center. (Wider beds should have a path down the middle so you can work both sides.)

Turn the packs upside down and tap them lightly on a hard object, such as an upside-down flower pot, to loosen the root balls. Don't yank them out by the stem. Some plants, such as marigolds, get very rootbound in containers. Butterfly each of these halfway up from the bottom: Stick your thumbs in the bottom of the root ball and tear those tough roots apart. With plants that have tender roots, such as pansies, just fondle the roots a little to loosen them, so they won't get into the ground and sit there thinking they're still in a container.

Make a hole with the trowel and put in the plant; in the case of butterflied roots, spread them over a central mound. Cover the roots with soil up to the original depth of the plant in the container. Press down gently on top of the roots with your palms to give them good contact with the soil. Water deeply after planting. Space the plants according to package directions. (If you're transplanting them to containers, they can be put closer together without ill effects.)

How to Plant Straight in the Ground from Seed. In Southern California many, though not all, annual flowers and vegetables can be planted straight in the garden from seed. Soil must be more thoroughly prepared for seeds than for transplants. Dig deeply and add enough organic amendment so the top won't bake hard. Then rake and cultivate until the ground has a smooth texture with no lumps.

Sow and cover seeds to the precise level recommended on the package. Some seeds, such as larkspur, impatiens, and stock, need light in order to sprout. Sprinkle these on top of well-prepared ground and press them down gently with the back of the hoe, a flat board, or the palm of your hand so they make contact with soil. (To keep them moist in hot inland areas, cover them with a floating row cover that lets light through, such as Reemay, and remove it as soon as they germinate.) Other seeds, such as those for many wildflowers, can be lightly raked into the ground.

✸ QUICK TIP

The "Hat Trick." *When planting transplants on a hot day, don't let tender roots get dried out and damaged. After removing one transplant from a pack, lay an old straw hat over the remainder to shade them from the sun.*

Cover seeded areas with netting to protect them from birds; remove the netting when sprouts are 4 inches high. After seeding, keep the seedbed damp by sprinkling it once or twice daily—even three or four times in hot interior valleys—until sprouts emerge. Then water it regularly and deeply when rains aren't adequate. Bait against snails with Sluggo, and, if cutworms are a problem, try sprinkling dry earthworm castings on top of the ground or working them into the ground. Earthworm castings repel many insects.

PRUNING

No one can prune a plant correctly without knowing how it grows. The best way to learn how plants grow is to refer to a good pruning manual for western plants. Some plants need frequent pruning, others little or none. Some have latent buds lying dormant under the bark; others don't. Some bloom on buds that last from year to year; others bloom on new wood or wood that's hardened for a certain number of seasons. Brief instructions for pruning many of our most common plants are given in the month-by-month chapters, but here are some general guidelines.

Prune to Stimulate Growth. One pruning technique is to clip off the growing tips of plants in order to make the plants bushier. This is called pinching or pinching back. Fuchsias, azaleas, and some annual and perennial flowers are good examples of plants that benefit from this type of pruning.

Pinch off the tip of a branch, and the side shoots will grow longer. Pinch the side shoots but leave the growing tip unpinched, and the branch will grow longer. Pinch all but one side tip, and the branch will change direction. (This technique can be used to train pine trees into graceful shapes.)

Stimulating growth within a tree, vine, or shrub by cutting back the top or the growing end of a whole branch or branches is called heading back. The interiors of shrubs, such as hibiscus, can be stimulated to fill out by heading back selected branches (as described on page 124). Some young trees grow stronger when headed back. Bare-root fruit trees (trees sold without earth, when dormant in winter), for example, always need heading back at planting time to make up for the loss of roots and encourage the growth of correctly spaced scaffold branches on a sturdy trunk. Some large shrubs that grow in the shape of a fountain, such as oleander and cotoneaster, benefit from having branches cut down to the ground to encourage new branches to grow.

Shear Plants to Shape Them. Shearing is similar to pinching, but, instead of removing individual tips one by one, you evenly slice off the entire tip or sides of the plant with hedge shears or, in the case of lawns, a lawn mower. One reason to shear is to keep a small-leafed plant at the same size indefinitely. With some plants, this method can be used to remove spent flowers and stimulate growth. It's also used in topiary, the art of training stylized shapes. One of the best uses of shearing is to maintain hedges.

Thin by Cutting Out Branches. Cutting out whole branches or parts of branches at the point where they join another branch or trunk is called thinning or thinning out. Thin with a pruning saw, ratchet pruner, or long-handled lopper. Do this to remove dead or diseased branches, to let light into the interior, and to keep a tree "laced out," so that plants growing underneath will have adequate sunshine.

Brittle shrubs such as acacia should be thinned in fall to prevent top-heaviness and consequent storm damage. Dense trees sometimes need thinning in order to let light in and permit wind to pass through. Plants can be made into special shapes, such as trained two-dimensional espaliers, by controlled thinning and training.

Finished cuts should be made flush with the outside of the branch collar, the swollen area surrounding the branch where it meets the trunk or larger branch. (If you cut off the branch collar, the wound won't heal properly.) In order not to tear the bark, start the cut from below. Then finish with a second cut from above. With very heavy limbs, make cuts at three places. Make the first cut on the bottom side about 1 foot out from the trunk. Cut halfway through the branch (this is the cut that keeps the bark from tearing). Make the second cut on top of the branch 6 inches out from the first cut, to remove the end of the branch. Then cut off the remaining stub at the branch collar, starting from below and finishing from above.

Prune to Encourage Flowers and Fruit. Almost all fruiting vines and fruit trees, especially deciduous fruit trees, require special pruning in order to encourage proper growth, fruiting, and flowering (as discussed on page 51). Many annual and perennial flowers will stop blooming unless they're deadheaded. (*Deadheading* means clipping off faded flowers before they can set seed.) Pruning hard after the bloom or removing seed capsules can encourage many flowering vines, shrubs, and, in some cases, trees to bloom better the following season, or even repeat bloom in the same year.

Prune to Control Size. Many gardeners do a great deal of pruning to keep plants down to desired size. This is probably the worst reason for pruning and produces the ugliest results. We all do it, however, because we choose plants that are too big for the spaces we put them in; then we have to chop at them continually to keep them in bounds. Most hedges, of course, need frequent pruning or they'll grow too tall and wide, but shrubs should be chosen so that, at full size, they will fit the spaces allotted to them.

CONTROLLING PESTS AND DISEASES

In Southern California we work in our gardens year-round, but so do the bugs. Pests such as caterpillars, mites, whiteflies, snails, and slugs are part of the environment we regularly deal with. Animal pests may be a challenge. Plant and soil diseases, too, sometimes present problems, especially with specific types of plants. Successful gardeners outwit animal pests and minimize diseases through good cultural practices. They balance the environment in order to live in harmony with a few pests without having a garden that looks like a chewed-up disaster. This book isn't a handbook on pests and diseases, though organic, chemical-free tips for controlling many problems are included in the month-by-month chapters. But here are a few basic principles and rules that will help you deal wisely with this aspect of gardening.

Control Pests through Integrated Pest Management. Prior to the 1960s, many Southern California home gardeners thought that regular spraying with pesticides was the right way to control pests. That was before Rachel Carson's book *Silent Spring* alerted our society to the dangers inherent in the irresponsible use of insecticides, especially DDT. Formerly, gardeners often sprayed with DDT to control caterpillars and ants, totally unaware of the hazard it posed to birds and other wildlife, not to mention humans. Today the approach has completely changed. Wise gardeners now know that toxic pesticides should never be purchased or used. Chemical sprays are possible health hazards, and their use upsets the balance of nature, killing beneficial insects and creating new strains of pests that are resistant to pesticides. The alternative is integrated pest management (IPM), a multipoint strategy. It involves spraying only when absolutely necessary and using specific organic sprays against specific pests instead of broad-spectrum sprays that kill the good guys along with the bad. IPM also involves working with nature and trying not to upset its balance—by using, for example, environmentally safe pest controls such as mechanical traps, Safer soap, and BT (*Bacillus thuringiensis*, a bacterium that kills certain leaf-eating caterpillars but nothing else).

Release Beneficials and Help Them Fight Pests. Our environment has not only a resident population of pests but also armies of beneficial organisms that are constantly on the hunt for caterpillars, beetles, and bugs. These creatures—often lumped together under the catchall term "beneficials"—include spiders, ladybugs, praying mantises, several nematodes, various types of predatory mites, green lacewings, syrphid flies, various whitefly parasites, and many types of wasps, including trichogramma wasps. Gardeners who practice IPM help nature along by releasing additional populations of beneficials; they also take care not to kill such conspicuous helpmates as birds, frogs, lizards, and toads, as well as the nearly invisible larval forms of beneficial insects and arachnids that may occur in their gardens.

In my garden, I've found that releasing ladybugs, trichogramma wasps, and lacewings several times beginning in early spring reduces pest problems to such an extent that spraying is unnecessary. It's not the adult ladybug or lacewing that kills the pests but the immature, larval stage of the insect. Although ladybugs are sold mainly as a control for aphids, it's been my experience that they may also control immature stages of whiteflies and mites, including fuchsia gall mites. Prior to releasing ladybugs, I always chill them in the refrigerator (see the Quick Tip on page 160). Every year millions of other types of beneficials are released by botanical gardens, zoos, and governmental and agricultural agencies. Because all beneficials travel from place to place, we can cooperate with nature by not killing those that settle in our gardens.

To work with nature in this way, one needs to understand that some pests must be allowed to coexist along with the beneficials; otherwise, the beneficials would have nothing to eat! The goal is to work toward a natural balance between pests and predators. Gardeners who release several types of beneficials and talk their neighbors into adopting IPM as well may see dramatic results.

Ladybugs, green-lacewing eggs, and the egg cases of praying mantises can be purchased at many local nurseries in spring. Many other types of beneficial insects, arachnids, and nematodes can be purchased by mail. Because birds, too, can be a help in controlling caterpillars and other pests, encourage them to set up housekeeping. Provide shrubs for nesting, birdhouses of correct design and placement, and a safe source of water for them to drink. Water in motion—a fountain or a birdbath with a dripper, for example—is more attractive to birds than still water in a birdbath.

Control Disease through Good Cultural Practices. Plant diseases are caused by microscopic organisms in the air and the soil that attack plant tissues. There are many different kinds of diseases. Fungal diseases, such as rust, mildew, and botrytis, are usually the most readily observed and easily diagnosed by gardeners because they disfigure leaves, stems, or flowers. These diseases tend to occur at particular times of year, during certain kinds of weather, and on some host plants more than others. They

can usually be controlled by such good cultural practices as growing resistant plants, watering early in the day, not planting sun-loving plants in shade, and keeping a clean garden.

Viral diseases are sometimes caused by pests that carry the disease from plant to plant. Leafhoppers, for example, can carry viral diseases that infect tomatoes and other plants. Bacterial diseases are caused by single-celled organisms that prey on larger plants. Fireblight, a bacterial disease that causes blackening and dieback of members of the rose family, can be controlled by cutting off diseased portions 12 inches beyond the damage and by maintaining healthy growth.

Soil diseases, such as various root rots and crown rots, can be caused by overwatering and by growing plants in insufficient drainage. Therefore, when you adjust lengths of watering times, take into consideration the time of year and the weather. Good cultural practices that help cut down on root rots include improving soil, providing good drainage, and growing resistant plants. Wilt diseases, such as verticillium wilt and fusarium wilt, can affect entire plants (such as tomatoes), gradually causing death. The best solutions are crop rotation and growing resistant varieties.

Learn to Diagnose Plant Problems. The first step in proper pest and disease control is always to inspect the ailing plant carefully and make an intelligent diagnosis of the cause. Once you've found out what's wrong with the plant, you can then choose an appropriate organic solution.

For example, if leaves are chewed, leaving large holes, go out at night with a flashlight to find out what's doing the damage. Nine times out of ten, the problem is slugs, snails, or caterpillars. Control slugs and snails with an OMRI-labeled product, such as Sluggo or other organic controls (as described on page 115); spray caterpillars with BT or introduce beneficials such as trichogramma wasps. If plants show telltale signs of sickness, such as mottled or browning leaves, wilting branches, or lesions oozing sap, the source of the problem might be either pests or disease, or even animal damage, depending on the specific plant, the time of year, the place where the plant is growing, and the precise appearance of the damage.

One good way to diagnose a problem is to list the signs of damage, wrap a sample leaf in plastic, and compare these with the text and pictures in the *Ortho Problem Solver* (edited by Michael D. Smith). This thick volume can be used for reference free of charge in most nurseries, discount stores, and garden-supply centers. It contains hundreds of color photographs of pest and disease problems on specific plants. It also suggests controls, including proper cultural practices and chemical sprays. Once you've diagnosed the problem, you may want to compare the accompanying solutions with those in other sources—for example, an organic guide. You might also consult with a local Cooperative Extension office regarding the wisest course of action. You could also ask advice from a knowledgeable nurseryperson at a nursery specializing in organic products, but much wrong advice is handed out by nursery employees who, though they may love plants, may know nothing whatsoever about growing them.

CONTROLLING WEEDS

The best and safest way to get rid of weeds is by pulling, hoeing, or digging them up before they make seeds. Black plastic mulch can also be used, especially in the vegetable garden and under paths, to shade out many weeds. (This is one way

How to Clean Up a Vegetable Garden or Flowerbed That's Entirely Overrun with Devilgrass

When an entire vegetable garden or annual flowerbed has been taken over by devilgrass (common Bermuda grass), sacrifice the area in late August. Pull up all the flowers or vegetables. Hoe and pull up all top growth. Bag it and send it to the dump; don't compost it. Follow up with soil solarization, as described in detail on page 295. Basically, the steps are to water the ground to 24 inches, cover the ground with clear plastic, weight it down securely, and wait 6 to 8 weeks in the heat of summer. In full sun, this process effectively nukes Bermuda grass, but it also kills all the good bioorganisms along with the bad. Before replanting in October, bring the soil back to life by amending it with aged horse or chicken manure and products containing beneficial microbes and rhyzobia as well as fertilizing and treating the ground with humic acid.

to get rid of Bermuda grass.) Landscape fabrics can be installed under mulch and pathways to control weeds. However, when planting seeds, sod, or a whole garden in an area known to be full of weed seeds, it's possible to get rid of the problem before you plant. One way is to water the ground first to germinate the seeds, wait until the plants grow, and then kill them by tilling them under or applying an organic herbicide. (See the box above.) Or you may opt to use a preplant or preemergent herbicide that's recommended for use prior to planting vegetables or flowers. The problem with most organic preemergents, however, including corn gluten meal, is that they also inhibit growth of vegetable and flower seeds.

No pastime provides better exercise or is more rewarding than gardening, especially in Southern California—if you know what to do and when to do it. After a year or two of combining the information in the month-by-month chapters of this book with practical application in your own home garden, you'll be a seasoned, experienced, and knowledgeable gardener. What's more, you'll get results and have fun. And isn't that what it's all about?

January

THE BARE-ROOT MONTH

Aloe striata

In cold-winter climates, gardeners rest from their labors in winter, but in Southern California, we garden year-round. Our gardening year starts in January, and it begins with a flurry of activity. Many tasks throughout the year are seasonal, so if you don't get to them one month, you can do them the next. But January's jobs can't be put off. The main tasks—pruning deciduous fruit trees if you haven't already done so, pruning roses, dormant spraying, and bare-root planting—must be done now. February will be too late. Coastal gardeners can start to feed their citrus trees this month. (If you live in an inland valley, wait until March.) There are also many flowering plants to care for and, as in every month, chores for keeping up lawns and vegetable gardens.

Even though January is our coldest and sometimes wettest month, it's often one of the nicest times to work outdoors. Good days are crisp and clear, perfect for gardening and for making the gardener feel even more optimistic than usual. So rejoice that the holidays are over, dig in, and enjoy the promise of the New Year, which to the true gardener is always the same: this year the garden will be better than ever before.

BARE-ROOT PLANTING

January is often called the bare-root month because a great many plants are available at local nurseries during January in bare-root form. *Bare-root* describes a plant that has had all the soil taken off its roots before shipping. Only plants that go dormant in winter can be sold in bare-root form. In our region, the major items sold this way are roses (discussed in a separate section, page 56); cane berry bushes; deciduous fruit trees; ornamental deciduous trees and vines, including wisteria; strawberries; and a few vegetables, including artichokes, asparagus, horseradish, rhubarb, and short-day onions.

There are definite advantages to buying bare-root plants. Not only are they usually cheaper than plants in containers, but the selection of plant material, especially of roses and fruit trees, is also far greater. (See the boxes for how to plant bare-root trees, page 52, and roses, page 57.) But before you dash out and start recklessly filling your car with bargains, a word of caution: more mistakes are made in plant choice now than at any other time of year. Unfortunately, some local nurseries, discount houses, and do-it-yourself centers still carry bare-root varieties that are poor choices for our climate. Asking for help may do no good, because the salesperson may know less than you do about gardening and may never have heard of a chilling requirement.

Choose Low-Chill Varieties. *A chilling requirement* is the number of hours spent at temperatures between 45°F and 32°F that a deciduous plant needs in order to grow, flower, and fruit. It applies particularly to deciduous fruit, nut, and ornamental flowering trees and to berries. It's not the depth of cold that does the job, but the number of hours that the plant undergoes the cold temperatures. Lengths of time necessary for proper performance may vary, according to variety, from hundreds to even thousands of hours.

If a plant does not receive its required winter chill, buds won't open properly or will open unevenly. Leaf buds need even more winter chill to break their dormancy than flower buds do. If a tree doesn't have enough leaves, it won't grow well, and its fruit will sunburn.

Fortunately, there are many fine varieties of deciduous plants with low chilling requirements, those that need few, if any, hours of cold in order to bloom and bear. Refer to the lists in the encyclopedia section of the *Sunset Western Garden Book*.

Choose Cane Berry and Blueberry Bushes Adapted to Our Climate. Bare-root cane berries, grapevines, and blueberries are available at many nurseries now, but again, some nurseries still sell varieties that won't bear fruit in Southern California. Look especially for rabbiteye or southern highbush blueberries. These were developed in Florida and Georgia and bear delicious berries here. You'll need at least two bushes for cross-pollination. Plant them so the root ball is slightly high. They need acid soil mix, acid fertilizer, good drainage, and ample moisture—in short, care and planting much like that for azaleas, except with full sun.

Check Whether You Need a Pollinator. Pollination is the transfer of pollen from the anthers (the male part of flowers) to the stigma (female part). Some fruit plants are self-pollinating; bees and other insects carry the pollen from flower to flower on the same plant. Others are cross-pollinating; they need another plant, called a pollinator, in order to bear fruit. The lists in the *Sunset Western Garden Book* will tell you which these are.

Don't Let Bare-Root Plants Dry Out. Purchase bare-root plants early in the month. The early shopper gets the best plants. If you buy them with roots wrapped by the shipper, leave them in their containers, and keep them in a shady place until you're ready to plant. The packages usually contain enough moisture to keep the roots in good condition until the end of the month, but the sooner you plant, the better. (Beware of packaged plants on display in full sun, since the roots may be dried out or damaged by heat.)

If you purchase your bare-root plants at a nursery that sells them loose in a bin of shavings, you have the benefit of choosing specimens with good, strong root systems but also the responsibility to keep them moist. Once you get the plants home, soak the roots in a pail of water for an hour or two and then plant right away. If that's impossible, heel the plants in. To *heel in* means to dig a shallow trench in a shady spot, lay plants on their sides with their roots in the trench, cover the roots thoroughly with soil up to the soil line, and water well. Heeled-in plants can survive at least six weeks, though it's best not to leave them that long because by then they'll have started to grow.

DECIDUOUS FRUIT TREES

All deciduous fruit trees need to be pruned for good shape from "childhood" on, and to bear well they need to be pruned at least once a year. The time to do the major pruning is January (unless you already did the job in December). The **Rule of Thumb:** *Deciduous fruit trees should be pruned during winter while the trees are dormant, after the leaves have fallen to the ground but before new buds have swelled.*

Each type of fruit tree needs to be pruned differently, so it's important to know which kind of tree you're pruning and how to prune it properly. For example, apples bear their fruit on spurs that bear again and again, sometimes for as long as twenty years. If you whack off all the spurs, you'll have no fruit. In general, apple trees need very little pruning once a main framework of branches has been established.

It's important, however, to cut off all the leaves even from low-chill varieties, such as 'Anna', that may not lose all their foliage in winter. Leaving old leaves hanging on while new ones form can lead to apple scab, a fungal disease that causes black blotches on leaves and subsequently causes the fruit to rot. Apple scab is at its worst during rainy years. Dormant spray also helps prevent apple scab.

Plums also bear on spurs. The pruning of mature European plums is minimal, as it is for apples, but Japanese plums grow so vigorously that they need heavy pruning of new growth. Apricots bear partly on one-year-old wood and partly on spurs that continue to bear well for four or five years. The older branches must be headed back so that one-fifth of the bearing wood will be replaced. Peaches and nectarines need the heaviest pruning of all: their fruit is borne on one-year-old wood. By pruning them hard, you encourage new growth to replenish fruiting wood. Figs need very little pruning at all except to control tree size and the density of foliage.

Not only different varieties but also individual trees vary in the pruning they need. And no two trees can be pruned exactly alike; basic guidelines should be applied differently according to the placement of their branches, their age, and their overall vigor.

Only an expert can keep all the complications of pruning clearly in mind. If you're not an expert, follow a pruning manual that applies to mild climates and contains charts. (Martin's *How to Prune Fruit Trees* is one, but I often consult more than one book, since the wording in one book may be better explained in another.)

After pruning deciduous fruit trees, clean up the ground under the trees and follow up with dormant spray, as explained on page 57.

How to Plant a Bare-Root Deciduous Fruit Tree

▶ Choose a spot in full sun with good drainage and adequate space for the tree to grow. (If space is limited, choose a dwarf tree or plant so you can espalier, training it on wires, on an arbor, or against a wall.)

▶ Prune off any damaged or broken roots, and plunge the remaining roots into a bucket of water to soak while you dig a hole.

▶ Dig a planting hole and check the drainage (as described on page 40).

▶ If you are planting in heavy clay, work at least 2 pints of gypsum into the soil in the bottom of the hole. It will do no harm, and it may improve drainage (see page 23 for explanation).

▶ If gophers are a problem, line the hole with a basket made of chicken wire (sometimes sold as "poultry wire") to protect the roots while the tree is young.

▶ Hold the tree in the hole so that the bump on the bud union faces north, to shade it from the sun, and the original soil line (look for it below the bud union) is 2 inches higher than the surrounding ground. (The bud union is the location where the variety was grafted onto the rootstock; on trees it usually appears as a slight bend in the trunk or a change in its width.)

▶ Backfill the hole by sifting the native soil you took from it back into the hole around, through, and over the roots. (Don't add soil amendment unless you're planting in pure sand.) Plant high, so that as the tree grows the area where the trunk meets the ground will be high and dry.

▶ Press down with your hands to compact soil around and over the roots.

▶ Make a watering basin. Mulch the ground around the plant and in the basin.

▶ If the tree does not already have a good branching habit, prune it immediately after planting: cut the tree to a height of 30 to 36 inches above ground. Remove most of the side branches (if present) except those needed for main-scaffold limbs. You can produce a low-branching tree by choosing to keep three low branches that are not exactly opposite one another.

▶ Water deeply by laying the hose on the ground and allowing water to trickle into the hole until it penetrates around the roots. In fast-draining sandy or decomposed granite soil, water often until the tree is established. If drainage is poor or if the soil is heavy clay, check once a week and water when the soil begins to dry out. Gradually lengthen the intervals between waterings.

ROSES

January is an important month for rose care: this is the time to choose and plant bare-root roses, prune and fertilize the ones you already have, and spray with dormant oil, if desired. (Some organic gardeners no longer use dormant spray.)

Why Organic Gardeners Feed Roses Now. Roses are gluttons for nutrients. They need nitrogen, phosphorus, and potassium, plus iron, magnesium, sulfur, and other minerals in smaller quantities. Gardeners who use synthetic rose fertilizers should never feed roses in January because all synthetic rose fertilizers contain strong forms of nitrogen that burn immature leaves. Organic rose foods are different. Though some generic fertilizers can burn—blood meal is a good example—most organic fertilizers need time to take effect. Thus, they need to be applied early in the season. Fertilize with organic fertilizers as soon as you finish pruning, but choose a day when the ground is damp, not bone dry. Don't dig fertilizers into the ground; digging around roses can harm the delicate feeder roots that are close to the surface. However, organic fertilizers need to make actual contact with the soil, so it's okay to scratch them lightly into the ground with a long-handled cultivator. (I personally don't do this, but many gardeners do.) Follow up by watering deeply and then cover the ground under each rose with a layer of organic mulch 2 to 3 inches thick. Use homemade compost, bagged or trucked organic soil amendment, or aged manure. (Bark pellets have no place in the organic garden; they subtract nitrogen from the soil in order to rot. Shredded bark is good for mulching paths and shrubberies but is not the best choice for mulching roses.)

Choose from Three Ways to Fertilize.

Throughout the monthly chapters, you'll find three ways of fertilizing roses from which you can choose. The first and easiest system is to purchase a ready-made organic rose food and immediately after pruning apply the amount per feeding recommended on the package. The second system for feeding roses is what I call the Rose-Pro Method. Based largely on the work of San Diego organic rosarian Jack Shoultz, it's outlined in a chart on pages 418–421. (Some gardeners photocopy this chart and hang it in their potting sheds.) The Rose-Pro Method uses a variety of organic commercial and generic products. It gives you a routine to follow, but some of the products called for

may be expensive. A third system for fertilizing roses is to create your own homemade combinations of generic products. You can use the Rose-Pro Method as a general guide but substitute generic products of your own choosing. This can save money but requires more thought. (For help, refer to the charts on generic fertilizers and soil amendments on pages 28–30. The monthly chapters also mention many options as we progress through the year.)

Using the Rose-Pro Method.

If you decide to fertilize your roses according to the Rose-Pro Method, wait until you've finished pruning all plants and cleaned up the soil under each rose. Then immediately after pruning, apply the following to the ground in the watering basin surrounding each rose: 2 tablespoons of John and Bob's Soil Optimizer, 2 cups Dr. Earth Organic 3 Rose & Flower Fertilizer (5-7-2) or another balanced organic rose fertilizer of your choice, and 2 cups Biosol Mix (7-2-3). (John and Bob's Soil Optimizer contains iron, calcium, and humic acid. Dr. Earth contains organic sources of nitrogen, potassium, and phosphorus plus soil microbes and mycorrhizae to release natural nutrients in soil. Biosol Mix is an organic dry fertilizer that provides slow-release nitrogen. It is made from fermented soybean meal, cottonseed meal, and sulfate of potassium mixed with the mineral bentonite. Humic acid is discussed and explained below.)

Using Free and Generic Fertilizers.

If your choice is generics, first consider free items. The best free soil amendment is your own homemade compost; it teems with microorganisms, and you can find many free ingredients to heat up the pile and increase its nutrient value. Most managers of health food stores and juice bars, for example, would rather save you a box of carrot, apple, and green vegetable fiber than throw it out. When you pick up your latte, bring home a bag of used coffee grounds for mulching acid-loving camellias, azaleas, and blue hydrangeas as well as roses to counteract our alkaline water. Supermarkets will save lettuce leaves and vegetable trimmings for composters. Among the most valuable and quick-acting free nitrogen sources are all the outdated fish and fresh fish trimmings tossed out daily by supermarkets, fish markets, and restaurants, which can be recycled straight into the earth. Just one dead fish placed under a rose at planting time can provide enough nitrogen, phosphorus and potassium for a year. It's the outdated, usually wasted stuff you want to get, not good fish. (I forgot to mention that in a lecture years ago, and one woman went out and bought swordfish steaks.)

Human hair is another nitrogen source that might sound a bit off-putting, but it's free for the asking at hairdressers and has been used for centuries as a slow-release nitrogen fertilizer. Similar in composition to gelatine (20-0-0), hair is mainly keratin. It decomposes quickly in moist soil and moist compost piles but, as Egyptian mummies demonstrate, slowly or never in dry soil. Some gardeners cut hair into short pieces and till it into garden soil prior to planting or bury it beside existing plants, such as roses. I know of a French gardener who buries a big handful of hair in the bottom of each planting hole in spring before planting tomatoes. Other than manure, that's the only fertilizer he uses. And don't ever throw out banana peels. Lay them under the mulch to provide calcium, magnesium, sulfur, potassium, phosphate, and silica. A word of warning, though: unless deeply buried, banana peels can attract raccoons and roof rats. Work a crowbar back and forth to make deep holes on the edge of the

watering basins without damaging rose roots, then stuff the banana peels down the holes and fill them with earth. Or chop and ferment the peels for a week in a jar of water and pour the solution over rose roots; this won't attract pests. Wood ashes from your fireplace are a potassium source, and charcoal absorbs nutrients and then doles them out slowly. Unfortunately, ash is highly alkaline, but it can be used in small quantities on fast-draining soils. (Charcoal and ash from barbecues should never be used; these can kill plants.)

Ada Perry's Magic Formula. Many years ago, the respected San Diego newspaper columnist Ada Perry invented a formula for feeding roses. Her mix contained generic fertilizers that can be bought in bulk. Rose lovers have used this homemade mix for many years. The original recipe calls for 1 cup gypsum, 1 cup Blood and Bone (no longer available), 1/4 cup soil sulfur, 2 tablespoons Iron Tonic (no longer available), and 1 tablespoon Epsom salts. It gave great results, especially if you added banana peels for potassium, needed by many Southern California soils. (An updated version of Ada Perry's Mix in the box on page 56 contains potassium as well as products available today.) Gardeners using generics could apply this formula twice a year, in January and June, and then feed with various forms of organic nitrogen in all other months through September. (Organic nitrogen sources are listed in the chart on pages 28–30.)

Apply Humic Acid. Humic acid is the best-kept secret of the gardening world, and a wonder-working organic fertilizer to apply to soil any time for remarkable results later on. It contains micronutrients, it frees up the nutrients in soil, promotes active roots, and

The Basic Categories of Roses

Hybrid teas are the most popular garden roses. They usually produce one flower per stem, on plants from 2 to 6 feet high. Grandifloras are bigger and taller, sometimes 8 to 10 feet high. Floribundas produce quantities of flowers in clusters on bushy plants that are usually shorter than hybrid teas. Polyanthas have smaller flowers than floribundas and are carried in larger bunches on many canes.

Climbing roses come in several types. Some, such as climbing "sports" (mutations exactly like the parent except for growth habit) of hybrid teas, are everblooming. Many old-fashioned climbing types bloom mainly in spring. Climbing roses send up long, bendy canes that usually don't end with a flower bud like standard roses; most of the flowers occur on side shoots that spring from the canes. Some types of climbers can be used as ground covers, and some can be grown as large freestanding shrubs, but most need support, such as a large tree, a fence, or an arbor. Pillar roses are similar to climbing roses. They have tall canes that are less bendy than those of climbing roses. They can be trained straight up a post or pillar or the corner of your house and will bloom all the way from the ground to the tops of their canes.

Miniature roses are natural dwarf versions of all the above types of roses. The only difference is that their canes, stems, flowers, and leaves are scaled down in size.

Heirloom old roses are favorites of the nineteenth and twentieth centuries prized for their hardiness, fragrance, romantic flower form, disease resistance, and rugged constitutions. Some old roses bloom only once a year; others repeat bloom. Species roses are those that were originally discovered in the same or similar form in the wild.

David Austin's English roses are an entirely new class of roses that combine the romantic flower form, fragrance, and other good qualities of old shrub roses with the bright colors and everblooming flowers of modern hybrids. Modern landscape roses, another somewhat vague category, include shrub roses, ground cover roses, and romantica roses. Romanticas, developed in the south of France by the House of Meilland (introduced here by Conard-Pyle Co.), blend the best qualities of old roses with those of modern ones. Romanticas have disease resistance and bright or unusual colors; several have compact growth habits that fit into small gardens. Flower carpet roses, developed by hybridizer Noack Rosen, are easy-care, disease-resistant, free-flowering ground covers or tree roses that require no fancy pruning.

improves overall plant health. Humic acid is a concentrated, dark-brown substance that technically could be extracted from compost or peat moss, but is usually derived from leonardite, a soft brown coal found in surface deposits in North Dakota, Utah, China, Russia, and many other places. Leonardite is made up of ancient terrestrial plant matter (with perhaps a few decomposed dinosaurs mixed in) and is composed of at least 85 percent humic acid. Though leonardite was discovered in 1919, the beneficial effects of humic acid on plants were discovered only in the 1960s, and it was only during the past fifteen years that products containing it have become readily available to gardeners and farmers. Today you can purchase humic acid in dry or liquid form, either pure and unadulterated or combined with other ingredients. When transplanting or planting, you might as well toss out the vitamin B1, long ago proven to be absolutely worthless, and use diluted humic acid instead. It's the best-ever planting fluid to stimulate roots.

Apply Earthworm Castings. A quart or two of earthworm castings per rose or earthworm-castings tea, applied before month's end, adds nutrients and microorganisms as well as repelling insect pests, including aphids and rose slugs. In interior zones, earthworm castings may dry out and harden like a cake in warm weather. If this happens, scratch or wash them into the ground, mix them with compost, or mix them with water and pour them over plant roots. (See the recipe for earthworm-castings tea on page 163.) Fertilizing with generics takes more thought and work, but often saves money. It also allows you to skip around and try various nutrients that benefit roses. Keep a notebook so you remember what you did and the results from year to year.

Ada Perry's Magic Formula (Updated)

1 cup mined gypsum
½ cup blood meal
½ cup fishbone meal
¼ cup soil sulfur
¼ cup Sul-Po-Mag (0-0-22)
2 tablespoons chelated iron, or iron sulfate
1 tablespoon Epsom salts

Multiply the amounts above by the number of roses to be fed. Wear gloves and a dust mask and mix all ingredients together. Feed 2½ cups of mix to each rose after January pruning. Repeat in June.

Select Bare-Root Roses. To get the best choice of rose varieties and plants, go to the nursery as soon as possible this month, but study a good handbook first. (Also see the lists on page 55.) Choose not only for color and fragrance, but also for basic categories of growth habit, disease resistance, vigor, and your climate zone. Some roses are more heat resistant than others. Roses with fewer petals generally do better along the coast than those with many, because there isn't enough heat for many-petaled roses to open completely. It's possible to save money by purchasing old varieties that are no longer patented, but it's not wise to skimp on grade, which is determined by law and labeled on each plant. Always buy No. 1 grade plants. They have more roots, bigger canes, and a better shape, so you end up with healthier and more vigorous plants.

Also consider water conservation. Limit the number of roses you plant to the amount of irrigation you'll be able to give them. Grow roses in a zone devoted to plants that have similar high requirements for water; don't put them close to drought-resistant plants. One way to irrigate roses is to provide a watering basin for each rose plant and flood it by means of bubblers (rather than sprayers) connected to a conventional irrigation system. Another way is to install a drip irrigation system with a header (main line) leading to each rose. Surround each plant with a circle 1 to 2 feet in diameter, depending on the size of the plant, of water-emitting hose, such as Drip-In, a $1/4$-inch soaker line. Place Drip-In on top of the ground but under the mulch. Drip-In won't clog when covered with mulch, but roots might invade it if you bury it in the ground. There is also a $1/2$-inch Drip-In Dripline that will deliver a larger volume of water in less

How to Plant a Bare-Root Rose

▸ Examine the roots. Prune off any broken or damaged portions. Then place them in a bucket of water to soak while you dig a hole.

▸ Choose a spot in full sun, and dig a hole approximately 1½ feet deep and 2 feet wide.

▸ Be sure to check the drainage (as described in the box on page 40), making sure it's adequate. It's possible to grow roses in red clay or adobe—they thrive in heavy soil—but they won't grow in a swamp.

▸ Unlike with trees, you need to amend the soil before planting roses because their root system is smaller. So unless your soil is superior loam, you'll need some good organic soil amendment, either a bagged commercial type or homemade compost, to mix with the earth you take from the planting hole. (Manure can be used as mulch but not in the hole.) Mix into the soil on the bottom of the hole: 1 cup fish-bone meal, steamed bone meal, or soft rock phosphate. Ensure it is right under the roots but does not touch them.

▸ Build a cone of mixed soil on the bottom of the hole, firming it with your hands. Set the plant on top, and spread the roots out over the cone. They shouldn't bend on the bottom of the hole. If they do, start over and dig deeper.

▸ Check your soil level with a stick. The bud union should end up 2 to 3 inches *above* ground level. Most roses do better with the bud union (that knob at the base of the plant) above ground, so don't bury it as they do in the East and Midwest. Plant high, because if you add mulch yearly, as you should, the bud union can get buried.

▸ Backfill the hole to the correct planting depth, firm the ground around the roots with your gloved hands, mulch the ground over the roots, and build a watering basin.

▸ Place the hose into the watering basin and let the water trickle in slowly to water the roots thoroughly. In fast-draining soil, water daily for the first three days and twice a week for the next three weeks. In moist, heavy soils, check the soil twice a week and water when needed. Thereafter apply adequate water—preferably by means of a drip system—to saturate the root zone once or twice a week, depending on the weather, your climate zone, and your soil.

time, but you may need to order it. For a hedge of roses, use one Drip-In line on each side of the hedge.

Prune the Roses You Already Have. Prune your rosebushes in January before new growth starts. (See the large box on pages 60–62 for directions.) Assemble your tools. You'll need pruning shears (the blade type that slices like scissors, not the snap-cut type that can squash the bark), long-handled shears, a keyhole saw, a pair of leather gloves, and some knee pads. You'll also need to know what kind of roses you've got.

DORMANT SPRAY

Dormant spray is any insect or disease-control spray, such as horticultural oil mixed with lime sulfur or fixed copper, that's applied in winter after a deciduous plant has gone dormant and dropped its leaves. (Deciduous plants are those that drop their leaves during dormancy. Many other plants, such as azaleas, are said to be dormant in winter even though they may not be deciduous. Don't spray these with dormant spray, since strong concentrations of oil sprays would damage the plants and burn their leaves.)

Using Dormant Sprays in the Organic Garden. Dormant sprays are used to control overwintering mites and insects, such as scale and certain caterpillars, by coating their bodies and suffocating them. When used appropriately, they are among the best, safest, and most effective of all pest-and-disease controls in the organic gardener's arsenal, but this doesn't keep them from being controversial with some organic gardeners. On the plus side, a dormant spray can stop pests and diseases in their tracks during winter, when there is no fruit on trees, and can do so without harming beneficials. On the negative side, you do need to take all precautions suggested on the label, but this is true of many botanical, nonsynthetic sprays as well, including neem oil and pyrethrins. Even if you are a dyed-in-the wool organic gardener, you probably should use dormant spray in winter on a few specific plants, especially to control peach leaf curl on peaches and nectarines ahead of the season.

Bonide Organic Lime Sulfur Spray is an example of a dormant spray approved for use by organic gardeners and farmers to kill overwintering pests as well as the spores of many fungi and diseases. Lime sulfur, made by boiling sulfur with hydrated lime, is one of the most time-honored controls for insects, fungi, and diseases on deciduous fruit trees, roses, berries, grapevines, and even some deciduous ornamental shade trees. It has largely replaced the older copper sprays, such as Bordeaux mix, which is made from copper sulfate and hydrated lime

and was first used in France in 1885 to control a disease decimating the vineyards. (Copper can build up in the soil and cause problems, so limit use of fixed copper sprays.) Most disease-resistant roses don't require dormant spray, but a few favorite, though troublesome, varieties could benefit from it, especially if you're aiming for exhibition blooms. (I no longer bother with dormant sprays myself, but at least one of my roses would be better off if I did.)

Substitutes for Dormant Sprays. Many organic gardeners claim their plants no longer need dormant sprays because soils rich in organic matter are filled with beneficial fungi and bacteria that destroy plant diseases. Agricultural scientists have now isolated some of these beneficial organisms and created biofungicides, extracts of the beneficial organisms in soil. Some, such as Serenade Garden Disease Control (*Bacillus subtilis*), control a wide range of plant diseases. Others control specific diseases: for example, AQ-10 (*Ampelomyces quisqualis*) controls powdery mildew. Rootshield (*Trichoderma harzianum*), SoilGard (*Gliocladium virens*), and Mycostop (*Streptomyces grisea-viridis*), used as drenches, control such problems as damping off, fusarium wilt, and seed, stem, and root rots. None of these products harms bees or beneficial insects. New biofungicides are being developed all the time, but home gardeners may have difficulty purchasing them. If so, try using organic products containing some of the same ingredients that might accomplish the similar results. For example, if you read the label on PROBIOTICS 4 Plants' Defensor Bacterial Inoculator, you will see that it contains *Bacillus subtilis* as well as *B. cereus*, two beneficial fungi known to attack or parasitize harmful fungi. The label suggests spraying a solution of it onto plants for the purpose of improving plant health. Gardeners have to read between the lines to guess that "improving plant health" may mean getting rid of fungus diseases. PROBIOTICS 4 Plants also makes Defensor Rhizo-Boost, Bacterial Inoculant BioStart, which provides naturally occurring beneficial microbes to enhance the biodiversity of garden soil. Use this one as a soil spray or drench to make plants more productive and healthier. Purchase these products when you need them, and use them right away, because live cultures don't live forever.

The Use of Horticultural Oils. The old, nonorganic way to apply lime sulfur in winter was to combine it with Volck Oil for a dual-pronged attack, smothering overwintering pests while controlling disease spores, but Volck is a petroleum product and thus not certified organic. "Summer oils" are lighter forms of horticultural oils suitable for year-round use, and these can be substituted for the stronger Volck. Vegol Year-Round Pesticidal Oil, for example, is an all-organic, biodegradable horticultural oil made from canola oil that has been heated to make it longer-lasting and more effective. If you decide to use a dormant spray, be sure to study the label directions carefully and use safety measures when handling it, including wearing protective clothes, boots, rubber gloves, and a mask.

Spray Peach and Nectarine Trees against Peach Leaf Curl. All conventional gardeners and many organic gardeners choose to use dormant spray on peach and nectarine trees to control peach leaf curl in winter after pruning. Dormant spray controls this disease in winter without damaging fruit or harming beneficials, which are less active in cool weather. Peach leaf curl is a fungal disease that thickens, curls, and reddens leaves in spring, especially in wet

> ✸ **QUICK TIP**
>
> **How to Keep Skunks out of Flowerbeds.**
> *Protect your spring bulbs and annual flowers from being crushed by skunks and other animals. Don't throw away the thorny canes you prune off climbing roses; bend them around the borders of your flowerbeds to make a low fence. Peg them in place with bent sections cut from coat hangers. The canes will soon be hidden by foliage and flowers, but skunks won't cross the thorny barrier.*

weather. It can kill whole shoots and branches of peach and nectarine trees and eventually may weaken and kill the tree. Despite the devastating consequences of this disease and its prevalence in mild climates, many organic gardeners claim that their trees no longer need dormant spray treatment because the bioorganisms that flourish in well-maintained organic soils keep plant diseases at bay. If you are new to organic gardening, it would be wise to continue dormant spray on these trees until you are confident in the disease-destroying capabilities of your soil. Spray your peach and nectarine trees with a product such as Bonide Organic Lime Sulfur Spray once after leaves fall in November or December and again in January before the buds begin to swell. As described above, you can mix lime sulfur spray with horticultural oil and smother overwintering pests at the same time. Organic gardeners also have other options, such as biofungicides and similar products that have already been discussed.

If you didn't spray in November or December, spray twice in January, once early in the month and again two weeks later. If you use lime sulfur and rain occurs within forty-eight hours, treat again. It's best not to spray if a heat

How to Prune a Rose

The Basic Principles

If you moved to Southern California from a cold-winter climate, forget what you may have learned there about rose pruning. In the East and Midwest, roses are pruned hard in fall—down to 12- or 18-inch stubs—so they'll survive the winter. Here, we should never shorten a healthy, productive cane. The more good wood left on the plant, the earlier it flowers and the longer it lives—so don't cut your plants way down. Try never to cut lower than your knee. Many of our roses can be left 4 feet tall after pruning, but the canes that remain should be thick and healthy ones. When making all cuts, in order to slice cleanly, put the blade of the pruner, rather than the anvil, next to the part of the plant that will remain. Cut closely above a promising outside bud, so new growth will point outward. Cut ¼ inch above the bud, or even closer if you can do so safely. Make sure you cut straight, not slanted. A sharp angle can dry out wood and kill the bud.

Bush Roses

▶ Start by removing all wood that is dead, damaged, or diseased.

▶ Remove all twiggy growth (smaller than the thickness of a pencil). It simply won't produce.

▶ Remove all old, spent canes. These are the ones that look tired and woody and produced nothing but spindly wood and inferior flowers last year. Get down on your knees and saw off the old canes right at the bud union—here's where your keyhole saw and knee pads come in handy. Saw off any old stubs, too. Sawing is not only easier than cutting, but also stimulates production of new canes. However, if you have a great many roses and not much strength, it's better to use a ratchet-type pruner than to not take off old stubs and canes. (Ratchet-type pruners are long-handled blade-cut pruners with a built-in ratchet device that makes it easy to cut through thick hardwood branches.)

▶ Leave all the good, strong canes in place, at least four or five per plant (five to seven for plants over five years old; more for some floribundas).

▶ For all bush roses, remove all branches that cross. Try to open up the centers so each plant takes the shape of a vase. In interior valleys, it's a good idea to leave a few branches that cross the center in order to provide shade, but gardeners elsewhere should cut off all branches that cross the center.

▶ For floribundas, cut out the center branch from each cluster of branches, and cut the other ones back to three or four eyes (undeveloped buds). On floribundas, leave more twiggy growth—you can even use hedge shears on them to get the right shape.

▶ For tree roses, cut back the branches to between 1 foot and 18 inches in length, depending on the age of the rose. (As tree roses age, leave their branches longer.) Remove all sprouts arising from the roots or trunk. Aim for symmetry: a rounded bush on top of the upright trunk.

▶ Miniature roses resemble large roses in every way except size, so for these follow the instructions for full-sized roses but scale down proportionally. Shape ground-cover types with hedge shears.

How to Prune a Rose (continued)

▶ For full-size roses, remove about one-third of all growth that was new last year, but don't cut into any new growth that's thicker than your thumb.

▶ For English roses and old roses, during the first two years after planting, remove dead wood and leaves only. Allow the shrub to build its size and strength with no pruning until it is three years old. As the rose matures, remove enough old growth to keep the plant producing young and vigorous growth. Prune Romanticas like floribundas or hybrid teas according to the growth habit of each rose. Prune Flower Carpet roses by simply shearing off one-third of their growth.

Remove the Suckers. Suckers on roses are canes that spring from below the bud union. Instead of growing from the bud union like the canes of the variety you want, they grow from the rootstock. Suckers are usually easy to recognize because they're thinner and more prickly than the canes that arise from the bud union, and their leaves are usually smaller and shaped differently from the other leaves on the plant. If allowed to persist, they'll sap strength from your varietal rose.

Suckers are easiest to reach after the major pruning is complete. The best way to get rid of one is to grasp it firmly with a gloved hand, work it back and forth and around and around to loosen it, then pull it off with a mighty yank. If you can manage this, you'll get the bud cells along with the stalk, but if instead you cut it off, two or three more suckers are likely to spring from the same spot.

Let Them Stand Tall. Finish the major pruning by cutting the tops of the canes so they're roughly equal in height. If any leaves remain on your plants when you are through pruning, clip—don't pull—them off. Removing the leaves prevents the buildup of disease.

After pruning:

▶ Your hybrid teas should stand 2 to 3 feet tall.

▶ Grandifloras should be approximately 4 feet tall.

▶ Floribundas and polyanthas should end up about knee-high, with a round, bushy shape.

▶ Miniature roses should be between 6 inches and 3 feet tall, depending on their age and variety.

▶ Old roses, English roses, and shrub roses vary greatly in height and size. Never cut old roses and English roses short; they may never recover.

Finish Up. Some gardeners paint all cuts made on the bud union with white glue. This is an unnecessary step, since if the cuts are made properly, they will heal naturally. Whatever you do, don't use a pruning compound, since this can prevent the development of buds on the bud union from which arise new canes.

Clean up the ground under and around the plants. Destroy all leaves and debris. Then mulch under your plants with steer manure or—better yet—compost. Follow up with a dormant spray (as discussed on page 57), such as Bonide Organic Lime Sulfur Spray. Wait until new growth unfurls and turns from red to green before feeding with a fertilizer containing nitrogen.

Climbing and Pillar Roses

Young climbing roses (particularly those less than two years old) should be pruned little or not at all. Do prune all everblooming climbing roses that are more than three years old now.

Climbers that bloom only once a year should be pruned when they finish blooming, but if this task was neglected, old spent canes and all sucker growth should be removed now. Clean up and apply

continued . . .

How to Prune a Rose (continued)

dormant spray to those that drop their leaves in winter. (Before spraying, clip off any leaves that remain except from species roses that are evergreen in mild climates, such as Lady Banks' rose *[Rosa banksiae]*. Do not prune these now; see page 188.)

Climbers that are arranged sideways on arbors and fences and espaliered on walls can bloom for many years on the same old canes. If this is the method you choose, be sure to remove unwanted canes as they arise throughout the year. Eventually, if the roses decline in vigor, allow new canes to grow and replace the old ones. With pillar roses, it's better to cut out one or two old woody canes yearly and allow new, vigorous canes to replace them.

Here's the procedure:

▸ Remove all dead or twiggy growth extending from the bud union.

▸ Leave all good, well-placed canes on the plant.

▸ Remove any suckers that arise from below the bud union.

▸ Cut back all laterals (side branches) to two or three buds each.

▸ Clip off all remaining leaves. (In cold climates, rose leaves fall in winter. Here, we often have to defoliate most or all by hand.)

▸ Untie the rose and reposition it on its support. Climbing roses bloom mainly on laterals that spring from the canes. In order to encourage them to put out more laterals and thus to bloom more, train the canes as horizontally as possible, either onto a fence, into an existing tree, over an arbor, espaliered on a wall, or with the tips of the canes pegged to the ground, giving the plant the shape of a fountain. Pillar roses are an exception. You can tie all the canes of a good pillar rose in a vertical position, onto a post, say, or the corner of your house, and it will bloom massively all the way from the ground to the top of its canes.

▸ Clean up and mulch the ground, and follow up with a dormant spray, such as Bonide Organic Lime Sulfur Spray and horticultural oil, if desired.

wave is expected, because if temperatures rise above 90°F soon after treatment, lime sulfur may injure buds. Use a proper sprayer—one that allows you to aim the spray onto the tree rather than broadcasting it into the air—and go over the tree carefully, reaching all parts (see page 382).

Dormant Spray for Sycamore Trees. Sycamore trees (*Platanus* species) are hosts to a flock of pests and diseases, among which sycamore scale (*Stomacoccus platani*) is one of the

worst. Sycamore scales overwinter on bark as eggs, then in spring attach themselves to the undersides of leaves and suck out plant juices. This creates yellow spots that eventually turn brown and cause leaves to drop prematurely. The scales also feed on young twigs and limbs, causing dieback and weakening the tree.

To find out whether your tree suffers from scale, look for cottony white masses of material bulging from cracks and crevices in the bark. This cottony substance protects overwintering eggs. Affected trees may be thoroughly sprayed now with a high-volume, high-pressure spray in order to get rid of the eggs. It's best to hire a reputable company with professional equipment to do this job. The procedure is to use dormant oil at the rate of 2 gallons of oil to 98 gallons of water, with a wetting agent (surfactant) also mixed into the spray. Make sure all precautions are followed during the spraying, and finish by cleaning up fallen leaves, twigs, and debris. (See page 87 for more about sycamores.)

CITRUS TREES

Start Fertilizing Citrus in Coastal Zones. If you live in a coastal zone, January is the time to start feeding your citrus trees. (See the box on page 64 for directions.) By fertilizing your trees now, you'll promote more blossoms in February and thus a more abundant crop. If you live in an interior zone where frosts continue through February and sometimes into March, don't start feeding your citrus trees until March. Feeding too early might encourage a flush of growth that could be damaged by frost.

Citrus trees are heavy feeders. It is often said that a mature tree growing in clay soil needs 1 pound of actual nitrogen per year, but the main task of organic gardeners is to build the humus content of soil by regularly adding organic soil amendments, such as compost, and other organic materials, including humic acid. This process alone will result in nitrogen being released to citrus roots as an effect of the microbial and mycchorizal (fungal) activity in soil. There is no way for the organic gardener to measure the amount of nitrogen created in this way. The proof is seen in the results. That said, citrus trees are heavy feeders, and their main need is nitrogen, but they also require phosphorus, potassium, and secondary nutrients,

especially iron, as well as trace minerals, including zinc. Citrus trees bloom in February, so you need to begin this month to feed citrus with an organic fertilizer recommended for citrus or with a mix of your own devising, as is suggested below.

Feeding Citrus with Generic Organic Fertilizers. Here is an example of how you could feed citrus organically using generic fertilizers: Choose a day early in the month after a rain or after an irrigation and begin by sprinkling mined gypsum over the ground, using enough to make it look as if a light snow had fallen; scratch it in and then apply chelated iron according to package directions. Give each mature tree 2 cups of fishbone meal or steamed bone meal (or another source of phosphorus) and 1 cup of Sul-Po-Mag (0-0-22) or another source of potassium. (You can omit this step for trees growing in decomposed granite, since they most likely have all the phosphorus and potassium they need.) During the last week of the month, give each mature tree 2 cups of blood meal or another nitrogen source of your choice. (Adjust the quantities of the material used according to the amount of nitrogen it contains. Several pounds of chicken manure, for example, are needed to yield the same amount of nitrogen as 2 cups of blood meal.) Sprinkle the nutrients over the ground beginning 1 or 2 feet away from the trunk and ending just beyond the drip line (the edge of the canopy.) All this is a lot of work, but some gardeners do it. Others simply mulch their trees with horse manure once a year in October or November, after the first rains, and that's the end of it. By spring the trees have everything they need.

But if you are applying the fertilizers as described above, be sure to cover the ground over the fertilizer and under the tree canopy with a layer of organic amendment, such as homemade, bagged, or trucked compost and follow up with a deep irrigation. Mulch can reduce weeds and maintain moisture. Begin the layer of mulch 2 to 3 feet away from the trunk so that the trunk itself stays high and dry. The suggestions above regarding the amounts of fertilizers are for mature, full-sized trees; younger trees and dwarf trees need proportionally less. A week after applying the fertilizers, drench the ground with a solution of humic acid mixed according to package directions. Continue to feed citrus every two months through July, as described in the accompanying box.

⚙ **QUICK TIP**

How to Keep Mulch and Water Away from the Trunk of a Citrus Tree. *Cut the bottom out of a 5-gallon plastic plant container. Use a can cutter to make a slit up the side. Slip the container upside down around the trunk, with the slit side facing away from the water source. The container will keep the trunk high and dry.*

Correct Chlorosis. As mentioned above, give iron and zinc to citrus trees now if they show signs of chlorosis (iron deficiency). Plants suffering from chlorosis have light-green leaves with dark-green veins. Don't use iron sulfate. It can't be absorbed by the tree because it combines with minerals in the soil and becomes insoluble. Get the chelated kind that's combined with zinc. Apply it, according to package directions, evenly to the ground around the tree, with the fertilizer. For faster results, purchase a product for foliar application and spray it onto your tree. Overwatering can cause chlorosis, so proper irrigation is often the best treatment.

How to Fertilize Citrus Trees

▸ Determine how much fertilizer a tree will need during the year and divide this quantity by the number of applications you want to make during the year.

▸ Measure the amount of commercial, organic, citrus food, or generic fertilizers needed for one application into a small paint bucket. (See page 82.) When using generic fertilizers, wear a dust mask and mix them together in the bucket.

▸ Scatter the contents of the bucket evenly on the ground in a 3- to 4-foot-wide, doughnut-shaped band centered under the drip line (an imaginary line directly under the branch tips). The main feeder roots of a mature citrus are in the top 2 feet of soil, beginning 2 to 3 feet from the trunk and extending out twice as far as the drip line. You can, if you wish, distribute the fertilizer over this entire area.

▸ Water the fertilizer deeply into the ground right away. (Don't work it into the soil.)

Irrigate Citrus. Water mature citrus deeply and infrequently—perhaps once every two or three weeks depending on the weather and your soil type and drainage—rather than shallowly and often. Frequent shallow watering can harm citrus; it encourages shallow rooting and causes root and trunk rot.

Make sure sprinklers don't hit the trunk of any citrus tree. A wet trunk can lead to gummosis (oozing sap and sunken lesions on the trunk, caused by fungal disease). (See the Quick Tip, at left.) The **Rule of Thumb** for watering citrus: *Apply water so it sinks into the ground* *around the tree in a broad doughnut-shaped band beginning one-third of the distance from the trunk to the drip line and extending an equal distance beyond the drip line.* The ground next to the trunk of the tree should be kept high and dry, with no soil pushed up against the trunk. If water is collecting in the wrong places, build a wide double-walled watering basin around the tree at the drip line to keep the irrigation water there and away from the trunk.

Control Citrus Pests. Check trees for insect and disease damage (as described on page 45). Be on the lookout for snails. In inland valleys, snails often spend the winter snuggled together in the crotches of orange trees. You can clean your entire tree of snails now by picking them off, tying them into a plastic bag, and tossing them into the trash. Once snails have been removed, clip off bottom leaves that brush the ground. Some gardeners find that surrounding the trunk of each tree with a copper band prevents snails from crawling back up it. (These and other snail and slug controls are discussed on page 115.)

CAMELLIAS AND AZALEAS

Select and Plant Good Varieties. Camellias and azaleas are two of our most prized plants for permanent winter color in semishade. Both camellias and azaleas have a long bloom cycle that starts in fall and lasts through spring, but not all varieties flower at the same time. Some varieties may open as early as October; others don't flower until April or May.

As a general rule, you can safely plant any camellia or azalea during a cool winter month, including this one (see the box on page 66 for directions). But the best time to plant them is while they're actually bearing flowers. This is because the roots and branches of camellias and azaleas rest rather than grow during their bloom cycle, and the minute they finish blooming they start a spurt of growth. If you plant them while they're in bloom, they get off to a good start; planting later disturbs roots and interferes with normal development.

When you shop for azaleas, don't just fall for a pretty face; select good varieties. To find them, refer to lists in the *Sunset Western Garden Book* and ask experts for recommendations. Belgian indicas, developed for florists, are often difficult to grow. 'Alaska', 'Phoenicia', and 'Formosa' are easy for beginners. (The last two, sometimes taken to be identical, are not the same. 'Formosa' has larger leaves and is often used as understock.) Don't be misled by the term "sun azalea." These varieties can take more sun and interior heat than most azaleas, but they will die if you put them in full sun. The exception is in the fog belt along the coast. Some camellia and azalea varieties can stand full sun along the coast if grown in the ground, not in pots.

☼ QUICK TIP

Prune Camellias as You Pick Them. *Whenever you leave the house, break off a few blossoms, each with a short piece of stem and a few leaves. Give them to whomever you meet at work, the bank, the store—you name it. It's all the pruning most camellias need.*

Protect Camellias from Petal Blight. Pick up dead and fallen petals and flowers from camellias, daily if possible, in order to prevent petal blight. Petal blight is a fungal disease that causes brown, discolored, rotting blooms—not

How to Plant Camellias and Azaleas

▸ Choose an area in semishade. Most camellias and azaleas need some sun in order to bloom. Morning or evening sun is best—not midday. Good spots are in dappled light under lath, shade cloth, or an open tree, or to the north of a house, hedge, or wall.

▸ Choose an area with good drainage, especially for azaleas. If you don't have such an area, use raised beds or tubs filled with an acid-type potting mix.

▸ Dig a planting hole one and a half times as deep and twice as wide as the root ball.

▸ Amend the soil removed from the hole by mixing it with one-half acid-type soil amendment, such as commercial camellia-azalea mix, or leaf mold.

▸ Slide the shrub out of the container and plant it high. Camellias and azaleas can't stand to have soil collecting around their trunks. Measure the height of the root ball and the depth of the hole. Add as much amended soil as needed to bring the top of the original root ball 2 to 3 inches higher than the surrounding soil.

▸ Gently lift the plant into the hole, position it with the best side to the front, and backfill the hole with amended topsoil.

▸ Use your hands to press the soil mix firmly around and over the roots.

▸ Form a watering basin, and cover the entire bed with an acid mulch, such as 2 to 3 inches of pine needles.

▸ Place the hose, running gently, into the watering basin and allow the water to thoroughly penetrate the root ball and the surrounding ground while you go on to the next plant.

▸ Water daily for the first three days and frequently thereafter until the plants are established. Then lengthen the periods between irrigations.

just at the petal tips, as can be caused by wind or rain, but brown to the center. Blighted

 QUICK TIP

A Time-Saving Way to Foil Petal Blight. *Cut shade cloth in circles, with a hole in the center and a slit from the outside of the circle to the center hole. Place under potted or ground-grown camellias during the flowering season. When blossoms fall, pull out the fabric, shake it into a waiting trash can, and replace it under the bush.*

blossoms that fall to the ground permit the fungus to live and reproduce in the soil for years. Spores can be carried by the wind from nearby gardens.

Cleanliness is the best way to avoid petal blight, but if you're troubled with a serious outbreak, spray with the biofungicide Serenade, which does not harm bees or other beneficials. (Follow package directions.) Add a spreader-sticker such as Spraymate, according to package directions, when you mix the spray. (A spreader-sticker is an additive that decreases surface tension of water, making sprays cover plant surfaces more evenly and effectively.)

Protect Azaleas from Petal Blight. Petal blight also attacks azaleas. To control it, remove dead and brown blossoms—and while you're about it, snap off the little seed capsule inside each flower with your thumbnail rather than leaving it on the plant. Long-blooming varieties, such as 'Alaska', 'California Sunset', and 'Nuccio's Happy Days', will be stimulated to produce even more flowers.

WATERING

It's tempting to neglect watering chores when the weather's cool and plants aren't growing, but properly irrigated plants stand up better to frost than plants with dry roots. Even when it rains, don't forget those specimens under the eaves that aren't getting a drop. Many a poor camellia or tree fern has died an untimely death just because the gardener forgot that no winter rains could reach them.

COPING WITH FROST

Move Container Plants to Safety. Many a balmy December is followed by a sudden cold snap in January. Protect tender container-grown plants such as impatiens, fuchsias, and cymbidiums from frost by moving them under the eaves of your house or beneath a sheltering tree. Injury is more likely for plants exposed to open sky. Cold air can often be trapped in an atrium or a courtyard surrounded by walls, or even hedges, and can build up like water in a swimming pool. So don't choose these spots for sheltering treasured tropicals. Move them to places from which cold air can escape.

Cover Plants in the Ground. Protect tender plants growing in the ground, such as agaves, aloes, Natal plum *(Carissa macrocarpa)*, bougainvillea, and cineraria, by throwing old sheets, towels, canvas dropcloths, car covers, or cardboard boxes over the plants. In interior zones, use tall pea stakes (as described on page 354) or hoops of heavy-gauge wire to support cloth above the plants, since the fabric may sometimes become cold enough to damage the foliage it touches. Dash out first thing in the morning and uncover the plants before sun strikes. Heat builds up quickly under covers and can burn foliage as badly as frost.

Don't Prune Off Frost Damage. If, despite all your care, some tropicals are damaged by cold, resist the urge to prune off the unsightly dead parts. The frost-burned portions will protect the rest of the plant. Removing frost-burned leaves and twigs now can be disastrous, causing the plant to grow and then be hit again, worse than ever, if more cold follows. So hold off until the weather warms up and all danger of frost has passed. (Then, you may find plants not as badly damaged as you think.) The **Rule of Thumb:** *Wait until you see signs of regrowth before cutting off frost-damaged growth.* Large branches may not recover until summer.

EPIPHYLLUMS

Start feeding epiphyllums (orchid cacti) phosphorus and potassium to encourage spring and early summer bloom. Begin now by using a liquid organic bloom fertilizer, such as Meta-naturals (1-5-5) Organic Bloom Fertilizer, and feed every two weeks until plants bloom. Or if you prefer to feed with generics, you could, for example, give each 1-gallon plant 1 tablespoon of fishbone meal or steamed bone meal and 1 teaspoon Sul-Po-Mag (0-0-22) or soft rock phosphate and water into the soil mix. For hanging baskets, use 1 tablespoon of each. (One feeding with these generic bloom ingredients should provide adequate amounts for the year. Drenching with humic acid or adding 1 teaspoon of John and Bob's Soil Optimizer to a 1-gallon-size plant, or 1 tablespoon to a hanging basket, will green up the plant and make the fertilizers even more effective.) Even if you've neglected them and they look scruffy, don't feed with higher than 2 percent nitrogen now or you'll trigger growth instead of flowers.

Don't prune epiphyllums until after the bloom cycle. It's all right to cut off badly diseased or rotted branches, but like excess nitrogen, extensive pruning will make your plants grow rather than bloom. Plants should have some sun now, not solid shade.

CYMBIDIUMS

Purchase cymbidium orchids now, while they're in bloom. Most cymbidiums sold by supermarkets are growers' discards with ordinary colors and too few flowers per spike, but you can find outstanding varieties with superior colors and many blooms per spike at specialty nurseries, orchid clubs, plant shows, or even small mom-and-pop growers at outdoor markets. (What you buy is what you get. Proper fertilizing and care can increase the number of spikes, but not the number of flowers per spike of a particular variety.) Continue to feed cymbidiums with a balanced fertilizer high in bloom ingredients but containing some nitrogen for growth; for example, use AgSafe (6-30-30) or make your own mix. (Since cymbidiums

grow year-round, they need some nitrogen even during the bloom season.) Stake bloom spikes, and protect the plants from snails and slugs. Once blooms open, stop feeding the plants but keep them well watered. Put blooming plants in a cool, shady spot to lengthen flower life.

Enjoy some cymbidiums in the house, too, but don't let them sit in puddles. Put gravel in plant saucers and cachepots to hold roots safely above water that drains out the bottoms of the pots. (For more on cymbidium care and characteristics, see pages 179 and 318.)

COLOR FROM PERMANENT PLANTS

A well-planted garden in our area can have perennial color year-round. If your garden needs some pepping up, consider adding one or more of the following January-blooming plants. Among drought-tolerant plants that give color now are many named varieties of New Zealand tea tree (*Leptospermum scoparium*), Bailey acacia (*Acacia baileyana*), Kaffirboom coral tree (*Erythrina caffra*), and many species of aloe. By choosing aloes with care, you can have varieties in bloom any month of the year, but most of the aloes we grow here are from South Africa, so they flower in winter, a time when the insects that pollinate them are most active.

Less drought resistant but still beautiful are deciduous magnolias, such as saucer magnolia (*Magnolia soulangiana*) and star magnolia (*M. stellata*). These trees stay small for a long time and are good in flower and bulb beds, entryways, and small-space gardens, against a dark wall, and in Oriental gardens. A striking shrub for winter bloom is the pink powder puff (*Calliandra haematocephala*), at its best espaliered on a sunny wall. Marmalade bush

(*Streptosolen jamesonii*) needs plenty of water but gives bright-orange bloom at this time of year in frost-free zones. (It's lovely when planted above a retaining wall and allowed to cascade down it.) Outstanding choices for purple bloom are the drought-resistant vine *Hardenbergia violacea* 'Happy Wanderer' and the Brazilian shrub called princess flower (*Tibouchina urvilleana*). The trick with princess flower is to plant it in acid soil and give it acid fertilizer and ample water. *T. heteromalla* is 3 feet tall and easier to grow with ordinary soil and watering. It bears spectacular 18-inch-long clusters of flowers on branch tips and looks good near swimming pools.

ANNUAL AND PERENNIAL FLOWERS

Mulch, Cut Back—Perhaps Even Plant—Perennials. Perennials are working on their roots in winter; those you planted in fall are getting established now. Fix up the soil by adding a mulch before the tops start growing and spread out to cover the ground. Continue to deadhead plants such as pentas that may bloom year-round. Cut back to the ground, or almost to the ground, plants that bloomed in fall and winter, such as Japanese anemones (*Anemone japonica*), perennial marigold (*Tagetes lemmonii*), perennial asters, and Russian sage (*Perovskia* 'Blue Spire'). Trim back the woody branches of yellow flax (*Reinwardtia indica*) that have bloomed; it will keep putting out its golden, trumpet-shaped flowers into March. If you haven't cut back fringe flower (*Hypoestes aristata* 'Lavender Cloud') do it now; cut stems that have bloomed to 16 inches. Young buddleias can be cut almost to the ground, but old woody ones will probably die if you cut them too short. Wait until they sprout new growth,

then cut off the old wood just above strong new sprouts. This keeps buddleias from becoming leggy. Some plants, such as Mexican sage (*Salvia leucantha*), make *basal foliage* (new foliage sprouting from the plant's base). Once the fresh basal growth is 8 to 12 inches tall, it is safe to cut off all the tall, old woody growth in order to renew the plant. When you see bushy basal growth on *Verbena bonariensis*, for example, you can cut off the old woody growth above it and leave the fresh basal foliage to make a new plant. Common sneezeweed (*Helenium autumnale*), false dragonhead (*Physostegia virginiana*), veronica, gayfeather (*Liatris*), balloon flower (*Platycodon grandiflorus*), and California fuchsias (*Zauschneria*) are among other perennials and subshrubs that can be cut back to the ground or nearly to the ground now. The easiest way to attack mounds of Santa Barbara daisy (*Erigeron karvinskianus*), Mexican evening primrose (*Oenothera berlandieri*), and botanical geraniums, including *G. sanguineum*, is with hedge shears. Shear lavender into nice rounded forms now in January, and you won't interfere with its spring bloom.

All this cutting will leave plenty of bare spaces to mulch. Maybe you can even add a few new varieties. So if you're just dying to visit nurseries to see what they've got, there's no need to resist. But what perennials to plant now? The answer is simple: whatever you find.

Plant Cool-Season Annual Flowers. If you planted winter and spring bedding flowers in September and October, you can congratulate yourself now because many should be flowering, especially in coastal zones. But in January nurseries are brimming with cool-season flowers (annual and perennial bedding plants that bloom in winter) already in bloom. These include foxgloves (*Digitalis*), cyclamen,

English primroses, malacoides or fairy primroses, obconica primroses, calendulas, pansies, Johnny-jump-ups and other violas, stock, and snapdragons. So if you didn't plant earlier and your flowerbeds and pots need sprucing up, or if you have bare patches in your beds, use nursery transplants to fill them with instant color.

Fertilize Cool-Season Flowers. The trick with cool-season flowers, other than wildflowers, is to give them plenty of nitrogen for strong growth, as well as high phosphorus for bloom and some potassium for general plant health. The reason for the extra nitrogen is that it tends to leach from the soil during the rainy season. Also, fungi and bacteria in the soil are less active in cooler weather, so nutrients are not released as quickly from organic matter. This is especially true of plants growing in containers. (In general, use liquid or slow-release fertilizers for winter flowers in containers, and pellet, powdered, or granulated fertilizers for plants in the ground.)

Feed Cineraria. Continue to feed cineraria (*Senecio x hybridus*) weekly for growth with an organic liquid fertilizer high in growth ingredients, such as fish emulsion, but begin in January to fertilize with an organic high-bloom fertilizer to stimulate the growth of buds in preparation for February bloom. Tiger Bloom (2-8-4), for example, is a fast-acting organic fertilizer that stimulates flowers and can be used toward month's end as buds are forming. When using a slower-acting bloom formula, either your own mix or a commercial preparation, begin to apply it earlier so it has time to take effect. At the beginning of the month, sprinkle 1 tablespoon earthworm castings into each 1-gallon pot or sprinkle a handful on top of the ground around each plant to ward off leaf miners. Organic sprays against leaf miner include pyrethrum.

(Pyola Insect Spray is one such product. Follow package directions and warnings.)

Should You Plant Seeds? January isn't one of the best times to plant seeds, but that doesn't mean it's impossible. Seeds of California poppies (*Eschscholzia californica*), lupines, and other wildflowers, gaillardia, clarkia, godetia, and sweet alyssum (*Lobularia maritima*) will sprout and grow if sprinkled onto well-prepared ground and raked in prior to rain. It's better, however, to plant wildflowers in fall (as described on pages 354 and 355–356). (When rains aren't adequate, water seeded areas daily to keep them damp.)

CORAL TREES

Prune Naked Coral Trees. The naked coral tree (*Erythrina coralloides*) is one of the best coral trees for local gardens in Zones 21 to 24. Though slower to start, it's a much better choice for home gardens than Kaffirboom coral tree (*Erythrina caffra*). It blooms spectacularly in spring on tip growth. Once a tree has become established, prune it judiciously in January (heavily, when specimens get out of hand), during its brief dormancy, in order to bring out its artistically bizarre shape and stop it from becoming a tangled mess. Cut out branches that cross. Control size by cutting out unwanted branches. A word of caution: Don't whack off all the tip growth or you'll lose all the flowers.

Don't Prune Kaffirboom Coral Trees Now. Many Kaffirboom coral trees are pollarded in winter—all branches are cut back so hard that only stubs are left at the top of a bare trunk. Pollarding coral trees permanently ruins their shape, makes them subject to rot, and prevents them from ever blooming. Prune Kaffirboom coral trees, if necessary, by thinning out a few unwanted branches back to a main scaffold branch or trunk while leaving all desired growth in place, and do the job after rather than before bloom.

Kaffirboom coral trees eventually become giants, 30 feet high and 40 feet wide. Plant them in places where they'll have room to grow to full size, and don't plant them on lawns. The frequent watering lawns need is bad for Kaffirboom coral trees; it causes overly rapid growth with dangerously brittle, top-heavy branches. Most coral trees do better and bloom more beautifully when subjected to benign neglect once they are established. When winter rains are adequate, and depending on the soil, mature trees in coastal zones can often go without irrigation until late summer before showing stress and needing a deep application of water.

JOBS FOR A COLD OR RAINY DAY

Start a Garden Notebook. If you don't know much about gardening, keep a notebook to help yourself learn. If you're a seasoned gardener, keeping notes can help you remember things you'd otherwise forget. There are several printed gardening diaries on the market, but any notebook or calendar will do as long as there's plenty of room to write.

Clean Out the Potting Shed. Another good task for a rainy day is to clean out the potting shed or tool shed, if you have one. If you don't, this is a good time to consider building one and getting the messy accumulation of garden supplies and equipment out of the garage. A serviceable shed for supplies and tools can often

do more to promote domestic harmony than flocks of psychiatrists.

Order Seeds from Catalogs. Most seed catalogs arrive in January. (See the list of seed and plant sources on pages 416–417.) Order now so you'll have the seeds in time for spring planting. If you've ever gardened in a cold-winter climate, you probably remember the joy and temptations of poring over a seed catalog on a snowy day.

The danger of ordering from catalogs when you live in Southern California is ordering not only too much but also the wrong items for our climate zones. Check all new-to-you ornamentals by looking them up in the encyclopedia section of the *Sunset Western Garden Book* so you won't be disappointed by trying to grow something that isn't suited to your climate zone or that needs to go through a freezing winter in order to perform.

The plus side of catalog buying is that you can sometimes find rare items that aren't locally available. If you care about color schemes and don't always want a mixed packet, you can get flowers in specific colors. Many gardeners order vegetable seeds because they enjoy growing gourmet varieties that they can't buy in the grocery store. Don't forget to add a package of nitrogen-fixing bacteria, such as Legume-Aid, to your order. If you plan to plant beans in March, you'll need this product, which usually isn't available in local nurseries (see page 137).

Studying seed catalogs can help beginners learn about annuals and vegetables, but be forewarned: many cool-season plants and flowers that are planted in early spring in the East are planted in fall here. When you live in Southern California, you should think ahead and order seed for fall planting now along with the seed for spring. (Keep the seed cool and dry during the summer.) Or, if you prefer, order from catalogs again in summer for fall planting, though by then some items may be sold out.

LAWN CARE

Cool-Season Lawns. Cool-season lawns, such as bluegrass, tall fescue, and ryegrass, are at their best now, so keep mowing them regularly and feeding them, at intervals of one month to six weeks, with an organic lawn fertilizer or with other products as directed. (Bluegrass unmixed with other grasses is a poor choice for Southern California, but some such lawns survive from an earlier era.) Water all cool-season lawns when rains aren't adequate.

One of the most positive steps you can take toward the well-being of our environment is to reduce the size of your lawn and stop feeding it with synthetic fertilizers and chemicals. Switch now in January to an all-organic system. Begin by raising the level of your mower blades to the top setting. Mow often, keep the mower blades sharp, and if possible cut the grass on a dry, sunny day, leaving the grass tall and allowing the clippings to remain where they fall. The clippings will return quick-acting organic nitrogen to the soil from which they came and build the humus content of the ground. A mulching lawn mower can help by chopping up the clippings and distributing them evenly so they can dry quickly and sift to the ground.

A healthy, well-fed lawn is resistant to disease. If you notice unsightly red-brown pigment on grass leaves plus red dust on your feet after walking across your lawn, it's suffering from rust. This is a sign it needs feeding. You don't need to spray—just fertilize with nitrogen and mow regularly to remove the older, infected portion of the grass blades. The rust will disappear and the lawn will green up like magic.

Feed Cool-Season Lawns. Fertilize cool-season grasses such as tall fescue and ryegrass with a quality organic lawn fertilizer. There are many brands to choose from, including Ringer All Natural Lawn Restore (10-2-6), which gives outstanding results but contains feather meal, which may attract animals; Agrowinn-All-Natural Organic Lawn Food (5-3-4), made in Southern California; or Safer Brand Lawn Fertilizer (8-1-1). Alternatively, by studying their ingredients, you could devise your own mix. For example, alfalfa powder or pellets won't burn but can provide a lawn with almost all nutritional needs. (Alfalfa may attract rabbits and other animals until it's washed into the ground.) Aged chicken manure, available bagged, contains phosphorus and potassium as well as nitrogen and makes an excellent and inexpensive organic lawn fertilizer without attracting animals. Apply it when the ground is moist but grass blades are dry, and follow up with deep irrigation. Cockadoodle Doo Lawn and Garden Fertilizer and Jong's GroBetter All Purpose Organic Fertilizer (2-4-3) are pelletized and easier to apply but more expensive. All nitrogen fertilizers are slower acting in winter, so it may take a few weeks before you can see the results. Treating the lawn with humic acid in solid or liquid form at month's end will help by improving the efficiency of fertilizers, and in the long run will produce a healthier, more disease-resistant lawn. Many types are available, both liquid and solid, some of which are combined with other ingredients, such as kelp for soil conditioning and *Yucca schidigera* to enhance water penetration.

Warm-Season Lawns. Warm-season grasses, such as Bermuda, St. Augustine, 'Adalayd' (seashore paspalum), and zoysia, are dormant now. They need no feeding or mowing. ('Adalayd' may continue to grow in areas along the coast; if so, mow it.)

Control Crabgrass with a Preemergent Herbicide. If you had a problem with crabgrass last fall, it's time to begin dealing with the seeds it left behind. If there has been no frost this winter, crabgrass, usually an annual, can even grow year-round. So the first step is to look around and pull out any errant plants you find. Luckily, by using an organic preemergent herbicide, you can stop the seeds of crabgrass and other weeds in their tracks without using dangerous chemicals. The best-known organic preemergent is Corn Gluten Meal (9-0-0), which prevents germination of weed seeds and feeds the lawn at the same time. You can even buy organic bagged lawn fertilizers that contain corn gluten meal in the mix. (Don't use corn gluten as a vegetable fertilizer, since it would prevent your vegetable seeds from sprouting and effects may be long lasting.) Spread an organic preemergent on the lawn according to package directions in mid-January along the coast and in early February inland. (Use a soil thermometer if you like. When the soil temperature reaches 63° to 65°F, that's when the seeds germinate, so it's the time to apply.) To control weeds and feed at the same time, some gardeners feed lawns lightly every month with Wow!, from Gardens Alive! Wow! feeds the lawn and keeps it weed-free; Wow! Supreme is a complete organic lawn food with weed control.

Check the Lawn Mower. January is also a good time to check over the lawn mower and make sure the blades are sharp. If necessary, have them sharpened.

Consider an Electric Mower. Another environmentally friendly idea is to replace your gas-powered mower with a mulching cordless electric mower, or even with a push mower. New push mowers are lightweight and easy to use and provide good exercise. Most electric mowers have a rechargeable battery that can be recycled. Electric mowers cause no gas spills, start instantly, are quieter than gas-powered ones, and give off no carbon emissions. (Lawn mowers and gas-powered tools are among our worst offenders against air quality. There are millions of them, but they aren't smog-tested.) On the negative side, electric mowers cost more than gas-powered types, they don't work well on wet grass, and in most cases they are not self-propelled. You do the pushing while they do the cutting, but their light weight makes the job easy. Electric mowers with cords are more powerful, but dealing with a cord is not easy unless you are the type who never gets tangled in the cord of a vacuum cleaner.

VEGETABLE GARDENING

Fill in with Transplants or Seeds. As you harvest rows in your vegetable garden, refill them with winter vegetables; use either transplants of broccoli, Brussels sprouts, cabbage, cauliflower, celery, lettuce, parsley, peas, and Swiss chard or seeds of beets, carrots, lettuce, mesclun, peas, radishes, and turnips. Short-day onions, artichokes, asparagus, strawberries, rhubarb, and horseradish can be bought bareroot. I list the last three with reservations. November is a better time to plant strawberries (see page 383), and rhubarb is difficult in Southern California. I don't recommend growing it, because along the coast it doesn't get the frost it needs to develop good flavor, and inland it usually succumbs to root rot during the summer. (See page 106 and 141 for asparagus and artichoke planting directions.) Horseradish grows like a weed here. It's well worth planting but needs ample water plus room to grow. Confine it in a special place, such as a raised bed, or it could become a noxious and invasive pest.

Side-Dress Vegetable Rows with Fertilizer. Nitrogen is less active in winter, and rains wash soluble nutrients down to deeper levels where plant roots can't reach them. This makes it doubly important to remember to side-dress

Fava beans

your vegetable rows with more organic fertilizer if you didn't do so in December. *Side-dressing* simply means to sprinkle fertilizer on top of the ground around individual plants or down the sides of rows.

When fertilizing vegetables, you have a wide range of choices. You could choose a ready-made commercial organic vegetable fertilizer and use it according to package directions, or, if you prefer, you could use manure for side-dressing rows. Aged rabbit and chicken manures are particularly good for this purpose, and they don't attract animals. Alternatively, you could mix up a homemade fertilizer. Study the ingredients of bagged products and use them as a guide, or try one of the mixes in the box on page 77. Homemade fertilizers can work well, and you can change the formula to fit your soil and plants, but some generic organic materials, particularly nitrogen sources, bring animals. Use these mainly prior to planting so you can dig them into the ground, and then use aged manures for side-dressing rows.

Feed for Continued Crops. Spread the fertilizer just before a rain, or water it into the ground. Harvesting is also a cue to fertilize. For example, after cutting the central head from broccoli, feed the plant so it can produce good side sprouts. After cutting all the outside leaves from a row of lettuce, side-dress the row so the plants can keep producing. Onions also need regular fertilizer now to make them produce plenty of green growth. With onions, the trick is to feed them early in the season so they'll have lots of sturdy green leaves, and then to stop fertilizing them a month or two before they're ready to make a bulb; otherwise, their skins will split open and they may rot instead of keeping well after harvest. Liquid fertilizers,

How to Plant, Grow, and Harvest Lettuce from Seeds

▸ Plant in full sun. (Lettuce can take some shade in summer but not in winter.) Don't plant it in the same spot twice, or it may succumb to wilt.

▸ Dig deeply prior to planting. Mix in organic soil amendment and add organic fertilizer that's recommended for vegetables to the top 6 inches of soil, according to package directions.

▸ Distribute the seed down a wide row, or broadcast it on a raised bed at the approximate rate of three seeds to every 2 square inches of soil surface.

▸ Cover the seed very lightly with potting soil (about ¼ inch), and water by sprinkling lightly. Use a misting valve. Continue to keep the seedbed damp by sprinkling daily until the seeds sprout—three to seven days. Then lengthen the watering times and water more deeply. (If your lettuce seeds don't germinate,

your soil may be too salty. Give the soil a long, deep soaking to leach out salts. Plant again with fresh seed.)

▸ Stimulate fast growth with plenty of water and fertilizer. (Fast growth means sweet, crunchy lettuce, while slow growth makes it tough and bitter.)

▸ Protect the plants from slugs (pages 115–116).

▸ Thin seedlings according to package directions. Either eat the little thinnings or transplant them to an adjacent row.

▸ If you'd like to grow lettuce but don't have space, plant it in pots and half barrels filled with potting soil. Feed every two weeks with liquid fertilizer recommended for vegetables.

▸ Harvest whole heads of lettuce, leave the roots in the ground, and feed and water them; they will grow new heads. Or lengthen your harvest by taking off only the outside leaves as needed.

such as fish emulsion, are the safest way to feed onions now because liquids don't hang around in the soil.

Plant Lettuce. This is the best time for lettuce. It's easy to grow and a money saver. Plant either from transplants, which will give you a faster harvest, or from seeds (see box, above), which will give you more lettuce over a longer period of time. Lettuce seeds germinate within a wide range of soil temperatures (from 35° to 80°F) but sprout quicker at cooler temperatures than at warm ones, so this is a good time to plant them. Growing from seeds also gives you more interesting varieties to choose from, such

as 'Rouge d'Hiver', a red romaine, or mesclun, a mixture of various lettuces, salad greens, and herbs that are expensive to buy in the grocery store but easy to grow in your garden. (For instructions, see page 108.)

Force Fava Beans to Bear a Crop. If you planted fava beans last October, by now they should be waist-high. Protect them from being pushed over by rain or wind by adding a few bamboo stakes and connecting them with twine.

In some climate zones, fava beans will bear crops without the aid of the gardener, but for a variety of reasons (including too much shade, water, or fertilizer), they may bear flowers but no beans. If that happens, pinch off the growing tips of the stems. It's all right to then side-dress the rows with vegetable fertilizer according to package directions; gently cultivate it into the ground and water deeply. Within a week of pinching, the favas will start to bear beans. Wait until the pods are between 5 and 8 inches long and filled with beans before you begin to harvest. (The tips of the stems you pinched off are very good to eat; steam or stir-fry them.)

Harvest Cole Crops. The term *cole crop* refers to all members of the cabbage family. They all descended from one common wild, Mediterranean ancestor and became different from one another through spontaneous mutations occuring over many centuries, aided by human beings selecting plants they liked and saving seeds. Thus, each one grows differently and requires special harvesting. Here's how to harvest cauliflower, cabbage, and Brussels sprouts. When it's done correctly, all but cauliflower will continue to produce.

As soon as you see the white curd (head) beginning to form on cauliflower, tie the leaves together over the top to protect it from sunshine. Sun turns cauliflowers green. (Even "self-blanching" types are best treated this way in our strong sun.) Untie and check them every few days. When a head suddenly starts to fill out, check that one daily for readiness.

A head of cauliflower is a flower in the bud stage. Harvest it just when the snowy white buds are all filled out but before they open. When you see the sections just beginning to loosen up and separate around the outside, cut the head with a knife below the curd. If you wait too long, it will be overdone and ricey.

Homegrown cauliflower cooks more quickly than bought. Steam the whole head for three to five minutes; then test with a fork. No need for sauces; it's a tasty treat straight from the garden, one of the best vegetables.

After harvesting, pull out and compost the plant. Replace it with something else, such as bare-root short-day onions, carrots, or lettuce, not another cole crop; they all share the same diseases, so you shouldn't plant them in the same spot for two or three years.

Broccoli is another edible flower bud that needs checking daily. Harvest by cutting stalks with a knife when the buds are filled out but still tight. Don't pull up the plants when you harvest; leave them in the ground and side-dress the row with fertilizer. Unlike cauliflower, broccoli will branch and give you more crops. The farther down on the stalk you cut, the fewer but the fatter will be the side branches you get. Many home garden varieties—'Bonanza' is one—are known for their ample manufacture of such second, third, and fourth crops.

Harvest cabbage as soon as the heads fill out and feel firm to the touch. If they give when you squeeze them, they're not quite ready. As soon as they feel as hard as a bowling ball, pick them by cutting just below the head. If you wait too long, they'll split.

To keep the plants going, cut off the outer leaves but let the roots remain in the ground. Fertilize and water them and they'll form three or four baby heads. Though these have a stronger flavor than the first harvest, they're good for soup.

There's a trick to harvesting Brussels sprouts, and unless you practice it you may not even get a crop. As soon as the plant begins to manufacture sprouts, pull off its lower leaves with a few downward twisting motions, and take off a few of the tiny sprouts at the bottom of the stalk. This stimulates sprouts farther up on the stalk to grow faster. As the sprouts grow, pull off all the remaining lower leaves that have sprouts above them, leaving a topknot of leaves at the peak of the stalk, rather like a mini palm tree. This provides more room for sprouts and forces the energy of the plant into sprout production.

Harvest Brussels sprouts as soon as they're big enough to eat. Always take them from the bottom to the top. Side-dress the row with fertilizer and continue to water the plants when rains aren't adequate. They'll grow and continue to produce sprouts throughout cold weather.

Two Homemade Organic Vegetable Fertilizers for Western Soils

You can mix your own organic fertilizer for vegetables. Here are two sample formulas for western soils. Wear gloves when mixing, and irrigate thoroughly after use. For light feeders, such as carrots, apply 4 quarts of either mix to 100 square feet and work into the top 6 inches of ground prior to planting. For heavy feeders, such as corn, apply 6 quarts per 100 square feet. (These mixes can also be used to side-dress rows, but be aware that blood meal, feather meal, alfalfa pellets, and seed meals may attract animals when left lying on top of the ground and not dug into the soil.)

Pre-Plant Vegetable or All-Purpose Fertilizer

2 cups blood meal or 4 cups alfalfa pellets, feather meal, or seed meal*

2 cups fishbone meal, steamed bone meal, soft rock phosphate, or high-phosphate guano

1 cup naturally mined gypsum

1 cup kelp meal

½ cup Sul-Po-Mag (0-0-22)

1 cup humic acid powder or pellets

High-Nitrogen Mix

1 cup alfalfa meal

1 cup cottonseed meal or soy meal (or other seed meal*)

1 cup feather meal

2 cups fish meal

2 cups fishbone meal

2 cups kelp meal (or Kelzyme)

1 cup Sul-Po-Mag (0-0-22)

1 cup humic acid powder or pellets

* Note: Seed meals are available at animal feed stores and pet stores.

JANUARY CHECKLIST

PURCHASE/PLANT

{ } Purchase and plant bare-root roses, trees, vines (including wisteria), berries, and vegetables, *49*

{ } Choose and plant camellias and azaleas, *65*

{ } Purchase cymbidiums, *68*

{ } Purchase and plant cool-season flowers to fill in bare spots, *69*

{ } Plant seeds of warm-season flowers for transplants to put out in spring, *69*

{ } Continue to plant winter vegetables from transplants and seeds, *72*

{ } Many succulents, including cacti, bloom in winter and spring; purchase new types now, *270*

TRIM, PRUNE, MOW, DIVIDE

{ } Prune deciduous fruit trees, *51*

{ } Prune roses, *57, 60*

{ } Pick camellias, *65*

{ } Deadhead azaleas, *67*

{ } Don't prune off frost damage, *67*

{ } Prune naked coral trees, *70*

{ } Mow cool-season lawns. Most warm-season lawns are dormant now and don't need mowing, *72*

{ } Cut back Japanese blood grass, *328*

{ } Prune conifers, *267*

FERTILIZE

{ } Choose a system for fertilizing roses and begin feeding, *53*

{ } Begin to feed citrus trees in coastal zones only, *63*

{ } Treat citrus trees to correct chlorosis, *64*

{ } Start feeding epiphyllums for bloom, *67*

{ } Continue to fertilize cymbidiums that have not yet bloomed with a high-bloom formula, *68*

{ } Feed cool-season flowers (other than wildflowers), *70*

{ } Feed cineraria, *70*

{ } Fertilize cool-season lawns, *72*

{ } Side-dress vegetable rows with fertilizer, *74*

{ } Treat the ground under royal purple brunfelsia with nitrogen fertilizer mixed double strength, *403*

WATER

{ } When rains aren't adequate, water all garden plants according to their individual needs (succulents don't need water now, but native plants will perform better if given water in dry weather during their growing season), 67

{ } Irrigate citrus trees if rains aren't adequate, 64

{ } Remember to water plants under eaves where rains can't reach them, 67

{ } Water cool-season lawns when rains aren't adequate, 72

CONTROL PESTS, DISEASE, AND WEEDS

{ } Apply dormant spray to roses and deciduous fruit trees, 57

{ } Apply dormant spray to sycamore trees, 62

{ } Pick up dead camellia blossoms to prevent petal blight, 65

{ } Protect cymbidiums from slugs and snails, 68

{ } Control rust on cool-season lawns, 72

{ } Control crabgrass with preemergent herbicide, 73

{ } Check trees, shrubs, and ice plant in coastal zones for overwintering whiteflies. Control by spraying, 58

{ } Pull weeds, 46

{ } Spray peach and apricot trees for peach leaf curl, 59

{ } Control ants, 84

ALSO THIS MONTH

{ } Protect tender plants from frost, 67

{ } Stake cymbidium bloom spikes, 68

{ } Start a garden notebook, 71

{ } Clean out the potting shed, 71

{ } Order seeds and supplies from seed catalogs, 71

{ } Check the lawn mower; have the blades sharpened if necessary, 73

{ } Pinch tips of fava beans if they fail to bear crops, 75

{ } Harvest cool-season vegetables as they mature. Harvest cole crops by individual methods, 76

{ } At month's end in coastal zones, begin to check bamboo to see if it's time to propagate, 128

February

A MONTH FOR WAITING

Clivia miniata
(Bush lily)

In Southern California, February feels like spring. Acacias decorate the roadsides, orange blossoms scent the air, the first bulbs come into bloom, and gardens smell inviting after rain, which may be frequent this month. Native plants are in a season of growth, and cool-season garden flowers such as primroses, cyclamen, linaria, annual African daisies, pansies, and cineraria are at the height of their beauty. But despite appearances, it's still winter. Most plants are growing slowly now, and the wise gardener knows never to rush the seasons. February is not a major planting month. If spring is in your blood, concentrate on putting in those few items that can be planted now.

Though there are many interesting jobs to be done in February, it's also a time for waiting. Certain plants can be pruned now, but wait until the weather warms up before cutting off frostbitten branches. In cold low-lying gardens and interior valleys, wait until all danger of frost has passed before you move those tender plants now safely sheltered under eaves. Fertilize deciduous fruit trees—and avocados too, in coastal zones—but wait until next month to feed most of the landscape. Throw off your coat, dig in the garden, prepare the soil, spread manure, and start a compost heap, but wait until March to put in summer vegetables and flowers.

AVOCADO TREES

Fertilize Avocado Trees. Begin feeding avocados now; they are heavy feeders. A mature avocado fed with synthetic fertilizers needs at least 2 pounds of actual nitrogen per year and varying amounts of other nutrients, such as phosphorus and zinc. When feeding organically, however, you do not need to go by the weight of nitrogen, since additional nitrogen and other nutrients are provided by the breakdown of organic matter in the soil, as explained on pages 25 and 30–36. Organic soils also team with natural rhizobia (nitrogen-fixing bacteria) that make additional nitrogen available to roots.

◉ QUICK TIP

Use Paint Buckets for Garden Tasks. *Keep a supply of small, lightweight plastic paint buckets on hand for measuring, mixing, and carrying fertilizer. They're perfect for carrying kitchen peelings to the compost pile and birdseed to the feeder. When planting, use one to hold potting mix for covering your seed rows, another to carry a little sand for mixing with small seeds, and a third to keep your seed packets high and dry, along with a pair of scissors to cut them open and a few paper clips for closing up the packets still containing seeds.*

Choose a Fertilizing Method. When feeding organically, you have a choice of methods and of fertilizers. One option is to apply bagged or boxed organic citrus and avocado food or any all-purpose organic fertilizer for food crops according to package directions. Look for products whose ingredients provide the main nutrients avocados need: nitrogen, phosphorus, potassium, and, to a lesser extent, zinc. A second method is to make your own mix of basic organic ingredients that provide the necessary nutrients. For help with choosing generic and commercial organic fertilizers, consult the lists on pages 28–30. For a sample formula, see the "Pre-Plant Vegetable or All-Purpose Fertilizer"

in the box on page 77. Spread the fertilizer or fertilizers of your choice over the ground beginning a foot or two from the trunk and extending as far out as the branch tips. One way to spread a product evenly is to use mined gypsum to mark the area under the tree into four pie segments, weigh the total poundage of fertilizer needed on a bathroom scale, and divide the total among four small paint buckets. Spread the contents of each bucket evenly over each pie segment.

Know Your Soil Type. When choosing a fertilizing method, it's wise to take into consideration the type of soil in which your tree grows. Many of our local soils, especially sandy ones, are poor. Sandy soil may contain almost no natural nitrogen or minerals needed by plants. On the other hand, decomposed granite soil may be rich in phosphorus, potassium, calcium, and trace minerals, and clay soils are usually rich in iron and other minerals. A soil test might show that your land contains sufficient quantities of most nutrients other than nitrogen. Building the humus content of soil by adding organic matter and humic acid, discussed on pages 18–19, can help unlock the natural mineral content of soils so that plant roots can access them.

A Tried-and-True Method. To give you an idea of how to work with generics, here is the way that one gardener fed his avocado trees, with excellent results. First, in February, he purchased bagged, aged chicken manure at his local nursery and spread 25 pounds of it under the canopy of each mature tree. He fed his younger trees proportionally less. Beginning in March, he gave each mature tree two cups of blood meal and one cup of bone meal every six weeks through August. (If you prefer, use fishbone meal, which is even higher in phosphorus than bone meal. Use a mask when spreading bone meal.) If mulch is thick, rake it aside and spread the fertilizers evenly over the ground under the tree and then replace the mulch on top. Unless heavy rain is expected, follow up with ample irrigation from the hose, not just a drip system.

Another home gardener, who grew avocados and citrus trees in old agricultural loam (a mixture of red clay, sand, and silt), fed his grove with nothing but aged horse manure applied once or twice a year, every year, in fall and sometimes also in summer. The trees were productive and healthy. (When using horse manure, be sure your tetanus shot is up to date.) Regardless of your fertilizing method, it is wise to jot down products, amounts, and dates in a garden diary. By keeping a record of methods and results, you can gradually adjust your system to fit your requirements and soil.

Other Basic Requirements of Avocados. The main requirements of avocados are rich soil, excellent drainage, and a thick layer of mulch over the roots. Allow the leaves that fall to remain under the tree; don't rake them up. (Avocados are best planted at the back of the garden, where their large leaves won't look untidy.) Unless you are fertilizing with a bulky soil amendment such as horse manure, mulch the ground under the canopy of the tree at least twice a year with homemade, bagged, or trucked organic compost.

Water avocados deeply but infrequently, applying an inch of water at a time. In winter when rains are adequate, established avocado trees may not need additional irrigation. Low-impact sprinklers and drip systems have been used successfully for avocados. They use less water, though they water more frequently—perhaps every other day in hot weather. One irrigation method is to place a circle of laser-cut drip hose around the tree under the mulch, enlarging it gradually as the tree grows. Another way is to install individual drippers onto a drip line encircling the tree, with one 1-gallon-per-half-hour emitter next to the tree when it's first planted. When the tree is two months old, increase the 1-gallon emitters to two on opposite sides of the trunk, at a distance of 2 to 3 feet from the trunk. Thereafter, gradually move the ring outward while increasing emitters until you have eight emitters under the drip line of a mature tree. (Drip irrigation is not without problems; emitters can clog, and animals sometimes chew the lines. Foil animals, including gophers, which attack from below, by putting a layer of chicken wire flat on the ground around the tree. Overlap the edges of the wire and fix it to the ground with landscape staples. Install the drip lines on top and bury the whole thing under a thick layer of mulch. To stop clogs, look for drip lines equipped with turbulent flow emitters designed for subsurface use. When fertilizing through drip lines, use hydroponic fertilizers, such as Nature's Nectar Nitrogen (5-0-0), Nature's Nectar Phosphorus (0-2-0), and Nature's Nectar Potassium (0-0-5). These are OMRI-labeled and totally organic but contain no sediment that could clog lines or emitters.

Never cultivate or dig under avocado trees, because that would damage the roots and all your fruit might fall off. It's best not to grow anything under an avocado tree, especially if that plant needs frequent irrigation. Wet soil promotes root rot in avocados.

CITRUS TREES

Control Citrus Pests. Citrus pests often step up their activity now. Books such as the *Ortho Problem Solver* contain colored photographs that help you recognize specific pests and diseases. Use a magnifying glass to identify such pests as aphids, which cause curly leaves and sooty molds; mealy bugs, which also cause sooty mold; and woolly whitefly, which can be recognized by fuzzy white residue under leaves. Rust mites (which are the same pest as silver mites on lemons) cause reddish-brown fruit that spoils easily. Various scales attach themselves to trunks, twigs, and fruit.

Wash Citrus Trees. One of the pleasures of growing your own fruit is knowing it hasn't been sprayed. Fortunately, many calamities can be avoided by keeping trees clean. It's been proved that beneficial insects can't reach and destroy harmful ones if the latter are hidden beneath a layer of dust. If your trees are dusty, even after rain, spray them with water mixed with an insecticidal soap, such as Safer soap, using 10 tablespoons per gallon of water—soft water is best. Or use a solution of 1 to 2 tablespoons of dishwashing liquid—the kind you use in the sink, not in a machine—per gallon of water. (Before spraying, cut off the tips of branches that brush the ground, as described below, because they're a ready highway for ants.)

Washing trees can also help rid them of certain pests directly. Aphids, woolly whiteflies, and mealybugs can be washed to the ground with a soapy spray. An even better job can be done if you're willing to get right under the leaves and manually scrub off aphids and other pests with a sponge or paintbrush. I've done this myself, and it doesn't rank high on the list of my favorite jobs, but rubber gloves, a rain suit, and boots can make it bearable.

Cut Ants Off at the Pass. Although washing and sponging under the leaves can get rid of most pest problems on citrus, the problems will come back if you don't get rid of ants. Ants are determined little dairy farmers that manage immense herds of sucking insect "cows," such as aphids, mealybugs, woolly whiteflies, and scale. Ants protect pests from predators, carry them from plant to plant, and milk them for the honeydew they produce. If you can get rid of ants, your pest problems will be almost completely gone. This requires a special strategy.

Before washing the trees, carefully cut away any branches that are resting on the ground. (Don't cut up too high. It's good for a citrus tree's branches to hang low, not only because of all the extra fruit they bear, but also because this "skirt" of low branches protects the trunk from sunburn.) Now the only avenue left for ants is up the trunk. You can cut off that route by applying a sticky product such as Tree Tangle-foot Pest Barrier. Don't put these products directly onto the bark. Wrap quilt batting (available at fabric stores) around the trunk so that ants can't climb under it, cover it with a strip of plastic, and apply the substance over the plastic. Wear an old pair of rubber gloves to keep the product off your skin—it's quite hard to get off! Renew the coating frequently to keep it sticky.

Use Worm Castings to Repel Ants and Other Pests. Most ant baits, even homemade ones, do not comply with the organic method since they contain poisons. (The active ingredient of most homemade baits is boric acid, a poison.) I personally don't use ant baits outdoors. My method for controlling ants and many other pests in the garden is to spread a 1-inch-thick layer of worm castings under affected plants and renew the layer every year or two. I have successfully used this method to control greenhouse whitefly on tomatoes and mint and giant whitefly on begonias and hibiscus, as well as weevils (some gardeners say worm castings control fire ants, too). Worm castings do not seem to repel caterpillars, but they may help control rose slugs, which Spinosad, an organic pesticide made from a soil fungus found in an old rum distillery, also controls. (Though Spinosad has the OMRI label of approval, it's toxic to bees. If you use it at all, carefully follow package directions. See page 152 for more on rose slugs.) Worm castings do not upset the balance of nature, and they don't kill bees or other beneficial insects, but they require a little patience. Their pest-control effects kick in one month after spreading, but results are long-lasting. Spread or respread worm castings annually in February or March, since pests speed up their activities in April.

It may seem almost too good to be true that simply spreading a layer of worm castings over the roots of plants can repel so many pests. Though no specific study has been made, there may be a scientific explanation. Worm castings contain chitinase, an enzyme that can break down chitin. Chitin is an abundant natural biopolymer that forms the hard shell of arthropods, including the protective exoskeletons, or shells, of crustaceans and insects. Chitin also protects parasites, fungi, and spiders. (There's nothing bad about chitin; it even has beneficial effects on the human body, and applications in health sciences.) Chitinase occurs naturally in plants and helps them to fight off insect attack, but plants with worm castings over their roots apparently contain a higher amount of chitinase than normal, which improves their ability to repel pests and fungi. (Since chitin is also found in the cell walls of fungi and some algae, manufacturers have even created organic fungicides from earthworm castings, or you can make your own.) Worm castings also act as a good organic soil amendment and mild fertilizer. They help sandy soils retain moisture, and they add soluble nutrients as well as humus and various bioorganisms to any soil. In my experience store-bought brands and home-grown castings are equally good pest repellants, though the homegrown ones are sticky and thus more difficult to spread than the dry powdered types. On the plus side, homegrown or farm-raised ones contain live earthworms and eggs, thus adding live worms to soil and containers. (In hot, interior climates, home-grown castings sometimes bake into a hard layer that sheds water. If this occurs, mix the castings into the soil or cover them with mulch. (Also use the alternative remedy for ants in the following Quick Tip.)

☀ QUICK TIP

Use Cornmeal to Control Ants. *Sprinkle cornmeal on ant trails or near their nests. Some ants will ingest the cornmeal, which swells up inside them, thus stopping them in their tracks. Other ants carry the grains back to their nests where it grows a fungi that emits a gas toxic to ants, thus destroying the nest.*

Release Ladybugs to Control Aphids.
Citrus trees are a favorite food of aphids, which are sluggish, green-colored sucking insects. Unless you've spread a layer of dry earthworm castings under your tree, as described above, now's the time when aphids are likely to appear like magic on its fresh tip growth. Ants deposit the slow-moving aphids onto the juiciest parts of favorite plants, and pretty soon the plant becomes a sticky messy of aphids, ants, honeydew, and black sooty mold. One way

to protect plants from aphids is to wash them off, as described previously. Another way is to release ladybugs. (For instructions, consult the Quick Tip on page 160.) Gardeners who occasionally release ladybugs find that aphids and sticky mildew disappear, along with some other pests, including greenhouse whitefly.

Encourage Beneficials and Protect Bees.

Gardeners can purchase many other beneficial insects, including lacewings, to release in gardens. Even if one does not remember to do this often, a well-kept garden, free from poisonous sprays, will be home to a host of helpful creatures. It is remarkable how well beneficial insects and arachnids can control pests, including difficult pests such as scale and mites.

Citrus fed in January should be covered with blooms in February and swarming with bees. One of the worst mistakes any gardener can make is to spray citrus—or anything else, for that matter—with malathion. Malathion is a poisonous, broad-spectrum chemical insecticide that does indeed kill aphids, but it also kills bees and many other beneficials. If there are no bees, there will be no fruit. (See page 280 for more about bees.)

Hand-Pollinate If You See No Bees.
It's a sad fact that bees have had problems in recent years; some are unable to find their way back to their hives. This may be caused by a pesticide many people use on lawns to kill grubs. The pesticide confuses the grubs, but it also confuses bees. (See page 278 for more about bees and their problems.) If despite your good care, you see no bees on your citrus blossoms in February, it would behoove you to hand-pollinate the flowers. (This applies to deciduous fruit trees too.) Use a soft sable paintbrush and play bee, going from flower to flower, twirling

the paintbrush much as a bee's body moves. The idea is to pick up pollen from one blossom and deposit it into another. On a large tree, you might be able to use a clean feather duster to spread the pollen all over the tree, but the paintbrush method, though time-consuming, works best. Do this several times as long as new flowers are opening. The best time of day to hand-pollinate is early morning, after the sun is up and the dew has dried. With luck, you should get fruit. Also, make sure there's a water source for bees. A fountain or a pond will bring bees as well as birds. A birdbath near your orchard may attract more bees than birds.

DECIDUOUS FRUIT TREES

Feed and Mulch Deciduous Fruit Trees.
In cold-winter climates, gardeners fertilize and mulch deciduous fruit trees in late summer and fall. In our mild Mediterranean climate, it's unwise to fertilize deciduous fruit trees in fall with any synthetic fertilizer or fast-acting organic nitrogen fertilizer, because this could upset dormancy. On the other hand, slower-acting organic amendments work better if added in fall. Many organic gardeners find that simply mulching the ground over the roots in fall with a layer of horse manure, or with 4 to 6 pounds of chicken manure covered with homemade or bagged compost, provides the trees with all they need for the year. By springtime, the winter rain has washed the nutrients into the ground and the trees are all ready to grow and bear fruit.

But let's say you're new to the organic method and you didn't mulch with manure last fall. In that case, you can apply balanced organic fertilizer suggested for fruit trees early in February, in time for the tree to absorb some nutrients before its flowers open, and then cover the fertilizer with a layer of organic mulch. Or feed with generics, such as 1 cup blood meal, 1 cup fishbone meal, and ¼ cup Sul-Po-Mag (0-0-22) sprinkled over the roots of each mature tree, covered over with organic mulch, and watered into the ground. Deciduous fruit trees are not heavy feeders, but if you provide rich organic soil and a little extra fertilizer prior to bloom, you will get a more flavorful and abundant crop. Next fall, begin the new system of mulching with horse manure—the best choice, if you can manage it—and thus take care of all the tree's needs at once and in the easiest way.

Feed young trees very lightly, and don't overfeed mature trees with products containing nitrogen or they will produce leaves at the expense of fruit. When applying mulch and fertilizer, begin a foot or two from the trunk and end at the drip line or beyond, and always follow up by watering deeply when rains aren't adequate. Tests have indicated that fruit grown with organic fertilizers can be more nutritious than fruit grown with synthetic products, but their taste, a factor that can't be measured, may also be superior. One has to grow one's own fruit to discover that apricot trees bear much more flavorful fruit when fed with organic fertilizers than when they're fed with synthetics.

SYCAMORE, ASH, AND ALDER TREES

Sycamore trees (*Platanus*) are prized for their golden fall color, statuesque trunks, handsome branches, and lovely mottled bark. As they grow, their old bark, instead of stretching like that of most trees, flakes off in irregular patches, revealing fresh white bark beneath.

The California sycamore (*Platanus racemosa*) also tends to take on striking shapes, making it a favorite subject of California plein-air painters. The London plane tree (*Platanus x acerifolia, P. x hispanica*) is more erect. It grows fast, provides a shady green canopy spring to fall, and puts up with dust, smog, any kind of soil, and even reflected heat from roads, walls, and sidewalks, all of which makes it a fine street tree. The buttonwood or American plane tree (*P. occidentalis*), native east of the Rockies, is the largest of all, with smooth white branches and leaning, often multiple trunks. Planted streamside, these can become giants. In nature, sycamores grow on bottomland over an aquifer or on stream banks, with their trunks high and dry and their roots in water. All sycamores prefer deep, fertile, moist soil.

Clean Up Sycamore Trees. Unfortunately, sycamore trees are subject to a host of pests and diseases. Sycamore anthracnose (*Gnomonia platani*), a fungus disease often called sycamore blight, causes dieback of young shoots and fresh leaves, brown or scorched mature leaves, and cankers that can girdle branches, causing them to die and fall to the ground. In damp weather, sycamores can also fall prey to mildew. To avoid anthracnose and other diseases, feed sycamores now with EnviroTree, a safe, organic, and revolutionary liquid fertilizer that you spray directly onto the bark. When EnviroTree is diluted and applied according to package directions, the cambium layer, which lies between the outer bark and sapwood of the tree, absorbs the fertilizer directly and distributes it throughout the tree, quickly greening up leaves and helping the tree to fight off disease. Sycamore lace bug (*Corythuca*) and bark beetles also attack the trees. Despite all these obstacles, some ancient specimens survive many centuries by living off their own refuse. They grow huge, hollow out, rot away, fall to the ground, and spring up again as a circle of trunks rising from their own roots to repeat the process. But in a garden, instead of allowing fallen sycamore limbs and leaves to rot under the tree, it's better to keep the ground clean. By removing refuse, you prevent dormant pests as well as mildew and blight spores from over-wintering under the tree and migrating back up the trunk in spring. Rake the ground under sycamores now, bag fallen leaves, twigs, and branches, and send them to the dump. Don't add them to the compost pile. This will go a long way toward keeping your tree pest- and disease-free.

Plant, Feed, and Mulch Sycamores. When selecting London plane trees, always choose a disease-resistant variety. 'Colombia' is resistant to anthracnose and mildew, 'Bloodgood' resists anthracnose, and 'Yarwood' resists mildew. When planting native varieties, place them in appropriate locations, next to a stream or on the bottom of a canyon. Provide adequate space, and choose a specimen that already has an unusual shape in the nursery can. Plant it at an angle to encourage an artistic, leaning habit of growth. Unless the tree is growing in a wild native landscape, keep the ground clean, encourage the help of birds and beneficials, and build up the organic structure of the soil. When growing a sycamore tree as a street or lawn tree, mulch the lawn annually in fall with screened cow manure or fine-grained compost. (If you failed to do this job last fall, do it now.) Besides feeding stressed trees with EnviroTree, drench their root zones now with a product containing humic acid.

Feed and Mulch Ash and Alder Trees.
People plant ash (*Fraxinus*) and alder (*Alnus*) trees because they want a leafy tree like something they grew back east. Developers plant them because they're green, inexpensive, and fast-growing. In many cases, ash and alder trees are planted in incorrect climate zones. (Before purchasing a variety, always look it up in the *Sunset Western Garden Book* to make sure you live in a zone to which it's adapted.) Be aware, also, that many ash trees are host to pests and diseases, and that alder trees need so much water that they're poor choices unless planted by streams. Most ash trees are prone to borers, and in some areas they also fall prey to ash whitefly, though released beneficials have successfully controlled this pest in most areas. Despite their negative characteristics, some ash and alder species and varieties can fill certain needs. Italian alder (*Alnus cordata*) makes a good avenue tree in hot inland areas where roots can access adequate water. Arizona ash (*F. velutina*) can withstand hot, dry conditions in the desert but needs regular water. F. v. 'Rio Grande', also called 'Fan-Tex' ash, resists windburn and thrives in alkaline soil and hot, dry climates.

Control Ash Anthracnose and Tent Caterpillars. Most communities have crossed off Modesto ash (*Fraxinus velutina* 'Modesto') from their recommended tree lists because of its disease problems, but there are still some isolated specimens around. If you happen to have one of these survivors in your garden and you notice its leaves going brown and falling off in spring, your tree is most likely suffering from ash anthracnose (*Gleosporium aridum*). Trees usually leaf out again in summer, but the disease can totally kill a tree. If you've seen signs of this disease in the past, cut out any dead branches now and clean up the ground under the tree, removing and destroying diseased wood and old leaves. Feed early this month by spraying the tree's bark with the liquid fertilizer EnviroTree, diluted and applied according to package directions. EnviroTree, mentioned above in the section on sycamores, is recommended for all trees but is especially helpful to stressed or diseased trees since it gives them natural vigor, allowing them to fight off disease and in some cases even pests. Feeding EnviroTree annually takes care of nutritional needs and disease problems in one fell swoop.

Alder trees' main pest problems are aphids and alder flea beetles. To control them, clean up the ground, mulch, and release beneficials. Given adequate water, mature alders need little fertilizer unless they are growing in poor soil.

Kiwi vine with fruit

Later in summer, tent caterpillars may be a problem. Be on the lookout in summer, and if they appear, pull off and destroy the protective tents, scrape off and destroy eggs, and spray the foliage surrounding the tents with Spinosad to kill any caterpillars that may have escaped. (Spinosad is a selective organic pesticide effective against caterpillars, but don't broadcast it, and be careful to use it according to label instructions, and only at times when honey and native bees are not active. Despite its OMRI label, Spinosad is toxic to all bees and, unfortunately, is much overused.)

KIWI VINES

Prune kiwi vines in February, during dormancy. Kiwis bear mostly on new canes arising as laterals from fat buds on canes that grew last year. Prune young kiwis lightly to develop a primary trunk and to create a structure on a pergola, overhead wires, or espalier. Head back canes to create fruiting wood. Prune mature kiwis hard to remove old wood and produce fresh fruiting growth. Here are the basic steps for mature plants:

- Remove all twiggy, dead, diseased, and tangled growth.
- Remove a few two- or three-year-old branches each year to reduce crowding and encourage growth of new branches for the future. (These cuts won't produce much fruit this year but are necessary for renewal.)
- Cut off all but twenty-eight or thirty canes with smooth wood (those that grew last year). Shorten the remaining canes to four or five buds.
- Shorten fruiting spurs (short side branches) to two buds each.

CAMELLIAS

Continue to buy, plant, and transplant camellias now, while they're still in bloom and before they start to grow. (See the box on camellias on page 66 for instructions on how to plant them.) Most people choose camellias simply by picking out something that looks pretty. It's better to select them for your climate zone and for ease of growing. Some are slow growers, others vigorous. Some are good along the coast, others better inland. Many varieties need extremes of temperature in order to open their blooms and thus do better in inland valleys than they do along the coast.

Among varieties that do well inland but have difficulty opening in coastal gardens are 'Mathotiana', 'Ballet Dancer', 'Mrs. Charles Cobb', 'Chandler Elegans', 'C. M. Wilson', and 'Shiro-Chan'. Easy to grow either on the coast or inland are 'Debutante', 'Pink Perfection', 'Herme' ('Jordan's Pride'), 'Professor Sargeant', 'Lady Clair', and 'Ace of Hearts'. ('Ace of Hearts' can take full sun when grown close to the coast.)

As a general rule, singles and semidoubles do best in milder areas, though many formal doubles will open there, too. Anemone-form and peony-form camellias usually won't open in coastal gardens, because the winters are too warm. Get more information from knowledgeable gardeners, nurseries that specialize in camellias, and your local camellia society.

DECIDUOUS MAGNOLIAS

Purchase deciduous magnolias now, while they're in bloom (before leaf-out). Saucer magnolia (*Magnolia soulangiana*) and star magnolia (*M. stellata*) eventually become large, but they grow so slowly they're good choices for small gardens. Use them as focal points in corner beds. They're best against a dark background. They grow best in interior valleys and the Los Angeles basin, where they get some winter chill. A pink saucer magnolia underplanted with spring-flowering bulbs can be breathtaking.

CLIVIA

Purchase clivia now, while they're in bloom, to get the shade of orange or yellow and the size of flowers you want. Belgium hybrids are more handsome than chance seedlings, and there are several exciting new varieties and colors, including white and yellow. 'Flame', developed by a local nurseryman, has unusually wide, shiny foliage and brilliant flaming-orange blooms, with twenty-four individual flowers in each cluster instead of the usual fourteen. (Your local nursery can order it from Monrovia Nursery.)

Clivia are easy to grow in pots or the ground and are good multipliers. They flower most when crowded, and they'll bloom in northern exposures under overhangs that have too much shade for almost all other winter flowers. If you grow enough of them, they make dramatic, long-lasting cut flowers.

Fertilize Clivia and Control Slugs and Snails. Feed clivias early in the month with any fast-acting, balanced organic fertilizer for flowers, or your own concoction, either liquid or solid, and then water it into the ground. Blood meal is said to intensify flower color. The result will be more and much bigger flowers. As soon as you see the flower spikes but before the flowers open, treat for snails and slugs. They won't damage the foliage of clivia, but they'll hide among it and sneak out at night to ruin your flowers. The best organic product for controlling slugs and snails in thick drifts of flowers is Sluggo, a blend of iron phosphate and bait additives. Sprinkle the pellets around the plants and in among the leaves. (See pages 115–116 for more on slugs and snails.)

GERBERAS

Plant Transvaal daisies (*Gerbera jamesonii*) now through April. New varieties are freer-blooming and have a wider range of colors than older types.

Gerberas are easy to grow in pots or the ground but need good drainage, sun along the coast, and partial shade inland. When planting, take care to bury all the roots but not the crown (the place where the roots join the leaves). They rot if planted too deeply. Allow gerberas to dry out slightly between waterings. Protect them from snails, and feed often with a complete fertilizer.

GLADIOLI

Start planting gladioli early this month. By continuing to plant a few more every week between now and the end of March, you will have a continual display lasting from early June through summer. The ones that go in now will be less subject to thrips. This rasping insect that disfigures leaves and flowers particularly favors gladioli, but it's most active in hot weather. Beneficial insects, especially lacewings and ladybugs, can keep thrips under control. Also, try covering their root zone with earthworm castings. Add a handful to gladioli in pots. Thrips are less likely to attack gladioli growing in a mixed flowerbed, especially if the glads are kept well watered.

Gladioli are easy to grow if you give them what they need: full sun; light, sandy loam; bone meal worked in under the corms and covered with a handful of earth; plenty of water; and good drainage. Buy the best corms and plant them in drifts at the back of beds—they look gawky in rows. Or use dwarf types up front. Plant small corms 3 to 4 inches deep, larger corms 4 to 6 inches deep. (Mark the spots so you won't plant something else on top.) They do well in pots if you shade the containers from burning sun. A few giant red ones can spark up a patio.

ROSES

Water and Fertilize Roses. Keep roses irrigated with at least 1 inch of water per week beginning at mid-month when rains aren't adequate. This is the time of year when roses are forming new shoots, leaves, flower buds, and canes. You want to see new canes springing from the bud union, but roses can't push up this succulent new growth without regular and adequate irrigation. As the weather warms up, give your roses enough irrigation to keep them actively growing. Roses in fast-draining soil need more frequent irrigation than those in water-retentive soils such as clay.

If you've chosen to fertilize your roses with a commercial organic rose food, continue to feed according to package directions. Throughout this book, I also recommend an alternative method for fertilizing roses, the Rose-Pro Method (summarized on page 53). If you've chosen the Rose-Pro Method, you won't need to fertilize this month since you fed all your roses last month. Organic fertilizers are long-lasting and slow-acting; thus their effects continue for months. If you did not begin feeding

Easy, Disease-Resistant Roses

Hybrid Tea Roses
'Mellow Yellow'—light yellow
'Color Magic'—pink to red
'First Prize'—pink blend
'Just Joey'—fragrant coppery apricot
'Veteran's Honor'—red

Floribundas
'Betty Boop'—red-bordered yellow blend
'Carefree Beauty'—rich pink
'French Lace'—white
'Knock Out'—cherry red
'Outta the Blue'—fragrant magenta/lavender
'Bonica'—pink

Climbers
'Lady Banks'—yellow or white
'Royal Sunset'—fragrant apricot
'Sombreuil'—white
'Sally Holmes'—white single; pink tinges
'Altissimo'—red single
'Fourth of July'—red and white

English Roses
'Belle Story'—apricot blend
'Mary Rose'—dark pink

Hybrid Musks
'Cornelia'—coral pink
'Penelope'—light shell pink

Grandiflora
'Gold Medal'—yellow, with pink touches
'Tournament of Roses'—pink

your roses last month, follow the directions given for January on pages 52–53. Organic fertilizers applied now may need a little while to take effect, but their benefits will increase as soon as warm weather wakes up beneficial bacteria and fungi, which are always less active in winter.

Protect Roses from Pests and Diseases. It's an unfortunate fact that roses, one of our most loved garden plants and the national flower of the United States, are also host to a flock of pests and diseases. It's almost impossible to grow healthy roses without spraying them with chemicals. It can be done—I've done it myself for years—but to do so you have to grow only the most disease-resistant roses and be content with somewhat ratty-looking plants for the second half of the year.

If you're not satisfied by anything less than pristine rose plants unblemished by pests or diseases, you probably should give up growing roses except for Lady Banks, discussed below. On the other hand, if you can put up with a few imperfections in summer and fall, why not enjoy roses for their fragrance, drama, and romance? Through the years, gardeners have discovered many organic controls for pests and diseases. If you belong to the Rose Society and enjoy exhibiting roses, you will want to try out all these controls and use them at the times and in the manners recommended both by the Society and by this book. Environmentally friendly disease controls include Summit Year-Round Spray Oil and the Cornell Fungicide Formula. (See the Quick Tip on page 95.)

Grow Roses the Easy Organic Way. You may be looking for the easiest organic route that will produce good results. If so, here's what to do: Instead of growing roses in a plantation, mix them in with everything else in the garden. This confuses the bugs. Release beneficials, especially ladybugs against aphids, as described on page 44, and if you find any large aphid colonies, wash them off with a spray of water in the early morning. Also, help roses repel pests by placing a layer of earthworm castings over their roots now. (See the explanation on page 56.) This will get rid of ants and most other pests except for caterpillars. (Caterpillars are discussed in the March and April chapters, since they are not active this early in the year.)

Plant Disease-Resistant Varieties. Lastly, but most importantly, plant disease-resistant varieties (see the list on facing page) and yank out the troublemakers. Almost every All America Award–winning rose developed within the past ten years is easy to grow and resistant to diseases, but the healthiest of all roses is the ancient spring-blooming climber Lady Banks (*Rosa banksiae*), available in yellow double (*R. banksiae lutea*), fragrant white double (*R. banksiae banksiae*), and several rare forms, some of which are fragrant. All forms of 'Lady Banks' are drought-resistant, free from pests and diseases, and thornless, except for the white double banksia, 'Fortuniana' (*R. b. fortuniana*), which has thorny canes, larger leaves, and larger flowers born singly rather than in clusters.

Begin Disbudding. Besides keeping plants healthy and watering when rains aren't adequate, rose growers who wish to exhibit roses can begin corrective pruning as plants grow. Clip or rub off unwanted shoots heading in the wrong direction, such as toward the center of the plant, and disbud the side buds on hybrid teas and grandifloras so there will be only one large flower per stem. Allow the larger central bud to remain, and clip or pinch off the smaller ones on the sides. Disbud florabunda and old polyantha varieties, if desired, by removing the large central bud of each flower cluster. This will cause all the flowers in each cluster to open at the same time. Many modern climbing, ground-cover,

and landscape shrub roses do not need this attention, since they are grown for a big splash of color in the landscape rather than for cutting. Some, like the disease-resistant 'Betty Boop', have buds that open almost simultaneously in warm weather. Gardeners who don't desire exhibition roses or single-stem roses for cutting may not want to spend time disbudding.

Cut Off Blind Shoots. A blind shoot is a short and disappointing stem that sprouts a few small, oddly shaped leaves on its tip rather than ending in a flower bud. Blind shoots beset all rose growers and sometimes occur in great number. Some varieties, such as 'Peace', habitually make many blind shoots, but any rose variety may suffer from blind shoots when the weather is unstable—hot one day, cold the next—or if skies are heavily overcast, or if both problems occur at once. Roses often sprout blind shoots if they are getting too much nitrogen and not enough phosphorus and potassium—a climbing 'Cécile Brunner', for example, if it's grown on a fence, wall, or arbor next to a lawn that's fed with sulfate of ammonia. Inspect all roses now, and cut each blind shoot back to the first five-leaflet leaf. It will then grow a new shoot that will end as it should—with a bud. Throughout spring, remain on the lookout for blind shoots and cut them back as soon as you find them.

BULBS

When rains aren't adequate, keep spring bulbs well watered. Dryness can damage flowers. After ranunculi are 3 to 4 inches high, remove the netting (see page 42) that's covering them. Birds love the sprouts when they're young and tender but turn up their beaks at them later.

How to Cut Back Standard and Shrub Fuchsias

▸ Cut back standard and shrub fuchsias now. Look at the bark. The twiggy growth with smooth bark is what grew last year. The bark with darker color and rougher texture is the old wood. Cut off the twigs along with an inch or two of the older wood.

▸ Go easy on very old specimens that haven't been pruned in years. Cut these back by one-third now. Then wait a month to six weeks for the plants to regrow. When they're leafed out, cut back a third more, and wait for that to regrow before finishing the job. (If you cut back a venerable old fuchsia all at once, you might kill it.)

▸ Clean up the ground beneath the plant. Water, fertilize, and pinch back as described in the accompanying box on hanging-basket fuchsias. Fertilize plants in the ground once a week with fish emulsion, or use a dry organic fertilizer recommended for flowering plants according to package directions, or use 2 cups of aged chicken manure to start and 1 cup monthly thereafter. Follow up dry fertilizer with irrigation. At month's end, drench the root zone with humic acid.

▸ As plants regrow, pinch them to make them bushy, as described in the last point in the box on hanging-basket fuchsias.

How to Cut Back Hanging-Basket Fuchsias

▸ Cut back fuchsias growing in hanging baskets to pot level or 4 inches above the soil. If the plant is young and vigorous, take off all green growth.

▸ Turn the basket on its side and, with your gloved hand, clean off the surface of the soil. Remove all old leaves and debris.

▸ Dig out and remove about one-quarter of the old potting mix, roots and all. Replace it with fresh fast-draining acid soil mix. Press it down firmly. Rehang the plant in semishade.

▸ Water well after pruning. Don't let the roots dry out.

▸ Start to fertilize immediately, and fertilize regularly thereafter, with a balanced fertilizer high in growth ingredients. For example, drench the soil of each hanging basket once a week with fish emulsion mixed according to package directions. (Fish emulsion is an ideal fertilizer for fuchsias since it promotes growth; fuchsias can't bloom unless they grow.)

▸ As plants regrow, pinch them to make them bushy; when a sprout has made three pairs of leaves, clip off the top pair. This makes the plant branch. When it's really full, stop pinching and let it bloom.

Try growing lilies-of-the-valley (*Convallaria majalis*). You can buy prechilled roots, called pips, at nurseries now. Plant the pips in pots of high-quality potting mix, water them, and keep them in a warm eastern window. Give the pots a quarter turn daily. They'll bloom fragrantly in three weeks. (Once in bloom, keep them in bright light with no sun, and give them cool nights.)

QUICK TIP

Control Rose Diseases with the Cornell Fungicide Formula. *To control blackspot, mildew, and several pests on roses and to control early blight on tomatoes, try this formula: Mix together 1 tablespoon baking soda, 1 tablespoon light summer oil (such as Summit Year-Round Spray Oil), and 1 gallon of water. Spray once every four or five days, shaking the mixture frequently as you work.*

FUCHSIAS

Fuchsias bloom only on new wood. They need to be cut back annually to stimulate growth (see directions in boxes on facing page). In mild, frost-free coastal zones you can cut them back in November and allow regrowth during the winter, but for most other Southland gardeners, February's the time to cut them back. Wait until you see some green growth begin, and then prune and begin fertilizing with your own mix or a balanced organic product that will stimulate growth as well as bloom.

THE USE OF MANURE AS MULCH

Manure has been much criticized for its high salt content. If you've ever had a problem with salt damage on plants or had a soil test showing a high salt content in your soil, don't use it. But bagged steer manure is an inexpensive and readily available soil amendment that has some good applications when used wisely. On certain plants, it can be beneficial, especially when they're growing in fast-draining soil and when the application of manure is likely to be followed by rains. (Some plants, such as asparagus, are more resistant to salt than others.)

Horse or cow manure adds low-level nitrogen and life-giving humus to soils. Horse manure picked up daily by a conscientious owner is free from chunks of salt from broken salt licks, which cow manure often contains. Also, cattle feed is heavily salted, unlike the alfalfa hay commonly fed to horses. I often lay horse manure straight on top of sandy ground, over the roots of plants, as mulch and let it age right there while winter rains wash the nutrients into the ground. In a month or two I cultivate it into the ground prior to planting flowers or vegetables. Manure is especially good for fast-draining soils, but it improves clay soils, too, if rains or irrigation is adequate and the manure isn't salty. Rabbit manure is not salty and doesn't burn.

A few cautions: Every gardener should have an up-to-date tetanus shot, but particularly those using manure. Always wash vegetables carefully prior to eating them. Hog manure is unsafe for vegetable gardens; dog and cat manure contains dangerous pathogens. Hot composted manures, including bagged cow manure, contain fewer pathogens than fresh manure. Some experts say that pregnant women and people with low immune systems shouldn't eat raw vegetables grown in manured soils, but also say that cooked vegetables are fine. Cow and steer manure may contain hormones. Pig manure should never be used in gardens because of the pathogens in it: in one case, run-off from a pig farm where the animals were raised in crowded conditions infected an adjacent vegetable field with *E. coli*. "Good" types of manure, however, are often discussed inaccurately in news reports about vegetable contamination. In a recent example, thousands of tomatoes were pulled off supermarket shelves because the water in which they were washed was contaminated with *Salmonella st. paul*, a fairly mild but rare strain of *E. coli* that comes only from the droppings of frogs, lizards, snakes, and alligators. Yet the media reported the problem arose from "manure," without explaining that it was an exotic type of manure never used in farming.

These reports naturally frighten people who are not familiar with organic gardening and farming. Those who know about organic practices realize that the process of adding organics, including aged manure, to soil awakens beneficial organisms that in turn digest and change the structure of the newly added organic matter. Eventually it all ends up as humus. The chemical and biological processes by which soil organisms work are incredibly complicated, even miraculous. By the time manure and other organic matter have become humus, the chemical and biological structure of the original ingredients has been changed into totally different formulae and substances. (These are organic substances, not metals.) Healthy soil is thus a transforming and even, in a sense, a cleansing material.

The practice of manuring the ground is centuries old. When humans eat plants grown in soil that contains manure, they are not eating the manure itself but the transformed nutrients created as the organic material breaks down in soil and the resulting nutrients are absorbed by plants. Gardeners need to make up their own minds on these matters. Those who have grown up on farms and lived near farm animals all their lives are likely to feel differently from the city-born. It may be wise to refrain from using cow or steer manure on edibles unless you know its source, and to use only aged horse, chicken, or rabbit manures in the vegetable garden and on fruit trees.

Observing these precautions, spread manure over the roots of the following: bananas, ginger, cannas, asparagus, perennials, and old clumps of geraniums. Also spread it under bushes, trees, and ground covers, especially gazanias, ivy geraniums, and small-leafed ivy. (Don't use manure on camellias, azaleas, ferns, or succulents.) Water thoroughly after spreading.

PRUNING CHORES FOR WASHINGTON'S BIRTHDAY

Washington's birthday is the time-honored day for cutting back certain tropical and subtropical plants, including begonias, ginger, and cannas. Gardeners in mild areas, such as Rincon, Malibu, Long Beach, Laguna, and coastal San Diego County, can do these jobs a week earlier, on Lincoln's birthday. But if you live in a low-lying interior valley where you may still get a late frost, it's safer to wait until early March.

Prune Begonias. If you did not cut back the begonia 'Richmondensis' last fall, do it now. Cut them back to pot level or 4 inches above the ground to keep the plants from getting leggy in summer. Or you may opt to use progressive pruning, which means cutting back a few of the longest branches every month throughout the growing season. Feed lightly with a balanced fertilizer mixed at half-strength. They'll soon regrow. Richmondensis begonias grow best in the ground or in large containers—they dry out too soon in small ones. When ground grown, they can be used as a tall ground cover and can go two or three years before being cut back, if desired. Cut back container-grown angel-wing and other cane begonias to pot level now for a bigger flower display in summer. Spectacular varieties such as 'Irene Nuss', which bears the largest bunches of flowers of any cane begonia, especially benefit from this treatment. Flowers will be larger and plant size more controlled.

Clean up old-fashioned, tall-growing cane begonias, and cut out one or two old canes to encourage new canes to arise. Cane begonias can be grown in moist acid ground away from invasive tree roots or, if trees are a problem, in large tubs.

Prune Ginger, Cannas, Asparagus Fern, Ivy, and Pyracantha. If you live in an interior valley, remember to hold off pruning these plants until the weather has warmed up for good and there's no more chance of a late frost.

Ginger is monocarpic, which means it blooms just once on a stalk and then dies. If you don't cut back stalks that have bloomed, the clump will tend to stop sending up new growth. You won't get much, if any, bloom.

- **Algerian Ivy** (*Hedera canariensis*). Renew thick, woody stands by cutting them to the ground by hand or rented machine. Follow up with aged manure.
- **Cannas.** Cut all stalks that have bloomed down to the ground now to encourage new stalks to grow and make plants look as good as new. Deadhead them throughout the year (remove individual dead blossoms after bloom).
- **Kahili Ginger** (*Hedychium gardneranum*). Cut back to ground level now all stalks that have bloomed, to encourage growth of new stalks that will bloom this year. Leave stalks that have not yet bloomed.
- **Pyracantha.** Cut off branches that have borne fruit this year to the base of the plant or to strong side branches. Pyracantha bears only on one-year-old wood. Clip to shape and keep it growing, but don't cut off all of last year's wood, which will flower this spring and bear fruit next winter.
- **Shell Ginger** (*Alpinia zerumbet*). Beginning now, cut down to the ground all blooming stalks after their blooms have finished. Continue this throughout the year. After blooms fade, some varieties make little plantlets that you can use to propagate more plants.
- **Sprenger Asparagus Fern** (*Asparagus densiflorus* 'Sprengeri'). Renew ratty-looking clumps by cutting them to the ground now. Fertilize for quick bounce-back. (If you're not already growing Sprenger asparagus, don't plant it. It's invasive and almost impossible to eradicate. Meyers asparagus [*A. densiflorus* 'Myers'] and shrub asparagus [*A. retrofractus*] are better forms. Both are highly attractive and long-lived but noninvasive.)

COMPOST

A compost pile can be a great way to use up vegetable wastes from garden and kitchen and return them to the soil. In general, there are two ways to go: slow (cold) composting and rapid (hot) composting. Slow composting requires much more time and space but less effort than rapid composting, and it works eventually even if you don't have the perfect combination of ingredients. (Serious composters should consider purchasing a garden chipping machine, since small particles decompose much faster than large ones.) Rapid composting is indeed fast but takes considerable work; it kills most diseases and pest organisms, but you need scientific know-how and a ready supply of the necessary ingredients.

Slow Compost. Choose a hidden area at least 10 feet square. Dig within it a hole 1 to 2 feet deep and 3 to 4 feet square, and pile in such garden refuse as leaves, vegetable peelings, lawn clippings, and chopped remnants of garden plants. If you find you have too many dry materials and not enough wet ones while you are making a pile, sprinkle on some blood meal or mix in fresh grass clippings or wet organic kitchen wastes to provide extra nitrogen and speed up decomposition. Wet the pile often to keep it damp.

When adding such wet materials from the kitchen as fruit and vegetable peelings, first dig a deep hole in the pile and pour them into it; chop them up a bit with a spade and then completely cover them with other materials to prevent odors. Topping a cool compost pile with a thin layer of moist earth can also destroy odors and prevent flies from laying their eggs. Technically, the best compost is made without adding earth, but if an occasional topping of it

saves you from the horror of finding maggots in your compost pile, changing the rule in this case is worthwhile.

Keep adding to the pile until it is about 3 feet high and 3 feet wide; then start another. Leave the first for another six months or a year to rot. Slow composting is hit or miss. Some slow compost piles occasionally heat up due to the ingredients that have gone into them, and thus decompose faster than others. Some never go through a hot stage. Many cold compost piles become earthworm factories; the worms slowly devour all the organic materials and eventually turn them into rich soil. Sooner or later you'll end up with a heap of finished compost, and it will be about half the size of the pile you started with. When your compost has become even-textured, soft, crumbly, dark brown, and sweet smelling, and you can no longer discern what went into it, then it's sufficiently decomposed to safely add to garden soil. Use homemade compost like any other soil amendment—it's better than most you can buy. (This pit system of making compost is unconventional, but it's an excellent way to make a low-profile compost pile and keep it damp in our dry climate.)

Suburban and Small-Space "Composting"

Even without room for a compost pile, you can get some of compost's benefits. Mix vegetable wastes from the kitchen with unsoftened water, and purée them in a blender. Dig a hole with a trowel, and pour the contents of the blender straight into the garden soil. Cover it with earth to discourage flies. (This is a good way to feed earthworms and increase their numbers.)

You can also chop up vegetable and fruit wastes from the kitchen and bury them in flowerbeds and under the paths in your vegetable garden. They will slowly decompose, adding soluble nitrogen straight into garden soil.

Rapid Compost. Choose an area for composting or build a system of three wooden bins. A plan for bins is included in Sinnes's *All about Fertilizers, Soils and Water*. University of California Leaflet #21251, *The Rapid Composting Method*, tells you how to make compost in one to two weeks.

Basically, to make a good, active pile, it's necessary to mix equal amounts of carbonaceous wastes with nitrogenous wastes until you have a pile approximately 3 feet square. Carbonaceous wastes are woody materials, such as dry leaves, cornstalks, hay, and wood shavings. Nitrogenous wastes are fresh manure and damp green or wet plant materials, such as grass clippings, green leaves, and kitchen peelings. (Grass clippings do an excellent job of heating up compost, but don't layer them like other materials or they'll stick together in a leathery wet mat that won't properly decompose. Instead, separate them with dry materials; thoroughly mix grass clippings with an equal volume of hay or dry leaves.) Don't add earth to hot compost piles; earth only slows down the composting process and makes the final product too heavy.

Keep the pile damp. Covering the pile loosely with a sheet of black plastic can help hold in moisture and discourage odors that could attract flies. (With hot composting, flies are usually not a problem; all their eggs are killed by heat.) As soon as the pile heats up to approximately 160°F, begin to toss and turn it with a garden fork every day or two to keep it from getting too hot. (If the compost heats to over 160°F, the microorganisms that break down the organic materials will be killed and the process will have to start over.) As you work, try to get the inside portions onto the outside and the outside portions into the middle. Tossing also aerates the pile, which keeps the decomposition process functioning. In two to three weeks, when your compost has thoroughly cooled down and is fine-textured, dark, and sweet smelling, stop tossing it and use it in the garden as a soil amendment.

Warning: Never add cat or dog manure to compost since they contain dangerous pathogens. Meat, bones, and fat should not be added since they attract animal pests, including rats.

Enclosed Plastic Compost Containers.

Gardeners on small lots in suburban areas may prefer to compost in enclosed plastic containers, such as the Bio-Stack Bin, Soilmaker/

Soilsaver, or my personal favorite, the Green Cone Solar Digester, manufactured by Solarcone. The Green Cone is easy to set up and works as its manufacturer claims. It uses solar power to quickly decompose all kitchen wastes into the ground, is fully enclosed so it doesn't attract animals, and can safely take all kitchen scraps, even fish, meat, bones, and fat. It's easy to use, makes the garbage disposal unnecessary, saves precious water, and, when used in combination with a conventional compost pile, can make the conventional pile less attractive to animals. One Green Cone installed in full sun is reputed to take care of all kitchen wastes for a family of four. (Worm composting, discussed on page 410, is another way to get rid of kitchen waste and create organic soil amendment at the same time.)

How to Keep Wild Animals and Tree Roots Out of Compost Bins

Once wild animals, such as raccoons, opossums, mice, and roof rats, discover an open compost pile or wooden compost bin, they may use it as a convenient larder, visiting nightly to devour worms and freshly added kitchen peelings. To foil them, cover the floors inside your compost bins with concrete pavers. To prevent tree roots from invading from below, bury a sheet of heavy-gauge plastic beneath the pavers. Cover the sides of the compost bins with ½-inch galvanized-wire hardware cloth. Complete the project by building a hinged frame for the top of each bin. Cover these too with ½-inch hardware cloth. In rainy weather or to provide shade, throw a tarp over the top.

ANNUAL AND PERENNIAL FLOWERS

Deadhead and Feed Cool-Season Flowers.
If you planted cool-season flowers in October, they should have started to bloom before Christmas and will be in full bloom this month. If you got them in late, they'll start to bloom this month.

Continue to feed with a balanced organic fertilizer, and deadhead the plants or pick the flowers to promote bloom. Nitrogen is less active in cold soil, so choose a fertilizer with a high first number as well as bloom ingredients. Most of the new pansy varieties with smaller flowers don't need deadheading, but larger-flowered varieties look better if seedpods are removed. Older varieties need this care to keep them blooming. Among winter flowers that need to be deadheaded or picked to promote continuous flowering are calendulas, tall varieties of cineraria, foxgloves, Iceland poppies, linaria, snapdragons, and stock.

Plant More Flowers If Necessary. Fill bare patches and containers with transplants of such cool-season flowers as calendulas, evergreen candytuft (a perennial), foxgloves, primroses, pansies, and violas. If you planted these and other cool-season flowers at the right time (September through November), you won't need to plant many flowers now, because all available space will be taken. People who fill whole beds this late don't get their money's worth, because their flowers won't bloom for long. But there are some exceptions. Evergreen candytuft (*Iberis sempervirens*) is often available only in spring when in bloom. The corm *Oxalis purpurea* is a lawn weed in South Africa, but here it's a tidy, charming, pink-flowered, gray-green foliaged plant, super as a winter

and spring path-edger or rock-garden plant. It's adapted to our climate and dies down in summer, but it multiplies, and you can find it now only when it's in bloom. There's another one with dark purple foliage, but it's less prolific. Paludosum daisy (*Chrysanthemum paludosum*) is another small plant you can buy now in bloom, and you will never need to purchase more than one. Its tiny yellow-centered white daisies cover a compact 8-inch globe of green foliage nonstop for a month or two, and then the whole plant is likely to suddenly die—a disaster for those who don't realize that paludosum daisy is a cool-season annual. But this tragedy has a happy ending after all. This small, pretty daisy reseeds itself with abandon. In fall you'll have many seedlings to move around for edging beds. Feed them a bit, water when dry, and this time they'll bloom nonstop from winter until cut down by hot weather. Also available now are new varieties of viola and pansy that are both heat- and cold-resistant. They go through winter better than the old varieties and last longer in hot weather.

It's too early to plant most warm-season flowers, such as lobelia, marigolds, and salvia. They won't get off to a good start. One exception is petunias. They won't bloom in February but will create strong roots for better bloom later. So if you still have a whole flowerbed or tub to fill in a hot spot in full sun, choose petunias. Protect them from frost and snails. Feed for growth.

If you've been feeding cinerarias with nitrogen all winter, they should be large and healthy. Watch them now for the first flower buds, and continue to feed every two weeks until flowers open with a product to stimulate flowering, such as Tiger Bloom (2-8-4) or another fast-acting organic fertilizer high in bloom ingredients. This will give you a huge display. Then stop fertilizing but continue normal watering. Bait for slugs and snails; control leaf miners, if necessary, with earthworm castings or Vegol Year-Round Pesticidal Oil. (Beneficial wasps, once established, also control leaf miners.) Control aphids with insecticidal soap.

Cut Back Woody and Overgrown Perennials.

By midmonth you can cut back perennials that are woody and overgrown to basal growth (fresh new growth springing up close to the roots). Mexican bush sage (*Salvia leucantha*), for example, may die if you cut it back in fall, when the basal growth is only an inch or two high, but by February basal growth should be 6 to 8 inches long and actively increasing. Now you can safely cut all the woody parts off, leaving the new growth. Follow up with a little balanced fertilizer, add a layer of fresh mulch over the roots, and you'll soon have a fresh new plant on the old roots.

Any plant that has a similar show of fresh basal growth can be cut back safely now. *Artemisia* 'Powis Castle', for example, grows huge, flops open in the middle, and looks ugly. Cut it back now if you see new growth springing from the middle. You can keep artemisia from flopping open by cutting the bottom branches off from below in spring and fall (as described on page 266), but once it's happened, you have to attack it from the top. Also cut back to basal growth plants that bloomed late last summer and fall, including penstemon and *Verbena bonariensis*. It's too late to cut back plants that bloom mainly in spring, such as lavender. With lavender, just pinch back its rangy tips to keep it compact and bushy, but wait until after it blooms to shear the whole plant. Achillea (also called yarrow) and New Zealand brass buttons (*Leptinela squalida*) will bloom soon, but you can cut back outer portions of these and other creeping plants that are overwhelming their neighbors; transplant some if desired. Clean up coreopsis, cutting to the ground those short stalks that stick up above the rest of the leaves and have plantlets on top, sometimes with roots that you can stick into the ground.

Plant Perennials and Biennials.

Many fine perennials and biennials reach nurseries this month, and some are in bloom. The following selections, all available now, will give you an almost instantly colorful perennial border in hues of pink, yellow, blue, lavender, gray, and white: Gaura lindheimeri 'Siskiyou Pink', yarrow (*Achillea filipendulina* 'Gold Plate'), blue marguerite (*Felicia amelloides*), Salvia 'Indigo Spires', Santa Barbara daisy (*Erigeron karvinskianus*), French lavender (*Lavandula dentata*)— one of the easiest lavenders to grow here—and wallflower (*Erysimum* 'Bowles Mauve'). The last, a fine filler, makes a mound of gray-green foliage 2 to 3 feet tall and often 6 feet wide with nonstop mauve flowers arranged at equidistant intervals all over the top. In three years it wears itself out from flowering and suddenly dies, but by then you'll be bored with it.

If you didn't plant California poppies last fall, don't despair; you'll find them in nurseries by month's end. (Though usually treated as annuals, they're actually perennials.) Orange California poppies won't mix well with the colors of the border suggested above, but you could create a stunning arrangement in another spot with three 5-gallon Spanish lavenders (*Lavandula stoechas* 'Otto Quast') planted in a triangle and a drift of seven 1-gallon California poppies in front. Deadhead both these plants to keep them blooming.

Delphiniums are perennials that are usually treated as annuals here. When planting delphiniums, prepare a rich planting hole; put plenty of compost with some fertilizer mixed into it under their roots. Add a sprinkling of organic fertilizers of your choice, such as bone meal for phosphorus, greensand for potassium, and blood meal or cottonseed meal to provide nitrogen. Along with the fertilizer, I once put wet kitchen clippings—mostly papaya peels—into the planting hole, covered them with a little soil, and plopped a delphinium on top, which took off almost immediately with growth resulting in spectacular bloom. (Dry organic matter such as sawdust or coarse mulch rots slowly in soil and robs nitrogen from the soil in order to rot, but soft, wet organic matter is nitrogen-rich and rots quickly, though anaerobically [without air], when buried. This may create a smelly situation underground, but the process gives off fast-acting nitrogen that roots can immediately absorb. See below for more about fertilizing perennials.) After delphiniums have bloomed, cut them back; they may bloom again in summer. Foxglove is another biennial to plant now, though they may bloom later than if you'd put them in last fall.

Divide Plants That Die Down in Winter.

In late February, divide plants, such as saponaria (rock soapwart; *Saponaria ocymoides*), that act like true perennials and die down to their roots in winter. Saponaria is a low-mounding plant for the front of the border and interior zones with bunches of pink, phlox-shaped flowers blooming over a long season through summer and fall. It's a real workhorse, blooming long with little care. Other plants that can be divided now include Japanese anemones (*Anemone x hybrida*), true, or botanical, geraniums, and Stokes' aster (*Stokesia laevis*), which thrives in interior gardens given adequate irrigation, good drainage, and full sun. Wait to divide until you see little plants coming to life

and sprouting up; you may have plenty to share with friends. If rudbeckias live from year to year in your garden—they don't for everyone—divide these now or as soon as you see growth begin again. Do the same with clumps of echinacea and gaillardia. *Gaillardia x grandiflora* 'Yellow Queen', which is yellow throughout and great for bouquets, may still be in bloom now. Nevertheless, if the clump is too large, this is the time to divide and replant it. 'Yellow Queen' reestablishes quickly and keeps right on blooming. There's a **Rule of Thumb** that applies to all these plants, and perhaps some others I haven't thought of: *When perennials begin to grow again and show some life, it's safe to divide them.*

Fertilize Perennials.

In good years, winter rains will have washed nutrients to lower levels, so fertilize all perennials now in preparation for spring flowers. Alstroemeria, daylilies, pelargonium, and penstemon are among the plants that will reward you with much finer displays. One of the best things to use is cottonseed meal. Buy a sack and sprinkle it around (it's difficult to prescribe exact amounts when discussing organic fertilizers, but because they're milder, they're also less likely to burn). Organic gardeners eschew strong nitrogen fertilizers because they kill earthworms, and swear that organically nourished plants suffer less from pests and disease. Meanwhile, build up the humus content of your soil with homemade compost and other organic amendments. For nitrogen, rely on manure, cottonseed meal, and alfalfa meal. When a liquid fertilizer is called for, use fish emulsion. Sandy soils may be deficient in phosphorus and potassium. Bone meal and Sul-Po-Mag (0-0-22) or greensand can correct these deficiencies and should be added early in the growing season. Provide trace minerals by spraying with seaweed emulsion, and spread chelated iron. (For all these products, follow package directions regarding amounts.)

Also feed Madeira geranium (*Geranium maderense*) to keep it growing strongly now in readiness for flowering in late March or early April. Give it organic fertilizer for bloom and growth. (For more about Madeira geranium, see page 164.)

SEEDS FOR FLOWER AND VEGETABLE TRANSPLANTS

Although February is too soon to plant warm-season annuals and vegetables in the ground, it's not too early for seeds. Ambitious gardeners with lots of space to fill can grow their own transplants in flats or peat pots filled with sterilized potting soil. Cover the potting soil with a thin layer of chicken grit (available at seed and pet stores); this prevents damping off. (*Damping off* is a term used for the action of several funguses that can kill seedlings.) Use bottom heat (70°F) from a heat cable to germinate seed. (Alternatively, a 12- or 20-watt bulb in a "trouble light," protected from moisture by several layers of plastic, can be used under flats raised on bricks or flower pots.) Bright light for healthy transplants can be provided by a fluorescent shop light hung 7 to 10 inches above your flats. Leave it burning from fourteen to sixteen hours per day.

As soon as plants have developed two true leaves, begin feeding them at weekly intervals with fish emulsion diluted according to package directions. Give plants a gentle transition into the garden—first a week in the shade, then one in full sun, during daytime only. The third week, leave them out at night, too, to harden them off. Grow varieties, colors, and sizes not found in the nursery.

 QUICK TIP

How to Test the Thickness of Thatch. *With a sharp knife, cut a small triangle into the soil and pull out the resulting plug of turf. A layer of thatch between* $1/4$ *and* $1/2$ *inch thick is normal. Thatch thicker than* $1/2$ *inch will harm the lawn.*

LAWN CARE

Check Warm-Season Lawns for Thatch. Thatch is a layer of partially decomposed leaf sheaths, stems, and roots that forms between the earth and the grass blades. It's not made up of grass clippings. Certain subtropical grasses

How to Reduce Lawn Thatch and Landfill Waste

▸ Follow the **Rule of Thumb** for mowing: *Never mow off more than one-third to one-half of the leaf length of grass at any one time.*

▸ Instead of using a grass catcher, allow your lawn clippings to fall where they are mown. The lawn clippings will fall through the grass and decompose quickly.

▸ This continual mulching will actually help nourish your lawn with an organic source of nitrogen, reducing its need for fertilizer by almost a third, and slowing the growth of thatch.

▸ By not tossing out your grass clippings, you will do your part in alleviating the serious problem of urban waste.

How to Dethatch Warm-Season Lawns

▶ Wait until the weather in your area has definitely warmed up and your lawn has greened up and begun to grow. This happens in mid-to late February in coastal areas and in early March in inland valleys.

▶ Rent a professional renovator or dethatching machine, called a vertical mower, which cuts down into the thatch. (It may be necessary to reserve one in advance.)

▶ Mow the lawn short at least twice, first mowing back and forth in one direction and then across it from side to side. Adjust the blades lower with each pass.

▶ Drive the vertical mower over the area. Go in both directions and then diagonally. Start on the highest setting; then lower the level of the blades. (If the thatch is very deep, don't try to do the job all at once. Renovate the lawn by degrees over one or two years; with each treatment, remove ½ inch of thatch.)

▶ Rake up the thatch, bag it, and send it to the dump. Don't compost it—it would take a blow-torch to kill the stolons (above-ground shoots or runners that produce roots at their nodes.)

▶ Follow up by leveling, if necessary. (See directions in the box at right.)

▶ Evenly sprinkle on an organic fertilizer recommended for lawns, such as Biosol Mix (7-2-3,) applied according to package directions, or apply 6 pounds of chicken manure for each 1,000 square feet of lawn, using a spreader if you have one. A week later, spray the lawn with an organic product containing humic acid.

▶ Follow up by watering thoroughly. Keep the lawn well watered until it has completely regrown.

that spread by runners, such as Bermuda, make lots of thatch. Bluegrass is intermediate in thatch production, while tall fescue and perennial ryegrass make little, if any. If thatch is more than $1/2$ inch thick, it harms the lawn by preventing water and fertilizer from passing through (see the Quick Tip on page 103). Roots may even "move upstairs" and live in it. Thatch dries out fast, causing dead patches of lawn in summer. A thick layer gives a lawn a springy texture and makes mowers bounce, causing scalp marks.

Dethatch warm-season lawns, such as Bermuda (see directions in the box above) every two or three years, when they wake up and start growing again in late winter or early spring. If you dethatch your lawn just after it greens up, it will bounce back quickly. (Dethatch cool-season lawns in early fall, as described on page 360.)

CONTROLLING NUTSEDGE IN LAWNS AND FLOWERBEDS

Nutsedge is a troublesome weed that thrives in waterlogged soils in lawns and flower-beds; once established, it can survive drought. Though often called nutgrass, nutsedge is a true sedge. (Sedge stems are solid and triangular; their leaves are thicker and stiffer than most grasses and are in sets of three at the base. Grasses have round, hollow stems, and grass leaves are in opposite sets of two.) Two types

How to Level Your Lawn

When you mow your Bermuda lawn in summer, do you end up with brown, scalped areas? These mower marks may result from the machine bouncing on a thick layer of thatch, but many times they result from dips and bumps in the grade. Golf courses are kept smooth and their hills gently rolling by topping them with sand at least once a year and letting grass grow up through it. You can correct bumpy lawns in the same way, and you won't need to do it as often. Do this job just after the grass begins to grow; your lawn should bounce back fast and won't have scalp marks after mowing. Here's how:

▸ Measure the lawn and order sand and soil amendment. For each 200 square feet of lawn, you'll need at least 1 cubic foot of good washed plaster sand and 1 cubic foot of dark-colored, fine-textured soil amendment, such as ground nitrolized wood shavings or ground bark. (The dark color attracts heat and speeds growth.)

▸ Totally scalp and, if necessary, dethatch the lawn (as also described in this section).

▸ Mix the sand with an equal portion of soil amendment by putting a shovelful of one, then a shovelful of the other, into a wheelbarrow and mixing the contents.

▸ Arrange the sand mixture in piles all over the lawn. (This will look like the attack of a giant gopher.)

▸ Attach a 4-foot piece of 1-by-4 lumber to a garden rake (not a grass rake) to construct a leveling device. Drive half a dozen nails into the lumber and bend them over the teeth of the garden rake. Push and pull your leveler evenly over the lawn, filling in the depressions.

Follow up with fertilizer and keep the lawn well watered until the grass comes through, as described in the box on dethatching on the facing page.)

---

of nutsedge grow here: yellow nutsedge, which has light brown flowers, and purple nutsedge, which has reddish flowers and black or dark brown seeds. Both produce tubers on rhizomes that can be 8 to 14 inches underground. Because buds on the tubers sprout into new plants, patches grow to 10 feet or more in diameter. Nutsedge may arrive in your garden with a load of topsoil, unless you specified weed-free soil, or in potted plants. Hoeing or digging can get rid of the tops but spread tubers farther. Hand-pulling takes off the tops, but the tubers stay in the ground to sprout again, though repeated pulling can weaken the tubers.

The only organic control for nutsedge in lawns is to pull out all plants as soon as you see them. Treat now and again in March with a product containing corn gluten meal if plants have gone to seed. Keep pulling the plants when they reemerge; eventually you'll win out. (Chemical herbicides for nutsedge do exist but are poisons and thus not appropriate for an organic garden. Roundup, another more common chemical product that should never be used by organic gardeners, does not control nutsedge.)

Get rid of nutsedge in flowerbeds by continually weeding until the tubers are weakened, by shading the ground with a layer of mulch, and by maintaining an abundant growth of plants. Another method is to weed out the tops and then use a weed-block fabric to cover the ground between plants. (Nutsedge can pierce some fabrics; inquire when purchasing.) Place the weed-block fabric flat on the ground

How to Plant Bare-Root Asparagus

▸ Choose a good variety that will produce reliable crops in our mild climate. (Most asparagus varieties need freezing winters, which we don't have.) 'UC 157', 'UC 157F1', and 'UC 157F2' were especially developed for conditions in California and are available bare-root in February. These varieties are mostly male and will thus produce all, or almost all, fat, tender spears and lots of them. (Female spears make the berries and are more stringy.) 'California 500' is another fine variety but only for coastal gardens. It produces good crops in frost-free zones, but it cannot abide summer heat.

▸ Put the plants in a bucket of water to soak while you prepare trenches in well-drained soil, making them 1 foot deep, 1 foot wide, and 3 feet apart. (Add organic amendment if necessary.)

▸ Put 4 inches of well-aged manure mixed with one handful of bone meal per linear foot in the bottom of each trench, or mix in 15 to 20 pounds of 5-10-10 or 5-10-5 fertilizer per 100 feet.

▸ Cover the bone meal with 2 inches of soil, and form mounds 4 inches high and 18 inches apart in the trench.

▸ Place the plants on the mounds with their roots arranged out over the sides. Cover them with soil so that each crown is an inch below the soil surface.

▸ Water the plants well when rains aren't adequate. As they grow, add more soil to cover them until the trench is filled.

▸ Mulch with manure in February. Wait two years before starting to harvest.

around ornamental plants, or cover bare ground with it prior to planting, fixing it to the ground with landscape staples. Cut X-shaped holes in the fabric and plant through them. Finish by hiding it under a thick layer of organic mulch. Or create your own inexpensive, organic weed block by spreading newspapers 6 plies thick around plants, overlapping the edges. Cover the newspapers with mulch. Eventually they'll biodegrade; worms love the paper, and by the time it's gone, weeds will be, too.

Mow, Feed, Aerate, and Spread Mulch on Cool-Season Lawns. Cool-season lawns are still growing fast this month. Water them regularly when rains aren't adequate to keep them growing. Mow them frequently with the mower blades set long to 2 to 3 inches. Fertilize every six weeks, or less frequently with a slow-release formula. To increase the humus content of the soil, top cool-season lawns with a fine-textured organic soil amendment.

Grass that's mulched now will better withstand hot weather in summer. You'll need about 1 cubic foot of mulch for each 100 square feet of lawn. In fast-draining soils where salt damage has not been a problem, it's probably all right to use steer manure, despite its possible high salt content. If you have clay soil, it's wiser to use fine-textured nitrolized wood shavings or nitrolized ground bark. If soil compaction has been a problem, rent an aerator prior to mulching and run it over the lawn to remove plugs of earth and sod. Rake up the plugs; then spread the soil amendment and rake it into the holes. After aerating, mulch with nitrolized ground bark or nitrolized wood shavings, not manure. Water thoroughly after spreading it.

Continue to Control Crabgrass. In inland areas, control crabgrass by treating your lawn with an organic preemergent herbicide in early February and once again two weeks later (as described on page 73). If you live in a coastal zone and you failed to use a preemergent in late January, it may be too late now for preemergent control. Remember to start earlier next year.

If plants are already up and growing, you can still win the war against crabgrass. By pulling up the plants in fall (as described on page 360), using preemergent herbicide earlier next year, and applying it again in April, you will eventually get rid of the problem.

VEGETABLE GARDENING

February offers the last chance for planting winter crops. Whether to plant more at this time depends on how much ground you have, how close to the ocean you are, and how much your family likes winter vegetables. If you're crowded for space, it's much easier to continue to pick and eat the winter vegetables you have this month and hold off on major planting until March. That way most of the garden can be dug up, the soil prepared, and the first planting of summer vegetables put in all at one time. But if your family adores a specific winter vegetable, such as peas, a last crop could be put in now, especially if you live near the coast. Hot temperatures will ruin peas, but cool coastal conditions will permit much later harvesting. (When planting peas this late, be sure

to choose a disease-resistant variety. Mildew problems increase as the weather gets warmer.)

Other vegetables that can be planted now are lettuce, mesclun (see box, page 108), beets, broccoli, cabbage, carrots, cauliflower, celery, kale, kohlrabi, potatoes, radishes, spinach, Swiss chard, and turnips. Asparagus, artichokes, horseradish, and rhubarb can be put in bare-root. With asparagus, equally good and sometimes better results can be had from planting in March from seeds. To do so, dig and prepare the trench as described in the box on the facing page for bare-root planting, plant the seeds in the bottom of the trench according to package directions, and fill in with soil as the plants grow. The main difference is you'll have to wait three years instead of two before harvesting.

Harvest your winter vegetables regularly. Continue side-dressing the rows with fertilizer to keep them growing (as described on page 74). Water when rains aren't adequate, and vigilantly protect your crops from slugs and snails. Blanch your celery now (as described on page 412), and don't let slugs climb inside the stems or they'll ruin your crop. Lettuce also needs special protection from those slithery marauders (see page 115 for ways to control them).

How to Plant, Grow, and Harvest Mesclun

Mesclun (pronounced "mess-cloon") is the collo-quial term for "mixture" in Provence and refers to mixtures of young lettuces and salad greens. Traditional Provençal mescluns contain chervil, arugula, lettuce, and endive in precise proportions. American mescluns and those from northern France include a wide selection of exotic greens and even edible flowers.

▸ Purchase ready-made mesclun mixes or individual packages of salad greens for making your own mix. Choices include lettuces, arugula, endives, mustards, purslane, chicory, cresses, parsleys, fennel, escarole, mâche (lamb's lettuce), miner's lettuce (*Claytonia perfoliata, Montia perfoliata*), and others. (The Cook's Garden carries seeds. Address is listed on page 416.)

▸ Prepare a wide row in full sun. Or plant in a raised bed, a half barrel with holes drilled in the bottom, or pots. Dig wide rows or raised beds deeply, and mix in a 4-inch-thick layer of well-aged homemade or bagged compost. Apply organic fertilizer recommended for vegetables according to package directions, working it into the top 6 inches of ground, and rake smooth. For barrels, cover each drainage hole with a piece of broken crockery and fill with potting soil appropriate for vegetables. Mix in 1 gallon of commercial bagged chicken manure and an organic vegetable fertilizer according to package directions. Fill other containers with the same mix. Water seedbeds and containers deeply and let the ground settle overnight.

▸ Divide the seeds into two or three batches so that you can plant successive crops. (Store remaining seeds in a cool, dry place.) Thinly broadcast the first planting of seeds in a block and rake gently into the ground, or cover seeds lightly by sprinkling the ground with fine compost or potting soil. Pat down.

▸ Some greens, including mustards, kale, chicories, and certain lettuces, grow larger and more vigorously than others. Plant these separately so you can harvest some when they are young to add to mesclun and let others grow larger for use in salads and other dishes.

▸ Sprinkle the bed and bare areas surrounding the bed with an organic bait labeled for the control of slugs, snails, and cutworms in the vegetable garden. Or use other organic controls (as described on pages 115–116).

▸ Optional step: Cover the seeded area with a floating row cover, such as Reemay, available by sheet or roll at garden centers or through mail-order catalogs. Peg down the edges to protect against wind and birds, or build a lightweight, reusable wooden frame the size of the seeded area. (Use a staple gun to attach the floating row cover to this frame.) Remove the row cover when the plants are 1 to 2 inches high.

▸ Sprinkle daily or twice daily to keep seed moist. Water regularly by drip system, overhead watering, or hand-watering. Continue to control slugs and snails.

How to Plant, Grow, and Harvest Mesclun (continued)

▶ Begin harvesting by thinning according to package directions (pulling up whole plants) when they are 2 to 3 inches tall. When the plants are up 5 to 6 inches, begin regular harvesting by shearing the green 1 inch above the roots; the plants will regrow and you can continue harvesting for several weeks. Or, for slightly larger plants that are 5 to 6 inches tall, harvest by picking individual leaves from the outside edges of plants.

▶ Feed the bed once a week with a balanced liquid fertilizer such as fish emulsion, diluted according to package directions. Alternatively, apply dry organic fertilizers to the ground around the plants after harvesting and before rain. When rains aren't adequate, wash the fertilizer into the ground by watering overhead.

▶ Plant another patch for future harvests. Meanwhile, your first seeding of mesclun will provide salads for several weeks.

FEBRUARY CHECKLIST

PURCHASE/PLANT

{ } Continue to purchase and plant camellias and azaleas, 65, 90

{ } Choose and plant deciduous magnolias, 90

{ } Purchase clivia, 90

{ } Plant gerberas, 91

{ } Begin to plant gladioli, 91

{ } Plant lilies-of-the-valley, 94

{ } Fill in beds and pots with cool-season bedding plants, if necessary, 100

{ } Start seeds for flower and vegetable transplants, 103

{ } Plant more winter vegetables, including mesclun, if desired, 107

{ } Plant bare-root asparagus (but wait until March to plant seeds), 106

{ } Many succulents, including cacti, bloom in winter and spring; continue to purchase colorful types, 270

{ } Purchase and plant perennials in coastal zones, 101

TRIM, PRUNE, MOW, DIVIDE

{ } Prune kiwi vines, 89

{ } Cut back fuchsias after they begin to grow, 95

{ } In coastal zones, prune begonias, cannas, ginger, ivy, pyracantha, and Sprenger asparagus, 96

{ } Deadhead cool-season flowers to keep them blooming, 100

{ } Mow cool-season lawns, 106

{ } Check warm-season lawns for thatch. Dethatch if necessary, but wait until the lawn begins to grow, 103, 104

{ } Level Bermuda lawns that need it to prevent scalp marks from mowing, 105

{ } Propagate running (usually hardy) bamboos in coastal zones, 127

{ } Cut back Mexican bush sage, 101

{ } Cut back woody and overgrown perennials, 101

{ } Mow to reduce thatch and cut down on landfill waste, 103

{ } Finish pruning conifers, 267

FERTILIZE

{ } Continue to feed citrus trees in coastal zones, 63

{ } Continue to fertilize epiphyllums, 67

{ } Begin to fertilize avocado trees in coastal zones, 81

{ } Feed deciduous fruit trees, 86

{ } Fertilize roses, 91

{ } Begin to fertilize fuchsias, 95

{ } Spread manure over the roots of asparagus, bananas, cannas, ginger, and old clumps of geranium, 96

{ } Feed cineraria to promote bloom, 100

{ } Fertilize cool-season lawns, 106

{ } Fertilize raspberries and other cane barriers when they begin to grow, 405

{ } Fertilize perennials, 102

WATER

{ } Water all garden plants according to their individual needs; don't water succulents, *36, 270*

{ } Water roses, *91*

{ } Keep bulbs well watered, *93*

{ } Water cool-season lawns as required to keep them growing, *106*

CONTROL PESTS, DISEASE, AND WEEDS

{ } Continue to bait cymbidiums for slugs and snails, *68*

{ } Control pests on citrus trees, *65, 83*

{ } Control pests on ash, alder, and sycamore trees, *87, 88*

{ } Bait clivia for slugs and snails, *90*

{ } Protect roses from pests and diseases, *92*

{ } Protect cineraria from leaf miners, aphids, and slugs and snails, *100*

{ } Control crabgrass with preemergent herbicide, *107*

{ } Hand-weed flowers and vegetables, *46*

{ } Trap gophers, *385*

{ } Protect celery from slugs, *115, 412*

{ } Control nutsedge, *104*

ALSO THIS MONTH

{ } Continue to harvest winter vegetables, *107*

{ } Mulch young avocado trees, *83*

{ } Make a compost pile, *97*

{ } Mulch cool-season lawns, *106*

{ } Aerate cool-season lawns if compaction has been a problem, *106*

{ } Blanch celery a month prior to harvesting whole heads, *412*

March

THE FIRST SPRING-PLANTING MONTH

Wisteria Sinensis
(Chinese Wisteria)

Our spring planting season begins on the first of March, so roll up your sleeves and pitch in. People who set aside extra time for gardening in spring and again in fall find that their gardens require less maintenance during the cool winter and hot summer months. Sometimes weeks go by when the landscape seems to get along all by itself with only an occasional boost from the gardener. At other times, especially in March and April and again during September and October, good gardeners often spend whole days working outdoors. These are the months when most of the planting is done.

During March, you can plant most summer annuals and perennials, warm-season and cool-season lawns from seed, some cool-season and most warm-season vegetables, and almost all permanent garden plants, such as trees, shrubs, ground covers, and vines. (Wait a month or two to put in tropicals. They'll take off better in warmer weather.) If you've never gardened before, you couldn't choose a better time to start, because you'll soon see results. One of the wonderful things about our sunny climate is how quickly it makes the garden grow. Gardeners with low-lying or mesa-top gardens should still be aware of cool temperatures at night and the possibility of frost until March 15, or even late April in some foothill locations, but for most of us the weather has certainly warmed up. Winter is over; spring has arrived.

THE BASIC LANDSCAPE

Inspect. Fertilize the basic landscape if necessary. Gardeners who mulched the entire garden with horse manure last October or November are likely to find this one step is enough to take care of all their plants' nutritional needs for the year. Other gardeners would be wise to check now to make sure all bare ground (except for a foot or two around the trunks of trees) is covered with a 3- to 4-inch layer of organic mulch consisting of homemade, bagged, or trucked compost or manure. If trees, shrubs, and ground covers, such as gazanias, look as if they're struggling to stay alive, this is a cue to apply an organic fertilizer, such as Biosol Mix (7-2-3), over the roots of plants and follow up with mulch and water. Treating the ground with humic acid, kelp, and rhyzobia (discussed on page 130) will speed results. If, on the other hand, you've been adding organics all along and perhaps in addition feeding certain plants with specific organic fertilizers meant just for them, your plants should already have everything they need to take off with healthy growth now.

Many plants fall into the broad category of specialty plants because they require special handling. Some specialty plants, including cacti, succulents, and native plants, have little or no need for fertilizer. Others, such as camellias, azaleas, begonias, ferns, fuchsias, orchids, epiphyllums (orchid cacti), roses, fruit trees, and vegetables, have unique requirements. Follow the directions for them in this and other monthly chapters.

There are other exceptions, too. Old, overgrown gardens in rich soil sometimes become virtual jungles, feeding on their own refuse. To fertilize such a garden when there's no sign of nitrogen deficiency, such as stunted growth, yellow leaves, or disease, may simply contribute to more growth, which will require constant pruning. And such invasive plants as blue gum eucalyptus (*Eucalyptus globulus*) and old stands of Algerian ivy (*Hedera canariensis*),

once established, make one wish one had never planted them. Feeding them would make them more rampant.

Plant New Permanent Specimens. March is one of the two best times of year to plant almost anything we grow in the permanent landscape, such as trees, shrubs, vines, and ground covers. The other time is October. Planting in fall is traditionally considered to be just a bit better than planting in spring, but after a year or two, you'll never know the difference. Now through mid-June is the time to look your garden over, assess its strengths and weaknesses, replace troublemakers you don't like, and add permanent specimens where needed. Choose drought-tolerant plants over heavy water users. Be sure to group plants according to their needs for water, for sun or shade, and for soil type. Before purchasing any plant, research its requirements and growth habits.

FROST DAMAGE

If you have a cold, low-lying garden or live in an interior valley, beware: there's always the possibility of a late frost striking suddenly in early March. Keep a garden diary from year to year and listen to the evening news to help anticipate temperatures. Protect tender plants such as tomatoes with commercially available frost caps at night. Remove them during the day. If you grow tomatoes in cages, surround them with plastic. On cold nights, throw a cover over the top.

Once all danger of frost has passed, take tender tropicals out from under eaves and the spreading trees where you've sheltered them. At last you can cut off the unsightly frost-damaged portions of trees, shrubs, and vines. Control the urge to clean up too soon, though; the damage may not be as bad as you think. As soon as leaves start showing, you can safely cut off dead portions without destroying more than necessary. With bougainvillea in particular, wait until you see growth resume; then cut back to it. (Follow up with food and water to hasten its regrowth.) Bougainvillea blooms on new wood, so spring pruning often results in more summer bloom.

CONTROL OF SNAILS AND SLUGS

Warm spring rains keep snails and slugs on the prowl. Our common garden snail is actually the edible European snail *Helix aspersa*, an important food source since ancient times. One can grow them in cages, purge them, and eat them. (Picart's book *Escargots from Your Garden to Your Table* listed in the bibliography tells how.) But if you're more interested in simply getting rid of them, strike early and mount a multiflank attack. Here's a selection of controls:

- Go out at night with a flashlight and rubber gloves, handpick the snails, bag them, and dispose of them in the trash. (Look for them by day under leaves of amaryllis, agapanthus, agave, cannas, clivia, daylilies, and dracaena.)
- Wear rubber boots and squash them under foot (though eggs may survive).
- Clean up the garden; get rid of undergrowth and other hiding places.
- Surround trunks of citrus trees with copper collars. Snails won't cross them. Cut off low-hanging leaves that brush the ground.
- Lay on the ground such traps as upside-down grapefruit rinds, loose lettuce leaves, upside-down flower pots, and flat boards with 1½-inch wooden runners at each end to raise them off the ground. Next morning, throw away the lettuce leaves and grapefruit rinds, pests and all. Lift the boards and flower pots daily and dispose of the slugs and snails lurking underneath.
- Fill yogurt cartons with 1½ inches of beer (or a solution of 1 cup water, 1 teaspoon sugar, and ¼ teaspoon baker's yeast). Make entry holes in the sides. Sink the cartons upright in the ground, up to the holes. (Slugs will be attracted to them, become inebriated, and fall in and drown.)
- Keep ducks; they eat slugs and snails, though they also eat many garden plants. Chickens, guinea hens, jungle fowl, and bantams are also good at cleaning out slug and snail eggs, and they have varying appetites for plants. Other natural predators include ground beetles, skinks, snakes, starlings, frogs, toads, opossums, and—yes— rats. (If you live in an area free from snails, chances are it's infested with roof rats.)
- Introduce the African decollate snail, a carnivorous snail that eats young helix snails. (Their best use is in citrus groves rather than in home gardens since they damage new seedlings and transplants. They aren't legal in all counties.)
- Use baits. Ordinary bran is highly attractive to snails and slugs. Some gardeners sprinkle it on paths and open areas; wear gloves the following morning to gather and destroy the slithery creatures it attracts. Drop them in a small brown paper bag, cut short, or fold them into a half-sheet of newspaper, beat sharply with a brick, and bury deeply as slow-release fertilizer. This quick death may be unpleasant for the perpetrator but is kinder than using an organic commercial bait. The latter are harmless to people, pets, and wildlife but are death on mollusks; they include Sluggo Snail and Slug Bait and

Garden-Safe Organic Slug and Snail Bait. Both contain the fertilizer iron phosphate as their active ingredient. Safer's Ready-to-Use Slug and Snail Bait contains a patented form of ferric sodium hydroxy EDTA (ethylene diamine tetraacetic acid, an amino acid and chelating agent) together with carbohydrates, said to be fast-acting.

The **Rule of Thumb** for all baits: *When using snail and slug baits, bait once thoroughly; wait ten days or two weeks and bait again.* (The first treatment gets the parents; the second gets the offspring.)

ANNUAL AND PERENNIAL FLOWERS

Plant Warm-Season Annual and Perennial Flowers. March is the first month to plant seeds or transplants of warm-season annual and perennial flowers outdoors. If you weren't able to take advantage of fall planting, fill all beds and pots with warm-season flowers now. If you planted last fall, however, most beds will be full to overflowing with cool-season flowers. There's little if any room to plant more. The only planting to be done is to plant seeds in flats—for bedding plants to be set out later, to fill bare patches as they occur—and to plant pots and hanging baskets.

Continue to feed container-grown cool-season flowers with a liquid organic fertilizer for growth and bloom. Fertilize cool-season flowerbeds with a granulated organic fertilizer if growth or flowering slow down. Water it in well afterward. Deadhead flowers to keep them blooming.

Though nurseries are filled with such cool-season flowers as calendulas, Iceland poppies, nemesia, pansies, primroses, snapdragons, stock, and violas, wise gardeners remember that these are the flowers that should have been planted in fall. Planted now, cool-season flowers, for the most part, will give only a short season of bloom, especially inland. The height of their bloom season is April, though in coastal gardens some will last through May. Stock, snapdragons, calendulas, and Iceland poppies are particularly unhappy choices to plant now. Heat or disease knocks them down fast. Cyclamen, pansies, polyanthus primroses, and violas can be popped into blank spots, but don't fill whole beds with them. Polyanthus primroses and small-flowered cyclamen will bloom through June in cool coastal gardens, however, and can be kept alive to bloom another year. And newer varieties of small-flowered pansies are floriferous and heat tolerant. They may last into August.

If you're filling whole beds with annuals, prepare the ground thoroughly and choose mainly warm-season flowers. Good annual-flower choices to plant now from pony packs for color in sunny spots all summer long include ageratum, cosmos, marigolds, nierembergia, petunias, salvia, sweet alyssum, and verbena. In semi-shade, put in transplants of begonias, coleus, fuchsias, impatiens, and lobelia. (Bedding begonias and lobelia can take full sun along the coast when grown in the ground. Impatiens can take full sun only if they're in a cool, breezy spot next to a lawn rather than hot pavement.)

A large number of warm-season flower species can be planted successfully now from seeds. They include achillea (yarrow), ageratum, anchusa, balsam, ornamental basil, browallia, calliopsis (*Coreopsis tinctoria*), celosia (plume flower), cleome (spider flower), coleus (*Solenostemum*), cosmos, gaillardia, gazanias, geranium, globe amaranth, gloriosa daisy (*Rudbeckia hirta*), helipterum (everlasting), hollyhock, impatiens, lobelia, marigold, morning glory (be sure to nick morning glory seeds with a file so they'll sprout), salvia, sanvitalia, sunflower, strawflower (*Helichrysum bracteatum*), sweet alyssum, thunbergia, tithonia, and verbena. (Ageratum, coleus, impatiens, lobelia, and scarlet sage need light in order to germinate. Sprinkle seeds on top of prepared soil, and anchor them by pressing gently into the soil surface—don't cover them with earth. Keep them moist with frequent misting.)

Desert gardeners can plant Jerusalem cherry (*Solanum pseudocapsicum*), Madagascar periwinkle (*vinca; Catharanthus roseaus*), nicotiana, portulaca, and zinnias from seeds, but the rest of us had better not plant them yet. These heat lovers can't stand cold feet. They'll do much better if we wait for warmer weather.

Choose and Plant Perennials. An incredible number of perennials can be put in now, including achillea (yarrow), agapanthus, basket-of-gold (*Aurinia saxatilis* or *Alyssum saxatile*), campanulas (bellflowers and cup-and-saucer plants), carnations, marguerites (*Chrysanthemum frutescens* [*Argyranthemum frutescens*]), columbine, coral bells, coreopsis, daylilies, delphiniums, dianthus, dusty miller, evergreen candytuft (*Iberis sempervirens*), gaillardia, geum, penstemon, perennial forget-me-nots (*Myosotis scorpioides*), Pride of Madeira (*Echium candicans*), Shasta daisies, and statice. Most of these have been grown in California since Victorian times, but in recent years a tidal wave of new perennials has swept into our gardens, and every year brings more. Botanical geraniums, salvias, and ornamental grasses have become so numerous they deserve separate treatment. (See pages 165, 260, and 326 for discussions of these.) It's an exciting time to be gardening, but also a bewildering one. Sometimes the only way to discover whether a new

plant will work for you is to try it out. Here are a few facts about perennial gardening to keep in mind.

Technically, a perennial is a nonwoody plant that lives more than two years on the same roots, dies down in winter, and comes to life again in spring. In Southern California, however, this doesn't often happen. Many perennials that die to the ground in winter won't succeed in the mildest gardens along the coast. Other perennials turn into woody shrubs; some even flower year-round (making it difficult to decide just when to cut them back). Thus, the typical Southern California perennial garden or border is a conglomeration of soft-tissued plants and flowering shrubs. It's usually tall and billowy and needs frequent pruning to keep the plants in line.

When choosing plants, try to find out their eventual size so you can space them properly. Planting a perennial bed correctly requires the gardener to place tiny plants so far apart that enormous gaps remain between them, to be filled for the first year with nothing but mulch and human patience. If yours is in short supply, fill in with annuals. Beware of plants that are too large for your garden. Cape mallow (*Anisodontea*) and *Westringea fruticosa*, for example, are dense shrubs that will grow inexorably to 6 feet tall and wide, crowding out smaller adjacent plants. For small spaces, choose W. 'Morning Light'; it's finer-textured with nice variegated foliage, a good substitute in small gardens for sprawling Artemisia 'Powis Castle'.

Allow the shapes, colors, and heights of plants to play against one another, just as you would in a flower arrangement. Even if space is limited, the tall, airy, purple-flowered stems of *Verbena bonariensis*, white *Gaura lindheimeri*, and the spikey *Salvia* 'Indigo Spires' are easily controlled and will add welcome relief to lower mounded plants such as pink scabiosa (*Scabiosa africana* is difficult to find but the best kind) and white Santa Barbara daisy (*Erigeron karvinskianus; E. karvinskianus* 'Moerheimii' has larger flowers). Try to find plants that succeed for you and bloom over a long season or at a time when especially needed. Strive for a garden with its own distinct flavor and big drifts of color rather than a bit of this, a bit of that. The uncertainties involved in plant choice add to the fun of gardening; you can always move things that don't work out. When the garden does at last fill in and bathe itself in flowers, the surprises and discoveries will increase your delight.

Once flowers fade, the need to deadhead takes over. Timely pruning and fertilizing plus replacement of plants as they die can keep a perennial garden going for many years. Left untended, a California perennial bed will soon become an overgrown tangle. By the end of March, for example, plants that bloom only in winter, such as yellow flax (*Reinwardtia indica*), need cutting back. Once it stops flowering, cut all the woody stems that have flowered down to the ground. Also, when you see new growth at ground level on blue lily turf (*Liriope muscari*), variegated liriope (*L. muscari* 'Variegata'), and other, similar plants, use sharp, one-hand lawn shears to cut off the faded foliage above the new growth, so the old leaves won't be mixed in with the new.

ROSES

Water Roses Deeply. Give roses plenty of water this month so they can grow plenty of leaves, stalks, and buds for next month's flowers. In interior zones, they may need as much as 2 inches of water per week at weekly intervals in fast-draining soil.

Fertilize Roses. Continue to fertilize your roses this month according to the system you've chosen. If you're feeding with a complete fertilizer recommended for roses, check your calendar to see when you did the job last month, and fertilize at the suggested interval; once again, mark the date on your calendar. By now most roses will be making buds, and a few may begin blooming. If you're feeding with generics, your choices this month include compost tea, manure tea, and alfalfa tea, sometimes called witches' brew because of its unpleasant odor. (See the box on the facing page.) It's labor-intensive but inexpensive, and homemade liquid fertilizers such as this one really do work wonders. Carrying watering cans and buckets of liquid fertilizer can be a daunting task, but if you dilute the concentrate with water in a clean drum or trash container you can apply it with a siphon device attached to the garden hose. Little paint buckets are much lighter to use than watering cans when scooping out the sludge, or skip the whole tea-making system and feed roses with dry alfalfa powder or pellets and simply water these into the ground. Though not quite as effective as the liquid form, these work too. (Cost-free fertilizers are discussed on page 53. Also see the chart on page 28.)

Rose-Pro Fertilizing. Rose-Pro gardeners can fertilize this month with a product containing humic acid. Additionally, when roses have 4 to 6 inches of growth, drench the soil with one or two bucketsful of alfalfa tea. (See the suggestions above and the recipe in the box on the facing page.) Or apply any organic liquid fertilizer of your choice, such as compost tea or fish emulsion diluted according to package directions. Some recipes for alfalfa tea include Epsom salts for magnesium, but gardeners who have already fed with John and Bob's Soil Optimizer and/or kelp and humic acid don't need to add Epsom salts since these products provide a good supply of trace minerals, including magnesium.

Recipe for Alfalfa Tea

▸ Place a sturdy, lidded 30-gallon trash can in a sunny area near roses and fill halfway with water from the hose.

▸ Add approximately 4 gallons of dry alfalfa meal or pellets. Stir with a broom handle to combine. Tightly cover the trash can and steep for four days.

▸ Stir daily with a broom handle. (The smell will be increasingly pungent.)

▸ On the fourth day, don't stir, but feed the liquid to your roses, scooping it up with a bucket or watering can or using a siphon device attached to the garden hose. Leave the sludge in the bottom of the can.

▸ On the fifth day, stir up the sludge in the bottom of the can and pour or scoop bucketsful of it evenly among your roses. (The high smell will dissipate, and roses will respond with vigor.)

Control Pests and Diseases. Control pests by handpicking, by spraying with insecticidal soap, and by releasing beneficials, including lacewings and ladybugs. Purchase fresh, healthy ladybugs at your local nursery; it's not necessary to send away for a special kind. Spread them after prechilling and in the evening (as described in the Quick Tip on page 160). Some ladybugs will fly away by morning. Others will lay eggs, and still others may settle down and stay, especially if the garden is moist, contains pollen-bearing plants and a pond or fountain,

and has not been sprayed with poisons. Disease control can be partially accomplished without spraying by growing disease-resistant roses exclusively and by spraying with Cornell Fungicide Formula (see page 95) against mildew.

After a few months of feeding roses organically, you may find they respond not only with darker leaves and more flowers but also with better resistance to pests and disease. If you also banish the troublemakers and replace them with disease-resistant varieties, you'll have no disease problems whatsoever and mighty few pests. But who can give up the delightfully fragrant 'Mister Lincoln' or 'Double Delight'? These two and a few other favorites are mildew magnets, but even they will fare better than before.

Begin or Continue Disbudding. If you're interested in growing roses for show or if you prefer your roses to bear only one large flower per stem, begin disbudding your hybrid tea and grandiflora roses early this month. To disbud a rose means to remove the secondary, or side, buds on the flower stem shortly after these appear. Secondary buds sap strength from the primary buds. By removing them, you allow the center bud to grow to full size. (An exception is when roses send up new canes. In this case, allow them to "candelabra": to grow naturally without disbudding in order to get maximum height.)

In most cases, there are only one or two side buds to remove, and some roses have none, but a few hybrid tea and grandiflora roses make so many secondary buds that none of the flowers can fully open. Disbud florabundas and polyanthas, if desired, by removing the larger central bud, so all the buds in a cluster will open at once. Easy-care landscape roses, including many modern shrub roses, climbers, and ground covers, need no disbudding, and most home gardeners never bother to disbud their roses.

How to Grow Tuberous Begonias from Tubers

▸ Fill flats with moist acid potting soil. Roll the tubers in soil sulfur and sink them into the potting soil so that each one is barely covered, with the bumpy concave side up, the rounded bottom down.

▸ Place the flats in a warm, shaded spot with early-morning sun or in a lath house or gazebo. Keep them damp, but don't fertilize them yet.

▸ When growth is 2 to 3 inches high, plant in well-drained acid soil in pots, hanging baskets, or the ground under an eave or noninvasive tree, preferably facing east. (Plant them with leaf points facing the front of the bed; the flowers will face the same direction.)

▸ Wait until growth is 3 to 4 inches high, then start feeding the plants regularly, every time you water, using fish emulsion diluted according to package directions.

▸ Control mildew with PROBIOTICS 4 Plants' Defensor Bacterial Inoculator. (See pages 58 and 187 for explanation.)

▸ Always allow plants to dry out a little between waterings. Begonias are far more drought-resistant than they appear.

BULBS

Spring-Flowering Bulbs. Unless rains are steady and frequent, continue to water spring-flowering bulbs. After they finish blooming, cut off the flower pods and feed the plants with a organic fertilizer—it's an investment in next year's performance. Don't cut the leaves off until they go brown and die back. (If their floppy appearance bothers you, tie them in knots.)

Tigridias. Bulbs of tigridias, or tiger flowers, can be found at local nurseries now. Plant them 6 inches apart and 3 inches deep in full sun along the coast, or wherever they'll get afternoon shade inland. Fertile loam or sandy soil is best. If you have clay soil, mix in plenty of soil amendment or plant in pots or raised beds. The colorful blooms appear in July and August. Each flower lasts only one day, but others follow on the same branch, so the bloom season is quite long.

Gladioli. Tie gladioli planted in February to stakes installed at planting time. Protect them from slugs and snails, and keep them well watered. Feed potted glads with liquid organic fertilizer. Continue to plant gladioli, though if planted now, they will need more protection from thrips in summer.

Dahlias. Prepare planting holes for dahlias by mixing plenty of organic matter into the soil. Some aged chicken manure can be added to the soil now, along with bagged organic soil amendment or homemade compost, in preparation for planting in April. Dig the organics deeply into the ground—as much as a foot deep—and keep the soil damp.

Tuberous Begonias. Start tuberous begonias this month. If you kept some tubers from last year, take a look at them now to see whether they're showing signs of life. If so, bring them out of hiding and start watering them. Buy new ones at local nurseries. Some tubers are slow to sprout, so choose those that already have a sprout or two.

Tuberous begonias aren't easy to grow, but if you have rich acid soil in an east-facing area, not too many snails, and a knack for growing begonias, they can be one of the most rewarding plants for summer color in semishade. Years ago they were considered suitable for coastal zones only. Heat-resistant varieties such as 'Non-Stop' have made it possible for gardeners in interior zones to try their hand at this most colorful and exotic-looking garden plant. If growing them from tubers sounds too involved, wait until summer and visit a "dig-your-own" nursery, such as Weidner's Begonia Gardens in Leucadia, San Diego County.

HERBACEOUS, OR SOFTWOOD, CUTTINGS

March is the best month for rooting herbaceous cuttings, also called softwood cuttings, to make more plants. Good candidates include 'African Blue' basil, cane and 'Richmondensis' begonias, chrysanthemum (*Chrysanthemum x grandiflorum*), marguerite (*Chrysanthemum frutescens, Argyranthemum frutescens*), euryops, pelargonium, russelia or coral fountain (*Russelia equisetiformis*), ornamental salvias, roses, and any perennial plant that has been cut back in winter and has new growth springing up close to the ground. To make softwood cuttings correctly, take them early in the day. For each cutting, clip 3 to 5 inches of succulent bendy growth from the tip of a branch. (It snaps when bent even though it is soft and flexible.) Remove the lower leaves of each cutting, leaving two or three leaves in place. (Russelia cuttings may have no leaves, but sections root easily.) Cuttings that are taken low on the plant, close to the roots, contain more natural rooting hormone than others and root quickly. Some may even have root hairlets attached; leave these on. Dip the cut end in a rooting hormone, such

as RooTone or Dip'N Grow, and plant in pots or flats of fast-draining potting mix to which you've added about 10 percent perlite. As soon as they're rooted, transplant them into pots or the ground. Feed them often. When they start to grow, pinch them back to make them bushy. Chrysanthemums root easily but once rooted require more care than most plants, including regular feeding, pinching, pest control, and staking. Given this care, they can reward you with masses of old-fashioned color in fall.

CITRUS AND AVOCADO TREES

Now's a good time to plant citrus and avocado trees. They'll have all spring and summer to get established before winter's cooler temperatures slow their growth. Provide them with good drainage and choose varieties that are right for your area. If you wrapped the trunks of young trees last fall, unwrap them now.

In interior zones, also begin fertilizing citrus and avocado trees this month (as described on pages 64 and 81). In coastal zones, continue to fertilize them.

MACADAMIAS

As with citrus and avocado trees, this is a good time to plant macadamias and to unwrap the trunks of young trees if you wrapped them for frost protection last fall.

Two species of macadamia are grown here, the smooth-shelled integrifolia (*Macadamia integrifolia*) and the rough-shelled tetraphylla (*M. tetraphylla*); both are from Australia. These trees are attractive, slow-growing evergreens with glossy green foliage and white flowers. The trees can survive drought well, but in order to bear a good crop, they need about the same amount of water that avocado trees require. Overwatering is seldom a problem. Macadamias bear round nuts that are notoriously difficult to crack; a special nut-cracker is a necessity. The kernels have a high oil content and delicious flavor; in stores they're a luxury item.

Fertilize Macadamias.

Macadamias' precise fertilizer requirements are not yet known; over-fertilization may actually harm the tree. When these trees are grown in fertile garden soil well mulched with aged compost or manure and are given adequate water and full sun, they'll increase in size and produce crops with no fertilizer whatsoever. However, if you're growing a macadamia tree in poor soil, or if it's stunted in size and bears poor crops, feed it very lightly with a complete organic fertilizer. The safest way to feed a macadamia is to apply a solution of fish emulsion over its roots twice monthly during any month of the year when the average minimum temperature is in excess of 50°F. Mix 5 tablespoons of fish emulsion into 5 gallons of water, and sprinkle the solution all over the ground under each tree.

Select and Plant Macadamias.

When purchasing a macadamia tree, don't buy a seed-grown tree, which may or may not bear nuts. Be sure to choose a proven, grafted variety. Most varieties are hardy to 27°F, but all grow best in frost-free zones. Integrifolias and hybrids are more cold-resistant than tetraphyllas. ('Cate' and 'Elimbah' are tetraphyllas, and 'Beaumont', a good backyard tree, is a hybrid between *M. tetraphylla* and *M. integrifolia*.) If gophers live in your vicinity, line the planting hole with a basket of chicken wire to protect the young roots from gopher damage.

Harvest Macadamias.

The nuts on macadamia trees ripen at different times of year depending on variety. When the nuts are ripe, they usually fall off the tree over a period that may last several months—ninety days is common. The nuts from 'Cate', for example, ripen from September through mid-December, and those of 'Elimbah' ripen from December to April. 'Beaumont' is an exception to this rule; it hangs on to its crop long after the nuts are ripe, so you must pick them off. If you're growing a 'Beaumont', strip all the nuts from the tree during the first week in March. Unfortunately, most gardeners leave them hanging on the tree because they don't realize that 'Beaumont' nuts stick tight. Leaving the ripe nuts on the tree makes 'Beaumont' bloom throughout the year, eventually dropping its yearly crop of nuts over about nine months—from October through June—and over several years this will make the nuts successively smaller until all you get are "peewees" (undersize nuts). But if you pick the nuts off by hand during the first week in March, the tree will put all its energy into the new crop, and you'll get a good harvest of large nuts the following year. With all other varieties, wait until the nuts fall to the ground—don't ever pick them or shake them from the tree—and then gather them up at least once a week.

Some varieties of macadamia are self-husking—the husk, or outer covering of the nut, splits open when the nuts ripen. 'Cate' is somewhat self-husking, 'Beaumont' is reasonably self-husking, and 'Elimbah' and some integrifolias are less so. But with many varieties, the gardener must manually remove the nuts from the husks.

Macadamia nuts require considerable processing. After harvesting and husking, it's important to properly and slowly dry macadamia nuts; otherwise they'll be sticky or gummy (see the box on the facing page for directions).

How to Harvest, Husk, Dry, and Roast Macadamia Nuts

People who take the time to perform the following tasks can produce homegrown nuts that are every bit as good as those grown commercially. Because of the chemical makeup of macadamias, slow drying is essential for a good product.

▶ **Harvest Ripe Nuts.** If your tree is a 'Beaumont' variety, pick all the nuts from the tree during the first week in March. With all other varieties, you know that the nuts are approaching ripeness when they start falling from the tree. In the case of varieties other than 'Beaumont', the first few nuts that fall (during the first two weeks) may not be completely ripe. Open some up; if they're wrinkled or discolored, throw them out and wait until good nuts start falling. Once they do, rake them up every day or two and separate the nuts from the leaves. (The nuts are likely to spoil if left lying on the ground for more than a week.)

▶ **Husk the Nuts.** Use a large pair of pliers to remove the husks (the outer coverings of the nut that may or may not remain attached to the nuts). If your tree bears nuts that are difficult to husk, let the unhusked nuts sit several days in shade, and then they'll be easier to remove. It's best to husk the nuts from 'Beaumont' immediately.

▶ **Air-Dry the Husked Nuts in Their Shells.** To do this, spread them in shallow, screen-bottomed trays and put the trays on a rack or other support in a dry, shady place. Leave them there for two or three weeks.

▶ **Finish Drying the Nuts in Their Shells over Low Heat.** Do this by placing them in a screen-bottomed container over a furnace register for three or four days. Or dry the nuts at 100° to 115°F for twelve to forty-eight hours, or more, in a shallow pan in the oven. (The lowest possible setting on an electric oven may dry the nuts in as little as twelve hours. The heat given off by the pilot light in an old-fashioned gas oven is ideal; it will dry the nuts in three or four days.) From time to time crack open one or two nuts to test their progress. When the shells are dry and brittle rather than bendy—even though still hard—and the nuts are loose in the shell and approaching crispness, they're done.

▶ **Store the Nuts in Their Shells.** Enclose the dried nuts in sealed heavyweight plastic bags to prevent them from absorbing moisture, and store them in a cool place.

▶ **Remove the Shells.** Crack open the hard nutshells with a special macadamia-nut cracker, available from the California Macadamia Society, P.O Box 1298, Fallbrook, CA 92088.

▶ **Store the Nutmeats.** Store the nutmeats in tightly covered containers in the refrigerator or freezer. (Roasted nuts may also be stored this way.)

▶ **Roast the Nutmeats.** Shelled macadamia nuts are ready to eat or to use in cooking, or you can roast them. In a preheated conventional oven, roast whole and half nuts for 40 to 50 minutes at 250°F. (To avoid burning, don't roast broken pieces that are smaller than halves.) Watch them carefully, and stir them occasionally to prevent burning. Remove them from the oven as soon as you see them start to turn from white to light tan.

To use a convection oven, first make a basket from folded quarter-inch hardware cloth. Fill it with shelled nuts of all sizes—wholes, halves, and pieces—and roast at 300°F for 20 minutes.

EPIDENDRUM

Epidendrum orchids are easy to grow in pots or the ground, are inexpensive, bloom almost year-round in frost-free zones, and are almost immune to pests and disease. Grow them in full sun along the coast, in partial shade inland. They're spectacular in raised beds flanking swimming pools and worth hunting for in specialty nurseries.

Once an epidendrum stem has borne its clusters of cattleya-shaped flowers, it won't bloom as well a second time. Cut it back to the second leaf joint from the ground. Stick the cuttings in the ground or in pots filled with potting soil and you'll soon have new plants. Feed them often with organic liquid fertilizer for growth and bloom, or choose a granulated type and follow package directions.

CAMELLIAS

Improve the shape of camellia bushes now by judicious pruning, and bring the cut branches inside to enjoy, leaving on the flowers and leaves. Look at the structure of your camellias; cut where you want to increase bushiness. If you look closely at a branch, you'll see the bump where last year's growth began. The new wood is a different color. Make your cut in this new wood just beyond the bump. This will produce branching and more flowers next year.

AZALEAS

The more vigorous an azalea, the easier it is to grow. But some that are robust and easy to grow—Southern Indica azalea varieties such as 'Pride of Dorking', 'Formosa', and 'Phoenicia';

Rutherfordianas such as 'L. J. Bobbink'; and even some heat-resistant Brooks hybrids—sometimes throw out extra growth in awkward places. Don't do all-over pruning yet, but now is the time you can improve an azalea's shape by cutting out undesirable, crossing, or old woody branches that have ceased to bear well. These unwanted branches make lovely cut flowers to take into the house. Choose and plant azaleas while they're flowering, but don't feed them until the bloom season is over. Overfeeding azaleas is a cardinal sin. It's possible to kill them with kindness as well as neglect. They also mustn't be overwatered, but never let an azalea dry out completely or it will die.

FUCHSIAS

Continue to feed and pinch back fuchsias. They bloom on new wood only. Every tip will produce flowers, so the idea is to make the plant produce as many tips as possible. As soon as each sprout grows three pairs of leaflets, pinch out the top pair. Take some of the bendy new unpinched growth for cuttings (see the box on the facing page).

HIBISCUS

Start to prune tropical hibiscus (*Hibiscus rosa-sinensis*). Hibiscus flowers only on new wood; if you never prune it, the flowers appear ever farther from the center until they're out of sight on top of a leggy shrub. Young plants need little or no pruning. Plants more than five years old should be pruned a little every month from now until August. Don't chop hibiscus all over like a hedge, because that would slice the large leaves in two. Here's what to do:

- Choose only three or four woody branches to remove now. For symmetry, they should be on opposite sides of the shrub. Reach into the hibiscus and prune out the whole branches, back to two or three growth buds from the center of the plant. This will encourage bushiness and regrowth from within. (With very vigorous varieties, such as 'Agnes Galt', prune harder now, taking out as much as one-third of the old woody growth.)
- In a month or six weeks, remove three or four more old branches in the same way, and proceed thus throughout summer. Note the schedule on your calendar. This progressive pruning will result in lots more growth and flowers. (Don't prune hibiscus in winter.)
- To keep hibiscus shaped as a screen or large hedge, head back one-third to one-fourth of the tip growth 1 to 2 feet into the shrub, working here and there all over the sides and top of the hedge. Come back in a month and head back another third. Continue throughout summer. When you walk away, no one should be able to see you've pruned.
- Follow up with organic fertilizer and water.

CONTROL OF GIANT WHITEFLY

Be on the lookout for giant whitefly (*Aleurodicus dugesii Cockerell*). Adults are approximately 3/16 inch long, slightly larger than other whiteflies. Look for infestations on aralia, avocado, begonia, bird of paradise, blue dawn flower (*Ipomoea indica*), citrus, eugenia, ginger, hibiscus, mulberry, orchid tree, xylosma, and all broad-leafed tropicals.

Giant whiteflies hide under leaves in large colonies. Females lay their eggs in a spiral pattern, usually on the bottom of leaves but sometimes on top. The eggs soon hatch into

How to Start a Fuchsia from a Cutting

▸ Clip from an established fuchsia a soft, bendy growth tip with two or three pairs of leaves.

▸ Clip off the bottom pair of leaflets.

▸ Dip the cut end of the stem, including the node from which you have clipped off the leaves, in a rooting compound, such as RooTone or Dip'N Grow, and knock off the excess. (A node is the place on a plant stem from which one or more leaves grow.)

▸ With a chopstick, make a hole in a 4-inch pot filled with fast-draining acid potting mix.

▸ Take your first "pinch": clip off the top pair of leaves so the plant will branch as soon as it begins to grow.

▸ Write the variety name on a plant label and stick it on the pot.

▸ Keep the plant moist in semishade. Begin feeding with diluted fish emulsion as soon as growth begins.

▸ As soon as the roots fill the container, pot the plant on—repot it in a container one size larger—and pinch it back to keep it bushy.

immature whiteflies, called nymphs. Both nymphs and adults feed by inserting needle-like mouthparts into leaves and sucking on the plant's sap. The nymphs excrete sticky honeydew and exude long hairlike filaments of wax up to 4 inches in length that rapidly become a sticky and unsightly mass. Heavily infested plants are severely weakened and look as if they have been bearded or flocked.

Release Beneficials. To bring giant whitefly under control, entomologists have released legions of parasites and predators known to attack it, including two minute Mexican wasps (*Ideoporus affinis* and *Encarsiella noyesii*). Giant whiteflies are not a problem in Mexico, their country of origin, because they coexist in balance with these and other beneficial creatures. Gardeners can help bring about a similar balance here by purchasing beneficial insect allies from nurseries and insectiaries and by not spraying with broad-spectrum pesticides that can kill the beneficials. Beneficials you might start releasing now or next month against giant whitefly include delphastus beetles (*Delphastus catalinae*) and, if available, nonstinging parasitic wasps of the genus *Entedononecremnus*. If you refrain from spraying with pesticides and if you also provide moisture and flowers for pollen in your garden, beneficials will settle down there and increase year by year, thus helping to control whiteflies (for more on beneficials, see pages 160–161).

Wash Plants and Spread Earthworm Castings. Besides releasing beneficials, one of the best ways to help keep this pest under control is to wash off the affected plants with strong jets of water at weekly intervals (see page 84). Birds also love to eat giant whiteflies, especially on hibiscus, but they don't like all that sticky white stuff. Placing a layer of bagged earthworm castings over the roots of susceptible plants, such as begonias, will banish giant whiteflies from your garden, even if there is a hibiscus across the street so loaded with whiteflies it looks as if it was caught in a blizzard. It takes a month or six weeks for the castings to take effect. Renew them every year or two. If you live in a dry interior zone, apply the earthworm castings by mixing them with water and pouring the slurry over the roots, or

mix them with mulch or compost so they can't bake into a hard crust on top of the ground. Also release delphastus beetles. Their numbers will build gradually if you provide for their needs, as described on page 160.

QUINCE, GUAVA, AND CHERIMOYA TREES

Quince, guava, and cherimoya not only are ornamental but also bear delicious fruit, and they grow well here. But even though they have many flowers, they don't always bear much fruit because we don't have the right insects here to pollinate them efficiently. You can help the local bees and ensure a larger crop by hand-pollinating. With quince and guava, choose a warm, dry morning and simply dab the centers of the flowers with a small sable brush to distribute the pollen. If there are too many flowers for this, use a long-handled wool duster. Dust the pollen into the flowers all over the outside of the tree.

Pollinating cherimoya requires two steps because the flowers are both female and male. In the morning hours, when the flowers aren't fully opened, they're in the female stage. In the afternoon, the flowers open fully and become male. First, collect pollen in the afternoon; hold a 35mm film canister under each fully opened flower and brush the pollen and strawlike anthers into it with a small paintbrush. Close the container and keep it in a cool, dry place. The next morning, find flowers in the female stage. Spread the petals with your fingers, dip the brush into the canister of fresh pollen, and apply it to the conelike pistil with an even, swirling motion. It takes cherimoya fruit five months to mature, so if you pollinate ten or twenty blossoms once a week year-round, you should have a far more abundant harvest, with fruit ripening throughout the year instead of only in November.

BAMBOO

For thousands of years bamboo has been among mankind's most economically useful plants, but modern gardeners prize it most for its serene beauty and for the tropical or Oriental atmosphere it lends to the landscape. Nonhorticulturally minded people are often surprised to learn that bamboo is actually giant grass: like Bermuda grass, bluegrass, and wheat, bamboo is a member of the Poaceae (Gramineae) family. There are well over a thousand different species of bamboo (members of the Bambuseae tribe of grasses), and these are further divided into numerous genera, their actual number depending on which botanist you consult. Some bamboos grow 120 feet tall with individual stems (called culms) a foot in diameter; some bamboos are low-growing ground covers a foot or less tall; and there's every size between these extremes. Most bamboos are evergreen; some are hardy, and others are tropical.

There are two main types of bamboo: those that grow in a clump and those that send out long runners. The ones with runners can eventually spread all over your property, and they often invade your neighbors' gardens, too. Control these invasive types by planting them above ground in containers, or grow them in the ground enclosed in drain tiles, bottomless containers, or a buried barrier of poured concrete or stainless-steel sheet metal, or use a manufactured root barrier, such as Deeproot 48/30 Water Barrier/Bamboo Barrier. Another option is to grow them in a raised bed surrounded by a 1-foot-deep trench filled with fir bark; police the trench often to cut off escaping runners as they enter it.

Most bamboos are monocarpic: once they bloom and bear seeds, they die. Some species flower at various times, and many of this type bloom without dying. But other species don't flower for many years, and when they do, it's on a specific schedule—perhaps at intervals of 7, 12, 30, 60, or 120 years, or possibly even several hundred years. (Some types have never been known to flower.) Amazingly, when members of many species flower, bear seeds, and die, they do so all at one time, just as if they were one plant. Sometimes an entire species dies within a year or two all over the world. Eventually this bamboo species will come back from seed, and in some cases the rhizomes stay alive and put out new growth after a few years. This fascinating habit can be a tragedy if you're a giant panda bear and depend on a particular species of bamboo for food—or a gardener whose species reaches the end of its cycle.

Choose Unusual Bamboos and Feed Them Like Grass. A number of bamboos, including Mexican weeping bamboo (*Otatea acuminate aztecorum*), a graceful, drought-resistant variety that lives for thirty-five years, are well suited to Southern California gardens (consult the list and detailed discussion in the *Sunset Garden Book*), but only the most common ones can be found in most nurseries. Unusual bamboos can best be found in specialty nurseries, such as Endangered Species in Perris at botanical-garden sales, or through the American Bamboo Society.

Most bamboos require good soil and plenty of water to look their best. They also appreciate a layer of mulch over their roots. Since bamboo is giant grass, lawn food is its ideal fertilizer. Hence, feed bamboo occasionally with

How to Propagate Bamboo from Rhizomes

Bamboos grow from branching rhizomes that have joints on them, called nodes, from which spring the fibrous roots and the bamboo stems or canes, called culms. The rhizomes of running bamboos are elongated, while those of clumping kinds are short and thick. The right time to separate bamboo is when new culms are just ready to sprout (when the underground buds have swelled but not yet begun to grow).

Starting now, from time to time dig down carefully with a trowel and see whether buds are forming. Hardy bamboos (these are mainly the types with runners) usually begin to grow in early March, sometimes as early as late February along the coast. If the new shoots have already emerged from the ground, it's too late; they will abort if you separate their rhizomes now (in which case, try again next year). Tropical bamboos (most clumping types are tropical) tend to sprout a little later. Divide the running and clumping types according to the methods described below.

Divide Running Bamboo.
Look for a place where several mature culms emerge from the ground. They should be near each other.

▶ With a saw or long-handled loppers, cut off a section of rhizome that contains at least two nodes and two to four existing culms (plus visible buds that are about to sprout).

▶ Dig up the rhizome with its roots.

▶ Cut back the culms by one-third to one-half of their height to compensate for the loss of roots.

▶ Plant the rhizome immediately in rich organic soil in a container or the ground, positioning it at the same depth at which you originally found it.

▶ Cover the roots with an inch or two of mulch; stake the culms, if necessary, to prevent them from being pushed over by wind; make a watering basin; and water thoroughly.

▶ Keep the roots moist until the new plant is well established.

▶ Beginning one month after planting, start fertilizing regularly with an organic fertilizer recommended for lawns.

Divide Clumping Bamboo.
▶ Look on the outside of the clump for a bulge of growth containing at least three or four culms and some rhizomes with buds on them. (This can be difficult since growth is often dense.)

▶ Slice down around the chosen bulge of growth with a sharp spade or cut through the rhizomes with a pruning saw to separate them from the parent plant. Then, with a trowel or spade, dig up the entire clump with the rhizomes and roots attached.

▶ Proceed to cut back, plant, water, and fertilize the new plant as described above for running bamboos.

any commercial organic lawn food according to package directions, or with Biosol Mix (7-2-3) or aged chicken manure, or feed for a whole year by applying aged horse manure in fall.

Divide Bamboo in Spring. The easiest way to propagate bamboo is by separating rhizomes from the parent plant in spring, just before the plants begin to grow. Bamboo can be propagated from seeds, but they aren't always viable. (See the box on the facing page for directions on using rhizomes.)

LAWN CARE

March is the time to feed all types of established lawns and to plant new ones from seed. You can also plant lawns from sod this month. First, though, decide whether you actually want a lawn.

Consider the Lawn-Free Landscape. March is an excellent month for gardeners to ask themselves, "Do I really need a lawn?" Green grass is soothing to the eye, it cools the atmosphere, and it is great as a play space for children, but lawns create more strain on water supplies than any other feature in a landscape. No real gardener wants to waste water creating a Never-Never Land of stage-set gardening, yet for the past century Southern Californians have been doing just that. A landscape of drought-resistant Mediterranean and native plants can provide the soothing atmosphere we crave as well as the feeling of living in tune with nature. So, if your children no longer need the lawn to play on, why not consider replacing the lawn with something more colorful, useful, and satisfying?

Ways to Replace the Lawn. One way to go is simply to brick in the lawn. It might be a shock the morning after you've finished, but once decorated with a splashing fountain, tubs of flowers, comfortable furniture, and an arbor drenched in fragrant roses, your patio may prove itself far more useful and attractive than the lawn it replaced. Or instead of a rose arbor in the patio, build a pergola and festoon it with wisteria or 'Lady Banks' roses; both are

drought-resistant and provide cooling shade. If the patio is in front of the house, a 3-foot wall with potted plants on top might provide adequate privacy, especially if you live on a cul-de-sac. A higher wall fronting a busy street with one or two barred and shutter-flanked windows can combine a sound barrier with the atmosphere of Spain or Italy, as well as providing support for a brilliantly colorful bougainvillea and a charming glimpse inside for passersby. Other lawn substitutes include colorful succulent gardens anchored by boulders, dry streambeds, and water-thrifty ground covers, shrubs, small trees, and perennials interwoven with meandering paths. Or edge a sunny front lawn with a flower-decked picket fence, and fill the space inside with raised beds for vegetables separated by gravel. This bold option can use less water than the lawn while providing food for the family. Build a rose arbor over the garden gate, and what began as an economy might end up giving your home more street appeal than the front lawn ever delivered.

Mow All Lawns. Warm-season grasses, such as Bermuda, St. Augustine, and zoysia, are waking up from winter dormancy in March. As soon as they start growing, begin mowing weekly with a reel mower to the correct height for each. Mow common Bermuda to 2 inches, hybrid Bermuda to $1/2$ to $3/4$ inch, St. Augustine to between $3/4$ and $1^{1}/4$ inches, and zoysia to $3/4$ to 1 inch in height. Cut 'Adalayd' or Excalibre grass with a rotary mower to between $3/4$ and 1 inch in height. Cool-season grasses, such as fescue, ryegrass, and bluegrass, are still growing fast; mow them weekly with a mulching rotary mower set high, to 2 to 3 inches for tall fescue and $1^{1}/2$ to $2^{1}/2$ inches for perennial ryegrass and bluegrass. (Bluegrass is not adapted here but is still used in some seed mixes.) Let the grass blades fall where they are mown to return the nitrogen they contain to the lawn from which they came, as described on page 72. If some grass blades fall in lumps, just spread them around a bit with a grass rake. On a sunny day, they'll soon dry out and sift down to the ground. (It's all right if the ground is damp when you mow, but the grass blades should always be dry.)

Feed Lawns the Organic Way. If you still have a lawn, one of the best things you can do for the environment, and especially for bees, is to fertilize it organically and never again use synthetic lawn fertilizers, chemical pesticides, or chemical disease controls. If you hire a company to care for your lawn, ask them at least to fertilize with a semiorganic product such as Gro-Power, a humus-based fertilizer that contains no pesticides or herbicides, instead of using products containing dangerous pesticides. Above all, avoid products containing imadacloprid (manufactured by Bayer and included as a grub killer in many lawn fertilizers). According to European agriculturists, imadacloprid might be causing CCD (Colony Collapse Disorder) in bees. A properly fed organic lawn will be thick and healthy, with plenty of vigor to withstand pests and fight off diseases.

The old conventional method for feeding lawns was to fertilize them in March with one pound of nitrogen per 1,000 square feet, usually combined with phosphorus and potassium and other elements that are included in synthetic lawn fertilizers. When a lawn is fed in this way, much of the nitrogen and other ingredients end up in our groundwater instead of being used by plants. Current fertilizer instructions are better—they now tell gardeners to use as little fertilizer as necessary to keep the lawn healthy and growing. Slow-release fertilizers are another improvement, but even they cause runoff. Worse still, the synthetic ingredients they contain kill the natural organisms in soils that can create natural nitrogen while also building up various microorganisms and biological processes that control pests and prevent lawn diseases.

An organic lawn depends upon the gradual buildup of organic matter in the soil to feed the grass and fight disease. Organic fertilizers recommended for lawns bind themselves into soil and cause far less runoff than synthetics. Since organic fertilizers need time to take effect, most organic gardeners will have already fed their lawns in February, and by now the grass will be beginning to show results. But if you are new to organic gardening and did not fertilize earlier, now is the time to apply Biosol Mix (7-2-3) or any other organic lawn fertilizer, such as Ringer All Natural Lawn Restore (10-2-6), Lawns Alive, or Cockadoodle Doo Super-Premium Organic Lawn Fertilizer, according to package directions. A less expensive choice is to apply chicken manure at the rate of 6 pounds of dry, aged manure for each 1,000 square feet of lawn, using a spreader if you have one. (When feeding with chicken manure, be sure to fertilize when the ground is damp but the grass blades are dry, and follow up by watering deeply, in order not to burn your lawn.) Another option is to feed lawns with your own compost tea. A week after fertilizing, spray the lawn with an organic product containing humic acid or spread on a dry product containing humic acid. Products containing kelp and rhyzobia are also beneficial. Humic acid and kelp contain micronutrients, and rhyzobia fix nitrogen in the soil and help roots access nutrients.

Water Lawns. Irrigate all lawns now, according to their individual needs, when rains aren't adequate.

Choose the Best Time to Plant. Both warm- and cool-season grasses may be bought as sod, and cool-season grasses can be planted from sod any month year-round. When planting from sod, ask for and file the names and proportions of the grass varieties in it so that you can duplicate the mix if you ever need to reseed a bare patch. Although you can plant both warm- and cool-season grasses from seed this month, wait if you possibly can to plant cool-season grasses. October is a better time to plant them because fall planting gives cool-season grasses planted from seed more time to establish a root system before summer heat arrives. When planting warm-season grasses, wait until the weather has warmed up in your area. (If you plan to plant zoysia, it's best to wait until June.)

Study Lawn Types before Planting. How do you choose which grass is right for you? Begin by looking around your neighborhood. Talk to the owners of good-looking lawns. Don't just choose for appearance, though. Consider how much traffic your lawn will have to take and how willing you are to fuss over it. Also consult your Cooperative Extension office and reference books on lawns to choose a grass that's right for your area and needs. Above all, consider drought resistance.

Weigh the Pros and Cons of Warm- and Cool-Season Grasses. If water were plentiful, the majority of gardeners would never choose to plant such warm-season grasses as Bermuda and zoysia, because of their bad habits: they go brown in winter, and they invade borders. Most people prefer cool-season lawns because they stay green all year and look more like eastern lawns. But periodic droughts, dwindling water supplies, and forced cutbacks have made

gardeners realize that it's totally unrealistic to expect a lawn to look like a golf green; the ideal lawn is one that can survive. Cool-season lawns aren't invasive, but they need more water than Bermuda or zoysia, which can look good on only 18 inches of irrigation a year, and you can cut that amount by two-thirds and still keep them alive. If you're forced to let them go brown in a drought, they'll pull in their horns and may live through it. The very characteristics that make Bermuda invasive and devilishly hard to get rid of are the same ones that help it live through tough times. (If you want to keep it from creeping into your flowerbeds, install a continuous concrete curb.)

Seashore Paspalum. Seashore paspalum, or 'Adalayd', grass (*Paspalum vaginatum*) is heat and drought resistant, has the look of bluegrass, and has remarkable salt resistance—it can thrive in ocean spray. But it turns brown in winter, it requires use of a reel mower, and its wiry stems can look unsightly after cutting. Currently there's a breeding program for seashore paspalum, so better varieties may some day emerge.

Tall and Dwarf Fescues. Among gardeners in coastal zones, cool-season lawns are still the favorite. The most popular choice today is one of the newer dwarf fescues. These grasses give you the look of a cool-season lawn but require less water and fuss than old-style cool-season grasses. They have fairly good shade tolerance, and they don't invade flowerbeds. Dwarf fescue grasses are more drought-resistant than other cool-season grasses, but eventually, increased water restrictions will undoubtedly push them off the market. If lawns are part of our future, the most likely candidates will be drought-resistant Bermuda grass, zoysia, and most especially buffalo grass, discussed following. But until that inevitable day, many types of tall and dwarf fescue continue to be sold as seeds or sod.

The story of tall fescue lawns began when agricultural scientists saw the potential of several coarse pasture grasses and bred them to create turf-type tall fescues for use as lawns. Continued breeding led to the development thirty years ago of the popular dwarf fescues. These cool-season grasses have shorter, finer blades and a wide range of individual characteristics. You can plant dwarf fescues either from seeds or sod, and every major sod farm in Southern California has its own names for the blends it sells. Before purchasing, study the available brands and compare their characteristics in light of your special requirements. For example, Pacific Sod Farms sells fescue grasses under the names Medallion Tall Fescue. The toughest variety, Medallion Plus, contains some bluegrass and stands up well to wear. Medallion Bonsai, containing 'Bonsai' dwarf fescue, is known for its disease resistance and dark color, with some shade tolerance, and Medallion Dwarf Green Carpet has the finest texture of the Medallion series but is a little less tolerant of wear. Southland Sod Farms sells the Marathon Family of grasses, including Marathon, an improved tall fescue that's rugged and rapid-growing, with some shade tolerance, which can fill in fast when damaged; Marathon II, with shorter, deeper green blades and greater density; and Marathon III, which is still shorter, denser, darker green, and slower-growing. It has the finest texture of the three but is less tolerant of shade and wear. (These varieties can also be planted from seeds.)

When planting from seed, choose a good named variety. Some new varieties with improved characteristics include 'Chapel Hill', 'Jaguar III', 'Insignia', and 'Redcoat'. 'Chapel Hill', 'Success', and 'Pedestal' stand up better than most to heat and drought. 'Insignia' and 'Redcoat' have fine blades. RTF (rhizomatous tall fescue) is the name of a new group of tall fescues, such as 'Labarinth', that make rhizomes—that is, they creep enough to heal spots on the lawn made by dogs—and are included in some mixes. Good seed mixes combine several varieties so you benefit from a range of good characteristics. Avoid buying cheap seed, outdated seed, seed marked "uncertified," and seed bearing the letters VNS (variety not stated). Check the expiration date printed on the box, and don't buy seed that's been sitting on the shelf too long. Plant your seed within a year of the germination test date given on the package.

Other Cool-Season Grasses. Among other cool-season grasses, perennial rye uses more water and is usually more subject to pests and diseases than tall fescue. Nevertheless, people still plant lawns of perennial ryegrass mixes from sod or seed. Bent grass is thirsty, disease-prone, and ill-adapted to our climate. Don't plant it. Kentucky bluegrass is often blended into ryegrass mixes to reduce fusarium wilt, but when planted here by itself, it is a troublemaker and a water hog.

Grasses for Special Needs. Another group of grasses promises the atmosphere of a lawn with less upkeep. Creeping red fescue (*Festuca rubra*) is sold as seed under the name 'Slopesaver', among other names, and due to its shade tolerance it's a frequent ingredient in cool-season lawns. Planted for erosion control, it cascades down steep wooded hillsides like long green hair. It grows best in shade and in cool, coastal climates, but needs plenty of water. A similar grass sold as sod by Pacific Sod

Farms, called 'No Mow', is a fine fescue blend, a mix of hard fescue and chewings fescue intended to create good color and growth. This easy-care, bunching, fine-textured grass can provide the atmosphere of an informal meadow in country gardens and has more drought tolerance than creeping red fescue alone. It's popular for covering hillsides, "green" roofs, and the rough edges of golf courses. There are a number of other drought-resistant grasses, but many of them grow in tufts too bumpy for lawns.

The grass with greatest promise for the future is the warm-season grass called buffalo grass (*Buchloe dactyloides*), a short prairie grass native to the Great Plains that makes flat sod instead of tufts. Buffalo grass has roots that grow as deep as 3 feet, and it can survive on as little as $1/4$ inch of water a week. The variety best adapted to Southern California is 'UC Verde', developed by the University of California and released in 2003. 'UC Verde' is available only as plugs, but it will grow a dense, finely bladed, bright green turf in full sun and stands up to blistering heat in interior zones. In inland areas, it goes dormant in winter, like Bermuda grass, but some new varieties stay green all year along the coast or in warm desert locations, and they have better shade resistance and save up to 75 percent of your water bill. A few other new buffalo grass varieties, such as 'Legacy' and 'Prestige', developed by Ohio and Nebraska State Universities, offer promise in special locations, such as the mountains and high deserts.

Warm-Season Grasses. Bermuda grass (*Cynodon dactylon*) is currently the best-suited species for full sun in Southern California. It goes dormant in winter (except for 'Tifgreen' when planted on the coast), but the advantage of winter dormancy is that it allows gardeners a rest from mowing and saves water,

too. If there's a Bermuda grass golf course in your area, there's no point in growing any other grass, since birds will seed Bermuda into whatever you've got. New varieties from seeds, including 'Contessa', 'Riviera', 'Sovereign', 'Yukon', 'Vera Cruz', and 'Princess', have improved early spring color and other special characteristics. Mixes of these varieties offer a range of good qualities, but in most cases hybrid grass is a better choice since it won't seed itself into flowerbeds or vegetable gardens. Hybrid Bermuda grasses and many other subtropical grasses can be planted from sod, rhizomes, sprigs, plugs, or stolons (sections of stem that creep along the surface and root into the ground.) Modern varieties to grow from sod include 'Tifway 419' (a tough, durable, fine-textured grass for golf courses, parks, and home gardens), 'Tifway II' (a medium-fine-textured grass, resistant to sod webworm and nematodes, and slightly coarser than 'Tifway 419'), 'GN-1' (a sports-field grass named for golfer Greg Norman, good for home gardens with kids and pets), 'Premier' (a fine-bladed, darker green sport of 'Tifgreen' discovered in Seal Beach), and 'Bull's Eye' (a tough variety for hot interior valleys that uses 30 percent less water than tall fescue; it goes brown in winter but can take some shade).

Old-style zoysia grasses had a slightly grayish-green hue and grew so thick they felt bouncy underfoot, but zoysia has always been beloved by a few gardeners for its stunningly smooth appearance all summer long and its greater shade tolerance than Bermuda grass. 'Meyer', for example, which grows flatter than the old types, looks remarkably like bluegrass even when grown in blistering heat, but it uses a fraction of the water any cool-season lawn would require; on the negative side, it goes brown early in fall and is slow to green up in spring. By contrast, the UC releases 'El Toro' and 'DeAnza' often stay green year-round in warm-winter zones or when grown near the coast; inland, they stay green longer in fall and green up quicker in spring. Hold off until June to plant zoysia unless you're planting from sod. When you plant it from plugs, zoysia takes off better in summer (see page 249). St. Augustine grass is the most shade-tolerant of all lawn grasses, but you have to pour water on it to keep it looking good, especially in the hot interior. It's a warm-season grass popular in the desert, but as water restrictions increase, this may be the first lawn to be replaced with buffalo grass, at least when it's grown in full sun. Old types of St. Augustine grass made a bouncy, coarse-bladed turf with trimmed edges as thick as a brick, but newer varieties, such as 'Palmetto' and 'Sunclipse', have a finer texture and a smooth, flat growth habit, more like other lawns.

Plant New Lawns. Regardless of the type of grass and method of planting you choose, be sure to prepare the site thoroughly. Edge invasive grasses, especially Bermuda grass and zoysia, with a continuous concrete strip prior to planting so they can't creep into flowerbeds. Where gophers are a problem, plant all lawns on top of a layer of overlapped chicken wire laid flat on top of prepared ground (as described on page 358).

For all lawns, rototill deeply, add plenty of soil amendment, and level and lightly roll the ground. Sprinkle seeds evenly and cover them with mulch. Either roll stolons with a cleated roller to press them into the soil or partially cover with topsoil. Keep your freshly planted lawn damp until established. Sprinkle it twice or three times daily, but avoid watering late in the day.

Mow your newly planted lawn for the first time when it has grown to one and a half times the normal cutting height of the grass variety you've chosen. Letting it grow longer before mowing will reduce the health of the lawn. Always follow the **Rule of Thumb** (mentioned in the box on page 103): *Never mow off more than one-third to one-half of the leaf length of your grass at any one time.* When you mow for the first time, be sure that the grass is dry and the blades on your mower are sharp.

VEGETABLE GARDENING

Start planting summer vegetables now. If you've never before grown a vegetable garden, now is the best time to begin. The first week in March is the earliest time to put in warm-season crops. The sooner you plant, the sooner you'll have a harvest.

A wide range of crops can be put in now. Summer vegetables that can be planted in March include artichokes, chayote, corn, green beans, New Zealand spinach, and tomatoes. In coastal zones and warm, south-facing gardens, cucumbers and both summer and winter squash can be planted by midmonth. If you have room, there's still enough cool weather left to plant a few cool-season crops, such as broccoli, cabbage, head lettuce, kohlrabi, mesclun, and potatoes. And, of course, you can plant crops that grow year-round, such as beets, carrots, chard, radishes, and turnips. Wait until April to put in the real heat lovers, such as eggplant, lima beans, melons, okra, peppers, and pumpkins.

Create a No-Dig Garden. Conventional vegetable gardening calls for turning over the soil to the depth of your spade and breaking up the clods, and then mixing in organics and fertilizers

134

How to Install a No-Dig Garden

▸ Measure a level area in full sun, and use a planning pad to draw a plan for installing raised beds, with each printed square representing 1 square foot.

▸ Allow for beds from 6 to 8 feet long, from 1 to 2 feet high, and no wider than 4 feet across. Narrow ends should face north and south, wide sides should face east and west.

▸ Plan paths at least 2 feet wide surrounding at least three sides of each bed.

▸ If access is from one side only, the bed should be on the south side of a wall or fence to allow for full sun, and should be no wider than 3 feet so you can reach all parts of it without stepping on the soil. (In this case, the wide side can face south, if necessary.)

▸ Assemble materials for raised beds or order a ready-made kit. (Optional step: Purchase enough lumber to surround each bed with a seat, if desired, by nailing a 6-inch-wide board on the upper edge of each raised bed, mitering the boards at the corners.)

▸ When using lumber or a kit, turn the finished bed upside-down and nail a sheet of ½-inch-gauge galvanized hardware cloth on the bottom to keep out gophers. (When using masonry, place the hardware flat on the ground so it extends through the footings with the rebar extending up through it, and build the walls on top.)

▸ Provide for an automatic watering system to be added later, if desired, by burying PVC pipe with a connecting pipe leading under the wall of each bed and up to the center of one end of the bed. (See text for more information.)

▸ To kill weeds, cover the ground surrounding the beds and beneath each bed with 10 layers of newspaper, and overlap edges.

▸ Cover the paths surrounding the beds with gravel, decomposed granite, or coarse mulch such as tree-trimmers' chippings. (Place landscape fabric under gravel to prevent it from sifting into the ground.)

▸ Fill beds with layers of organic matter measuring 3 to 4 inches thick, working as follows: a layer of straw, a layer of alfalfa hay, a layer of horse manure, 5 cups of fishbone meal and 5 cups of blood meal sprinkled over the horse manure, and a layer of organic homemade, trucked, or bagged compost on top. (The mound will sink as it ages.)

▸ Water thoroughly. Let stand for three months before planting vegetables, watering once every week or two to keep the beds damp. Install a timer and drip system by attaching Apex or some other brand of recycled-rubber soaker hoses to the PVC pipes and arranging the drip hoses on top of the beds.

▸ As the beds decline in height, add more organic materials on top. Soak the beds by hand or with the irrigation system at intervals of one week to ten days, depending on the weather.

▸ As soon as the organic materials have settled down, cooled, and turned into usable soil beneath the top layer of mulch, plant the beds, adding organic fertilizers as needed and more organic materials on top of the pile whenever they become available.

▸ Do not ever dig or work the pile. Pull out plants when they are finished, add more layers of organic materials on top, and plant straight into the beds.

twice a year prior to planting vegetables for each new season. Having done this myself for fifty years, I can attest it's good exercise but can be hard on the back and knees. Another way is called no-dig gardening, first promoted by Ruth Stout in *How to Have A Green Thumb Without an Aching Back*, published in 1955, and later augmented in other books including Esther Deans' *Gardening Book: Growing without Digging* and Patricia Lanza's *Lasagna Gardening*. Ruth Stout practiced her style of no-dig gardening in her large, cold-climate vegetable garden on open ground. In dry Mediterranean and Southwest climates, gardeners have found that raised beds work better. A gardener in the Hollywood Hills, for example, raises vegetables in raised beds according to a no-dig method he learned in Australia. He begins by lining the beds with sheets of newspaper to eradicate weeds and attract worms. Then he fills the beds with layers of organic materials, lasagna style, in a system I've adapted and outlined step by step in the accompanying box.

No-dig gardening has many advantages. It overcomes poor soil and invasive weeds, uses earthworms already existing in the ground to work the beds, saves the backs and knees of gardeners, and reduces the amount of irrigation plants need in order to grow and produce a crop. Necessary irrigation is reduced because raised beds filled with organics retain moisture like a sponge. Watering is usually necessary only once a week or every ten days and can be accomplished by hand, soaking the beds, or automatically, by installing an irrigation timer and PVC pipes leading to each bed, with Apex or some other brand of recycled-rubber soaker hoses laid on top of the soil. (After a couple of years, these hoses may clog; if so, make holes where you need them with a large wooden-handled needle used for leather work.) Worms

also mix up the organic materials, and as they devour them, they increase the moisture content of the ground, as anyone who has raised worms in a box knows. Additionally, the system is self-balancing, so after the beds get going, plant needs are provided for without the gardener needing to figure out precise amounts of fertilizers required by specific plants. Depending on the materials one chooses for building them, the beds themselves can be environmentally responsible. Free and recycled materials include broken concrete, used brick, or on-site cobbles or rocks—even old rowboats and bathtubs, given a coat of paint and adequate drainage holes in the bottom. One can also build rot-free beds from recycled lumber substitutes like Trex, or by putting together a ready-to-build kit guaranteed for fifty years, such as the type offered by Abundant Earth and other companies. Regardless of the materials you choose, construct the beds no wider than 4 feet across so you can reach the center without stepping on the bed. It's also wise to nail, or otherwise affix, a layer of galvanized, $1/2$-inch-gauge hardware cloth on the bottom of the box, under the newspapers, to keep out gophers. (For more about gophers, see page 358.)

Plant Herbs. Culinary herbs are the hallmark of a good potager, so plant some along with your vegetables. Herbs add beauty and atmosphere to the garden, health to surrounding plants, and pizzazz to summer dishes. But not all herbs are edible, and a few are dangerous to ingest (for more information, see page 409). Among edible herbs to put in now are basil, dill, marjoram, mint, oregano, parsley, rosemary, sage, summer savory, and thyme. Most of these can be interplanted with vegetables. Plant basil between tomatoes, for example, and dill next to cucumber. Or plant herbs separately in a raised bed or herb garden, in large ornamental pots, or as an edging surrounding the vegetables, where you can reach them easily. Rosemary is not a good selection for interplanting because it soon grows large and woody. Grow it elsewhere in the garden. Mint can also be planted now, but it's invasive; confine it in a 5-gallon can or other container nestled near a hose so you can water it frequently. To keep pests at bay, release ladybugs and lacewings onto mint. Clip leaves often and fertilize it regularly.

Provide Adequate Light. Plant vegetables in full sun. Without it, they'll succumb to disease and fail to flower, and you won't get a crop. Lay out your vegetable garden to make the best use of sunlight. The **Rule of Thumb:** *Plant tall crops to the north and short crops to the south, and arrange your rows from north to south so the sun goes from side to side across them.*

If you're dying to grow vegetables but don't have full sun, try asparagus, lettuce, potatoes, and herbs—parsley, for example. In a pinch, these choices will take partial shade. (For lettuce, it's sometimes better.) Tomatoes will bear a crop with just four or five hours of midday sun in a warm, sheltered location, especially if it also provides reflected heat.

Provide Good Soil and Drainage. Vegetables need deep, fertile soil with adequate drainage. Sandy or decomposed-granite loam is best. But if you have red clay, adobe, or almost pure sand, don't despair. Good vegetables can be grown in heavy clay soils or highly sandy soils if plenty of organic soil amendment is added. Don't attempt to grow vegetables in areas clogged with tree roots, since they sap the water needed for healthy growth. If your soil is rock hard or drainage is nil, plant in raised beds that are filled with topsoil mixed with organic amendments,

or use the no-dig method outlined earlier in this chapter (page 135). If roots are a problem, plant in large containers with paving stones underneath them.

How Farmers Discovered That Legumes Need Inoculation

All legumes (plants such as peas and beans that have a pod shaped like a pea pod) have the ability to take nitrogen out of the air. They do it by means of nodules on their roots and a symbiotic relationship with tiny bacteria called rhizobia. Centuries ago, farmers noticed that certain patches of peas or beans produced better crops than others. They discovered that a handful of soil from one of these good patches mixed with the seed of legumes could improve growing conditions in less-productive areas. Unbeknown to themselves, they were actually inoculating their seed.

Modern inoculants are available by mail from seed companies and come with directions for their use. Most kinds can be applied by sprinkling them into the bottom of the furrow before planting seeds. When planting many seeds, mix them in a bowl with enough table syrup or honey to make them sticky. Then add inoculant and stir the seeds until each one is thoroughly coated. If you inoculate your seed, don't use nitrogen fertilizer; the plant will manufacture all the nitrogen it needs, and adding more will make the inoculant less effective.

Install a Drip System. Decide on a watering system. The furrow method is good, especially for heavy soils, but it wastes water. Overhead sprinkling can work early in the day, but it can be bad along the coast, where excess moisture

How to Grow Pole Beans

- ▸ Choose a spot 6 feet square in full sun.

- ▸ Dig up and loosen the soil to the depth of 1 foot, and cultivate a 4-inch layer of organic soil amendment (but not manure) into it.

- ▸ Work in 1 pound fishbone meal, and provide nitrogen by inoculating your seed with nitrogen-fixing bacteria. (The box on inoculation on page 137 describes the origin of this technique.)

- ▸ Tie together at one end four 8-foot-long bamboo poles or green plastic-covered garden stakes. Set up this teepee with the legs spread about 4 feet apart and the ends shoved 3 to 4 inches into the ground.

- ▸ Plant five or six beans 3 inches apart, with the scar side down, around each pole. Plant 1 inch deep along the coast, 2 inches deep inland. Cover the seeds with commercial potting soil and pat it down gently.

- ▸ Water deeply after planting. Don't water again until the beans come up, unless the soil begins to dry out. (Sometimes beans rot instead of coming up. If the problem is heavy soil, see box on page 139 on how to plant seeds in heavy soil. If the problem is cold soil—below 60°F—presprout the seed before planting it. See page 172.)

- ▸ Once the plants have emerged, keep them well watered and protect them from birds and snails.

- ▸ When the plants are 3 to 4 inches tall, thin to the best three on each pole. (Snip the others off with scissors.) Give the young plants a helping hand to start them winding around the poles. Once started, they'll keep going with no further help from you.

on leaves, cool temperatures, and a moist atmosphere may encourage the growth of fungal diseases.

The best way for modern Southland gardeners to water vegetables is with a drip system. Most vegetables need the equivalent of an inch of rain per week for healthy growth. Drip systems use 40 to 60 percent less water by putting it where roots are. Choose a system designed for row crops, such as nonclogging Drip-In $1/4$-inch soaker dripline, which can be buried under mulch. The time taken now to install a drip system will save untold hours later.

Plant for Successive Crops. When planting vegetables that mature all at the same time,

such as carrots and beets, don't plant the whole package at once. Plant quantities no bigger than your family can eat at one time, and save the rest of the seeds to plant at intervals for continued crops. The same goes for lettuce. If you continually harvest outside leaves, you can lengthen the harvest, but if you plan to take out whole heads, plant at shorter intervals. With mesclun, cut sections with scissors and allow them to regrow (see page 109).

Make Space for Planting in Established Gardens. If you grow vegetables year-round in an established garden, begin now to make space for summer crops. When you plant winter vegetables in fall, you can usually pull up

How to Plant Large Seeds in Heavy Soil

Heavy soils such as red clay or adobe often bake to a hard crust on top. Large seeds—beans and squash, for example—may not be able to break through it. Take these precautions to keep them from rotting under the ground.

▸ Make a trench of the right planting depth. Soak the trench deeply at least two or three times, and let the water drain out.

▸ Place seeds in the bottom of the trench. (In the case of beans, place them with their scar side pointing down. The root will go straight down, and all your beans will come up at the same time.)

▸ Cover the seed with an inch of dry potting soil in coastal zones, or with 2 inches of dry potting soil inland. Pat down gently, and don't water again until the beans pop through. The dry potting soil will act like a mulch and draw just the right amount of moisture to the seed for it to sprout.

just about everything and start out fresh. But when you plant summer vegetables in spring, it's not quite that easy, because the seasons for many crops overlap. It's often necessary to plant now among some winter vegetables that are still going strong and to pull out others—even if they aren't quite finished—in order to make room for summer vegetables.

The smaller the space, the more important it is to schedule your fall planting so that your cole crops, such as cabbage, broccoli, and cauliflower, will be finished by now. If they're still going, plant them earlier next year. Peas are often getting ratty-looking and mildewy by now, so pull them out and replace them with

tomatoes and corn. Harvest the last of the fava beans and pull up celery, which by now is usually going to seed. Onions and garlic stay in the ground to mature as the days lengthen. Be sure to weed your onions often; their small root systems can't compete with the rapacious roots of weeds. Replace parsley now or next month. A good place for it is east of a row of trellised cucumbers, where it will get some shade on hot afternoons. By cleaning out most winter crops now and cultivating and amending the soil, you help prevent a carryover of pests and diseases.

Plant Green, Wax, and Purple Beans. Green beans are often called snap beans or string beans, though modern varieties are almost stringless. Wax beans are similar but turn yellow as they mature and usually have a milder flavor. Colorful varieties are available, including a delicious purple bean—'Royal Burgundy'—that turns green when it's cooked. All these beans do best when planted now.

✹ QUICK TIP

How to Protect Bean and Corn Sprouts from Birds. *Birds, especially mockingbirds, love your bean and sweet corn sprouts. Pop a green berry basket (the kind that strawberries and cherry tomatoes come in) over each planted seed. After sprouts have touched the top of the baskets, you can safely remove them; by then the birds will have lost interest.*

For the earliest harvest, plant bush beans—choose a good variety, such as 'Venture' from Park Seed or 'Pencil Pod', a wax bean. If you have limited space, plant pole beans. (See the

Creating Visual Vegetable Excitement

Vegetables can be food for the eyes as well as for the body, and designing the vegetable garden is as much fun as picking the crops. Here are a few ways to spark up your potager.

▸ Separate your beds with geometric paths, edging these with low walls, hedges, clipped herbs, and dwarf espaliered fruit trees. (Meandering paths are an option but more difficult to use among vegetables.)

▸ Create vegetable parterres. Plant colorful crops, and crops with various textures, in patterns intended to be viewed from above. Cut a square bed into quarters, for example, edging the four pie-piece triangles that result with 'Spicey Globe' basil. Then fill in two facing triangles with chives or onions and the other two with colorful leaf lettuces. Many colorful vegetables can be planted this month, including 'Bright Lights' Swiss chard, red Swiss chard, 'Red Sails' lettuce, 'Green Zebra' tomato, and, from Renee's Garden, Cajun Hot Sauce Chiles, Rainbow Radishes, and Tricolor Pole Beans, (These seed mixes by Renee allow you to try out several colorful named varieties of one crop without purchasing a whole packet of each variety.)

▸ Plant annual flowers, such as marigolds and nasturtiums, in sections of your vegetable garden, or edge the vegetable garden with flowers. (Marigolds are reputed to have a beneficial effect on vegetables; nasturtiums are edible. Other edible flowers include bee balm, borage, calendula, chives, daylily, Johnny-jump-up, scarlet clover, scarlet runner bean, scented geranium, society garlic, and violet.)

▸ Grow a few favorite vegetables, flowers, or herbs in ornamental pots, barrels, and other containers; use these as focal points among the vegetables or at path intersections.

▸ Make ornamental plant supports of bamboo, willow branches, grapevine prunings, and other discarded plant materials. (Sculptural plants like the squash 'Tromboncino', with 8- to 18-inch hanging fruits, from the Cook's Garden, are dramatic hanging from overhead arches.)

▸ Add your own signature with tastefully selected birdbaths, statuary, and topiary.

box on page 138 for directions.) You'll get a bigger and longer-lasting harvest and, in most cases, a better-tasting bean. Brown-seeded 'Kentucky Wonder' is one of the finest and easiest varieties for our area because it's resistant to rust. White-seeded 'Kentucky Wonder', also rust-resistant, is actually a different strain and not quite as prolific. (Try both and compare.)

Plant Potatoes. Seed potatoes can be bought now at local nurseries. Plant them if you have room; they're fun and easy and delicious when homegrown. Cut seed potatoes in half so there are two eyes per section, roll them in RooTone or soil sulfur, and let them stand a day or two for the cuts to callus over before planting. Or, if you prefer, plant the seed potatoes whole. Tests indicate you may get a bigger harvest that way. (Potatoes can also be grown from seed, but until better varieties come along, it isn't worth the trouble.) Plant them 3 to 4 inches deep and 2 inches apart.

QUICK TIP

How to Keep Seeds Dry. *Fold over the openings of partially used seed packages, secure the folds with paper clips, and place the envelopes in a dry screw-top jar. Add a homemade desiccant of 2 tablespoons dried skim milk powder wrapped in tissue and secured with a rubber band. Seal the jar tightly, and store it in the refrigerator or in a cool, dry place.*

Potatoes grow best in fertile, sandy, slightly acid soil. Before planting them, amend your soil with acid soil mix—for example, nitrolized redwood shavings or peat moss. Also apply a complete organic vegetable fertilizer according to package directions and work it into the top 6 inches of soil. As the plants grow, mound the soil up around their stems until you have formed a row that is mounded approximately 6 inches higher than the surrounding ground. Keep the ground moist by giving it an occasional deep watering.

Plant Artichokes to Grow as an Annual Vegetable. Globe artichokes (*Cynara scolymus*) are edible thistles that have been cultivated since the time of the ancient Romans. They grow well in Southern California, particularly close to the ocean. They're usually planted bare-root in fall to grow as a permanent plant that will produce a crop the following summer. (Bare-root plants are the commercial variety 'Green Globe', which is the same kind you most frequently see for sale in your grocery store.) If you plant these in spring, you can't be sure of a harvest the first year. Now, however, newer seed-grown varieties of artichoke, plus proper fertilization and care, can guarantee a

harvest the same year, even if you plant as late as March. To plant now and grow artichokes as an annual, buy transplants already growing in pony packs or 4-inch containers. These are the seed-grown plants, and they'll produce a harvest as early as June. (If you live in a hot interior valley, wait until mid- to late summer to plant seed-grown plants for a late winter and spring harvest. Flower buds are woody if they mature during hot weather.)

Dig the soil deeply. To grow rapidly, artichokes need good drainage, plenty of fertilizer, and deep watering. Add a generous quantity of organic soil amendment and choose a good-quality organic vegetable fertilizer. Measure the dimensions of the ground to be fertilized and follow package directions. Cultivate the fertilizer into the top 6 inches of soil. Space plants 4 feet apart—don't crowd them—and plant high to avoid crown rot. Cover the roots thoroughly with soil; then make a watering basin slightly deeper than the crown of the plant. As the plant grows, pile a little more soil around the main stalk to prevent irrigation water from touching it.

QUICK TIP

How to Foil Cutworms. *Save the cardboard tube from holiday wrapping paper. Cut it into 2-inch sections to make protective collars. When you plant tomatoes, first slip the leaves of each plant gently through a cardboard collar; then anchor the sleeve 1/2 inch into the soil around the transplant. Cutworms won't climb over the collar.*

Water artichokes twice a week for the first two weeks and then deeply once a week, or use a drip system that provides ample water. (The

How to Plant and Grow Tomatoes

Tomatoes are the favorite vegetable for home growing. If you want to grow a special variety you can't find in nurseries—'Sweet Million', for example—you can sprout the seeds indoors (they germinate readily) and grow your own transplants. But it's easier and quicker to grow your tomatoes from transplants you buy at the nursery, so that's the method given here.

▶ For ease of growing, select a disease-resistant variety such as 'Champion', 'Husky Red', 'Better Boy', 'Ace Hybrid', or 'Celebrity' that's appropriate for your needs and climate zone. For a quick harvest when planting in March, also plant an early variety—'Early Girl Improved', 'Fourth-of-July', or 'Enchantment', for example. If you prefer, choose heirloom varieties such as 'Brandywine', 'Cherokee Purple', 'Green Zebra', 'Brown Derby', and 'Black Krim', but these types are more difficult to grow. (To reduce damage from nematodes, grow heirlooms in highly organic soil or release beneficial nematodes. Don't prune them, since pruning opens up stems to disease, and don't plant them in the same spot year after year. Raised beds or even large pots work well. Before planting pots, dig out and replace the top layer of old potting soil with fresh mix.)

▶ Choose a spot in full sun, and prepare the soil by digging it deeply with a spade and adding organic soil amendment, such as aged homemade or bagged compost.

▶ Use either an organic vegetable fertilizer or one especially recommended for tomatoes.

▶ Plant transplants deeply. Most are leggy, so snip off the lower leaves, make a little trench with the trowel, lay the plant in sideways, and bend the stem up gently. Roots will form all along the buried stem.

▶ Choose a staking system (see the box on the facing page).

▶ Water deeply using the garden hose, and allowing the water to sink into the ground. Gradually lengthen times between waterings, until you are watering deeply every 1 to 2 weeks along the coast, more frequently in interior zones. This is the best way to keep the soil evenly moist. (Drip systems do not work well for tomatoes since they cause uneven moisture and this can cause blossom-end rot. See page 250.)

ground must be constantly moist, so don't grow them during drought years.) Artichokes grow quickly when watered and fed, and they tend to send up many offshoots or side shoots, sometimes called suckers. Break them off as they occur. If you have room, stick them elsewhere in the garden; they'll grow. Or plant them in gallon containers to give to friends. (Artichoke plants in pots are amusing on a patio, but they'll bear only small artichokes.) Protect plants from snails, which love artichokes.

How to Stake Tomatoes

Don't let tomatoes sprawl on the ground; they'll rot, or pests will get them. Here are three staking methods. Each works for a different group of tomatoes, gives different results, and requires different training.

▶ Bend a 6½-foot length of 5-foot-tall, 6-by-6 hardware cloth or cement-reinforcing wire to make a round cage 2 feet across. Place a cage over each plant. Stake it down firmly to withstand wind.

Pruning and Training: Don't prune at all. The tomato will climb up inside the cage by itself and need no staking

Results: This method will give you the most fruit but the smallest.

Areas and Growth Habit for Which Method Is Recommended: Any zone, but especially those in hot interior climates (because it keeps the fruit well shaded). Best for non-determinate varieties. (Nondeterminate varieties continue growing in height all season.)

▶ Construct a trellis of 6- or 8-foot-tall hardware cloth or cement-reinforcing wire supported by three or four 8-foot stakes shoved a foot into the ground.

Pruning and Training: Prune out lower branches so that only two or three main stems are left to grow. You don't need to tie up the vines; just weave them gently in and out as they grow. The trellis will support them.

Results: The fruit will be bigger than cage-grown fruit, and more numerous than those grown by the single-stem method that follows. (However, pruning cuts may allow entrance of stem diseases.)

Areas and Growth Habit for Which Method Is Recommended: All zones—both coastal or inland. Good system for non-determinate varieties.

▶ Support each tomato with a single 8-foot stake that you embed 1 to 2 feet in the ground.

Pruning and Training: Tie up the tomato plant as it grows. With nondeterminate varieties, remove all suckers allowing only one main trunk to grow. With determinate varieties (those that grow about 4 feet tall and then stop growing), no pruning is necessary.

Results: This method takes more work but yields large fruit and an early harvest.

Areas and Growth Habit for Which Method Is Recommended: Best method for all determinate varieties. Can be used for non-determinate varieties in coastal zones only (because fruit will sunburn inland).

A word of caution: If your tomatoes have ever been stricken with blight, a fungal disease that causes blackening of stems and rotting of fruit, do not prune out suckers. (Despite disease problems, most commercial growers prune nondeterminate tomatoes in the early weeks of growth, in order to produce larger tomatoes in smaller space. Tomato blight diseases are discussed on page 171.)

MARCH CHECKLIST

PURCHASE/PLANT

- { } Plant drought-resistant plants, 39
- { } Plant asparagus from seeds, 107
- { } Don't plant tropicals, 113
- { } Plant trees, shrubs, vines, and ground covers, 114
- { } Plant flowerbeds with warm-season flowers, if you have space, 116
- { } Plant perennials, 117
- { } Plant tigridias, 120
- { } Continue to plant gladioli, 120
- { } Start tuberous begonias, 120
- { } Plant herbaceous, or softwood, cuttings, 121
- { } Plant citrus, avocado, and macadamia trees, 121
- { } Purchase epidendrums, 124
- { } Start fuchsias from cuttings, 125
- { } Plant lawns, 129
- { } Start planting summer vegetables. Plant more cool-season crops if desired, 134
- { } Replace parsley now or next month, 200
- { } Plant green beans, 139
- { } Plant potatoes, 140
- { } Plant artichokes from seed-grown transplants, 141
- { } Plant tomatoes, 142
- { } Plant culinary herbs, 136
- { } Plant edible flowers, 140

TRIM, PRUNE, MOW, DIVIDE

- { } In interior valleys, prune begonias, cannas, ginger, ivy, pyracantha, and Sprenger fern, 96
- { } Dethatch warm-season lawns just after they begin to grow, 104
- { } Deadhead annuals and perennial flowers, 118
- { } Start to disbud roses if you are growing them for show, 119
- { } Tie floppy leaves of bulbs in knots (don't remove them before they go brown), 120
- { } Tie gladioli to stakes as they grow, 120
- { } Cut back epidendrum stems after bloom, 124
- { } Prune camellias, 124
- { } Take cut flowers from azaleas while they're in bloom, 124
- { } Pinch fuchsias to make them bushy, 124
- { } Start to prune tropical hibiscus, 124
- { } Propagate bamboo, 127
- { } Mow all grass lawns, 129
- { } Cut back blue hibiscus (*Alyogyne huegelii*) progressively from now until fall, 206
- { } Cut back clumps of *Festuca glauca* now or in fall, 328

FERTILIZE

- { } Fertilize citrus trees, 121
- { } Continue to fertilize epiphyllums, 67
- { } Fertilize avocado trees, 121
- { } Fertilize fuchsias, 124
- { } Fertilize ornamental trees, bushes, lawns, and ground covers, 113
- { } Feed container-grown flowers with liquid or slow-release fertilizer, 116
- { } Fertilize cool-season flowers if growth or flowering slows, 116
- { } Fertilize roses, 118
- { } Begin to fertilize macadamia trees, 122
- { } Feed all lawns, 130
- { } Feed blue hydrangeas with acid organic fertilizers. Mulch with tea leaves and coffee grounds, 320

WATER

{ } When rains aren't adequate, water all garden plants according to their individual needs, *67*

{ } Keep fuchsias well watered, *208*

{ } Water roses, *118*

{ } Water spring-flowering bulbs when rains don't do the job for you, *120*

{ } Don't let azaleas dry out, *124*

CONTROL PESTS, DISEASE, AND WEEDS

{ } Control slugs and snails, *115*

{ } Control pests and diseases on roses, *119*

{ } Protect gladioli from slugs and snails, *120*

{ } Control cutworms, *141*

{ } Pull weeds, *46*

{ } Plant French marigolds *(Tagetes patula)* solidly and leave them for a full season of growth to control nematodes, *296*

{ } Spray cycads for scale, *303*

{ } Control giant whitefly, *125*

ALSO THIS MONTH

{ } In interior zones, protect tender plants until all danger of frost has passed, *114*

{ } Once all frost danger is over, take out tender tropicals you sheltered during winter, *114*

{ } When frost-damaged plants resume growth, cut off damaged portions, *115*

{ } Prepare holes for planting dahlias next month, *120*

{ } Unwrap trunks of young citrus and avocado trees, *121*

{ } Harvest 'Beaumont' macadamia nuts and cure them correctly, *121*

{ } Hand-pollinate quince, guava, and cherimoya, *126*

{ } Install a drip system for irrigation of vegetables, *137*

{ } Continue to harvest winter vegetables, *139*

{ } Inoculate legumes, *137*

{ } Choose a staking method for tomatoes, *143*

{ } Desert flowers begin to bloom in late March; see them now or next month, *147*

{ } Make an herb garden, *136*

{ } Consider the lawn-free landscape, *129*

April

THE HEIGHT-OF-BLOOM MONTH

Eschscholzia californica
(California Poppy)

April is a magic time, the height of spring in Southern California, and in the back-country native plants deck the hillsides with color. So get out and take an observant walk around an old neighborhood, visit botanical gardens, go on garden tours sponsored by local clubs, and enjoy wildflowers in their moment of greatest glory. Take along a camera and notebook to record ideas. See native plants in bloom at such locations as Rancho Santa Ana Botanic Garden in Claremont; Torrey Pines State Reserve, near Del Mar; the Theodore Payne Foundation in Sun Valley; and the Antelope Valley California Poppy Reserve near Lancaster. (The last week in March is usually the height of desert bloom, but the first two weeks in April are often the best time for seeing wildflowers carpeting hillsides on back-country roads, especially after wildfires have cleared away brush in fall. Unless homes were destroyed or lives lost, this is the positive side of wildfire destruction.)

Southern California gardens are also in full bloom this month. We pride ourselves on year-round flowers, but we have more in April than at any other time of the year. Cool-season annuals planted in September and October reach their zenith early this month, and by mid-month, countless permanent landscape plants are in full bloom. April is our second spring-planting month but is less demanding than the first. If you did most of your spring planting in March, relax now and enjoy the fruits of your labor. If not, there's still time to catch up on jobs that went undone.

It's warm enough to sprout seeds quickly but not hot enough to scorch seedlings. Stormy days—often bringing heavy rains—alternate with sunny days, speeding growth and opening flowers. Pests also enjoy the warming trend. Cabbage butterflies, thrips, mites, and tobacco budworms speed up activities and need to be controlled. Despite this one negative note, April is a month to relish.

VALLEY AND DESERT DWELLERS

If you live in a hot inland valley or desert area, do your last planting this month, before the onslaught of summer heat. This is the last moment for you to plant ground covers without risking development of ugly gaps, and it's not too late to plant tropicals and subtropicals—palms, for example. Local nurseries have assortments of heat-loving bedding plants that can go into the ground now, including balsam, Madagascar periwinkle (vinca; *Catharanthus roseus*), marigolds, petunias, portulaca, and zinnias. (In desert areas, plant petunias in fall.)

Mulch plants after setting them out, and protect them from the hot noonday sun until they're well started. A shot of well-diluted fish emulsion after planting can get plants off to a good start.

AZALEAS

April is the best month of the year in which to plant azaleas, though not the first possible month. (Precise directions are given in January, page 66.) The largest number of azaleas are in bloom now, and while they're in bloom their roots are dormant, so you can safely plant them. As soon as they finish blooming, they'll take off and grow. Above ground they'll start putting out fresh leaves, and below ground they'll sprout tender young roots that shouldn't be disturbed.

Plant azaleas in tubs or the ground and in partial shade—a northern or eastern exposure is best. For easy care, water with a drip system. Use a ring of laser-cut drip tubing adjusted to keep roots evenly moist—neither soggy nor dry.

WISTERIA

Choose wisteria vines now, while they're in bloom. There are two main types: Chinese wisteria (*Wisteria sinensis*), which blooms all at once on bare branches, and Japanese wisteria (*Wisteria floribunda*), which has a longer period of bloom, more fragrance, and flowers that open from top to bottom as leaves appear. Besides the familiar violet-blue, there are white, pink, and purple wisterias, some with 3-foot-long blooms. Always purchase named varieties or grafted plants. These have characteristics superior to those of chance seedlings.

Wisteria is one of our most satisfactory vines because, though it's easy to grow and highly drought resistant once established, its blooms are among the most romantic of flowers in color, shape, and fragrance. It's deciduous, so if you grow it on an arbor, it can give you welcome shade in summer and sunshine in winter. And it flourishes anywhere from desert to beach. Plant the vines in full sun, provide strong support, and water and fertilize them often for the first year or two to get them started. Once a wisteria is well established, you can subject it to benign neglect, but not before.

EPIPHYLLUMS

Epiphyllums, orchid cacti, are true members of the cactus family but are native to open jungles rather than deserts. They like semishade and well-drained soil, and, because most are epiphytes, or tree-dwelling plants (and because they're particularly delicious to snails), they do well in hanging baskets. There are more than nine thousand named varieties to choose from. Real fanciers fill entire backyards with these plants and have blooms year-round, but most gardeners grow them for a spectacular show beginning now and lasting through June. Begin looking for them in nurseries. Watch the newspaper for epiphyllum shows in May. Ask friends to save you a branch of this or that admired variety. They're easy to start from cuttings (the box below tells you how).

For most of the year, epiphyllums are the ugly ducklings of the garden. They can be kept tucked away in a semishady spot, watered once a week in dry weather, pruned of dead branches to encourage growth, and fed occasionally with a complete fertilizer such as fish emulsion during the summer and with an organic high-bloom formula such as Tiger Bloom (2-8-4) liquid organic fertilizer from January until they flower. Now's the time to move plants to center stage and enjoy the exotic blooms. Make sure you face the plants in the same direction they're used to, or the flower buds may fall off.

Each flower lasts only a day or two, but more keep opening. For best appearance, cut off the faded blossoms; otherwise their wilted petals will hang on for a long time. Mist "epis" frequently in dry weather, but don't overwater them. Though less drought resistant than almost all other cacti, epiphyllums use little

How to Start an Epiphyllum from a Cutting

▸ Cut off a branch from a plant you wish to propagate, making the cut at the narrow intersection where it joins another branch.

▸ Use a permanent broad-tip marker to write the variety name in block letters directly on one side of the cutting.

▸ If the cut branch is wide, trim off excess flesh to make a point. Dip the cut section in a rooting hormone such as Dip'N Grow or RooTone, knock off the excess, and allow the cutting to dry and callus off for a day or two.

▸ Plant in a 4-inch pot of dry—not wet—potting soil to a depth ½ inch above the two lowest areoles, or spine cushions. (On epiphyllums, these are found in the notches on the stem.) Tamp the soil down firmly around the cutting; then stake the cutting with wood or bamboo and tie it securely.

▸ Mist the cutting daily, but take care not to water the soil until the cutting has rooted, which will happen in about a month. (You can check by pulling gently on the cutting; once roots have sprouted, it will resist. Or you can feel the thickness of the cutting; when the roots begin to grow, it will get plumper.) Once it has rooted, start regularly watering. Feed lightly with diluted fish emulsion when it has grown 2 to 3 inches tall. When roots fill the container, repot into a larger size.

▸ A good soil mix for epiphyllums is light and airy, drains well, and contains agricultural charcoal. The following works well: 1 gallon good-quality acid commercial potting soil mix recommended for "jungle" plants, 1 cup perlite, and 1 cup agricultural charcoal.

water, especially if you irrigate them with a drip system instead of a hose. Test whether plants are ready for watering by sticking a finger an inch or two into the mix. If it feels damp, don't water. If it feels dry, turn on the drip system until you see water drain out the bottoms of the containers; then turn it off. During the rainy season, don't water at all.

What's an Epiphyte?

An epiphyte is a plant that lives by attaching itself to another plant, typically a tree, or in some cases to a rock. They often root in pockets of soil that gather in the crotches of trees and are fertilized by a regular sprinkling of bird droppings, dead insects, and the occasional dead animal. Unlike parasites, epiphytes don't take nourishment from the host plant. Most are native to humid tropical or subtropical regions. Many aroids, orchids, ferns, cacti, and bromeliads are epiphytic. They're good choices for our gardens because so many of them have developed built-in reservoirs, thickened leaves, or other devices to see them through drought.

All epiphytes prefer loose, acid, airy, well-drained soil. They're often grown in hanging baskets. Some are grown on slabs of bark, and all can be naturalized (made to grow and multiply as they would in the wild) on tree branches if kept moist with an automatic mist system.

PRUNING

Cut Back Poinsettias. After poinsettia flowers have faded, sometime between now and the end of May, prune garden-grown plants back to two or three dormant buds. (These look like swellings or scars close to the bottoms of the branches.) Poinsettia (*Euphorbia pulcherrima*) is best known today as a Christmas potted plant, but old varieties such as 'Hollywood' make easy-care garden plants, requiring only average watering in summer. (Among indoor varieties, 'Annette Hegg' grows best outdoors.) Order garden varieties from nurseries or purchase them at plant sales. They grow easily from cuttings. Fifty years ago, before modern varieties and growing techniques made poinsettias so popular for Christmas, they were a staple of California gardens in frost-free zones, and they're still useful for hard-to-reach sunny spots, such as a south-facing garage wall.

Control Shrubs That Would Like to Be Trees. Hedges and shrubs start fast growth now. Any green shrub that has an eventual size of over 6 feet needs frequent pruning during the warm months if you want to keep it as a shrub. (Remember to prune flowering shrubs that bloom for a specific season after, rather than before, bloom.) Many shrubs would like to shoot up and become trees; it's all right to let them—some make fine specimens—but when it happens by accident, you end up with a crowded garden. (A more sophisticated approach is to use dwarf plants that will always be the right size for the space.)

With shrubs in particular, work for a billowy, sloping form, wider below than above (so lower branches won't die from shade). There are three main ways to prune them:

1. Plants with small leaves can be clipped on the outside like a hedge, with shears or loppers.
2. Plants with large leaves are best cut from the inside, with branches cut out deep within to renew growth from inside out. This gives an informal look and is often necessary to keep

heavy trunks from growing taller. (A saw or ratchet pruner can make this job easier; the built-in ratchet in particular increases your strength manyfold.)

3. Plants that grow from the ground in the shape of a fountain, such as oleander and heavenly bamboo (*Nandina domestica*), are best pruned by taking out entire branches to ground level after bloom. Pittosporum, myoporum, and photinia are among the shrubs to prune beginning now.

- **Victorian Box** (*Pittosporum undulatum*). This is useful as a fragrant, drought-resistant informal shrub in coastal zones. (It requires more water in interior regions.) It frequently starts as a volunteer. Victorian box rapidly becomes a 12-foot tree if allowed, then gradually grows to 30 or 40 feet in height and width—a nice-looking tree, but drippy with leaves and sticky fruit. It can be kept as an informal hedge or screen indefinitely by cutting it back, mainly with loppers, beginning in spring and continuing occasionally throughout summer. A 9-foot hedge can be cut to 3 to 4 feet but will take a year or two to recover.
- **Tobira** (*P. tobira*). The standard variety of this pittosporum can grow slowly to tree height, but it can easily be kept small or pruned into artistic shapes with shears and loppers. 'Wheeler's Dwarf' is compact; it grows eventually to only 2 to 3 feet, with a mounded shape and no pruning necessary.
- **Myoporum** (*Myoporum laetum*). For a century, myoporum has been a useful, though invasive, coastal shrub growing quickly to 30 feet tall unless planted in the teeth of the ocean wind or controlled by pruning. (Compact varieties also exist.) Currently, myoporum thrips (*Klambothrips myopori*) are

contorting the leaves and new shoots of myoporum and even killing the plants. Until some biological control is introduced to control this pest, replace dead and dying myoporums with a better screen plant, such as pink melaleuca (*Melaleuca nesophila*).

- **Fraser's photinia** (*Photinia x fraseri*). This plant naturally grows as a shrub—as tall as 10 feet if you don't cut it shorter—or you can prune it into a small tree while it's young by choosing a single trunk and cutting out all others. Prune it often with loppers to maintain the size you choose and encourage fresh growth. New growth is red—dull when front-lit but exciting when planted on the west so that afternoon light shines through the leaves. If you are growing it as a shrub, don't let it get wide on top, or the bottom section will become bare and ugly. If it gets too tall, cut it to the desired size this month. It will soon bounce back.

DECIDUOUS FRUIT TREES

Deciduous fruit trees that are overloaded with fruit always drop a lot of it later in the year, in a natural process called June drop (described on page 243). You can permit your fruit to grow larger and decrease June drop by starting to thin it now. Thin out the fruit lightly this month, removing one or two fruits from heavy clusters all over the tree. Thin the fruit again four to six weeks later. (Mark it on your calendar so you won't forget.)

BULBS

Plant Dahlias. Dahlias are the best-kept secret in the garden. With just a little care, they're easy

How to Plant Dahlias

▸ Choose a spot in full sun along the coast or in afternoon shade inland, in rich, well-drained soil. Work in soil amendment if you didn't prepare planting holes in March.

▸ Dig holes 7 to 8 inches deep for large tubers, or 5 to 6 inches deep for small tubers, and 1 to 3 feet apart according to size. Work into the bottom of each hole a handful of fishbone meal or some other organic high-bloom fertilizer. McGeary Organics 2-3-4 is one choice. (High nitrogen cuts down on bloom.) Cover this with 2 inches of fast-draining soil or sand.

▸ Place the tuber on top with the eye (the growth bud) up.

▸ Cover the tuber with 2 inches of soil. As the plant grows up through this soil, continually cover it with more.

▸ Stake tall varieties at planting time, with the stake next to the growth bud. Tie them up later. (Bedding varieties don't need it, but a stake will help you remember where the tubers are.)

▸ When plants are up 3 inches, begin to fertilize with an organic fertilizer recommended for flowering plants.

▸ When the plant has three sets of leaves, pinch off the top set to encourage branching. Some gardeners like to pinch again when plants are 1½ to 2 feet high. This will produce more but smaller blooms.

to grow and so flamboyant they'll make any gardener look like an expert. Grown in rows, they're unpleasantly stiff, so plant dwarf and bedding types in drifts among other flowers and tall ones at the backs of beds (see page 315).

Feed Irises. Fertilize irises with a low-nitrogen, high-phosphorus, and high-potassium plant food—Tiger Bloom (2-8-4), for example—to encourage bloom. Solid fertilizers are the easiest to use on plants growing in the ground. Use liquids in containers. Protect irises from slugs and snails, which will ruin the plants if allowed.

Tie Up Leaves of Spring-Flowering Bulbs after Bloom. Continue to water spring-flowering bulbs when rains aren't adequate. Feed those that have bloomed with a balanced liquid fertilizer or solid bulb food watered into the ground. This will help them flower better next year. Don't cut off the green leaves until they go completely yellow; tie them into knots to make them look neater, and plant summer flowers around them.

ROSES

Control Pests and Diseases, Fertilize, and Irrigate. Continue to control pests and diseases on roses, and release beneficials, especially ladybugs, against aphids (as described on page 44). Also, wash off any aphids you see with a spray of water in the early morning, and increase your roses' ability to repel pests by placing a layer of earthworm castings over their roots. Earthworm castings will get rid of ants and most other pests except caterpillars and loopers, and they may also have an effect on rose slugs. (See an explanation on page 85.)

Caterpillars and budworms usually become active by month's end. Use BT against caterpillars and loopers. Spinosad controls budworms, caterpillars, and rose slugs and is longer-lasting than BT, but despite its OMRI label, it kills bees. Package directions say to spray after the bees leave the plants in the evening, and to make sure the spray dries before bees return. But how is one supposed to do this—use a hair dryer? Post warning signs? Even if bees could read and obey signs, they couldn't avoid carrying pollen back to the hive after the spray has dried, and when pollen treated with Spinosad is fed to larvae, it kills some larvae and weakens the rest. The only safe way to use Spinosad is to mix a couple of cups of spray at a time in a small hand sprayer—the kind used for spraying laundry—and spray the undersides of leaves in the evening, keeping spray far away from flowers. Broadcasting Spinosad with a ready-to-use spray container, in which it is often sold, cannot help but kill bees.

If you have been fertilizing and caring for your roses organically, you may find they are largely free from diseases and pests, even including the mites that are such a problem for gardeners who feed roses the conventional way. Those new to organic gardening are often flabbergasted when they see the unsightly damage from mites disappear after a few months. If, however, you still see telltale signs (whitening foliage and small, dense webs), try controlling them with Summit Year-Round Spray Oil or insecticidal soap. Control mildew with Cornell Fungicide Formula (see page 95).

Fertilize your roses regularly. Either feed this month with an organic commercial rose food or, if you're following the Rose-Pro Method, feed with Dr. Earth Organic 3 Rose & Flower Fertilizer (5-7-2), or any other organic commercial rose food during the first week in April, applying the product according to package directions. One week later, sprinkle 2 cups Biosol Mix over the roots of each rose. Also in April, unless you did the job earlier in the year, apply 2 tablespoons of John and Bob's Soil Optimizer around each rose and follow up with irrigation.

If you're using the above instructions as a guide to help you choose free or generic fertilizers, you have several choices. Look at the suggestions on pages 53 and 118, and choose fertilizers according to your budget and the plants' appearance. If your roses are putting out too much growth at the expense of flowers, hold back on generic sources of nitrogen and increase bloom ingredients. If plants have a lackluster appearance, give them a boost with earthworm castings, seaweed, humic acid, or compost tea. If by month's end none of your roses show signs of throwing up new canes, give each plant one or two tablespoons of Epsom salts to provide magnesium and promote new canes. However, if your budget has allowed you to apply humic acid or kelp, your roses already have trace minerals, making Epsom salts unnecessary.

In interior zones and fast-draining soils, irrigate roses deeply with up to $1\frac{1}{2}$ inches of water per application, and increase the frequency of irrigations now from once to twice a week. (One inch of water applied twice a week may be adequate in coastal climates and water-retentive soils.)

Prune Roses by Picking, Deadheading, and Disbudding. Roses start blooming in April, and when you pick them for cut flowers, you're doing a kind of pruning. Roses naturally flower in flushes of bloom, but how you cut them affects both the time elapsed between consecutive flushes and the length of their stems. The longer the stems you cut, the more time it will

How to Keep Cut Roses Fresh

▸ To Prevent Neck Droop of Cut Roses: In early evening, pick full buds that are beginning to open. Wrap them in a black plastic trash bag so no light can enter, and store them overnight in the refrigerator (between six and twelve hours). The next morning, take out the roses and treat them as follows.

▸ To Make Cut Roses Last Seven or Eight Days: Immerse them in a sink filled with lukewarm water (100°F) for twenty to thirty minutes. Clip off the lower leaves (but not the thorns); then recut the stems underwater. Arrange the roses in a vase filled with either of these solutions: 1 quart water, 2 tablespoons fresh lemon juice, 1 tablespoon sugar, and ½ teaspoon bleach; or 1 pint regular 7-Up, 1 pint water, and ½ teaspoon bleach.

take for the rose to rebloom, though the flowers will be good ones on long, strong stems. If you always cut your roses with short, stubby stems, the bush will bloom again much sooner, but with inferior flowers on short, weak stems. So unless you're growing exhibition roses, choose the middle ground: cut neither down too far nor up too high.

The easiest way to encourage roses to put out strong, healthy growth while allowing them to bounce back into bloom within a few weeks is to follow this general **Rule of Thumb:** *Cut flowers from rose plants that are over one year old just above the first five-leaflet leaf that points away from the center of the plant.* (Leave more greenery on a first-year plant to make the bush stronger.) When flowers have been allowed to

fade on the bush, deadhead them at the same point. This method of cutting roses quickly brings flowers back on long stems. (An exception should be made for varieties that naturally bear long-stemmed roses and are, in any case, more appropriately raised for their cut flowers than for their beauty in the landscape. You can cut these longer, but always leave at least two leaves on the plant at the bottom of each stem. New growth will arise above them.)

For one-to-a-stem and show-quality roses, continue to disbud hybrid teas and grandifloras (as described on page 119).

WATER GARDENING

Fish and lily ponds are one of the most exciting yet tranquil elements of horticulture. Water can provide sound from fountains and waterfalls; movement from fish, birds, dragonflies, and sky reflections; a paradisiacal atmosphere; and colorful flowers. Ponds can be of any size or shape. You can grow a dwarf water lily or dwarf exotic lotus even in a half wine barrel.

Water lilies *(Nymphaea)* are among the most intriguing flowers we grow. There are two main kinds. Hardy water lilies, which are easy to grow, bloom during the daytime in summer and have flowers that float on the surface of the water; tropical water lilies, which have a longer bloom season, carry their blossoms high above the water surface. Tropical lilies come in a rainbow of colors, including blue, with flowers often as big as dinner plates. Some are night blooming. Lotus (Neumbo), an exotic plant sacred to the Hindu and Buddhist religions, requires much the same care as water lilies.

There are many other aquatic plants. Some grow like water lilies and lotus, with their roots in mud or soil and their foliage either floating

How to Plant a Water Lily

▸ Purchase a water lily planting tub from a mail-order company specializing in water gardening, or make your own from a plastic or cardboard plant container that is 14 or 18 inches in diameter and 6 to 12 inches deep. (Both are lightweight and hold up well under water.) Plug the drainage holes with wads made of two layers of newspaper.

▸ Plant water lilies in rich garden soil; fertile loam is best. Make sure it contains no manure (which encourages growth of algae) and no peat moss, compost, commercial potting soil, perlite, wood shavings, or other lightweight soil amendment that might float to the surface of the pond. Or plant in Profile Aquatic Plant Soil according to package directions (it will not foul pond water).

▸ According to package directions, mix into the soil a complete, organic, granulated fertilizer that's recommended for aquatic plants and contains trace elements to enhance growth and flower color. Or choose a fertilizer in pellet or tablet form, such as Organic Aquatic Plant Tabs.

▸ Fill the container to 2 inches below the top with fertilized soil, and then water it so that it settles. Add more soil if necessary. Plant one lily at a time, keeping the others moist and in the shade. Don't let their roots dry out.

▸ In the case of hardy water lilies, plant them when the water temperature is 60°F or higher. Place the tuber with the bud facing up, and with the end that contains the bud pointing toward the center of the container and the other end of the tuber gently touching the inside of the container. Plant so that the crown or growth bud is ¼ inch below the surface of the ground and so that the tuber slopes down at a 45-degree angle from the bud end to the place where the tuber touches the container.

▸ Cover the top of the container with a circle of ½-inch galvanized chicken wire that's cut 2 to 3 inches wider than the diameter of the container. Bend it down over the sides to keep out fish. The lily will grow up through the wire. Alternatively, cover the surface of the soil with a 1-inch layer of pebbles or sand.

▸ Immediately after planting, submerge the container in the pond so that the top of the soil is 6 inches underwater. When the plant is thoroughly established, lower it so the soil surface is 12 to 18 inches underwater. Use bricks or cement blocks under the container to adjust the height.

▸ Plant tropical water lilies when the water temperature is 70°F or higher. Place the round chestnutlike tuber of each tropical water lily upright in the center of the container with its roots buried and its crown, the place from which the foliage emerges, protruding slightly above the soil.

▸ If your tropical lily has foliage, make your circle of chicken wire 2 inches larger than for hardy lilies. Cut a hole 4 inches in diameter in the center. Then cut the circle of wire straight through the middle from side to side, dividing it into two equal halves. After planting the lily, fit the two halves over the surface of the soil so the plant is growing up through the middle, and tie the two halves together. Bend down the edge around the sides.

▸ Immediately after planting, carefully submerge the tropical lily in the pond with 4 to 6 inches of water above soil level. When the plant grows to 8 inches in diameter, lower the container so there are 12 to 18 inches of water above it.

on the surface of the water or standing above it. (Most aquatic plants that are rooted in soil are best grown in containers for ease of maintenance. See the box on page 155 for guidelines on planting water lilies.) A second group of plants floats freely on the surface of the water, while a third type is completely submerged and adds oxygen to the pond.

Water gardening is romantic and beautiful, yet, like all other types of gardening, it has its practical requirements. First, the pool should be properly balanced, which means it should contain the right ingredients to prevent the water from becoming stagnant. The **Rule of Thumb** for balancing a pond: *For each square yard of water, you need two bunches of submerged oxygenating grasses, twelve water snails, two 5-inch-size goldfish or koi, and 1 medium to large water lily.* (In water barrels, substitute several guppies or mosquito fish for the goldfish or koi.) Don't feed your fish. If you don't feed them, they won't overproduce or grow too large. They'll get all they need from the pond and act as natural gardeners, helping to keep the water clean. In an ecologically balanced pond, fish eat bugs, various organic materials floating on the top of the pond, submerged oxygenating grasses, and algae. Even though you don't feed your fish, they'll get to know you, and they'll come to you when you approach the pond or touch the water.

Even if you've provided all the elements for balance, the water may turn green with algae, a diverse group of primitive flowerless plants, but it will eventually settle down and become clean and clear most of the time. There are two kinds of aquatic algae: filamentous, which attach themselves to walls and plants, and floating, which turn ponds green. Algae grow fast in unseasonably warm weather, and many balanced ponds go green for a while in spring.

If this happens to your pond, don't worry; just wait. When the weather cools, or when the water is adequately shaded by lily or lotus leaves, it will clear up by itself. If your pond stays green throughout the warm months, it may not be properly balanced, it may need more submerged oxygenating plants, or it may need more water lilies to shade the surface. Sixty to seventy percent of the water surface should be shaded by leaves during summer, less in winter.

Feed the Plants. For a pond, this means getting in there bodily. You'll need to wear hip boots, protective clothing, and long rubber gloves for this job because some forms of algae can be absorbed through the skin and may produce allergic reactions. Fertilize water lilies and lotus in April. They're gluttons for food and won't bloom or grow well without adequate nourishment. Beginning now, feed one aquatic plant pellet (the 6-gram slow-release type—10-5-5, for example) to each container per month. Use a wooden dowel to shove each pellet deeply into the soil mix as close to the crown of the plant as possible. While you're about it, scoop up some of the muck from the bottom of the pond. (Some gardeners report good results when using this pond by-product as a fertilizer on roses and other plants. You can try this if you wish, but use it sparingly at first because it may contain harmful salts.) Don't be concerned about muddying the water as you work. It will clear again, and the fish won't come to harm.

If you don't have a pond, consider the several easy ways to add one to the landscape, including ready-made pond liners. Both shaped and flexible pond liners are available. Be sure to put your pond in full sun. Also take into consideration animal threats to fish and plants. Unless your pond is correctly designed, the local family of raccoons will throw a pool party, trashing your plants and eating all the fish in one jolly night. To avoid this, place plant containers away from the edges and make sure the sides of the pond plunge straight down for 3 feet. (Raccoons will not enter water unless they can step down into it.) In the early morning or late afternoon, blue herons, too, might stake out fishing rights, but goldfish and koi can escape herons if you provide a hiding place for them, such as a cave on the bottom of the pond. For more information, order the magazinelike catalog from Van Ness Water Gardens in Upland, or refer to books on water gardening—for example, Sunset's *Garden Pools, Fountains & Waterfalls*; Paul and Rees's *The Water Garden*; or White's *Water Gardens*.

PEST CONTROL

Spray for Caterpillars and Worms. This is the month when caterpillars and worms wake up and begin serious munching. In a shrub-surrounded garden with many beneficials, tree frogs, and birds in residence, it may not be necessary to spray. But if caterpillar and worm damage is out of control, spray with BT, the bacterial disease that affects certain caterpillars but no other pests or insects. It's sold as a liquid or powder under the Safer and Attack brands and such trade names as Thuricide. (Read the labels to make sure it's BT you're getting.) When mixing powders into sprays, add a spreader-sticker, such as Summit Year-Round Spray Oil. It will make mixing easier and increase the effectiveness of the spray.

Some gardeners claim that BT no longer works, and this is encouraging them to change to another, newer biological product called Spinosad. Spinosad is made from the fermented

juices of the soil bacteria *Saccharopolyspora spinosa*. It doesn't kill many beneficials, such as butterflies, but it is toxic to bees. As explained in more detail on page 379, if the bees visit plants while the spray is still moist, they will die. Spinosad lasts in the environment up to four weeks, which is why people like it, but this is the very reason we should not use it often, if at all. Use it only in small amounts in controlled spaces away from pollen-bearing flowers, or use it on specific plants, such as geraniums, that bees never visit.

If your BT no longer works, purchase a fresh container; check the date on the new container to make sure it hasn't been sitting on the shelf too long. BT contains live fungi and lasts only a year, if that long, but it doesn't kill bees. BT lasts on a plant for only up to four days, so you may need to spray frequently. The important thing is timing, as the section below on budworms will make clear. On the other hand, you may not need to spray at all; some years, there won't be any budworms. A lot depends on the weather, climate zone, and the varieties of plants you grow.

Caterpillars are the immature stage, or larvae, of butterflies and moths. Butterflies are usually brightly colored and fly in the daytime; most moths fly at night, and their wings are dull colored. In their mature stage, butterflies and moths aren't harmful; some are even beneficial pollinators. But after mating, females lay their eggs singly or in groups on plants or other chosen food. When the eggs hatch, caterpillars emerge, and these are what do the damage. When the larvae of moths have grown to full size, they pupate within the plant or spin a silky cocoon in the soil or debris beneath it. When the caterpillars of butterflies pupate, they attach themselves to a branch or other support and form a protective shell called a chrysalis to protect the soft pupa, or third stage of metamorphosis. After metamorphosing inside the chrysalis for a few days or over the winter, the mature butterfly or moth emerges, mates, and lays eggs.

Fortunately, most butterflies and moths are selective about where they lay their eggs, making it possible to choose which plants to spray with BT and which ones to leave unsprayed. Parsley, for example, is host to the larvae of swallowtail butterfly, milkweed to monarch butterfly, and passion vine to Gulf fritillary. Don't spray these plants. But, obviously, when you see cabbage butterflies, you need to spray your cabbages. And redhumped caterpillars, the larvae of a brown moth, always begin their attack on broom *(Genista)* in April. These yellow caterpillars have a red hump, a red head, and red stripes. Working in large numbers, they quickly devour all flowers and sections of foliage in repeated generations. So spray broom with BT weekly.

Control Budworms. Tobacco or geranium budworms also get going this month. Budworms drill a little round hole in the flowers of geraniums and bore out the inside, ruining the blossoms. They also munch on leaves. In order to control budworms with BT, you need to spray the plants before the budworms climb inside the flowers. In this particular case you can, if you prefer, use Spinosad in controlled situations. As mentioned before, it is probably safe to use Spinosad in a small, laundry-type hand sprayer to control budworm on zonal geraniums *(Pelargonium x hortorum)*, including on their flower buds, because bees don't visit them. This month, you can time the treatment correctly because the night-flying moth that is the parent of the tobacco budworm usually makes its first egg-laying foray with the first full moon in April. So spray or dust all your geraniums with BT a day before the full moon, and repeat the process three or four days after the full moon. Or if you decide to use Spinosad, spray only once and only on plants such as zonal geraniums that are subject to looper and budworm damage but are never visited by bees. This will cut down the pest population at the beginning of the season and catch the budworms before they are safely ensconced inside the flowers. (If it rains hard on the night of the first full moon in April, you will have a month's reprieve. Budworms won't fly that night; they will wait a whole month until the next full moon to fly and lay eggs, which is when you will need to spray.)

Control Fuchsia Gall Mites. Fuchsia gall mite *(Aculops fuchsiae)* attacks new growth on fuchsias, twisting and distorting the buds, foliage, and flowers and turning leaves red. In many areas, predacious mites keep this pest under control.

By far the best control for fuchsia gall mites is to grow resistant varieties and take good care of the plants. Provide them with regular fertilizer (as discussed on page 208), the correct light (50 percent sunshine in coastal zones under lath or shade cloth), and daily irrigation by a drip system with mini-sprinklers concealed overhead to adequately moisturize the soil and wash off the foliage. I never spray the fuchsias in my garden. In early spring, I start applying ladybugs and lacewing larvae to the foliage. I also release spiders onto them, which I catch with damp facial tissue elsewhere in the garden. I also concentrate on growing resistant varieties. Here are a few: 'Baby Chang', 'Chance Encounter', 'Cinnabarina', 'Dollar Princess', 'Englander', 'Golden West', 'Iris', 'Miniature Jewels', 'Mendocino Mini',

'Nonpareil', 'Ocean Mist', and 'Pink Marshmallow'. I've also had good luck with 'Lisa', 'Swingtime', and 'Voodoo'. ('Voodoo' is susceptible to fuchsia gall mites in some areas but not in others.)

Control Spider Mites. Now through summer, watch for spider mites; they're most active in warm weather. Spider mites are members of the arachnid family that live on pine needles and under the leaves of other favored plants, including roses, fuchsias, primroses, and cyclamen. They suck out plant juices and cause whitening, yellowing, stippling, and loss of color in the foliage that can sometimes mean death to the plant. If you think a plant has mites, place a sheet of white paper under the foliage and tap the branch. Look with a magnifying glass for tiny black or reddish spiderlike creatures scurrying around on the paper. Another telltale sign, which is easier to see, is fine, hairlike webbing—like spiderwebs but messier—around, over, and under leaves and twigs. Suspect spider mites on roses or azaleas when their leaves turn yellow and fall off. Rub a yellowing leaf on a white cloth; if a smudge results, mites are to blame.

In conventional gardens, spider mites are dreaded pests. Some plants, including azaleas and moosehorn ferns (*Platycerium superbum*), can be so weakened by them that they die. Roses won't die from them, but they can be set back. Healthy, well-fed plants in any garden will be less likely to suffer a bad mite attack, but the most dramatic improvement in plant health occurs when a gardener switches from chemical and synthetic controls to organic ones. Simply by fertilizing with organic fertilizers, building the organic content of soil, and forgoing chemical sprays an organic gardener can banish spider mites from the yard and allow a whole army of beneficial creatures to take over the job of pest control.

Beneficials that kill spider mites abound in our environment. These include brown and green lacewings, spider mite destroyer ladybeetle (*Stethorus picipes*), six-spotted thrips (*Scolothrips sexmaculatus*), and several predacious mites. Predacious mites are long-legged and colorless, more active and faster than pest mites, stopping only to feed. Look for them with a handheld lens under plant leaves. Two of these mites—*Phytoseiulus persimilis* and *Typhlodromus occidentalis*—are commercially available, as are lacewings. (Biocontrol Network is one such source.)

Attacking spider mites with chemical sprays only increases problems, since mites quickly develop resistance to sprays, and when you spray, you destroy all their natural enemies. The best ways to control mites are to conserve their resident natural enemies, control ants, refrain from applying pesticides, and wash off plants to remove dust.

In addition to beneficial mites, organic gardens teem with other beneficial insects and arachnids, including hover flies, tiny black ladybugs, garden spiders, lacewings, and tiny parasitic wasps, all of which help keep the bad guys under control. Beneficial mites that parasitize pest mites abound in the top layers of organic soils, so if you have been building up your soil with homemade compost, manure, and other organic matter, you have also been fighting pest problems all along. You don't need to spray, and in fact your very decision never to spray is saving your plants from mite damage.

Control Eugenia Psyllid. For over a hundred years, eugenia (*Syzygium paniculatum*), also called Australian brush cherry, has been Southern California's most valuable hedge plant for

QUICK TIP

How to Encourage Ladybugs to Stay Put.
Before releasing ladybugs, chill them for an hour or two in the refrigerator; this slows their metabolism. Release them at dusk. Place them low on plants so they can walk up. When the weather is dry, provide dishes of water on the ground at the base of plants; place a rock within each for ladybugs to land on. Remember, ladybugs can't swim, but they do need water to drink.

frost-free zones; one can grow it to any needed height and clip it as narrowly as 1 foot. But at some point during the late 1980s, the eugenia psyllid *(Trioza eugeniae)* was accidentally imported from Australia, and it has since rendered its namesake practically useless for new plantings. Eugenia psyllid is a small flying insect that lays eggs under new foliage on eugenia shrubs and trees. The larvae suck out the juices from fresh leaves, stunting, twisting, and distorting the foliage, but they don't kill the plants. Young plants show more damage than old ones, and in the early spring the psyllid is active on new growth. Fortunately, government agencies have released beneficial insects to control eugenia psyllid. When the weather warms up slightly, these existing beneficials become active and wipe out the psyllid population. Gardeners who spray with pesticides kill the psyllid but also kill the beneficials. Hose off the plants now, and put up with a little leaf damage, knowing that the plants will look much better as the year progresses. If you're planting a new hedge, substitute another plant, such as Carolina laurel cherry *(Prunus caroliniana)*; Japanese yew *(Podocarpus macrophyllus)*; fern pine *(Podocarpus gracilior)*; native holly leaf cherry *(Prunus ilicifolia)*,

which provides food and habitat for birds; Italian cypress *(Cupressus sempervirens* 'Stricta' or *C. v.* 'Glauca'); or finally, Icee Blue yellow wood *(Podocarpus elongatus* 'Monmal', *P.* 'Icee Blue')*, a drought-resistant South African tree with stunning blue-gray foliage for sun or shade.

Release Beneficials and Encourage Animals. Start releasing beneficial insects this month. Ladybugs are available at many nurseries now. Keep the packages damp with a few drops of water. Prior to releasing ladybugs, place them in their packages in the refrigerator for a least an hour; this slows down their metabolism. Meanwhile, sprinkle the garden with water to provide an inviting environment. And then apply the insects by small spoonfuls here and there around the garden at dusk. Fewer fly away when prechilled and introduced into a moist garden in the cool evening hours. Put a few on each of your fuchsias. Also send away for other beneficials, including lacewings and predatory mites and wasps. Encourage birds—they eat many insects—and, though it may sound eccentric, also install homes for bats. Bats eat night-flying moths whose larval forms, such as cutworms and budworms, are so destructive in the garden. Welcome spiders into the garden. Spiders, beneficial insects, and animals can help the gardener keeps pests under control better than poisonous sprays. Try to interest your neighbors in your new methods.

We have seen on a grand scale what beneficial creatures can accomplish. The ash whitefly has been almost eliminated, the pine tip moth and eucalyptus long-horn borer greatly reduced (though now another species of long-horn borer has arrived). These triumphs should give gardeners hope, but working with beneficials to control pests takes patience and requires following a few rules. One rule is to get rid of ants;

Plants That Attract Beneficials

Many beneficial insects feed on pollen and nectar, so to attract beneficials, grow old-fashioned annual and perennial flowers, wildflowers, and flowering herbs; these bear more pollen and nectar than modern hybrids. Push whole carrots from the kitchen down into the ground here and there in the garden and they will flower. When annual herbs such as parsley, cilantro, and arugula start going to seed, don't pull them up; let them also flower. Do the same with a few cole crops, such as mustard and broccoli. Here's a list of plants that are especially rich in nectar and pollen:

Achillea	Gypsophila (baby's breath)	Signet marigold
Aster	Honeysuckle	Silver sage
Carrot	Lantana	Sunflower (many kinds)
Chamomile	Lavender	Sweet alyssum
Cilantro	Lemon balm	Thyme
Cleome	Nasturtium	Valerian
Clover (white and scarlet)	Nepeta (catnip and catmint)	Wild buckwheat (*Eriogonum sp.*)
Cosmos	Parsley	Wildflowers
Daisy (many kinds)	Queen Anne's lace	Zinnias
Daylily	Roses (with few or single petals)	
Dill	Scented geraniums	

they kill the larvae of beneficial creatures while protecting and spreading aphids and other pests in order to milk them for their honeydew. To control ants, spread earthworm castings under affected plants, or try sprinkling corn meal near ant nests and on their trails. Don't spray chemical pesticides, and try to guide your neighbors onto the same path. There will always need to be a few pests for the beneficial creatures to eat, and beneficials are easily killed by pesticides. Our aim should be a landscape of healthy plants within which pests and predators live side by side, in balance with each other. Provide water in the garden for the beneficials to drink. A fish pond or small garden fountain, an Indian grinding stone, or the top section of an old birdbath nestled down into the ground can do the trick. Containers with sloping sides work best since insects can reach the water without falling in. Finally, make sure there are pollen-bearing flowers, such as sweet alyssum or daisies, in the garden throughout the year, because when there aren't enough pests to eat, beneficial insects keep themselves alive by eating pollen and nectar. (See the box above for a list of pollen-bearing flowers.)

ANNUAL AND PERENNIAL FLOWERS

A Word about Timing. April is an ideal month to plant warm-season annuals and perennials for summer color. In actual practice, however, most gardeners who planted cool-season flowers last fall have no room to plant in. All sunny beds are filled with flowers at the height of bloom at least until midmonth and typically until May.

(Maintain these areas by deadheading, staking if necessary, and watering when rains aren't adequate.) The only beds bare of blooms now are those that were filled with cineraria or bulbs, now faded and ready to be replaced. If all your flowerbeds are bare of blooms in April, it's probably a sign that you didn't plant the right things at the right time. Don't despair; this fall you'll get another chance (see page 324).

For now, resist the urge to stock up on masses of spring flowers in bloom at the nursery, because they'll soon fade. It's very confusing to first-time local gardeners that in April nurseries are overflowing with cool-season flowers in full bloom. (The correct way to use them is as fill-ins where something has died or faded. Or fill a pot or two for a party or special occasion.) Examples of items *not* to fill beds with now are calendulas, cineraria, dianthus, foxgloves, Iceland poppies, primroses, snapdragons, stock, violas, and pansies (except the newer heat-resistant varieties, such as those in the Universal series).

Annual Flowers to Plant Now. Seeds of warm-season flowers to plant now include ageratum, amaranth, anchusa, calliopsis, celosia, coleus, cosmos, marigold, nicotiana, portulaca, scarlet sage, sweet alyssum, and verbena. (Except in the hottest areas, wait until May to plant zinnias. They languish when planted in cold soil.) Save money by starting your own bedding plants from seeds that are easy to grow, such as ageratum, cosmos, marigolds, and scarlet sage, in flats of potting soil. Start them in semishade, cover them with a sheet of plastic, and keep them moist until germinated. As soon as they're up, remove the plastic, move them into sun, and water daily. When they've made two true leaves, start feeding with diluted fish emulsion for healthy growth. You'll have plenty of transplants to fill beds.

This is the best time of all to dress up patios with tubs and hanging baskets of warm-season annual flowers from nursery transplants. Annual flowers, and plants we treat as annuals, to put in now from pony packs and color packs include ageratum, globe amaranth, bedding begonias (*Begonia semperflorens*), bellflowers (campanulas), dusty miller, gaillardia, impatiens, lobelia, Madagascar periwinkle (vinca; *Catharanthus roseus*), marigolds, mealy-cup sage (*Salvia farinacea*), nierembergia, petunia, and Swan River daisy (*Brachycome iberidifolia*). Marguerites (*Chrysanthemum frutescens*) can be planted now and will last until the end of June inland and up to three years in coastal zones, but they need watering every day. Euryops 'Green Gold' (*Euryops pectinatus* 'Viridis'), a permanent flowering shrub, is infinitely more drought resistant than marguerite. It's useful inland or along the coast. Some annual flowers, particularly daisy types such as cosmos, tend to shoot straight up on one stem and pop a bud on top. Pinch off this bud to encourage branching. It takes self-control to do this, because you destroy flowers, but it pays off later with more bloom on bushier plants.

Enjoy Your Perennials. As with annual flowers, perennial beds are usually filled to overflowing with color now. So place outdoor furniture strategically, on the grass if need be, so you and your friends can drink in the pleasures you've planted for. Also, pick bouquets of long-stemmed flowers to keep plants blooming and in bounds. If some of your alstroemerias are just a mass of foliage with many leafy, perhaps weak and droopy, stalks and few or no flower buds on them, it's time to shock the plants into blooming. Get down on your knees and yank off all those green leafy stalks. Don't clip them off. Take hold of each one low down on the stalk, give it a twist, and pull it off. Then water and fertilize the plant; almost immediately it will put out a mass of strong new stalks, each with flower buds on it. (Use this yanking method to deadhead or pick alstroemerias, instead of cutting off the stems, which will stop the plant from blooming.)

If you've just moved into a new house, or for some other reason have bare beds to fill, you'll find masses of perennials and flowering subshrubs in nurseries now, often in bloom. Even if you plant from 4-inch containers, they'll soon grow to larger sizes. Among plants in nurseries now are achillea (yarrow), alstroemeria, artemisia, 'African Blue' basil (a sterile hybrid that is a cross between *Ocimum* 'Dark Opal' and African camphor basil [*O. canum*], courtesy of the bees in Athens, Ohio), bishop's weed (*Aegopodium podagraria;* plant in shade), border penstemon (*Penstemon gloxinioides*), botanical geraniums, brachycome (*Brachycome multifida*), candytuft (*Iberis sempervirens*), Canterbury bell (*Campanula medium*) and cup-and-saucer (*Campanula medium Calycanthema*), much loved by children, and Italian bellflower (*C. isophylla*), catmint (*Nepeta faassenii*), columbine, convolvulus, coral bells, coreopsis, cranesbill (*Erodium*), crown pink (*Lychnis coronaria*), delphinium, dianthus, gaura, ladybells (*Adenephora liliifolia*), lavender (many kinds), licorice plant (*Helichrysum petiolare*), ornamental oreganos (*Origanum dictamnus* and others), pincushion flower (*Scabiosa*), rudbeckias, Santa Barbara daisy, scented geraniums (*pelargoniums*), star clusters (*Pentas lancerolata*), strawflower (*Bracteantha bracteatum*), thrift (*Armeria*), twinspur (*Diascia*), and wallflower. Another plant available now is New Zealand brass buttons (*Cotula squalida*), an easy plant to cover the ground under an open tree or cascade over a wall. It has spreading gray foliage with yellow button

flowers that attract snails and caterpillars but not bees; bait cotula for slugs and snails and spray it with BT or Spinosad against caterpillars. Bellflowers (*Campanula*) also harbor snails and slugs. These and caterpillars are the main pests to watch for in the perennial garden this month. Unless you're vigilant, tiny caterpillars can vacuum all the petals off a mound of Santa Barbara daisies overnight.

How to Make Earthworm-Castings Tea

Use this tea as a mild fertilizer and foliage spray to improve overall plant health and fight rust and other fungal diseases.

▸ Place 1 quart earthworm castings in a bucket and cover with 3 quarts water.

▸ Stir mixture and let stand for twenty-four hours.

▸ The next day, stir again, allow mixture to settle five minutes, and scoop the tea into a sprayer.

▸ Apply earthworm spray in the early morning under and over plant leaves.

▸ Stir up leftover tea and pour both water and sludge over roots of plants.

GERANIUMS (AND ERODIUMS)

What we commonly call a *geranium* is not a geranium at all—it's actually a pelargonium. Geranium is the botanical name of an entirely different group of plants. The flowers of true, or botanical, geraniums look symmetrical and have five separate overlapping petals. Pelargonium flowers also have five petals, but they are usually showier and have two petals pointing in one direction and three in another. Erodiums also look much like botanical geraniums, but they have only five stamens; geraniums have ten.

The botanical names for geraniums, erodiums, and pelargoniums came from the shapes of their fruits (seed containers), which were thought to resemble cranes, herons, and storks, respectively. The botanical name *Geranium* comes from the Greek word *geranos*, meaning crane; *Erodium* from *erodios*, meaning heron; and *Pelargonium* from *pelargos*, meaning stork. This is why geraniums are known as cranesbills and why erodiums are called heronsbills. It's a shame pelargoniums didn't get the common name storksbill instead of geranium, which has confused so many gardeners, especially now that dozens of geranium species and cultivars have been introduced in Southern California and several have become stalwart favorites. Here's a selection:

- **Geranium incanum.** The most popular true geranium, with a number of varieties and cultivars. It has ferny foliage, reseeds freely, spreads rapidly to about 4 feet, and reaches about 18 inches high. Good in hanging baskets, it blooms year-round in coastal gardens. As it expands in size, it flowers less freely; when that happens, cut it to the crown or dig it up and start over. (Best advice: if you don't love it, don't plant it.) It grows in full sun along the coast, needs some shade inland, and goes dormant in frost.
- **G. 'Jolly Bee'.** A Proven Winners company introduction with dark green foliage and bright blue flowers with white centers that withstands our long, hot summers. More upright and airier than 'Rozanne' (see right), but equally long-blooming, colorful, and heat resistant.

- **Madeira geranium** (*G. maderense*). An astonishing plant in full bloom now, best in coastal zones. Biennial or occasionally perennial, it grows for the first two or three years as a foliage plant in full sun or partial shade, creating a rosette of attractively shaped fanlike leaves on strong stems splaying out from a central woody stalk. When the plant is ready to bloom, a massive inflorescence 3 or more feet in diameter and 4 feet tall emerges in March. Masses of purplish-pink, $1\frac{1}{2}$-foot flowers are displayed on sticky and hairy purple stems. Each flower lasts a day, but new ones constantly arise for a month to six weeks. The plant then dies, though offshoots may remain and many seedlings will spring up. (You can keep the flowers blooming for a special event in early May by deadheading the sticky little seed capsules daily.) Never prune off Madeira geranium's leaves or the plant will fall over. As the leaves fade, their stems bend down to support the plant.
- **G. x riversleaianum 'Mavis Simpson'.** Mid-pink flowers blooming on annual flowering stems in a low mound; good in a large container or spilling over a wall; takes heat.
- **G. robustum.** Has the same cultural requirements as above but is larger and more vigorous than other geraniums; makes a mound 2 to 3 feet tall and wide with slightly larger leaves and more substance than the others, plus blue-gray foliage and nonstop flowers. Good for embankments.
- **G. 'Rozanne'.** Has more and larger flowers than most other cultivars. Blooms more and takes heat much better than formerly popular 'Johnson's Blue'. Good in hanging baskets or the ground. To rejuvenate clumps, prune back by half. Seldom needs dividing.

✹ QUICK TIP

Make an Easy Hanging Basket with a Continental Look. *In each hanging basket plant one 1-gallon-size, heat-resistant ivy geranium* (Pelargonium peltatum) *with tiny flowers, such as those from the Balcon or Fischer Cascade series. (These are the ones seen spilling out of window boxes in Europe as far south as Italy.) Fill around them with good potting soil. Sprinkle the top of the soil with a few seeds of trailing blue lobelia or, for a quicker start, add one transplant of lobelia from a pony pack to each corner of the container. Hang it in full sun or partial shade, keep it damp, and feed it occasionally with a complete organic fertilizer.*

PELARGONIUMS (GARDEN GERANIUMS)

Begin spraying pelargoniums (garden geraniums) with BT for budworms in April (see page 157). Pelargoniums are the plant most people call geraniums, thus creating a confusion between them and the true geranium (discussed in previous section). Like their cousins the geraniums, pelargoniums are members of the geranium family *(Geraniaceae)*. These tough, colorful, drought-resistant natives of South Africa are perfectly adapted to our climate. In cold-winter climates, pelargoniums are the treasured aristocrats of the greenhouse, bought at precious price for the summer garden. Here they bloom year-round in frost-free zones, flowering happily on the edges of vacant lots or covering entire slopes in place of a lawn. There are many different kinds and four main categories:

- **Common or garden geraniums** *(Pelargonium hortorum)* are the popular upright variety, usually having double or single flowers in large, rounded clusters. Most frequently grown from cuttings, though some can be grown from seeds, these are often called zonal geraniums for the dark or faint pattern, or "zonal" marking, on the leaves (some modern varieties have no zones). Most zonal geraniums are grown for their spectacular year-round flowers, but more than fifty fancy-leaved varieties are grown mainly for their colorful leaves in bright shades of pink, red, white, and yellow. Zonal geraniums are outstanding in containers and window boxes and in pots on steps and balconies.
- **Ivy geraniums** *(P. peltatum)* are a largely disease-free and pest-resistant species with trailing stems and ivy-shaped leaves and a wide variety of flower shapes and colors. Excellent in hanging baskets, as ground covers in frost-free zones, and in flowerbeds. They need to be cut back and replanted occasionally, but their color display, peaking in spring and summer, is nearly year-round. There are also a number of crosses between zonal and ivy geraniums that combine the good qualities of each, are heat resistant, and stay compact in containers. 'Balcon' and 'Cascade' are among the best varieties for ground covers or in hanging baskets.
- **Martha Washingtons** or **regals** *(P. x domesticum)* bear flowers reminiscent of azaleas. When in full bloom they are spectacular in pots, beds, and borders. But they bloom mainly in spring and early summer, peaking in June, which is when you see large numbers in nurseries. In July their flowers fade, and bloom is sparse until the following spring.

How to Grow Geraniums (Pelargoniums)

Here we discuss those plants that gardeners usually call geraniums, even though their correct botanical name is *Pelargonium* (as explained in the text). (In order not to confuse them with botanical geraniums I am calling them pelargoniums in this box.)

▶ Plant pelargoniums in the ground or in containers in full sun along the coast, in partial shade inland. Most pelargoniums need at least four hours of sunlight every day, with the exception of peppermint-scented geraniums and golden-leafed zonals, which can take light shade.

▶ Plant pelargoniums in well-drained soil. (A mildly acid soil is ideal; at pH 5.5 and below, poor growth will result.) When planting in clay soil, dig up the planting area and mix in a generous quantity of organic soil amendment. Then plant high, putting each plant on a slight mound so its crown will always be dry. A good mix for pelargoniums in containers is two parts Supersoil to one part perlite. Also mix in an all-purpose organic fertilizer.

▶ Provide irrigation when rains aren't adequate. Keep plants on the dry side; when the soil is dry, irrigate to an inch or two from the surface.

▶ Fertilize once a month with diluted fish emulsion or other liquid organic fertilizer, such as Earth Juice Grow (2-1-1). Scented geraniums need little or no fertilizer unless you are growing them in containers; then feed half-strength. Martha Washingtons will flower better if fed before spring bloom.

▶ Control budworms with BT or Spinosad. Begin spraying every year at the time of the first full moon in April (see page 158). Control rust by practicing good sanitation and by feeding with Crab Shell (2-3-0), which contains chitin; by spraying the leaves with a home-made earthworm-castings fungicide that contains chitinase (see the box on page 163 for the recipe); or by spraying with an environmentally responsible commercial fungicide, such as Soap-Shield Fungicidal Soap, which contains fixed copper and is available from Gardens Alive!. (Crab shell, rich in chitin, attracts organisms that control fungus problems. Earthworm castings are rich in chitinase, which protects plants from fungus problems. Chitin and chitinase are explained on page 85.)

▶ Plant fresh, not old, cuttings of pelargoniums year-round. For optimum success, dip shears in alcohol prior to taking 2- to 3-inch tip cuttings. Dip the lower end of the cutting into rooting compound such as RooTone or Dip'N Grow and plant in sterile soil mix in a sterile container.

▶ Prune pelargoniums according to their bloom schedule.

Zonals, ivy-leafed geraniums, and some species of geraniums bloom year-round and thus should be pruned progressively year-round. Each month, cut back a few ungainly stems by two-thirds of their length. With a ground-cover planting of ivy geraniums, shear all over when the plants grow lanky and heavy-flowering. Martha Washington geraniums bloom in spring and summer. Cut these back progressively, beginning after bloom and stopping in November.

- **Scented and species geraniums** are a group of over seventy separate species of pelargoniums with scented leaves, most of which are edible. Increasingly popular in recent years, scented geraniums are beloved for their charming appearance, fragrance, and usefulness as ground covers, in herb gardens, and as fillers in the perennial border. Several are good subjects for the drought-resistant landscape. Many are categorized as herbs because their leaves are used to flavor jellies and sauces and to decorate platters of food. Good landscape subjects include peppermint-scented geranium (*P. tomentosum*), an excellent ground cover spreading 2 to 4 feet wide in partial shade; rose geranium (*P. graveolens*), a taller and rangier bush; lemon geranium (*P. crispum*), which grows 2 to 3 feet tall; and nutmeg-scented geranium (*P. x fragrans*), which has small leaves and makes a mound 1 to 2 feet high. *P. siddoides*, which comes in several colors, including gray with burgundy, is much admired among perennials. Many others can be found in nurseries and the gardens of friends; in the latter case, ask for a cutting.

Other groups of pelargoniums are less well known and not widely grown. Some sport a weird, cactuslike appearance prized by collectors. Others are miniatures, and a few are best adapted for use as bonsai. For pelargonium culture, see the accompanying box.

LAWN CARE

Feed, Water, Mow, and Plant. Feed all lawns this month, and water them thoroughly after feeding. (See page 130 for a choice of fertilizers.) Warm-season grasses are speeding up growth now and will need regular fertilizing throughout the warmer months. Water warm-season grasses deeply and infrequently to encourage deep rooting. Most cool-season grasses need more frequent and shallow watering.

All warm-season lawns can be planted from sod or stolons now, and common Bermuda can be planted from seed. Cool-season lawns can be put in from sod, although it's best to wait until October. (See page 196 for advice on lawn selection.)

Mow all lawns once a week to keep them at their proper height, as described on page 129.

VEGETABLE GARDENING

Continue to Plant Summer Vegetables. Did you plant summer vegetables last month? If so, you'll get an early harvest. If not, don't be discouraged; it's not too late. Many vegetables prefer being put in now. Among vegetables to plant now from seeds are green beans, beets, carrots, corn, endive, leaf (not head) lettuce, New Zealand spinach, pumpkins, radishes, salsify, squash, sunflowers, Swiss chard, and turnips. (Don't plant New Zealand spinach unless you love it, because if you tear it out, it will quickly pop up again from seeds, especially in interior zones.) Put in transplants of cucumbers and tomatoes.

⚙ QUICK TIP

How to Secure Plastic Mulch to the Ground. *With wire cutters, cut the bent ends off wire coat hangers to make arched sections approximately 5 inches long. Shove them through the plastic down into the ground all around the edges and here and there on the paths (taking care not to spear drip lines). These can last for several seasons.*

How to Get a Huge Harvest of Sweet Corn

▶ Choose a good variety, such as the super-sweet All America Award–winner 'How Sweet It Is' or 'Kandy Korn'. Buy seeds for successive plantings of twelve to twenty plants at a time.

▶ Spade the ground deeply in a square area that gets full sun, north of shorter crops. (Corn is pollinated by wind. Pollen from the male flower must fall on the female silks, so plant in a block of several short rows rather than in one long, skinny row.) Mix organic soil amendment into the ground and cultivate organic vegetable fertilizer (6-12-6, for example) into the top 6 inches according to package directions.

▶ Set up a drip system designed for row crops. Run the rows north to south, 3 feet apart (18 inches apart if space is at a premium). Mound the rows 4 inches high and 8 inches wide between furrows that are to be used as paths.

▶ Except in the hottest areas, cover the entire area with black—not clear—plastic sheeting as mulch, to increase heat and yields.

▶ For supersweet varieties, presprout the seeds indoors over bottom heat. (The box on page 172 tells how.) Supersweet varieties have a "shrunken gene" that causes their seeds to be shriveled and difficult to germinate if soil is cool.

▶ As soon as the seeds sprout, plant them 2 inches deep and 12 to 18 inches apart in each row. (If the rows are only 18 inches apart, use the wider spacing within rows for a bigger harvest.) For each, use a razor blade to slice a 4-inch-square X in the plastic mulch, make a 2-inch-deep hole with your finger, and put the seed in with the root pointing down and the sprout pointing up. Press the soil gently back together. Fold the cut edges of plastic under and slip the lower edge of an upside-down berry basket into the slit area to protect the seed from birds. (The berry basket will exactly fit the square space you have cut and be held firmly in place.)

▶ Water with a drip system—daily in sandy soil or twice or three times weekly in clay soil—until sprouts emerge. Gradually lengthen spacing between waterings until you're watering deeply and well about every three days in sandy soil, once a week in clay.

▶ When leaves reach the tops of the berry baskets, remove the baskets. Plant more corn in two weeks, and feed the first batch with fish emulsion.

▶ When the corn tassels out, give it extra water and feed it thoroughly with a balanced liquid fertilizer—for example, fish emulsion containing the whole fish, such as Neptune's Harvest (2-4-1), mixed double-strength, or alfalfa or manure tea. (See the recipes on pages 119 and 317.) Pour it around plants with a watering can, or, using a water wand attached to a siphon, soak the ground under the plastic with it. If you prefer to use granulated fertilizer, apply organic vegetable fertilizer according to package directions when the corn is 12 to 18 inches high and again when it is 24 to 30 inches high. Or use fish meal, an ideal fertilizer for corn (as we know from Squanto's advice to the pilgrims). (See pages 74, 198, and 249 for other suggestions.)

▶ For full ears in a small plot, hand-pollinate: when tassels bloom with dusty pollen, break off sections and whip them on the silks at the tops of the ears. (To activate growth in every kernel, each silk needs one grain of pollen.)

Why Some Sweet Corn Varieties Must Be Isolated from Other Varieties

Because each kernel is individually pollinated by wind, corn easily crossbreeds when different varieties that mature at the same time are planted closely together. Sweet corn, popcorn, field corn, and ornamental varieties can all interbreed. For this reason, it's best to plant only one variety of sweet corn in staggered plantings or to plant an early, a mid-season, and a late variety so that they will not produce pollen at the same time. Be particularly careful when planting AE and SH2 varieties. (See the accompanying box.) Also, when planting popcorn and ornamental corn, make sure maturity dates are different from all other corn varieties you'll plant. Pollination between two different types of corn will make your corn starchy and bland tasting.

This is the last month to plant seed potatoes (as described on page 140; also see the section later in this chapter on mounding and harvesting potatoes). In hot interior zones, plant sweet potatoes beginning this month. This is the first month for putting in the heat lovers: eggplant, peppers, okra, lima beans, cantaloupe, and watermelon. If you live in a fog bank, wait until May to plant cantaloupe. In this case, it usually isn't worthwhile to plant watermelons at all; they grow better inland.

Plant Herbs among Your Vegetables. Continue planting culinary herbs in April. Put in basil, oregano, parsley, rosemary, sage, summer savory, and thyme from nursery transplants. (You can also plant parsley and basil from seeds.) Cilantro and arugula can be grown throughout the summer in semishade in some gardens, but they prefer cooler weather. Grow French tarragon (*Artemisia dracunculus*), horseradish, and mint in containers; they're invasive. (Don't be fooled into buying tasteless Russian tarragon [*Artemisia dracunculoides*] by mistake.)

Plant for Successive Crops. If you planted vegetables last month, continue to put in seeds now for additional crops. Many gardeners plant too much at one time; then it all matures at once, and they're swamped. A similar problem is planting too much of one crop; zucchini, for example, can easily overwhelm the unwary. Two or three plants are plenty for a family of four. A row will feed an army. Vegetables to plant successively are those that you harvest over a short period (a week or two), such as corn and bush beans, or those in which individuals are harvested wholly, such as carrots or beets. Lettuce can go either way; you can take just the outside leaves to extend the harvest or cut whole heads. When planting successively, use a quarter or a third of a package of seed at intervals of two to three weeks. Choose interesting varieties. Carrots, for example, come in many sizes, sweetness levels, and degrees of crunchiness. Grow several and taste-test them with your family.

Thin Those Rows. Don't forget to keep thinning your vegetable rows according to package directions. When you thin leafy vegetables such as lettuce, transplant the extras into another row, but don't try this with carrots; they split when they're transplanted. Thinning seed rows—and flowerbeds, too—is a task too often neglected by first-time gardeners. People hate to do it because it seems so wasteful. Actually, the reverse is

Understanding Sweet Corn Varieties and High-Sugar Genes

Sweet corn varieties are available in white, yellow, or bicolor kernel colors and in tall or short sizes. They also come in varying maturities that are categorized as early (sixty to seventy days), mid-season (seventy to eighty days), or late season (ninety or more days). Additionally, you can choose varieties for their genetic heritage. These are explained below.

▶ **Open-Pollinated Varieties.** Old sweet corn varieties such as 'Gold Bantam', 'Early Gold Bantam', and 'Country Gentleman' are "open pollinated," meaning that the seed was derived from a natural pollination process, such as insects or (in the case of corn) wind, and that it will breed true, or nearly so. (Open-pollinated varieties change gradually as the years pass through natural or human selection.) You can save and plant seed from these.

▶ **SU,** or **Standard Varieties,** or **"Normals."** The seeds of these modern F1 hybrids—including 'Silver Queen', 'Golden Midget', and 'Early Sunglow'—are derived from a cross between two other varieties; thus they are the first generation (F1) after the cross. Hybrids have what is called hybrid vigor. They provide the gardener with such characteristics as high yields, disease and pest resistance, sweetness, and dependable harvest.

▶ **SH2** or **Supersweet Hybrids.** This genetic type (SH2), including such varieties as 'Illini Extra Sweet', 'Early Extra Sweet', and 'How Sweet It Is', has sugar content twice as high as that of standard sweet corn at peak maturity. SH2 types are called supersweet, ultrasweet, or extra sweet. The term SH2 stands for "shrunken 2" because when the kernels dry, their seed coats shrink, giving the seeds a shriveled appearance. Supersweet varieties retain their sweet flavor longer than ordinary sweet corn both on the stalk and after the harvest. But SH2 varieties must be isolated from other types of sweet corn, or else foreign pollen will make hard, ugly, dented kernels on the SH2 ear. (See the box on isolation on page 169.)

▶ **Sugary Enhanced (SE) Hybrids.** Varieties in this class, including 'Kandy Korn', 'Earli Glow', and 'Snow Queen', are the result of a cross that produces a sweet flavor and tender texture. This genetic type (SE) contains genetically high sugar levels, revolutionary in the flavor of sweet corn. The seed coat of this type is not shrunken like that of supersweet, so it sprouts more easily in the ground. It is also much sweeter than regular sweet corn and retains its flavor before and after harvest. SE hybrids must be isolated from SH2 hybrids, but not from other SE varieties or SU varieties.

true. You won't feel sad about thinning rows if you remember that overabundant plants act like weeds; by competing with one another, they stunt your crops. This is especially true of plants such as onions that have shallow roots.

Prune Tomatoes and Avoid Problems. You can train tomatoes several ways (as described on page 143). If you plan to grow them on stakes or a trellis, prune each plant now to one or two major vines by pinching off the suckers

⚙ QUICK TIP

Vegetable Space Saver. *To plant three crops in one space, interplant corn with pole or lima beans and one or two pumpkins or the kind of winter squash that grows on a sprawling vine, such as 'Sweet Mama'. The beans will climb up the corn and need no support. The squash or pumpkins will give you another crop on the ground (and incidentally will discourage raccoons from stealing your corn if these masked bandits live in your neighborhood).*

that grow as side branches above leaf joints. Check them weekly; they grow fast. (Be aware that pruning tomatoes may allow diseases to enter stems. However, plant diseases are less likely to attack plants growing in soils rich in humus, chitin, and beneficial fungi.)

Occasionally, gardeners complain of getting no fruit. This can happen if the plants are growing in shade. Sometimes plants have green growth but no flowers. This is the result of too much nitrogen (treat the ground around the plants with a liquid organic high-bloom fertilizer, such as Tiger Bloom [2-8-4] or Earth Juice Bloom [0-3-1] to correct it). If the plants flower but the blossoms drop off without fruiting, they may have been allowed to dry out completely. Tomato buds also fall off if the temperature ever drops lower than 55°F or rises higher than 75°F during the night or higher than 105°F in the daytime. Desert dwellers should grow tomatoes during the fall, winter, and early spring months.

If low temperatures are the source of your problem, grow early varieties until the weather warms up, or try using a tomato blossom-set spray. Use it exactly according to directions:

use one slight burst of spray about 10 inches from each bunch of flowers only three times, at intervals of ten days. Sometimes flowers drop off because they weren't pollinated. This can happen in wet weather or in greenhouses. Tomatoes have "perfect," or self-pollinating, flowers. The pollen has to go only a short distance within the flower, from the anthers onto the sticky stigma. Wind does the job more than bees, so if there's no wind, there won't be any fruit. You can improve your tomatoes' pollination by rapping a hammer on the tomato stakes or cages in the middle of the day, when the weather's warm and dry.

Watch for Tomato Blights. Early blight and late blight are two major blights affecting tomatoes in foggy or rainy weather. Late blight causes downy mold on lower surfaces of leaves, drying and shriveling of leaves, water-soaked spots on stems, and grayish water-soaked spots on fruit. Rotting fruits have an offensive odor. Infected fruit is inedible. Early blight causes dark spots with light centers with concentric rings on leaves and stems, browning and dying back of the lowest branches, and discoloration of fruit. Severe blight can cause almost complete defoliation, exposing fruit to sunscald. You can eat the fruit if you cut off the diseased portions. If your plants were infected with either of these blights last year, the spores may have endured in the soil; therefore, this year, do not prune plants, because infection can enter the plant through pruning cuts. Treat infected plants with PROBIOTICS 4 Plants' Defensor Bacterial Inoculator to improve their health. (This product contains *Bacillus subtilis* as well as *B. cereus*, two beneficial fungi that attack or parasitize harmful fungi, though the label does not say so. See pages 58 and 187 for further

How to Presprout Seeds for a Fast Start with No Rot

Some seeds, planted in the ground, may rot instead of growing. Examples are any beans planted in cold, wet soil, some varieties of sugar peas that have shriveled-looking seeds, and supersweet varieties of sweet corn that have shriveled seeds caused by the "shrunken" gene that makes them so sweet. In these cases, it's easy, timesaving, and worthwhile to sprout seeds indoors. Here's how:

▸ Wet a paper towel. Squeeze it out and spread it flat. Place a few more seeds than you need on half the towel, arranging them so they don't touch one another. Bend the other half over. Put the whole thing, flat, in a zip-locked plastic bag and seal it up.

▸ Place the plastic bag containing the paper towel and seeds over bottom heat at approximately 70°F. Possible heat sources include low-wattage light bulbs; radiantly heated floors; antidampness bars used to keep closets, towels, and pianos dry; heat vents;

water heaters; or even the tops of TVs or VCRs. (If a light bulb or heating bar is used, elevate the seeds on a cookie sheet or metal tray to diffuse the heat.)

▸ Check your seeds daily; add moisture if needed. Bean seeds sprout in about three days, corn and peas in four or five. As soon as they sprout, plant them in the garden. Handle them gently; don't break their roots.

▸ To plant, make a hole with your finger deep enough for the thin white root to go straight down; the thicker, yellowish sprout should point up. (In cool weather, plant the seed only an inch deep. After the sprout comes up, you can mound the soil higher around it.) Press the soil gently but firmly from the sides to make good contact. If some sprouts fail to come up, presprout more and replant to fill gaps in the row.

---

discussion.) Dusting with sulfur can also be helpful. (Crab shell [2-3-0] can add beneficial chitin to soil and fight nematodes as well as fungus disease, but may be too alkaline for our local soils.)

Mound and Harvest Potatoes. Until potato plants have grown 10 inches high, use a hoe to mound soil up around the stalks, but leave the leafy portion sticking out of the top. This increases the harvest and keeps the potatoes cool and dark. (Potato skins turn green if they're exposed to light; all green portions of potatoes are poisonous, including stems, leaves, fruit, and sprouts.) If before mounding soil around the stems you first mix it with nitrolized wood

shavings or homemade compost, harvesting becomes much easier. Stop mounding the soil when the mound is 5 to 6 inches high or when the plants begin to flower.

When flowers appear, some tubers have grown. You can then gently push the soft, amended soil aside and use a trowel to dig up just the number of small new potatoes you want for dinner. Replace the mound so the remaining potatoes will be protected from heat and sunlight. When the leaves begin to turn yellow with age, you can harvest as many full-grown new potatoes as desired. Leave smaller tubers in the ground to continue growing. Once the tops of the plants have completely withered and died, harvest the remainder by digging up the whole row with a garden fork. Leave these mature potatoes on top of the earth to dry for two or three hours; then store them in a cool, dark place at 40° to 45°F. If you store them at over 50°F, they'll sprout and eventually spoil.

Protect Lettuce Against Pests. Bait lettuce against slugs and snails with an organic product. Watch for leafhoppers; they spread viral diseases. (Spray for them with insecticidal soap, or control them with diatomaceous earth if you feel it's absolutely necessary, but the latter will kill ladybugs and other beneficials, including spiders.)

Introduce beneficials, as discussed in the preceding section on pest control. Ladybugs, lacewings, trichogramma wasps, and other beneficials are especially important in the vegetable garden because most gardeners prefer not to spray vegetables with pesticides. Be sure to put ladybugs where you see whiteflies and aphids. Control caterpillars with BT, or Spinosad if your flowers are not visited by bees. (See pages 153 and 379 for more about Spinosad.)

APRIL CHECKLIST

PURCHASE/PLANT

{ } Continue to plant drought-resistant plants, *39*

{ } Choose and plant azaleas while the greatest number of plants are in bloom, *148*

{ } If you live in the desert or in a hot inland valley, finish all spring planting this month, *148*

{ } Choose and plant wisteria while it is in bloom, *148*

{ } Purchase epiphyllums, *148*

{ } Plant dahlias, *151*

{ } Plant water lilies, *155*

{ } Plant warm-season flowers, *162*

{ } Plant tubs and hanging baskets, *162*

{ } Continue to plant summer vegetables, *167*

{ } Plant corn, *168*

{ } Plant herbs, *169*

{ } Plant tropicals in inland valleys, *148*

{ } Start perennials from seeds in interior zones, *246*

{ } Purchase, plant, and transplant succulents, including cacti and euphorbias, *270*

{ } Now through summer, choose, plant, and naturalize bromeliads, *274*

{ } Plant geraniums and erodiums, *163*

{ } Plant pelargoniums, *165*

TRIM, PRUNE, MOW, DIVIDE

{ } Break off suckers from artichokes, *141*

{ } Remove suckers from tomatoes and tie up the vines, *170*

{ } Take cuttings from epiphyllums, and root them to make new plants, *148*

{ } Cut back poinsettias, *150*

{ } Trim hedges and screens, including pittosporum and photinia, *150*

{ } Thin out fruit on deciduous fruit trees, *151*

{ } Prune roses by picking, deadheading, and disbudding, *153*

{ } Mow lawns, *167*

{ } Thin vegetable crops (including beans) planted last month, according to package directions, *169*

{ } Stop pinching fuchsias when plants are well filled out and bushy. Remove seedpods often after flowers fall, *124*

{ } Start to prune and train espaliers as they begin to grow, *291*

{ } Propagate daylilies by planting their proliferates, *344*

{ } Divide and plant dahlia tubers you lifted from the ground in December, *398*

FERTILIZE

{ } Feed citrus trees, *63*

{ } Feed avocado trees, *81*

{ } Feed fuchsias, *208*

{ } Feed tuberous begonias, *260*

{ } Feed irises, *152*

{ } Fertilize roses, *152*

{ } Feed water lilies, *156*

{ } Fertilize lawns, *167*

{ } Fertilize peppers when flowers first show, *279*

{ } Feed and water cycads, *303*

{ } Treat blue hydrangeas with acid fertilizer, *320*

{ } Do not fertilize onions after they begin to make bulbs, *74*

WATER

{ } Water all garden plants according to need when rains are inadequate, *67*

{ } Keep all vegetables well watered, particularly globe artichokes, *141*

{ } Water roses, *152*

{ } Water lawns, *167*

{ } Don't let tomatoes dry out, *171*

CONTROL PESTS, DISEASE, AND WEEDS

{ } Control crabgrass with a final treatment of corn gluten meal as a preemergent herbicide, *73, 107*

{ } Continue to control slugs and snails, particularly on irises and lettuce, *115, 173*

{ } Control rose pests and diseases, *152*

{ } Spray with BT against caterpillars if necessary, *157*

{ } Control fuchsia gall mite, *158*

{ } Control spider mites, *159*

{ } Control eugenia psyllid, *159*

{ } Release beneficials, *160*

{ } Protect corn from raccoons, *171*

{ } Control leafhoppers, *173*

{ } Cultivate to remove weeds among shrubs and trees, *46*

{ } Control weeds among vegetables and flowers by hand-pulling, *46*

{ } Release ladybugs, *160*

{ } Watch for tomato blights, *171*

ALSO THIS MONTH

{ } Move tuberous begonias started in flats into pots or beds, *120*

{ } Keep bamboo from running into your neighbor's garden, *127*

{ } See spring flowers, including wildflowers and native plants, in full bloom, *147*

{ } Continue to tie up leaves of bulbs that have bloomed, *152*

{ } Treat cut roses to keep them fresh, *153*

{ } Consider building a garden pond, *154*

{ } Avoid problems with tomatoes, *170*

{ } Begin to harvest potatoes, as needed, when blossoms show, *172*

{ } Presprout hybrid corn if it won't germinate, *172*

{ } Harvest vegetables while they're young and tender, *199, 281*

{ } Save branches from pruning to use as pea stakes to support flowers, *355*

May

THE FAST-GROWTH MONTH

Cymbidium
(Orchid)

If you finished your spring planting in March or April, May is the month to watch everything grow. In good years, when seasonal rains have been generous, excess salts have been washed down into the ground and the entire landscape has been well watered. Seasoned organic gardeners have helped things along by mulching the ground with aged horse manure or compost in fall and by fertilizing with organic generic or commercial fertilizers in January, February, or March. Many folks will have used other soil amendments too, including products containing humic acid and kelp. All these organics are now actively working in the ground to deliver abundant health and nutrition to your plants. Now, as the weather gets warmer, all growth systems go full speed ahead. You can almost see some plants expand, especially the trees and bushes put in last fall.

May is also a month for catching up on neglected tasks. If you didn't finish spring planting in March and April, do it now. Heat-loving plants take off even better in May. If you live in an interior valley, waste no time getting your final planting done. Interior-valley gardeners can safely expect occasional spells—two or three days long—of scorching heat this month.

But what if the rosy picture painted in the first paragraph above fails to happen? If your plants fail to grow and flower, if they suffer from pests or diseases, if they have small, colorless, or yellow leaves that fall to the ground, first check irrigation and drainage to make sure you're neither over- nor underwatering. Stunted plants with small leaves that turn yellow and fall off usually suffer from a lack of nitrogen. (Yellow leaves with green veins are different; these come from chlorosis, as explained on pages 27 and 64.) To correct yellow leaves coupled with lack of growth and lackluster appearance, increase applications of balanced organic fertilizer with a high first number (nitrogen). If necessary, switch products, trying something better. All too often, a gardener new to the organic method will buy one 5-pound box marked "All-Purpose Organic Fertilizer," sprinkle the contents around the garden, and think that that's enough. It's not. Digging compost into the ground before it's well rotted is another problem. It's fine to put a layer of uncomposted organic materials, such as shredded bark or chipped tree leaves and branches, on top of the ground, but if unrotted carbonaceous materials, such as dry leaves, plant stems, or wood chips, are mixed into garden soil, they will rob nitrogen from the soil in order to rot. This can stunt or even kill garden plants. The solution is to apply more nitrogen.

As already noted in the introduction and early chapters of this book, there is a wide range of powdered, granulated, and liquid plant foods from which to choose. These include concoctions you can mix up yourself, dozens of commercial organic fertilizers and soil amendments, and even some free substances. But all these products must be applied in sufficient quantity to produce appreciable results. In most cases, the chance of overfeeding with organics is far less than the chance of underfeeding. Problems from overfeeding apply mostly to bone meal, Sul-Po-Mag (0-0-22), Epsom salts, alfalfa, and chelated minerals. Apply these substances twice a year only, in January and June, unless they are listed as ingredients in a bagged commercial organic fertilizer, in which case it's okay to use them according to package directions. Use caution also when feeding with blood meal, one of the few organics that can burn if you apply too much at one time. Most organic fertilizers are nonburning, but all organic fertilizers and soil amendments need to be thoroughly watered into the ground in order to take effect. They also need time—a few weeks or even months—to work. So if you are doing everything right but were late starting your work, if you are using a variety of plant foods and plenty of them, and if you are mulching with well-aged compost in ample quantities, and if you are watering sufficiently, then a certain amount of patience may be all that is necessary before you'll see results.

While conventional landscape plants, most of which are imported, are now beginning a season of fast growth, native plants are in a season of withdrawal. The chaparral is drying up, and most wildflowers are going brown and setting seed. Many wild plants pull in their horns and let leaves fall as nature prepares for a long dry season. Those who live in interior valleys or near a canyon or wild hillside may sense a bit of nostalgia in the air this month, similar to that sensed in fall back east.

DEEP WATERING

From now until November, the gardener's main task is to water deeply and appropriately for each plant whenever available water supplies and local regulations allow it. In drought years, some plants may suffer during the late spring and summer from inadequate water. Identify such plants, and consider replacing them with better choices. If you grow native plants, learn which ones can accept summer water shortages and which cannot. All native plants need irrigation to get started. Some, such as monkey flower (*Mimulus* species and Verity hybrids), can be kept blooming longer by gradually replacing rainfall with some summer water. Others, including bush poppy (*Dendromecon rigida*) and woolly blue curls (*Trichostema lanatum*), may succumb to root rot if watered at all. Take the cue from nature and begin to taper off on watering these plants. The best way to help native plants, especially newly planted ones, through a long hot spell is not to water them but simply to spritz the foliage once in a while with a spray from the hose. Do this in the early morning or evening, just wetting the foliage of plants, cooling them down, and barely damping the dust. Simulate the heavy dew or brief summer downpour that occasionally visits us with the edge of an interior-southwest monsoon. Watering certain chaparral plants in summer—flannel bush (*Fremontodendron*) and woolly blue curls, as noted above, are good examples—can rot their roots, but washing off their leaves with a quick spray of water may give them just enough moisture to absorb through their leaves and pull them through.

Because the price of water continually rises and domestic cutbacks occur whenever there's a drought, wise gardeners think of ways to make the garden less thirsty. If you haven't already installed a drip system to water everything you otherwise would water with the hose, such as container-grown plants, now's a good time to do the job. Also, study your sprinkler system and see whether adjustments can be made to conserve water in the months ahead.

IRISES

Bearded irises, those with a hairlike tuft on the falls, or lower petals, bloom this month. Whether or not you're growing them now, enjoy them in bloom, and consider planting some; the rhizomes can be found at nurseries in fall. They're among our best perennials—good in all zones, easy to grow, and not overly thirsty. See displays

of them at botanical gardens and nurseries, and watch for newspaper announcements of shows.

Hybridizers have developed many kinds and heights of iris, but the tall bearded ones are the easiest to start with, and they're the most frequently grown. They prefer rich, humusy, well-drained soil but will accept almost any soil as long as they have full sun along the coast, six hours of sun inland, moderate irrigation, and protection from snails. If you have irises in your garden that aren't blooming, chances are they're growing in too much shade or need dividing (page 241 tells how).

Among other rhizomatous irises to consider growing are the spuria irises, which make tall clumps, bloom in June and July, and need little summer water, and in light shade the native Pacific Coast irises (*Iris douglasiana*), which are spring blooming, drought resistant, low growing, and good for naturalizing.

CYMBIDIUMS

Now begins the main growing season for cymbidiums, terrestrial orchids that are usually grown in containers. The quality and number of flowers you get next winter will depend partly on good summer care.

Although cymbidiums shouldn't be soggy, don't let them dry out. Move those that have finished blooming into less-conspicuous places for a season of growth. Through midsummer, keep these Asian orchids in semishade, such as under an open tree; then in late summer (see pages 257 and 319), bring them out into more light. Or keep them year-round under 50 percent shade cloth (35 percent in coastal zones).

As blossoms fade, cut off the bloom spikes and start feeding the cymbidiums with a complete fertilizer high in growth ingredients.

How to Divide and Repot a Cymbidium

Cymbidium orchids need dividing when they overcrowd their containers or get too heavy to carry.

▶ Water plants well before dividing them.

▶ Use a can cutter or sharp knife to cut off the plastic container.

▶ Use a large kitchen knife kept for gardening to cut between the pseudobulbs (the bulb-like structures growing above ground) and down through the roots. Aim for at least three productive pseudobulbs and four or five back bulbs per division. (Back bulbs are fully grown pseudobulbs that once bore leaves and flower spikes but now are bare. They act as storage containers for the remainder of the plant.)

▶ Trim off all roots that are diseased, damaged, or simply messy. In all, you should remove about one-third of the roots.

▶ Optionally, soak the divisions in a solution of 1 quart bleach to 10 quarts water for ten minutes to kill any fungus or rot. Allow them to dry.

▶ To replant, choose plastic containers that have plenty of holes in the bottom and are the next size larger than the old pots, or approximately 4 to 6 inches wider than the top of the root ball. (Oversize containers slow growth.)

▶ Hold the plant so that the bottom of the pseudobulbs is level with the top of the container. Fill around the roots all the way to the top of the container with the smallest size of bark chips, a product often labeled "pathway bark." Purchase this instead of the product labeled "orchid bark" (which is more expensive and usually moldy). In interior zones, cymbidiums do better in a homemade mix, such as 2 gallons pathway bark, 2 gallons ground nitrolized wood shavings, and 1 gallon commercial sterilized potting soil (Supersoil is one such brand). Make sure the roots are completely covered with soil mix and the pseudobulbs totally above ground. (If pseudobulbs are buried, they'll rot; if roots are exposed, they'll dry out.)

▶ Water the cymbidiums thoroughly after planting, keep them in semishade, and wait two or three weeks before starting to fertilize.

Cymbidiums prefer the kind of organics they would get in nature, where they often grow in little pockets of rotted organic matter fertilized with bird droppings and the occasional dead lizard or frog. Since one cannot buy ground-up lizards and frogs, feed plants with the closest approximations, fishmeal or bat or seabird guano—a handful per plant once a month—or drench the soil with diluted fish emulsion, such as Atlas or Neptune's Harvest, every two weeks. If you have many orchids and prefer using a siphon attachment to draw fertilizer solution out of a bucket directly into the hose, then choose a nonclogging product such as Nature's Nectar or try Fox Farms (6-4-4).

Transplant cymbidiums that have outgrown their containers no later than the end of June, in order not to destroy the next flowering cycle. They can flower well even when crowded, so wait until they're pushing against the sides of the container to repot them into the next size of container. Don't be in a hurry to divide them. A huge plant with twenty bloom spikes can be a showstopper in a home garden. (A half whiskey barrel makes a fine container, but plant only one variety per barrel.) Divide them (see the box on facing page) when plants become too big to handle.

CAMELLIAS AND AZALEAS

Feed, Mulch, and Prune Camellias. Fertilize camellias after they finish blooming. Camellias aren't gluttons; they need only a light application three times a year. The **Rule of Thumb:** *Feed camellias for the first time as soon as they've finished blooming, feed them again four to six weeks after that, and feed them for the last time six weeks later.* Mark these times on your calendar. Use an acid-type, organic commercial fertilizer especially recommended for camellias and azaleas, or use cottonseed meal, the choice of many professionals. At each feeding, apply ¼ to ½ cup for a newly planted 1-gallon plant, ½ to 1 cup for a newly planted 5-gallon plant, 2 to 3 cups for plants from 3 to 5 feet tall, and 5 to 6 cups for large trees. Also treat with iron chelates (Bonide Chelated Iron is one such product), following package directions. If you prefer, apply products containing kelp or humic acid to provide trace minerals plus microorganisms that can free up nutrients in the soil. Sprinkle the fertilizer all over the ground under the branches but especially in a wide band under the drip line, and water it into the ground.

Never cultivate under camellias. Cover the ground with a fresh layer of mulch, such as fir bark or pine needles, to keep the roots cool and happy. To save water, install drip systems for camellias and azaleas, using circles of laser-cut drip tubing surrounding each plant and hidden beneath the mulch. As the plant grows, increase the size of the circle so that the drip tubing is directly under the plant's drip line (the outer edge of the foliage). You should run drip systems about 20 minutes three times a week for newly planted camellias and azaleas, or long enough to moisten the entire root zone. Longer or more frequent irrigations may be necessary in interior zones, shorter and less frequent ones in coastal zones, depending on your water and soil. Monitor the watering to make sure plants get enough moisture, and then gradually lengthen the time between irrigations. (Never let an azalea dry out completely, or it will die.)

If you haven't yet pruned your camellias, do the job now to maintain the size you want, improve their shape, and increase bloom. Look closely at the tip of a branch. Notice the bump where last year's growth began and then the growth of the year before that. You can cut back into last year's growth or that of the year before and cause buds farther back on the branch to send out shoots. If you do this right after flowering, there'll be no loss of flowers next year; in fact, there'll be more. You can even cut back into smooth gray-barked wood to renew an old plant that's gotten out of hand, but in such cases flowering won't resume for a year or two.

Feed, Mulch, and Prune Azaleas. Fertilize azaleas as soon as they've finished blooming. The **Rule of Thumb:** *Azaleas need fertilizing only twice a year, once as soon as they've finished blooming and again in late September.* Some people feed them more often—and it's all right to give a lackluster plant a shot of liquid humic acid in midsummer—but many an azalea has been killed by overfeeding.

Feed with a dry pelletized or powdered commercial fertilizer especially recommended for camellias and azaleas and follow package directions, or use cottonseed meal and iron as recommended above for camellias. Sprinkle the fertilizer in a wide band under the drip line.

You can, if you wish, work it down through the mulch with a gloved hand, but as with camellias, don't ever cultivate under an azalea, even with your fingers. Delicate feeder roots lie right under the surface and can easily be damaged.

It's also time to clean up and prune azaleas. Leaves can remain where they fall, but be sure to remove all dead blossoms to prevent blossom blight from getting a foothold. Azaleas take well to pruning because the dormant buds that will respond to it are hidden under the bark all the way to the ground. Cut out old or ungainly branches and pinch back tips to promote bushiness. The easiest way to get a really professional look is to give azaleas a butch haircut now. Start by watering the plants deeply. Then, using hedge shears, shear off all the tip growth. Next year you'll have a solid blanket of flowers all over the top of the plant.

ROSES

Continue to control rose pests and diseases and to water, fertilize, and prune your roses by picking flowers and disbudding. If you're fertilizing your roses with commercial organic rose fertilizers, continue to follow package directions. If you are following the Rose-Pro Method, feed roses twice this month, by soaking the root zone once every two weeks with one or two gallons of fish emulsion diluted according to package directions. Do this job on a day after the roses have been irrigated so the ground will be damp, but since you are using fish emulsion, you do not need to water the fertilizer into the ground afterward, as with dry fertilizers. Also this month, give plants a foliar application of seaweed or compost tea. Seaweed products contain micronutrients, so also pour some on the ground to benefit soil

organisms. Products such as humic acid and earthworm castings may be applied whenever plants appear to need a boost.

As is true every month, gardeners who are using generic fertilizers have a wide range of choices. Refer back to the recommendations on pages 53 and 118 and apply the products of your choice. Fishmeal, for example, could be substituted for fish emulsion and watered into the ground. It decomposes rapidly. Or see the accompanying box for another homemade all-purpose fertilizer that can be used now for feeding roses, once every two weeks at the rate of 1 cup for each rose shrub and 2 cups for each large climbing rose. A couple of cautions: Don't overuse alfalfa, since it contains triaconatol, a plant hormone and fatty acid that is a growth stimulant but can have the opposite effect if applied too often. (Two or three applications a season should be fine.) Blood meal is one of the few organic fertilizers that can burn; it's difficult to get wet; and it scares away rabbits, which is fine, but it also attracts dogs, who may want to roll in it, which can be a pain. To avoid such problems, put these products under the mulch, and then wash them into the ground by watering deeply. If you wish, use a product containing *Yucca schidigera*, a natural wetting agent, to help moisten blood meal as you irrigate. (When considering generic nitrogen fertilizers, it may be of interest to note that up until the 1920s, the only food most roses ever got was animal manure over their roots plus human urine, which is chock-full of nitrogen and phosphorus, but also contains salts, fine in areas with plentiful rainfall, such as the Pacific Northwest, but risky in our dry climate.)

You can also plant canned roses this month. Prepare planting holes as for bare-root roses (as described on page 57), but omit building a mound on the bottom of the hole.

Homemade Rose Food

- 2 parts blood meal or alfalfa meal
- 3 parts fishbone meal
- 1 part kelp meal

Mix all ingredients, and give 1 cup to each shrub rose or 2 cups to each large climbing rose. Scratch lightly into the ground under the mulch, and replace the mulch on top. Follow up with ample irrigation from the garden hose.

TROPICALS

Late spring is an excellent time to put in tropicals of all kinds, including citrus and other tropical fruit trees, tropical flowering trees, palms, philodendrons, and flowering vines such as bougainvillea. (See page 199 for dwarf citrus harvest times for year-round fruit, and page 207 for instructions on planting bougainvilleas.) Tropicals are planted during their active growing season. If you live in a hot interior valley, April is an even better month to plant tropicals, because the weather can become scorching by late May and may burn your newly planted specimens.

Many tropicals don't actually have a built-in dormant season. In hot climates and jungles, they grow year-round, sometimes in spurts to coincide with the alternating wet-dry seasons that last two or three months in their native habitat. Here in Southern California, it's up to the gardener to get tropicals to grow fast during the warm months and rest from growth in winter—even though it's our rainy season. The way to do this is to feed and water your tropicals in spring and summer but withhold fertilizer in early fall and water less when the weather cools

down. Putting tropicals in the ground in spring gives them a chance to get established all summer long, then slow down and harden off in fall so they can survive light frosts.

FERNS

Start feeding ferns once every two or three weeks now, and continue until fall. Native ferns that sprang to life with the first rain last fall, beneath toyons and on canyon walls, are dying down and dropping fronds now. They need no fertilizer. But most of the ferns we grow in our gardens and houses have awakened from winter torpor and are well into their season of fastest growth.

Ferns are ancient plants with poor plumbing systems. Most require shade, perfect drainage, and acid soil, and they have to be fed with care. Feed most ferns every three or four weeks during spring and summer with a well-diluted complete liquid fertilizer. (Feed staghorn ferns less frequently, as discussed below.) High nitrogen often spells "good-bye fern" if the fern is dry before you feed it. The safest food is fish emulsion, mixed according to package directions, because it's nonburning. Cottonseed meal is another good organic fertilizer for ferns. Ferns appreciate high phosphorus and potassium plus trace elements; thus a liquid product containing seaweed, such as Neptune's Harvest Fish/Seaweed 2-3-1, diluted according to directions for container-grown plants, is another excellent fertilizer for them. Ferns love humus-filled acid soil, so humic acid is good for ferns too. Ferns growing in containers need to be fed on a regular basis since typical fern soil mixtures contain no nutrients.

Now's the best time to transplant ferns that have overgrown their pots. When their roots fill their containers, repot 'Dallas', 'Kimberly

Queen', and 'Chino' to the next sizes, in fast-draining acid soil mix. 'Dallas' and 'Kimberly Queen' are varieties of Australian sword fern (*Nephrolepis obliterata, N. cordifolia*), similar in appearance to Boston fern (*N. exaltata 'Bostoniensis'*) but more vigorous and able to flourish in lower light. ('Fluffy Ruffles', 'Roosevelt', and 'Whitmanii' are forms of Boston fern, fun to collect and grow but not quite as vigorous as the Australian sword fern types. Repotting an ordinary Boston fern usually kills it unless it's growing in a greenhouse.)

How to Renew a Hanging Squirrel's Foot or Bear's Foot Fern

▸ Using a keyhole saw, clippers, and long-handled loppers, saw and cut out the entire center of the root-filled basket.

▸ Rebuild the sides of the basket with fresh, damp sphagnum moss.

▸ Fill the cavity you've made with fresh, well-drained potting mix.

▸ Cut the growing tips from the removed portion of fern, dip them in a rooting compound such as RooTone or Dip'N Grow, knock off the excess, and plant them in the top of the basket. (Use leftover cuttings to start a new basket.)

▸ Attach a fresh set of wires or chains strong enough to hold up the plant.

▸ Keep the plant damp and in a shady, protected spot for two or three weeks until it's rooted; then feed it with diluted fish emulsion every week or two to speed its growth until it's well established.

Footed ferns, such as squirrel's foot fern (*Davallia trichomanoides*) and bear's foot fern (*Humata tyermannii*), are best adapted to growing in hanging baskets. Eventually the baskets become filled and covered with a solid mass of unproductive roots, and the plants begin to look distinctly ratty. Now's the time to renew them (see the box at left).

Collect Easy-Care Staghorn Ferns. Staghorn ferns (*Platycerium* sp.) are a group of about seventeen species of strikingly shaped, tropical, epiphytic ferns that are prized by plant collectors. (Certain of them are also called elkhorn, giant staghorn, or moosehorn ferns.) They attach themselves to the bark, branches, or crotches of trees by means of hairlike roots, and they grow two distinctly different kinds of fronds. The sterile fronds, which are at first green but go brown with age, are shaped like shields; they support the plant by accumulating organic matter and by wrapping themselves around the tree or branch on which the plant grows. The fertile fronds are green regardless of age and shaped like antlers; they jut out from the plant and bear spores on their undersides. (A spore is a microscopic, spherical, single-celled reproductive unit that's used in place of seeds by some primitive plants, including ferns, fungi, moss, and algae.)

The various common names of platycerium ferns match their striking shapes. The true staghorn fern (*P. bifurcatum*) has fertile fronds shaped like stags' antlers and is the easiest one to grow. (Individual specimens have withstood temperatures as low as 20°F when protected by a shade structure, and the species is widely grown as an ornamental patio plant in both coastal and inland gardens.) Elkhorn ferns (*P. hillii, P. veitchii,* and *P. willinckii*) are very similar in appearance to staghorn ferns but generally less hardy. There are also several species of giant staghorn ferns. All are spectacular, but moosehorn fern *(Platycerium superbum)* is the easiest one of these to grow. It's highly decorative, well adapted to coastal gardens, bears 3- or 4-foot-long fertile fronds shaped like moose's antlers, and has majestic bright green sterile fronds that often grow 4 to 5 feet wide. Moosehorn ferns are usually raised in greenhouses and adapt to gardens best when purchased and put outdoors now.

Keep all staghorns in bright, indirect light or in filtered sunshine. Protect them from hot sun, winds, and cold weather. When you water them, drench them thoroughly, but then allow the moss (or soil) to dry out before you water again. Platyceriums are much more drought resistant than their lush tropical appearance might lead you to think. In dry interior zones, water staghorns thoroughly about twice a week during the summer and once a week in winter. Along the coast, water them once a week in summer and once every two weeks in winter. (In any zone, a heat wave or a Santa Ana may make more frequent watering necessary, but feel with your finger to make sure. It's important not to overwater your staghorn ferns, because they'll rot.)

Staghorns are easy-care plants. They need to be fed only once every two or three months, beginning in spring. Don't feed them during winter. One way to fertilize staghorns is to drench them with a complete organic liquid fertilizer such as diluted fish emulsion. The easiest and most effective way to feed moosehorn ferns is simply to place banana peels behind the fronds once you've eaten the bananas inside them. If your platycerium ferns are hanging high up, on the trunks of palm trees, for example, use a bamboo pole or a long-handled cut-and-hold pruner to drop the peels behind the fronds so

they don't show. Each fern can absorb 4 to 8 peels a month, but more won't hurt. Pour water from the hose behind the fronds at least once a week. It will drain right through, but enough moisture will remain to irrigate the plant and activate the nutrients. Banana peels are an excellent source of phosphorus, potassium, and just enough nitrogen to provide moosehorns with everything they need for a magnificent appearance. You can feed them banana peels whenever you want throughout the year. (Children love this job. Give them a long bamboo pole so they can place a peel on its tip and reach up to the plant.)

Moosehorn ferns aren't easy to propagate, but you can do it with a combination of luck and patience. First, wait until one of the brown spore patches under the fertile fronds flakes off easily when you lightly rub it. This means these spores are ripe. Sterilize a clear plastic shoebox

---

✹ QUICK TIP

How to Sterilize Potting Soil, Peat Moss, or Coir. *Thoroughly moisten 1 gallon potting soil or peat moss. (Moisten peat moss by mixing it with 3 cups boiling water.) Spoon the soil, peat moss, or coir into a plastic cooking bag; make a hole in the top of the bag, and place it in a baking pan. When using a conventional oven, bake at 350°F for fifteen minutes. When using a microwave oven, cook on high for three minutes per quart of soil. (Cooking times may vary depending on your oven, so watch over this process closely. When the soil or peat moss is steaming hot throughout, it's done.) Place the bag outdoors and allow the contents to cool to 70°F before you use it.*

by washing it in a solution of 1 quart water and 2 tablespoons bleach. Allow the shoebox to air dry, and then fill it with a 3-inch-deep layer of damp, sterilized peat moss or coir. Hold the prepared shoebox directly under the spore patch, and with clean hands sprinkle some of the ripe spores—they're like fine brown dust—onto the surface of the damp peat moss. Close up the box and keep it in bright light but out of direct sun and in a warm place (with daytime temperatures of 72° to 80°F and nighttime temperatures about 10 degrees cooler). Use distilled water to keep the contents damp but never soggy, and in six months to a year you may be lucky enough to have some tiny 1-inch-wide platycerium ferns, big enough to plant in paper cups filled with a light acid soil mix. Keep them warm and in filtered light, feed them lightly, and pot them on into the next size pot occasionally as they grow. Eventually you can mount them on boards, as described in the accompanying box for the more common variety of staghorn fern.

Many staghorn and elkhorn ferns not only have spores but also make a great many offsets, called pups. You can propagate these very

How to Separate and Mount the Pups of Staghorn Ferns

Once the pups (offsets) of staghorn ferns have sprouted and grown at least 4 inches long, you can separate them from the parent plant to make new specimens.

▶ Soak some green sphagnum moss in a bucket of water while you prepare the planting base. To the back of an appropriately sized piece of wood or plywood (flat cork bark or a fern trunk can also be used), attach a plastic-covered wire for hanging. (Use screws or nails to fix it firmly in place.)

▶ Cover the front of this base with a 1- or 2-inch-deep layer of premoistened sphagnum moss, and hold it in place by winding nylon fishing twine around it, or, alternatively, cover the entire face of the sphagnum moss with a piece of gardener Bird-X netting. Secure the netting by stapling the edges to the back of the base. Turn the base over and cut a horizontal slit 1 to 2 inches long in the center of the netting. (Wear rubber or surgical gloves when handling wet sphagnum moss; it harbors spores that can cause serious skin infections.)

▶ With your fingers, carefully pull off a clump of pups from the mother plant. For each new plant, use between one and four pups; each one must have a sterile frond as well as at least one fertile frond. (If possible, remove a small portion of the sterile frond of the mother plant to help hold the new plant together.)

▶ Wrap the roots of the pup (or pups) in damp sphagnum moss, and seat them in the center of the base you have made. Tie them in place with fishing twine, being careful to wrap the twine under but not over the face of the sterile fronds.

▶ Hang the new plant in a shady, protected spot in bright light, and keep it moist for two or three weeks until it's rooted. Then begin to feed it once every two weeks with diluted fish emulsion throughout the warm months.

▶ For even faster growth, mist your young staghorn with water once or twice a week. Occasionally add diluted fish emulsion to the water you use for misting.

easily by dividing them off at any time in spring after they reach the proper size (see the box on the facing page).

VOLUNTEERS

Look around the garden now for plants that have seeded themselves in the wrong places, and weed them out. Admittedly, some plants are weedier by nature than others, but any plant can be a weed if it's growing where you don't want it. Even a native Torrey pine, live oak, or Washingtonia palm can be a weed if it seeds itself between the sun and your vegetable garden.

Develop the eye of an artist as you assess what to keep and what must go. If shade draws your sensibilities and your need is a forest retreat, you can achieve it easily by planting well-chosen trees, but don't let it happen by accident. If there's something you really don't want, grit your teeth and pull it up now, or you'll find yourself in a few years chopping it down at great expense to pocketbook and conscience.

CONTROL OF MILDEW

Moderate temperatures combined with damp oceanic air make May the worst time for mildew. If you're still growing peas and you don't want to pull them out yet, try dusting the plants with sulfur at intervals of one week. Roses and tuberous begonias are particularly sensitive to mildew, though organically grown plants tend to be much more resistant to fungus diseases such as mildew than are plants grown with chemicals. Soils supplied with organic fertilizers and amendments are chock-full of beneficial fungi that parasitize or consume harmful fungi, while synthetic or chemical fertilizers kill all the good guys and thus allow damaging organisms to proliferate. You can even speed up the growth of beneficial bioorganisms by spraying plants with a biofungicide containing beneficial fungi. (These are discussed on page 58 but may be difficult to obtain.) So why not try a nonspecific, OMRI-labeled product containing the same or similar fungi? PROBIOTICS 4 Plants' Defensor Bacterial Inoculator, for example, contains *Bacillus subtilis* as well as *B. cereus*, two beneficial fungi known to attack or parasitize harmful fungi. Directions suggest mixing 1 teaspoon per gallon of water with 2 teaspoons molasses or sugar and applying the spray to soil or foliage. (Molasses stimulates microbial action in soil and accelerates the decomposition of organics. Adding yucca, kelp, humic acid, or compost tea is not necessary but will increase the spray's effectiveness.) Spray the solution on foliage, being careful not to breathe it into your lungs. This product is not labeled for controlling mildew, so use it as the directions suggest, for the purpose of "increasing plant health," and the result should be plants with no mildew or other fungus disease. (PROBIOTICS 4 Plants makes another innovative product, Defensor Rhizo-Boost, Bacterial Inoculant BioStart, which provides naturally occurring beneficial microbes to enhance the biodiversity of garden soil. Mix it according to label directions and spray it onto soil or drench the root zone of plants with the diluted product. It makes plants more productive and healthier.)

PRUNING

Prune winter- and spring-flowering vines, bushes, trees, and ground covers after they finish blooming. A **Rule of Thumb** that applies in almost all cases: *Prune flowering plants that* *bloom once a year after they bloom, not before they bloom, or you'll prevent them from flowering.* Refer to a pruning manual for additional directions by plant type; I especially recommend the *Sunset Pruning Handbook*, listed in the bibliography. Here are a few examples of plants to be pruned now:

- **Trailing African Daisy** *(Osteospermum fruticosum)*. Give osteospermum a yearly haircut in early May after bloom to prevent the buildup of thatch, which could lead to death from summer fungus. Clean up the ground; remove clippings and dead leaves. Then spread aged manure on the ground under the plants to provide both mulch and fertilizer, or, alternatively, sprinkle the ground with an all-purpose organic commercial fertilizer or a generic or homemade all-purpose fertilizer—see the recipe on page 77, for an example—cover the fertilizer with a layer of organic mulch, and follow up by watering deeply. You'll get another show of bloom.
- **Geraldton Waxflower** *(Chamelaucium uncinatum)*. One of our loveliest drought-resistant plants, this one responds well to heavy pruning after bloom. Cut back whole sprays—not all the way down to the ground, but into the body of the plant and back to the trunk. If you have room, let it grow big, like a small shaggy-barked tree, but if it has outgrown its space, it can be chopped back to 2 feet high now. Fresh shoots will spring from apparently dry wood below the cuts, and you'll have a whole new plant by fall. (Don't ever give this plant manure. It hates the stuff.)
- **Polyanthum Jasmine** *(Jasminum polanthum)*. Lightly cut back this fragrant, winter-blooming vine after bloom to remove unsightly dead blossoms and produce a second wave of bloom. Then cut it back hard—almost to bare wood—to clean up the plant, prevent it from building up a tangled interior, and produce new wood to bloom next year.
- **Lady Banks' Rose** *(Rosa banksiae)*. Cut this rose back lightly right after bloom to stimulate another, though lighter, wave of bloom. Next month, in June, cut mature specimens back hard to produce new wood that will grow during the summer and bloom next year. (Never prune this rose in winter or you'll have no spring bloom.)
- **New Zealand Tea Tree** *(Leptospermum scoparium)*. Shape this large shrub or small tree during bloom by cutting sprays for cut flowers. After bloom, you can further shape it by cutting out whole unwanted branches and by heading back tips of selected branches to increase bushiness and develop a natural billowy shape. Don't ever shear this plant like a ball—this practice ruins its growth habit and prevents proper flowering.
- **Wisteria.** Train young plants onto a strong support. For the first three years, choose strong new shoots, gently straighten them out, and tie them down loosely just where you want them to grow. Cut off all unwanted ones. Train young growth straight, or wind it around posts: clockwise for Japanese wisterias *(W. floribunda)*, and counterclockwise for Chinese wisterias *(W. sinensis)*. On top of the pergola or arbor, arrange the shoots straight, instead of twining them, and allow spaces between them. This will form the basic structure of your wisteria. Once your arbor or pergola is covered, wisteria will continue to grow many new shoots every summer that will try to twine around anything they touch. Begin now in May to cut off all unwanted shoots back to two buds, leaving a stub with one or two leaves attached. (A long-handled Japanese grab-and-hold pruner is useful for this task.)

The stub you leave on the plant will become a spur. (Spurs are flowering or fruiting wood that live many years and bloom every spring; don't cut them off.) Pruning this way produces more spring bloom as well as sporadic summer bloom.

BULBS

Plant Tuberoses. If you're especially fond of fragrant plants, try planting tuberoses (*Polianthes tuberose*)—known in Hawaii as lei flowers—in early May. Choose tubers with a green growth tip, and place them so that the tips are level with the soil surface, 6 inches apart, in acid, well-drained soil in pots or the ground. Choose a warm spot, in full sun along the coast or slightly shaded but with reflected heat inland. Water them and wait for a sprout to appear; then water often and well. Feed them monthly with an acid organic fertilizer for bloom and growth, such as Pro-Holly (4-6-4). (Cottonseed meal is also acidic but is slower acting.)

The heavily scented white flowers will appear in August or September. After the plants die down, you can leave the tubers in the ground, though if you do, they'll sometimes skip a year before repeating bloom. For surer results, lift them and store in perlite until next May.

Care for Spring-Flowering Bulbs as the Bloom Season Ends. Continue to keep spring-flowering bulbs well watered during and after bloom. If you grew some in pots and want to reuse the containers, slip the bulbs out carefully and plant them as clumps in a sheltered spot. A shot of fish emulsion diluted according to package directions after bloom will help your bulbs store up strength for next year. Don't cut off leaves before they go brown.

These instructions apply to bulbs grown in pots filled with potting soil. Bulbs that were forced in pebbles and water should be thrown out right after bloom; these usually will not bloom again.

ANNUAL AND PERENNIAL FLOWERS

Clean Up and Replant Annual Flowers as They Finish Blooming. In Southern California, we grow annual flowers year-round by planting with the seasons, twice a year. Beginning in September, but mainly in October, we plant cool-season annuals that bloom all winter and peak in April. This makes May the logical time to replace them with warm-season annuals for blooms all summer long. (If you planted ahead from seeds in flats, as suggested in the March chapter, you'll have plenty of homegrown transplants all ready to go into the ground.) So now's the time to pull out all cool-season annuals that have finished blooming, such as calendulas, cineraria, Iceland poppies, malacoides (fairy) primroses, snapdragons, and stock. As you clear the beds, also clean them up, then dig in some well-rotted homemade, bagged, or trucked compost, sprinkle on an organic all-purpose organic fertilizer or one that is recommended for flowering plants, applied according to directions, and work it into the top 6 inches of soil. Replant the bare spaces with summer annuals, including cosmos, gomphrena (globe amaranth), marigolds, petunias, verbena, and zinnias in full sun, and begonias, impatiens, and lobelia in partial shade. (Semperflorens, 'Richmondensis', and 'Dragon Wings' begonias can be planted in sun or shade in coastal zones.) Plant scarlet sage in partial shade inland, in full sun along the coast.

Follow up with a layer of mulch and then thoroughly water the new plants. Follow the same basic recommendations for annuals in containers, but in this case you will plant in fresh potting soil mixed with organic fertilizer and will not mulch the top of the ground. (For more, see the "Annual and Perennial Flowers" section in April, beginning on page 161.)

Keep Plants That Are Still Going Strong.

May border planting isn't like October's, when every summer annual can be pulled up by the roots to make way for cool-season flowers. Some of the seeds and transplants we put in during fall or early spring, such as cosmos, Shasta daisies, and the new heat-resistant pansies and violas, will continue to bloom all summer long in most coastal and some inland zones. Clarkia, larkspur, lavatera, and many wildflowers will bloom through June and perhaps into July. Pull out dead plants to make way for slower-growing seedlings of summer-blooming flowers that may be hidden underneath, ready to fill in the gaps.

Many gardeners have become so dazzled by perennials that they've forgotten how easy and colorful annuals can be. The widespread dwarfing of bedding plants hasn't helped. To get the tall and showy varieties, grow them from seed. Try using them as fillers among your perennials or purposefully, as English gardeners do, to pep up your flowerbeds with added color and excitement. Annuals are actually much easier to grow than perennials; just plant, feed, water, and deadhead them or pick them for bouquets, and when they get ratty, pull them out.

Plant Heat-Lovers from Seed.

At last it's time to plant heat-loving annuals, such as zinnias, from seeds. Modern hybrid zinnias bounce back quicker after transplanting than old varieties do, but as a rule zinnias do best when planted from seeds right where you want them to grow. This allows you to choose varieties not usually found in nursery packs. 'Benary's Giant Zinnia', a mildew-resistant variety developed for the cut-flower industry, is the best tall, strong-stemmed variety. Order from catalogs, including Johnny's Seeds. Park Seed Company sells individual colors under the name 'Park's Picks Giant Zinnias'. Pick or deadhead flowers to keep them coming.

Foil Cutworms. If you've ever had a problem with cutworms, treat the ground prior to planting with an organic cutworm control, such as the one described in the box on how to grow zinnias from seeds. Cutworms are gray or dull-brown fat caterpillars, 1 to 2 inches long, with shiny heads. They hide in the ground during the day, emerge at night, and cut down stems of young tomatoes or zinnias at ground level. Beneficial nematodes control cutworms in moist soil, but these nematodes, unlike the harmful ones, die in sandy soil that dries out between irrigations. When using transplants, stop cutworm damage by surrounding the stem of each plant with a 1-inch-tall cardboard collar cut from the cardboard tube inside a roll of gift wrap. One can even plant seeds inside these rings. Use your fingertip to press each seed onto the top of damp soil so it makes good contact with the ground. When planting inside rings, don't cover the seeds, or they won't get enough light. (Zinnias need light to germinate.) Keep the seeds and the ground around and inside the collars damp by watering daily, or twice a day in hot weather. The shade provided by the rings slows the seedlings' growth a little, but once up, they'll be safe from cutworms. After they have two real leaves, feed with diluted fish emulsion to speed growth. Once the leaves are higher than the collar, zinnias

A Foolproof Way to Plant and Grow Zinnias from Seed

▶ Choose a spot in full sun that is not hit by overhead sprinklers. Also choose a good variety. 'Benary's Giant Zinnia' is today's best tall, open-pollinated variety developed for the cut-flower trade. (You can save seed of open-pollinated varieties but not of F1 varieties.) For compact FI varieties, choose All America Award winners 'Profusion Cherry', 'Profusion White', and 'Profusion Orange', or compact tall varieties, 'Zowie! Yellow Flame' or 'Magellan Coral'. All are mildew resistant and drought tolerant. Profusion varieties need no deadheading. Magellan varieties and 'Zowie! Yellow Flame' will bloom better if you cut off faded flowers.

▶ Dig the ground deeply and mix in a generous layer of organic soil amendment. Add a complete organic fertilizer recommended for annual flowers according to package directions, and mix it into the top 6 inches of soil.

▶ Use a garden hoe to make a dike of soil 3 to 4 inches high all the way around the seedbed; it will hold in the water when you irrigate. Rake the seedbed level inside this dike. Or first rake the seedbed level and then install a drip system that will water the bed at ground level. (Drip systems make water basins unnecessary.)

▶ To kill cutworms one week prior to planting, thoroughly mix 2 cups of wheat bran with ½ cup *Bacillus thuringiensis* powder and sprinkle the mixture evenly over the prepared flowerbed, or apply Sluggo Plus according to manufacturer's instructions.

▶ Pour some seeds into the palm of your hand. Grasping them one by one, place each seed right where you want it to grow, in a continuous diamond pattern all over the bed or drift. (As for all bedding plants and ground covers, alternate the rows when planting so that the plants will grow evenly all over, rather than standing like soldiers in foursquare rows.) Follow the package directions on spacing. (Large varieties should be spaced about 12 inches apart, small varieties, about 6 inches.)

▶ Cover the seeds very lightly with about ¼ inch of soil—zinnias need light in order to germinate—and pat it down gently. (If you're planting in clay soil, cover the seeds with potting mix rather than soil so they won't have to break through a hard crust.)

▶ Mist the seedbed thoroughly after planting. Continue to mist it twice daily (more often in interior zones) until the seeds germinate. (Covering the bed with a floating row cover, such as Reemay, can help keep seeds damp and speed germination in hot interior valleys. After seeds have germinated, take off the row cover.)

▶ Once the zinnias are up and firmly rooted, stop misting and start irrigating with the drip system or by putting the hose on the ground inside the dike. (Aim the hose into a sideways-set flower pot to mute the force of the water.) The **Rule of Thumb** for zinnias is: *Always water zinnias by soaking the ground; never use overhead sprinklers, or you'll ruin the foliage.*

▶ When the plants are 3 to 4 inches high, start watering them more infrequently and deeply until you're applying 1 to 2 inches of water per week, depending on your soil and climate zone.

▶ To encourage branching, pinch out the first flower bud on each plant or pinch above the third set of leaves.

▶ Pick and deadhead zinnias throughout the summer.

will grow at regular speed. Plant leftover seeds off to the side or in a flat, so if some don't germinate in the bed, you'll have transplants for filling in gaps.

If you've never grown anything from seeds but would like to try, zinnias are a good first choice (see the box on page 191). Other flowers you can plant now from seed include calliopsis, celosia (cockscomb or plume flower), Madagascar periwinkle *(vinca; Catharanthus roseus)*, marigold, nicotiana, portulaca, scarlet sage, sunflower, sweet alyssum, verbena, and morning glory (see the Quick Tip on page 194).

One of the best old-fashioned, easy-to-grow plants to put in now from seeds is spider flower *(Cleome hasslerana)*. Old-fashioned varieties, such as 'Rose Queen' (deep rose-pink) and 'Helen Campbell' (white), thrive in interior zones with sun and heat. They hate wet, soggy soil, make great cut flowers, and bring hummingbirds. The spiny-stemmed plants grow 4 to 6 feet tall and 5 feet wide and need staking; they self-seed and are fragrant but mildew in coastal gardens. New compact varieties 'Senorita Rosalita', by Proven Winners, and the 'Spirit Series' grow 2 to 3 feet tall, thrive in full sun in all zones, need no staking, and are resistant to mildew. Although they share the drought resistance and tough constitutions of the old varieties, they have no spines and don't set seeds, so you won't need to deadhead. What's more, they're perennial, surviving through winter in frost-free zones, though flowering less in cold weather. Plant these types now from transplants, not from seeds.

If you need to fill more space, plant cleome F1 'Sparkler Blush' from seeds. This 3-foot-tall All America Award Winner needs no staking but will need picking or deadheading. Before planting cleome seeds, prepare the ground by digging up and turning over the soil, working in some well-rotted homemade or bagged compost and balanced organic fertilizer, and then raking the area smooth. Sprinkle the cleome seeds on top of the prepared soil and use the back of the hoe with its handle held upright to press them into contact with the soil. (Don't cover the seeds; they need light to germinate.) If you notice birds watching you plant, cover the area with bird netting, or they'll steal your seeds as soon as your back is turned. Keep the seeded area damp by sprinkling daily until plants are established, then water deeply but infrequently. (Pick or deadhead these plants so they don't self-seed; the seeds of F1 hybrids will sprout and grow but they will yield inferior plants, called F2 hybrids, that have lost the vigor, uniformity, and other good characteristics of the parent plant; some will be oddly shaped; none are worth growing.)

Use Nursery Transplants for Instant Color.
Pony packs of many summer annuals can be planted now; they'll soon fill out in size. Or, for instant flowerbeds and patio pots chock-full of plants, use the more expensive but larger-rooted color packs. Arrange them in your shopping cart to see which color combinations look good together.

Years ago it was preferable to purchase flowers before they bloomed, but new varieties are made to bloom in the pack—even in tiny pony packs—and continue to perform spectacularly in the garden. The one thing the gardener must remember is to loosen up the roots when planting, or they'll just sit there for months, thinking they're still in the container. May is a good time to plant red, white, and blue flowers for the Fourth of July. Begonia 'Dragon Wings' and fan flower *(Scaevola aemula* 'New Wonder') make a great combination for a patio tub. 'Dragon Wings', an easy plant, can live many years in a pot with non-stop bloom year-round. 'New Wonder' scaevola is compact and doesn't go bare in the middle as older types do. For flowerbeds in full sun, choose the bright orange-and-yellow compact blanket flower *Gaillardia* 'Arizona Sun', one of the best new easy-to-grow, drought-resistant plants for long bloom in containers or the ground. Buy the 1-foot-tall compact plants now, or fill a whole bed from seeds next fall. (Supposedly, no deadheading is needed, but my seed-grown plants bloomed better through August when I removed seedheads weekly.)

In partial shade, try shiso, or beefsteak plant (*Perilla frutescens*), a 3-foot-tall Himalayan plant with colorful leaves like those of coleus. Varieties include the 'Fancy Fringe' series and 'Magilla Purple', dubbed Magilla perilla by gardeners. Shiso thrives in heat in full sun on the coast, in partial shade inland, but needs regular irrigation. For full sun in interior zones, plant *Rudbeckia* 'Cherokee Sunset'; it dies or does badly on the coast, but blooms through summer into winter inland. Lions tail (*Leonitus leonurus*) blooms year-round in coastal zones and likes warm-weather planting. Older varieties are 6 feet tall and good for the back of a border; newer compact types work well in drought-resistant beds.

Gardeners who are alert to new plants and styles are switching away from old-fashioned plants, such as the Shasta daisies so beloved fifty years ago, that bloom briefly and need much water. Today's perennial gardeners are on the lookout for improved, tough, long-blooming varieties of wild drought-resistant plants, such as *Agastache* 'Heather Queen', *Penstemon* 'Liliput Rose', and Ozark primrose (*Oenethera* hybrid 'Lemon Drop'). 'Lemon Drop' blooms its head off on a hot bank all summer long with little care or water. The best-looking gardens combine a variety of shapes, including tall, spiky plants resembling exclamation points. Verbascum would fill the bill, but it takes more water than a plant such as old-fashioned blue sea holly (*Eryngium alpinum*), which is easy to grow from seeds planted now and looks lovely in backlit drifts in the evening.

Deadhead, Cut Back, and Plant Perennials.
When those gorgeous spikes of bloom on Pride of Madeira (*Echium candicans*) are spent and begin to look unsightly, it's time to cut them off down to the plant's gray foliage. New growth will then sprout farther down on the stalks that have bloomed. In a month or two, cut down to this new growth and the plant will branch. In midsummer, cut out unwanted branches so the spring blooms will be larger. Allowing too many branches to grow will result in smaller flowers.

Deadhead coral bells (*Heuchera*) after bloom, and cut back columbine (*Aquilegia*). If happy in their location, a stand of coral bells will last for many years, but when columbine is grown here, it usually ignores the fact that it's perennial and dies in summer from root rot. Be not dismayed; it's an efficient self-seeder. Unless you've deadheaded it with amazing regularity, you should find many progeny to dig up and move around in fall. (Unfortunately, hybrid plants cross-pollinate and do not come true from seeds, thus seedlings of the highly desireable McKana Hybrids, for example, will be far inferior to your original plants.) Other plants that die after bloom—but for a different and more acceptable reason—are Canterbury bells (*Campanula medium*) and the ever-popular cup-and-saucer (*C. medium* 'Calycanthema'). These are biennials, so the end of their bloom season naturally signals their demise. They're prone to mildew and need cool temperatures, moist soil, and good drainage and thus are fussier, scarcer, and more expensive than foxglove, another biennial. But just for fun, why not try planting the variety 'Cup-and-Saucer Mixed Colors' (available from Park Seed Co.) from seeds next fall? It grows 1½ feet high and may reseed itself after bloom next year.

Perennials aren't always what their name implies. Cast-iron plants such as achillea, gaura, and Santa Barbara daisy settle down and live for years. Others, such as lavender, live several years, then die. Clipping them back helps keep them going, but eventually you'll have to go out and buy more. Some gardeners can keep certain plants, such as coral bells, alive year after year; others can't. And then there are the "perennials" that most gardeners here treat as annuals, never expecting them to last a second year—delphiniums are the best example.

Aster x frikartii 'Mönch' and *A. x frikartii* 'Wonder of Staffa', long cherished for ease of growing and long bloom season, are widely available now. *A. ericoides* 'Monte Casino' (white) does well in coastal or inland gardens, blooming spring and fall with tall, airy spikes— a good substitute for boltonia, which won't grow here. Another cut flower is *Verbena rigida*. Drought resistant, it makes a spreading mat of growth with spikes of violet blooms 20 inches tall in summer and fall. And then there's *Hypoestes aristata* 'Lavender Cloud', which blooms in fall, but planting now gives it a chance to get established. (Perhaps you have a friend with seedlings.) Grow it from the beach to inland valleys, in sun or shade, and with only ordinary care. Cut it back lightly after bloom, then heavily in January or February, down to the new foliage springing from the ground or close to the ground. Cut 1 or 2 feet off the top of the whole plant now and you will get more bloom on sturdier stems and a shorter plant, 4 to 5 feet tall instead of 6 feet tall.

 QUICK TIP

How to Scarify Seed. *Some seeds with hard coats, such as morning glory (Ipomoea tricolor) and lupine, have to be scarified (nicked) prior to planting, or they won't sprout under garden conditions. To scarify a seed easily, grasp it with pliers and use a small three-cornered file to carefully file through the edge of the seed at any spot other than the "eye" from which it will sprout. Soak scarified morning glory seeds overnight in warm water before planting.*

Cut Back Kool-Aid Plant. Another, somewhat rare, self-seeding plant for semishade is blue spurge pea, or Kool-Aid plant (*Psoralea pinnata*). This is a short-lived shrub or small, leaning tree, riparian in South Africa but drought resistant here. It combines beautifully with azaleas or camellias and blooms at the same time that they do. Look for the seedlings now, and move them to spots where you want them to grow, or plant them into gallon cans to share with friends. In spring, this plant is solidly drenched with azure-blue pea-shaped blooms that give off a strong but pleasant fragrance like grape Kool-Aid. Cut Kool-Aid plant back hard now, after bloom, to encourage longer life; pinch tips as it regrows. (Blue broom [*Psoralea affinis*], from Annie's Annuals, is more erect, bearing blue and white blooms on drooping branch tips, and is said to be even more fragrant.)

CLEMATIS

Clematis is a climber needing rich, damp, slightly alkaline soil that is well drained but never dries out, plus frequent applications of organic fertilizer and, in most cases, at least a dash of winter chill. It's fair to say clematis is better adapted to southern England or Paris, where magnificent specimens grow, than to our mild, dry Mediterranean climate. Nonetheless, some gardeners grow handsome clematis, and right now you can find varieties that grow fairly well here at nurseries and botanic gardens. The finest specimen I've ever seen in Southern California was a 15-foot-tall, 8-foot-wide, C. 'Jackmanii,' and every inch of it was smothered with purple bloom. Knowing that clematis climbs by twisting leaf petioles (the small stalks attaching the leaf to the stem) around a thin support (usually twigs of another plant), the gardener had arranged netting for the clematis to climb on by nailing the netting onto the wooden rail of an exterior stairway and balcony. The entire front and top of the plant were in full sun and reflected heat, but its roots were hidden in a flowerbed under the stairs, thus fulfilling the old **Rule of Thumb:** *Plant clematis with its feet in shade and its head in full sun.* It bears mentioning that the gardener who raised this plant has now moved to Hilo, Hawaii, where she can grow spectacular flowering plants without water restrictions. English gardeners often put a flat rock over the roots of clematis to provide a cool root run, but thick mulch works too. If you wish to grow clematis, find out which type you are buying before you purchase it. There are three main categories: (A) spring blooming, (B) summer or fall blooming, and (C) repeat-blooming, and each type requires different pruning. The A group blooms on old wood that grew last year, so it needs little pruning except to shape and clean out dead growth. If you prune hard in spring, you get no flowers. The B group blooms on new growth that grows this year, so prune in fall along the coast or in spring inland when you see new leaf

buds emerge, cutting the whole climber down to 12 or 18 inches from the ground, just above a good bud. The C group blooms in late winter or spring on old wood formed last year and again in fall on new wood that grows this year, so cut back more heavily after the first wave of bloom and very lightly after the second wave of bloom. Consult the *Journal of the American Clematis Society* (c/o Edith Malek, PO Box 17085, Irvine, CA 92623-7085; clematis.org) for articles on the choice, cultivation, and pruning of clematis. Malek's *Simply Clematis: Clematis Made Simple* (see the bibliography) takes the mystery out of growing clematis.

LAWN CARE

As mentioned in other months' chapters, sweeping greenswards are a carryover from garden styles that were prevalent in the 1930s, '40s, and '50s, when Southern California gardeners thought they had plenty of irrigation water. But before the Los Angeles Aqueduct was built, lawns were of little importance. During the golden age of California gardening (1910 to 1920), few lawns were planted. The romantic ideal of that era was the Italian, Spanish, or Mediterranean garden, which uses steps, paths, patios, pergolas, flowerbeds, and shrubberies instead of lawns to cover ground. Today, as drought worsens and water crises mount in our state, it's more necessary than ever to find a better garden model than England, the East Coast, or a tropical jungle. Several ideas for substitutes are discussed on page 129, but the possibilities for creating a drought-resistant but satisfying landscape are as endless as your imagination. Unless you have a worthy reason to own a lawn, don't plant one, even though the subject of how to plant lawns is discussed below. For those who still have lawns, the best plan is to keep them small, fertilize them organically, and adjust the irrigation system so that it waters adequately but not wastefully.

Plant Warm-Season Lawns and Dwarf Fescue. St. Augustine and Bermuda get off to a fast start when planted in May. (Hold off until June to plant zoysia; see page 249.) It's too late to plant most cool-season grasses from seed, but dwarf fescues can be planted from sod.

Lawns can be planted in several ways: from seeds, plugs grown in flats, or sod rolled out like an instant carpet. Bermuda and zoysia can also be planted from stolons (creeping stems with roots attached). Whichever method you use, be sure to prepare the ground properly. Before beginning, decide whether to plant a warm- or cool-season lawn (as discussed on page 131), and choose a variety appropriate for your area and needs.

Select the Best Variety for You. When you research grass types, be sure to consult with successful local gardeners and the nearest University of California Cooperative Extension office. Consider these factors:

- St. Augustine is better adapted to shade than other lawn grasses but needs a lot of water.
- Dwarf fescue is now the most popular lawn grass in coastal regions. Good varieties are disease resistant and more drought resistant than perennial ryegrass and a lot less troublesome.
- If you live close to a Bermuda golf course, Bermuda will seed itself eventually into your ryegrass lawn, making it look ratty. To minimize this, plant a hybrid or selected strain of Bermuda for your own lawn in the first place. (See descriptions of varieties on

page 133.) You'll need a reel mower, not a rotary one, to cut Bermuda.

- As mentioned earlier in this book, don't plant such troublemakers as bent grass or Kentucky bluegrass—they'll die in the first drought. Common Bermuda and deeply rooted varieties of hybrid Bermuda grass are the two most drought-resistant choices.

Mow and Water Lawns; Feed If Necessary. Warm-season lawns, such as Bermuda grass, zoysia, and St. Augustine, are speeding up this month, while cool-season lawns, such as ryegrass, bluegrass, and fescue, are slowing down. Fertilize all warm-season lawns this month with a commercial organic fertilizer recommended for feeding lawns, such as Biosol Mix (7-2-3) or with chicken manure or a homemade or generic product. Some gardeners find that a liquid lawn fertilizer works faster than a powdered or granulated product and is easier to apply. If you are switching from synthetic fertilizers to organics for the first time, liquid fertilizers can help wean the lawn from chemicals by jump-starting growth with fast-acting, though still gentle, organics. AGGRAND (4-3-3), a concentrated fish and kelp liquid, is one such type, or combine liquid kelp, liquid fish, and humic acid to create your own spray-on fertilizer. (A screw-on siphon device may clog less often than most hand-held sprayers. Shake or mix the solution as you spray so solids don't collect on the bottom of the container.)

Make sure mower blades are sharp, and allow the grass blades of all lawns to fall back onto the grass. They will soon dry and fall to the ground, feeding the lawn with organic nitrogen year-round. If your mower leaves lumps of clippings behind, spread them around with a grass rake so they can dry out more easily. An organically fed lawn will withstand diseases far better

How to Grow a Cantaloupe in a Tire

Gardeners in cool coastal areas often have problems growing cantaloupes. Here's a successful heat-increasing method.

- In early May, plant a cantaloupe variety that will ripen at relatively cool temperatures, such as 'Ambrosia'.

- Dig a hole 2 feet wide and 1 foot deep in full sun. Mix together aged manure, compost, organic soil amendment, and some of the native soil from the hole to make a rich organic soil. Into this mix a cup of complete organic vegetable fertilizer or balanced generic fertilizer, and refill the hole.

- Lay an old auto tire over the hole, pack native soil into the sides of the tire with your hands, and fill the center of the tire up to its inside edge with more manure, compost, soil, and a handful of the same fertilizer you mixed into the hole below. Finish with a layer of potting soil and water deeply. (The bulging tire makes a perfect watering basin.)

- Plant five or six seeds, 1 inch deep, spacing them evenly around the top.

- Water deeply and daily until the seeds sprout. When the seedlings are up 4 inches, choose the strongest two. Clip off or pull out the others. For continued harvests, plant in other tires. Separate them from the first by 3 to 4 feet.

- Cover the ground all around the tires with a layer of black plastic mulch to raise the temperature of the melon patch. (Peg it down.) The vines will grow out over the plastic, which will keep the fruit clean.

- Once the plants are established, water deeply; lay the hose in the tires and let water soak in slowly. Do this twice a week when the plants are young, once a week when they're full-grown. (If plants wilt, water them right away.)

- Water less as the fruit nears maturity. (Too much water at this time makes fruit less sweet.)

- Pick at "full slip," meaning there's a crack around the vine so that the melon slips off easily when it's lifted. Enjoy the sweetness and flavor.

than one that has been continually forced into fast growth with synthetic fertilizers.

Organic gardeners with cool-season lawns have been feeding them throughout fall, winter, and spring to build up the soil and promote growth. On these lawns, slower-acting organic fertilizers may still be working to keep them looking good. Nonetheless, if you live in a coastal zone, you may wish to give your cool-season lawn a final boost of liquid organic fertilizer, such as diluted liquid fish emulsion mixed with liquid kelp and humic acid, to see it through summer. Interior-zone gardeners should quit feeding cool-season lawns now. Fertilizing cool-season lawns during the warm season of the year subjects them to unnecessary stress. Experts advise feeding all lawns as little as possible to keep them in good health, but this advice applies more to chemical fertilizers than to organic ones. Organic fertilizers work mainly by building up a humus-filled soil so that microbial action will provide all the nutrition that grass needs.

Mow all lawns frequently enough that you're removing no more than one-third of their height at a time. Lawns need to be long enough for photosynthesis to work, but short enough that they don't mat down or look unsightly. Mow cool-season lawns, such as tall fescue, once a week with a rotary mower set at the highest setting of 2½ to 3 inches, and mow warm-season grasses according to type. Mow Bermuda grass planted from seeds to 1½ inches in length. Mow zoysia grass and hybrid Bermuda to 1 inch. (Keeping hybrid Bermuda and zoysia grasses an inch instead of ½ inch long can help them withstand foot traffic and drought.) Mow seashore paspalum (*Paspalum vaginatum*) to 1½ inches and tall St. Augustine grass to 2 inches, but cut dwarf St. Augustine varieties shorter, to 1 inch.

Also check the irrigation system now to prevent waste. Check for leaks, making sure sprinkler heads are working properly and that sprinklers are not over- or underwatering or hitting pavement. Sometimes it's worth calling in an expert to fix that troublesome soggy spot. Spread out irrigations so that you're watering deeply but infrequently instead of shallowly and often. Some new climate-activated sprinkler systems have water-efficiency settings that change with the temperature and other factors. A low-tech way to lengthen times between your

◉ QUICK TIP

Why It's Okay to Plant Melons Next to Cucumbers or Squash. *Gardeners who watch bees visit squash flowers and then melon flowers sometimes fear that cross-pollination will affect the sweetness of the fruit, but it has no effect. The flesh of the melon will be just as sweet and the texture of the squash will be just as true as if they were self-pollinated. What is affected is the seed. Do not save the seeds, as the next generation of plants from this mixed parentage will be totally unpredictable.*

irrigations is to watch how grass looks and acts. When grass blades fail to spring back after you step on them, that's a sign it's time to water. Set the sprinkler schedule accordingly. Minimize fungus problems in coastal zones by setting sprinklers to water in the early-morning hours, before dawn if possible. In the desert and hot, dry interior regions, set sprinklers to irrigate in the evening after dark, thus saving water.

VEGETABLE GARDENING

Irrigate and Fertilize Summer Crops. Summer vegetables grow fast this month, and watering is the most important task. Vegetables aren't drought resistant—they need plenty of water, but you can cut down on the amount you use by installing drip irrigation. Raised beds also reduce the amount of irrigation vegetables need, as does the no-dig system of gardening described on page 135. Plan your system now, and switch to it before fall planting. Short-day onions, such as 'Grano' or 'Granex', are the exception to steady watering that most crops need in May. As soon as these sweet onions begin to expand into sizeable bulbs in late April or early May, you can begin harvesting big ones as you need them for cooking and to slice for sandwiches throughout the month. Don't take more than you need, so the others can continue to grow and cure. When necks weaken and they begin to fall over, usually by month's end, stop watering to let them cure. (I accomplish this by pulling the drip line for each row of onions out of the header and plugging the hole in the header with a "goof plug.") Don't worry if some necks don't fall over, and don't knock them over, as some books say to do. Dig up the remainder when the tops die, which should happen during the first week or two of June. If any crop shows signs of slowing, side-dress the row with organic vegetable fertilizer, following package directions. But don't overfertilize beans or tomatoes with nitrogen, or you'll risk encouraging leafy growth at the expense of harvest. (If you've already done that by mistake, soak the ground with Tiger Bloom (2-8-4) or Earth Juice Bloom (0-3-1) to stimulate flowering.) Don't use high-bloom fertilizers except occasionally to stimulate flowering. They are useful for this purpose, but plants need nitrogen to grow. I once met a misguided gardener who fed everything in the garden with Super Bloom (0-10-10), a synthetic liquid fertilizer containing no nitrogen. The result was sick, stunted plants with small leaves. Even the flowers were small. (For an explanation of fertilizers, see "What You Need to Know First," page 24.)

Continue to Plant. For continuous crops of vegetables, keep planting summer crops in whatever spaces you may have. By staggering plantings, you'll get longer harvests and more manageable quantities. All the vegetables for summer plus the ones that can be planted year-round can be put in now, including beets, carrots, chayote, corn, cucumbers, eggplant, green beans, leaf lettuce, lima beans, melons, New Zealand spinach, peppers, pumpkins, radishes, summer squash, winter squash, Swiss chard, tomatoes, and turnips, as well as many herbs.

Harvest Regularly. Once beans and squash begin to bear, pick them daily to keep them coming. Picking vegetables is a type of pruning, like deadheading flowers to keep them blooming. Most crops, including root vegetables, should be harvested when young and tender. Hunt for zucchinis daily, or you'll be tripping over giants as big as blimps. Eat the little ones flowers and all. Some oversized zucchini are

Dwarf Citrus Harvest Times for Year-Round Fruit

Most citrus trees for home garden use are "dwarf." But there are no truly dwarf citrus varieties. When a citrus tree is called "dwarf," it simply means that a full-size variety has been grafted onto a dwarf rooting stock, such as trifoliate orange, *Poncirus trifoliate*, or 'Hiryu' ('Flying Dragon'). Dwarf citrus trees are good choices for home gardens, and by selecting the right varieties according to their harvest times, you can have year-round fruit. Here are good choices:

Winter
'Robertson' navel orange
'Owari' satsuma and 'Clementine' tangerines
'Rangpur' lime

Winter and Spring
'Ruby Pink' and 'Marsh' seedless grapefruits

Spring
'Kinnow' tangerine
'Sampson' tangelo
'Shamouti' orange

Late Spring
'Nagami' kumquat

Spring through Summer
'Kara' tangerine

Late Spring through Summer
'Minneola' tangelo

Summer
'Summernavel' and 'Valencia' oranges

All Year
'Eureka', 'Lisbon', and 'Improved Meyer' lemons
'Bearss Seedless' and 'Mexican' limes
'Eustis' limequat

good for nothing but laughs, but if you catch them in time, they're delicious sliced, breaded, and fried, or in cold zucchini soup.

Pick herbs to keep them in bounds, and plant more to discourage pests. (There's little reliable research on the value of herbs as pest traps or pest repellents, but many home gardeners find that planting herbs among their vegetables creates a more pest-free garden.) Among herbs to plant or replace now is parsley. If you planted a row last year, it will probably go to seed now because it's biennial. Pull it up (don't throw away the roots; cook them in soup), and plant a new row in another spot. You may also want to leave a few plants in the ground, as I do, to go to flower and eventually to seed. The flowers attract beneficial insects. The seeds often sprout and grow new plants.

Care for Tomatoes. Continue to tie up tomatoes growing on stakes and trellises (as described on page 143). Except on cage-grown plants, pinch out the suckers to maintain one or two main trunks per plant, according to your preference. After indeterminate tomatoes (the ones that keep growing and bearing until they're cut down by cold weather) reach the top of 8-foot stakes, stop pinching out the suckers, and tie bamboo or wooden stakes horizontally overhead between the vertical stakes to hold up

flopping vines. (Determinate varieties usually don't grow this tall because they're genetically programmed to grow only to a certain height, which differs according to variety.)

A word of caution about pruning: If your tomatoes have ever suffered from early or late blight, it is better to grow them in cages or on stakes or trellises without pruning out the suckers. The disease can enter the plant through the cuts you make when you prune. (Early and late blight are discussed in detail on page 171.)

Keep the soil evenly moist in order to avoid blossom-end rot (discussed on page 250). If you want plenty of evenly shaped, big tomatoes with many seeds in them, continue to hit tomato stakes and cages with a hammer at midday, or vibrate the individual flower clusters, to increase pollination. If you prefer meaty fruit with few seeds, you can stop this practice now because warm temperatures, breezes, and insect activity will give you ample fruit anyway; if the fruit is not well pollinated, it may be somewhat strangely shaped, but it will contain fewer seeds. For best flavor, pick tomatoes when they're red and ripe.

Control Pests and Diseases. Continue to use organic methods to control pests and diseases on vegetables. Interplant with herbs to confuse the bugs. (A diverse collection of plants helps prevent pests from specializing, as they can do when only one crop is grown.) Introduce ladybugs, green lacewings, and other beneficials. Handpick bugs and caterpillars, catch slugs and snails with raised boards (as described on page 115), and go out at night with a flashlight to gather snails. (Just be sure to sing out a warning to any grub-digging skunks you might accidentally surprise.) If you feel you must spray, stick to a biodegradable insecticidal soap such as Safer, and use BT against

---

⚙ **QUICK TIP**

Enlist the Help of Scrub Jays. *Nail an empty tuna can on top of a tomato stake. Stock it with a few unshelled peanuts to attract scrub jays. They'll take the peanuts, notice the caterpillars, and come back for them.*

How to Grow a Giant Pumpkin

There's time to grow a giant pumpkin for Halloween if you plant it now.

▶ Choose a giant variety, such as 'Big Max' (it's actually a squash).

▶ Dig a hole in full sun. Add the organic matter and fertilizer prescribed for cantaloupes on page 197. Include horse manure if it's available.

▶ Build a hill of amended soil that's 18 inches wide at the base and 4 to 6 inches high. Make a small watering basin on top for starting the seeds; also make a large watering basin in amended soil on the north side for watering the mature plant. (Later arrange the vines so they grow away from the basin.)

▶ Plant four to six seeds 1 inch deep on the top of the mound. Water them daily until sprouted. When the plants are up 4 inches, choose the best one and clip off the others. Start watering deeply in the basin.

▶ Allow many fruits to reach grapefruit size. Then choose the best one—the one closest to the roots and with the thickest stem and best color, size, and shape. Clip off all the others.

▶ Feed the pumpkin monthly with a high-nitrogen fertilizer. Fill the watering basin regularly so that total water is equal to an inch of rain per day.

▶ While you can still lift your pumpkin, slip a piece of plywood under it to keep its bottom dry and protect it from rot and pests.

▶ Here's an optional step for even larger growth and contest-size fruit: Force-feed the pumpkin by means of a woolen wick that you enclose in a plastic tube. Insert one end into a gallon of milk, the other into the stem of the pumpkin. Replace milk bottles as necessary until the pumpkin stops growing (or perhaps until you hear a giant burp).

caterpillars. Don't use Spinosad against caterpillars, since it will almost surely kill bees when used in a vegetable garden, regardless of your climate zone. If you've been purchasing zucchinis or cucumbers at your local farmers' market or grocery store, you may notice that many of them contain no seeds and some have a narrow blossom end and bitter flavor as a result. This occurs because bees did not pollinate the flowers, and it may be a result of farmers using Spinosad or other products that kill bees. You don't want that to happen in your home garden. In dry interior zones, many gardeners use a floating row cover such as Reemay to protect plants from cabbage butterflies and night-flying moths. Close to the coast, floating row covers rot the leaves of vegetable plants because dew collects atop and beneath the fabric.

Many diseases can be controlled by keeping the garden clean. Cut off any diseased leaves (dip the clippers in alcohol between cuts to disinfect them), keep the ground clean, and pick up rotting fruit. Don't pick beans when the dew is on them, in order not to spread rust. And always rotate your crops: when you harvest a row, plant something different in its place. Prior to replanting, dig in some well-rotted compost and organic vegetable or all-purpose fertilizer. Water the ground and let it settle overnight.

MAY CHECKLIST

PURCHASE/PLANT

{ } Plant irises, *179*

{ } Plant canned roses, *182*

{ } Plant tropicals, *183*

{ } Plant tuberoses, *189*

{ } Transplant potted bulbs into the ground, *189*

{ } Replace cool-season bedding flowers with flowers to bloom in summer, *189*

{ } Plant zinnias and other heat-loving flowers, *190*

{ } Plant morning glories, *192*

{ } Plant warm-season lawns, *196*

{ } Continue to plant summer vegetables, *199*

{ } Plant melons, *198*

{ } Replace parsley if you haven't already done so, *200*

{ } Plant a giant pumpkin for Halloween, *201*

{ } Start perennials from seed in interior zones, *246*

{ } Purchase, plant, and transplant succulents, including cacti and euphorbias, *270*

{ } Plant cleome and nicotiana, *192*

{ } Plant perennials, *193*

{ } Plant clematis, *194*

TRIM, PRUNE, MOW, DIVIDE

{ } Stop pinching fuchsias if you did not do so last month, *124*

{ } Mow all grass lawns, *195*

{ } Thin out fruit on deciduous fruit trees, *151*

{ } Pinch dahlias back when the plant has three sets of leaves; tie the plants up as they grow, *152*

{ } Continue to pick and deadhead roses; disbud them if desired, *153*

{ } Divide and repot cymbidiums that have outgrown their containers, *179*

{ } Cut off bloom spikes from cymbidiums after flowers fade, *179*

{ } Prune camellias if you have not already done so, *181*

{ } Clean up and prune azaleas, *181*

{ } Divide and mount staghorn ferns, *186*

{ } Prune winter- and spring-flowering vines, shrubs, trees, and ground covers after they finish blooming, *187*

{ } Continue to tie up tomatoes, *200*

{ } Remove berries (seedpods) from fuchsias after flowers fall, *208*

{ } Continue to prune and train espaliers, *291*

{ } Propagate daylilies by planting their proliferates; cut off spent bloom stems, *344*

{ } Remove the seed pods from white fortnight lilies, but leave the bloom stalks on the plant; they'll bloom again, *293*

{ } Deadhead yellow fortnight lilies by cutting down entire stalks after each one has finished blooming, *293*

{ } Deadhead and cut back perennials, *193*

FERTILIZE

{ } Feed citrus trees, *63*

{ } Feed avocado trees, *81*

{ } Feed fuchsias, *208*

{ } Feed tuberous begonias, *260*

{ } Feed water lilies, *154*

{ } Fertilize corn, *168*

{ } Feed cymbidiums that have finished blooming, for growth, *257*

{ } Fertilize camellias after bloom, *181*

{ } Feed azaleas after bloom, *181*

{ } Feed roses, *182*

{ } Feed ferns, *183*

{ } Feed flowerbeds, *100*

{ } Fertilize lawns, *195*

{ } Side-dress vegetable rows with fertilizer, *198*

{ } Feed all container-grown succulents with a well-diluted complete liquid fertilizer, *270*

{ } Fertilize peppers when flowers first show, *279*

{ } Feed and water cycads, *303*

WATER

{ } As the weather becomes drier, water all garden plants regularly, *178*

{ } Wash off foliage of California native plants that do not accept summer water, *178*

{ } Water cymbidiums, *179*

{ } Water roses, *182*

{ } Water vegetables, *198*

{ } Do not water succulents, *270*

CONTROL PESTS, DISEASE, AND WEEDS

{ } Control rose pests and diseases, *92*

{ } Control mildew, *187*

{ } Control pests on vegetables, *200*

{ } Control weeds among permanent plants by mulching or cultivating, *181*

{ } Control weeds among vegetables and flowers by hand-pulling, *46*

{ } Control gophers before planting lawns, or trap them, *358, 385*

ALSO THIS MONTH

{ } Keep bamboo from running into your neighbor's garden, *127*

{ } Keep cymbidiums in semishade but ensure they get some sun, *179*

{ } Mulch camellias and azaleas, *181*

{ } Renew overgrown fern baskets, *184*

{ } Remove volunteers that are growing where they aren't wanted, *187*

{ } Pull out cool-season annuals that have finished blooming, *189*

{ } Harvest vegetables regularly, *199*

{ } Harvest bananas whenever they are ready, according to type, *302*

{ } Begin to harvest short-day onions to slice and eat raw, *388*

{ } Harvest citrus, *199*

MAY

June

THE EASYGOING MONTH

Epiphyllum
(Orchid cactus)

June is the month when we're most aware of our proximity to the ocean. As the continental air mass warms in early summer, it has a tendency to rise and pull cool oceanic air inland. There's always a chance that this year may be different, but if the weather behaves in a normal manner damp ocean air now often extends inland beyond the first range of hills, well into Zones 20 and 21. The weather forecaster's familiar "night and morning fog along the coast" often lasts all day, and even gardeners in the interior may experience some overcast.

It's an easygoing month in the garden. Most of the spring planting should be done by now, and the hot, dry days of summer haven't yet arrived. Gardeners in interior valleys face the onset of scorching heat by month's end, but early in June, except for an occasional hot spell of two or three days in the hundreds, it's still pleasant enough to garden in the middle of the day.

JUNE BLOOM

In Southern California, it's possible to have color year-round from permanent plants. If your garden lacks color now, notice what's in bloom in local gardens, botanical gardens, and nurseries. Consider adding one or two of the following plants that bloom during June:

- **Lemon Bottlebrush** (*Callistemon citrinus*). Among our finest drought-resistant small trees or shrubs, lemon bottlebrush grows slowly to 25 feet. Named cultivars have the best color and largest flowers.
- **Chinese Fringe Tree** (*Chionanthus retusus*). White flowers shaped rather like lilac blossoms cover the entire tree in June.
- **Fuchsia, Hydrangea, and Lantana.** All these are at the height of bloom in June. Fuchsias need regular water but adapt well to drip systems. Hydrangeas also need

plenty of water, but they make good container plants or choices for moist canyons with damp but well-drained soil. Lantana is one of the easiest full-sun, drought-resistant plants to grow and is a great bank cover.

- **Jacaranda with Agapanthus.** Jacaranda is a spectacular tree. Try planting white agapanthus, also in bloom now, at its feet. Or use blue agapanthus for a mirror effect—blue on the tree "reflected" on the ground as well.

- *Puya berteroana.* This spiky accent plant, drought resistant once established, has flower stalks like huge asparagus, 3 to 6 feet tall, that open to red, lavender, turquoise, and white flowers. Use puya to complement areas of cacti and succulents, in a spot where they can get slightly more water.

- **Vines.** All of the following bloom in summer and can be purchased and planted now:

    Bower vine (*Pandorea jasminoides*) is pink ('Rosea') or white ('Alba'). Protect it from wind.

    Mandevilla 'Alice du Pont' is bright pink and a good choice to espalier on an east wall.

    Violet trumpet vine (*Cytostoma callistegioides*) is easy, disease resistant, and gorgeous in its late-spring, early-summer bloom.

    Blood-red trumpet vine (*Distictis buccinatoria*) does best near the sea but can be grown in the interior, though it will suffer frost damage.

    Royal trumpet vine (*D.* 'Rivers') is a strong grower, disease resistant, with flowers ranging from mauve to royal purple.

    Vanilla trumpet vine (*D. laxiflora*) is violet fading through lavender to white.

TROPICALS AND SUBTROPICALS

Fertilize tropical and subtropical plants, according to their individual needs, during summer while they're growing. Continue to plant them except in interior valleys, where scorching days may burn their foliage if they're planted this late. Tropicals and subtropicals give us our distinctively Southern California atmosphere, and not all are great water users—some are drought resistant.

Among the numerous tropical and subtropical plants that like to be planted in June (in all but the hottest interior zones) are bougainvillea, gardenia, ginger, hibiscus, Natal plum, palms, tree ferns, and many flowering trees, such as cassias, coral trees, crape myrtle (*Lagerstroemia indica*), Floss silk tree (*Chorisia speciosa*), golden trumpet tree (*Tabebuia chrysotricha*), pink trumpet tree (*T. heterophylla*), and orchid trees (*Bauhinia*).

Also plant blue hibiscus (*Alyogyne huegelii*), a splendid dry-climate shrub from Australia with eye-catching bright blue flowers that bloom on and off year-round in full sun. Plant it in your hottest spot or it won't bloom. It's widely available either in its natural shrub form or as a standard, with a 3- to 4-foot trunk. The only fault of blue hibiscus is that it's rangy and open and doesn't branch freely. You can remedy this and also keep the plant blooming if, once a month from spring to fall, you cut back two or three of its longest branches by half or two-thirds their length.

Other choices to plant now include tropical fruit trees, such as avocado, banana, cherimoya, citrus, pineapple guava, and white sapote. (As mentioned in other chapters, some of these species can be planted happily at other times as well.) In most areas—other than the warmest

How to Plant a Bougainvillea and Get It Growing

Bougainvilleas are drought resistant, free from pests and disease, romantic, glowingly colorful, and easy to grow—but not easy to plant or get started. Use them as large ground covers on banks and have them pouring over walls, roots, fences, and arbors. Here's how to plant them.

▸ Choose plants with the color, eventual size, and growth habit you desire. Some are vines and some shrubs. Some are more vigorous than others. Five-gallon sizes make a faster start in the ground than 1-gallon sizes do.

▸ Choose a spot in full sun, preferably where the root run—the area where the roots grow—is also hit by full sun. (In the desert and hot interior valleys bougainvilleas will bloom in light shade.)

▸ Dig a hole twice as wide and the same depth as the container. Loosen the soil in the bottom of the hole, and work in 2 or 3 cupfuls of bone meal. (If the soil is heavy clay, also work in gypsum.) Cover this with enough soil so that when you set in the plant, the top of the root ball will be level with the surrounding ground. Add slow-release organic fertilizer packets, such as Happy Naturals Organics' (3.5-3.5-3.5), or make your own by neatly folding ¼ cup of all-purpose organic fertilizer inside one-quarter sheet of newspaper and sealing with paper tape. Distribute 4 packets around the outer edges of the bottom of the planting hole.

▸ Bougainvilleas are fragile when young and often killed when they're planted because their roots and crown are broken. Turn the plant on its side. With sharp pruning shears,

cut around the bottom of the container and look to see whether it's well rooted. If it is, slip the plant out sideways by pushing from the bottom. Lower it carefully into the hole while supporting the roots with your hands. Backfill with native soil.

▸ Press the soil down around the plant with your hands. The top of the root ball should be even with the surrounding ground.

▸ Make a watering basin, and water deeply right away. Then, in fast-draining soils, water once a day for three days; for the next two weeks water three times a week; and for the following month water twice a week. Thereafter, for the first three years, water once a week. In clay soils you should water enough to keep the root ball damp but not soggy for the first three weeks to a month. Thereafter, water deeply after the ground dries out. (Bougainvilleas are drought resistant not because they don't need water, but because their roots extend into the ground until they find an underground water source. When young they take all the water they can get, as long as drainage is adequate.)

▸ For the first three years after planting, fertilize bougainvilleas once a month between April and August. After three to five years you can stop fertilizing in summer, stop watering in winter, and reduce the frequency of summer watering to once a month or every six weeks—or perhaps never, depending on placement and variety. (Container-grown vines will always need regular fertilizer and water.)

interior valleys—the early-summer weather stimulates growth but isn't yet hot enough to dry them out. Keep them well watered until established.

MORNING GLORIES

Perennial morning glory, more correctly called blue dawn flower (*Ipomoea indica*), gets started rapidly when planted now. Grow this vine in full sun and in ordinary or poor soil, with no nitrogen fertilizer added. Water regularly to get the plants started; then irrigate occasionally thereafter. These vines are invasive, drought resistant, and permanent once established. Use morning glories for an old-fashioned, colorful, countrified look and to camouflage chain-link fences. They're not for formal gardens but can be an eye-catching ornament in the right spot and in old neighborhoods, sometimes clambering into trees and covering neglected hedges.

BEARDED IRISES

If your irises don't bloom, they're either growing in too much shade or they need dividing. (They need full sun along the coast and six hours of daily sun in the interior.) After bearded irises have been in the ground for three or four years, they become crowded: Their roots intertwine, the clumps rise ever higher out of the ground, and if they're not divided they'll stop blooming. In coastal zones, divide irises as soon as flowering is finished, in June. If you don't finish the job in June, you can continue into July in most areas. In the hottest interior valleys wait until October. Sometimes, in old gardens, irises have been neglected for years and it's a big job to divide them.

FUCHSIAS

Fuchsias should be covered with a blanket of bloom this month. Feed them often with a balanced fertilizer that's high in nitrogen as well as bloom ingredients, such as fish emulsion or your own mix or a balanced organic product that will stimulate growth as well as bloom. When the individual flowers of most fuchsia varieties fade they fall off the plant, but they leave their seedpods still attached to the branch. Pinch off these seedpods—or berries, as they're often called—daily if possible, after the flowers fall. This keeps the plants blooming. If you don't have time for removing seedpods, grow single varieties, which are self-cleaning, such as 'Ballerina Blau', 'Belle of Salem', 'Display', 'Gartenmeister Bonstedt', 'Nonpareil', 'Orange Drops', or 'Red Spider' rather than double varieties. (The top four, often upward curving, petal-like parts of fuchsias are called the "sepals." The true petals hang down in the center and are called the "corolla." Varieties with five or six petals in the corolla are considered single. Flowers with big, fluffy, many-petaled corollas are double.)

Water fuchsias regularly to prevent them from drying out, but don't overwater. Soggy soil can lead to root rot, fuchsias' worst bugaboo. Be on the lookout for pests, and spray if necessary with BT for cabbage loopers.

In my garden I control all other pests on fuchsias by beginning to place garden spiders, ladybugs, and lacewings onto them in spring. People often ask me why my fuchsias don't have whiteflies. The answer is that I release beneficial insects, locate them in places with the right light for fuchsias, and provide adequate fertilizer and daily automatic watering with a drip system leading to a minispray head hidden over each basket. Spraying against

PREVIOUS PAGE *Orange flowers have extra pizzaz when seen against a background of lavender or gray as proved by this California poppy (Eschscholzia californica) naturalizing next to the old fashioned, drought-resistant Mediterranean plant, Dusty miller (Senecio cineraria).*

LEFT *Supported by a wooden trellis and cascading over a red tile roof bougainvillea 'Camarillo Fiesta' shows off at its stunning best in this warm, south-facing location with plenty of reflected heat. Next to the weathered front door, a potted* Mandevilla splendens *'Red Riding Hood' echoes the hot color scheme and blooms nonstop, year-round. (Design by Brian Capon and Don Terwilliger.)*

ABOVE *A stucco-covered, concrete-block retaining wall next to the sidewalk transforms a steep bank into a flat terrace that makes plant care easier, saves water, prevents runoff, and showcases a wide array of drought-resistant plants, including (clockwise from foreground),* Senecio mandraliscae, Euphorbia tirucalli *'Sticks-on-Fire',* Sedum ssp., Aloe striata, *tea tree (*Leptospermum scoparium *'Crimson Glory'), bougainvillea 'Camarillo Fiesta', river stars (*Gomphostigma virgatum*), and* Aloe plicatilis. *(Design by Brian Capon and Don Terwilliger.)*

LEFT *This spectacular spring show makes use of winter and spring rains. (Clockwise from foreground: lacy phacelia (*Phacelia tanacetafolia*), scarlet flax (*Linum grandiflorum 'Rubrum'*), California poppy (*Eschscholzia californica*), Madeira geranium (*Geranium maderense*), Shirley poppy (*Papaver rhoeas*). Background plants, left to right: Rosa 'Grusse en Aachen', Rosa 'America', yellow daylilies, paludosum daisies (*Chrysanthemum paludosum*).*

TOP RIGHT *Sea holly (*Eryngium amethystinum*) is easy to plant from seeds and similar to Miss Wilmott's Ghost, but more successful in our climate and uses less water.*

BOTTOM RIGHT *To create this display in late February, I purchased bulbs of King Alfred daffodil and corms of giant Dutch hyacinths in September. I planted the daffodils in November (as described on page 375), but chilled the hyacinths in the refrigerator for 6 weeks before planting them in late December (as described on page 397.) Pony packs of Iceland poppies planted in October bloomed all winter and spring.*

LEFT *Climber 'Joseph's Coat' provides a whole color scheme in one rose and shows up well against a solid green background of star jasmine (*Trachelospermum jasminoides*) and Victorian box (*Pittosporum undulatum*) with easy-care sea lavender (*Limonium perezii*), for contrast.*

ABOVE *Caught in a ray of evening light and exuding charm and fragrance, the David Austin English rose 'Abraham Darby' grows well in coastal or inland zones and works well when trained upright like a small climber on an iron, obelisk-shaped tuteur.*

ABOVE *Thousands flock to Descanso Gardens in La Cañada every spring to view the magnificent annual display of tulips, here captured at the height of bloom in early April. To grow them in gardens, refrigerate the corms for six weeks prior to planting in late December or early January; they begin blooming in February along the coast, March inland. In the background, is a drift of hybrid St. Brigid, poppy-flowered anemones. Low growing garden verbena (*Verbena x hybrida*) makes a good bulb cover.*

RIGHT *Iceland poppies are easy to grow from transplants, not from seeds. Plant them from pony packs in October, fertilize often, and water when rains are inadequate; they will bloom for seven months throughout winter and spring. The hairy leaf on the left is borage, an herb that seeds itself every fall in my garden. I use its blue flowers on salads. Baby snapdragons (*Linaria moroccana 'Northern Lights'*) grew from seeds tossed on the bed in November.*

LEFT *A basket of just-harvested vegetables in my summer garden includes 'Celebrity' tomatoes, 'Royal Burgundy' purple beans, 'Patty Pan' white squash, 'Hungarian Yellow Wax' peppers, 'Kentucky Wonder' green beans, and 'Japanese Burpless' cucumbers. In the background are dwarf zinnias.*

ABOVE, TOP LEFT *By hunting in catalogs for good seed varieties like All America Award winner, 'Peter Pan Hybrid' you can grow vegetables with superior flavor. 'Peter Pan' is meaty, never watery, and easy to grow from seeds. Harvest some flowers at the stage shown in the photo; they're delicious stuffed with feta cheese and sautéed.*

ABOVE, BOTTOM LEFT *I plant my peas in two rows providing them with a stout support of metal posts and wire hardware cloth and protecting them on each side of the row with an A-frame house of bird netting (as described on p. 329). On the right is Mammoth Melting Sugar Pod, a Chinese-type pea, and on the left is Snappy, a mildew-resistant snap pea that you eat, pod and all, when the peas inside the pod are plump. The lettuce in the center row is large enough now to begin harvesting the outer leaves or taking whole heads if desired.*

ABOVE, RIGHT *Edging the kitchen garden with flowers and using handmade supports can transform a ho-hum vegetable patch into an artistic creation. Here are summer vegetables shortly after planting, with paths mulched, tomatoes supported by wooden obelisks, and cucumbers climbing a trellis of bamboo.*

TOP LEFT *When a small white curd begins to grow at the base of cauliflower leaves, as seen here, then tie up the leaves to shade (blanch) the curd, as I've done to the plant in the background.*

BOTTOM LEFT *After you tie up cauliflower as shown here (described on page 76) to blanch the head, be sure to untie the leaves once a day to peek inside. Cauliflower expands rapidly and is often ready within a week of first blanching.*

ABOVE *Once a head of cauliflower has filled out and the edges of the flower have barely begun to loosen up, harvest it by cutting it off just beneath the flower, as described on page 76. Pull up and compost the remains of the plant. (A head that has loosened up too much will taste "ricey.")*

LEFT *Anna apples in summer, including a bright red one that's ready to pick and eat, on a young espaliered tree on a south-facing fence in my garden. (An east-facing fence or wall is better in interior zones.) Espaliered fruit trees are attractive, space saving, and practical; branches trained horizontally produce more fruiting spurs. Anna often provides two crops per year and performs best with a pollinator (as discussed on page 50).*

ABOVE *The best cantaloupe variety for coastal zones is 'Ambrosia' melon, growing here over black plastic mulch to increase warmth. When cantaloupes look like this, stop watering them and they'll be sweeter. Harvest at full slip, described on page 281.*

ABOVE *The color scheme I call "Sun Colors" uses all the colors of sunshine—many shades of red, orange, yellow, and pink and adding white for the clouds and blue for sky. By carefully selecting cinerarias, ranunculus, marguerites, geraniums, pansy, and kalanchoe in these colors Jack and Louise Tyler created a prize-winning arrangement of pots for their Coronado Island home.*

RIGHT *California lilac, Ceonothus 'Joyce Coulter' attracts bees and birds and makes a fine bank cover. It's well adapted to growing in gardens, withstands heavy soil and pruning, and can take some summer irrigation.*

LEFT *In Lani Freymiller's garden, a mulched area under a California sycamore serves as an informal patio much used by a little group of friends who enjoy painting in each other's gardens. Plants, clockwise from foreground, include: White hydrangeas (*Hydrangea macrophylla*), variegated hydrangeas (*H. macrophylla 'Variegata'*), Pelargonium 'Gerald Porter', montbretia (*Crocosmia crocosmiiflora*), Rosa 'Iceberg', skyflower (*Duranta erecta 'Geisha Girl'*), and low hedges of boxleaf euonymus (*Euonymus japonicus 'Microphyllus'*).*

ABOVE *Azalea 'Red Wing' is a Brooks Hybrid azalea. Brooks Hybrids were bred in Modesto, California, for heat and drought tolerance, large flowers, and compact form. This one has thrived in semishade on a north-facing bank for over twenty years, with its roots mulched with pine needles and watered by a drip system.*

ABOVE *In the garden of Greene and Greene's iconic Gamble house in Pasadena, Eulalia or silver grass (*Miscanthus *'Morning Light') demonstrates that evening light is as good as morning to create a magical effect, especially against a background of Mexican sage (*Salvia leucantha*), as seen here. (Cut back ornamental grasses after bloom as described on page 327.)*

ABOVE, LEFT *In a handsome Pasadena garden designed by Chris Rosmini and filled with Mediterranean-climate plants, this elegant, bird-attracting fountain provides cool air, pleasing sound, and water circulation for the fish beneath.*

ABOVE, TOP RIGHT *A secluded pond filled with tadpoles, frogs, and fish creates an enchanted world in Lani Freymiller's garden of many rooms.*

ABOVE, BOTTOM RIGHT *The edges of Laurie Connable's garden pond in Poway go straight down for 2 feet or more around the edges (as described on page 157) in order to discourage the local raccoon family from using it as a swimming pool. This pond is correctly located in full sun with all necessary shade provided by water plants.*

ABOVE *Chinese wisteria (W. sinensis 'Cooke's Special'), highly drought-resistant once established, took about two years to cover this pergola. Notice how I trained all growth straight down the top of the pergola and how I am continuing to train young twiners on the left all in counterclockwise direction up the post, instead of allowing a rat's nest of growth to form. Once wisteria has covered its support, cut all new sprouts in summer back to two buds. This encourages more flower-bearing spur wood to grow, all the way to the ground, if you wish, as shown here and explained on page 188.*

RIGHT *Flame vine* (Pyrostegia venusta), *a native of Brazil that blooms in winter, is reputed to be at its spectacular best in full sun and in the hottest spots, but its sheets of orange flowers here provide a magnificent ornament a few blocks from the sea. Inland it needs an average amount of summer water, but along the coast very old and deeply rooted vines have been known to survive on groundwater alone.*

ABOVE *This well-designed drought-resistant suc-culent garden is near Silver Lake in Los Angeles. (Front to back: echeveria hybrids,* Senecio mandraliscae, *golden barrel cacti (*Echinocactus grusonii*), and* Agave desmettiana *'Variegata'.)*

RIGHT *Chalk dudleya (*Dudleya pulverulenta*) is native to our coastal scrub and chaparral where it likes some shade and often grows on steep cliff faces and rocky ground. In gardens, plant it next to rocks. It comes to life in fall, flourishes through winter and spring, but detests summer irrigation.*

PREVIOUS PAGE *Since the earliest days of gardening in California, cacti have been used as barrier plants, so if there is a section of ground you really wish people, dogs, or wild animals would leave alone, consider installing some well-chosen cacti, such as this handsome drift of golden barrel cactus (Echinocactus grusonii) combined with rocks. Your problems will be over.*

LEFT *On a dry roadside bank within a block of my home an old flame eucalyptus (Eucalyptus ficifolia) gets little water or care, but every year in late July and early August bursts into magnificent bloom. If you have a similar place for this tree, generations of people to come will be thanking you.*

TOP *In a sunny location with little or no irrigation, Brazilian flamebush (Calliandra tweedii) is a shrub or small tree that makes a stunning accent for a dry garden. Ferny foliage lights up in spring and fall—or all winter if warm enough—with bright scarlet blossoms bringing hummingbirds.*

ABOVE *Pink powder puff (Calliandra haematocephala) is a natural espalier graced with spectacular bloom from fall to spring. It's an elegant plant for sunny entryways, where you can often clip off the faded flowers to keep it looking its best.*

LEFT COLUMN FROM TOP *For many years I used this 12' x 10' raised bed for growing wildflowers as described on page 354. Here is the bed (top) in November after the soil has been tilled and amended, with the drip lines on top. (The stepping-stones make it possible to care for the bed without compacting garden soil.)*

To grow wildflowers this way, bury drip lines, sprinkle seeds onto the bed, rake the seeds lightly into the ground, and then push pea stakes (twigs cut from shrubbery) into the ground and cover the pea stakes *with bird netting, weighing down the edges with rocks to keep out animals and birds.*

By the time wildflowers are up 4 inches, the birds won't bother them. Keep skunks out by wrapping the long thorny rose canes around the raised bed.

Wildflowers can be grown for spring bloom or almost year-round. When planting for spring only, I replace them with summer vegetables or flowers, such as Benary's Giant Zinnia, shown here (bottom) growing from seeds planted in May, as described on page 191.

ABOVE *Here is the display in April, a riot of California poppies and scarlet flax that have totally hidden the pea stakes. The white flowers around the edge are sweet alyssum and paludosum daisies that self-seed every year (as described on page 100.) Clockwise from birdbath: paludosum daisy (Chrysanthemum paludosum), Scarlet flax (Linum grandiflorum 'Rubrum'), California poppy, borage, and Madeira geranium (Geranium maderense).*

NEXT PAGE *Pride of Madeira (Echium candicans) holds steep ground and provides dramatic spring bloom on large, drought-resistant, sunny banks. Perfectly adapted to our climate, it survives with little or no irrigation, and produces seedlings, but never too many. For a magnificent large-scale bank cover, combine it with red bougainvillea 'La Jolla'.*

How to Divide Irises

▸ With a garden fork dig up an entire clump, shake off excess soil from the roots, and then squirt it with a hose to wash all soil from the rhizomes. (A rhizome is a thickened stem that grows horizontally underground or on the surface of the ground.)

▸ Using a sharp knife, from the outside of the clump cut vigorous, healthy divisions. Each division for planting should have one fan of leaves, a section of young, healthy rhizome approximately 2 to 6 inches long, and some roots coming out the bottom. It may also have one or two new growth buds, or eyes, bulging out on the sides.

▸ Discard the following: the old, woody center of the clump that has no leaves, anything that is diseased or rotted or has been attacked by pests, any thin or spindly growth, and all immature rhizomes with no leaves.

▸ Cut off the tops of the fans at a neat right angle, with the center point 4 inches higher and the sides 2 to 3 inches higher than the rhizome.

▸ Cut back the roots by about one-third and allow them to dry and callus off in the sun for two or three hours.

▸ Dig up the bed or prepare individual planting areas, in full sun along the coast or where there's six hours of sun inland. Work in compost and bone meal.

▸ Replant the rhizomes on the same day, three to a clump, with the leaves pointing out from the center. Irises keep growing in the direction of each fan of leaves. On hillsides plant them with the bare rhizomes pointing downhill and the leafy part pointing up hill.

▸ For each rhizome use a trowel or small spade to dig a hole approximately 4 inches deep and 8 inches wide. Make an elongated mound in the planting hole. Arrange the roots over the mound with the rhizome resting on top so that the top of the rhizome is level with the surrounding soil. If the roots bend on the bottom, dig the hole deeper. Cover the roots with soil and press it down firmly with your hands. When you're finished, the top of the rhizome should still be level with the surface of the soil.

▸ Water the bed thoroughly after planting and keep it damp, but not soggy, until the plants are rooted.

whiteflies is a two-edged sword: You kill the beneficials and don't control the whiteflies (see the detailed discussion on page 125).

Visit nurseries to pick out new fuchsia varieties this month, and you'll have a whole summer and fall to enjoy them. Choose them according to the environment you'll provide. White and pastel colors usually need more shade. Reds, purples, and small single varieties

usually can take more sun. No fuchsia can bloom in solid shade; all need partial sun, such as under lath, shade cloth, or an open tree. In interior zones concentrate on growing heat-resistant varieties such as 'Angel's Earrings', 'Bonanza', 'California', 'Carnival', 'Checkerboard', 'Display', 'Papoose', and 'Swingtime'. Such upright varieties as 'Gartenmeister Bonstedt' are best in the ground or tubs. Trailers, such as 'Lisa' and "Pink Galore', are best in hanging baskets. Some, like 'Swingtime', one of the easiest fuchsias to grow, can go either way.

EPIPHYLLUM CACTUS AND CYMBIDIUM ORCHIDS

Some epiphyllums (orchid cacti) are still in bloom, so it's not too late to choose these undemanding and dramatic plants at nurseries. After they finish blooming, prune off diseased and desiccated branches and feed them occasionally with a weak balanced formula, such as fish emulsion. Keep them in semishade.

Prune off ungainly branches and root them to make new plants (see directions in the box on page 149). For a faster start, root four cuttings of the same variety in one 6-inch plastic container. (Never mix two varieties in the same container. The more vigorous one will soon crowd out the other, and you'll lose a prized color.) Pruning stimulates growth more than fertilizer alone, so if you desire to hasten growth of a sluggish variety, cut off all unsightly branches and feed it often. If you want to keep plants the same size, however, don't prune them too much and never overfeed with nitrogen.

June is also your last chance for dividing cymbidium orchids. Do the job this month or wait until next year, otherwise you will get no flowers. (See page 180 for instructions.)

GARDENIAS

Gardenias (*Gardenia augusta*, *G.* jasminiodes) are among our most-grown and least-understood plants. They're often put in the wrong spots, such as small, shady patios, where they invariably get whiteflies. Wrong locations can also cause bud drop, especially in warm coastal zones. Gardenias need acid soil, good drainage, adequate moisture, full sun along the coast or part shade inland, protection from thrips, and also regular fertilizing for growth and flowering with an acid-type product that contains trace elements to prevent chlorosis. However, you can meet all these requirements and still have gardenias that drop buds instead of blooming. The reason is that if night temperatures get over 60° to 62°F, the buds won't develop. They'll stay on the plant but won't grow. Then if suddenly a few cool nights occur, they'll all drop off. So don't grow gardenias where they'll be subjected to warm night temperatures—for example, on patios or porches or close to house walls. Put them where temperatures are colder at night—away from the house and out under the open sky; with the daily temperature spread they'll bloom.

Summer is the time to choose and plant gardenias. It's tempting to grab the first heady-scented beauty one sees, but instead, choose a good variety that will fit your needs, and then read the tag to make sure it's grafted. Gardenias that have been grafted onto strong, disease-resistant rootstocks are light years ahead of cheaper plants growing on their own roots. Choice large-flowered varieties include old-fashioned, 6- to 8-foot 'Mystery'; long blooming, 6-foot, double 'Miami Supreme'; and hardy, 4-foot high and wide 'Chuck Hayes'. There are many other choices including dwarf plants, and a wide range of flower sizes and times of bloom. Fine growers, including Monrovia Nursery, graft several choice varieties onto the roots of the sturdy South African gardenia (*G. thunbergia*), which is resistant to root rot. This, too, is a good garden plant if you can find it and bears single 4-inch fragrant flowers in winter. It's easy to grow in frost-free zones. Old ones are sometimes pruned like small trees.

DECIDUOUS FRUIT TREES

Do the last thinning on deciduous fruit trees after June drop has occurred. June drop is nature's way of getting rid of an overload of fruit. It may occur at any time between early May and July but is most likely to happen around the first of June. One day you visit your apple, peach, or apricot tree and find a circle of immature fruit lying on the ground under the branches. These trees often set more than twice the amount of fruit they could possibly ripen properly, so they simply drop off part of it.

If you followed the advice for April and thinned out the fruit on your trees then and again four to six weeks later, you enabled the remaining fruit to grow larger—and thus less fruit will drop off now. Nevertheless, you may need to remove even more fruit than naturally drops in order to space your crop evenly down the branches. Inspect other deciduous fruit trees that are less subject to June drop—plums, for instance—and thin out their fruits also.

Clean up the fallen fruit under the tree before it has time to rot and spread disease. If it's healthy, chop it and add it to the compost pile (cover it with earth to protect against flies and rodents). Also water deciduous fruit trees well in June and July.

ROSES

Continue pruning, spraying, irrigating, and fertilizing roses as you did during the month of May (follow the chart on page 418 and explanations on pages 91 and 118).

You can plant canned roses now, but be sure to purchase them from a reputable nursery. Canned roses may harbor rose pests whose larvae live in the soil under the rose. The safest way to buy roses is bare-root.

SHRUB DAISIES

Two groups of shrub daisies, marguerite and euryops, are often sold side by side in nurseries. Because of their similarities, these plants are frequently confused, but they actually have different characteristics and needs. Marguerites are shorter lived than euryops, they need ample water, and will die if you cut them back too hard. Euryops are long-lived, highly drought resistant, and will sprout new growth even if you cut them back into hard wood. Now is the time to prune both.

Marguerites. For many years gardeners have grown and loved marguerite daisies, a flowering shrub native to the Canary Islands and Madeira, in the Atlantic Ocean. About ten years ago taxonomists changed the botanical name of marguerite from the familiar *Chrysanthemum frutescens* to *Argyranthemum frutescens*, because marguerites differ genetically from chrysanthemums. Botanists sent up a hue and cry, so now the international experts have switched the name back again. By whatever name you call them, newer hybrid marguerites (*C. frutescens*) are a great improvement over the old ones. New varieties come in dwarf, compact, or tall sizes; single, double, or semidouble flowers; and many shades of white, yellow, pink, and red. They're more heat resistant and drought resistant, and less likely to die if accidentally cut back too hard, but still bloom most heavily in spring and need midday shade inland and full sun in coastal zones. Deadhead marguerites often to keep them blooming, though some varieties like 'Moliba Helio White' will keep right on blooming even if you don't. All need regular irrigation, will live longer in coastal zones than inland, and make excellent container plants. If all the flowers on your marguerites go dead at once in June, give them a butch haircut by shearing the top of the plant into a rounded shape, cutting off all the flowers and an inch or two of foliage. Don't cut a marguerite back hard into old bare wood or it may die. Follow up with organic fertilizer for flowering plants, water thoroughly, and it will soon bounce back.

Euryops. Euryops are yellow shrub daisies native to South Africa. They're much more drought resistant than marguerites. Also, euryops have dormant buds hidden under their bark all the way to the ground. This means you can, if you wish, prune them hard, into old bare wood, and they'll grow back, though it's always best to leave a bit of foliage on each branch. Follow up with water and fertilizer. Two euryops cultivars are widely grown in Southern California. Both can withstand drought but need some irrigation for best appearance. One has gray foliage and bright lemon yellow flowers with narrow petals: *Euryops pectinatus*, which blooms mainly in fall, winter, and spring. Cut back this type in June after bloom. Shear the plants all over with hedge shears. Remove dead flowers and 3 to 4 inches of tip growth to shape and renew the plant.

The other most commonly grown cultivar is green-gold euryops (*E. pectinatus* 'Viridis'). This has golden yellow flowers, wider petals, and dark green foliage. It blooms year-round but a little less in summer than in the cooler months. It can be pruned, if necessary, at any time of year, but now's the best time to shear and shape it.

ANNUAL AND PERENNIAL FLOWERS

Annuals. It's a little late for planting seed for summer annuals, but there's no rule against it. You'll simply get a shorter season of color than if you'd planted earlier. Seeds will sprout fast now. So if you've just moved into a new home with oceans of bedding space to fill but no money for transplants, planting from seeds is the way to go. Just don't skimp on soil prep.

Annuals that can be planted from seeds now include anchusa, coleus, cosmos, lobelia, marigold, portulaca, sunflower, sweet alyssum, and zinnia. For the fastest and easiest results choose zinnias and marigolds, perhaps with an edging of sweet alyssum. Dwarf sunflowers are equally easy and even faster to grow, though the splash of color they give you is soon gone. They're worth growing simply because people find them so amusing. (Pull the plants out after their flowers fade or they'll ruin the look of your border.) In semishade, sprinkle seeds of impatiens onto well-prepared ground and blue lobelia along the edge. Don't cover them with soil. Press them into the ground with the back of your hoe. They need light in order to germinate. Keep the ground damp.

For quicker results and to fill empty spots in existing beds purchase nursery transplants. Madagascar periwinkle (vinca; *Catharanthus roseus*) is a good choice for filling bare spaces in the hottest spots in full sun. It's easy to grow and mixes well with other flowers. Cosmos is good for the backs of beds. It blooms into fall and, in coastal zones, often seeds itself so new plants bloom through winter.

Deadhead and pick summer annuals to keep them going. Keep an eye out for stem borers on zinnias. These worms enter the stem and cause the top of the plant to die and sometimes fall over. Open the stem and find and squash the worm. If the plant is high enough, it will branch and continue to bloom.

✺ QUICK TIP

Keep a Bag of Polished Pea Gravel on Hand. *Use this small-gauge ornamental gravel to mulch the bare spaces when planting between flags and stepping-stones on a terrace or walkway. (Press them down lightly so they won't be dislodged by foot traffic.)*

Perennials. Be on the alert for interesting summer-blooming perennials at your nursery. More are for sale in June than at almost any other time of year because many perennials bloom in June. Some of the best are sold only when flowers are on the plant, so now's your chance to find some treasures. But be wary of buying plants that are not right for your climate zone or the conditions in your garden. I often overhear gardeners say they prefer English garden style to any other, but if that sounds like you, why not create the atmosphere you love while using drought-resistant plants that do well here? Some of our best so-called "perennial" gardens are not English-style borders at all, but whole gardens of drought-resistant shrubs, perennials, and bulbs native to hot dry climates in our own and other countries, often intertwined with winding paths or dry stream beds. And here we don't stick with perennials that die down in winter; we freely mix in flowering shrubs like lavender and cape mallow (*Anisodontea x hypomandarum*). Thirty years ago cape mallow debuted on the garden stage with a shape like a blimp; today's examples like Anisodontea 'Elegant Lady' have larger flowers

on a compact shrub and a more graceful shape. Plant breeders eager to catch onto new trends are finding tough, water-thrifty wildflowers from dry areas of our own and other countries. Western sundrops (*Calylophus hartwegii* 'Sierra Sundrop'), and the gray-foliaged Australian strawflower (*Chrysocephalum apiculatum* 'Flambe'), for example, will smile through heat and drought in full sun. Two new pimpernels, *Anagallis monelli* 'Wildcat Blue' and *A. arvensis* 'Wildcat Orange', began life as weedy European wildflowers, but now grab center stage. Improved varieties of kangaroo paw (*Anigozanthos*) 'Big Red', 'Pink Joey', 'Harmony', or any of the 'Bush Gems Hybrids' are colorful sun-lovers from open clearings in eucalyptus forests in Australia. They're happiest in fast-draining soils and don't mind going dry between irrigations. (Mulch them, control slugs and snails, but withhold phosphorus—Aussie plants don't like it. Cut spent blooms to the ground now to encourage another long-lasting wave of bloom.)

Other heat-resistant plants available now are the self-cleaning Calibrachoa hybrids, 'Superbells' and 'Million Bells'. These need regular moisture but thrive in large patio containers. And among old staples, look for purple coneflower (*Echinacea purpurea*), *Scaevola* 'New Wonder' (best in coastal zones), *Verbena bonariensis*, and *Rudbeckia fulgida* 'Goldsturm', a superior garden variety of black-eyed Susan. *R. Laciniata* 'Hortensia' (golden glow) is difficult to find but especially useful for hot interior gardens. Its yellow flowers with yellow centers continue to bloom right through October. *Gaillardia x grandiflora* 'Yellow Queen' also isn't easy to find but worth hunting for; it blooms into September and is excellent in the interior. For shade, try the graceful meadow rue (*Thalictrum*) and *Bergenia ciliate*, but bait them for snails. 'Victoria Falls' iris is a fine repeat bloomer with tall flowers. Add charm to the garden by creating little lawns in flat areas and filling small spaces between rocks or stepping-stones with chamomile, creeping oregano (*Origanum laevigatum* and *O. vulgare* 'Compactum'), creeping thyme, pennyroyal, and *Dymondia margaretae*, a drought-resistant, dwarf, matlike relative of zinnias.

You probably fertilized all your perennials in early spring. Now it's time to clean up, deadhead, and lightly cut back plants that have bloomed or grown floppy, fertilizing them again to encourage those summer flowers. Use an all-purpose fertilizer such as the homemade formula on page 77 or a commercial organic fertilizer recommended for flowering plants, such as Dr. Earth Organic Rose and Flower Fertilizer (5-7-2). Anything further you wish to add, such as humic acid, kelp, or John and Bob's Soil Optimizer, applied according to package directions, will help your plants perform better throughout summer. If you're into generics, don't forget soft kitchen waste like fruit and vegetable peelings, which rots so quickly that instead of subtracting nitrogen from the soil, it gives off a quick—though rather smelly—shot of it. You can bury a cup or two of this sloppy waste in the bottom of any planting hole, add a little all-purpose organic fertilizer, cover it over with a handful or two of soil, and pop the plant on top. The plant will thrive and earthworms proliferate. When top-heavy plants split open in the middle or flop over to reach light, stake them with pea stakes (twiggy branches cut from Victorian box [*Pittosporum undulatum*], corkscrew willow [*Salix matsudana* 'Tortuosa'], or other shrubs. Be sure to pull willow branches out at season's end, or they'll sprout roots and before you know it you'll have an unwanted thicket.) Deadhead coreopsis by grabbing handfuls of faded flowers

and shearing them off with one-hand grass shears. For large clumps, use hedge shears. (A few buds will bite the dust, too.) Follow up with water and fertilizer; coreopsis will bounce right back with another wave of bloom. Shear off faded flowers of dianthus.

Cut back perennials that bloom in winter and early spring—for example, *Euphorbia characias wulfenii*. A good plant for gardens in which the soil goes dry between irrigations, it has blue-green foliage delightfully complemented by chartreuse flowers. Flowers are followed by long-lasting seedpods. When the pods fade and begin to look ratty with yellow stems, cut them down to the base, but leave the basal foliage—the new shoots you should see sprouting below—which will bloom with chartreuse flowers next year. Look for young euphorbia plants in nurseries now through fall, usually among the succulents.

June is the best month to start perennials from seeds in coastal zones. (Gardeners in the interior can start a month or two earlier.) Warmer temperatures help seeds sprout faster. This is an enthralling undertaking that can save money and give your green thumb the acid test, but it takes perseverance—almost a whole year of it.

First choose and purchase seeds, taking care to select plants that are recommended for your climate zone. Fill flats with sterilized soil and plant the seeds according to package directions. (Some are easy to germinate, others not.) Mist the flats to moisten them, cover them with glass or plastic, and keep them in semishade. As soon as seeds sprout, remove the cover and replace it with bird netting to protect the seedlings from birds and cats. Water regularly, and after the plants form two true leaves, start fertilizing with a weak solution of complete fertilizer or fish emulsion. As the seedlings grow, gradually move them into more light, protect them from pests and disease, transplant them into 4-inch individual containers, and pot them on throughout the year. If all goes well, by next spring or summer you'll have sturdy, gallon-size plants to go into the ground.

PEST CONTROL

Many pests are active in June. Spider mites, caterpillars, slugs, and snails are just a few of the usual pests that you are continuing to watch for now. But among the pests that seem to rear their ugly heads most avariciously this month are thrips and whiteflies. If your garden suffers from an infestation of whiteflies, you probably know it already because they're highly visible, but if it's inhabited by large population of thrips, you may be aware of the damage they're causing but not know which culprit you should blame.

Thrips. Thrips are small, slender, black, rasping insects that often step up activities in June. They're difficult to see, so be on the alert for signs of their damage—distorted flowers on marguerites, roses, and gardenias, and scratched stems and leaves on gladioli and beans. The best solution is to use organic controls that don't upset the balance of nature. These include insecticidal soaps and Summit Year-Round Spray Oil, as well as keeping a clean garden, destroying weeds, growing resistant plants, and rotating crops. Continue to introduce beneficial insects to your garden and neighborhood to control pests.

The larvae of green lacewings, available from Gardens Alive! and other sources, eat thrips. Several years ago I released lacewings in my garden, but on two occasions I put ladybugs onto infested daylilies at the first sign of damage—with surprising results. I spread the ladybugs because though their larvae prefer

aphids, they're omnivorous and will eat any small insect pests they find. One week after I released the ladybugs onto the daylilies, the live thrips were gone, but they probably were not eaten by ladybugs or even the lacewings. The tiny black thrips had indeed disappeared, but their empty white cases remained on the plant, a clue that minute pirate bugs (*Orius tristicolor*) had done the job. These tiny beneficials pierce the bodies of thrips with their pointed mouthpart and suck out their insides, leaving behind the empty exoskeletons. When you refrain from spraying, beneficial insects blown in from other places may settle down and call your garden home. Then miracles can happen right under your nose. Spreading a layer of fresh organic mulch early in the season will also help reduce the number of thrips since their larvae live in the ground and the adult thrips will have trouble emerging. Organic soils help too, by harboring beneficial nematodes and other organisms that attack the larvae of thrips and other pests in the ground. Despite these good practices, any organic garden might harbor a few thrips, but they simply become dinner for beneficial creatures already living in the garden. Once beneficials are fully established in your garden it may never be necessary to add to their numbers.

Whiteflies. Of all the pests that plague gardeners, greenhouse whiteflies (*Triaeurodes vaporariorum*) seem the most maddening. These tiny—$1/16$-inch—winged insects skulk under the leaves of favored plants and fly out in an embarrassing cloud every time someone brushes past the foliage. (The giant whitefly is different and is discussed on page 125.) Lift a leaf gently and you can see them hiding underneath. It's actually not the flying insect but their microscopic larvae that do the damage, sucking plant juices, weakening plants, and excreting a sticky honeydew that's attractive to ants. Some of whiteflies' favorite plants are tomatoes, cucumbers, mint, fuchsias, and neglected patio plants such as ferns and gardenias that grow in too much shade.

Whiteflies are bad news for gardeners who spray with chemicals because the whiteflies always win. This insect multiplies rapidly and goes through five different stages of development between egg and adult, each of which is susceptible to a different insecticide—or to none at all. Thus if you wipe out one stage, all the other stages remain to proliferate. The more a gardener sprays against greenhouse whitefly with a product such as Malathion, the more resistant this pest will become. Spraying with poisons also kills the tiny helpers that would get rid of whiteflies if only permitted to do so.

On the other hand, gardeners who follow the rules of organic gardening and refrain from spraying soon discover that greenhouse whiteflies pose no problem at all. A healthy organic garden is home to all manner of beneficial creatures including ladybugs, lacewing larvae, delphastus beetles, garden spiders, and many types of parasitic wasps, all of which are on the prowl for pests such as whiteflies. You can even purchase and release tiny encarsia wasps (*Encarsia formosa*) that specialize in killing greenhouse whiteflies. As with all beneficials, you will need to provide a welcoming environment with an absence of poisons and their residual effects. Beneficial insects also need food other than pests in order to survive. For example, parasitic wasps of many shapes and sizes lay their eggs on caterpillars. When the eggs hatch, the larvae invade the body of the caterpillar and eat it from the inside out—not a pleasant thought—but once they metamorphose into adult wasps, they live on pollen from flowers. Beneficial insects also need water from

a fountain or other water source. If you put all these steps into operation, as outlined in the accompanying list, you may never see a single whitefly in your garden again.

How to Get Rid of Greenhouse Whiteflies

▶ Grow plants in adequate light.

▶ Fertilize and water plants sufficiently.

▶ Mulch the entire garden with organic mulch.

▶ Spread earthworm castings over plant roots.

▶ Use no chemical sprays or synthetic fertilizers.

▶ Release beneficial insects in your garden.

▶ Plant pollen-bearing flowers.

▶ Install a fountain or at least a birdbath.

▶ Try to convince your neighbors not to spray.

LAWN CARE

Cool-Season Grasses. If you haven't yet reset the cutting height of your lawn mower, do it now. Cool-season lawns such as ryegrass, bluegrass, fescue, or a mix of cool-season grasses should be allowed to grow longer during the summer. Longer leaves give them more resistance to hot weather. So set the blades of your lawn mower to 3 or even 4 inches. If your lawn is an improved tall fescue, such as Medallion or Marathon I, II, or III, set the mower to its top setting, and be sure to keep the blades sharp. The **Rule of Thumb:** *Never cut off more than one-third of your lawn's height at one time.* (This rule applies to all lawns, but it's particularly important for tall fescue.)

Keep cool-season lawns well watered according to the needs of each type. From now until fall feed them lightly with a liquid fertilizer such as diluted fish emulsion, worm castings tea, or compost tea, when and if needed to maintain color. (See page 317 for how to make compost tea.)

Warm-Season Grasses. If your lawn is a warm-season grass, such as Bermuda, zoysia, or St. Augustine, start now to mow it as short as possible. Set the mower blades lower in order to cut common Bermuda to 1 inch. Cut hybrid Bermudas shorter, to 1/2 or 3/4 inch, with a reel mower. Cut zoysia and St. Augustine to between 3/4 inch and 1 inch, and cut kikuyu to 1/2 inch. Feed all warm-season grasses regularly during their growing season except for 'Adalayd' grass (*Paspalum vaginatum*; called Excalibre in sod form), which can be fed in June and July, but during the heat of August and early September, only lightly if at all. Kikuyu grass is another exception; because of its invasive qualities, don't feed it unless you notice poor color or stunted growth. Continue to water warm-season lawns deeply and as infrequently as possible while still maintaining good appearance.

Zoysia. Late spring or early summer is the best time to plant zoysia from plugs or stolons. When you plant from stolons or plugs in June, zoysia grass will take off faster and have less competition from weeds than when it is planted at any other time of year. (For fast coverage, plant stolons at the rate of 12 bushels per 1,000 square feet, double the commercial rate, or plugs spaced on 9-inch centers.)

Zoysia makes a tough, good-looking turf that's tolerant of drought, heat, salinity, and heavy foot traffic. It has few, if any, pest problems and is largely disease free, especially when grown in hot, dry interior zones. Once established it's practically immune to weeds. Newer varieties, such as 'De Anza', have finer leaf blades, a faster rate of coverage, a nice springy texture underfoot without building up thatch, and, best of all, stay green year-round.

As zoysia fills in, water it regularly for fast growth, and keep weeds pulled. Feed mature zoysia grass once every two months beginning in March and continuing through September. (Organic fertilizers applied in March won't affect the growth of zoysia until May or June, but they will contribute to an organic soil that will release nitrogen and other nutrients as soon as temperatures rise.) Use an organic fertilizer recommended for lawns such as Biosol Mix (7-2-3), chicken manure, organic commercial lawn food or a generic lawn food of your choice. Follow up with thorough irrigation. Additionally, spray the lawn in June with a product containing humic acid, yucca, and kelp, or make your own spray. (What you want is a deep green color. When lawn color declines it means time to feed.) Mow zoysia regularly to a height of 5/8 inch with a reel mower.

VEGETABLE GARDENING

By now the summer vegetable garden should be in full swing. Harvest root and leaf crops regularly while they're still young and tender. Pick the outside leaves of lettuce as needed. Pick beans and summer squash daily while they're still small, but pick tomatoes when fully ripe.

As crops reach the midpoint in their growing seasons, if you didn't do the job last month, side-dress the rows with organic fertilizer to keep them going. Most crops need additional nitrogen at some point during the growing season. Beans are an exception; don't fertilize them unless they show signs of nitrogen deficiency (slow or stunted growth), because too much nitrogen can prevent them from bearing. Beans that were inoculated at planting time need no fertilizer. Corn needs additional nitrogen and plenty of water when it starts to tassel out. The best time to side-dress tomatoes with additional nitrogen is when they start to bloom. Corn and tomatoes respond with visible results when fed with a fish emulsion like Neptune's Harvest Fish (2-4-1) or Neptune's Harvest Fish/Seaweed (2-3-1). Or use your own homemade compost or manure tea or other generic or cost-free alternatives. If you are regularly squishing snails, don't throw out their bodies; bury them under plants as a source of nitrogen, similar to whole fish.

Water regularly and deeply. Overhead watering is all right inland but must be done early in the day. Ground-level soaking or subterranean irrigation with a drip system is best in all areas. Most vegetables require the equivalent of 1 inch of rain per week. It's especially important not to let cucumbers or tomatoes dry out. Thirsty cucumbers turn bitter. Watering tomatoes unevenly can cause blossom-end rot, a black discoloration on the bottom of fruits. Overwatering tomatoes can cause root rot and wet, rotting fruit.

It's not too late to put in seeds, either to fill in for continued harvests or to plant a whole garden. As with annual flowers you'll simply get later results. Seeds that can be planted now run the gamut of summer vegetables, including corn, cucumbers, green beans, lima beans, leaf lettuce, okra, peppers, pumpkins, New Zealand spinach, summer squash, and winter squash; melons; and also the vegetables we plant year-round, such as beets, carrots, Swiss chard, radishes, and turnips. Heat lovers such as eggplant and peppers do well and grow rapidly when put in from transplants this month. For a fall crop of tomatoes, plant seeds now or put in transplants next month.

Rotate Crops. Crop rotation is important, not only because it prevents soil depletion, but also because it cuts down on pest damage. If you plant the same thing in the same place time after time, pests and fungus organisms and other diseases build up in the soil. Wireworms (the larvae of click beetles), for example, are fond of onions and carrots, and will settle down and multiply in rows where these crops are repeatedly planted. If you clear out two rows at the same time, crop rotation is easy; just switch when you replant. When you clear only one row look for the next item that's likely to be harvested and replant with that, or with something totally new and different. Branch out and try exotic vegetables you haven't tried before.

Control Vegetable Pests and Diseases. As in the ornamental garden, concentrate on keeping the garden clean and keeping an eye out for pests and disease. Also continue to introduce beneficial insects and arachnids (spiders and beneficial mites), still our best and most enlightened defense against pests. Release delphastus beetles, lacewing larvae, and ladybugs in the vegetable garden. Resist the temptation to spray, which can upset the balance of nature. Now is a great time to observe all the fascinating wild insects and spiders that are helping you. To identify them, use a book like Charles L. Hogue's *Insects of the Los Angeles Basin* or "Mac's Field Guide of Good Garden Bugs of California," a laminated sheet you can hang in the potting shed or take into the garden that shows the good bugs on one side and bad bugs on the reverse.

Don't pick beans early in the day when plants are wet with dew, because doing so can spread rust and mildew. Wait until midday or late afternoon when the vines are dry. Wash off aphids with soapy water. Handpick large bugs and beetles. If caterpillars are a problem, spray with BT or introduce beneficial wasps. Mint, basil, and dill are said to protect tomatoes from hornworm. (Confine mint to 1-gallon cans; don't let it loose in the garden. Like horseradish, it will take over.) Attract scrub jays (see the Quick Tip on page 200).

Leafhoppers on tomatoes, beans, and cucumbers spread mosaic virus diseases. Spray with insecticidal soaps or homemade sprays of onion or garlic. Personally, I never bother with homemade pesticides, preferring to rely on the balance of nature to control pests. Organically grown vegetables have a natural vigor that helps them withstand pests. Pulling weeds and cutting off brown or damaged leaves as they occur also helps control pests and disease.

Mix vegetables as much as possible and interplant them with herbs and marigolds to muddle and confuse insects. Solid plantings of anything, whether ornamental or vegetable, always get hit more severely by pest and disease problems than plants grown in a mixed landscape.

Harvest, Cure, and Braid Short-Day Onions.

Once the tops of sweet 'Grano' or 'Granex' or other globe onions die down, pull or dig them up with a garden fork, brush the soil off the roots, and spread out the onions on sheets of newspaper in a cool, shaded place for a week or two to finish curing. While the tops are still flexible and before they become paper dry, braid the onions, beginning by tying three together on the bottom, and then adding onions as you braid until you have a handsome string of them weighing 8 to 10 pounds. (If the onion tops are brittle, strengthen your braid by blending in some strands of raffia as you work.) Tie the tops and raffia into a loop on the top of each string so it's easy to hang, and suspend them from hooks in a cool, shaded place under the eaves or in the kitchen. When you need an onion, simply cut it off the string with scissors, leaving the rest in place. Mild onions don't keep as long as pungent onions, but last several months when properly cured. Cure and braid garlic the same way.

Help Strawberries Bear More Fruit.

Strawberries tend to grow vegetatively in June by sending out runners instead of blooming and bearing fruit. Clip off the runners as they occur. A shot of fish emulsion (2-4-6) now will help prolong the harvest.

Unless you're growing strawberries on plastic, keep the ground deeply mulched with pine needles or straw. Sprinkle bait underneath organic and plastic mulches against snails, slugs, and sow bugs. Sow bugs do little harm to most crops but can ruin soft fruits like strawberries. Sow bugs don't attack strawberries growing in strawberry pots, but abound in mulch. Control sow bugs by sprinkling diatomaceous earth under the mulch, but beware of the dust; it's harmful if breathed into lungs. Once diatomaceous earth gets wet, it loses its effectiveness. A better way is to apply dried earthworm castings under the mulch to repel sow bugs. Sluggo Plus is a third option; it contains Spinosad and controls earwigs, pill bugs, sow bugs, cutworms, slugs, and snails. (Keep Sluggo Plus away from flowers, including strawberry flowers visited by bees, and don't put this product near puddles or muddy ground that bees visit for a drink of water. Spinosad is highly toxic to bees.) Don't let the plants go dry now, or fruiting will stop.

JUNE CHECKLIST

PURCHASE/PLANT

{ } Continue to plant drought-resistant plants, 39, 206

{ } Continue to plant melons, 250

{ } Plant tropical and subtropical plants, 206

{ } Plant bougainvilleas, 207

{ } Plant perennial morning glories, 208

{ } Purchase fuchsias, 208

{ } Continue to purchase epiphyllums, 242

{ } Plant seeds of heat-loving annuals, 244

{ } Use bedding plants for quick color, 244

{ } Purchase perennials in bloom now at nurseries, 245

{ } Start perennials from seeds in coastal zones, 246

{ } Plant zoysia grass, 249

{ } Continue to plant summer vegetables, 250

{ } Plant exotic vegetables, 250

{ } Purchase, plant, and transplant succulents, including cacti and euphorbias, 270

{ } Purchase alstroemerias throughout summer while they are in bloom, 293

{ } Plant papayas and bananas, 301

{ } Plant and transplant palms, 302

TRIM, PRUNE, MOW, DIVIDE

{ } Continue to pick and deadhead roses, 153

{ } Pinch back chrysanthemums to make them bushy, 381

{ } Divide and repot cymbidiums that have outgrown their containers, 180

{ } Remove berries (seedpods) from fuchsias after flowers fall, 208

{ } Divide bearded irises if necessary (but wait until October in hot interior valleys), 208

{ } Prune epiphyllums, 242

{ } Thin out deciduous fruit trees after June drop, 243

{ } Give marguerites a "butch" haircut, 243

{ } Cut back euryops, 244

{ } Deadhead and pick summer flowers to keep them going, 244

{ } Mow cool-season lawns longer, 248

{ } Mow warm-season grasses short, 249

{ } Clip runners off strawberries, 251

{ } Prune climbing roses that bloom once a year in spring, but wait until flowers fade, 258

{ } Continue to prune and train espaliers, 291

{ } Continue to remove spent bloom stems from daylilies and to propagate the types that make proliferates, 293

{ } Deadhead alstroemerias often by pulling off the stalks with a sharp tug, 293

{ } Clean up, deadhead, and cut back perennials, 244

FERTILIZE

{ } Feed citrus trees, 63

{ } Look for yellow leaves and green veins indicating chlorosis in citrus, gardenias, azaleas, and others; treat it with chelated iron, 270

{ } Feed avocado trees, 81

{ } Feed fuchsias, 208

{ } Feed tuberous begonias, 260

{ } Feed bamboo with organic lawn food, 127

{ } Feed water lilies, 154

{ } Fertilize corn, 168

{ } Fertilize cymbidiums for growth, 257

{ } Give camellias their second feeding for the year, 181

{ } Fertilize roses, 182

{ } Feed ferns, 183

{ } Fertilize tropicals, 206

{ } Feed epiphyllums, 242

{ } Fertilize marguerites after pruning, 243

{ } Feed container-grown annuals and perennials with a complete fertilizer, 30

{ } Fertilize cool-season lawns lightly, 249

{ } Fertilize warm-season lawns according to type, 249

{ } Side-dress vegetable rows if you didn't do it last month, 198

{ } Give strawberries a shot of high-phosphorus fish emulsion, 251

{ } Feed all succulents growing in containers with a well-diluted complete liquid fertilizer, 270

{ } If peppers look yellow despite adequate nitrogen, spray them with Epsom salts, 279

{ } Feed cycads, 303

{ } Fertilize perennials, 102

WATER

{ } Water all plants except some well-established drought-resistant plants and some native plants, *178*

{ } Give newly planted or stressed native plants a quick spritz of water from the hose, to wet foliage but not ground, *178*

{ } Water cool-season lawns more often and shallowly, *249*

{ } Water warm-season lawns deeply and infrequently, *249*

{ } Water corn well as it tassels out, *250*

{ } Water vegetables, *250*

{ } Don't let strawberries dry out, *251*

{ } Water cyclamen occasionally, though they are semidormant now, *316*

{ } Most succulents growing in the ground need no water this month, *274*

CONTROL PESTS, DISEASE, AND WEEDS

{ } Control slugs and snails, *115*

{ } Watch chrysanthemums for pests, *247*

{ } Control rose pests and diseases, *243*

{ } Control pests on fuchsias, *208*

{ } Watch for stem borers in zinnias, *244*

{ } Control thrips and whiteflies, *247*

{ } Control pests and diseases on vegetables, *250*

{ } Protect strawberries from slugs, snails, and sow bugs, *251*

{ } Control weeds in the vegetable garden and flowerbeds by hand pulling, *46*

{ } Control weeds among permanent plants by mulching or cultivating, *181*

{ } Control mildew on tuberous begonias, *260*

{ } Protect English primroses from caterpillars, slugs, and snails, *115*

{ } Control corn earworm, *306*

ALSO THIS MONTH

{ } Hand-pollinate corn growing in small plots, *168*

{ } Prevent bud drop from gardenias, *242*

{ } Reset mower blades for cool-season lawns, *248*

{ } Harvest vegetables regularly, *249*

{ } Practice crop rotation, *250*

{ } Put bloomed-out cyclamen and English primroses in a shady spot for the summer, *261, 401*

{ } When the tops of globe onions fall over, stop watering them; allow them to cure, then harvest, eat, and store them, *386*

July

THE FIRST REAL
SUMMER MONTH

Aechmea fasciata
(Silver-vase)

In July the weather starts getting hot even along the coast, and we like to spend as much time as possible outdoors. In hot interior valleys the early morning and evening hours are the best ones for sitting, playing, or working outdoors, but in coastal areas outdoor living is comfortable all day long if we've taken steps to make it so. Because we're in the open air so much this month, it's a good time to notice whether our landscape is as attractive and useful as we want it to be. We may find garden improvements taking root in our minds. July is not a particularly good month for planting—spring and fall are much better— but it's a great time for planning ahead. Do you need to plant another shade tree? Except in the hottest areas, tropical and subtropical plants can still be planted early this month (as well as in June). Perhaps you have space for a romantic vine-covered arbor or pergola or an additional patio. Think about these options now when you can see just where shade and comfort are most needed. (For detailed advice on shade planting, consult this chapter's section on shade plants.)

Hot, dry weather makes regular watering the most important task now through September. And because there are right and wrong ways to water, summer is a good time to plan as well for water conservation. Now more than ever before it's wise to plant a basic landscape of drought-resistant plants, watered by drip systems and low-impact sprinklers, and confine plants that need more water to containers and small areas near the house. A drip system with hidden tubes can do more than save time and water; it can also banish from the patio the unsightly garden hose.

WATERING

Except for some California native plants and a few well-established drought-resistant plants from other parts of the world, all plants need regular watering now. Water large trees deeply but infrequently, to encourage deep and healthy roots. Allow the soil to dry out somewhat between irrigations, to permit air to enter the soil pores and provide the oxygen that roots need. When drought is inevitable, trees with deep, healthy root systems are better able to survive it. The best, most water-saving time to do regular watering is early in the day.

Mist systems that pulse on briefly throughout the day in shady areas enhance the environment for some plants and use little water. Many shade plants, including bromeliads, orchids, ferns, epiphyllums, and fuchsias, either absorb moisture through their foliage or appreciate the cooling evaporation of a fine spray of water. Native plants, also, appreciate an occasional spritz of water from the hose, applied in the morning or evening to wet the foliage only of those natives that would die if irrigated in summer, as explained on page 288.

MULCH BARE GROUND

Look around the garden for areas of bare soil and cover these with a 2- or 3-inch-thick layer of organic mulch. Organic mulch keeps the ground cool, conserves water, keeps many weeds from growing, and adds valuable organic matter to the soil. Mulching is one of the easiest ways to gradually improve your garden's soil. In general, stick to smooth-textured mulches in flowerbeds and vegetable gardens because these decompose fairly quickly and can be safely dug into the ground when replanting. Rough-textured

mulches are longer lasting and thus work well under permanent shrubs, trees, and vines and on pathways. Be alert to slugs and snails, which can find hiding places in some rough-textured mulches. Unfortunately, though mulch is a hallmark of organic gardening, dry or woody organic mulches can be a fire hazard. If your home borders on wildlands or is located in a "shelter-in-place" community (as described on page 299), substitute gravel or river rock for organic mulch. and cover informal paths with decomposed granite instead of shredded bark. While gravel and rocks don't add organics or help control weeds, they can reduce water needs by cutting down on evaporation and giving drought-resistant plants a place beneath which to hide roots. To add the benefits of humus, spray the ground with humic acid diluted according to package directions and immediately after spraying, wash it off the gravel or rock and down into the ground with clear water to prevent staining. (Before spreading rock or gravel, cover prepared ground with a layer of water-permeable weed barrier. Fit it around tree trunks, and cut X's for pulling smaller existing plants up through it and for planting new ones. To stop new weeds from springing up from seeds, also apply under the fabric a pre-emergent weed killer containing corn gluten meal, which performs a dual role since it also acts as a fertilizer.) (For more on mulch and a list of organic materials, see page 22.)

CITRUS AND AVOCADO TREES

Don't let citrus and avocados dry out in July or August or a great deal of fruit may fall off. This doesn't mean you should keep the trees in a boggy condition. They don't like that either. Established trees in most soils need deep watering every two or three weeks depending on soil type and weather conditions. Newly planted trees usually need deep watering once a week. (The best way to know when trees need water is to use a soil auger or a tensiometer; see page 38.)

Citrus need water in a broad band starting one-third of the distance from the trunk to the drip line and extending an equal distance beyond the drip line. This is where their feeder roots are, not next to the trunk. Put the hose on the ground and let it run slowly, filling a well-placed watering basin. The bark of citrus trees must be kept dry to prevent the fungal disease gummosis, which can infect their trunks.

Avocados need water all over the ground under their branches, up to a foot or two from the trunk. The best way to water them is slowly, with a sprinkler They can also be grown with drip systems installed at planting time and gradually enlarged, as described on page 83. Avocados are highly prone to phytophthora root rot (a fungal disease that's spread by infected plants and favored by wet or poorly drained soil), but they're not susceptible to gummosis.

CYMBIDIUMS

This is the time of year when cymbidiums are growing new leaves and pseudobulbs. Continue to feed them for growth every two weeks with diluted fish emulsion, such as Atlas or Neptune's Harvest, or with Fox Farms Grow Big (12-7-7). If dry fertilizers work better for you, apply to each container a handful per month of fishmeal, or bat or seabird guano. These types of fertilizers most closely resemble what cymbidiums might get in the wild. Organic fertilizers tend to break down the bark in soil mixes, so if necessary add more bark on top, so that the roots of the plants are covered but the pseudobulbs are above

ground—if they're buried they rot. Pull out weeds sprouting in containers, but it's too late to divide plants. Disturbing the roots of cymbidiums later than June will prevent them from blooming the next winter or spring. Keep them in filtered shade for the summer, and don't let the roots dry out. In interior gardens a drip system is ideal. Misting the foliage can be beneficial in the dry interior, but it's not necessary in coastal regions. Along the coast watering once or twice a week suffices. Overhead sprinklers are fine, but don't allow them to run for a long time— and avoid overwatering in general—since these practices can cause fungal problems, especially when the irrigation is done late in the day.

Sometimes cymbidiums are kept in too much shade, such as under a dense tree—a frequent mistake in home gardens. Black marks on the leaves and pseudobulbs are signs of fungal problems. The plants don't die, but they won't bloom as well. It's probably best to get rid of stricken plants so they don't spread the disease to healthy specimens. Some varieties seem more resistant to disease than others. Stick with those, and grow plants in a coarse, fibrous potting soil that drains well and in appropriately sized plastic containers. Don't put a cymbidium in a container that's too large for its roots or you'll drown it with soggy soil.

ROSES

Continue to control rose pests and diseases, and to water, and to prune the plants by picking the flowers, but stop disbudding them now. If you have been feeding your roses this year according to one of the organic systems suggested in this book, they will have adequate nourishment in July. Wait until next month before fertilizing again. Follow the basic guidelines given in

March (page 118) and expanded in April and May (pages 153 and 182). In hot interior zones step up the frequency of irrigations now to three times per week at the rate of 1 1/2 inches of water per irrigation. (In coastal zones, twice a week may be sufficient. In hot interior valleys and depending on your soil more frequent irrigation may be necessary.) Keep the ground around the plants well mulched.

Prune Climbing Roses That Bloom Only Once a Year. Most modern climbing roses bloom continuously from April to January. These should be pruned along with your other roses in January. But some roses bloom only once in spring. The **Rule of Thumb:** *Established climbing roses over three years old that bloom only once in spring or early summer should be pruned after bloom.* These roses bear their flowers on wood that grew during the previous year. If you wait until winter you risk cutting off new canes that will bear next year. There are several kinds of spring-blooming climbers, among which are the following:

- **Ramblers.** Rambling roses have thin, bendy canes and massive clusters of small, flattish flowers no bigger than 2 inches in diameter. Older types bloom magnificently but only once, in spring or early summer. Newer types bloom several times during the year. Where there's room, ramblers can be allowed to sprawl over the support of mature trees, large shrubs, or house or shed roofs, and they'll continue to grow larger and bloom massively without ever being pruned. (If they've been allowed to mound and climb for many years, clean out as much as possible of the dead interior after bloom.) If you want to control the size of old-fashioned rambling roses, prune them immediately after their bloom

finishes by cutting out old (gray) wood and canes that have bloomed this year. But don't cut out any fresh green canes. You have a choice of options: You can cut all the way to the ground, or you can keep a structure of main canes over a support and cut back the laterals that have bloomed to two buds, or eyes. New growth starts now, in summer. Tie up the abundant new canes as they grow, but cut off weak, twiggy ones at ground level. All new canes will bloom the following year.

- **Spring-Blooming, Large-Flowered Climbers.** Large-flowered climbers have thicker canes than ramblers and larger flowers, with fewer per cluster. Some old types flower once in spring; many repeat the bloom once again in summer. Several, such as 'America', 'Don Juan', and 'Handel', three of the best, bloom continuously from April through December; prune these in January, not now.

  Don't prune young plants. Prune established plants that bloom only once, right after the bloom finishes, by cutting out old woody canes more than three years old but leaving all younger canes and as many succulent ones that grew this year as you have room for. (Two- and three-year-old canes bloom best.) Cut back laterals on canes that have flowered to two or three buds each. These will bloom next year. Rearrange them and retie them onto their supports. Remove any suckers that sprout from below the bud union.

- **Spring-Blooming Species Roses.** These old-fashioned roses were originally found in the wild, though some selections, such as the Chinese species known as Lady Banks' rose *(Rosa banksiae)*, have been cultivated for centuries. In some areas Lady Banks' rose continues to bloom through June. In early July, or as soon as blooming stops, cut back the outsides of established plants hard, to shape and control them, and to encourage lots of new growth that will bloom next year. Follow up with a balanced organic fertilizer, and water deeply.

✸ QUICK TIP

Instant Shade for a Hanging Basket.
Fuchsias, begonias, and other shade plants are often burned by afternoon sun when hung from west-facing shade structures or porches. For these, spray a Japanese parasol with clear plastic to weatherize it, and shove the handle into the soil at a low angle to provide shade.

SHADE PLANTS

How to Garden in Shade. Every garden is bound to include a certain amount of shade, and now's a good time to study these areas while their relative coolness is most appreciated. Well-designed and properly planted shade gardens are the most refreshing parts of any landscape, but you can't plant them properly unless you understand the characteristics of shade.

How Shade Occurs. Many homeowners start out with mostly full sun but then either plant too many trees or let volunteers grow wherever they plant themselves. After a few years on this course, a sunny garden can become a shady or even gloomy one. It takes real courage to cut down mature trees, but sometimes this is the only way to reclaim the sun. In some cases you can lace trees out (remove twiggy branches and interior growth) to let adequate light through. The best shade is that which

you create yourself, either by building a shade structure or by planting an appropriate number of well-chosen trees in the right places. The most difficult shade is that which you can't control—solid shadows of buildings or walls, sometimes alternating with an hour or two of burning hot sun.

How Shade Moves and Differs in Degree. Shadows don't stand still; every day they move from west to east as the sun moves across the sky from east to west. They also lengthen northward as the sun moves south during fall and winter, and then they gradually shorten again as the sun moves north in winter and spring. These factors make gardening in the shade a lot trickier than gardening in full sun. So if you're interested in shade gardening, begin by observing and understanding the shadows in your own garden; notice where they occur, how dense they are, and their duration.

Not all semishade or even dense shade is alike. It differs widely according to what caused it and its exposure (the direction it faces). So before you plant, it's important to learn how to distinguish between these various degrees and exposures of shade and to learn which plants are most likely to succeed in each of them. Shade plants vary greatly in shade tolerance. Most shade plants, particularly flowering ones, need semishade, which by definition means part sun. Only a small number of plants will grow with no sun at all, yet many gardeners have to contend with total unmitigated shade in some areas. (See the box on page 261 for a list of the main types and exposures.)

How to Create a Restful Atmosphere. A peaceful shade garden can remind you of a cool forest glade even if you've housed it in lath or covered it with manmade shade cloth. So when

✺ QUICK TIP

Keep Impatiens from Wilting in the Afternoon. *If your impatiens wilts every afternoon and your neighbor's impatiens across the street are beautiful all day long, it's because your house faces west and theirs faces east. For success and water savings, grow impatiens in east-facing beds; never plant them in beds or on balconies that face west.*

you design your shade garden, work for a natural and informal feeling. Accent your plantings with rocks, driftwood, and stepping-stones—perhaps surrounded by moss or baby's tears. Pools and waterfalls lend a cooling atmosphere, and in some cases they use less water than heavily irrigated plants. The sight and sound of a splashing fountain can make a hot day seem cooler. Create charm and interest by adding rustic seats and wandering paths, and use pastels and color tones from the cool half of the spectrum: They're more restful than bright colors.

Tuberous Begonias. If you planted tuberous begonias in March they'll be in full bloom now. They're heavy feeders, so feed them regularly with balanced liquid fertilizer, such as Bioform (4-2-4) or fish emulsion, every week. Don't overwater. Let them dry out between waterings. Always remove spent blossoms but leave the stems on the plant: They'll fall off in a few days and can then be removed.

Control mildew with Serenade Garden Disease Control or increase plant health with PROBIOTICS 4 Plants' Defensor Bacterial Inoculator (as discussed on page 187). If you didn't raise these flamboyant flowers yourself, you can find them in bloom now at some specialty and dig-your-own nurseries.

Impatiens. Impatiens fill dappled shade with color faster than any other flower. For the most color and easiest care choose the regular single variety. New Guinea impatiens have colorful leaves as well as flowers. They need more light than other types, and plenty of water. Water impatiens daily now, especially when growing them in containers. They like loose acid soil but aren't as fussy about drainage as other plants. You can buy small bedding sizes of impatiens to transplant into tubs or the ground, or purchase them in hanging baskets and keep them in the containers they come in. Feed regularly but lightly for growth and bloom. Prune progressively (see Quick Tip below).

✺ QUICK TIP

Correct Leggy Impatiens with Progressive Pruning. *Each time you feed impatiens, select the two longest shoots on opposite sides of the plant and cut them back by two-thirds. By pruning progressively in this manner, the plants will remain full, well branched, and bushy at all times.*

SALVIAS

Tough, ornamental, easy, sometimes fragrant, often drought tolerant, and seldom bothered by pests, the members of the *Salvia* genus, commonly called sages, have been beloved by local gardeners for years. Recognize them by two-lipped flowers in almost any color of the rainbow, arranged in whorls evenly spaced or in tightly massed spikes on single or branching stems. Some salvias are shrubs; some are native plants; others are annual bedding plants, culinary herbs, or good subjects for the perennial garden. Many are old garden favorites. Varieties

The Kinds of Shade and Some Plants to Grow in Them

Some shade plants are adapted to several of the areas described below, others to only one or two. So use the following list as a starting point rather than as a set of immutable rules. You can learn more by experimenting with the shade in your own garden.

▶ **Full Shade.** This occurs under thick evergreen trees and north-facing overhangs and in some patios, atriums, and covered porches.

Characteristics: Virtually no sunshine hits full shade, at any time of year. This is the most difficult kind of shade to cope with, since few plants survive in dark places. (If these areas get some reflected light they're easier to plant.) The ground in full shade is cold and often poorly prepared. When it gets wet it stays wet, unless it contains tree roots. Yet if it's under an overhang it's often neglected, and in that case it's watered too seldom.

Special Tips: Prepare the soil by first removing some of it. Then dig up the ground deeply and replace the removed soil with large quantities of acid soil amendments (most shade plants are acid loving). Add 1 to 3 pounds of soil sulfur per 100 square feet. Check the soil often to make sure it's moist but not soggy. Cover bare ground with a smooth-textured mulch or cloak it with a ground cover. Accent gloomy areas by digging holes in the mulch or ground cover and slipping in potted, seasonal plants already in color or bloom, including caladiums, calceolarias, chrysanthemums, cymbidiums, cineraria, and cyclamen. Rely heavily on design elements, like bromeliads mounted on driftwood, stepping-stones, and fountains. Illuminate at night with soft light.

Plants That Grow in Full Shade: Paradise palm (*Howea forsteriana*); fatshedera (*Fatshedera*

x lizei); Japanese aucuba (*Aucuba japonica*), including gold dust plant (*A. japonica* 'Variegata'); monstera; many houseplants, including philodendron, dracaena (*Dracaena fragrans*), Swedish ivy (*Plectranthus verticillatus*), aspidistra (one of the best for difficult, dark shade, including windy exposures); ferns, including leatherleaf fern (*Rumohra adiantiformis*), sword fern (*Nephrolepis exaltata*), *N. exaltata* 'Dallas', and *N. obliterata* 'Kimberley Queen'; liriopes and ophiopogons, including mondo grass; baby's tears (*Soleirolia soleirolii*); small-leafed ivy, including 'Needlepoint'; cryptanthus; and—where there's plenty of reflected light—clivia.

▶ **Filtered Shade.** This occurs—though rarely—as dappled shade under an open-branched tree. More often it's found inside a structure built especially for shade plants and covered with wooden lath or shade cloth.

Characteristics: From morning to night at all times of year small shadows move from west to east over the plants. This is the ideal situation for most shade plants because it cuts the intensity of the sun, which otherwise could burn leaves or flowers. Plants stay cool and comfortable, but they get plenty of sunshine for growth and bloom.

Special Tips: Shade houses are best built in areas that were originally in full sun. When using wooden lath, always arrange it so the individual slats run north and south. When using shade cloth, choose its degree of shade according to your climate zone and the plants you wish to grow under it. In general, use cloth that casts 25 to 30 percent shade in coastal zones and 50 to 75 percent shade inland.

continued . . .

The Kinds of Shade and Some Plants to Grow in Them (continued)

Plants That Grow in Filtered Shade: All shade plants without exception. Some plants that are especially well adapted to filtered shade include camellias; azaleas; bromeliads; all ferns, including staghorn; fuchsias; impatiens; epiphyllums; all orchids that can grow outdoors in your climate zone; tuberous begonias; and shade-loving annuals, particularly coleus.

▸ **East-Facing Partial Shade.** This occurs on an east-facing porch, under an east-facing overhang, or to the east of a house, wall, or tree.

Characteristics: This is one of the finest kinds of shade to plant in. Cool morning sun shines into these areas, but they're protected from the burning hot sun of midday and afternoon hours.

Special Tips: Grow plants that must have sunlight in order to bloom but can't stand the burning rays of hot midday or afternoon sun. Plants that need partial shade inland but full sun along the coast will usually do well in eastern exposures. Hanging-basket plants such as fuchsias will be one-sided. Don't attempt to turn them, since that would deprive them of necessary light.

Plants That Grow in East-Facing Partial Shade: Tree ferns; mahonia (*Mahonia japonica* Bealei Group and *M. lomariifolia*); Tobira pittosporum (*Pittosporum to bira* 'Wheeler's Dwarf'); Japanese privet (*Ligustrum japonicum*); euonymus; abutilon; acanthus (*Acanthus mollis*); daylilies; agapanthus; snowbrush (*Breynia nivosa*) and bergenia; fuchsia; impatiens; cymbidiums; epiphyllums; begonias, including tuberous begonias; coleus; geraniums (pelargoniums); calla lilies; hydrangeas; so-called sun azaleas; and all shade-loving annuals and perennials.

▸ **West-Facing Partial Shade.** This occurs to the west of a house, wall, or tree or under a west-facing overhang.

Characteristics: Plants are totally shaded throughout the morning and hot noonday sun, and then suddenly in the afternoon the sun strikes them in all its fury. When this condition is combined with a heat wave or Santa Ana, all west-facing plants get fried. (The problem is at its worst in inland areas.)

Special Tips: Unless you live near the coast, don't even try to grow shade plants in unprotected western exposures. Instead choose plants that are capable of growing in either sun or shade. Cut the force of the afternoon sun by planting open trees and shrubs or by building a patio overhang, view garden, or shade structure that will allow you to grow a wider selection of plants.

Plants That Grow in West-Facing Partial Shade: Pittosporum; Indian hawthorn (*Rhaphiolepis incica*); nandina; breynia; aeoniums and other succulents; Madeira geranium (*Geranium maderence*) in coastal zones only; daylilies; euryops; fortnight lilies (*Dietes*); agapanthus; geraniums (pelargoniums); abutilon; 'Richmondensis' begonias; simperflorens begonias; 'Gartenmeister Bonstedt' fuchsia; any plant described in *Sunset Western Garden Book* as being suitable for sun or shade in your climate zone.

▸ **North-Facing Partial Shade.** This occurs to the north of a house, wall, or tree but not directly beneath a north-facing overhang, porch cover, or tree. (These areas are in full shade.)

Characteristics: North-facing shade changes with the seasons. In winter such areas enjoy

The Kinds of Shade and Some Plants to Grow in Them (continued)

full bright shade under the open sky, sometimes called "skyshine." Unless shaded from the side, they get full sun for a month or two in late spring and early summer, when the sun reaches its northernmost position. The shadows to the north of houses and trees will be shortest at the summer solstice (June 21 or 22).

Special Tips: Make sure these areas get adequate water in summer while they're exposed to more sunshine. If shade plants get burned by summer sun, install removable panels of lath or shade cloth. Provide more shade in summer for a north-facing backyard by building a freestanding shade structure or pergola, and growing a deciduous vine, such as wisteria, over it.

Annual flowers and vegetables can be grown in north-facing flowerbeds that are shaded in winter but sunny in summer. In fall, plant them with winter-blooming flowers for shade; in summer switch them to sun-loving flowers or vegetables, like zinnias or tomatoes. You can also plant bulbs if you plant them where sun will hit them when it's time for them to bloom. Raised beds can increase the speed of the returning sun by lifting plants above the shadow of the house.

Plants That Grow in North-Facing Partial Shade: Camellias; azaleas; clivia; many ferns, especially tree ferns; Japanese maple (*Acer palmatum*); leopard plant (*Farfugium japonicum* 'Aurea maculatum'); billbergia; bergenia; cineraria (plant in October for late-winter bloom); bulbs, including daffodils and pre-chilled hyacinths and tulips (also for fall planting); and annual flowers and vegetables as described above. (For a discussion of a north-facing perennial bed, see above).

▶ South-Facing Partial Shade. This occurs under a deep south-facing overhang, under a south-facing porch cover, or under the branches of a south-facing tree. (Areas to the south of a wall, a tree, or your house that are open to the sky or under a very narrow overhang—1 to 3 feet—are in full sun.)

Characteristics: South-facing shade exists in summer but not in winter. In winter the area under the branches of a large, dense, south-facing tree or under a deep south-facing overhang, solid-roofed patio, or porch will be flooded with sun in the middle of the day. In summer these same areas will be in total shade in the middle of the day. Thus the comfort level for people in south-facing shade is first-rate, but plant choice is difficult.

Special Tips: In general, south-facing shade is a prime place for a patio or porch. Pave these areas wherever possible and you'll have an ideal spot for sitting comfortably outdoors in both winter and summer. Decorate south-facing covered patios and porches with containers that can be moved or replanted according to the seasons.

Plants That Grow in Full Shade: Winter-blooming annuals for full sun or partial shade, including primroses, violas, pansies, and snapdragons, can be switched in summer to such houseplants as Swedish ivy (*Plectranthus verticillatus*) and African violets—those that like extremely bright light but no direct sun. Or grow succulents year-round. They like sun in winter and don't mind shade in summer, and many, such as *Kalanchoe blossfildiana*, have the added attraction of winter or spring bloom.

from South America, Mexico, Asia, Europe, and Africa lend an air of relaxed sophistication to every garden in which they're grown. Here are some good choices for local gardens:

- **Autumn Sage** (*Salvia greggii*). Usually red blooms, occasionally yellow or purple. Needs full sun, good drainage; very drought resistant, it needs no water along the coast once established.
- **Cleveland Sage** (*S. clevelandii* 'Pozo Blue', 'Aromas', and the compact 'Allen Chickering' and 'Winnefred Gillman'). California native that can take some garden water without dying.
- **Hot Lips Sage** (*S. microphylla* 'Hot Lips'). Eye-catching white flowers with red lips attracting hummingbirds turn solid red in hot weather; blooms dot compact foliage from early spring to winter; best in full or west-facing sun; low water requirement.
- **Pitcher Sage** (*S. spathacea*). Another native; forms a dense mat; can take some shade and attracts hummingbirds.
- **Purple Sage** (*S. leucophylla* 'Point Sal Spreader', 'Figueroa', or 'Mrs. Beard'). A good bank cover and native that needs no summer water once established.
- ***S. chiapensis.*** Attractive, airy upright plant to 1 to 2 feet with bright fuchsia, nonstop-blooming flowers. Needs moist, well-amended soil with good drainage; responds well to organic fertilizer. Reseeds.
- ***S. confertiflora.*** Richly colored, foot-long, velvety orange spikes on a 6-foot shrub for large gardens. Prune after spring bloom and tie to pea stakes to support heavy fall bloom.
- ***S. involucrata.*** Hot pink flowers late summer and fall; a good combination with 'Indigo Spires' in large gardens; dense velvety foliage on a shrub 5 feet tall.

- ***S. patens* 'Oxford Blue'.** Does well in inland or coastal regions; 2 to 3 feet tall.
- **White Sage** (*S. apiana*). Native with flat leaves; good for making smudges.

⚙ **QUICK TIP**

How to Revive a Wilted Impatiens. *When an impatiens wilts from too much heat, sun, or dryness, don't despair. Plunge the entire container up to the stems of the plant in a bucket of water. Come back in half an hour; the plant will have recovered.*

ANNUAL AND PERENNIAL FLOWERS

Plant Annuals. You can still plant annuals this month, especially in coastal zones. You'll just get a shorter season of bloom. The best choices are the heat lovers, such as Madagascar periwinkle (vinca; *Catharanthus roseus*), marigolds, portulaca, zinnias, and, early in the month, celosias. (If you plant the last too late, it won't make a proper head.)

Care for Coleus (*Solenostemon scutellarioides*). We grow coleus for its colorful leaves and not for its flowers. Once considered a Victorian plant, it is coming back into favor thanks to new varieties with brighter colors and interesting characteristics. You can have success with this potentially fine annual if you give it what it needs.

Coleus sickens in full shade and burns in too much sun, so grow it in filtered or half-day sun. Plant it in porous, slightly acidic soil, either in containers or in beds, away from the roots of invasive trees and protected from snails. Keep the soil damp but not soggy; too much water will cause the leaves to drop off. When the flowers appear, pinch them off; they sap the plant's strength. Feed coleus lightly with fish emulsion or a complete organic fertilizer. (Don't overfeed it or you'll get all stalk instead of leaves.) Many of the newest varieties grow larger and more vigorously than old varieties, and accept more sun, thus making them far better as single-specimen plants for patio containers.

Shiso or Beefsteak Plant. Another stunning member of the mint family is shiso (*Perilla frutescens*). A group of introductions called 'Magilla Perilla' are often confused with coleus due to their brilliantly colorful leaves in iridescent hues of purple, red, bronze, green, and black. Shiso hails from the Himalayas and eastern Asia, and it's fast growing—up to 3 feet tall in tubs or ground. Grow it in full sun along the coast, half shade inland. Sometimes called Chinese basil, shiso is a dual-purposed plant, both edible and ornamental, but to grow it for food, look for green shiso (*P. frutescens* var. *japonicus*). Dip the sweet-flavored flowers of green shiso in batter and fry them tempura style. Chop or slice the young leaves to use raw in place of basil or to add a pleasant ginger flavor to salads, mesclun, or stir-fries. Varieties with colorful leaves are used for staining foods and coloring pickles, and some have strong flavors. Don't eat ornamental varieties purchased in nurseries in case they were sprayed with pesticides.

Start Biennials. Now's the time to start biennials from seed. These are plants that take two years to bloom, such as foxgloves (*Digitalis*), sweet William (*Dianthus barbatus*), Canterbury bell (*Campanula medium*), and cup-and-saucer (*C. m. 'Calycanthema'*). Foxgloves are well worth growing from seed because tall varieties aren't always available in nurseries, especially in fall when you most want to plant them. (Dwarf

 QUICK TIP

A Timesaving Way to Grow Foxgloves from Seed. *Sprinkle seeds on any warm, semi-shaded section of bare ground kept continually moist by a drip system, such as the top of a hanging basket under a mister or a vegetable row between stalks of a tall crop, like tomatoes. Dig up and transplant the resulting seedlings in late summer or early fall.*

foxgloves, such as 'Foxy', bloom soon after fall planting instead of waiting until spring, and the bloom usually doesn't last long.) Tall varieties take up no more space than short ones and give you a bigger display for the same amount of effort. Take these steps to grow them from seed:

- Provide rich, fertile, well-dug soil. Alternatively, use a flat filled with damp, sterilized potting soil.
- The seeds are tiny, so mix them with a little sand and sprinkle them on the surface of the soil. Press them gently into the soil surface with a flat piece of wood. Don't cover them with soil; they need light to germinate. Mist them with water.
- Put flats in a warm, shady spot. Cover them with a plastic sheet to keep them moist until the seed germinates. Once they sprout, remove the cover.
- After the plants have developed two real leaves, start feeding them with a well-diluted solution of fish emulsion. Transplant them in the garden in late August or September.

Deadhead and Water Perennials. Continue to deadhead perennials. Keep them well watered now and cut back spring bloomers that stopped blooming at the arrival of hot weather.

Border penstemons (*Penstemon hybrids*) are bloomed out by now, so cut back the stems that have bloomed, leaving two green leaves at the bottom of each. Leave any basal foliage in place. (With plants like penstemon that don't go woody, you shouldn't cut their stems all the way to the ground.) Penstemon will then flower again on side branches in late summer.

When gaura has its midsummer "downtime," shear off all the dead flowers and a bit of foliage, so plants stand 12 to 15 inches tall; in a month or less it will be back in bloom.

If artemisia 'Powis Castle' has grown too fast, keep it in a smooth, compact mound by pruning. Shear it all over now or cut back the tips of branches and shorten the longer ones by cutting them back harder, down to lower joints without exposing bare wood. (Don't overfeed or overwater artemisia. If it grows too fast, lush, and tall, it will split open in the middle exposing ugly bare wood. The center will sprout eventually but is slow to regrow.)

Deadhead pentas (star clusters; *Pentas lanceolata*); if you do, its white, pink, lilac, or red flowers will bloom for months. Grow pentas in full sun, cover its roots with mulch, and give it frequent fertilizer, regular water, and good drainage. It doesn't do well in sandy soil that dries out between waterings or where tree roots are a problem. Strengthen and shape lavender shrubs by shearing them after bloom. Licorice plant (*Helichrysum petiolare*) looks good spilling over the hard edges of a path; shear it back to keep it from sprawling too far, and cut off faded blooms.

CONTROL OF BARK BEETLES ON CONIFERS

Most vigorous and healthy conifers, such as cypress and pine trees, can withstand numerous attacks from bark beetles. But trees such as Monterey cypress and Monterey pine, if they are already stressed from lack of care, may suddenly die in summer, or at least portions of them. If a tree's looking sick, inspect the trunk. Look for drill holes, frass (boring dust), or "pitch tubes" of frass and sap mixed together. Peel back the bark around a drill hole, and you may see galleries excavated by beetles right under the bark, where they live and reproduce. Once damage has girdled the trunk, the tree will die. Preventive measures and solutions include the following:

- Maintain healthy trees: Don't plant pines and other conifers in wet, poorly drained areas; water deeply at least once a month during the summer months, more frequently in fast-draining soils and hot, dry weather. The best way to water is to place a sprinkler under the drip line of the tree, running as low as it will go, and move it every two or three hours to another spot until you have watered all the way around the tree.

- Spray tree bark with EnviroTree to give trees adequate nutrition and vigor to fight off pests and diseases. (A less expensive option is to fertilize under the drip line with organic fertilizer.) Two weeks later, spray the ground and trunk with earthworm-casting tea, which can help if you catch the problem early. (In a test performed on drought-weakened forest trees attacked by bark beetles, earthworm-casting tea was sprayed on the ground surrounding the trees and on their trunks. One year later this treatment appeared to have saved from beetle attack those trees that looked healthy at the beginning of the test, but did not save trees already severely damaged at the time they were sprayed.)

- Remove badly infested or dying trees promptly. Don't pile the wood or tree trimmings near conifers, or the beetles may spread to healthy specimens. (If you want to save the wood for your fireplace, remove its bark so it will dry quickly; this will prevent the larvae from maturing.)
- Wait until cool weather (November through February) to prune conifers. Warm-weather pruning increases beetle activity and stresses the trees.

CONTROL OF PINE PITCH CANKER AND CYPRESS CANKER

Monterey pines on the Monterey Peninsula have recently been attacked by a relatively new disease, pine pitch canker. This disease causes sunken areas on branches, branch dieback, a tremendous amount of dripping sap, and the eventual death of the tree. Unfortunately, the canker is not restricted to Monterey pines but has been found on virtually every other pine species we grow in California, including the Torrey pine. Another canker disease, cypress canker, has for many years infected Monterey cypress trees and sometimes juniper.

Unfortunately, there is no known cure for pine pitch canker or cypress canker. Your only options are to remove and destroy infected branches to slow the disease, cut down trees that are dead or dying, and avoid planting species that are poorly adapted for local conditions. Until a solution is found for pine pitch canker, do not plant new pine trees in California. Meanwhile, maintain the health of your pine and cypress trees by watering and fertilizing them. An unusual footnote to this problem may offer hope for a future cure: Trees in an area that was gassed for one week by a black cloud of carbonaceous smoke from wildfires showed remarkable health, growth, and the ability to withstand existing pine pitch canker, cypress canker, and beetles for an entire year after the smoke was gone.

DON'T KILL ALL THE BUTTERFLIES

Caterpillars, loopers, and worms—especially green loopers, tomato hornworms, and cabbage worms—are the bane of many gardeners. If necessary, control them with BT. But butterflies, with the possible exception of white cabbage butterflies, are the floating flowers of the garden. So why kill them all? In fact, why not encourage them? Gardeners who plant meadows filled with wildflowers often provide perfect habitats and never notice the depredations of the attendant caterpillars, a necessary stage before you get butterflies.

If you like swallowtail butterflies, grow parsley, plenty for you and for them. (Common fennel [*Foeniculum vulgare*] also attracts swallowtails, but invades wildlands. If you grow it, cut off the seeds to prevent birds from spreading them.) The caterpillars are attractively striped and not overly voracious. They do, however, like willow trees, poplars, and sycamores. If you grow these trees, you're likely to have a resident population already.

Attract monarch butterflies by planting red milkweed (*Asclepias curassavica* 'Red Butterflies', *A. incarnata*). Butterfly weed (*A. tuberosa* 'Gay Butterflies') is often sold to attract butterflies and may do so, though not as reliably as *A. curassavica*, which is better adapted to our climate. Large-flowered passion vine will attract Gulf fritillary, a red-orange butterfly with black-to-brown markings and silver spots under the wings. The fuzzy black caterpillars

How to Make Cut Hibiscus Flowers Stay Open at Night

Most hibiscus flowers close up at night. You can keep them open this way:

▸ Pick blossoms just as they're barely open at 9 or 10 a.m., and slip each one into an empty Sno-Cone cup to protect it. (Pick them right under the flower rather than at the base of the stem in order not to tear the bark.)

▸ Put the Sno-Cone cups containing the flowers in a plastic bag and place them in the refrigerator for the day.

▸ Take the flowers out in the evening. They'll soon open fully and then stay open all night without water. (Some new varieties will stay open for three days.)

▸ Since water isn't needed, you can use these methods to arrange them: Spear the blossoms on toothpicks, and stick the toothpicks into arrangements. Or, to use the flowers in vases, spear them on long bamboo barbecue skewers and arrange the skewers. Or instead of the stiff bamboo skewers, substitute the center veins of fronds cut from a pigmy date palm (*Phoenix roebelenii*). Cut off the individual leaflets from each vein to bare stem and then spear a flower with its sharp tip. Your hibiscus will be transformed into cut flowers with long, graceful, arching stems.

will decimate leaves of passion vine but not touch much else in the garden. The mourning cloak butterfly is attracted to newly mown lawns and is often fearless enough to sit on a gardener's moist outstretched palm.

HYDRANGEAS

Once hydrangea flowers have faded to brown or green, cut back each stalk that has bloomed, leaving only two buds or leaf scars, from which new wood will grow to bloom next spring. (Cut back young plants lightly.) Don't cut off green stems that haven't yet bloomed because they'll bear flowers next year—or later this year if the plant has a north-facing exposure. (Hydrangeas perform best facing east.) Feed for growth and according to the color of hydrangea you are growing.

Hydrangeas come in pink, white, red, and blue, and the colors of some varieties are influenced by the acidity or alkalinity of the soil in which they grow. Some pink and white varieties won't change color no matter what soil they grow in. In order to keep a red hydrangea red, keep the soil pH to 7.0 or higher by feeding it with a balanced organic fertilizer containing phosphorus. If you begin with a good red variety this should not be difficult to accomplish. To keep a blue hydrangea blue keep the soil pH below 5.5; as low as 4.5 is even better. This is a much more difficult task due to our alkaline soil and water. The easiest way to give a blue hydrangea everything it needs to stay blue is to fertilize it often with aluminum sulfate, or with "Blue Hydrangea Fertilizer," which is the same thing, but never with phosphorus, since phosphorus prevents plants from absorbing aluminum.

Keeping blue varieties of hydrangeas blue with aluminum sulfate creates a dilemma for organic gardeners since aluminum phosphate is a synthetic fertilizer; some of them bend the rules and take the easy route. The purely organic way to maintain the color of blue hydrangeas is to increase the acidity of the soil by planting them in acid soil in the beginning,

Layer Camellias and Azaleas to Make New Plants

Treasured varieties of camellia and azalea that you cannot find commercially, plus many other woody ornamental plants, can be propagated now. To layer them (i.e., bury an attached branch in the ground to allow it to root, so it can be cut off as a plant in its own right), follow these steps:

▸ Choose a low-lying branch that bends easily to the ground.

▸ With a sharp knife carefully cut halfway through the chosen branch, making your cut beneath the branch and several joints from the tip.

▸ Brush the cut with a powdered rooting compound, such as RooTone or Dip'N Grow.

▸ Insert a sliver of wood or a small pebble into the section that is out to hold it open.

▸ Bury the cut section in damp soil. Firmly peg the branch down on both sides—"elbows" cut from coat hangers work well—and place a brick on the ground over the cut section to hold it down. Keep the soil damp throughout the summer.

▸ Check the branch in the fall. When it's thoroughly rooted, sever the new plant from the parent branch, dig it up, and plant it in a suitably sized container.

Note: Air-layering is a method of propagation similar to layering, but it's done above ground. In this method, first wrap a section cut as above in damp sphagnum moss. Then cover the moss with plastic sheeting, and wind tape around the plastic and the branch both above and below the cut section to keep the moss damp. In a few weeks, after roots grow, sever the branch below the cut. This system is very easy to use on some houseplants, especially corn plant (*Dracaena fragrans*).

fertilizing them exclusively with acid organic fertilizers containing no phosphorus, mulching them with tea leaves and coffee grounds, and applying soil sulfur annually to the ground around their roots. (Soil sulfur doesn't do any good unless it is actually combined with the soil.) Some organic gardeners counteract the alkalinity of our water by putting one teaspoon of vinegar into every quart of water they use for watering hydrangeas, or about a tablespoon per gallon. They claim this keeps the soil acid enough to maintain blue flowers. (Too much vinegar can kill plants. Undiluted vinegar is often used as a weed-killer, though usually it's the leaves of weeds that are killed, not the roots.)

HIBISCUS

Continue to prune, water, and fertilize hibiscus. Continue also to release beneficials onto them and wash the plants off with water to control giant whitefly. (For a full discussion of this pest, see page 125.) Now's a good time to plant these showy garden shrubs. There are about thirty varieties available in a wide range of shapes, sizes, and vibrant colors. Fancy-flowered varieties are less vigorous, lankier in growth, and need more protection from frost than common garden varieties. Grow them for their flowers, prune them lightly, train them as espaliers, or grow them as large perennials at the backs of beds.

CAMELLIAS AND AZALEAS

Feed camellias for the third and last time between one month and six weeks after their last feeding. (Feeding is discussed on page 181.) Use an acid organic fertilizer that's recommended for camellias and azaleas, and follow package directions exactly. Avoid overfeeding camellias; neither they nor azaleas are heavy eaters. Keep the roots damp but not soggy. Check to see that soil is not collecting around the trunk.

Give azaleas that bloomed through June their first feeding of the year immediately after blooming stops. Don't feed them again until late September unless one or two fail to respond. If this should occur, treat these sluggish growers once or twice with humic acid.

Check all your camellias and azaleas for signs of chlorosis (a deficiency in iron evidenced by yellow leaves with dark green veins). Treat the soil around chlorotic plants with a chelating product that contains iron, manganese, and zinc. Liquid formulas can also be sprayed on leaves. (Humic acid contains trace elements, so when you treat sluggish growers with it you also correct chlorosis, especially when you spray it on the foliage as well as pour it around the roots.) To start new plants, layer camellias and azaleas (see the box on page 269).

CONTROL OF BOUGAINVILLEA LOOPER

During the summer of 2006 an exotic 1-inch long caterpillar called the bougainvillea looper (*Disclisioprocta stellata*), accidentally introduced into California, began decimating the foliage of bougainvilleas, a plant previously immune to pests. This new pest is the larvae of a moth called the somber carpet moth, which lays its eggs on bougainvilleas and steps up its activities in warm weather. Bougainvillea looper prefers fresh young leaves but eats older growth too, working from the outside edge of leaves inward, leaving a scalloped effect. Look for these telltale signs now and control if necessary. This pest caused huge damage during the first year or two of its arrival, but now appears to be largely controlled by environmental factors, birds, and other beneficials. If damage is slight, hold off and let the beneficial creatures do their work. If damage is severe, control them by handpicking at night with a flashlight. (Loopers are also called inchworms for the way they loop their bodies and inch along twigs and leaves; this habit makes them easy to see.) Another option is to spray at night with BT (*Bacillus thuringiensis*). Handpicking is best since overusing BT gives caterpillars a chance to develop resistance to it, as is already happening with a number of species. Spinosad also controls this pest but, as explained on page 379, kills bees.

SUCCULENTS AND CACTI

Succulents and cacti are such a basic part of the Southern California landscape that almost all gardens contain at least one or two. But despite our familiarity with them, many people don't know the difference between a succulent and a cactus. The difference is simple: All plants that store water in their leaves or stems are called "succulents," while "cactus" actually is the name of just one large family of plants within the succulent group. All cacti have spine cushions, called "areoles," out of which spines arise, but many succulents—crassulas from Africa and echeverias from the Americas, for example—have no spines at all.

A Good Soil Mix for Succulents and Cacti

Choose a commercial mix especially formulated for succulents and cacti, or make your own by combining these ingredients.

▸ 6 to 7 parts pumice

▸ 2 parts commercial potting soil (such as Uni-Gro)

▸ 1 part sterilized oak leaf mold

Euphorbias are another large group of mostly succulent plants that are often confused with cacti because, at first glance, there's considerable resemblance. But whereas many euphorbias have spines, none of them have spine cushions. Other differences are that cacti are nonpoisonous and their sap is clear, while euphorbias are usually poisonous and their sap is white and cloudy. Also, all but a few cacti are native to the Americas, and most euphorbias are from Africa or Madagascar. Many of the vast number of tender succulents we're fortunate to be able to grow outdoors are houseplants in the rest of the country.

Choose Succulents for Widely Varying Conditions. Succulents have playful shapes, lovely flowers, undemanding and drought-tolerant natures, plenty of variety to keep one interested, and the ability to draw enthusiastic comments from anyone who sees them. If you live in a place where it's difficult to garden, they're ideal plants. One plus to growing succulents in containers is their portability. If you move, you can take them with you. But for the easiest care, grow them in the ground.

Your garden needn't look like a desert scene for succulents to fit in. Many have a lush, green look; some make good accent plants, and others can be used as ground covers. They're good choices for rock gardens, and they mix well with other drought-resistant plants.

Create a Whole Landscape of Succulents. As garden styles change to drought-resistant schemes, sophisticated gardeners are reawakening to the full potential and statuesque beauty of succulent plants. Before the building of the Los Angeles Aqueduct succulents were treasured garden plants, but after water became abundant, drought-resistant plants like succulents fell out of favor to be replaced by tropical jungles, or an East Coast look of water-soaked lawns and annual flowers. Now that water scarcity is upon us again, people are rediscovering the possibilities of succulents, and magazines are filled with photos of large-scale plants and smaller species combined into stunning designs. Today you can create an instant garden of succulent plants, including trees, shrubs, climbers, and ground covers. Among succulent trees are the dragon tree (*Dracaena draco*), tree aloe (*Aloe barberae, A. bainesii*), quiver tree (*A. dichotoma*), and pencil tree (*Euphorbia tirucali*). (The sap of a pencil tree can cause severe sight damage if it gets into eyes, which perhaps explains why so many old specimens are still standing. No tree trimmer will touch it.) Some aloes, though not exactly trees, grow as tall as small trees but with upright shapes that fit in small spaces. Their eye-catching shapes and arresting winter flowers make these plants choice accents, either arranged alone or in a group of three, five, or seven. Two of the best are coast aloe (*A. thraskii)* and cape aloe (*A. ferox*).

Succulents of shrub size include all the large but ground-hugging agaves such as non-spiny foxtail agave *(Agave attenuata)*, the perilously spiny, and invasive but nonetheless handsome, blue-gray *A. americana*, with its many variegated spinoffs, as well as variegated Mauritius hemp *(Furcraea foetida var. mediopicta)*, tree aloe *(A. arborescens)*, elephant food *(Portulacaria)*, and jade tree *(Crassula ovata)*. Climbing succulents include night-blooming cereus *(Epiphyllum oxypetalum)* and climbing aloe *(A. ciliaris)*, which blooms all winter if deadheaded and is often seen in old neighborhoods hiding the bases of palm trees. Trailing succulents work best in containers slung from the branches of trees. These types include bundle of strings *(Rhipsalis capilliformis)*, donkey tail *(Sedum morganianum)*, and string of beads *(Senecio rowleyanus)*. Succulent ground covers complete the picture by drifting over banks, cascading over the edges of walls, covering bare ground, and tucking themselves around larger plants in places that humans can't even reach. (For names of succulent ground covers, consult the list on page 374.)

Today, gardeners with a flair for design are combining succulent plants with other design elements including rocks, boulders, dry streambeds, art objects, and hardscape, sometimes with edgy touches—freestanding walls, for example, painted in shocking colors. Like perennials and annuals in borders, succulents look better when arranged in solid drifts of one variety at a time so that the drifts play off one another in color and shape. For example, the brilliant orange flowers of aloes look particularly stunning when seen against a vivid blue-gray carpet of blue fingers *(Senecio mandraliscae)*, which also contrasts well with red pork and beans *(Sedum x rubrotinctum)* and black aeonium *(Aeonium arboreum 'Zwartkop')*.

How to Transplant Cacti and Spiny Euphorbias

Most spiny succulents can be safely handled with leather gloves, but all cacti and a few euphorbias have spines that are either sharp enough to penetrate leather or, in the case of some cacti, are barbed so they can permanently attach themselves to it. To avoid ensnarement, try this method:

▸ Hold tiny plants gently with barbecue tongs. To grasp a small plant, roll a sheet of newspaper in the shape of a tube, flatten it, and wrap it around the cactus. The jutting ends of the newspaper provide a handle. Grasp large plants with rolled burlap. Tie the burlap ends together with twine. Use these handles to securely hold and support the plant as you dig up its roots and lift it out of the ground or container. (More than one handle may be necessary for large specimens.)

▸ Transplant the cactus into loose, well-drained soil mix appropriate for cactus and other succulents. Use a chopstick to work the soil mix down around the roots.

▸ Cover the roots completely with soil mix up to the original soil level. Tamp gently but firmly with a blunt stick. Stake and tie tall specimens.

▸ Cover the soil mix with a layer of ornamental gravel or volcanic rock. Water thoroughly. Keep potted plants in semi-shade for a month.

This aeonium and others, as well as hybrid echeverias, often become leggy within only a year or two after planting. Designing and planting a succulent garden may be a daunting task at first glance. It is a fine art like making an English perennial border, and even though the end result is dramatically different, some of the same rules apply. One of the best ways to overcome timidity and get ideas for good combinations is to consult books on the subject. (Debra Lee Baldwin's *Designing with Succulents* is chock-full of garden photographs and is especially useful since it identifies all the plants in the photos.)

Clean Up, Feed, and Water Succulents.

Choose and plant succulents year-round. Some take full sun; others need semishade. Most container-grown specimens do best in partial shade. They're perfect for dressing up a balcony or a condo patio—places where hot sun alternating with solid shade makes survival difficult or impossible for almost all other plants.

The colorful blooms of succulents occur mostly in winter and spring. After plants have finished flowering, cut off the spent blooms and seedpods if they are unsightly. This applies also to cacti—epiphyllums, for example—unless you wish to propagate the seeds or eat the fruit. (The fruit of some cacti and both the young leaves and fruit of prickly pear cactus [*Opuntia ficus-indica*] are edible. But remember: All parts of African euphorbias are poisonous.) Clean up all succulents by pruning off diseased or desiccated portions.

Feed all cacti and euphorbias in July and at intervals of one month throughout the growing season. Most succulents growing in the ground need little if any fertilizer unless growing in something akin to pure beach sand. But plants in containers have nothing to grow on other than what is in the pot and need fertilizers throughout the warm season of the year. However, if for any reason you wish to fertilize succulents growing in the ground organically, first try to imagine what they might get in the wild. I have noticed succulent plants growing in wild places in Mexico and seen how they grow in well-drained soils on mountainsides, rich in minerals and sometimes volcanic, but almost always poor in organic matter. Most likely the only fertilizer they receive, if any, would be scat from snakes, lizards, birds, or rodents. Well-diluted bat or bird guano mimics this most closely, and bat and bird guano are both available commercially at a reasonable price. Dissolve these in water and apply a weak solution to the ground and to the plants themselves. Ordinary manure is not good for succulents and can rot or kill them, but humic acid is beneficial since it can help release nutrients already existing in soil. John and Bob's Soil Optimizer can also boost health and growth while doing plants no harm. Products containing yucca can help moisten overly dry or sandy soils. Feed plants in containers once every two months with a solution of 1 tablespoon high-phosphorus fish emulsion per gallon of water. On alternate months give them liquid seaweed or kelp fertilizer diluted according to package directions. If growth seems sluggish increase the frequency to every two or three weeks, but be careful not overfertilize succulents with fish emulsion since too much may damage roots.

✺ QUICK TIP

How to Remove Cactus Spines from Your Skin. *Some cactus spines are easy to see and remove with tweezers. But fine, almost invisible, hairlike spines, called "glochids," have hooks on their tips and are painfully irritating when embedded in human flesh. To remove them, glob on rubber cement and let it dry. Then rub it off, spines and all.*

Most succulents growing in the ground need no irrigation during the winter. Those in containers need water only during dry spells. The **Rule of Thumb** for watering container-grown succulents, including cacti and euphorbias: *If the soil is dry 1 inch below the surface, it's time to water.* But all begin to need irrigation this month. Depending on the weather and your climate zone, water them every one to three weeks throughout summer and fall. The exception to this rule is lithops, or "living rocks." More lithops die from overwatering than from any other cause. Water lithops from March 1 to July 1 and withhold water in July and August. Resume watering September 1 and continue until they finish blooming in mid-November. Allow lithops to go dry in winter, putting them under cover so they don't get rained on. Allow plants to dry out slightly between waterings. Good drainage is important.

BROMELIADS

Like cacti, bromeliads are native to the Western Hemisphere, except for a lone adventurer found in Africa. The bromeliad family includes such widely differing plants as the pineapple and Spanish moss, but most family members share the basic shape of a rosette of leathery leaves, sometimes plain and at other times strikingly variegated. They can be brilliantly colored, striped, or mottled. Often these leaves are arranged in a cone that forms a natural reservoir to collect rainwater and see the plant through drought. Flowers either are hidden in the cone or arise from it on straight or cascading stems. Often the inflorescences are bizarre, exciting, and spectacularly colored.

Queen's tears *(Billbergia nutans)* was the first bromeliad to be widely grown in California

The Apple Trick to Make a Bromeliad Bloom

An event occurring sometime during the first third of the twentieth century altered the history of bromeliads in cultivation. As the story goes, smoke from a wood-burning heater accidentally escaped overnight into a greenhouse filled with bromeliads, including some species that had been there for years without blooming. Within six weeks to two months most of the plants—including those that had never bloomed—suddenly sprouted inflorescences. The smoke was analyzed and found to contain ethylene gas. This discovery enabled growers to make pineapples bear fruit year-round.

In our climate most well-grown bromeliads will naturally cycle into bloom at the right time of year for each species. But if desired, mature plants, particularly any recalcitrant ones that have never bloomed, can often be "gassed" to stimulate bloom on demand. One way to do so is to place a full-grown plant into a large plastic bag and drop in a whole 'Red Delicious' apple (a better source of ethylene gas than 'Golden Delicious'). Tie the bag closed and keep it in cool, solid shade for one week. Then take the bromeliad out and care for it as usual.

gardens; it thrives on neglect. In the 1970s, silver vase plant *(Aechmea fasciata)* took its place as the most popular bromeliad. Most bromeliads are experts at survival, and they thrive outdoors in Southern California, even naturalizing in some gardens.

Propagate Bromeliads. All bromeliads except one are monocarpic—they bloom but once and then die. But in the process they leave many

How to Divide and Multiply Bromeliads

When you propagate bromeliads, remember that spines from prickly varieties can enter your flesh and fester, so wear leather gloves when handling them. (If you do happen to get a spine in your flesh, see page 273.) You can divide a plant when the pup is at least a third or half the size of the mother or has formed root of its own. Here are two methods.

▶ Depending on what will work with the size and type of plant you're propagating, stick a serrated knife, keyhole saw, sharp hunting knife, or blade-type pruning shears down into the soil and cut off the pup as close to the mother plant as possible. Continue with the directions for pot planting that follow immediately, or skip to the last item.

▶ Fill a 4- or 6-inch plastic container with pre-moistened, fast-draining potting mix into which you have mixed 1 tablespoon of balanced organic fertilizer.

▶ Dip the cut section of the bromeliad pup in a rooting hormone, such as Dip'N Grow or RooTone, and knock off the excess. Make a hole in the planter mix. Insert the plant and press the damp soil mix around it.

▶ Water the bromeliad occasionally, and keep it in semishade.

▶ Most tillandsias are grown on a piece of wood or bark, with no soil at all. Vase-type bromeliads can also be grown in trees. To mount them this way, first cover the base of the bromeliad with two or three handfuls of potting soil wrapped in a piece of homegrown phoenix-palm fiber or a small coir (coconut fiber) basket liner. Tie up the bundle with nylon fishing twine. Then place the plant upright on a branch or in the crotch of a tree or on a large piece of driftwood, and attach it firmly in place by winding nylon fishing twine around the branch or driftwood, the palm fiber, and the plant base. The bromeliads will soon develop aerial roots. (Mature Australian tea trees [Leptospermum laevigatum] make particularly attractive settings for bromeliads because their branches are often at eye level and they have interesting, twisted shapes.)

progeny in the form of seeds and offshoots called "pups," which sprout from the mother's stalk. With proper care you can have plants for life. Now's a good time to propagate bromeliads by separating the pups from their parents to make new plants (see the box, above).

Give Them Proper Care. Bromeliads need good air circulation, fast-draining acid soil mix, and occasional watering. In interior zones hook up a mist system to keep their foliage and the air around them moist in hot, dry weather. It's not necessary along the coast. Most bromeliads need bright light—up to 50 percent sunshine in coastal zones, 25 percent inland. Once in a while let their center cups go dry. Flush them out occasionally to prevent mosquitoes from setting up housekeeping.

Feed and Flush Bromeliads. Feed bromeliads lightly with diluted fish emulsion, diluted bat or bird guano, or any balanced liquid

How to Repot Fragile Donkey Tails

The most attractive and best way to begin growing donkey tail plants *(Sedum morganianum)* is in small round Mexican pots, drilled for use as hanging baskets because they do not have the sharp edges of plastic pots that can break the branches. Once the plant has filled the pot and grown to several feet in length, it's time to transplant it into a large hanging basket. Once transplanted, the plants can attain stunning beauty and spectacular size—often growing to 5 feet or more in length.

▸ Purchase a sturdy, rust-proof metal hanging basket with chains strong enough to support approximately 75 pounds. Hang the basket briefly to test the chains' length and make sure it hangs level.

▸ Line the basket with the correct size of palm-fiber liner.

▸ Fill the lined basket with loose, highly organic, fast-draining potting soil. Make a hole in the middle.

▸ Gently place the plant, pot and all, into the hole, carefully spreading the long stems over the edge of the basket. (This may take two or three people.)

▸ Carefully break the pot in several places with a hammer. Pull out the shards. Fill in the gaps with more soil.

▸ Dip the ends of broken branches in RooTone or Dip'N Grow and plant these too. Hang the basket on a stout hook in semishade. Protect it from wind and birds. Keep it moist and feed occasionally.

organic fertilizer. Some hobbyists feed their bromeliads only three or four times a year, with fine results. Others fertilize once every two or three weeks in the summer months, which brings even better results. Pour some of the diluted fertilizer around the roots and a little into the cup. Mist tillandsias (air-plant bromeliads) with the solution. (Foliar feeding benefits all bromeliads regardless of type.)

LAWN CARE

Cool-Season Grasses. As in June, cool-season lawns such as perennial ryegrass and fescue are growing slowly now, so don't mow them short. Cut ryegrass 2 inches high now. Tall fescues should be left even taller—between 2 and 3 inches after cutting. (Use the top setting of your mower.) Mow tall fescues often, never cutting off more than one-third of their total height, and always be sure your mower's blades are sharp.

Extend the time between irrigations of tall fescue now, and water it deeply to encourage deep roots. Almost all other cool-season grasses need shallower and more frequent watering than warm-season grasses do. In hot weather most cool-season grasses need to be watered twice or three time a week in interior zones, and at least once a week along the coast. Early morning—any time between midnight and dawn—is the best time to irrigate both for water conservation and for lawn health except in the desert, where evenings are acceptable.

Don't fertilize cool-season grasses now in interior zones. Along the coast fertilize very lightly—one-half the normal amount.

Warm-Season Grasses. Warm-season lawns such as Bermuda, zoysia, kikuyu, 'Adalayd' grass, and St. Augustine thrive in summer and are growing at their fastest now. As in June, cut common Bermuda short, to between 1 and 1½ inches, and cut hybrid Bermuda to ½ or 1 inch. Cut zoysia to between ½ and 1 inch, and kikuyu grass to 1 to 1½ inches. (Slice down through and pull out escaped kikuyu stolons often, to thwart their tendency to creep into flowerbeds.) St. Augustine grows fast, so cut it often to 1 to 2 inches at least once a week.

All warm-season grasses should be watered deeply and infrequently—rather than shallowly and often—to encourage deep rooting. St. Augustine needs the most water; it can die if allowed to go dry. Water it at least once a week—more often in sandy soils. Bermuda, zoysia, and kikuyu can often go as long as two weeks between waterings, depending on the weather and your climate zone. Water deeply, and extend the time between irrigations as much as possible while still maintaining good appearance.

Feed most warm-season grasses every four to six weeks during the growing season. Feed 'Adalayd' half strength, early in the month. (Too much fertilizer in hot weather can stress it.) If kikuyu is growing well, don't feed it at all. Too much fertilizer can turn it into a monster. If you want to get rid of kikuyu or Bermuda as you would weeds, kill it now by using soil solarization. (This system uses the sun's rays to kill weeds, seeds, and pathogens and has been proven to kill kikuyu or Bermuda grass when done correctly, as described on page 295.)

Lippia as Lawn. Phyla nodiflora (*Lippia repens*) is a useful and attractive lawn substitute for interior and desert regions and on the beach front, where its deep roots recommend it for erosion control. It's tough, evergreen, and drought tolerant, and once established it withstands foot traffic. It creates a thick mat that blooms in early summer and fall with pink flowers that are pretty to look at and attractive to bees. To protect children and dogs from bee stings, mow the flowers off now. Follow up with lawn fertilizer and deep water (as a general rule, water lippia deeply but infrequently).

Renew Diseased Patches of Korean Grass. Korean grass (*Zoysia tenuifolia*) is one of our best drought-resistant ground covers for places that can't be mown with a lawn mower. Its creeping, undulating growth habit and fine mosslike texture make it a good choice for Oriental gardens and children's imagination gardens. It's stunning when used in modern landscape design to soften the hard edges of rectangular beds. It goes dormant in winter in interior zones but stays green year-round in frost-free zones. But Korean grass has a problem. After it fills a space and reaches its pinnacle of good looks, it then begins growing in height, developing bouncy hills of growth one-foot thick. Disease sets in, the lower layer rots and splits open and—voila!—your formerly gorgeous lawn is disfigured with ugly brown patches. Don't spray it with fungicides, or tear it out; these are the wrong solutions. Now in warm weather, simply cut it down to the roots. Use a weed-whacker to get it right down to the ground. Rake up and send the dead grass to the dump; don't compost it. Fertilize the bare ground with Biosol Mix (7-2-3) and follow up with irrigation. A week later, apply a solution of humic acid and kelp or Kelzyme. It will soon bounce back, and before the end of summer it will look even more handsome than before.

VEGETABLE GARDENING

As early summer vegetables are harvested, clean up the rows, add soil amendment and organic fertilizer, and then plant more crops. All summer vegetables can be planted now, but they'll have a shorter growing season. If you need the space in September for winter vegetables, don't plant crops now that won't bear until fall. (Read the seed packages and count the days to harvest.)

Where Are All the Bees? Perhaps you've noticed in recent years how few bees there are in your garden. If so, your fruit trees are probably bearing smaller crops than they used to and you're probably picking fewer peppers, cucumbers, and squash. No bees, no food, or a lot less. The fact is, about a third of the food on our tables comes to us as a result of the pollinating abilities of the lowly little honeybee. Any reduction in their numbers amounts to an environmental disaster, and unfortunately that's just what happened.

During the late 1980s two species of predatory mites, the varroa mite and the tracheal mite, which attack and kill honeybees, were accidentally introduced into California, destroying feral hives. Meanwhile, changes in the tax laws together with the expense of controlling varroa mites in managed hives forced many commercial beekeepers out of business. Now the Africanized honeybee, which is less susceptible to the varroa mite, has arrived in California and is interbreeding with the European honeybee in commercial hives, creating even more work and expense for beekeepers. The hybrid offspring swarm more frequently and defend their nests more aggressively than purebred European honeybees. Also, beekeepers must now annually replace the queens in all commercial hives with certified European bee queens. See the boxes on pages 280–281 and 283 for ways in which you can protect yourself from Africanized bees and increase the number of beneficial native bees in your garden.

Colony Collapse Disorder. On top of these problems, bees worldwide are now beset with CCD, Colony Collapse Disorder, a problem appearing from some accounts to have resulted from exposure to pesticides, especially imidacloprid and some other related pesticides produced by Bayer Crop Science. Imidacloprid is the active ingredient in Merit, contained in Season Long Grub Control made by Bayer Advanced, and an ingredient in many commercial lawn fertilizers for grub control. Merit is long lasting and gets into groundwater. It is also a systemic so it gets into other plants. Though European growers have been fighting the Bayer company about this problem for ten years, Bayer has so far refused to admit that their product as at fault. In the meanwhile, lawn owners, golf course managers, and agriculturists using commercial fertilizers containing grub control may be unwittingly killing bees. Whatever is killing bees is doing so to all of them; the wild bees and bumblebees are disappearing along with domestic, feral European, and Africanized bees.

 QUICK TIP

How to Keep Seed Rows from Drying Out in Hot Weather. *Cover a seeded row with a 4-inch-wide strip of burlap. Sprinkle it thoroughly to soak the row every morning. Pick up the edge of the burlap daily to check progress; remove it as soon as the seeds sprout. Floating row covers also work well for sprouting seeds.*

Crops You Can Still Plant. The best things to plant now are the heat lovers, such as corn, cucumbers, eggplant, peppers (in coastal zones only; see the accompanying box), and summer squash. Tomatoes and chard can also be planted. Continue to put in beets, carrots, and radishes in small quantities for successive crops. Green beans can be planted now but will be less vigorous and have more insect problems than those planted in March. It's too late to plant melons along the coast. Inland you can plant cantaloupe, pumpkins, and Crenshaw and honeydew melons early in the month, if you know from experience there'll be enough hot weather to ripen them in October. (Planting this late is much riskier than planting in May or June.) It's too late to put in winter squash and be sure of a harvest. For all these crops keep the seed rows damp. It's often necessary to mist them more than once daily (see Quick Tip, left).

Fending Off Problems. Watering and either cultivating or mulching (as well as harvesting) are the most important tasks in the July vegetable garden. There's no use in kidding ourselves—vegetables aren't drought resistant; they need a steady supply of water. If a cucumber plant goes dry the cucumbers will be bitter. If tomatoes go dry they'll drop flowers or get blossom-end rot (as discussed on page 250). (Tomatoes growing in heavy soil can go a long time between waterings if their roots are deep in the ground but not if they're shallow rooted, in very sandy soil, or in containers.) If drought forces the shutdown of your vegetable garden, or part of it, don't be discouraged. Work for solutions to our water problems, keep up your hopes, and plant again in fall. Drip irrigation is the most water-wise method for keeping row crops happy.

How to Have Success with Peppers

▸ Peppers are classed as hot-weather vegetables, but they perform best within a precise range of temperatures. The fruit sets best when night temperatures are between 60° and 75°F. Daytime temperatures near 75°F are best—when they top 90°F, they can cause blossom drop.

▸ Feed peppers lightly with a balanced liquid fertilizer as soon as you see the first blossoms open, and keep the ground evenly moist. A lack of dark green leaf color despite adequate nitrogen may come from lack of magnesium. In this case spray the leaves with a solution of 1 teaspoon Epsom salts to a pint of lukewarm water.

Continue to side-dress rows with organic fertilizer halfway through the vegetables' growing seasons. Use cotton seed meal and blood meal to provide extra nitrogen if crops show signs of nitrogen deficiency, such as yellowing foliage or a slowdown in growth. After harvesting out a row and before replanting with another crop, always work in a layer of aged homemade or bagged compost and balanced organic fertilizer into the top 6 inches of the ground. (Use a commercial vegetable fertilizer or mix your own; for example mix together 4 pints soymeal, $1/2$ pint fish bonemeal, $1/2$ pint kelpmeal, $1/4$ pint Sul-Po-Mag [0-0-22], and $1/2$ pint powdered humic acid. Work in 1 gallon per 100 feet of row prior to planting.)

All gardeners need to watch for pest problems now. Handpick caterpillars, get birds to help, or use BT. Continue to release beneficials.

Good Bees for Your Garden

Bees are one of the most important and necessary of all the insects. Bees pollinate most flowers and more than a hundred food crops and also produce honey and beeswax. Unfortunately, some people think of bees as enemies, and the arrival of the Africanized honeybee has not helped. But bees only sting in self-defense or when they sense their hive is threatened. Stinging is serious business to the honeybee because the process of stinging means death to the bee. Each honeybee can sting only once, and then it dies. So protect yourself from the Africanized honeybee (see the box on page 283), but also take steps to protect our precious bees of all species.

Fortunately, many types of native bees help with pollination. The ground-dwelling squash and gourd bee, for example, came to California along with these crops and starts pollinating early in the morning when the flowers open. Many native bees get going earlier in the morning than honeybees and even pollinate flowers in winter. Provide homes for native bees; purchase special houses from catalogs or make your own. Leave some bare ground in your garden—some moist and some dry—for ground-dwelling bees to nest in, perhaps between stepping-stones, where you can watch them come and go. Do not spray with pesticides, especially imidacloprid (the active ingredient in Merit and Bayer Advanced Complete Lawn Insect Killer); also avoid Spinosad. Every time you get rid of a pest this way, you're also killing bees. Keep some flowers blooming in your garden year-round to provide pollen for the bees and other beneficials. (See the list of pollen-producing flowers on page 161.) Here are a few beneficial bees to protect, enjoy, and encourage:

▸ **European Honeybee.** True bees of the Apidae family, these highly social creatures live in large colonies. They are our best pollinators; pollen from flowers clings to the special branched hairs that cover their legs and bodies and then gets brushed off onto other flowers. They also collect pollen in special sacs on their back legs and carry it from flower to flower while gathering nectar, from which they make honey.

▸ **Bumblebee.** Four local species of true bees, up to an inch long, also of the Apidae family, marked with furry black-and-yellow stripes. Excellent pollinators for all vegetables, bumblebees are actually better than honeybees at pollinating tomatoes and eggplants. They nest in small colonies in the ground or in tree hollows, or even—as happened at my house last summer—in an empty birdhouse. Catalogs carry ready-made bumblebee houses with built-in observation panels. Many flowers attract bumblebees, especially zinnias.

▸ **Carpenter Bee.** These large—almost 1-inch-long—black or dark blue, shiny creatures of the Anthophoridae family are also good pollinators, especially of tomatoes. Like bumblebees, they will sometimes hit you with their bodies without stinging in order to move you a little farther away from their nest. (Tell them you're just gardening; it calms them down.) The less-numerous males are spectacularly covered with golden hairs. The females nest solitarily, drilling round holes into soft wood. (The one that's nesting in my redwood patio table is apparently unconcerned that her progeny are covered by a tablecloth during mealtimes.) To increase pollination in your garden, you can purchase carpenter bee larvae and blocks of wood in which these amusing bees can nest. Wisteria attracts them.

Good Bees for Your Garden (continued)

▸ **Mason Bee.** Small, ⅜- to ½-inch bees of the Megachilid family, with long black hair and black legs, are better pollinators than honeybees for orchards and pollinate during winter when European bees are all buzzing inside their hives trying to keep warm. Mason bees are gentle and don't sting unless swatted. You can buy houses for them, wooden nesting blocks with holes drilled in them, and also their live larvae, which are shipped in winter, from several sources, such as Entomo-Logic—see page 416). Install these bees in your garden, and you'll get more apples and other fruits from your trees that bloom in winter.

▸ **Metallic Sweat Bee.** Bright green, shiny, housefly-sized bees that nest in the ground and are a good pollinator of melons, these sting if swatted but not as painfully as honeybees.

▸ **Leaf-Cutter Bee.** Several species of bees of the Megachilid family: Good pollinators, about ½-inch long, and hairy in colors of brown, gold, or black, they cut round pieces out of leaves to construct a nest. These bees will also make their nests in nesting boxes you can buy from catalogs. (Some catalogs may also carry larvae.)

When and How to Harvest Summer Vegetables. Pick summer vegetables when they're young and tender—it's half the fun of growing your own. They grow so fast that many crops need checking daily. Whenever possible, eat them the day you pick them.

- **Beets.** Harvest at any size, but they're best between tiny and golf-ball size.
- **Cantaloupe.** Pick at "full slip," when a crack forms around the stem next to the fruit and the fruit falls off in your hand with no pulling.
- **Carrots.** Ready to eat when finger sized. In sandy soils pull them up by the leafy crown. In clay soils loosen them first with a garden fork or trowel. (Be careful not to disturb others left in the ground.)
- **Corn.** When the tips of the silks go crispy brown and the ears are filled out, pierce a kernel with your thumbnail. If the juice is milky the ear is just right; if clear it's not yet ready; if dry or pasty you've waited too long.
- **Cucumbers.** Harvest at any size, but mature fruit with small seeds, dark green skin, and crisp texture taste best. Harvest often to keep the vines bearing.
- **Eggplant.** The fruit should be glossy, filled out, and big enough to eat. The flesh should not spring back when you press it with your thumb. If the seeds or skin are brown the eggplant has gone too far. Pick often; the more you pick the more you get.
- **Green Beans.** Pick often and pick young—as soon as immature seeds fill the pod but before the pods get bumpy, and while the outside's still slightly velvety. Wait until the leaves are dry before walking among the plants to pick beans. (Picking when the leaves are wet from dew can spread rust.)
- **Lima Beans.** Don't pick these too soon. Leave the full-grown pod on the plant until

Beware of Sleepy Bumblebees

Pole beans, dahlias, and zinnias are bedrooms for bumblebees. Watch for them when picking flowers and vegetables in the late afternoon or evening. These gentle creatures don't want to sting you, but they will if you grab them.

it fills with beans and you can clearly feel them inside.

- **Peppers.** Pick as soon as the fruit are well formed and full sized, with crisp, thick skins and seeds that are almost mature. Leave a few fruits on the plant to go red if desired, but not all, because the plants have a built-in fruit load. Once you reach their limit they'll stop blooming unless you pick some.
- **Radishes.** Plant often and pull daily in small quantities, as soon as they mature but before they split. (These tend to get very hot to the taste during summer.)
- **Summer Squash.** Pick while the skin can be easily pierced with your thumbnail. Try picking tiny ones with the blossom still on the plant and cooking them blossom and all. If crops get too overwhelming, slow them down by picking both male and female blossoms to batter-fry or add to ratatouille.
- **Tomatoes.** For the best flavor leave these on the vine until they're fully red and ripe, unless birds, animals, or caterpillars are getting them first.
- **Watermelon.** Harvest when the skin under the melon turns from pure white to a creamy color and the tendril on the stem starts to dry up. Thumping doesn't help. (When the sound changes from a sharp tap to a dull thud the melon is usually overripe.) Also

count the days since planting. Small varieties may ripen in late July; large varieties, maybe not until August.

Stop Removing Runners from Strawberries. Summer heat shuts down fruit production, so stop pinching off runners early in July. In fall you'll be able to use the runners that have grown to make new plants. Fertilize them to encourage growth. If you're growing strawberries on plastic mulch, remove it now so runners can root in the soil.

How to Live with the Africanized Honeybee

To an untrained observer, Africanized honeybees look exactly like their European cousins, and, if you are stung only once, their sting is identical. The problem is that Africanized honeybees anger more quickly and defend their hives more aggressively than European honeybees. When aroused, large swarms of Africanized bees pursue intruders up to half a mile from their nest. They also nest in more places, forming smaller colonies, storing less honey, and moving more frequently. Africanized honeybees are good pollinators and are no more prone to sting when you are working in your garden than European honeybees. You can safely work in the garden in close proximity to them. They are dangerous, however, if you come too close to a nest.

▶ Inspect your property. Bee-proof your home by removing possible nesting sites; seal openings larger than ⅛ inch with cork, foam, or stucco patch. Be alert to bees entering or leaving a particular location. Close openings to cavelike places under roofs or porches with ⅛-inch hardware cloth. If you find a nest, hire a professional to remove it.

▶ If attacked by a swarm, cover your face—Africanized bees will go for your face first—and run for the closest shelter in a house or car; do not jump into water because the swarm will wait until you come up for air. (However, one woman who was attacked by bees and denied entrance to a house survived the attack by holding a hose over her head and body with the water running full-force until help arrived.) Use a credit card or flat-edged object to scrape stingers out; do not squeeze them. Wash the stung area with soap and water and apply icepacks. Seek medical attention if you have been stung numerous times. If you are a member of the 1 percent of the population that is extremely allergic to bee stings, carry a bee-sting kit with you.

▶ For more information about the Africanized honeybee and how to live with it, call your local University of California Cooperative Extension Farm and Home Advisor's office and ask for the brochure *Bee Alert: Africanized Honeybee Facts.*

JULY CHECKLIST

PURCHASE/PLANT

{ } Continue to plant tropicals in coastal zones, 206

{ } Purchase tuberous begonias already in bloom, 120

{ } Continue to plant summer annuals, 264

{ } Start biennials from seeds, 265

{ } Choose and plant hibiscus, 269

{ } Choose and plant succulents, 270

{ } Transplant succulents, including cacti and euphorbias, 272

{ } Continue to fill in vegetable rows with summer crops, 279

{ } Continue to plant papayas, bananas, and palms, 206

{ } Transplant palms, 206

{ } Select and plant salvias, 260

TRIM, PRUNE, MOW, DIVIDE

{ } Continue to pinch back chrysanthemums, 381

{ } Continue to pick and deadhead roses, but stop disbudding them now, 153, 257

{ } Remove berries (seedpods) from fuchsias, 208

{ } Deadhead flowers, 265

{ } Prune climbing roses that bloom only once a year, 258

{ } Prune impatiens, 260

{ } Pinch flowers off coleus, 264

{ } Cut back hydrangeas, 268

{ } Pick hibiscus blossoms, 269

{ } Clean up succulents by pruning off diseased and desiccated portions and removing unsightly spent blooms and seedpods, 270

{ } Propagate bromeliads by dividing the offshoots from parent plants, 274

{ } Mow all lawns to their correct height, according to variety, 276

{ } Mow off the flowers from lippia lawns, 277

{ } Stop removing runners from strawberries, 282

{ } Continue to prune and train espaliers, 291

{ } Continue to propagate and clean up daylilies, 293

{ } When Martha Washington geraniums stop blooming, clip off their faded flowers and begin to cut them back progressively, 346

{ } Cut back penstemon, artemisia, and pentas, 266

{ } Renew Korean grass that has developed ugly brown patches, 277

FERTILIZE

{ } Feed fuchsias, 208

{ } Feed water lilies, 156

{ } Feed cymbidiums with a high nitrogen fertilizer for growth, 257

{ } Fertilize roses, 257

{ } Feed ferns, 183

{ } Fertilize tropicals according to need during the summer months, 206

{ } Feed tuberous begonias, 260

{ } Fertilize impatiens, 260

{ } Feed coleus lightly, 264

{ } Fertilize azaleas that bloomed through June, 270

{ } Check camellias and azaleas for chlorosis; treat if necessary, 270

{ } Give camellias their third and final feeding for the year, 270

{ } If an azalea fails to respond to spring feeding, treat it with humic acid, 270

{ } Fertilize cacti and euphorbias that are growing in the ground, 273

{ } Fertilize bromeliads, 275

{ } Fertilize cool-season lawns lightly along the coast; do not fertilize them inland, 276

{ } Feed warm-season lawns according to type, 277

{ } Feed and water lippia after mowing, 277

{ } Continue to side-dress vegetable rows with additional fertilizer according to need, 279

{ } Treat pepper plants that lack good green leaves with Epsom salts, 279

{ } Feed and water cycads, 303

WATER

{ } Water all bougainvilleas that are under three years old, paying particular attention to newly planted ones, 207

{ } With the exception of certain California natives, water all garden plants according to their individual needs. Don't neglect to water young drought-resistant plants, 256

{ } Water citrus and avocado trees, 256

{ } Water cymbidiums, 257

{ } Increase water for roses to as much as 1½ inches three times a week in fast-draining soils, 258

{ } Give plants in north-facing shade extra water now while sun hits them, 261

{ } Water impatiens daily, 260

{ } Begin to water succulents growing in the ground once every two or three weeks, 273

{ } Water lawns according to their specific requirements, 276

{ } Keep newly planted seed rows damp, 279

{ } Continue to water vegetables regularly; don't let tomatoes or cucumbers go dry, 279

{ } Keep transplanted palms well watered, 302

{ } Do not water lithops in July or August, 274

CONTROL PESTS, DISEASE, AND WEEDS

{ } Control weeds by cultivating, mulching, or hand-pulling, 46

{ } Continue to control rose pests and diseases, 257

{ } Control mildew and slugs and snails on tuberous begonias, 260

{ } Control bark beetles on conifers, 266

{ } Control bougainvillea looper, 270

{ } Don't kill all the butterflies, 267

{ } Kill unwanted kikuyu or Bermuda grass with soil solarization, 277

{ } Continue to control pests on vegetables, 250

{ } Control corn earworm if desired, 306

{ } Control pine pitch canker, 267

{ } Protect yourself from Africanized honeybees, 283

{ } Attract good bees to your garden, 280

ALSO THIS MONTH

{ } Spread mulch to cool the ground and conserve moisture, 256

{ } Study the shady areas in your garden with an eye to improving them, 259

{ } Create additional shade where it's needed, 259

{ } Replace plants that are dying or doing badly in full shade with better choices for dark places, 261

{ } Replace plants in west-facing shade with better choices if they are being burned by sun or wilting in the afternoon, 262

{ } Protect fuchsias from burning rays of sun, 208

{ } Propagate camellias, azaleas, and other woody plants by layering, 269

{ } Replant donkey tails, 276

{ } Flush out bromeliads occasionally to prevent mosquitoes from breeding, and allow the cups to dry out from time to time, 275

{ } Harvest summer vegetables according to special techniques for each, 281

{ } Beware of bumblebees as you harvest vegetables and pick summer flowers, 282

August

THE HEIGHT-OF-SUMMER MONTH

Musa
(Banana)

August may not always be the hottest and driest month of the year, since September sometimes shoves the thermometer higher, but August usually attacks the job with more persistence. Along the coast the weather's almost always sunny this month, with oceanic breezes to keep temperatures cool and comfortable, albeit drier than in early summer. Every few years, however, if you live along the coast, you can experience a disappointing August—either overcast skies or a blanket of fog. Thirty or forty years ago in interior zones there was seldom, if ever, a cool or moist August day and almost never a cloud in the sky. But in recent years, a reliable number of tropical storms have been wheeling up from the South Pacific and hitting various portions of Southern California.

We also get the edge of summer monsoons, a normal feature of summer weather in the interior Southwest. Sometimes these storms bring humid weather; at other times they simply bring clouds that have a cooling effect. Usually they don't bring a measurable amount of rain, so watering is still the major task in the garden, and pest control comes next.

Other than in coastal zones it's too hot to plant most permanent additions to the landscape, but it's a good time to start seeds. In the vegetable garden harvesting is important. For the most part August is a time to enjoy life, take it easy, and maintain what you've got. Go to the beach. And if you want, bring home a bag of seaweed to add to the compost pile or work directly into garden soil.

WATERING

When the weather's hot and dry and there's no measurable rain, even the most inept gardeners are aware that most plants won't survive without regular irrigation. Unfortunately, one response is to stand with hose in hand and squirt water on the plants or on the surface of the ground around them. This doesn't do much but dig up the soil. Wise gardeners give their plants the amount of water each one needs in ways that save time, effort, and water.

Use the Right Equipment. Much water can be saved in summer by using the irrigation method appropriate to each part of the garden. Briefly, hand-sprinkling is fine for sprouting seeds, and washing off the leaves of native plants with an occasional spritz of water, as described on page 372, can be helpful for them, but all other watering should be done with conventional irrigation systems or drip systems. In general, conventional irrigation systems work best for most of the basic landscape, including lawns, while drip systems work best for plants in containers and vegetable gardens. Reserve watering by hose for filling furrows and basins around trees and bushes, when these are not equipped with bubblers. (When you water this way, put the hose right down on the ground, and let the water sink in slowly.)

How Often Should You Water Now? For most plants it's best to irrigate deeply once a week or every ten days—even less for many plants, depending on your climate zone and soil. Lawns—with the exception of Bermuda and zoysia—vegetables, certain annual flowers, and some perennial shade flowers are the thirstiest plants in the garden. Water these as frequently as necessary to prevent wilting. Some plants, such as fuchsias and impatiens, need water daily when growing in containers. Some drought-resistant native and exotic plants need little summer water or none at all. (In general, native plants that are summer deciduous should never be watered during the hot summer months or they'll die from root rot. Some native plants that don't drop their leaves in summer, including flannel bush [*Fremontodendron*], should be watered only if they show severe wilting and, even then, sparingly if in clay soils. As pointed out before, simply wetting their foliage as if they were moistened by a summer monsoon may be enough to pull them through.)

Other plants recommended for their resistance to drought—Mexican fan palms (*Washingtonia robusta*), Torrey pines, and Aleppo pines are good examples—will look better if they are watered deeply at least once during August. Water all pine trees deeply as needed—usually once every three weeks—to prevent stress in hot weather, which invites attack from bark beetles. Subtropical trees—including coral trees (*Erythrina*) and floss silk trees (*Chorisia speciosa*)—should be watered deeply, early in the month. Allowing chorisia to go on the dry side in late August often contributes to more spectacular fall bloom.

Remember to look for signs of stress and think of each plant as an individual; water accordingly. With deep, infrequent waterings, teach them to send their roots far into the ground, so that when there's a drought they'll survive.

Check for Malfunctioning Sprinklers and Drip Emitters. The easiest way to supply plants with the water they need is with an automatic system controlled by a clock, but once it's installed you can't just walk away and forget it. Automatic irrigation isn't entirely trouble-free; when it malfunctions, it can cause havoc.

Broken sprinklers and buried drip hoses with holes in them waste water. Clogged sprinklers and drip emitters can kill plants. If you go away on a trip, be sure to ask a responsible person to watch your garden, and leave the phone number of an irrigation repair person in case something goes wrong.

Now's a good time to check out your irrigation system. Begin by installing a new backup battery in your timer. Then flush the filters and the header lines of drip systems. Also, check all the drip emitters and clean out or replace those that are either flooding plants or failing to give them adequate water.

Run each section of your conventional sprinkler system on the manual setting; look for broken or clogged sprinklers or bubblers, and replace or repair the culprits. If your sprinklers don't adequately reach all parts of the lawn, you may get brown spots, especially after fertilizing. Sometimes gardeners don't realize how little water is actually penetrating the top layer of soil. In lawns, insufficient penetration may be caused by thatch (discussed on page 103). Or the problem may be that sprinkling is done too often and not long enough at one time. Set out empty juice cans to see how much water your sprinklers deliver in the amount of time you let them run. Adjust the timer to deliver water sufficient to sink deeply into the ground.

Another possible problem is that the soil has gotten so dry it won't absorb water. (Dry, sandy soils often shed water.) Check now by digging down to take a look. If this is the problem, treat the soil with a surfactant or wetting agent containing *Yucca schidigera* to increase water penetration.

Renew Watering Basins and Terraces.
Creating a basin of soil to hold water around the roots of bushes and trees is a typical way

How to Keep Water from Pouring Off a Bank

When sloping ground is irrigated, water often runs off and pours down the street. It may run off because the ground is hard and dry or simply because it has insufficient time to sink in. Here are some solutions:

▸ Apply a layer of mulch over the roots of plants growing on the slope to catch and hold moisture and increase water penetration. (Be sure to irrigate enough that water enters the ground as well as the mulch.)

▸ Install a time-lapse control clock that pulses water onto the area in brief bursts; the water sinks into the ground during the shut-off periods. (Check the instructions for your existing timer; it may already have this option.)

▸ Install low-volume sprinklers and set them to run for a longer time.

▸ If the slope is planted with lawn, aerate it in the fall and follow up with mulch.

▸ If all else fails, terrace the area by installing retaining walls or Gardenblock mortarless garden wall (a patented concrete block used to create terraces in which to grow plants on a bank).

to provide efficient irrigation in the Southwest, particularly on sloping ground, and the basin can be made into a decorative feature. Loose rocks can be used to hold the mounded soil in place. (Early Californians used abalone shells.) In some gardens a permanent system of wooden, concrete, or rock walls can convert steep slopes into usable garden space.

If no rock or concrete mortar is used to hold the soil, eventually it will erode away. Now's a good time to check watering basins and rebuild them if necessary. (Get the children involved. Shaping the walls of the basins can be fun, especially if it's wet and muddy.) Sometimes it's best to haul in unwanted clay soil from somewhere else in the garden, if you have some, instead of digging into the soil on a slope and creating more erosion.

Be sure to make tree basins big enough. Water standing around the trunk can cause crown rot and will never reach the roots, which aren't near the trunk but out farther, under the drip line. If the walls of the basin are made high enough, the center can be filled with mulch to hold moisture and improve the soil.

Give Special Care to Plants in Containers. Plants in containers often suffer at this time of year. Water them frequently. (A drip system can save time plus all the water that's wasted when you go from plant to plant with a hose.) In interior zones containers often dry out as soon as they're watered. It's not only the heat; dry air literally pulls moisture out of the soil right through the sides of terra-cotta pots.

Terra-cotta containers add charm to gardens and patios, but, surprisingly, most plants actually grow better in plastic. The idea that plants are helped by a pot that "breathes" is a mistaken one. The soil mix itself should breathe. It should be light and airy, which can be accomplished by adding perlite or sponge rock (a natural volcanic product that hold air.) In containers that breathe, roots follow the water as it escapes through the sides of the pot, forming a solid mat that clings to the inside of the pot, dries out daily, and causes the plant to wilt. When plants are grown in plastic, roots tend to form more evenly throughout the mix.

(Eventually they congregate at the bottom and wind around the sides, but then it's time to repot them to the next size of container.) Before planting in porous containers, seal the insides with a double coat of black waterproofing tar to help prevent escape of moisture.

DECIDUOUS FRUIT TREES

Don't feed deciduous fruit trees now even if you happen to read a newspaper column advocating this practice. Such columns are syndicated for the country at large, and the advice doesn't apply here. It's difficult enough for us to get our fruit trees into dormancy in this area without stimulating growth so late in the season.

Prune Unwanted Sprouts. Water sprouts are tall shoots that grow in summer straight up from the trunk and branches in the centers of mature deciduous fruit trees. Their growth is so sudden and rapid they soon look like buggy whips. Spot this growth as it begins and cut it out flush with the bark. A tree in which water sprouts have been allowed to persist and take over is a sorry mess. They eventually thicken and bear branches just like miniature trees within a tree, taking energy from the parent and ruining its shape. Some deciduous fruit trees also send up suckers from the base of the trunk and from roots. Cut these off now too, so they don't sap the strength of the tree.

Water Fruit Trees Infrequently. Water deeply and infrequently to encourage deep rooting, but don't subject your trees to absolute drought unless it's unavoidable. The **Rule of Thumb:** *Mature deciduous fruit trees growing in hot interior valleys need two or three deep irrigations per month throughout the* *growing season in order to grow well and bear good fruit. Full-grown trees along the coast should be watered deeply once or twice a month.* Trees in sandy soil need more water. Young trees require more frequent water to get established.

Double-Potting Beats the Heat

Hot sun hitting dark-colored containers can burn roots and damage or kill plants. Use double-potting to grow plants in plastic containers, enjoy the artistic look of terra-cotta pots, and keep plants roots cool.

▸ Plant any item you wish to grow in an appropriately sized plastic container, or, when roots aren't crowded, leave it right in the nursery can.

▸ Sink the planted container into a terra-cotta pot large enough to hide it. (Spherical Mexican pots are ideal; they hide planted containers best.)

▸ Where tree roots are a problem, place the outer pot onto a large stepping-stone. This will prevent roots from entering from below.

Train Fruit Tree Espaliers. Throughout the growing season train the whippy new growth that you want to save into the shape you want, while it's still soft and pliable. Tie it gently but firmly into place. (Refer to pruning manuals such as Tanner's *Living Fences: A Gardener's Guide to Hedges, Vines and Espaliers* for detailed instructions.) While the branches are still flexible, try tying bamboo poles onto them to train them in straight lines. This method can be especially helpful if you're training your espalier onto a wire framework because wire bends but bamboo is rigid. Remove the poles when the wood has hardened. Also cut off unwanted water sprouts, flush with the bark, from espaliered trees now.

On trees that bear on spurs, such as apples, apricots, and pears, cut new growth back to two or three buds to stimulate production of fruiting spurs. (Apricots aren't ideal for espalier. After several years, when their old wood no longer bears as well as formerly, retain some well-placed fresh growth to replace it. Then, during winter dormancy, cut out the old wood; start training the new growth to take its place.)

POOL PLANTING

Replace or trim vines and trees that drop leaves, fruit, or petals near swimming pools. Tidy vines such as Carolina Jessamine (*Gelsemium sempervirens*), Madagascar jasmine (*Stephanotis floribunda*), and star jasmine (*Trachelospermum jasminoides*) do well in the special microclimate near pools, and they add fragrance. If a tall accent is needed, choose a tree that has a tendency to hang onto its foliage until it is trimmed, such as Mediterranean fan palm (*Chamaerops humilis*), Spanish dagger (*Yucca gloriosa*), giant bird of paradise (*Strelitzia nicolai*), or firewheel tree (*Stenocarpus sinuatus*). For color try epidendrum, succulents, hibiscus, canna lilies, kangaroo paw (*Anigozanthos*), gazanias, and verbena. Fill large tubs, watered daily with a drip system, with 'Richmondensis' begonias surrounded by *Scaevola* 'Blue Wonder'. These plants aren't messy, and they can stand the reflected glare at poolside. Kahili ginger (*Hedychium gardnerianum*) does well if given rich soil, plenty of water, and protection from burning hot sun.

FUCHSIAS

Most fuchsias look bedraggled and bloomed-out in August. Cut them back lightly and pinch the tips for a week or two; you'll have a second flush of bloom that will last until cold weather. Continue to feed them regularly and remove berries (seedpods).

Cuttings root quickly now. (Use the method described on page 125.) Take your cuttings from the fresh, succulent growth that results from pruning. Root them in small pots filled with the same potting soil that you grow your fuchsias in and the plants won't suffer root shock when they're repotted.

Watch for pest problems. If possible, avoid spraying with anything other than a soap spray, like Safer's Insecticidal Soap, in order to preserve beneficials. Well-fed plants that are free from ants and have an adequate supply of beneficials should never need spraying.

FERNS

Keep ferns well watered during August and September. Protect them from drying winds, which can turn fronds brown and subject the plant to disease. Most ferns like an atmosphere comparable to the floor of a Northern California redwood forest—shady, damp, and thick with acid mulch. The closer you come to it, in an atrium, shady entryway, or some other protected spot, the happier your ferns will be. Leatherleaf fern (*Rumohra adiantiformis*) and southern sword fern (*Nephrolepis cordifolia*) are valuable exceptions to the rule. They're drought resistant, unfussy, and easy. (Sword fern is invasive but useful in narrow beds surrounded by pavement so plants can't escape.)

Many ferns are sold mainly as houseplants, but few of them can actually survive long inside most homes. ('Dallas' fern [*Nephrolepis exaltata* 'Dallas'] and 'Kimberley Queen' [*N. obliterata* 'Kimberley Queen'] are exceptions; they can withstand lower light than most ferns.) The common type of Boston fern (*N. e.* 'Bostoniensis') is among the most often bought and quickly killed of all houseplants. Indoors they die within a few months, but they thrive outdoors in semishade in coastal zones (see Quick Tip, below). One way to have success with houseplant ferns is to grow them outdoors but cycle them into the house for a week at a time.

◎ QUICK TIP

How to Keep a Difficult Boston Fern Alive. *When you leave for work in the morning, take the fern out and hang it under a tree (like putting out the dog). Take it in when you return. One Southern California gardener used this method to keep her houseplant fern alive for seven years.*

ROSES

Continue to feed, fertilize, water, and control rose pests and diseases. If you're following the Rose-Pro Method, during the last week of August apply to the soil over the roots of each rose: 2 tablespoons of John and Bob's Soil Optimizer, 2 cups Dr. Earth Organic Rose Fertilizer, or other organic rose food of your choice, and 1 or 2 cups Biosol Mix (7-2-3) All Purpose Fertilizer, depending on your soil. (Sandy soils need more than clay soils.) Scratch these nutrients lightly into the ground and follow up with a deep irrigation.

Prune Lightly. Roses usually take a rest during the heat of August while they gather strength for a great burst of bloom in fall. You can cooperate by cutting them back lightly during the last ten days of August to promote fall flowering. Prune off as much as one-third of the growth of shrub roses. Remove spent flowers, dead twigs, and hips (the fruits of roses, which contain the seeds). Instead of cutting off stems that have bloomed just above the first five-leaflet leaf, as you do in other months, cut them down farther. Notice the joint at the bottom of the flower stem where it springs from thicker wood, and cut it off so you leave only two buds or leaves on the stem above that joint. This will stimulate new growth that in turn will produce good autumn bloom. Also, cut or yank off suckers sprouting from below the bud union.

DAYLILIES AND AGAPANTHUS

Clean up daylilies *(Hemerocallis)* and agapanthus now by removing stems that have bloomed. On most daylilies the stems go brown after flowering; simply yank these off. But many varieties, especially the newer everblooming ones, have stems that never go brown. Instead they stay green and continue to grow; don't try to pull them off or you'll uproot the plant. After these green stems finish flowering, they sprout leaves and form plantlets, or "proliferates," on the stem. As soon as the proliferates have formed one or two short roots, cut the stems off the mother plant, so they don't sap its strength. Gently snap off the pups and plant them elsewhere in the garden, or give them to friends.

Agapanthus stems have to be cut off. Some gardeners hang them upside down to dry and then use them in flower arrangements or dip them in glue and glitter for holiday decorations.

FORTNIGHT LILY

Fortnight lily *(Dietes iridioides, D. vegeta)* has white blossoms with orange blotches on them. It's good near swimming pools and is drought resistant, easy to grow, and one of our commonest plants—some people think it's much too common. There's also a yellow type *(D. bicolor)*. Both have clumps of upright narrow, pointed leaves and bear their flowers in flushes every two weeks or so, spring through fall, sometimes year-round. Keep them looking their best by feeding them lightly now and watering them well. After flowers fade from the yellow species, cut off the flower stalk at the base. Remove the seedpods of white fortnight lily to clean up the plants and promote continued flowering, but don't remove the stalks; they'll bloom for several years.

ALSTROEMERIA

Peruvian lilies, or alstroemerias *(Alstroemeria aurea, A. aurantiaca, A. psittacina, A. ligtu,* and hybrids) are members of the lily family whose azalea-like blossoms and many virtues have captivated the hearts of local gardeners in recent years. The plants are considerably drought resistant; the blooms have sturdy stems, and their cut flowers last two weeks. The craze for alstroemerias began when a photograph of the Berkeley Botanical Gardens' massive display of peach, orange, and gold ligtu hybrids was published on the cover of *Sunset* magazine. But ligtu hybrids have some drawbacks: It takes at least three years to get them going, and once established they're almost impossible to eradicate or transplant. Their tall flowers make a magnificent display, but they do so only once a year, in June and July. Many catalogs, including Thompson and Morgan (see the catalog list on page 416), carry seeds of ligtu hybrids, but these are difficult to germinate. A better way to start them is to purchase rooted plants from sales at botanical gardens, such as the annual Bulb Sale at the University of California at Irvine Arboretum. Nothing can beat a bed of ligtu hybrids in bloom, but Meyer hybrids are the kind we usually grow in Southern California.

Meyer hybrid alstroemerias are more heat resistant, easier to grow, and less invasive than the ligtu types. They also bloom longer and can be transplanted, divided, or moved in fall. They come in many shades of white, lavender, maroon, rose, and pink with stems ranging in height from $1^1/_2$ to $2^1/_2$ feet. They're available at nurseries throughout Southern California. If you let them go dry in summer they won't die, though they will stop blooming, but if you water, feed, and deadhead them regularly, many of them will bloom on and off year-round. The newest varieties like 'Tri-Color', 'Jupiter', 'Third Harmonic', 'Casablanca', and 'Jena' are 3-feet tall, vigorous, and everblooming, with abundant flowers on sturdy stems, that last two weeks in water. They need full sun or part-shade in hot inland valleys.

Look for Meyer hybrid alstroemerias in summer and plant them in fall in loose, well-drained soil with plenty of organic matter worked in. After a few years divide and transplant the clumps, handling the tubers gently to preserve their delicate roots. After the flowers fade, remove each spent stalk by giving it a sharp tug. By pulling off the stems singly you remove them cleanly and safely from the tubers, and this stimulates the plant to produce more bloom spikes. (Cutting off stems makes the plant stop blooming.) Follow up each wave of bloom with an application of complete organic fertilizer, and water it thoroughly into the ground.

WISTERIA

Continue pruning and training wisteria. Throughout spring and summer wisteria sends out many thin, long twining stems until it stops growing in mid or late August. If you haven't kept up on pruning, there's still time to do some corrective pruning on young plants. All growth you allow to stay will eventually be part of the structure, and in time become heavy wood requiring strong support. Never allow the young stems to twine around each other or they will form a "rat's nest" of twisted growth that can never be corrected. While wisteria is young, train it onto its support, such as a pergola. To grow a straight trunk, tie the young shoots gently but firmly straight up a post. If you prefer to have them wind around the post, arrange them all in the same direction, clockwise for Japanese wisterias and counterclockwise for Chinese wisterias, according to their natures, and tie them loosely into place. (All branches touching each other in the same direction will form a natural graft and become one thick trunk or branch.) Once a young wisteria has reached the top of its support, such as a pergola, climb a ladder every week or two throughout the growing season and loosely tie the best new shoots down flat on top of the pergola separating them from one another by one to two feet. Train these shoots in parallel lines down the length of the pergola, cutting all others off as explained below. Continue doing this with all good new shoots until these straight branches of growth cover the top of the entire pergola from one end to the other, which may take two and three summers to accomplish.

All summer long and every summer thereafter, cut off all unwanted new growth as it occurs, but don't cut it off flush. Instead, every time you make a cut, leave a stub with two buds (the same as two leaves) still attached to the plant. Every time you cut back a twiner to two buds, the stub you leave attached to the plant will become a spur. (Spurs are short, straight, or stubby growths that sprout fat flower buds in fall that bloom in spring.) Spurs can bloom repeatedly every spring for fifteen or more years; don't ever cut them off. Pruning this way in spring and summer hugely increases spring bloom and also makes wisteria sport a few blooms continually all summer long. A long-reach Japanese cut-and-hold pruner is ideal for pruning mature wisterias once they've covered their support. (These are indispensable, also, for pruning climbing roses and bougainvillea. You can purchase them from Wahmhoff Farms. See page 416 for the address.)

TREES FOR AUGUST BLOOM

Crape myrtle (*Lagerstroemia indica*) is an elegant, drought-resistant tree for small gardens in interior valleys. (It gets mildew along the coast.) It blooms in white and electric shades of pink and red from July through August. Its lovely gray-brown bark peels off yearly to soft pink. Look for the plant while they're in bloom. (People either love or hate some of the colors.)

The gold medallion tree (*Cassia leptophylla*) is the most dramatic of the cassias that can be grown here. It's best in a warm, sheltered spot and watered deeply and infrequently, but it will grow in lawns if it has excellent drainage.

Along the coast the flame eucalyptus or red-flowering gum; (*Eucalyptus ficifolia*) can grow in the teeth of the wind and still bloom magnificently. This is the time you may be able to pick out the color you want. (Young ones often won't bloom in the can.) The orangey red is gorgeous viewed against the sea. Grow it with a single trunk, or, if desired, cut it back to make

a huge, multibranched shrub. It blooms on and off all year. The eucalyptus beetle prefers blue gum eucalyptus (*E. globulus*) and usually doesn't attack this species unless it's under stress from drought.

CONTROL OF NEMATODES

Nematodes are especially active in warm weather. These are microscopic worms that bore into roots of susceptible plants, causing galls and knots and weakening the plant. Here are two ways to significantly reduce large populations of nematodes:

Solarize the Soil. Solarization—using the effects of the sun's rays—is the method to use only when nematode and fungal problems are acute and unbearable. It kills useful organisms, including worms and beneficial fungi, along with the bad ones. (This method works best where summer days are hot—90°F—and skies are clear.)

- If nematodes and fungus have rendered a vegetable or flower area unusable, sacrifice the plants now. Pull them out roots and all. (Don't compost the roots; destroy them.)
- Thoroughly soak the soil with water.
- Cover the area with clear (not black) polyethylene plastic that's 1- to 4-millimeters thick. Peg it down around the outside, and bury the loose edges. (A few round rocks in the middle will hold it down in case of strong wind.) Tests at University of California, Davis show even better results with two layers of clean 1-millimeter polyethylene film separated by a 6-centimeter air space. (Prop up the top layer here and there with wire hoops or bamboo frame.)

- Leave the plastic in place for six to eight weeks of hot, sunny weather. Test plots under a single plastic layer in the San Joaquin Valley reached 140°F at a depth of 2 inches and 102°F as far down as 18 inches. Almost all traces of harmful disease organisms were destroyed, including fungi. (Soil solarization also kills invasive plants, including devilweed [common Bermuda grass growing as a weed] and kikuyu. After solarizing soil, restock the ground with beneficial organisms by applying earthworm castings, manures, rhyzobia, compost, humic acid, and kelp meal.)

Plant Marigolds. Many people think marigolds repel nematodes, but the truth is they attract them. Root knot nematodes entering marigold roots are killed by a natural plant chemical before they have a chance to reproduce. Planting a single row of marigolds among vegetables won't get rid of nematodes, however. Marigolds can be used to rid the ground of these pests, but you have to start earlier in the planting season. Consider this method for next year.

- In March solidly plant the area to be treated with French marigolds *(Tagetes patula)*. Space the plants in a 7-by-7-inch pattern all over the bed.
- Leave the marigolds in place for a full 120 day season of growth.
- Systematically remove all weeds at their earliest appearance.

After this treatment the ground can be planted with any desired crop. Nematodes will gradually return, but they'll be discouraged if you regularly add organic soil amendment. They don't like humusy soil.

Harmful nematodes can also be controlled by releasing beneficial nematodes into the ground.

Beneficial nematodes can be purchased online. Unlike the harmful types, beneficial nematodes need moist soil to survive.

CONTROL OF FIREBLIGHT

Fireblight *(Erwinia amylovora)* is a bacterial disease of the rose family *(Rosaceae)* that infects such common garden plants as apples, pears, evergreen pear *(Pyrus kawakamii)*, pyracantha, cotoneaster, California holly or toyon *(Heteromeles arbutifolia)*, plum, cherry, quince, and loquat (though some varieties are resistant to fireblight). Fireblight first wilts the fresh green growth, then shrivels and blackens it, as well as twigs, branches, berries, and fruit, making the victim look as if it had been caught in a flash fire. Birds and insects carry the bacteria from tree to tree during the bloom period. Remove disfigured twigs and branches now to reduce the sources of infection. Cut out infected branches 8 to 15 inches below any visible damage, and destroy them. (Dip the pruning shears in rubbing alcohol after making each cut to avoid spreading the infection.)

OLEANDER LEAF SCORCH

Since 1994 oleanders *(Nerium oleander)*, particularly in interior valleys, have been stricken with a bacterial disease called oleander leaf scorch, caused by a new strain of *Xylella fastidiosa*, which in the late 1800s wiped out vineyards in Southern California. Xylella is a disease spread by glassy-winged sharpshooters, leaf-sucking insects native to the southeastern United States. Once a plant is infected, its leaf edges go brown, then whole branches die and finally the entire plant goes. At the present time there's no known cure for leaf scorch. Until a solution is found, maintain good plant health by watering and fertilizing regularly. Destroy infected branches and dying plants and don't plant oleanders. Boston ivy (*Parthenocissus tricuspidata*), Virginia creeper (*P. quinquefolia*), crape myrtle (*Lagerstroemia indica*), and periwinkle (*Vinca*) are potential hosts of sharpshooters and leaf scorch bacteria, so don't plant these near oleanders. (Be careful handling oleanders; all parts are extremely poisonous.)

ANNUAL AND PERENNIAL FLOWERS

Plant Cool-Season Annuals from Seeds.
Gardeners who want to grow their own transplants of winter flowers, particularly tall rather than dwarf varieties or single colors rather than mixed, should plant seeds of cool-season annuals now. Plant in flats, small pots, or peat pots. If you can't find the seeds you want locally, kick off your shoes, relax in the shade, study the seed catalogs, and send away for seeds. A few varieties may be sold out but most are still available, and service now is swift.

Seeds of such flowers as calendulas, cineraria, delphiniums, dianthus (pinks), Iceland poppies, nemesia, pansies, primroses, snapdragons, stock (discussed in detail below), and violas, planted in August, can give great numbers of transplants with which to fill beds in October.

Plant Stock.
Growing tall varieties of stock (*Matthiola incana*) is particularly worthwhile from seed, since you can be assured of disease-free transplants. (Stock is susceptible to stem and root rots, so don't plant them in the same place two years in a row.)

To grow stock, disinfect flats and fill them with sterilized potting soil. Place the seeds on top of the soil, carefully spacing them where you want them; press them down gently. (Stock needs light to germinate.) Keep them moist and in semishade. Cover the flats with plastic until the seeds germinate. Then take off the plastic, protect the sprouts with netting, and move the flats in stages—over a period of two or three weeks—into increasing light, eventually into full sun. Start to feed the plants lightly when each has two real leaves. Transplant seedlings into beds when they are 3 to 4 inches tall. The sooner you get stock in the ground the better, because early planting enables the plants to build big, strong root systems and hefty stalks. You'll reap a long-lasting and dramatic display.

Try to find seeds of the brand-new variety called 'Vintage', which may revolutionize stock for home gardeners and perhaps the floral trade. 'Vintage' produces large branching plants with three or four shoots, each as strong and as full of flowers as the main stem. Your color display will be much greater and last longer. Mixed-color seed packets of 'Vintage' include copper, a new color for stock.

The real problem with stock is disease, and yellowing leaves are the first symptom. To make stock more resistant, feed it when you plant it and treat it with humic acid. Fertilize often with fish emulsion. If you plant stock in September, you will have color in December. It's one of the best winter-color plants.

Pick Summer-Blooming Annuals.
Continue picking or deadheading warm-season annual flowers and feed and water them regularly. Tall varieties of zinnia and cosmos will bloom through September if you give them this care.

Maintain Perennials. In interior zones August is far from the best time to plant perennials. Continue to pick flowers, deadhead, and clean up as needed. Renew mulch. Water in the early morning hours. When summer phlox (*Phlox paniculata*) begins to look tired and bloomed out, cut off its main terminal flower heads. This will force the side branches to produce blooms that will flower into September. Continue to deadhead pentas. Every time you cut off a faded flower, two more pop out, but it can't do so without regular fertilizer and water.

Along the coast, gardeners will find many interesting and often new perennials in bloom in nurseries. Big blue lilyturf (*Liriope muscari*) is far from new but is a fine shade plant that blooms now. The benefit of finding plants now is that you know that they will bloom at this time every year. Some gardeners take their finds home but keep them in the containers for fall planting. Personally, I find it harder to keep a plant in good shape in a nursery container than in the ground.

In all zones you might find propeller plant (*Crassula falcata*) now among the succulents or ask for cuttings from a friend. A super plant for a tub, a bank, or well-drained bed, its bright scarlet blossoms against blue-green foliage will light up a patio or delight the sunbathers next to a swimming pool in late summer.

FIRE-RESISTANT LANDSCAPING

Fire is endemic to Mediterranean climates worldwide. Each of them is home to a brushy community of native, drought-resistant shrubs and small trees—different plants in each region but with similar attributes. Collectively these plant communities are called the Mediterranean Biome, but individually they are called *fynbos* in South Africa, *heathlands* in Australia,

Fire-Resistant Trees for Suburban Areas*

American sweet gum (*Liquidamber styraciflua*), Chinese banyan (*Ficus microcarpa*), Chinese mastic (*Pistacia chinensis*), crape myrtle (*Lagerstroemia indica*), flowering plum (*Prunus cerasifera* 'Nigra'), Italian alder (*Alnus cordata*), jacaranda (*Jacaranda mimosifolia*), Japanese maple (*Acer palmatum*), maidenhair tree (*Ginkgo biloba*), mayten tree (*Maytenus boaria*), strawberry tree (*Arbutus unedo*), tulip tree (*Liriodendron tulipifera*), Victorian box (*Pittosporum undulatum*), western redbud (*Cercis occidentalis*), Catalina cherry (*Prunus ilicifolia lyonii*), pomegranate (*Punica granatum* 'Wonderful'), callery pear (*Pyrus calleryana*), California live oak, coast live oak (*Quercus agrifolia*).

* *Fire resistant* in this context means "less flammable alternatives to cedars, palms, pines, and eucalyptus."

mattoral in Chile, *maquis* in the Mediterranean Basin, and *chaparral* in California. All of them periodically burn and regenerate through fire. Some hard-coated seeds in each of these plant communities only sprout after fire; many wildflowers and bulbs bloom after winter rains but only if wildfires first clear away dense brush. In California we think of fall as the traditional fire season, but when hot weather coincides with strong wind, parched plants, and lightning, wildfires can strike at any time. Gardens and houses on hillsides or next to canyons and wildlands are particularly vulnerable.

Lessons from Other Cultures. Some Mediterranean societies have found efficient ways to protect their homes from wildfires, and why shouldn't we copy some of these techniques? Australian communities pen herds of goats inside portable fences to clean out dense underbrush near houses. Goats are now clearing brush on Mt. Palomar in California. Goats quickly consume twigs, dead leaves, and foliage without killing the plants. Goats climb steep banks, work dawn to dark, and don't get paid overtime. Once the goats have cleaned one section or canyon, it's easy to herd them into another. Men with chain saws follow the goats pruning trees and removing low-hanging branches. In southern Italy and Greece, flat or tile-roofed stone houses are huddled together amidst a network of steps, roads, flower-decked patios, and small walled gardens. The surrounding hillsides burn repeatedly, but not the towns.

A new concept in Southern California called "shelter in place" surrounds fire-resistant homes with larger fire-resistant landscapes. In 2007, a newly constructed "shelter-in-place" community stopped a firestorm in its tracks. Every home was fire-resistant and surrounded by 100 feet of what is known as *defensible space* (a clearing surrounding a home that is planted with a fire-resistant landscape and can greatly help a home survive a fire). In another Southern California example, a Spanish home appeared to have been saved by its garden of mature succulent plants including agaves, aloes, crassulas, and euphorbias. The plants were singed but did not burn, nor did the house, though neighboring houses and gardens burned to the ground. Fire-resistant homes have fireproof roofs,

How to Create A Fire-Resistant Landscape

▸ Create defensible space on your property by removing combustible plants and materials from the 100-foot-wide area closest to your home. Replant with fire-resistant plants. (Choose succulent plants or shrubs and trees with lush green leaves.)

▸ If you live next to a canyon, chaparral, or wildland, divide your landscape into fire zones and plant defensively, choosing plants such as those on the accompanying lists. (See the description of the various zones in the text on page 300.)

▸ Keep the area surrounding your home well irrigated and neatly pruned.

▸ Plant fire-resistant trees, remove low-hanging branches of existing trees so their canopies are high off the ground, and make sure no branches overhang your roof.

▸ Space shrubs apart so they are well separated from one another and from trees. Remove plants that would give fire a ladder to climb from the ground into a tree.

▸ Make sure foliage is a least 10 feet away from rooftops, chimneys, decks, and outdoor barbecues.

▸ Surround your home with hardscape, including brick or concrete patios, masonry seats, decorative walls, and rock mulches. Construct shade structures and decks of fire-resistant materials.

▸ Remove combustible materials like dry leaves and pine needles from rooftops and surrounding ground. Mulch the ground with gravel, pebbles, and river rock instead of flammable materials.

Plants for Fire Zones

Succulent Ground Covers for Zone I Firebreaks

Bronze carpet stonecrop (*Sedum spurium* 'Bronze Carpet'), cobweb houseleak (*Sempervivum arachnoideum*), coral stonecrop (*Sedum album*), Disneyland ice plant (*Delosperma* 'Alba'), gold moss sedum (*Sedum acre*), gray fingers (*Senecio mandraliscae, Kleinia mandraliscae*), orange bush (*Lampranthus aurantiacus*), pork and beans (*Sedum x rubrotinctum*), pride of London (*Crassula multicava*), red spike ice plant (*Cephalophyllum* 'Red Spike'), Redondo creeper (*L. filicaulis*), rock purslane (*Calandrinia umbellata*), Rocky Point or yellow trailing ice plant (*Malephora lutea*), rosea ice plant (*Drosanthemum floribundum*), rose-flowered ice plant (*L. deltoides*), sweet aeonium (*Aeonium simsii, A. caespitosum*), trailing ice plant (*L. spectabilis*)

Perennial Ground Covers for Zone II Firebreaks

Beach strawberry (*Fragaria chiloensis*), California poppy (*Eschscholzia californica*), carpet bugle (*Ajuga reptans* 'Giant Bronze'), freeway daisy (*Osteospermum fruticosum*), golden barrel cactus (*Echinocactus grusonii*), green lavender cotton (*Santolina rosmarinifolia*), Indian mock strawberry (*Duchesnea indica*), lippia (*Phyla nodiflora*), miniature gazanea (*Dymondia margaretae*), Mother of thyme (*Thymus praecox arcticus*), Naked lady (*Amaryllis belladonna*), Peruvian verbena (*Verbena peruviana*), silver spreader (*Artemisia caucasica*), snow in summer (*Cerastium tomentosum*), Sonoma sage (*Salvia sonomensis*), spring cinquefoil (*Potentilla neumanniana*), trailing gazania (*Gazania* 'Sunglow'), woolly thyme (*T. pseudolanuginosus*), woolly yarrow (*Achillea tomentosa*)

Transitional Shrubs and Ground Covers for Zone III Firebreaks

Aaron's beard (*Hypericum calycinum*), Australian saltbush (*Atriplex semibaccata*), Catalina cherry (*Prunus ilicifolia* var. lyonii), common winter creeper (*Euonymous fortunei* var. radicans), creeping blue blossom (*Ceanothus thyrsiflorus repens*), creeping coprosma (*Coprosma x kirkii*), dwarf coyote bush (*Baccharis pilularis* 'Pigeon Point'), elephant's food (*Portulacaria afra*), Italian buckthorn (*Rhamnus alaternus* 'Variegata', syn. 'Argenteovariegata'), lemon bottlebrush (*Callistemon citrinus* 'Compacta'), lemonade berry (*Rhus integrifolia*), Monterey manzanita (*Arctostaphylos hookeri* 'Monterey Carpet'), natal plum (*Carissa macrocarpa* 'Green Carpet'), Point Reyes bearberry (*Arctostaphylos uva-ursi* 'Point Reyes'), rockrose (*Cistus crispus* 'Descanso'), toyon, California holly (*Heteromeles arbutifolia*), trailing myoporum (*Myoporum parvifolium* var. prostratum 'Pink'), Wheeler's dwarf pittosporum (*Pittosporum tobira* 'Wheeler's Dwarf')

boxed eaves, dual pane or tempered glass windows, residential fire sprinklers, and are built of fire-resistant materials. New ways for fireproofing existing homes include fire-resistant gels, but one of the best ways to protect a home from wildfires is to plant a fire-resistant garden.

Divide Your Property into Firebreak Zones. When planting a fire-resistant garden next to canyons and chaparral, experts recommend dividing your property into firebreak zones. Zone I refers to "defensible space," the 100-foot-wide, well-irrigated area closest to your home in which ideally there are no tall plants. Zone II, known as the "reduced fuel zone," is the next 35- to 100-foot-wide section, planted with low ground covers. Zone III is the "transitional zone" between a home garden and the wild landscape, containing a mix of low, drought-resistant Mediterranean and native shrubs. Zone IV refers to the existing native vegetation farthest from the house that has been cleaned out and thinned. (This is where the goats could help.) The width of the zones will differ depending on circumstances.

Some of the rules of fire-resistant gardening are at odds with the principles of organic gardening; especially in regard to organic mulch, protecting your home from wildfire may force hard choices. The closer one's home is to wildlands, the wiser it would be to sacrifice some ingrained ideas or even beloved plants to create a fire-resistant landscape. Most people don't want to cut down valuable old trees, but even without such drastic steps, much can be done to make an existing landscape safer. The first step is to remove plants that are a known fire hazard. Combustible plants include bamboo, cedar trees (*Cedrus* ssp.), palms, pines, eucalyptus, and most ornamental grasses, including fountain grass (*Pennisetum*), deer grass (*Muhlenbergia*), and Mexican feather grass (*Nassella tenuissima*). As an example of the damage flammable plants can do, in a recent firestorm flaming palm fronds blown loose from their trunks sailed through the air and jumped long distances to light new fires. For better choices, refer to the accompanying boxes and to the step-by-step method on page 299 for creating a more fire-resistant landscape.

TROPICALS

It's somewhat late for planting most tropicals this month, except in coastal zones. Among tropicals that can be planted along the coast now (or during any summer month) are papayas, bananas, and palms.

Plant Papayas and Bananas. Papayas (*Carica papaya*) and bananas (*Musa, Ensete*) will grow and bear fruit in all frost-free zones, but they do best near the coast, and thrive on sheltered south-facing hillsides. Papayas are tall, single-trunked, succulent trees with a palmlike cluster of leaves on top. It's a common misconception that bananas, like papayas, grow on trees; they actually grow on a large, green herbaceous perennial plant. The apparent trunk of a banana plant is actually a group of leaf stalks. Surprisingly, the fruits themselves are technically berries.

Plant Papayas from Seed or Plants. If you compost papaya skins and seeds, many papaya plants will come up here and there during the summer. Look for these seedlings now and plant a group of three to five of them in full sun, 4 to 6 feet apart. (You'll need both male and female plants to get fruit.) Provide papayas with moist, well-drained organic soil, and regular applications of complete organic fertilizer. Mulch with manure in fall.

The babaco papaya (*Carica x heilbornii pentgona*) is a popular type because, though expensive, it's hardy to 28°F, and the plant is small enough to grow in a whiskey half-barrel. Babaco papayas bear fruit when young, often while they're still in a five-gallon can, and you need only one plant to get fruit. The fruit is large—sometimes a foot long—and equal to other papayas in its health-giving properties, but it tastes more like a melon than an ordinary papaya. The fruit starts to ripen between now and fall. Pick it when it's yellow and gives slightly to the touch.

How to Tell When Homegrown Bananas Are Ripe

▶ Some varieties ripen on the plant. When the fruit of these begins to turn yellow, reach up with a long-handled fruit picker or pruning hook and pick one banana. If it's creamy yellow inside, and soft textured and sweet, it's ready. To harvest, cut off individual hands of fruit as they ripen or, if they're too far out of reach, cut the whole trunk down as described below.

▶ Most varieties don't ripen on the plant. Pick their fruit when they've lost their sharp edges and indented sides; wait until they lose their angularity. When the fruit is still green but has become rounded, filled out, and fat looking, it's ready to pick. (You will know if you have this type of plant because the fruit will not turn yellow on the plant.)

▶ Once ready, cut the whole plant down by nicking the underside of the trunk with a sharp knife or giving it a single whack with a machete. It will fall of its own weight. Ask someone to stand below and catch the fruit as it falls. Cut off the entire fruit stalk (scape) and hang it in a shady place to ripen, such as your front porch or patio overhang. When individual bananas go yellow, they're ready to eat.

▶ Chop up the remains of the stalk that's borne fruit; use it to mulch the rest of your bananas, or bury it and let it rot. Plant your next banana there.

Start Bananas from Plants You Buy at a Nursery. Begin with a good variety, such as 'Ice Cream' or 'Enano Gigante'. (The plants are small, but the fruit is giant.) Fertilize often with a complete organic fertilizer. Bananas are big eaters; they're also thirsty, so water them well. You can keep them barely alive with less water and fertilizer in drought years, but their growth will slow down and they won't bear fruit.

As suckers, or pups, form around the main trunk, use a sharp spade to slice off all but one, and plant them elsewhere in the garden. The one pup you leave will remain to replace the mature stalk after it has borne fruit. (Each stalk of a banana plant is monocarpic and won't bear fruit again.) At thirteen to fifteen months after planting you should have a scape covered with fruit.

Transplant Palms. Summer is a good time to plant or transplant palms because they take off

well when planted in warm soil. Before transplanting any palm, be sure it's a species that can be transplanted successfully. Most can; a few cannot. Trim off all faded fronds and cut back the remaining fronds by one-third to make up for the loss of roots. Bend these upright and tie them together on top with stout twine to protect the meristem layer (the area of actively dividing cells at the bud of the plant). Each single-trunked palm has only one bud; if it's damaged, the tree will die. After transplanting, leave the fronds tied for a month or two to shade the bud. (Be sure to water palms well after planting and keep them well watered for at least a year, until established.)

Palms can lend a tropical atmosphere to any garden, and not all are heavy water users; some are drought resistant. They're incredibly interesting and varied, so before choosing a palm, study the options and your requirements. Notice

Protect Canary Island Date Palms from Fungus

Before having Canary Island date palms (*Phoenix canariensis*) pruned, insist that the tree pruners sterilize all pruning tools by soaking the blades for 15 minutes in a solution of 1 part household bleach to 1 part water. (Request that a saw with a reciprocating blade be used—not a chain saw, which cannot be effectively disinfected.) Pruning with unsterilized saws causes healthy date palms to fall prey to fungal attacks, because it allows spores carried from infected palms to enter fresh cuts. As an additional precaution, remove only dead and dying fronds, not fresh green growth.

that some palms have fronds (leaves) shaped like feathers and others have fronds shaped like fans. Some palms form a clump while others are solitary. Some palms are self-cleaning—the fronds fall off without pruning. The fronds of others cling to the trunk after they're dead and need to be pruned off, or in some cases the old fronds look best left on the tree. Among those with persistent fronds, some have trunks that are easily cleaned off by pruning, while others have leaf bases that tend to stay on the trunk for many years. An important factor to consider if you have children is that some palms are armed with formidable spikes; others are unarmed.

CYCADS

Dating from the age of dinosaurs, cycads (Cycadaceae) are among the most ancient plants on Earth. They're also one of nature's first

attempts at making seeds. Male plants bear prominent cones that give off pollen, while female plants develop a sporophyll (a brushlike, spore-bearing organ) that can produce seeds if fertilized (though this is a rare occurrence in gardens). In appearance cycads look like ferns or palms, but they're not even closely related to either. The best known and most commonly grown cycad is often mistaken for a palm and even bears the confusing name of sago palm (*Cycas revoluta*). In gardens cycads are long-lived and slow growing. They grow well outdoors in most of Southern California if provided with some shade.

Water cycads well now; don't let their roots dry out. When cycads are neglected, their leaves may turn brown, pale, whitish, or yellow in color. Brown tips on leaves usually come from salt burn (sago palms are particularly sensitive to salts in the soil); drench the ground to leach out salts. Pale or brown patches on the leaves can come from sunburn; in this case, consider digging up the plant and transplanting it into more shade. All-over yellowing or loss of color most likely means lack of nitrogen or trace elements. To correct the problem, apply $1/4$ cup of John and Bob's Soil Optimizer and water into the ground, or mix fish emulsion with kelp and humic acid, diluted according to package directions, and drench the ground and the foliage with the solution. In addition to these steps, provide for the future needs of the plant by applying a balanced granulated or powdered organic fertilizer to the ground and watering it in. Feed again in spring. Cycads need good drainage and ample irrigation. They respond well to foliar feeding.

Yellowing and loss of color may also result from insect attack, though well-nourished sago palms, unless growing in solid shade, seldom suffer from pests. In the case of a neglected plant, scale is the worst offender. Look under the fronds for small, round, brown bumps—these are scale insects. The safest way to get rid of them now is to painstakingly scrub them off with a brush or sponge dipped in soapy solution; they come off easily. Oil sprays kill scale, so you could spray with Summit Year-Round Spray Oil. (Other oil sprays will damage foliage in hot weather.)

LAWN CARE

This is the time of year when warm-season lawns, such as Bermuda, zoysia, and St. Augustine, are looking their best, but cool-season lawns, such as Kentucky bluegrass, perennial ryegrass, and tall fescue are at their worst. Water warm-season lawns deeply and infrequently, and feed them every month to six

Sago palm (male and female)

weeks. As in June and July, mow common Bermuda to 1 to 1 1/2 inches; cut hybrid Bermuda shorter, to 1/2 or 1 inch; cut zoysia to between 1/2 and 1 inch; kikuyu grass to 1 to 1 1/2 inches; and St. Augustine grass to 1 to 2 inches in height. These heights are those recommended by UC Extension for mowing warm-season lawns. Ten years ago UC Extension recommended mowing warm-season lawns "as short as possible in summer." Neither system is perfect. Allowing lawns to grow longer helps them survive through drought and use less water. But allowing kikuyu to grow too long makes it more difficult to control, and allowing Bermuda and zoysia to grow too long in summer can contribute to the buildup of thatch. Cutting lawns short, on the other hand, means you have to mow more frequently and your lawn will need more water in order to survive. When you weigh the alternatives it's better to go with the UC lengths. Luckily, there's one fact about which there is no dispute: Allowing the cut grass leaves to fall on top of the lawn and thus feed and mulch the lawn will not contribute to the buildup of thatch. Regardless of how long you keep your grass, don't catch, rake up, or throw away the clippings. Allow them to remain on the lawn and sift down to soil level. Don't feed kikuyu or 'Adalayd' (Excalibre) in August. Continue to water cool-season lawns regularly, cut them high, and feed them lightly, if at all. (Overfeeding cool-season lawns now can stress them. See page 248 for basic guidelines on summer care for lawns.)

Control Pests and Diseases on Cool-Season Lawns. In August several pests and diseases often beset lawns that are fed with synthetic fertilizers. Well-maintained organic lawns are rarely attacked except perhaps in a few minor patches. In case you notice any damage from

pests or disease, here's how to diagnose the problem: If you see dead or brown spots, take hold of a tuft of grass in one of the bad patches and yank up on it. If the patch is circular and grass blades pull off at the roots but the roots stay in the ground, the problem may be brown-patch fungus. Some other fungal diseases cause variously shaped brown patches; with these the grass sticks tight when you pull on it. In some cases there's a dark green or grayish green line or circle around the damaged patch.

If you've noticed large numbers of moths fluttering in a zigzag pattern over the lawn in the evening and the grass blades are chewed off at ground level, look among the roots for silky white tubes with brown or gray black-spotted grubs in them. These are signs of sod webworm. If the grass is loose and comes up like a mat, roots and all, the problem is white grubs. Roll the turf back and look for curled white grubs living under the turf and eating the roots. (In our area these are not grubs of the Japanese beetle, as is the case on the East Coast and in the Midwest, but of several other beetles.)

The solution to all three of these problems—brown patch fungus, sod webworm, and white grubs—is a well-maintained, totally organic lawn. In most cases a thick, healthy lawn is adequate defense. Beneficial fungi are extremely efficient in controlling brown patch, which as a result is seldom a problem on organically fed lawns. In organic soils, beneficial nematodes and other naturally beneficial parasites keep the numbers of sod webworms and white grubs to a minimum. You can help these minuscule organisms do their job by adding to their numbers, and by maintaining a healthy organic lawn. If necessary, apply additional beneficial nematodes every couple of years, though these usually abound naturally in moist, humus-filled soils. Products containing milky spore disease can control Japanese beetle grubs, which we don't have here, but milky spore is also reputed to infect a few of the white grubs infesting California soils as well, so it might be worth a try. BT will kill soil webworms. (Spray the lawn with it late in the day once a week in August after mowing. Make sure you have a fresh bottle—BT is live stuff and doesn't live forever—and add a few drops of oil to the mix as a spreader-sticker.) Caterpillars ingest treated grass, stop munching, and later die from the fungus disease in BT. Birds also love caterpillars and grubs and will help control them if encouraged to frequent the garden by the presence of feeders, fountains, and birdhouses. Flocks of starlings sometimes settle on lawns in inland areas and voraciously devour almost all of the white grubs. We don't often think of moles and gophers as beneficial but both eat grubs, though gophers also eat plant roots. By planting lawns on top of chicken wire, as described on page 358, you benefit from the gopher's love of grubs without any mounds on the lawn. (They will be able to make air holes but no mounds.)

As most organic gardeners are aware, synthetic fertilizers kill the biological and microbial life in soil, leaving lawns without any protection from pests and disease. As a result, orthodox gardeners are forced to use pesticides and fungicides to control lawn problems, thus creating a vicious cycle—the more fertilizer the gardener applies, the sicker his lawn becomes, and the more dependent it will be on fungicides and pesticides. Problems with pests and diseases on artificially fed lawns are so common that lawn fertilizers often include these poisons among their ingredients. Meanwhile the organic gardener can relax in summer and take the easy course, happily letting beneficial nematodes, bacteria, fungi, protozoa, earthworms, and other organisms do the work of protecting the grass from pests and diseases. (For a full discussion of this subject, see Chapter 18 of Lowenfels, Lewis, and Ingham's *Teaming with Microbes: A Gardener's Guide to the Soil Food Web*.)

VEGETABLE GARDENING

The main jobs in the vegetable garden this month are watering, harvesting, and pest control. All summer vegetables can be planted now, especially the heat lovers, but most gardeners prefer to wait this month out and start planting winter crops in mid-September. Most vegetable gardens in interior zones get pretty well burned up by the end of August.

Start Seeds for Cool-Season Crops. By midmonth, seeds of bedding plants can be started in flats or peat pots for fall planting. (Keep them in semishade.) Good candidates are celery and all members of the cabbage family, including broccoli, Brussels sprouts, cauliflower, and cabbage. Homegrown transplants will be ready to put out in the garden in late September or October. If you need only a few it's much less trouble to buy transplants at the nursery.

Unfortunately, these plants bought at nurseries are usually labeled generically rather than by variety. Learn about good varieties for your zone, and ask your nursery to carry them as transplants. Patronize companies that grow "gourmet varieties." They're more expensive, but there's a good reason: The seeds cost more. If enough gardeners become informed buyers, bedding-plant growers and nurseries will gladly give them what they want.

Control Corn Earworm. If your corn is being badly attacked by corn earworm it's possible that you're waiting too long to harvest. Once corn silks turn crisp brown and the juice in the kernels is milky, it's time to harvest. (See details on page 281.) If you've had problems in past years, you might try using an eyedropper to apply a few drops of mineral oil into the silks at the top of the ears once the silks have begun to grow brown, which may or may not work. Some gardeners spray the silks with BT, but this too is an iffy undertaking. In my garden I don't even try to combat this pest since the worms usually do little more than disfigure the tops of a few of the ears. Varieties with tight husks often have no worms whatsoever, and beneficial wasps, including trichogramma wasps, control corn earworms along with other caterpillars. In a small organic garden where everything is working together, corn earworm problems are usually minor.

Corn needs lots of water while it's forming ears. Once you've picked them, cook the fresh corn no more than three minutes after the second boil.

Continue to Harvest, and Take Stock for Next Year. This is the time of year when people who love to can and freeze are happily stashing away jars and bags of produce for winter use, and those of us who don't are giving away armloads of vegetables and perhaps vowing to plant less next year. By now, first-time gardeners have learned that they don't need a whole row of zucchini to feed a family of four—three plants are plenty—but you never can plant enough corn—it goes fast.

AUGUST CHECKLIST

PURCHASE/PLANT

{ } Continue to plant tropicals in coastal zones, 206

{ } Transplant biennials you started from seed in July, when they are 2 to 3 inches high, into the garden, 265

{ } In coastal zones continue to purchase, plant, and transplant succulents, including cacti and euphorbias, 270

{ } Replace untidy plants growing near swimming pools with better choices, 291

{ } Choose crape myrtles in interior zones, 295

{ } Purchase cassias and pick out flame eucalyptus to plant in coastal zones, 295

{ } Grow your own transplants by planting seeds of cool-season flowers, 297

{ } Plant buffer zones between your home and native chaparral, 298

{ } Plant papayas, bananas, and palms, 301

{ } Transplant palms, 302

{ } If you want to grow your own vegetable transplants, start seeds of cool-season vegetables now, 306

{ } Plant stock from seed, 297

{ } Plant perennials in coastal zones, 298

TRIM, PRUNE, MOW, DIVIDE

{ } Cut off water sprouts and suckers from deciduous fruit trees, 290

{ } Prune and train espaliers throughout the growing season, 291

{ } Trim untidy trees and vines growing near swimming pools, 291

{ } Give fuchsias a light midsummer pruning, 292

{ } Give roses a light midsummer pruning; remove suckers, 293

{ } Clean up daylilies and agapanthus by removing stems that have bloomed, 293

{ } Propagate daylilies by planting the proliferates, 293

{ } Cut off bloom stalks from yellow fortnight lilies; take off seedpods only from white fortnight lilies, 293

{ } Prune and train wisteria, 294

{ } Clean out native brush; clear buffer zones, 299

{ } Remove only dead and dying foliage from date palms; use sterilized tools, 303

{ } Maintain perennials, 298

{ } Cut back any unsightly cool-season ornamental grasses to two-thirds height, 327

FERTILIZE

{ } Feed fuchsias, 292

{ } Feed tuberous begonias, 120, 260.

{ } Feed water lilies, 156

{ } Feed cymbidiums with a high-nitrogen fertilizer for growth, 257

{ } Feed ferns, 183

{ } Feed tropicals, 183

{ } Fertilize warm-season grasses, with the exception of 'Adalayd' and kikuyu, 305

{ } If cool-season lawns show signs of nitrogen deficiency (yellow leaves, stunted growth), fertilize lightly; otherwise not at all, 276

{ } Fertilize biennials started from seed in July with fish emulsion at weekly intervals, 265

{ } Feed all container-grown succulents with a well-diluted complete liquid organic fertilizer, 273

{ } Don't fertilize deciduous fruit trees now, 290

{ } Fertilize roses, 292

{ } Feed fortnight lilies lightly; follow up with water, 293

{ } Feed and water cycads, 303

WATER

{ } Reduce irrigation of cantaloupes when melons start to ripen, 282

{ } Water succulents, 270

{ } Water plants adequately during hot, dry weather, 288

{ } Don't water summer-deciduous native plants, 288

{ } Water drought-resistant plants, including Mexican fan palms and Aleppo pines, 288

{ } Water floss silk trees and coral trees early in the month, 288

{ } Study your irrigation system to see if it can be more efficient, 288

{ } Check for malfunctioning sprinklers and drip emitters, 288

{ } Install a new backup battery in your irrigation timer, 289

{ } Flush filters and headers of drip systems, 289

{ } If lawns develop brown areas, find out what's causing the problem and solve it, 305

{ } Renew watering basins, 289

{ } Water plants in containers, 290

{ } Water deciduous fruit trees in accordance with their age and your soil and climate zone, 290

{ } Water roses with up to 1 1/2 inches of water 3 times a week, 258

{ } Keep ferns well watered and protect them from dry winds, 292

{ } Give mature wisterias at least one deep watering, 294

{ } Keep transplanted palms well watered, 302

{ } Water warm-season lawns deeply at least once a week in most zones; water cool-season lawns more shallowly and frequently, 304

{ } Water vegetables, 306

{ } Don't water lithops, 274

CONTROL PESTS, DISEASE, AND WEEDS

{ } Continue to control weeds by mulching, cultivating, and hand-pulling, 46

{ } Control rose pests and diseases, 92

{ } Control pests on fuchsias, 292

{ } Control serious nematode and fungal problems with soil solarization, 295

{ } Control fireblight by removing disfigured branches and twigs, 296

{ } Protect Canary Island date palms from fungus, 303

{ } Check cycads for scale, 303

{ } Control pests and diseases that cause dead brown patches on cool-season lawns, 305

{ } Look for signs of sod webworm on lawns, particularly cool-season lawns; treat with BT if necessary, 305

{ } Control white grubs on cool-season lawns, 305

{ } Control corn earworm if desired, 306

{ } Release beneficial nematodes, 296

{ } Control oleander leaf scorch, 296

ALSO THIS MONTH

{ } Watch cantaloupes for signs of ripening; pick them at "full slip," 281

{ } Continue to harvest summer vegetables, 281

{ } Before planting in porous containers, seal the insides with a coat of tar, 290

{ } Use double-potting to keep roots of container-grown plants cool, 291

{ } Keep indoor ferns, including Boston ferns, alive in coastal zones by giving them equal time outdoors, 292

{ } Order seeds and supplies for fall planting from mail-order catalogs, 416

{ } If you live next to native chaparral, consider ways to minimize risks of fires, 299

{ } Harvest bananas when they are ready, according to type, 302

{ } Untie the fronds of palms transplanted in June, 302

September

THE FIRST FALL-
PLANTING MONTH

Lathyrus odoratus
(Sweet pea)

September marks the beginning of the fall planting season, one of the busiest times of year in the garden. This is when we switch gears in preparation for winter—and winter is a great time to garden here! Beginning now, we switch from summer-blooming to winter- and spring-blooming annual flowers and from warm-season to cool-season vegetable crops. Spring-flowering bulbs fill nursery shelves, some of which can be planted in September. It is also the best time for planting perennials and a good time for giving perennial beds an overhaul. Warm-season lawns can still be planted now, and cool-season lawns can be planted along the coast. In addition, most bushes, shrubs, trees, and ground covers, other than tropicals, do best when planted in fall before the winter rains.

This great flurry of activity doesn't happen all at once. Start now to clean out faded flowers and vegetables, but leave good ones in place to enjoy as long as they're still going. Prepare the ground and begin to plant—but keep in mind that October, the best planting month of the year, is still ahead.

Meanwhile, continue to water deeply and according to the individual needs of plants. Though nights may begin to cool off along the coast and shadows are noticeably lengthening, early September is largely a continuation of summer weather. Sunny, warm days are the norm. More often than not we get a blast of extremely hot weather and Santa Ana winds before midmonth. If this happens, water early in the day or in the evening. Also, check drought-resistant plants, other than summer-dormant natives, for signs of stress. One deep watering now can sometimes save the life of a tree or bush that's hanging on the brink of extinction and tide it over to the winter rains. Many mature trees, like Torrey (*Pinus torreyana*) and Aleppo (*P. halepensis*) pines, could be saved from beetle attack and other horrors if only people would realize that they need to be watered at least once now. Put a sprinkler under the canopy to the drip line and let it run for several hours, with the pressure turned low so the water sinks in. When water supplies are curtailed because of drought, use the precious water you have to irrigate mature shrubs, trees, and vines. Let your lawn and petunias die if you must, but save your valuable old plants—especially trees.

BULBS

One of September's most important and exciting jobs is to start buying and planting spring-flowering bulbs. Bulbs are easy plants to grow. They have a mystique bordering on the miraculous, but growing them here in Southern California is different from growing them on the East Coast or in the Midwest. Many bulbs need to undergo a cold winter in order to bloom. Some will bloom without cold weather but tend to rot during our hot, dry summers. Others can be grown here after being prechilled in the refrigerator, but in many cases they won't naturalize (come back year after year, bloom, and multiply). Countering these drawbacks, we're able to grow a huge number of charming and fascinating bulbs that are little known and rarely grown back East. Many of these naturalize readily, are drought resistant, and are almost unbelievably easy to grow.

Buy Bulbs Now to Plant Later. Begin purchasing spring-flowering bulbs in mid-September. They soon get picked over and sometimes put back in the wrong bins. A reliable local nursery is the best source of varieties that will do well in your climate zone, though some rare varieties can only be bought from catalogs. Choose the largest and fattest bulbs, because they produce the biggest blooms.

Among hardy bulbs (the kind grown in cold-winter climates), the best choices for Southern California are daffodils (*Narcissus*), hyacinths, Dutch and Spanish irises, and tulips. In inland gardens add grape hyacinths (*Muscari*). (*M. armeniacum* is best adapted to our climate.) Crocuses are difficult to grow in Southern California, though Dutch crocus (*Crocus vernus*) may succeed in inland valleys. Mediterranean species crocuses, such as *C. niveus* 'Bowles' and *C. goulimyi*, bloom in fall and are rare but can naturalize in some gardens. Most trumpet and large-cupped narcissus have to be replaced yearly, although several varieties, including 'February Gold', 'Ice Follies', and 'Fortune', will often naturalize and eventually form large clumps.

Look for daffodils with three or more divisions. Don't pull them apart. If they're still attached, each point will produce a bloom. Feel them gently to make sure they're firm to the touch; softness means rot. Hyacinths perform best and give the most bloom if you buy large bulbs. Tulips have to be bought yearly. (You could dig them in fall and rechill them, but those who try this find that, though the bulbs can attain great size, their flowers are tiny and on short stems because of our hot summer weather.) Don't buy "naked" tulip bulbs, ones that have lost their tunics (the brown papery skin)—they might be dried out.

Take anemones, crocuses, daffodils, grape hyacinths, hyacinths, ranunculus, and tulips home, but don't plant the bulbs yet. Getting them in the ground too early is a big mistake.

Keep them cool and dry: The garage is usually a good place. Crocuses, hyacinths, and tulips need to be chilled beginning next month or in November for six to eight weeks prior to planting. You don't have to put them in the refrigerator just yet. Exceptions to this rule are the species tulips (wild tulips), including candia tulip (*T. bakeri* 'Lilac Wonder', *T. saxitilis*), Florentine tulip *(T. sylvestris)*, and lady tulip *(Tulipa clusiana)*, which can be planted straight into the ground or in pots now. These will multiply and come back year after year. Grape hyacinths don't need prechilling, but as noted earlier, they usually don't grow well in coastal gardens. In interior zones grape hyacinth often comes back year after year. Anemones, daffodils, Dutch irises, and ranunculus need no prechilling.

Buy Bulbs to Plant Now. Some bulbs can and should be planted in September as soon as you buy them. Among these are some superb choices from the daffodil *(Narcissus)* tribe that naturalize readily and often spread over large areas. These are known as the Tazetta and Tazetta hybrids, and they include paper whites, 'Grand Soleil d'Or', 'Cragford', Chinese sacred lilies, 'Geranium', and others. Save some for forcing in pebbles later (page 377). They're popular and sell out early. Tazettas, especially paperwhites and 'Grand Soleil d'Or', are amongst the longest-lived and least demanding bulbs to grow in gardens. But plant all the various Tazetta hybrid narcissi you can find in drifts in perennial beds and shrubberies and next to paths. They'll reward you for years by springing to life in fall and blooming in late winter inland, fall and winter along the coast. Just when it's time to cut back and mulch beds of perennials and flowering shrubs, Tazettas burst into spectacular and fragrant bloom with practically no work from you.

Most important to purchase and plant now are the many captivating drought-resistant bulbs that are well adapted to our climate—so well they'll often naturalize even in areas that receive little or no summer water. Among these are various oxalis from the Western Hemisphere and many bulbs and corms from South Africa, such as babiana (baboon flower), *Chasmanthe aethiopica* and *C. floribunda*, crocosmia, freesia, ixia (African corn lily), *lapeirousia*, harlequin flower; *(Sparaxis tricolor)*; streptanthera *(Streptanthera cuprea, S. elegans)*, flame freesia *(Tritonia crocata)*, and watsonia. Most can take summer water if drainage is good. Some actually need it—for example the crocosmia hybrids, such as the famous 'Lucifer' and others, which multiply and bloom in June, but Chasmanthe *(Chasmanthe aethiopica)*—often incorrectly called crocosmia, tritonia, or montbretia—with tall, straplike leaves and orange flowers, is so drought resistant it naturalizes even under invasive eucalyptus. Arabian star flower *(Ornithogalum arabicum)* has long-lasting white flowers with unique shiny black beadlike centers that bloom later than other spring-flowering bulbs. Chincherinchee *(O. thyrsoides)* has white blooms on 2-foot stems. Both thrive in flowerbeds. Spring star flower *(Ipheion uniflorum)* is great for planting around the edges of beds. Once you get it going, it multiplies rapidly, comes back every year, and blooms for several months in winter and spring.

When purchasing your bulbs, jot down the planting directions for depth and spacing. A general **Rule of Thumb:** *Plant large bulbs at a depth that equals twice their height and small bulbs a little deeper than twice their height.* There are exceptions to this rule, so to be sure of correct depths and other care, refer to a bulb handbook. One of the best is Bryan's *Manual of Bulbs*.

When Is a Bulb Not a Bulb?

Many of the plants we call bulbs aren't bulbs at all. It's become common to lump together under this term not only true bulbs but all plants that grow from a thickened or bulbous storage organ. (Plants like clivia, daylilies, and iris are in a shady area between bulbs and perennials, so you find them discussed in books about both.) Here's how bulbs differ, so you can tell them apart:

▸ **True Bulb.** A modified subterranean leaf bud, the true bulb has a basal plate, above which are food-storing scales (rudimentary leaves) surrounding a bud that contains the magic makings of a plant. Some bulbs, like onions, tulips, and daffodils, are tunicate—they're covered with a papery skin. Others, like lilies, are imbricate—they have overlapping scales.

▸ **Corm.** A thickened subterranean stem that produces a plant. The inside is just a solid piece of tissue; the buds are on top. After bloom the old corm is used up, but new ones have grown on top or at the sides to take its place. Gladioli, sparaxis, and freesia grow from corms.

▸ **Rhizome.** A thickened stem or branch that grows on the surface of the ground or horizontally underground. Bearded irises and calla lilies grow from rhizomes.

▸ **Tuber.** A thickened stem that serves as a storage chamber but is usually shorter, thicker, and rounder than a rhizome. It grows totally or partially underground. Tuberous begonias, cyclamen, and potatoes grow from tubers.

▸ **Tuberous Root.** Growing underground, thus differing from a tuber in that it's a swollen root rather than a thickened stem. Tuberous roots have growth buds on top in the old stem portion, from which spring the plants. Dahlias and sweet potatoes grow from tuberous roots.

Consider the Lilies. Lilies are dramatic plants in the garden, but, while some gardeners swear by them, they have a reputation of being difficult to grow here. They need excellent soil, good drainage, and constant moisture—they're not good choices for drought years. There are many complicated differences among them. They're classified under nine divisions, within which are hundreds of varieties and species. In general, new varieties are easier to grow than old ones. Some may do well in one zone but not in another. The best way to find kinds adapted to your garden is through trial and error and by purchasing your bulbs at a local nursery that has a good reputation for carrying the right things. In general, if you live inland grow the early varieties, including native Humboldt lily *(Lilium humboldtii)* and the LA hybrids. If you live in a frost-free zone, you can grow any of the varieties that need no winter chill and bloom in midsummer, including the Aurelian hybrids and several species lilies like the fragrant and stunning *L. lankongense* from mountains in China. Probably the best and easiest lilies to grow anywhere in Southern California are the relatively new LA hybrids, including varieties like 'Trebiano', 'Royal Sunset', 'Red Alert', and many others. The name LA makes it easy to remember that these hybrids are easy to grow in Los Angeles and environs, but in this case the name doesn't stand for the city. When applied to lilies, LA stands for the word *longiflorum* combined with the word *Asiatic*. By crossing Easter lilies *(L. longiflorum)* with

Asiatic hybrids, hybridizers came up with the LA hybrids, which are easy to grow in many climates coast-to-coast and make great cut flowers with strong stems that needing no staking. I've also seen regal lilies (*Lilium regale*), a species discovered by the plant explorer "Chinese" Wilson and favored by Gertrude Jekyll, with flower stems 6 feet tall. They were thriving in a semishaded bed in Altadena, and the gardener claimed they were easy to grow.

Plant lilies as soon as you get them home. They never go completely dormant and must never be allowed to dry out. All lilies need loose, humusy, well-drained, moist soil (sandy loam is best) with plenty of bone meal worked in beneath the roots. Plant them at twice the depth of the bulb, unless instructions that come with the bulb say otherwise. (Madonna lily [*Lilium candidum*] should be planted near the surface.) Feed them when you plant them by mixing into the bed a slow-acting organic fertilizer recommended for flowering plants, applied according to package directions, or a homemade mix of your own. Feed them with 2-10-10 fertilizer when the first spouts show. Almost all lilies like to have their heads in the sun, their feet in the shade, a cool root run, and no wind. If you can provide these conditions plus protection from snails and slugs, in pots or the ground, perhaps lilies will do well for you.

Divide Irises. If irises aren't divided every three or four years, they'll stop blooming. If yours need it and you didn't divide them last summer after bloom, now, in mid-September through mid-October, is the time to tackle the job. Gardeners in hot interior valleys have no choice. It's do it now or wait another whole year (see page 241 for directions).

If your irises don't need dividing this year, clean up the bed now. Pull or cut off damaged leaves, clean up the ground, and mulch the bed. Bait for slugs and snails.

Purchase Cyclamen. In most of the country cyclamen are grown only as houseplants, but here they're one of our most aristocratic plants for cool-season bloom outdoors. Begin purchasing them now, either as tubers or as plants already in bloom. Grow them in pots, hanging baskets, or the ground.

How to Make Bulb Plantings Look Informal and Natural

Don't plant bulbs in rows; instead, plant them in drifts (the gracefully shaped areas that flow from back to front and from side to side in a flowerbed and are planted solidly with one flower). Do as nature does: Put many bulbs of one kind or one color together in a single drift, and then mix one or two of another kind or color in with them. To arrange a drift, mark the outline with gypsum and toss the bulbs onto the ground. Plant them where they fall.

When buying cyclamen tubers, look for those that are already beginning to sprout—they're the easiest to start—and plant them so the top half of the tuber protrudes above the surface of the soil. Put them in moist, humus-rich soil into which you have mixed a complete organic fertilizer recommended for flowering plants according to package directions. Keep them damp until the tubers are well rooted. Keep the plants in semishade; they prefer a cool spot, away from reflected heat. Once they're well rooted and leaves have begun to grow, begin feeding regularly with a complete fertilizer, such as well-diluted Tiger Bloom (2-8-4), or a high-bloom fish emulsion. Instead of watering them once a week, fertilize them once a week with a weak solution of liquid fertilizer.

Don't overwater cyclamen. Wait until the leaves slightly wilt and the plant looks as if it's dry; then water it, or as explained previously, instead of watering it, fertilize it. Cyclamen plants also wilt from overwatering. You can tell if wilting results from over- or underwatering by the condition of the plant's stems. If your cyclamen's stems are soft and wet you've over-watered it, but if the stems are dry, crisp, and firm—though wilted—you've underwatered it. Also, don't clip off the faded blooms; this too can lead to rot. Pull them off with a quick downward yank.

☀ QUICK TIP

Use Bulb Covers to Mark and Shade the Ground over Bulbs. *When planting bulbs, plant low-profile cool-season flowers over them. The bulbs will grow up through them and the ground will be ornamental while you wait. Nemesia, pansies, primroses, schizanthus (poor man's orchid; S. pinnatus), dwarf snapdragons, sweet alyssum, and violas, including Johnny-jump-ups, make good bulb covers.*

TROPICALS AND SUBTROPICALS

This is the last month of the growing season for tropicals, so it's also the last month when they can be fertilized, if necessary, in most zones. (If you live in an interior valley it's better not to fertilize them this late in the season.) Tropicals need to slow down in October and then harden off for winter during November. If you live in a largely frost-free zone you can give them a final

feeding of humic acid or compost tea early in the month to help their strength increase during this warm month and to eliminate any signs of nitrogen deficiency. But don't fertilize with a slow-release product. The idea is to strengthen the plants without triggering soft growth later in the fall, when it could be nipped by frost. (See the recipe for compost tea in the box on the facing page.)

In coastal zones this is also the last month for planting tropicals such as bougainvillea, hibiscus, lantana, natal plum (*Carissa macrocarpa*), philodendron, and tropical flowering trees. In the interior it's best to wait until spring to plant tropicals because fall planting will make them more subject to frost. But regardless of this, many fall-blooming subtropical trees are in nurseries now, and it will be impossible to choose the colors you prefer at any other time, when the trees aren't in bloom. Trees you can find now include Chinese flame tree (*Koelreuteria bipinnata* or *K. elegans*), floss silk tree (*Chorisia speciosa*), and Hong Kong orchid tree (*Bauhinia x blakeana*). Floss silk tree is one of our most spectacular large trees and reasonably drought resistant. The whole top of the tree turns vivid pink, magenta, or burgundy in fall. (There's also a white species, *C. insignis*.) The trunks are green and bear prominent, weirdly wonderful spines, but if you're planting in areas where children or animals might be endangered, choose a grafted kind without spines. Chinese flame tree is good near houses, is noninvasive, doesn't grow too large, and is quite drought tolerant. The display of salmon-colored pods in fall looks as if a bougainvillea got accidentally tangled in the top of the tree. (There's no choice of color with this tree, so you can wait if you wish and plant one next spring.)

Don't let fall-planted tropicals dry out in the almost inevitable September heat wave: Inland, hose off the area around them twice a day to

Recipe for Compost Tea or Manure Tea

▸ Save a perforated plastic or mesh bag from onions, oranges, or potatoes to use as a giant tea bag.

▸ Fill the bag with manure or homemade compost and tightly tie the top closed with string, leaving 3 to 4 feet of string attached.

▸ Place the filled bag in a 5-gallon bucket, allowing the excess string to fall over the edge.

▸ Place the bucket in the shade and fill it to the top with water.

▸ Cover the bucket loosely with a lid or with heavyweight aluminum foil, with the string on top so it doesn't act as a siphon.

▸ Allow the contents of the bucket to ferment for three days or longer. (The longer you leave it, the more fermented and odiferous it will become, but also the more effective.)

▸ When aged to your satisfaction, mix 1 cup of the dark brown concentrate with 2 gallons of water and pour over the roots of plants. (On overcast days, also pour diluted solution over plant leaves or use as a foliar spray.)

▸ After using up all the brown liquid, return the contents of the "tea bag" to the compost pile.

▸ To perk up your plants for a special party or event, apply manure or compost tea ten days prior.

raise the humidity during these spells. And come winter, remember that it's important to protect them from frost.

Don't prune hibiscus this month. But in frost-free zones several other heat-loving plants that bloom all summer, such as bougainvilleas, Cape plumbago (*P. auriculata*), and oleanders, can be pruned now after bloom. They'll regrow during winter for a big burst of bloom next spring and summer. (Pruning in spring instead of fall can cut down on spring bloom, but it's necessary in areas that suffer hard frosts.) Prune oleanders by taking out whole stalks that have bloomed—down to the ground. Take off several a year to renew the plants. Don't chop off the tops like a hedge. This fails to renew the plant with fresh growth from the ground and destroys all the flowers. (You could choose a much better green hedge, if that's all you want.) Don't prune New Zealand tea tree (*Leptospermum scoparium*) now, or you'll get no winter flowers.

CITRUS AND AVOCADO TREES

Make sure citrus trees are adequately and evenly watered during September. If their roots go dry now, the result can be fruit that splits. (Fluctuations in fertilizer levels can also cause fruit to split. Varieties with thin skins are more prone to the problem than those with thick skins.)

Continue Picking 'Valencia' Oranges. If you haven't eaten all your 'Valencia' oranges by now, you can continue picking them. 'Valencia' will turn green again in fall in a process called "re-greening," but it won't affect its flavor or sweetness. You can continue harvesting and eating 'Valencia' until navel oranges are ready to pick in winter. But do check over the trees now for old, corky fruit that may have hung on the tree for a year or two. Clip these off and eat or juice the good ones (see page 199).

Treat Lemon Trees for Brown Rot. Commercial growers pick lemons all at once, but most home gardeners leave lemons hanging on the tree until needed. If you do this, you'll have fresh ones year-round whenever you want them. The only problem is that fruit left hanging on the tree after it's turned golden-ripe sometimes develops brown blotches or turns brown all over. Brown skins can be caused by leaving the fruit on the tree so long that it becomes overmature. If the tree looks generally healthy and the brown fruits occur here and there all over the tree, then discoloration is most likely caused by leaving fruit on the tree too long. Pick the overripe fruit and leave the rest on the tree.

But brown blotches on the rinds of lemons (or fruit that turns brown all over) may also result from a condition called brown rot, which is caused by several fungi that live in the soil under the tree. You can tell if fungus is the culprit because, in this case, fruit of all sizes will be affected but the discoloration will occur primarily on fruit that's closest to the ground. Sometimes a white mold will appear on the fruit, and sap may ooze from the trunk of the tree, near the ground. Branches may also die back. Brown rot is at its worst in wet weather, when the fungi splash up onto the tree from the ground.

If your fruit has ever been affected this way, you have a chance to clear up the problem by spraying now with a biofungicide, such as Serenade Garden Disease Control, or spray with PROBIOTICS 4 Plants' Defensor Bacterial Inoculator, which contains *Bacillus subtilis* as well as *B. cereus*, two beneficial fungi known to attack or parasitize harmful fungi, and follow the directions on the bottle. Spraying with earthworm casting tea is another alternative. (Consult the recipe on page 163.) Most citrus growing in organic gardens are able to fight off fungus problems without being sprayed because the beneficial organisms in the products named above already exist in copious quantities in organic soils. It's also important to grow citrus in full sun and practice good garden hygiene. Cut out dead wood, prune off any branch tips brushing the ground, clip off mummified fruits when you see them, and pick up fallen fruit.

How Cymbidiums Came to California

Cymbidiums are largely terrestrial orchids native to cool tropical jungles, from the Himalayas eastward through southern Asia. For at least two hundred years they were hybridized and grown in cool greenhouses by English collectors. During the Second World War a great many varieties were sent to Santa Barbara to save them from the bombs. It soon became clear that cymbidiums flourish outdoors in Southern California. They multiplied so rapidly that when the loaned varieties were sent home after the war, many more plants were left here, to continue to grow in our gardens. They've since become one of our best plants for winter and spring bloom.

CYMBIDIUMS

Not all cymbidiums bloom every year. (You need three plants to be assured of annual bloom.) But some gardeners complain that none of their cymbidiums ever bloom. These plants are remarkably easy to grow, but they do have certain requirements. Here's how to make them bloom.

Switch Fertilizers in September. Beginning on the first of September switch fertilizers from a high-nitrogen formula for growth to a formula higher in bloom ingredients. One way to do this is to continue your regular fertilizing system (see page 24 for suggestions), while increasing bloom ingredients throughout fall by drenching the soil mix every two weeks with solution of 1 gallon of water into which you have mixed 2 tablespoons of Nature's Nectar Phosphorus (0-2-0) and 1 tablespoon of Nature's Nectar Potassium (0-0-5). Or, alternatively, feed with fish bone meal at the rate of 2 tablespoons per gallon size plant per month, and a handful for each larger container, once a month, beginning in early September, through December. A more conventional method is to switch fertilizers now to one of the commercial organic fish emulsions, commercial organic orchid foods high in bloom ingredients, or an all-purpose hi-bloom fertilizer, such as Meta-naturals (1-5-5) Organic Bloom Fertilizer or Tiger Bloom (2-8-4), applied as a drench every two weeks. Cymbidiums continue to grow year-round so they always need some nitrogen, but a higher percentage of phosphorus and potassium now will encourage development of bloom spikes.

Keep Cymbidiums in Bright Light. Don't keep cymbidiums in too much shade. If you've sheltered yours from hot sun under a tree during the summer, bring them out into more light now. Along the coast they can take full sun, though they'll need protection during the Santa Ana or sudden heat wave that almost always strikes sometime in September. Inland they need protection from the burning rays of midday sun—under 50 percent shade cloth or in a lath house is ideal. They often can take more sun than we give them. If your cymbidiums have dark green leaves, chances are you're keeping them in too much shade. Give them enough light to turn the leaves a yellowish color. Spread the plants apart, and allow sunshine to hit those pseudobulbs. Crowded plants won't bloom as well because the leaves shade the bulbs. (Trim off dead leaves and brown tips, but don't cut off or shorten healthy leaves. Cymbidiums need all their leaves to nourish the pseudobulbs.)

Provide a Wide Range of Temperatures. Large-flowered cymbidiums need a daily temperature range of at least 20 degrees during the hottest time of the year in order to trigger bloom. What they like best are nights that drop to 45° or 55°F and daytime temperatures of 80° or 90°F. Our gardens provide adequately warm days and cool nights, but our patios or porches often do not. They're too warm and sheltered at night. So situate your cymbidiums away from protective house walls and don't keep them indoors, or they'll never bloom.

This is a good time to throw away inferior plants. There's no point in wasting time and money caring for poor performers. Always begin with fine varieties. Good characteristics in cymbidiums include excellent flower color, many flowers per spike, and tall flower spikes that can be staked high above foliage or, in the case of miniature plants, allowed to cascade below the foliage, if desired, in a hanging basket. If you have a second-rate or third-rate variety that has stiff upright foliage hiding the blooms or bears few spikes with only two or three flowers on each, no amount of good care or fertilizer can correct these inferior growth habits. Also, certain classes of plants, such as miniatures, may perform better in your climate than others. Plants with flowers less than 3 inches across are classed as miniatures.

319

How to Stop Blue Hydrangeas from Turning Pink

▸ Start with a hydrangea that was blue when you bought it. (Some kinds never turn blue. White varieties always stay white. Some pinks turn purple instead of blue.)

▸ Plant and grow blue hydrangeas in acid soil mix. When planting in containers, use a commercial soil mix designed for camellias and azaleas. When planting in the ground, amend the native soil in the planting hole with camellia and azalea mix according to package directions.

▸ Check the root run of established plants to make sure the soil is acid. Use a soil test kit to assess the pH of the soil. A pH of 4.5 to 5.0 yields blue flowers, a pH of 5.5 to 6.5 yields mauve, and pH of 7.0 to 7.5 yields pink.

▸ The orthodox way to maintain the desired pH is with aluminum sulfate. Use 1 tablespoon aluminum sulfate per foot of plant height, or ¼ teaspoon per potted plant. Mix this in water and apply it as a drench several times in spring and fall, beginning in September. (Aluminum sulfate is not an organic fertilizer. See the explanation on page 268.)

▸ Organic methods for maintaining the desired pH include planting blue hydrangeas in acid soil; fertilizing with acid organic fertilizers; mulching the ground with leaf mold, tea leaves, coffee grounds, or cow manure; burying aluminum cans around roots; watering plants in containers year-round with 1 teaspoon vinegar per quart of water; or applying slate dust, which contains aluminum, to the soil. Or treat the soil spring and fall with 1 tablespoon of soil sulfur for each 8-inch pot, ¼ cup per 18-inch tub, and ½ cup per 3-foot plant growing in the ground. Use a garden fork to make holes into which to apply the sulfur; in pots use a chopstick. Soil sulfur has to actively contact soil in order to acidify it, and the action of sulfur is not permanent.

▸ Never use fertilizer that contains phosphorus. Phosphorus is alkaline, so the use of it will raise the pH of the soil and turn blue hydrangeas pink.

Miniatures tolerate hot weather better—up to 115°F—and will bloom when night temperatures in summer are as high as 65°F—higher than standard cymbidiums require to trigger bloom. Miniatures come into bloom in November and continue into March, while standards bloom from January to mid-May. So, if you have had problems getting cymbidiums to bloom in your climate zone or on your patio or porch, try the small-flowered varieties. They bloom more readily both inland and along the coast, and the bonus is that some of their flowers are highly fragrant.

Meanwhile, water cymbidiums enough to keep the pseudobulbs from drying out and shriveling. Water should always drain right through. Cymbidium roots can't survive in a puddle. As the spikes grow, stake them so they don't get broken, and protect the plants from slugs and snails.

CAMELLIAS

Keep camellias well watered this month. Letting them go dry now will make the buds go brown and drop off later, so you won't have any bloom this winter or next spring. Don't confuse this with natural bud drop. Some varieties form a great many more buds than they can open, and they always drop a lot of them of their own accord. These naturally dropped buds will be green, not brown. (Bud drop can also be caused by growing a variety that needs winter chill in a mild coastal zone where the buds can't open.)

Disbud Camellias. For the largest blooms start disbudding camellias now, by removing all but one flower bud from each tip or joint. Twist off all but one flower bud from each cluster, being careful not to remove the growth bud. (The flower buds are round and fat; the growth bud is thin and pointed.) Drop the buds in a plastic bag and dispose of them in the trash. Some gardeners don't disbud camellias, because they have too many of them or simply can't be bothered. When plants are as tall as trees it's almost impossible to disbud them. But all plants look better when they've been disbudded; the flowers become not only larger but better shaped and less prone to blossom blight.

It's a good idea to retain some forward-facing, but mainly downward-facing buds, especially when plants are tall or light colored. On tall plants downward-facing flowers will be seen better. On light-colored plants they'll be less prone to sun damage. In all cases they'll last longer; when it rains, water will pour off their backs instead of soaking into the center and causing rot.

AZALEAS

The time-honored method for feeding azaleas requires you to fertilize them only twice a year, once immediately after they finish flowering and again in late September. So give azaleas their second and last meal of the year during the last third of this month. The easiest way is to use an organic fertilizer especially formulated for azaleas or camellias, following package directions exactly, or to feed with cottonseed meal. Apply 10 pounds of cottonseed meal per 100 square feet of azalea bed. For individual plants, this translates to approximately $1/4$ cup for a one-year-old plant, $1/2$ cup for a two-year-old plant, and between 3 and 6 cups for plants five years and older. Amounts will vary depending on conditions. Azaleas are not greedy eaters, but they may not be the only plants at the dinner table. For example, if your azaleas are growing in the shade of pines or other trees, tree roots are also going to subtract some of the nourishment, and this means you need to satisfy the needs of the trees as well as the azaleas. If you simply toss cottonseed meal on top of a thick layer of mulch, it may help the mulch to rot but may never feed the azaleas. So after spreading the fertilizer, use a cultivator to gently worry it through the mulch so it's in contact with the ground. Then follow up with water. Also, at this time apply John and Bob's Soil Optimizer, or a liquid product containing humic acid and kelp—Neptune's Harvest is one brand—or mix your own. Drench the foliage as well as the ground. This can help keep azaleas healthy and disease-free, and also prevent chlorosis (dark green veins with yellow leaves, meaning the plants are deficient in iron, zinc, and other trace minerals).

ROSES

Continue to water roses with up to $1^{1}/_{2}$ inches of water each time you irrigate, but reduce the number of irrigations from three times a week to twice a week. (Amounts of water mentioned in inches in most chapters are meant to

How to Grow Thanksgiving, Christmas, and Easter Cacti

▸ Grow these cacti indoors or out. (They can grow as big as 3 feet across.)

▸ Start by buying small ones of the same color. Plant three or four cacti in a 6-inch container in good, porous potting soil, such as Jungle Growth, to each gallon of which you add 1 cup of agricultural charcoal and 3 cups of perlite. Pot them on as necessary.

▸ Keep the cacti in bright but not burning light. Filtered sun is okay, but hot rays through south or west windows are not. Keep them in natural light (away from electric lights at night) for the two months prior to bloom. (During bloom, flowers last longer when plants are kept cool.)

▸ Fertilize the plants year-round, once every two or three weeks or with a well-diluted solution every time you water. Feed with a balanced liquid organic fertilizer such as fish emulsion or Omega (6-6-6) for most of the year. Two months prior to bloom, switch fertilizers and begin feeding with a low-nitrogen, high-bloom organic formula, for example, Metanaturals 1-5-5 Organic Bloom Formula. Another way to boost flower production is to spray the plant weekly with Organica Organic Flower Booster, a product made entirely from giant sea kelp, which helps stimulate buds and bloom.

▸ Water regularly throughout the year. Keep the cacti slightly drier for a month or six weeks after bloom, but don't ever let the roots shrivel. In general, water well in summer, less in fall. (Some experts withhold water for one month after the weather cools in fall; others water year-round.) Always maintain good drainage—no soggy soil allowed.

be approximate guidelines, not hard and fast rules. Roses growing in fast-draining soils may need more water applied more frequently, while those in clay soils may flourish with less frequent irrigation.) Though roses fed according to the guidelines given in August should have all the nourishment they need now, some Rose Pro gardeners may wish to feed roses this month with a liquid solution, for example, alfalfa tea, compost tea, or a commercial organic product such as Soil Soup, which is made from earthworm castings and other beneficial substances. Gardeners using a commercial organic rose fertilizer can continue applying it according to package directions. Generic gardeners have many choices, from homemade compost tea to their own concoction of earthworm casting–based soil soup. But if your roses are growing well and looking healthy, you can let the job slide. Pick or deadhead the flowers according to your custom, but there's no need to disbud now.

Along with other fall planting, you can plant roses from nursery containers, if desired, from now through October.

THANKSGIVING AND CHRISTMAS CACTI

Zygocactus, or crab cactus (*Schlumbergera truncate*), is an epiphyte with "leaves" (actually thickened stems) shaped like crab claws. It's often sold a Christmas cactus, but it really

Plant Sweet Peas for Christmas Bloom

▸ **Plant Sweet Peas During the First Week of September.** In order to have armloads of fragrant sweet peas for Christmas, one must get the seeds of early varieties into the ground before the end of the first week of September and the seeds of day-length neutral varieties by mid-month. (*Day-length neutral* is a term used to describe plants whose cycles of growth or bloom are not influenced by the number of hours of daylight at a particular time of year.)

▸ **Purchase a Day-Length Neutral or Early Variety.** No matter how early you plant sweet peas, you will not achieve winter flowers unless you plant the right variety. Early varieties that will bloom prior to Christmas if planted now include 'Mammoth', 'Early Spencer', and 'Early-Flowering Multiflora'. Day-length neutral varieties bloom even earlier, often by the first of December. The first color mix of day-length neutral varieties developed for the florists' industry was 'Winter Elegance'. Newer varieties include the white 'Chiffon Elegance', and 'Velvet Elegance', a mix of deeper colors. (Renee's Seeds carries 'Velvet Elegance'.) The short varieties 'Snoopea' and 'Supersnoop' also bloom in winter and are easy to grow in a flowerbed or in pots and hanging baskets if planted in early September. (It's too early to plant old-fashioned, standard, or English varieties now, including the original Italian 'Cupani', famous for extra-strong fragrance. Plant them in early spring. Even if you plant them now they won't bloom until May.)

▸ **Dig a North-South Trench in Full Sun.** Make your trench 1½ feet deep and 6 to 8 inches wide. (For bush types prepare the whole bed.)

▸ **Provide Rich Soil.** Fill the bottom of the trench with one sack of manure per 8 to 10 feet of trench. Fork it in well. Then mix the soil from the trench with one-third homemade or bagged compost. Mix in an organic fertilizer that's low in nitrogen and high in phosphorus and potassium or work in fish bone meal and Sul-Po-Mag (0-0-22). Back fill to 1 to 2 inches from the top. Soak this with water, and let it settle overnight.

▸ **Provide Strong Support.** Tall varieties need some kind of trellis to grow on. Shovel metal posts or several 8-foot-tall metal plant stakes into the ground, and wire to them either hardware cloth or chicken wire. Or, alternatively, create an artistic support out of natural materials such as willow or bamboo. Be sure to anchor your trellises and arbors firmly into the ground (use a crowbar to make holes for the posts); also lash them tightly together so they will not be toppled by strong winds.

▸ **Soak the Seeds in Water Overnight.** Put the seeds in a jar and pour lukewarm water over them. Leave them overnight. Plant the next day.

▸ **Plant the Seeds an Inch Deep.** After you sow the seeds 2 inches apart, cover them with 1 inch of potting soil—sweet pea seeds need darkness to sprout. Pat it down gently. Sprinkle daily to keep the seeds damp until they sprout. Then water regularly. Or bury a deep tube under the row prior to planting.

▸ **Protect Sprouts from Birds and Snails.** Cover the row with bird netting or bent aviary wire. Once the sprouts are up 6 inches, remove it; the birds won't kill larger plants. Bait regularly for slugs and snails.

continued...

Plant Sweet Peas for Christmas Bloom (continued)

▸ **Thin and Pinch Seedlings.** When the plants are up 6 inches, thin them to 6 inches apart. Pinch their tips to force branching.

▸ **Add String If Necessary.** Sweet peas have tendrils and are often better at hanging on to their supports than edible peas, but if winds and rains are strong, tie twine around the row to hold up your vines.

▸ **Pick Frequently.** Once sweet peas begin to bloom, pick frequently to keep them flowering.

should be called Thanksgiving cactus because it blooms at Thanksgiving, sometimes staying in bloom until March. The true Christmas cactus *(S. x buckleyi)* has smooth "leaves." The flowers usually open on Christmas day. (There's also an Easter cactus [*Rhipsalidopsis gaertneri* or *S. gaertneri*], which blooms in April and May and often again in fall.)

These cacti can be so gratifying that people fall in love with them. Nevertheless, because of one characteristic they all share, they sometimes don't bloom: They are all "photoperiodic" (they respond to the length of the daylight hours). If you keep the plant indoors they often won't bloom, because house lights at night extend their days to a length that isn't right to stimulate flowering. So put your Thanksgiving and Christmas cacti outdoors now for six weeks or two months, in a shady place where night lighting won't strike them. Meanwhile, feed them with an organic fertilizer to stimulate bloom. (See the box on page 322 for year-round directions.)

ANNUAL AND PERENNIAL FLOWERS

If you were in Southern California last April, you know how delightful our spring gardens can be. If you want to achieve flowerbeds brimming with color—beds like those you noticed in the best gardens last spring—now's the time to plant for it. Don't wait until April and either regret not planting or try to plant then. That's one of the worst mistakes in local gardening. Start now; you have plenty of time—three whole months in most areas.

Plant Beds with Cool-Season Flowers. September is the first month in which you can plant cool-season annual and perennial flowers. The earlier you get them into the ground, the more likely you are to get them to bloom before Christmas. It's a race between you and the weather. Get them blooming in early December, and they'll stay in bloom all winter and spring. Otherwise, you'll have to wait until February or even March for flowers.

If you're a good gardener, even early October will not be too late, so you have a choice. If the summer garden is still looking presentable, you can keep it going through September by removing faded flowers, grooming plants, and feeding them with an organic fertilizer high in bloom ingredients; or if the flowerbeds look ratty, you can tear out summer annuals now, dig up the beds, add soil amendment, and replant in mid-September with winter and spring flowers.

When planting in large tubs, replace about one-third of the planting medium with fresh soil mix. When planting in small containers, or those that are chock-full of roots, replace all earth with fresh mix. Throw the old stuff in the compost. (Remember to place a piece of broken crockery over the drainage hole in the pot before refilling with potting soil.)

Among good choices to plant from pony packs now are calendula, candytuft (*Iberis*), foxglove, Iceland poppy (the smaller the better), nemesia, pansy, English primrose, malacoides or fairy primrose, obconica primrose, snapdragon, stock, sweet alyssum, sweet William (*Dianthus barbatus*), and viola. Plant seeds of annual African daisy (*Dimorphotheca sinuata*), calendula, cineraria, snapdragons, stock, sweet alyssum, Johnny-jump-ups and other violas, and wildflowers. (See page 354 for how to plant wildflowers.) Sweet peas are another good choice for planting from seeds now. You can have armloads of sweet peas (*Lathyrus odoratus*) in December if you plant them now, choose the right varieties, and do the job right (see the box on page 323).

A word of warning: The last of the year's summer flowers, such as French and African marigolds and petunias, are sometimes on sale now. There's nothing to be gained by buying them since they'll soon be out of bloom. Petunias will live through winter in frost-free zones (without flowers) and do better than ever next summer, but marigolds will die in October. However, September is one of the best times to plant euryops and marguerites (*Chrysanthemum frutescens*) because they bloom mostly in fall, winter, and spring. Plant them in full sun; they'll take off well in September's warm weather, and you'll enjoy their flowers throughout the cool months.

How to Keep Cats Out of Flowerbeds

Rake up the spiny pods of liquidambar (*Liquidambar styraciflua*) in fall, and store them in a basket. Use a gloved hand to sprinkle the pesky pods on a flowerbed and cats will get the message that it's not a litter box. Mulching lettuce and celery plants with the pods can discourage slugs, and a circle of seedpods surrounding a freshly planted bed will warn off cats, slugs, and skunks. (Don't worry about liquidambar seedlings popping up in your beds; their seeds don't readily sprout at local temperatures.)

Plant Perennials. Fall is the traditional time for planting perennials but the reality is that nurseries stock perennials whenever they're in bloom, and gardeners plant them when they find them. Nevertheless, many perennials are available now in nurseries. If you're just starting out there couldn't be a better time to plant. Beware of choosing plants that go totally dormant and die to their roots in winter. These get better established when actively growing in spring. Also avoid plants better adapted to the East Coast or Northern California. Instead, find similar plants that perform the same job here and need less irrigation. For example, instead of planting that Deep South favorite for shady beds, plantain lily (*Hosta*), choose heartleaf bergenia (*Bergenia cordifolia*), which is similar in size and shape and thrives in shade. Hosta grows well here, but it's a water hog, a magnet for snails, and dies down in winter. Bergenia is equally old-fashioned and also needs snail protection, but it's evergreen, easy to grow, bears long-lasting flowers, and won't croak in the first drought. Or choose wild ginger *(Asarum caudatum)*, a native plant for growing under oaks or in humus-filled soil in north-facing shade; it can survive with only occasional irrigation. Instead of planting the old East Coast favorite Solomon's seal *(Polygonatum)* under trees, choose bear's britches *(Acanthus mollis)* that grows to the same height with even more appealing spikes of bloom that attract hummingbirds. Acanthus is handsome, easy-to-grow, drought-resistant, and briefly summer deciduous, but springs back almost immediately from the ground. (It also needs snail bait.) For full sun, one of the most obvious switches is to plant *Euphorbia characias wulfennii* instead of lady's mantle *(Alchemilla mollis)*. Alchemilla is okay in England, but euphorbia delivers a similar splash of chartreuse more suitable for California on a cast-iron plant. For a combination with real punch, pop it in the ground next to a patch of spiky blue viper's bugloss *(Echium vulgare)*. They're both drought resistant and bloom at the same time in late winter or early spring.

Maintain Perennials. Maintain the perennials already growing in your garden. Cut back and clean out acanthus, removing those unsightly old leaves down to the ground. Almost immediately, new growth will leap up to replace them. Clean up the ground, treat for snails and slugs, renew mulch, and fertilize. Enjoy Michaelmas daisy hybrids, New England aster *(Aster novae-angliae)*, and New York aster *(A. novi-belgii)* while they're in bloom. These are fun to grow but best in moist, fertile, well-drained soil. Even with these advantages, you'll seldom see them perform as spectacularly here as they do in Oregon or England. *A. x frikartii* 'Monch' and *A. x frikartii* 'Wonder of Staffa' grow better here and bloom on and off from May to October. Now is the easiest time to find these plants in most

nurseries. 'Monte Casino' is worth a hunt. A choice aster that looks like boltonia, it thrives here (boltonia doesn't) and blooms spring and fall with masses of tiny, white, yellow-centered flowers on 3-foot-tall stalks.

Another plant that will be in bloom in your garden this month if you already have it is the perennial sedum *(Sedum spectabile)*. The light green foliage is pretty in the garden year-round and the flower colors gorgeous as long as they last. 'Autumn Joy', the most popular nationwide, starts out pale pink, then turns rose, and ends up deep terra-cotta. 'Meteor' is bright magenta. 'Brilliant' is rose colored. 'Carmine', soft pink, is most frequently grown here. Find it in bloom now in nurseries.

ORNAMENTAL GRASSES, SEDGES, AND RUSHES

The latest arrivals, as a group, onto our vast horticultural palette are the ornamental grasses, sedges, and rushes. A familiar, though often misquoted, rhyme can help gardeners tell them apart: "Sedges have edges and rushes are round, while grasses are hollow with nodes to the ground." True grasses are members of the Poaceae (Graminaceae) family and are "monocots." (Unlike most plants, which are "dicots"—that is, they produce two cotyledons, or seed leaves—the seeds of monocots produce only one seed leaf and their mature leaves have closely parallel veins.) The stems of grasses, which in some species are only visible when they flower, are usually round and are hollow with solid joints or nodes. Most sedges, on the other hand, have triangular stems filled solidly with pith, while most rushes have round pith-filled stems. Sedges and rushes prefer boggy soil, and many are highly invasive.

How to Use Them. The statuesque shapes, varied colors and textures, long-lasting inflorescences, and subtle qualities of ornamental grasses allow ample scope for creativity. Use them as focal points or foils for other plants, structural accents and screens, or major themes of entire gardens. Ornamental grasses have the reputation of being drought resistant, but many of the most attractive types actually prefer well-amended soil and look best when provided with occasional fertilizer and regular irrigation. Given these conditions, most grasses are easy to establish, easy to grow, and largely pest-free.

Know How They Grow. Almost all ornamental grasses need to be cut back annually, but first you need to know how they grow. Like lawn grasses, ornamental grasses can be divided into cool-season and warm-season types. Cool-season species grow vigorously in winter, bloom in late winter or spring, and go dormant or grow slowly in summer. Warm-season species grow vigorously in warm weather, bloom in spring or summer, and go dormant or grow slowly in winter. As anyone who has ever mown a lawn knows, you can cut back grasses, and they'll continue to grow. (This is because the growth center of grasses is close to the ground, thus allowing them to survive grazing.)

When to Cut Back. Cut back warm-season grasses that go dormant in winter, including the common red fountain grass (*Pennisetum sectaceum* 'Rubrum'), in fall or winter, so that they can renew themselves in spring. This will prevent unsightly plants with new leaves and blooms mixed in with the old. Keep a close watch on these grasses when rains begin in fall and winter. As soon as green growth commences at ground level, cut the whole plant down to a few inches above the ground. If frosts are frequent, wait until the weather warms up in spring and then cut back above the new growth (don't worry if you accidentally sear some off). Follow up with lawn fertilizer and water; the plant will soon bounce back. With evergreen warm-season types, remove faded and ratty flowers now after bloom or before new ones arise the following year; cut back or clean out the clumps of foliage when and if they become unsightly. Some evergreen grasses, such as pampas grass (*Cortaderia selloana*) rarely, if ever, need cutting back. For these types, cut off the flower stalks in winter or spring after last year's blooms get ragged-looking and before new blooms arise. (Leaves of pampas grass and some other grasses are razor sharp, so use long-handled loppers or a pole pruner; wear gloves, long sleeves, and pants.) The noxious weed purple pampas grass (*Cortaderia jubata*) and even ornamental pampas grasses have invaded wildlands. Some new pampas grass varieties are said to be sterile but may not be, so don't ever plant this invasive pest and pull out all seedlings you find.

When to Cut Back Cool-Season Types. Cut back cool-season grasses that go dormant in summer to two-thirds of their height for fire protection when they die back in summer or cease to be attractive. Or leave them standing until fall and then cut them back above new growth. In nature, the tops of clumping cool-season grasses would be grazed or burned off, leaving a stumplike growth too thick and airtight to burn through. Do the same as a fire would. Don't cut stipa grasses, for example, all the way to the ground. Their meristem layer (the growth center where cells divide) is in that section at the bottom; cut it off and they'll die. Now in fall (or any time after midsummer), deadhead the flowers of spring-blooming grasses, such as perennial quaking grass (*Briza maxima*), that look tattered. If you have planted a small meadow of cool-season ornamental grasses, use a weed-whacker to mow it two or three times a year.

The rage for grasses isn't just a California phenomenon; it's worldwide. Hence, while many of these plants do well here and are worth a try, finding those especially adapted to subtropical climate zones provides more of a challenge. No matter how pretty they are, avoid the invasive types. Greenlee's *Encyclopedia of Ornamental Grasses* offers a wealth of reliable information, including the virtues and vices of each grass. Here's a brief selection of ornamental grasses and tips for growing them:

- **Formosa Maiden Grass** (*Miscanthus transmorrisonensis*). Warm season. Big evergreen clump 3 feet tall and 5 feet wide. Red-brown flowers cascade to ground in summer. Likes full sun and moist, well-drained, fertile soil. Leaf tips go brown in dry soil.
- **Perennial Quaking Grass** (*Briza maxima*). Cool season. Clumping, with lovely nodding, spring-blooming flowers. Propagate by division; deadhead when blooms look ratty. Cut back if plant goes brown; fertilize and irrigate for quick rebound. Prefers moist, fertile soil and full sun; good with perennials.
- **Annual Quaking Grass** (*B. maxima*). Cool season. Charming seed heads on single stalks. Easy to grow from seed sown in fall in border or for cut flowers; seeds itself, but controllable.
- **Blue Fescue, Sheep Fescue** (*Festuca cinerea* or *F. glauca*). Cool season. Clumping evergreen grass that likes moist, well-drained soil but is drought tolerant. Grow in full sun on coast, partial shade inland. Cut back 3 to 4 inches above the crown once a year in fall or early spring. Replace clumps that die with fresh ones.

- **Foerster's Feather Reed Grass** (*Calamagrostis x acutiflora* 'Karl Foerster'). Warm season. Attractive flowers on long, straight stems can be cut for floral arrangements. Well mannered, with mound of green below. Prefers rich, moist soil, full sun.
- **Japanese Blood Grass** (*Imperata cylindrica* 'Red Baron' or 'Rubra'). Warm season. Upright foliage, up to 1 to 1 1/2 feet tall. Forms colonies that spread slowly, with no flowers. Foliage starts out green with wine-colored tips that turn redder as year progresses, vivid red by fall, copper in winter. Needs full sun, partial shade inland; loves moist, sandy soil, good drainage. Pull it out if it reverts to invasive green leaves. Cut back in winter above new growth.
- **Red Fountain Grass** (*Pennisetum setaceum* 'Rubrum'). Warm season. Most popular ornamental grass because of ease of cultivation, but prefers moist, fertile, well-drained soil in full sun. Flowers April or May until fall. Keep well watered in hot interior valleys. Pick flowers for arrangements. Cut to the ground in fall as described on page 327.

LAWN CARE

Maintain regular feeding of warm-season lawns, such as Bermuda and zoysia, but hold off on fertilizing cool-season grasses, such as ryegrass, bluegrass, and fescue for another month. (If you must fertilize, make it a very light feeding, and don't feed during or just before September's usual heat wave.) Continue mowing at summer heights. Also, mow off the fall flowers from lippia lawns to protect children and dogs from bee stings. Continue to water as you did during summer—deeply and as infrequently as possible for warm-season grasses, more frequently and less deeply for cool-season grasses except tall fescues (which are more drought resistant).

Plant Warm-Season Lawns. There's still enough warm weather to plant warm-season lawns now from stolons, with the exception of zoysia. It makes a much better start when planted in early summer. You can also plant warm-season lawns from seed, but it's better to wait until next spring, especially in inland areas. (Warm-season lawns can be planted from sod any month from spring through fall but not during winter dormancy.) Wait until October to plant cool-season lawns, unless you live close to the coast.

Dethatch Bermuda. If you didn't dethatch your Bermuda lawn in spring, or if the thatch was so thick it needs more than one treatment, now's the second-best time of the year to do the job. If you wait too long, the Bermuda won't have time to grow back, and you'll have to put up with a bare muddy area all winter long. Do the job now while there's still enough warm weather to stimulate a fast recovery. (See page 104 for full instructions.)

VEGETABLE GARDENING

Prepare Beds for Cool-Season Vegetables. Vegetable gardening is much like flower gardening this month: It's a matter of choice. Summer vegetables often keep on producing if given food and water, especially along the coast. If that's your case, wait until October to put in the winter garden. Or if everything is dead and dying, which usually is the case

inland, you can now pull up, clean up, chop up, and compost the remains and begin again, by planting the fall and winter garden on Labor Day weekend. Put in plenty of manure and soil amendment. Add organic fertilizer according to package directions. Choose a balanced fertilizer high in nitrogen as well as phosphorus and potassium or concoct your own mix. (For possible ingredients, see the list of generic fertilizers on page 24.) Nitrogen is less active in winter, so it's especially important to provide an adequate supply when growing most cool-season crops. (Legumes are the exception since they make their own nitrogen.)

 QUICK TIP

> **For the most even lawn appearance** *and to avoid the washboard look of mowing, mow the lawn in at least two directions.*

Protect Peas from Birds and Support the Vines

Make a narrow, A-frame tent of netting by stretching a 2- or 3-foot-wide strip of Ross Garden Netting down each side of a planted double row. Secure the strips by covering the bottom of each with earth and tying the tops to several small bamboo stakes. (Twist and Tie garden twine works well.) The peas grow up inside this tent; when they reach the top, untie it and let them grow beyond. Besides foiling birds, this system helps the plants cling to their trellis; there's no need to wrap the row with twine to hold up sagging vines.

How to Grow Peas

Peas are a good crop to plant early this month. Get them in before the usual heat spell; warm soil sprouts seeds fast to give you an early harvest.

▶ **Choose a Good Variety.** There are three basic kinds to grow: Chinese pea pods (also called snow peas), snap peas, and English peas. The first two are the easiest, and you can eat them pod and all. English peas are delicious, but you have to shell them, and they take up more space.

▶ **Prepare the Soil.** Thoroughly dig up the ground with a spade to the depth of 1 foot or at least 10 inches, adding organic amendment (but no manure). Work in a low-nitrogen fertilizer, such as Dr. Earth Organic 2 Starter Fertilizer (2-4-2) or your own low nitrogen, high phosphorus and potassium mix. (Legumes make their own nitrogen.)

▶ **Arrange North-South Rows.** Space rows so they run from north to south and are 18 to 24 inches apart. (Each row will be planted with a double row of peas, one on each side of the support.)

▶ **Provide Strong Support.** Even dwarf varieties need some kind of trellis to climb on. Shove metal posts or several 8-foot-tall plastic-covered metal plant stakes into the ground down the center of the row. Tie hardware cloth, chicken wire, or reinforcing wire to the stakes. Or create an artistic support using pea stakes cut from shrubs and trees. A teepee shape works well for shorter varieties.

▶ **Make Twin Furrows.** Space twin furrows (narrow grooves in the ground) 3 to 6 inches apart, one furrow on each side of the trellis. Make the furrows 1 inch deep in coastal zones, 2 to 3 inches deep in interior zones.

▶ **Inoculate the Seed.** Unless you've grown peas in the same place within three years or plan to fertilize with nitrogen, inoculate the seed with rhizobia for the largest possible harvest (as described on page 137).

▶ **Plant Close.** Plant the peas at intervals of 2 inches. (Or you can plant them 1 inch apart and thin them to 2 inches when the plants are 2 to 3 inches high.) Cover them with 1 inch of potting soil in coastal zones, 2 to 3 inches in interior zones. Pat it down gently.

▶ **Help Them Germinate.** Pea seeds germinate at soil temperatures from 40° to 75°F, but the warmer the temperature the faster they sprout. If you plant an old variety such as 'Mammoth Melting Sugar' in early September, they'll sprout fast, in three to six days. Some of the newer varieties of snap pea, such as 'Snappy' (my favorite) and the stringless 'Sugar Pop', don't germinate so easily. If they fail to come up, presprout more seed in the house, and put it in the ground as soon as it has sprouted. (Don't give up: presprouting is easy; see page 172.)

▶ **Foil Birds.** Cover the row with netting until the sprouts are 5 inches tall.

▶ **Water Regularly and Deeply.** Sprinkle the row daily to keep it damp until the seed germinates. Then water deeply and regularly, or use a drip system.

▶ **Tie Up the Vines.** Vines will hang on to supports with tendrils, but winter rains and wind can knock them down. Once they're 12 to 18 inches high and before the rains, wind twine around the rows periodically to hold up new growth. (See accompanying box for another method.)

Control Migrating Pests. A number of gardeners like to start planting in some areas while continuing to harvest in others. This works well if you grow vegetables on several levels or in raised beds. The only problem is you have less chance to get rid of all insect pests at once. Whiteflies in particular will tend to migrate off tomatoes onto something else. It's usually best to clean out the entire vegetable garden at one time and then wait a week or two before replanting.

If you've planted flowerbeds with seeds of wildflowers nearby, be careful when chopping up tomato vines. Tiny green worms can crawl right off them and journey across the ground to decimate your flower seedlings.

✳ QUICK TIP

How to Make a Straight, Shallow Furrow for Seeds. *Lay the handle of a hoe flat on its back on the prepared seedbed. Press it down evenly. Measure the furrow with a ruler for correct depth.*

Start a First Garden. If this is your first vegetable garden, start with careful planning. Choose an area in full sun. (This is imperative for winter crops.) Prepare the soil by cultivating deeply with a spade; don't just scratch the surface with a fork or hoe. In order to have success, you must dig up the ground with a spade to a depth of 1 foot or, at the very least, to 10 inches. With the handle of the spade upright, put your foot on the upper edge of the spade and shove it all the way into the ground; then pull the handle toward you and lift the spadeful; turn it over, and hit the resulting clod of earth with the back of the spade to break it apart. If the soil is too hard for you to accomplish this, build

raised boxes on it. Nail 1/2-inch-gauge hardware cloth on the bottom of the boxes to keep out gophers, and fill them with good topsoil mixed with a 4- to 5-inch layer of aged compost or bagged organic soil amendment. After working soil amendment into raised boxes or the ground, the next step is to sprinkle a complete organic vegetable fertilizer on top of the planting area according to package directions and then use a long-handled cultivator to work it into the top 4 to 6 inches of soil. The cultivator I use for this job, picked up years ago at a garage sale, has four thin, sharp, bent tines that reach down just the right distance. A gooseneck weeder also works. (While doing this and other tasks always stand on the paths between rows or between raised beds, never on top of prepared soil.) After preparing the bed as described above, set a sprinkler so it waters the area gently for about 20 minutes. Let the ground settle overnight, and the next day plant seeds or transplants of winter vegetables. This time-honored method of soil preparation works equally well for flowerbeds or vegetable gardens and needs to be repeated every time you replant beds with annual vegetables or flowers. In this way, you will be improving your soil on a regular basis twice a year, spring and fall. The result will be superior soil no matter what it was like when you began.

Another way to go, if you prefer, is to construct and fill raised beds according to the no-dig system of gardening described on page 135. No-dig gardening is easy and saves time, money, and water once you get it going, but you won't be able to plant the day after preparing the bed. After the initial construction of a no-dig garden, one must wait three months for the layers of organic matter in the beds to turn into compost before you can plant for the first time. But if you get no-dig beds started by mid-September, you will be able to plant them with winter vegetables in mid-December, choosing from the list on page 411.

Interplant Peas with Lettuce

If your rows of vegetables are 18 inches apart, skip a row between every two rows of peas. Plant lettuce in the skipped row. After the lettuce is harvested out, tie bamboo or twine across the tops of two rows of tall pea varieties, allowing them to grow across the gap. Children love going through the tunnel and picking peas.

Plant in late September or early October, and be sure to plant cool-season vegetables, not warm-season vegetables. These are the vegetables that are planted in earliest spring in cold-season climates, such as celery and all the cole crops (members of the cabbage family), plus the vegetables that can go into the ground year-round, such as carrots, beets, turnips, and radishes. When you go to the nursery, be careful to buy the right things, because this is one of those months when you can still find transplants of summer vegetables for sale side by side with winter ones. (Check the list in the following section to be sure.)

Fall is just as good a time to start a vegetable garden as spring. In fact, there are some advantages to planting now. Winter vegetables take less care, pest problems are fewer in winter, and irrigation water sometimes falls from heaven. Winter vegetables are fun, surprisingly easy to grow, and far more delicious than the counterparts you can buy in the market.

Begin Planting Cool-Season Vegetables.

Vegetables that can be planted now include beets, broccoli, Brussels sprouts, carrots, cauliflower, celery, fava beans, kale, kohlrabi, leeks, both head and leaf lettuce, mesclun, mustard greens, onions, parsley, peas, potatoes, radishes, rutabagas, spinach, Swiss chard, and turnips. (See the box at left for how to plant peas.) Technically, you could, if you wish, plant all these vegetables straight in the ground from seeds. In actual practice, however, it's easiest to plant broccoli, Brussels sprouts, cauliflower, and celery from transplants; plant potatoes from seed potatoes and onions from sets. (Wait until November to plant seeds of onions for slicing—the sets you plant now will give you scallions, not large onion bulbs.) Parsley and lettuce are also often grown from plants you buy at the nursery—parsley because the seeds are slow to sprout, lettuce so you can have a quick harvest while you're waiting for the seeded rows to grow. (Lettuce seeds sprout easily.) Wait until midmonth to put in transplants of cauliflower, and wait until October to put in transplants of cabbages and artichokes.

Make Carrot, Celery, Parsnip, and Parsley Seeds Sprout in Three Days or Less.

Despite the comments above, you really don't need to buy transplants of parsley. You can grow the flat gourmet type and plenty of curly parsley more inexpensively from seeds. Carrots, celery, parsnips, and parsley are all members of the parsley family, and their seeds are slow to sprout. Despite this problem, for many years I've been getting my carrot, celery, parsnip, and parsley seeds to germinate in three days or even less because I pour boiling water on them straight from the kettle. First I mix the seeds with a little sand in the palm of my hand and sprinkle them down the row.

(Since these seeds are so small, mixing them with a little sand makes them easier to distribute evenly.) Then I go indoors to boil a kettle of water. Once the water is boiling—and I do mean a fast boil—I carry the kettle out into the garden, and walk down the row while pouring the boiling water straight out of the kettle on top of the seeds in the row. Then I cover the seeds with a little potting soil and pat it down gently. (See page 361 for another reminder of this tip next month, and an additional method as well.) This boiling water treatment is a method of *scarification* (nicking, abrasing, or otherwise breaking through the seed coat of a hard-coated seed), and sometimes my parsley has even popped up the next day, but always

Harvesting celery

SEPTEMBER

within three days and all at once. Many people don't want to believe this tip, so I carry a big kettle when I give talks on planting seeds to convince my audience that it really works. But don't use this method on other seeds, only on seeds of members of the parsley family, including carrots, celery, parsnips and wild carrot called Queen Anne's lace, the seeds of which are notoriously difficult to sprout.

Use Humic Acid as a Transplant Fluid.

And here is another important tip: When planting transplants of vegetables, use a product containing humic acid as a transplant fluid. (Transplant fluids containing Vitamin B1 do absolutely nothing—zilch—as was proved by scientific research done many years ago. So throw yours away here and there in the garden just to get rid of it. It will do neither harm nor good; then purchase a product containing humic acid.) Dilute humic acid according to package directions and soak the ground surrounding every transplant at planting time. Cole crops in particular respond with astounding growth after this treatment. I pulled up one of my humic-acid treated Brussels sprouts once to show the results on camera. The roots were larger in circumference than those of untreated plants and much more numerous and branched, similar in appearance to a thick head of hair. Strong root systems result in a larger, more productive plant. Humic acid will also make the roots of peas and other crops more vigorous and plentiful so the stems will be stouter and stronger resulting in a more abundant crop.

Adventuresome gardeners might like to try growing broccoli, Brussels sprouts, cabbage, cauliflower, and celery from seeds. It requires a fuss—the seedlings need nursing along with frequent applications of a weak liquid fertilizer, such as fish emulsion—but it does allow a wider choice of varieties. If you're planting the seeds straight in the ground, a drip system will greatly increase your chances of success. Many gardeners grow their own transplants in flats or peat pots, but cole crops and celery actually don't like being transplanted; they form better roots when grown from seeds right where you want them. When planting broccoli, Brussels sprouts, cauliflower, and celery from seeds, plant them early in September for best results, but plant cabbage seeds about midmonth. (When planting celery from seeds remember to use the boiling water method of scarification, described above, to speed germination.)

Though it's too late to plant summer vegetables, some gardeners in frost-free zones have been experimenting lately with planting a last crop of tomatoes or beans early in September. Choose an early variety, such as 'Early Girl Improved' or 'Early Goliath' tomatoes ('Celebrity' works, too) or 'Venture' beans. Among vintage tomatoes, try 'Mortgage Lifter' and 'Big Red'; both are reputed to bear during cooler weather. Many gardeners keep a few tomato plants going until December.

Extend the Season for Tomatoes with Red Plastic Mulch.

Besides planting one of the early varieties mentioned above, you will undoubtedly have even greater success with fall-planted tomatoes if you mulch the ground surrounding the plants with red plastic mulch. (Red plastic mulch is available from Gurney's Seeds and some other catalogs.) Purchase a type with perforations in it to allow rainwater to pass through it or make holes in it after installation. Red plastic mulch is one of the most recent advances in agriculture, and besides increasing yields, it suppresses nematodes and reduces early blight. By reflecting infrared light upward as well as allowing infrared rays of

sunlight to pass through it, red mulch increases
the warmth of the air above it as well as warming the ground beneath it. In a three-year study,
tomatoes planted over red plastic mulch, com-
pared with black mulch, averaged a 12 percent
greater harvest. The current price of tomatoes
and healthy benefits of homegrown fruit justify
the cost of red plastic mulch. The problem is that
it's difficult or impossible to recycle. Whether to
use or not use plastic mulch is another of those
individual questions that can only be resolved
by comparing necessity with philosophy.

SEPTEMBER CHECKLIST

PURCHASE/PLANT

{ } Transplant the biennials started from seed in July into the garden, *265*

{ } Plant alstroemerias, *293*

{ } Begin purchasing spring-flowering bulbs, *312*

{ } Start planting bulbs, especially drought resistant ones, *313*

{ } Begin to plant lilies, *314*

{ } Purchase plants or corms of cyclamen, *315*

{ } Plant bulb covers over spring-flowering bulbs, *316*

{ } Finish planting tropicals in coastal zones, *316*

{ } Start planting cool-season flowers to bloom during winter and spring, *324*

{ } Plant sweet peas from seeds for Christmas bloom, *325*

{ } Plant warm-season lawns, except zoysia (though it's better to wait until spring), *329*

{ } Start planting winter vegetables, *332*

{ } Plant peas, *330*

{ } Plant cool-season lawns in coastal zones, *311*

TRIM, PRUNE, MOW, DIVIDE

{ } Continue to mow lawns at summer heights, *328*

{ } Divide irises that need division in interior zones, *315*

{ } Stop pruning hibiscus, *317*

{ } Prune oleanders by taking out whole stalks, *317*

{ } Don't prune New Zealand tea trees in fall, *317*

{ } Start disbudding camellias, *321*

{ } Resume picking and deadheading roses, but don't disbud them, *322*

{ } Dethatch Bermuda if it needs it and if you failed to do the job in spring or if you are correcting a serious problem with several treatments, *329*

{ } Mow off the flowers from lippia lawns, *277*

{ } Start fall cleanup for perennials, *326*

{ } Remove faded and ratty flowers from evergreen, warm-season ornamental grasses, *327*

FERTILIZE

{ } Feed fuchsias, *208*

{ } Continue to feed tuberous begonias, *260*

{ } Feed ferns for the last time this year, *183*

{ } Feed all container-grown succulents with a well-diluted complete liquid fertilizer, *273*

{ } Feed and water cyclamen, *315*

{ } Fertilize tropicals for the last time this year, only if they need it, *316*

{ } Switch fertilizers on cymbidiums to a higher-bloom formula to encourage flowering, *319*

{ } To maintain the color of blue hydrangeas, start treating the soil with aluminum sulfate, or use organic methods, *320*

{ } Fertilize azaleas at month's end for the second and last time of the year; correct chlorosis if necessary, *321*

{ } Fertilize Thanksgiving and Christmas cacti for bloom, *322*

{ } Continue to feed warm-season lawns; don't feed cool-season lawns until after midmonth, *328*

{ } Fertilize roses with compost tea if desired, *321*

WATER

{ } Continue to water all garden plants according to their individual needs (with the exception of certain natives), *288, 311*

{ } Check drought-resistant plants for signs of stress; give them a deep irrigation, if necessary, to tide them over to the winter rains, *288, 311*

{ } Don't let fall-planted tropicals dry out, *316*

{ } Keep citrus evenly watered to help prevent fruit from splitting, *317*

{ } Don't let camellias dry out now or buds will fall off later, *320*

{ } Water roses with up to 1 1/2 inches of water twice a week, *321*

CONTROL PESTS, DISEASE, AND WEEDS

{ } Treat lemon trees for brown rot, *318*

{ } Control rose pests and diseases, *92*

{ } Control migrating pests, *331*

ALSO THIS MONTH

{ } Untie the fronds of palms transplanted in July, *302*

{ } Start cleaning out flowerbeds and prepare the ground for fall planting, *324, 351*

{ } Make sure cymbidiums are in adequate light to produce bloom; also see that they get the range of temperatures necessary for bloom, *319*

{ } Put Thanksgiving and Christmas cacti into natural light for two months so they will bloom, *322*

{ } Prepare beds for cool-season vegetables, *329*

{ } Start new vegetable gardens, *331*

{ } Continue to harvest 'Valencia' oranges, *317*

October

THE YEAR'S BEST PLANTING MONTH

Ceiba speciosa
(Floss silk tree)

October is almost always one of the most pleasant months of the year. Though we sometimes get our first rains this month and occasionally they're torrential, the rainy season doesn't officially start until next month. For the most part the weather is clear and sunny, though cooler—cool enough for working outdoors in the middle of the day even in interior valleys. That's good news for gardeners because October is probably the busiest time of the year. It's the best time to plant almost all permanent additions to the landscape; the exceptions are tropicals (a bit late for them), bare-root plants (they get planted in January), native plants, and ground covers (wait until next month and they'll do slightly better). The idea behind fall planting is to get things into the ground ahead of the major rains. Roots get established during winter and reward you the following summer with a great surge of growth. It's the time-honored, easy, water-saving way to plant.

October, like March, is a pivotal month when we make the switch from one Southern California season to another. In March we switch to the summer scheme. In October we switch to winter. Gardeners who put aside extra time for gardening this month will be rewarded with better results and less work to do later. This is the time to pull up the last remnants of summer vegetables and flowers, and finish planting cool-season flowers and vegetables for winter and spring. Continue to cut back, clean out, plant, transplant, and revamp perennials. It's also the best time to plant most winter vegetables. Get them into the ground as soon as possible. Cool-season lawns can be seeded now, and it's time to prune, transplant, divide, and separate a great many garden staples. Continue to clean out the dead interiors of native plants. Cut out dead branches and shape the plants in readiness for winter growth.

FALL PLANTING FOR DESERT DWELLERS AND GARDENERS IN HOT INTERIOR ZONES

Those who live in the desert can plant a wide range of vegetables and flowers this month. Both summer and winter vegetables can be planted now, with the exception of corn and melons, which should be planted in late January or early February. (Wait until November to plant onions, but buy the seeds of short-day varieties now.) Many flowers, including ivy geraniums and petunias, which thrive in the spring and summer along the coast, can be counted on for winter color in desert areas. For more planting ideas, see the selection of bedding plants at local nurseries. Among permanent plants to put in now are flame vine (*Pyrostegia venusta*) and Easter lily vine (*Beaumontia grandiflora*).

Making a Desert Landscape. The only truly appropriate way to create a desert landscape is to use native desert plants, so why do so many desert dwellers still plant petunias and lawns? Perhaps the answer is that creating a well-designed landscape of desert plants is either expensive or challenging. The expensive option is to hire a professional landscape architect or designer and have the resultant design professionally installed. The challenging option is to study the subject in detail, draw a plan, purchase plants and supplies, and go it alone with hired help, an undertaking that requires a flair for design and a passion for native plants. Devoted desert gardeners who succeed usually

begin by visiting local and botanical gardens and collecting clippings, photographs, and books on the subject. Among recent books, Wasowski and Wasowski's *Native Landscaping From El Paso to L.A.* is chock-full of design ideas, photos, ideas for plant choice, and sample plans. Mielke's *Native Plants for Southwestern Landscapes* is an invaluable source of information on choosing, planting, and caring for plants for hot, dry interior regions.

These books cover dry-garden plants and gardening for all interior zones, including Southwest and Mediterranean climate zones, not just the desert climate zones. (People often call all Southern California a desert, but this is a misnomer. Only the areas east of the mountains can correctly be characterized as desert. Climate zones where native oaks, sycamores, and chaparral grow are more correctly called Mediterranean.)

Correct Soil Problems. Fall is the time to study one's soil, draw plans, and purchase plants and other materials. The best time to plant is late September through early December. First check the drainage according to the instructions in the box on page 40. If drainage is inadequate, modify plans so that all plants will grow on mounds or in raised beds. If caliche soil is a problem, consult your local UC Farm Advisor's office for solutions, which may include building raised beds and terraces, hauling away the hard cracked layer on top, breaking holes through buried hardpan. Gypsum can help correct compaction of clay soils resulting from alkalinity. (For details, see page 21.) Some desert gardeners begin by bulldozing and hauling away the top 1 to 2 feet of alkaline soil and replacing it with truckloads of sandy or loamy soil recommended for desert plants. (As described on page 19, mix some of the topsoil into the native soil that remains in order to avoid creating hardpan.) Organic amendments are seldom used when planting natives from desert regions.

Making a Garden Is Like Baking a Cake.
It may surprise you to know that with proper planning and enough hired help, you can install the bones of a fine desert landscape in one three-day weekend. Once having studied desert garden design and installation, fixed your soil, and drawn up a plan, the actual planting is like baking a cake. First you gather the ingredients, and then you put it all together. Gathering the ingredients is the part that takes time, but once all the ingredients are on site and you've made arrangements for delivery of bulky items on the weekend of construction, the job won't take long to install. Depending on the size of your property, here's a rough idea of what you might need for one front yard: enough landscape fabric to line the bottom of a dry streambed, two large balls of string, three crowbars, six shovels, and six garden rakes, several colors of stakes (each color will stand for a different size or category of rocks and plants), nine burlap bags and seven pairs of leather gloves for handling cacti and other spiny plants. Arrange for between three and five workmen to work for three days. Rent a backhoe for one day. Choose and tag three, five, or seven large, artistically shaped boulders ranging in size from about 3¹/₂ tons for the largest one and others in a variety of weights and shapes, to be delivered at 1:00 p.m. on Friday afternoon or first thing Saturday morning by a truck with a crane and an operator for installation. You will need sufficient flat rocks for one or two ornamental dry walls, if desired, and an adequate number of flagstones or pavers for paths; eight to ten sacks of fine pea gravel for filling the cracks

between the pavers; nine large, fifteen medium-size, and twenty-four smaller-size river rocks to create a natural-looking dry streambed, as well as enough pebbles or gravel to fill the bottom of the gully 8 inches deep as the base of the stream. (The purveyor will tell you how much to order for the area and depth.) You will also need a collection of native desert plants in containers including three boxed trees—for example, Palo verde (*Cercidium* 'Desert Museum'), desert olive (*Forestiera neomexicana*), and sweet acacia (*Acacia smallii*); three or five 15-gallon-size shrubs, such as black dalea (*Dalea frutescens* 'Sierra Negra'), violet silverleaf (*Leucophyllum candidum* 'Silver Cloud') and Apache plume (*Fallugia paradoxa*); and eighteen to twenty-five 1- to 5-gallon-size shrubs in three or four species including such cacti as purple-colored prickly pear (*Opuntia macrocentra* 'Tubac'). Purchase several plants—an uneven number—of each choice, and plant them in drifts. In addition, you will need three flats each of three varieties of ground cover, such as Goodding verbena (*V. gooddingii*), desert marigold (*Baileya multiradiata*), and trailing indigo bush (*Dalea greggii*). If the budget allows, invest in one large specimen desert plant, such as Joshua tree (*Yucca brevifolia*), saguaro cactus (*Carnegiea gigantea*), or ocotillo (*Fouquieria splendens*). Purchase these large items and such items as barrel cactus from reputable sources in order to ensure that endangered plants were not stolen from wild lands.

On Friday morning, use the backhoe to contour the ground according to your plan, digging out a slanting, undulating streambed that flows from left to right at an angle from backward to forward (or the other way around if it fits the space better). Use the native soil you remove from the gully to create two smooth mounds at the back and one on the left or right front. With the help of workmen, smooth and finish the shapes of the mounds with hand tools and dig holes for the boulders.

Measure the sizes of tree boxes, dig holes for trees, and fill them with water. (Two days should allow adequate time for the water to drain out.) Place one tree hole near the path or a wall, one off to one side and another in the streambed, so they form a triangle, not a row. When the boulders arrive have the crane operator place the boulders with the crane while the workmen stand back, and then use hand labor to nestle them into the ground in a natural manner. (At least one boulder should be set upright on end, as often occurs in natural desert landscapes.) To stop gravel from sinking into the ground, line the bottom of the gully with landscape fabric and fill the gulley with gravel. Insert colored stakes in the ground to indicate placement of rocks, walls, and plants. Measure, set stakes, and use string to outline dry walls and paths. Place the three sizes of rocks in the streambed, placing the large ones at the turns so that one can see that each curve in the stream took place because a rock, a tree, or other obstruction forced the water to change direction. (This technique results in a streambed that looks natural instead of fake.) Begin construction on walls. On Saturday finish the walls and set down the flagstones or pavers. Fill the spaces between the flagstones with pea gravel, retaining the rest for mulch. On Sunday plant the trees and the ocotillo or large cactus according to their placement on the plans. Dig holes for all plants and fill the holes with water. After the water drains out of the holes, loosen any roots winding around the container, and plant straight into the native soil. Plant the shrubs in the places you have staked so you are framing the house with a dramatic collection of desert plants. The final touch is to cover the

three mounds with ground cover, one variety for each mound. Follow up with irrigation once a week if necessary, allowing winter rains to take over whenever possible. Water desert plants in fall and winter when rains are inadequate, and occasionally in summer, when monsoons aren't enough to keep them going. Prune them in fall, just to remove dead foliage. As the years go by, fill in the design by adding more ephemeral plants such as firecracker penstemon (*P. eatonii*). (This bake-a-cake method of garden construction can be used to create a Japanese garden also, or almost any well-planned and prepared front yard.)

TREES, SHRUBS, AND VINES

Plant all trees, shrubs, and vines now to give them the best start possible. This is the finest time of the year to put in garden staples that last for years and become the backbone of the landscape. Tropicals are an exception: It's better to plant them in late spring or early summer, especially in interior zones. (Very tender plants like tropical hibiscus often die with the first frost when planted in fall.) But nurseries, understandably, may carry some plants only while they're in bloom, so fall may be the only time that you can find certain flowering trees and vines.

If you do plant tropicals now, don't fertilize them, do protect them from frost during winter, and ask your nursery if the plant you purchase is guaranteed to survive the winter. The reason fall planting benefits almost all other plants is that the soil is still warm enough to stimulate growth of roots, and winter rains will help them get established. You won't see much, if any, growth during the winter, but what you plant now will be ready to wake up and grow when the weather warms up in spring. Choose plants recommended for your climate zone, and take their eventual size and ability to withstand drought into consideration. Plant sun lovers in the sun and shade lovers in the shade, and always plant in zones, grouping plants with similar water requirements.

Among trees you might choose to put in now are all types of conifers, as well as Chinese elm (*Ulmus parvifolia*), mayten tree (*Maytenus boaria*), many melaleucas, cork oak (*Quercus suber*—the thick-barked tree that Ferdinand the Bull sat under), fern pine (*Podocarpus gracilior*), Australian and New Zealand tea trees (*Leptospermum laevigatum* and *L. scoparium*), and tipu tree (*Tipuana tipu*). Most shrubs used for hedges can be planted now, along with many shrubs used for accents and screens, including India hawthorn (*Rhaphiolepis indica*), photinia, pittosporum, lavender starflower (*Grewia occidentalis*), and yew pine (*Podocarpus macrophyllus*). Among vines and vinelike plants to put in now are Cape honeysuckle (*Tecoma capensis*), Carolina Jessamine (*Gelsemium sempervirens*), and lilac vine (*Hardenbergia comptoniana*). (Wait until next month to put in ground covers and California native plants.)

When purchasing India Hawthorne, be sure to choose a good variety. Flower color is poor on unnamed varieties. Among tall varieties, 'Dancer', 'Jack Evans', and 'Springtime' are good choices; 'Ballerina' is a stunning dwarf. Don't choose white varieties with single blossoms; their flowers go brown in rain and drop off in one week. If you don't specify to landscape companies which variety you want, you're likely to end up with inferior white or dull pink seedlings. (For more good varieties, refer to the list in the *Sunset Western Garden Book*.)

FALL COLOR

October is a good time to notice those plants that provide fall color year after year and perhaps add one to your garden. By purchasing now you can find the color that pleases you most. All the plants listed below can be put in now along the coast, and several can also be planted inland. (If you live in the interior don't plant tropicals this late in the season.)

For autumn leaves choose liquidambar for its colorful pink, red, yellow, or orange foliage, or maidenhair tree (*Ginkgo biloba*), which has golden leaves in fall. In order to avoid the sticky, malodorous fruit of mature female trees, plant only named male varieties, such as 'Autumn Gold' or 'Fairmount'. Liquidamber also drops seedpods, make practical use of them as described in the box on page 325. The Hong Kong orchid tree (*Bauhinia x blakeana*) has striking flowers ranging from cranberry to pink. Floss silk tree (*Chorisia speciosa*) blooms in burgundy or bright orchid to bright pink all over the top of the tree. (There's also a white species, *C. insignis*.) Nile tulip tree (*Markhamia lutea, M. hildebrandtii*) bears golden trumpet flowers from August through November. It's best near the coast. Flamegold tree (*Koelreuteria elegans, K. formosana*) is named for its salmon-colored seedpods, which follow less significant yellow flowers.

Vines include cup-of-gold vine (*Solandra maxima*), which grows well even on the oceanfront, and flame vine (*Pyrostegia venusta*), one of the best choices from the ocean to the desert for cloaking a tile roof, wall, or weathered wooden fence with a sheet of brilliant orange tubular blooms for several months in fall and winter. It will grow flat on top of a pergola and flow over the edge like a green curtain in summer, covered with bright orange blooms

OCTOBER

throughout fall and winter. Mexican flame vine (*Senecio confusus*) is a yellow-to-orange vine for coastal locations. (It dies down in frost.) It may be hard to find but can be grown from seed or cuttings. Cut it back hard after bloom.

DECIDUOUS FRUIT TREES

In mild zones it's sometimes a problem to get deciduous fruit trees into winter dormancy. Don't follow the erroneous advice to feed them now in fall, though you may read it in books, magazines, and even some local newspapers. Fall fertilizing is an accepted practice in cold-winter climates, but in our region it forces growth at the wrong time of year. After mid-month hold back on water, but don't let the soil dry out completely. Dry conditions may encourage trees to drop their leaves and go dormant for the winter, as is desirable.

PLANTS TO DIVIDE, TRIM, AND MULCH

October is the main month for dividing plants that tend to grow in a clump. Some of these plants—clivia, iris, daylilies, and ginger, for example—are bulblike in that they grow from thickened roots, or rhizomes. Others are true perennials. The reasons for dividing are to propagate more plants, to make plants look better, to keep them to a desired size, or to encourage bloom. (When crowded, some plants bloom better, but other stop flowering.) Always water thoroughly the day before dividing.

Kahili Ginger. Once the rhizomatous root-stocks of Kahili ginger (*Hedychium gardnerarum*) crowd the top of the pot, the plant will

How to Divide Daylilies

Divide daylilies every three to five years to keep them blooming. Old varieties bloom longer without division than new varieties.

▶ Dig up the clumps. Knock off excess earth. Separate large clumps by putting two garden forks back to back and prying them apart.

▶ To make individual sections, find the natural dividing point between two fans of leaves. Push downward between them with a large, old screwdriver kept for the purpose, so that the fans break cleanly in two.

▶ Throw away broken parts. Trim the leaves of good divisions to 4 inches. Trim off any broken or damaged roots. Shorten overly long ones.

▶ Dig up the bed and loosen the soil to a depth of 1 foot; mix in bone meal, fertilizer, and organic amendments.

▶ For each plant make a shallow cone of earth. Replant the daylilies 12 to 18 inches apart, with their roots spread over the cone and covered with 1½ to 3 inches of soil. Mulch and water the ground. Give excess plants to friends.

bloom less; this is a sign it needs to be either potted on or divided. Repot it, transplant it, or divide it now, to avoid destroying next year's bloom. To divide, slice down through the rhizomes with a knife or sharp spade to make large sections, 8 inches or more in diameter; trim off damaged roots only, and replant in pots or the ground, with the rhizomes just beneath the surface and the roots completely buried in humus-rich soil. Cut off faded blooms, but don't cut off the stalks or foliage: Kahili ginger needs its green leaves during the winter.

Clivia. October is the best time to divide clivia. They like to be rootbound, so don't divide them unless absolutely necessary (see the box on page 346.)

Iris. Clean up and mulch existing beds. Continue dividing and transplanting overcrowded irises (as described on page 241). They won't bloom when crowded.

Daylily. Renew all evergreen daylilies (*Hemerocallis*) by cutting the leaves back to 4 inches. Mulch the beds and clean up dead leaves. Bait for snails and slugs. (If ever-blooming daylilies are still flowering, wait until month's end or even November in coastal zones.) Follow up with organic fertilizer to bring out fresh growth. In interior valleys divide overcrowded daylilies now; along the coast do it now or wait until March (see the box on facing page for directions).

Fortnight Lily. Fortnight lilies (*Dietes, Moraea*) eventually make huge, ugly clumps with brown tips. Don't shear off the tops like rounded shaving brushes, as one often sees done; the tips will only go brown again, and new growth will stick up beyond the old in an ungainly fashion.

   If you must shear fortnight lily, cut them straight across with electric hedge trimmers 6 or 8 inches above ground. Follow up with organic fertilizer and water.

   A much better way to treat them is to dig up the old clumps now with a garden fork and divide them. (The roots aren't deep.) Cut back their tops to 4 to 5 inches and replant

How to Renew Gazanias

Gazanias are one of our finest drought- and disease-resistant ground covers. Divide the clumping kinds every three or four years to keep them like new.

▸ Dig up the clumps. Knock off excess soil.

▸ Divide the clumps by pulling and clipping them apart. Trim off any damaged roots and any dead leaves or flowers.

▸ Refurbish the bed by spading it deeply and adding soil amendment and organic fertilizer.

▸ Replant the divisions 8 inches apart. Keep them well watered until reestablished.

▸ You'll have plenty of plants left over; share them with friends or discard.

them. Throw away the excess. (These are too common to give away.)

Matilija Poppy. In the last half of September or the first half of October, cut down to the ground spent stems of Matilija poppy (*Romneya coulteri*) that have bloomed. You can if you wish divide the plant in late October or November. A friend of mine waits for the first rain and then cuts large (5-gallon-plant size) divisions with a spade. He uses a bucket for transporting the fragile roots, and plants them immediately, following up by watering deeply. He says small divisions don't work. By using the above method he has gradually created a magnificent display to hide 100 feet of chain link fence.

Bird of Paradise. Cut off the dead leaves of bird of paradise *(Strelitzia reginae)*. Pull out bloom stems after the flowers fade. Small plants can be divided with a sharp spade. They eventually make immense clumps that are almost impossible to divide. You may have to attack them with a chain saw. Replant salvageable sections.

Other Plants. Also divisible now, if necessary, are gazanias, ivy geraniums, lily turf, and all garden perennials that grow in clumps, including Shasta daisies, though it would be better to replace them now with a longer-blooming, less thirsty plant such as Alstroemeria 'Casablanca'. (Wait until November to divide and transplant agapanthus.)

GERANIUMS (PELARGONIUMS)

Prune Zonal (Garden or Common) Geraniums. Continue progressive pruning on zonal geraniums *(Pelargonium x hortorum)*. Remove dead and diseased leaves and branches. Cut back one or two of the longest branches, or, if you have been neglecting this job, take several. Make each cut straight across a branch and $1/4$ to $1/2$ inch from a joint. Leave one or two healthy leaves on the branches you've cut back. (Bare stubs won't recover.)

With potted specimens dig out some of the old soil and refresh it with fresh soil. Feed geraniums occasionally during the winter with an organic fertilizer. Continue to prune out one or two old leggy stems each month year-round. Save the most succulent cuttings to make new plants. Dip them in RooTone or Dip'N Grow and plant in fast-draining potting soil.

Cut Back Ivy Geraniums. Continue progressive pruning on ivy geraniums *(P. peltatum)*,

How to Divide a Potted Clivia

Clivia like to be rootbound. Plants in the ground can go almost indefinitely without division. But you must divide clivia grown in pots when no soil is left and the roots push up out of the top, because then drainage becomes a problem. To divide them, take these steps:

▸ Use a large knife to cut around the inside of the pot or tub. Place the pot on its side. Direct a strong water pressure up the drainage hole to loosen roots.

▸ To remove a plant that stays stuck, sit on the ground with your feet on the edge of the tub, grab the stalks close to the roots, and yank the monster out.

▸ Cut apart the individual stalks with a knife. Trim away some of the excess roots. Repot them in potting soil, three plants to an 18-inch container.

cutting back one or two of the longest branches once a month. If, however, you have not been faithful to this task, now is your chance to cut back all the long and ungainly growth to about 6 to 8 inches from pot level. Remove dead branches, leaves, and debris. Remove a little soil and replace it with fresh mix. Feed them for growth and water them. If your ivy geraniums are growing in the ground, cut them back lightly and clean up the ground around them. Then mulch, feed, and water them.

Prune Martha Washingtons. Martha Washingtons *(P. x domesticum)* can become floppy if not pruned, but don't cut them back all at once. It's best to begin right after spring bloom and do the job progressively. Prune one or two leggy stems back to the lowest pair of leaves. Then cut more when regrowth begins. In coastal zones, progressive pruning can be continued through October.

Prune Species and Scented Geraniums.

Cut back species geraniums lightly to keep them growing and in bounds. Some ground-cover types of scented geranium, including *P. tomentosum*, can be sheared with hedge shears. Remove dead and dying portions; clean up the ground. Follow up with a light application of a complete organic fertilizer like Dr. Earth or any other of your choice; water it in.

WATER LILIES

Lift Tropical Water Lilies in Interior Zones.

Tropical water lilies are the ones that hold their flowers high above the water and come in many exciting colors and a wide range of sizes. They usually can survive year-round outdoors in coastal climates, but if frost hits your garden every year they probably won't live through winter. If you know it's going to freeze, lift the tubers now, remove the soil, and store the tubers in damp sand in a garage or cellar for the winter. Plant them again in spring. If this sounds like a bother, buy fresh ones yearly. It's more expensive, but trying out new colors and sizes can add to the fun of growing these exotic plants.

Divide Hardy Water Lilies.
Hardy water lilies are frequently smaller and less striking than tropical ones, but they're easier to grow, and many people prefer the way they float on the surface of the water rather than standing high above it, as tropical water lilies do. For the best bloom, divide hardy water lilies or pot them on every three years in October. (You can also plant more now.)

To repot hardy water lilies, lift the containers out of the pool. (Wear protective clothing and rubber gloves to avoid contact with algae, which can cause allergic reactions.) Inspect the roots: If they fill the container and the plants look crowded, it's time to repot. To do so, first clean up the plants by removing dead leaves and debris, and also take off any baby plants. (Plant these in separate containers as described on page 155.) Then remove some of the old soil from the roots of the parent plant and pot it on, filling in around the roots in the new larger container with Profile Aquatic Plant Soil or rich garden loam that contains no manure, peat moss, bone meal, perlite, or wood shavings. To keep the water from getting muddy and prevent fish from nibbling on roots, either cover the surface of the soil with a 1- to 2-inch layer of washed sand (or pebbles) or galvanized chicken wire.

Hardy water lilies that don't look crowded but do have yellow leaves and fewer flowers may simply need fertilizing. (The best feeding regimen is once a month beginning in April, as described on page 156.) Feed now by pushing organic slow-release tablets recommended for aquatic plants beneath the soil surface, or mix 1 pound of slow-acting, granular organic aquatic fertilizer into the soil mix of every 5-gallon container. Replace the protective sand, pebbles, or wire netting on top. (Aquatic plants in containers are dependent on the gardener for nutrition, so one does need to feed them. Water lilies in ponds can't survive on native soil and droppings from fish as wild ones do.) Unfortunately, though the instructions above say to use an organic fertilizer, it's difficult or impossible to find one that would not have a negative effect on your pond, because organic matter in the water, or any loose fertilizer for that matter, promotes the growth of algae. There are many kinds of aquatic plant food tablets and spikes that will not pollute your pond or make algae grow in it, and each gardener needs to weigh alternatives and choose what fits in his or her priorities. For example, PondCare Aquatic Plant Food Tablets contains all the trace minerals and nutrients needed by aquatic plants, including water lilies, and it will not harm the pond or fish, but the formula of this fertilizer might not be completely organic in the sense of being totally derived from plants or animals.

BULBS

Shop for Spring-Blooming Bulbs. If you didn't purchase bulbs and corms last month, don't wait any longer. The early shopper gets the best bulbs. Always purchase bulbs at a first-rate nursery. You'll pay a little more, but it's worth it. Bargain bulbs sometimes won't even bloom. Some mail-order catalogs are excellent sources of rare bulbs; a few offer the convenience of premium-size prechilled tulips, but many mail-order bulbs of common varieties are just as expensive and much smaller than those you can find at the best nurseries.

You can still plant the South African bulbs, such as babiana, crocosmia, freesia, ipheion (spring starflower, *Ipheion uniflorum*), ixia, sparaxis, tritonia, and watsonia. You can also plant oxalis and all the Tazetta types of narcissus, such as 'China lily' (Chinese sacred lilies), 'Geranium', and paper whites. Lilies (*Lilium*) should be planted as soon as you get them home. (See page 315 for more information on these bulbs.)

Buy anemones, daffodils, grape hyacinths, Dutch irises, and ranunculus now, but wait until next month to plant them. Keep them in a cool, dry place such as the garage. (Don't refrigerate them.) The temperature of the ground and of soil in containers is still too warm this month in most zones for safe planting of these bulbs. (In interior valleys daffodils and Dutch irises can be planted by midmonth, but it won't hurt to wait until November.)

Prechill Hyacinth, Tulip, and Crocus Bulbs. Hyacinths, tulips, and Dutch crocus (*Crocus vernus*) bulbs can also be bought now. The **Rule of Thumb:** *To fool hyacinths, tulips, and crocuses into thinking they've had a cold winter, put the bulbs in the lettuce drawer of your refrigerator for six to eight weeks prior to planting.* Gardeners who live in interior valleys should start chilling these bulbs now for early December planting. Gardeners in coastal zones and air-drained, frost-free zones should wait until November to start the chilling process. Store them in a cool, dry place until then.

Before you refrigerate bulbs, put them in a brown paper bag, not plastic—it rots them. Write on the bag "not onions, don't eat!" If your lettuce drawer takes delight, as some do, in regularly freezing lettuce, it's too cold for bulbs; store them on a low back shelf. They must not freeze. Also, beware of fresh fruits that give off ethylene gas, including apples, bananas, and pineapples. When these are stored in the same refrigerator with bulbs, make sure they're in airtight bags or containers; if the gas escapes it can cause flower bulbs to rot or grow roots and sprout.

Divide Gladioli. When gladiolus stems have died, cut them off and dig up the corms. You'll probably be delighted, as I always am, to see how a new corm has grown on top of each old one. Sometimes you'll also find that several tiny new corms, called "cormels," have sprouted around the edges of it. Knock off the soil and

⚙ QUICK TIP

Off-Season Bulb Storage. *For tuberous begonias, caladiums, dahlias, gladioli, and other bulb and bulb-type plants, first line a wire basket with fly screen and a handful or two of perlite or sponge rock. Roll the bulbs in an organic fungicide, such as sulfur dust, place them in the basket, and cover them with more sponge rock. Hang them in a cool, dry spot high enough to be out of the reach of field mice. (They relish most bulbs and corms.)*

lay the entire thing, stem and all, on newspaper to dry for a few days in sun along the coast, a week or two in shade inland.

After they're thoroughly dry, the corms will separate easily. Keep the new smaller, fatter corms that have grown on top to plant next year. Throw away the stem, the roots, and the old wider, flatter corm on the bottom. It's now worn out. You can leave the cormels attached if you wish, or separate them from the parent and either discard or plant them, but cormels are often difficult to sprout. To avoid this problem, prechill them in the refrigerator for two months, as described above for hyacinths, tulips, and crocuses. Then plant them 1 inch apart in flats or the ground in late winter, and let them grow until they're big enough to bloom; the process takes a year or two. Lift them in fall and plant them 6 inches apart the following year. (Occasionally the genetic structures of cormels will be different from the parent plant, and you'll get a mutation, a flower unlike its parent.)

Roll the new corms and cormels in sulfur dust, as an organic fungicide. (This is optional. Use gloves and be careful not to breathe sulfur into your lungs.) Store them in a cool, dry place until next February, when once again it's time to plant glads. You can also treat the corms and cormels to control thrips before storage. To do so, soak the corms and cormels for six hours in a solution of 4 teaspoons of Lysol in 1 gallon of water. Dry the bulbs thoroughly before dusting with sulfur and storing.

Divide Naked Ladies. Naked lady (*Amaryllis belladonna*) is among our most valuable but least appreciated drought-resistant South African bulbs. Look for good hybrids now in nurseries. The cheerful pink flowers of the old wild (unhybridized) type are often seen in backcountry gardens arising in straight, awkward rows on bare stems from dusty ground. They look best massed or mixed with aeonium, aloes, and statice (*Limonium perezii*) to cover a windswept bank near the sea, but they make a fine, informal bank cover in any frost-free zone. Once established inland they need only occasional water. Along the coast (Zone 24) they need little or no irrigation.

Eventually naked ladies form big clumps that push up out of the ground and need dividing. The **Rule of Thumb:** *Divide naked ladies in early October, after bloom but while they're still dormant and before new roots or leaves have begun to grow.* If early rains stimulate growth, wait another year and dig them up a little earlier. They won't bloom for several years if divided during active growth.

Store Tuberous Begonias. Allow tuberous begonias to dry out after bloom. Slip the root ball out of the pot and let the whole thing dry in the sun. Leaves and stems will fall off by themselves. After the root ball is thoroughly dry, tear off the roots, roll the tuber in sulfur dust, and store it for the winter in sponge rock or perlite.

How to Force Poinsettias to Bloom for the Holidays

Potted poinsettias saved from last Christmas can be forced to bloom again this year, if you start now. In most cases the time involved hardly pays, but the large tub and tree-size plants produced by growers in recent years can make the trouble worthwhile, considering the plant's beauty and original cost.

▸ Place a healthy poinsettia plant in a warm, protected place where it will get four to six hours of direct sunlight daily. Turn it for even growth.

▸ Begin on October 1 to keep the plant in a totally dark, cool place (65°F) for fourteen hours every night for ten weeks. For example, you could place it in a closet or in the garage under an upside-down trash can or cardboard box from 5 P.M. to 7 A.M. Don't allow even the tiniest glint of light to hit the plant during the nightly dark period, or flowering will be delayed. (Temperatures below 60°F will also delay bloom.)

▸ Every morning return the plant to a place where it will get four to six hours of direct sunlight during the day.

▸ Meanwhile, water and feed the poinsettia often with a complete liquid fertilizer high in bloom ingredients, such as Tiger Bloom (2-8-4).

▸ When bracts on your plant begin to show good color, about the first week in December, discontinue the darkness regimen and enjoy the bloom.

If you prefer, you can try keeping the tuber right in the pot or in the ground. Lay the pot on its side in a cool, dry, shady spot. Simply ignore the ones in the ground. Some may rot, but a few may come back next year.

CHRYSANTHEMUMS

Stop feeding garden varieties of chrysanthemum (*Chrysanthemum x grandiflorum*) as soon as buds begin to open. Sit back and enjoy the flowers of your labor. Bait for slugs and snails. Visit nurseries that specialize in chrysanthemums. For example, at Sunnyslope Chrysanthemum Gardens in San Gabriel see how to grow chrysanthemums as spectacular cascades, hanging baskets, and bonsai. There are also annual displays at Descanso Gardens in Flintridge and the San Diego Wild Animal Park.

FLAX LILIES

Flax lily (*Dianella tasmanica*) a little-known, easy-to-grow plant, makes a clump of strap-like leaves and grows in semishade. The common green variety is well worth having, but 'Yellow Stripe' with yellow-striped leaves and 'Variegata' with white-striped leaves are more striking. Dianella grows from rhizomes that can sometimes be found in specialty nurseries, catalogs, botanical gardens, or in the old gardens of friends, who might be willing to share some roots now when the plant can be divided. This is the best time to get a division started, but don't worry if it doesn't bloom for a year or two after planting. Established clumps send up straight stems with star-shaped blue flowers in spring, followed by shiny berries in an arresting shade of blue that last two months and are lovely in flower arrangements. Dianella looks good near swimming pools and ponds, though not so close to water that berries fall in. Feed it occasionally with a handful of organic fertilizer, mulch the ground, and now in fall cut down spent stems and clean up the foliage. Watch that berries don't drop onto carpets; they stain.

ROSES

Continue to irrigate roses this month with an amount of water that would be equivalent to 1 1/2 inches of rain twice a week, or more in fast-draining soil. If rains begin this month, which occasionally happens, hold back on watering accordingly. (There have been years in the past when an unexpected October downpour delivered an inch of rain or more, but such events are rare and likely to become more so as the current dry cycle continues.) Continue to pick and deadhead roses this month to set the stage for a wave of bloom in November and December that's sometimes the best of the year. Gardeners who are using an organic rose fertilizer of their choice should continue to fertilize according to the package directions. Gardeners following the Rose-Pro method can fertilize their roses for the last time of the year this month by giving each plant 2 cups of Dr. Earth Organic 3 Rose and Flower Fertilizer (5-7-2). Gardeners using free and generic products can fertilize with any balanced product or concoction of their choice. (Consult the list of options on page 28, and the discussion on page 24.) Unless fertilizing immediately before rain or

a scheduled irrigation, wash the fertilizer into the ground by drenching it with water from the hose. (When fertilizers lie on top of the ground, some of the nitrogen in them escapes into the atmosphere.)

ANNUAL AND PERENNIAL FLOWERS

Cool-Season Flowers. Depending on your climate zone and the condition of your garden last month, you may or may not have started to switch flowerbeds and containers from summer to winter annuals, perennials, and biennials. An annual plant germinates, grows, blooms, sets seed, and dies in one season. Warm-season annuals begin life in spring and die when the weather gets cold in fall. Cool-season annuals begin life in fall and die when the weather gets hot in late summer. Biennials begin life in one year and then bloom, set seed, and die in the second year. Perennials are soft-bodied plants that make no permanent woody growth, but some are evergreen—they never die to the ground. Others are deciduous—they die down to the ground once a year and renew themselves from their roots. (Some plants, like impatiens, are technically perennials but sold and grown as annuals. Plants like lavender that make permanent wood are not perennials; these are flowering shrubs.)

One of the most important things a gardener can learn is that in Southern California we garden year-round, but we plant warm-season annuals and perennials in spring and cool-season annuals, biennials, and perennials in fall. Unfortunately, nurseries often leave warm-season annuals, such as marigolds or impatiens, on the shelves after it is too late to plant them, and they do the same thing in

351

spring with the winter-flowering plants, so it's important for gardeners to learn which are which and to choose the right plants to put into the ground or into pots at the correct time of year. (For more, see pages 116 and 324.) October is the best month to complete this job, so if you still have flowerbeds and pots filled with warm-season annual flowers, get them pulled out before month's end. Dig up, amend, and fertilize the soil, and transplant or sow flowers for winter and spring bloom.

Flowers to put in from transplants now for cool-season color include calendula, cineraria, cyclamen, delphinium, dianthus, evergreen candytuft (*Iberis sempervirens*), flowering cabbage and flowering kale, foxglove, Iceland poppy, nemesia, paludosum daisy (*Chrysanthemum paludosum*), pansy, malacoides (fairy) primrose, obconica primrose, polyanthus primrose, snapdragon, stock, sweet alyssum, sweet William, and sweet violet (*Viola odorata*), Johnny-jump-up, and other violas. Get them into the ground as soon as possible, provide them with adequate light, and feed them well for fast growth and bloom. The **Rule of Thumb:** *If you get winter annuals to bloom before the holidays, you'll enjoy their flowers throughout winter. If you don't, they'll just sit there doing nothing until the weather warms up in spring.*

Even this late in the year you can plant from seeds, bring some of the flowers into bloom before Christmas, and have abundant flowers in spring; some varieties will continue to bloom through summer. Flowers to plant from seeds now include African daisy (*Dimorphotheca*), pimpernel (*Anagallis monelli linifolia* or *A. monelli* 'Pacific Blue'), calendula, California desert bluebells (*Phacelia campanularia*), California poppy, clarkia, forget-me-not, globe candytuft (*Iberis umbellate*), godetia, hollyhock,

How to Grow Cineraria

Cineraria (*Senecio x hybridus*) are the aristocrats of the shade garden. Put in transplants now, and care for them through winter. They thrive on cold weather, as long as it doesn't freeze, and then bloom fabulously in February, March, or April.

▶ For the finest display purchase transplants of medium or tall—not dwarf—varieties, or grow your own next year by planting seeds in August.

▶ Choose a spot in open shade under trees or overhangs. (Under the open sky to the north of a tall tree or house is ideal, if you protect the plants from frost.)

▶ Provide deep, well-drained acid soil. If that's not available, plant in 8- to 12-inch plastic pots, and sink them into the ground.

▶ Plant in a solid pattern all over the bed at intervals of 8 to 12 inches, depending on variety. Water regularly. Don't let the roots dry out.

▶ Feed every two weeks with fish emulsion or Bat Guano 10-3-1 diluted with water according to package directions.

▶ Bait for slugs and snails, and use organic controls for leaf miners and aphids. (Beneficial insects or a spray of water controls aphids. Beneficial nematodes, earthworm castings in the soil, and Pyola Insect Spray from Gardens Alive! control both of these pests.)

▶ When plants are robust and flower buds begin to show, switch the fertilizer to Tiger Bloom (2-8-4) or other high-bloom organic fertilizer of your choice. Feed once a week until flowers open.

Johnny-jump-up, lavatera, linaria, nasturtium, Shirley poppy, snapdragon, sweet alyssum, and many wildflowers. Sweet alyssum, Johnny-jump-ups, and linaria are usually the first to bloom, closely followed by calendulas. (For the most rewarding show, grow tall calendulas such as 'Pacific Beauty', not the dwarf kinds.)

Permanent Perennials to Dig Up, Divide, and Replant, or to Mulch. Most perennials are permanent plants in the landscape and continue to grow and bloom for many years. However, many conventional perennial plants such as you might see growing in England or the Pacific Northwest and that die to the ground in winter, like columbine or summer phlox (*Phlox panicula*), are better adapted to cold-winter climates. They don't live long here because they don't get enough winter chill to go into true dormancy. (Phlox also mildews.) Gradually one learns to choose perennials that thrive here, like *Coreopsis grandiflora* 'Sunburst', yarrow (*Achillea*), *Verbena bonariensis*, and African daisy (*Arctotis*). Others, like Japanese anemone (*Anemone x hybrida*), for example, is a true perennial that dies to the ground in winter, but it's so successful here that it even becomes invasive and seeds itself in semi-shaded parts of the garden where it chooses to grow. The Mediterranean plant bear's britches (*Acanthus mollis*) is also a true perennial but it's a summer-deciduous one, dropping its leaves in late summer and springing back so quickly from the ground that you barely notice the changing of the guard. Many perennials make evergreen clumps, such as dianella, discussed on page 350. Some of these, like day-lilies or clivia (if it's growing in a pot) need to be divided occasionally. Others, like Peruvian lilies (*Alstroemeria*) and clivia (if it's grown in the ground) prefer to be left undisturbed.

 QUICK TIP

How to Make a Hanging Basket Hang Straight. *Your hanging baskets will always hang straight instead of crooked if, before you attach their plant hangers, you bend all of their wires simultaneously. Grasp a three- or four-wire plant hanger so all the wires are held tightly together, and bend the ends of the wires all at once into a hook, about 4 inches from the tips. Then spread the wires apart. Hook each plant-hanger wire under the top basket wire or through a hole in a wooden or plastic basket, and then twist the hook closed.*

Continue Fall Jobs. There's no better month than October for continuing the fall jobs begun in September—all the cutting back, pruning, mulching, moving, planting, and general cleanup that we do at this time of year. Here are some more specifics: Cut back Santa Barbara daisy (*Erigeron karvinskianus*) and pull it out when it's growing where you don't want it. Water and fertilize it for regrowth. Cut back *Gaillardia* 'Yellow Queen', *Rudbeckia fulgida sullivantii* 'Goldsturm', and goldenrod (*Solidago*). After Russian sage (*Perovskia* 'Blue Spire') and other late-summer and fall bloomers stop flowering, deadhead and trim them. Cut back pincushion flower (*Scabiosa*) now; if you don't, it gets to be a mess. *S. Africana* is the best one to grow here, and spreads well. *S. columbaria* is good in coastal zones (unfortunately, the one you usually find is *S. caucasica*).

Verbena bonariensis blooms through September. Cut it back now; it has wonderful basal growth underneath. Society garlic (*Tulbaghia violacea*) needs no cutting back; deadhead it if you haven't done it already, divide clumps that

353

A Foolproof Way to Grow Wildflowers

▸ Choose a spot in full sun. Spade or rototill the ground deeply, adding organic soil amendment but no fertilizer. (If you plant wildflowers for three years in the same bed, sprinkle the ground with a light application of complete organic fertilizer before planting for the third time.) Smooth and level the surface with a garden rake.

▸ Decide on a watering system. Drip tubes are best because they won't get the tops of flowers wet. I use a burial-type drip tape, called Bi-Wall, as illustrated and explained in the step-by-step photographs of the wildflower bed in my garden on pages 238 and 239 of the photographic section of this book.

▸ If the area you're planting is too wide for you to reach all parts of it from the edges, either make wandering paths through it or place stepping-stones here and there between the drip tubes so you can walk on the bed without compacting the soil.

▸ Sprinkle seeds of western wildflowers all over the bed. Sprinkle individual types in drifts, putting tall varieties at the back or in the middle and shorter varieties at the front or around the edges.

▸ Rake the seed lightly into the soil.

▸ Intersperse pea stakes throughout the bed (see the accompanying box on facing page).

▸ Protect the seeds and sprouts from birds: stretch Ross Garden Netting over the stakes. Fasten the edges down with rocks or wire staples. (After the plants are up 4 to 5 inches, take off the netting but leave the pea stakes in place to support the plants through wind and rain.)

▸ Sprinkle the bed by hand twice a day until seeds germinate. Then start watering with a drip system or by soaking the bed when rains aren't adequate.

▸ After the plants are up and growing, stand or lean your hands on your paths or stepping-stones to weed and thin the bed. Bait for slugs, snails, and cutworms. Later, use the stepping-stones when picking and deadheading the flowers.

▸ Use canes pruned from climbing roses to protect the bed from being smashed by skunks or other animals in spring (see page 59 for directions).

are dying in the middle, and throw away the brown parts. Crown-pink (*Lychnis coronaria*), which comes in white or cerise, comes up all over the place; move it around now. It looks good next to blue or purple plants, such as sea lavender (*Limonium perezii*).

Divide and replant perennials that bloomed in spring and summer. (Plants with fleshy roots that go dormant in winter—saponaria is an example—are better divided in late February.) Pull up and move, toss out, or give away plants that are coming up from seed in the wrong places. Gaura, verbena 'Bonny Blue', and some ornamental grasses are especially notorious.

If rains come early, keep a close watch on your ornamental grasses. Those that go dormant in summer need cutting back when they begin to grow again, which often happens with the first fall rain. Even warm-season ornamental grasses, including red fountain grass (*Pennisetum setaceum* 'Rubrum'), have such a short dormancy here that they often sprout fresh green leaves at ground level as soon as rains start. When you see growth begin, cut off all the old brown leaves and flowers just above the new growth. Follow up with an organic lawn fertilizer and water. (See page 327 for more about pruning ornamental grasses.)

Japanese anemones (*Anemone x hybrida*) are in full bloom now, brightening up the shade. If you don't already have this elegant plant that seeds itself in places where it's happy, look for it now in nurseries.

WILDFLOWERS

One of the greatest joys in gardening is growing wildflowers. Plant them early this month for a flower display that begins before Christmas and lasts through June—sometimes throughout summer. A good way to go about this is to purchase several packaged mixes of California or western wildflowers and add some choices of your own, such as extra linaria, California poppies, and larkspur. Put in some splashes of scarlet flax (*Linum grandiflorum* 'Rubrum') and an edging of nemophila. Notice that the labels of some mixes indicate whether the seeds are those of annuals or perennials and whether they're easy to grow. Labels often also tell the season when you can expect the flowers to bloom, whether they need dry or moist soil, whether they prefer sun or shade, and the average height of the plants.

Purchase seed from seed racks or catalogs. People often ask me where I buy my wildflower seeds, but I don't use the same source year after year. I look through seed racks first and then hunt through catalogs or on the Internet to find specific items I want. The benefit of planting one or two packages of mixed wildflowers every year along with your own favorites is that mixes change from year to year according to what is available. (Tree of Life Nursery is a good source of seeds for special situations.) Different items will flourish in your garden each year due to the weather or other factors. By trying out various sources for seeds you'll have the fun of discovering new plants to grow, and your wildflower bed will never look the same two years in a row. For example, one of the best performers in my garden this year was pimpernel (*Anagallis monelli linifolia*). Small, vivid blue flowers with red centers began blooming in early spring and are still going strong now in fall. (There is also a superior variety called *Anagallis* 'Pacific Blue'.) I had never grown anagallis before, but from now on will actively hunt for the seeds. It just goes to show the excitement and discovery that can come out of one little seed packet, in this case a small plastic bag of Stokes Seeds labeled "Wildflowers for Dry Soil in Full Sun," that I found on a local seed rack.

Use Pea Stakes to Protect Flowers from Heavy Rains and Wind

Use English pea stakes (originally devised to support peas) to prevent flowers from being damaged by wind or rain. Cut 2- to 4-foot-tall branches with many twigs from shrubs, such as Victorian box (*Pittosporum undulatum*).

If you want spring flowers, look for seed mixes that concentrate on spring-flowering annuals. If you'd like longer-lasting color, choose seed mixes that combine annuals with perennials. If you want long-lasting bloom in a sunny bed, your best bet is to choose a mixture of western wildflowers that contains both annuals and perennials and that needs dry soil in full sun. In good years when we have adequate rains, the wildflowers in these drought-resistant mixes can survive through winter and spring on little more than natural rainfall, but they perform better and last months longer when irrigated regularly once the rains cease. If you irrigate them once a week in hot weather, they'll provide an ever-changing and delightful flower display from Christmas until fall, at which time you can replant. Mexican hat (*Ratibida columnifera*) will come back year after year in a hot spot that it likes and give you masses of informal color all summer long with little care. (A word of warning: If you live in a suburban area, steer clear of wildflower mixtures that contain grasses along with the flowers. These are fine for country meadows, but they look weedy in suburban gardens, and the grasses may reseed themselves in lawns, ground covers, and shrubbery.)

Another way to plant wildflowers is to make your own mix of easily grown selections of California poppies, Shirley poppies (*Papaver rhoeas* 'Shirley'), Chinese houses (*Collinsia heterophylla*), godetia, or farewell-to-spring (*Clarkia amoena*) larkspur, linaria, nemophila, phacelia, Rocky Mountain clarkia (*C. unguiculata*) and scarlet flax (*Linum grandiflorum* 'Rubrum'). This mix of flowers will bloom through June. To make this mix last throughout summer until October or November when it's time to dig up the bed and replant, add pincushion flower (*Scabiosa atropurpurea*), gloriosa daisy (*Rudbeckia hirta*), and blanket flower (*Gaillardia x grandiflora*). The flowers grow and bloom in waves. If desired, dot the bed with seeds of tall orange calendulas. They'll bloom ahead of the California poppies to provide a happy contrast with the soft lavender tones of the linaria.

If you plant wildflowers in October, baby snapdragons (*Linaria moroccana*) and calendulas may bloom before the holidays. If you plant in November you'll have January bloom. If it freezes in your garden, wildflowers will act as if you'd pinched them back, but they won't die: They'll bloom a little later and may be a little shorter—but perhaps even stronger. As the year progresses you won't need to deadhead or pick bouquets, but if you do plants will bloom longer. After one species is finished, pull out their dead bodies to make room for something else. You'll have waves of nemophila, scarlet flax, and Chinese houses blooming for two or three months and then something else will take their place. In April many species will bloom all at once, including California and Shirley poppies. In May and June the whole bed may be taken over by farewell-to-spring (*Clarkia amoena*), tidytips (*Layia platyglosa*), or catchfly (*Silene armeria*). Summer may give you an even more exciting display. Wildflowers give so much in return for so little irrigation and such low cost. If you grow wildflowers you can't help having your heart go out to a gardener who lovingly takes home a single one-gallon plant from the nursery in summer when you have grown a whole bed full of flowers with a little patience and one or two packets of seeds.

LAWN CARE

Cool-season lawns such as ryegrass, bluegrass, and fescue are beginning to speed up now, and warm-season lawns such as Bermuda, zoysia, and St. Augustine are beginning to slow down. Mulch lawns with manure or a fine-grained soil amendment now, before the winter rains. This is also a good time to aerate lawns with a machine made for the purpose (see the box on page 358). Aeration aids growth by getting air to the roots.

Cool-Season Lawns. Continue to mow cool-season lawns at the same heights you cut them during the summer months. Mow tall fescue once a week with a rotary mower set at the highest setting of $1^1/_2$ to 3 inches and perennial ryegrass at $1^1/_2$ to $2^1/_2$ inches. Never cut off more than one-third of the height of the grass per mowing, and allow the clippings to fall onto the surface of the lawn, where they will dry and sift to the ground. This is called grass-cycling, and it's actually good for the lawn since it builds up organic matter and returns nitrogen straight back to the lawn from which it came. Only in wet weather, or if your mower has broken down and the lawn grown too long, should it be necessary to collect and bag the clippings. But please don't send them to the dump. Use them as mulch on flower beds and under shrubs, sprinkling them lightly or mixing them into the compost heap or directly into flowerbeds with a garden fork, prior to planting. (A heavy layer of grass clippings will stick together like a waterproof sheet.) Also help lawns to wake up and grow now by fertilizing them with a complete organic fertilizer recommended for lawns or with granulated or pellet-style bagged chicken manure or an all-purpose fertilizer such as Bio-Sol Mix (7-2-3). Thoroughly water fertilizers into the ground after spreading.

Help cool-season lawns wake up and grow by feeding them with a complete organic lawn fertilizer for both root and top growth.

Dethatch cool-season lawns and uproot any crabgrass in it in early fall. This is an annual task that can transform a lawn (see the box on page 360). Crabgrass can't get started in a thick, healthy lawn. It's nice to know that once you've dethatched and started a good program of water and fertilizer your problems will mostly be confined to the edges. October is also the best time of the year to plant a cool-season lawn from seed (see the box on page 359).

Warm-Season Lawns. Continue to cut warm-season lawns at the same height that you cut them throughout summer. Cutting them longer in winter, once a common practice, will simply increase thatch. Keep warm-season lawns green longer by continuing your feeding program through October.

In desert zones, feed St. Augustine now and continue throughout the winter. During the summer St. Augustine grass needs a great deal of water when grown in the desert, but the advantage is that you can keep it green throughout the winter by feeding it every six weeks with one of the fertilizers mentioned above. If you wish you can substitute for every third feeding a solution of compost tea, or of humic acid and kelp. Live organisms in the ground are less active in winter. Liquid fertilizers such as humic acid, kelp, and compost tea will give them an extra boost.

Overseed Bermuda grass with annual winter ryegrass, if desired, for a green lawn in winter. Cut Bermuda short before overseeding, and mulch with manure or a fine-grained, dark-colored soil amendment in a $1/_4$-inch layer over the seeds, to speed germination. Keep the ground damp until the seeds are sprouted. Be aware that in some areas, particularly warm coastal regions, there isn't enough summer heat to get the rye to completely die out in summer.

The result can be a shaggy-looking summer lawn. So before overseeding with winter rye, observe local lawns to see the final effects on your kind of Bermuda.

How to Aerate a Compacted Lawn

When the soil under a lawn becomes compacted from foot traffic or heavy equipment, it loses its springy texture and becomes hard as a rock. Water puddles or runs off, and lack of air to the roots causes the turf to deteriorate in appearance and vigor; it often develops thin or bare patches. To correct this condition take these steps:

▶ Mow the lawn; then make holes in the sod by running a rented aeration machine over it. Or do the job by hand with a tool made for the purpose.

▶ Rake up the plugs.

▶ Spread 40 pounds of gypsum and 15 cubic feet of organic soil amendment (such as fine-grained composted redwood or finely ground bark) over each 100 square feet of lawn.

▶ Apply a complete organic lawn fertilizer according to package directions. When the soil or thatch is hydrophobic (so dry it sheds water), also spray the lawn with a solution of water—mixed according to package directions—with a natural organic penetrant or wetting agent containing *Yucca schidigera*. (One such product is called Yuccah. Penetrants containing yucca are biodegradable and even more effective than many chemical products.)

▶ Rake these materials into the holes. Follow up by watering deeply.

Dethatch kikuyu grass now to keep it in bounds (see the box on page 104). Collect and bag the stolons. Don't put them in compost.

◉ QUICK TIP

How to Plant a Gopher-Proof Lawn.
Prepare and level the ground for planting. Reserve some amended soil. Cover the ground with chicken wire ($^1/_2$-inch mesh) laid flat, and wire the sections together. Cover the chicken wire with 2 to 3 inches of soil. Then plant the lawn from seed. When planting from sod simply cover the prepared ground with chicken wire, and overlap the edges of the wire strips by 1 to 2 inches. Lay the sod directly on top of the wire.

VEGETABLE GARDENING

It's time to put in the winter vegetable garden or, if you started planting last month, to continue the job. First, pull up and throw out or compost the remains of your summer garden. A thorough cleanup now really pays off in fewer bugs and diseases later. Dig up the soil deeply with a spade, turning it over, aerating it, and breaking up the clods as you do. Then use a garden fork to mix in such organic amendments as steer manure, chicken manure, seaweed, homemade or commercial compost, and whatever source of humus you've got.

Vegan Gardening. In addition to organic amendments, most cool-season crops other than legumes also need fertilizer, especially nitrogen, which is less active in winter. One of the strongest and fastest acting sources of nitrogen is blood meal, but a new class of gardeners called "vegan gardeners" avoids the use of

How to Plant a Cool-Season Lawn

If you want an instant lawn, order sod. (Be sure to prepare the ground thoroughly. Grade the soil ½ inch lower than walks to allow for the thickness of the sod, and, before installing it, level the ground carefully.) If you're going to plant from seed, take these steps:

▸ Choose turf grass adapted to your area. See page 196 for a discussion of varieties and cultivars.

▸ Amend the soil. Rototill the ground to a depth of 8 inches. Spread 3 to 4 inches of organic amendment on top and mix it in. Also, for clay soils apply gypsum at the rate of 10 pounds to every 100 square feet and mix it in.

▸ Level the ground, using a rented leveler or a homemade drag bar or leveler (as described on page 105).

▸ Install a sprinkler system.

▸ Rent a seed sower or use a handheld sower. Spread the seeds precisely according to the directions for the variety you're planting. Sow half the seeds while walking back and forth in one direction, the other half while walking at right angles to the original direction.

▸ Rake the soil lightly with a garden rake so the seed will be covered with no more than ¼ inch of soil. (Rake in one direction only so the seeds won't be buried too deeply.)

▸ Optional step: Instead of raking the seed into the ground use a "squirrel cage" (a rentable mulch spreader) to cover the seeds. Cover them with not more than ¼ inch of ground bark or screened manure, or the amount directed for the seeds you're using.

▸ Spread an organic lawn fertilizer according to package directions.

▸ Roll the lawn with a lawn roller one-third full of water. Erect a barrier, such as Weathashade Fence-It, to keep children and dogs out of the area.

▸ Use a fine spray of water to wet the soil at least 4 inches deep. (Be careful not to create puddles, because that will float the seed to the surface.) Then sprinkle lightly three or more times a day as needed to keep the surface soil moist until the grass sprouts. (Tall fescue and ryegrass germinate in about ten days. Bluegrass takes about one month. Bluegrass is not adapted here and should never be planted as a solid lawn, but is still included in some seed mixes.)

▸ When grass is about 2 inches high, mow it to 1½ inches. Use a sharp mower and mow when the soil is somewhat dry, so you don't tear out young grass plants.

blood meal, steamed bone meal, and bagged steer manure because these are by-products of factory farms and crowded feedlots. (For more on this subject, see Pollan's *The Omnivore's Dilemma.*) Vegan gardeners fertilize vegetables exclusively with compost, seed meals, manures from known sources, fish bone meal instead of steamed bone meal, and organic products that come from the ground, like mined minerals. It is possible, however, to grow healthy vegetables in full sun by fertilizing the soil exclusively with manure. A vegan box-farmer, that is, a farmer selling boxed vegetables by subscription, near my home uses no fertilizers

How to Dethatch Cool-Season Lawns and Control Crabgrass

Some cool-season lawns, such as bluegrass and the new, finer-textured tall fescues, make lots of thatch. Others, such as ryegrass, make little or none. (See page 103 for a description of thatch and how to gauge its thickness.)

▸ Annually dethatch cool-season lawns that need it in early fall.

▸ Mow the lawn short. Mow several times in different directions, adjusting the blades lower with each mowing. (This part of the process is much the same as that used on warm-season lawns in spring, as described on page 104, but don't scalp cool-season lawns right down to the ground.)

▸ If the thatch isn't very thick, you can dethatch a cool-season lawn by hand; rake vigorously with an ordinary metal grass rake or a special dethatching rake. Or do the job with a rented vertical mower, as described for warm-season lawns.

▸ Gather the poles of thatch into bags, and send them to the dump. Don't compost them, because they contain weed seeds.

▸ As you rake, you may notice certain grasses standing up much higher than your lawn grass. This is usually crabgrass. It grows low and crablike, spreading out into a thick clump, but when you rake it the stolons stand up taller than the lawn grasses. Pull it up by the roots now and throw it away along with the thatch. (Use organic preemergent herbicides in late winter.)

▸ Roughen up and reseed any bare spots left by crabgrass. Cover the whole lawn with dark-colored mulch, such as manure or ground bark. (If desired, also cover reseeded areas with Remay Grass Seed Starter, a spunbound polyester material you can reuse year after year.)

▸ Spread a slow-acting fertilizer such as Milorganite all over the lawn except on the parts you reseeded. (Fertilizers inhibit germination.)

▸ Water deeply and keep newly seeded areas moist.

other than horse, chicken, cow, goat, and rabbit manures from her own animals. Many organic gardeners, including vegan gardeners, mulch their whole garden with horse manure from a known source once a year in fall and find that is enough to keep most plants healthy for the entire year. Failure of winter vegetables to thrive sometimes happens because the gardener didn't realize that a heavy shadow falls across his or her vegetable garden in winter when the sun moves south. If this describes your vegetable plot and there's no better site on your property,

then it's even more important to fertilize winter vegetables to give them the vigor to continue growing until the sun moves north again. If you choose to add fertilizer, either choose an organic product recommended for vegetables and apply it according to package directions or mix your own. (See the list of ingredients on pages 28-30, and the homemade formulas on page 77.) Then use a garden rake to level the ground. Use a hoe to make furrows between rows in heavy soils.

The Easy Way to Make Carrot, Celery, Parsley, and Parsnip Seeds Sprout in Three Days

Seeds of the parsley family, including carrots, celery, parsley, parsnip, and the ornamental wild carrot, Queen Anne's lace (*Daucus carota*), have hard seed coats, which make them difficult to sprout. One must keep the seeded rows damp for two to three weeks to germinate the seeds (as described in the box on page 363). This may be difficult in interior gardens with fast-drying soil or in school gardens, which are untended on weekends. Here is a foolproof way to get the seeds to sprout in three days or sometimes even less:

▸ Prepare a seed row or seedbed and broadcast the seeds as described for carrots in the box on page 363 but don't cover them over.

▸ Go into the house and bring a kettle of water to a full rolling boil. (For a school garden, fill thermos jars with boiling water before leaving home in the morning.)

▸ Carry the kettle out into the garden and immediately pour the boiling water straight from the kettle or have the children pour the water from the thermoses onto the seeds in the seed row or all over the bed in a zigzag fashion first one way and then the other to make sure all the seeds are hit with boiling water. (This is called scarification, or breaking the seed coat.)

▸ Cover the seeds very lightly with about ¼ inch of potting soil (not garden soil).

▸ In order to make sure the seeds are in contact with the ground, pat down the row using the back of the hoe with the handle held upright. (In school gardens, have the children pat down the row or bed gently with the palms of their hands.)

▸ Sprinkle the seed row or bed with a light spray of water. Keep the seed row damp by sprinkling it daily.

▸ Seeds will come up all at once in three days or sooner. This technique shortens the days from planting to harvest by two to three weeks. (Boiling water from thermos jugs works equally well as boiling water straight from the kettle. Do not use this trick for other seeds, only for members of the parsley family mentioned above.)

Plant tall crops to the north and short crops to the south. Full sun is needed for all winter vegetables.

Plant Vegetables from Seeds and Transplants. Plants that can be put in from seeds now include beets, broccoli, cabbage, carrots (see boxes above and on page 363), cauliflower, celery, fava beans, kale, kohlrabi, lettuce, mustard greens, parsnips, green peas, snap and other edible-pod peas, radishes, rutabagas, spinach, Swiss chard, and turnips. Though all of the above technically can be planted from seed, it's better to put in celery and most cole crops, including broccoli, Brussels sprouts, cabbage, cauliflower, and collards, from transplants instead of seed. (It's a little late to plant these vegetables from seed.) Also plant lettuce from transplants for an early harvest; plant it from seed for later crops. (Send away for gourmet varieties—for example, mesclun.)

⚙ **QUICK TIP**

How to Prevent Green Shoulders. *Some carrot varieties tend to push up out of the soil as they grow. The exposed portions turn green or red and develop a bitter flavor. Prevent this problem by mulching the row or by mounding some soil around the base of the plants when the tops are 4 inches tall.*

Parsley grows well from seed, but it's slow to germinate. (Keep it damp for twenty days, or plant from transplants. Better yet, germinate the seeds in three days or less by pouring boiling water over them straight from the kettle onto the seeded row, as described in the box on page 361.) Put it in a row now, feed it well, and you'll have masses of parsley all winter—so convenient for stuffing turkey and garnishing your holiday dishes.

Plant curly cress, cilantro (coriander), and arugula (rocket) from seeds. All three grow rapidly, love cool weather, and are expensive to buy in markets. Garden cress tastes like watercress. Cilantro and arugula are unique, acquired tastes but delightfully addictive. Use cilantro in Chinese, Thai, and Mexican cooking, salads, soups, and lamb stew. (Add it at the last minute.) Use arugula in salads, as a sophisticated garnish, with Italian food, in sandwiches, and as a flavorful raw accompaniment to oxtail soup made from the dry mix. Both seed themselves if you let them.

You can now also plant potatoes from seed potatoes, raspberries (choose mild-winter varieties) from plants or bare roots, globe artichokes from seedlings or bare roots, and horseradish and rhubarb from bare roots (though rhubarb doesn't grow well here, so I don't recommend it). Onions can be put in from sets but, as explained on page 388, you won't get globe onions from them; you'll get scallions.

Confine horseradish in its own bed; it's an invasive though culinarily useful weed. If you've been growing it, now's the time to dig up the large roots. Peel the root, grind it (easily done in a food processor), and then purée it with a little water and a splash of vinegar. (Wear gloves, and don't get fumes up your nose.) Hand-mix a portion of the purée with sour cream and sugar to use right away, and freeze the rest in ice cube trays to use as needed.

Wait until early November to plant strawberries and globe onions. Look for seeds of short-day onion varieties, including 'Grano', 'Granex', or 'Crystal Wax', now if you didn't do it in September, so you'll have them on hand.

Cut Down Brown Stems of Asparagus and Plant New Beds. Leave the stems of asparagus on the plants as long as they remain green. When they've turned brown, which should occur sometime between now and January, cut them off at ground level and top-dress the bed with manure. Asparagus doesn't mind salty soil, but it needs rich and preferably sandy soil, full sun, good drainage, lots of water, and plenty of room.

Asparagus also can be planted now (as described on page 106). It's best to plant a variety developed for this area by the University of California, such as 'UC 157'. Asparagus is a reliable perennial vegetable, and once planted a bed of it can bear crops for as long as fifteen years if you give it good care.

Prechill Strawberry Plants for November Planting. In mid-October cut off the runners you've been encouraging your strawberries to grow (see page 282), thus severing them from the parent plants. Gently dig up these runners,

How to Grow Carrots

Carrots sprout at ground temperatures of 45° to 85°F—80° is best—and thus can be planted any month year-round. (The seeds sprout slowly.)

▸ Choose a gourmet variety, or choose several varieties for comparison.

▸ Dig and prepare a bed of deep, loose, well-amended soil—sandy soil is best. A raised bed works well. Or grow carrots in a half-barrel filled with planter mix. Add bone meal and low-nitrogen organic vegetable fertilizer but no fresh manure—it makes carrots fork or grow many hairy roots. Water the bed deeply and allow it to settle overnight.

▸ Plant the seeds all over a raised bed or in a straight row next to a buried drip tube. For the latter, press the back of a hoe handle into the soil to make a shallow trench.

▸ Carrots have tiny seeds, so mix them with a little sand in the palm of your hand to make them easier to sprinkle evenly. Pelletized seeds are available in some catalogs. You can grab these one by one and space them so they won't require thinning.

▸ Sprinkle the seeds thinly and evenly on the bed or down the row. Cover them lightly with ¼-inch potting soil. Pat it down gently to create good contact.

▸ Cover the bed with burlap strips or floating row cover if the weather's hot and dry.

▸ Sprinkle the bed once or twice daily with a fine spray for one to two weeks to keep the ground thoroughly moist until the seeds sprout. (Don't let it dry out. This is the conventional way to get carrot seeds to germinate. For a more efficient, time-saving method that will give you a quicker harvest, see the box on page 361.)

▸ If you're using burlap, peep under it daily. As soon as sprouts show, remove it.

▸ If you're not using a drip system, wait until the ground is dry 4 inches down or until the sprouts just begin to wilt before watering again. Then commence regular deep watering. (This encourages a taproot to go straight down and can produce a straight carrot even in clay soil.)

▸ Thin the carrots according to package directions. Eat the thinnings. Carrots cannot be transplanted; it makes them grow in inedible, forked, and twisted shapes.

and bare their roots by brushing or shaking off the dirt. Clip off all but two or three leaves from each new little plant. Gather them into bunches and tie them loosely together. Place the bunches in a plastic bag, and put it on a low back shelf of your refrigerator or, if your refrigerator doesn't freeze lettuce or other vegetables, into the lettuce drawer. Leave them there for twenty days before planting them next month, on or before November 10. Prechilling strawberries fools them into thinking they've had a cold winter. Once the plants have become reestablished in the ground, and as soon as the days lengthen and the weather begins to warm up in late winter, they'll be stimulated to produce fruit instead of more vegetative growth. Meanwhile, dig up the bed, throw away or compost all the old plants that bore this year, choose another spot for planting your new strawberry plants, and plant something else in the old bed.

OCTOBER CHECKLIST

PURCHASE/PLANT

- { } Plant transplants of cool-season flowers and vegetables in the garden now, 339
- { } Plant all types of permanent landscape plants other than bare-root plants, tropicals, and native plants, 339
- { } Desert dwellers can plant most summer and winter vegetables now, and many flowers, 340
- { } Plan and plant a desert garden using native desert plants, 340
- { } Plant flame vine in all mild zones; in the desert include Easter lily vine, 350
- { } Plant trees, shrubs, and vines, 342
- { } Choose and plant for permanent fall and winter color, 343
- { } Continue to shop for spring-blooming bulbs and plant the ones that can be put in now, 348
- { } Plant lilies as soon as you get them home, 348
- { } Buy anemones, daffodils, Dutch irises, grape hyacinths, and ranunculus; keep them in a cool, dry place until planting time, 348
- { } Purchase hyacinth, tulip, and crocus bulbs and prechill them in the refrigerator, 348
- { } Plant cool-season flowers for winter and spring bloom, 351
- { } Plant cineraria for late-winter and early-spring bloom, 352
- { } Plant wildflowers, 354
- { } Plant cool-season lawns, 359
- { } Overseed Bermuda grass with annual winter ryegrass, if desired, 357
- { } Plant cool-season vegetables and year-round vegetables, 358
- { } Plant celery, 412

TRIM, PRUNE, MOW, DIVIDE

- { } Thin out sweet peas and pinch them back to force branching, 323
- { } Divide, trim, and mulch plants that tend to grow in a clump and that need to be divided, including bird of paradise, clivia, daylily, gazanias, fortnight lily, iris, Kahili ginger, lily turf, and perennials, 344
- { } Continue progressive pruning of zonal, species, and ivy geraniums, 346
- { } Finish pruning Martha Washington pelargoniums, 346
- { } Continue to shape and clean out the dead interiors of native plants, 406
- { } Divide hardy water lilies, 347
- { } Lift, dry, separate, and store gladioli, 348
- { } Divide naked ladies, 349
- { } Dig up, divide, and replant perennials, or mulch them, 353
- { } Cut branches out of shrubbery to make pea stakes, 355
- { } Mow all lawns according to species and type, 357
- { } Dethatch kikuyu grass to keep it in bounds, 358
- { } Cut down asparagus stems after they go brown, 362
- { } Cut off runners from strawberries, gather them in bunches, and prechill them for November planting, 362
- { } Watch red fountain grass (*Pennisetum setaceum* 'Rubrum') for new growth, the sign to cut it back, 355
- { } Cut back clumps of sheep fescue (*Festuca glauca*) now or in early spring, 328

FERTILIZE

- { } Cut down to the ground spent stems of Matilija poppy (*Romneya coulteri*) that have bloomed, 345
- { } Feed fuchsias, 208
- { } Continue to treat blue hydrangeas according to the method you have chosen to keep them blue, 320
- { } Fertilize hardy water lilies that appear to need it, but don't fertilize tropical ones, 347
- { } Stop fertilizing chrysanthemums, and enjoy the blooms, 350
- { } Fertilize poinsettias with a complete fertilizer high in bloom ingredients, 350
- { } Feed roses early this month, 351
- { } Feed cool-season lawns with a complete fertilizer, 357
- { } Continue to feed warm-season lawns to keep them green longer, 357
- { } Feed St. Augustine grass in desert zones, 357
- { } Feed the basic landscape for a whole year, if desired, by mulching with aged horse manure now, 367

WATER

{ } Water all garden plants according to their individual needs, your soil, your climate zone, and the weather (reducing water if rains start early), *339*

{ } Water deciduous fruit trees more sparingly in fall, *344*

{ } Water roses with up to 1 1/2 inches of water twice a week, unless rains do the job for you, *351*

{ } Continue to water lawns when rains aren't adequate, *356*

CONTROL PESTS, DISEASE, AND WEEDS

{ } Treat gladiolus corms for fungus and thrips, *348*

{ } Create a gopher-proof lawn by burying chicken wire under it prior to planting, *358*

{ } Get rid of existing crabgrass by hand-pulling, *360*

ALSO THIS MONTH

{ } Harvest macadamia nuts when they fall to the ground, and cure them properly, *123*

{ } Lift tuberoses and store in perlite until next May, *189*

{ } Untie the fronds of palms transplanted in August, *302*

{ } Tie up sweet peas and edible peas to prevent them from being knocked down by wind or rain, *323*

{ } In interior zones where frost can be expected, lift and store tropical water lilies for the winter, *347*

{ } If you want to try growing the cormels (tiny sidebulbs) of gladioli, prechill them in the refrigerator, *348*

{ } Store tuberous begonias for the winter, *349*

{ } Begin forcing potted poinsettias for Christmas bloom, *350*

{ } Finish pulling out faded annual flowers and cleaning pots and beds for fall planting, *351*

{ } Straighten hanging baskets by attaching new wires if necessary, *353*

{ } Aerate lawns that are compacted from foot traffic or heavy machinery, *358*

{ } Thoroughly clean up the vegetable garden; pull up the last of the summer crops and compost the remains, *358*

{ } Dethatch cool-season lawns by hand or machine, *360*

{ } Harvest horseradish, *362*

{ } Continue fall maintenance of perennials, *353*

November

THE FIRST MONTH OF THE RAINY SEASON

Narcissus tazetta
(Bunch-flowered Narcissus)

Throughout most of the United States November signals the onset of cold and icy weather. After a short respite of late warm weather, the Indian summer, the sun dips low on the horizon and winter sets in for good. Gardeners throw mulch over tender roots and wrap up roses ahead of the snow. But in Southern California, November heralds the return of the rainy season.

This is an active time for us and for many of our plants. Out in the backcountry, in canyons and on hillsides, the native landscape wakes up from summer dormancy and starts to green up and grow. In our gardens we look forward to color from many flowering plants programmed by nature to bloom in winter. Roses give us some of their best blooms in November.

If you did most of your fall planting in October, November is an easy month in the garden. But if you didn't plant last month, don't wait any longer—do it now. Regardless, there are a number of plants—onions, strawberries, native plants, ground covers, and many bulbs—that are best when planted in November. Also, some organic gardeners mulch the entire landscape now with horse manure from a known source and find that this one step provides sufficient nutrition to last most plants for an entire year. Horse manure can age right where you put it on top of the ground. (If you have dogs, use aged manure.) The winter rains will wash nutrients into the ground, and by spring they will have been incorporated into the top layer of soil.

OUR CYCLICAL RAINS

Ever since certain events in the 1860s, it's been apparent that California's rains are not only seasonal (wet winters, dry summers), but they're also cyclical (several years of ample rains followed by several years of drought). In 1861–62 California had the heaviest rains ever recorded. In Los Angeles it rained for twenty-eight days without stopping, San Francisco had 49 inches, and the Central Valley turned into a lake. This disaster was followed two years later by the worst drought in California history. Tree rings tell the story, and they have longer memories than people—who tend to forget about bad years when the rains are good. Heavy rainfall makes them wonder, "What's all this fuss about drought?" But wise gardeners always remember, first, that it could happen again, and second, that they can never be sure how much rain there will be.

Some years the rains are torrential, smashing garden flowers and causing such bad botrytis (gray mold) that all gardeners wish they would stop. In the winters of 1997 and 1998 rainfall totals averaged 231 percent of normal, more than any years since 1883. Other years there's not nearly enough rain, and gardeners have to pour on water from the hose. Every year or two the media interprets a new scientific study to mean that our local weather pattern is changing. Of course, no one really knows the effects of global warming, but our wet-dry cycles, lasting about seven years for each phase, have existed for centuries and so have the warming and cooling ocean patterns, lasting roughly sixty years. Twenty years ago few people had ever heard of the weather phenomenon called El Niño that is now blamed for torrential rains. But El Niño is an ancient cyclical pattern; only our knowledge of it is new (see the box on the facing page).

Another factor, and one that's not so easy to forget, is that here in Southern California we're largely dependent on water brought from somewhere else. In the 1920s and 1930s there was an overabundance of imported water. Homeowners, gardeners, and industrialists became accustomed to using water in wasteful ways. Gardens took on the grassy New England or tropical jungle look. Now we're overcrowded and there's not enough water to go around. When you combine our cyclical rainfall with the fact that irrigation water is in ever shorter supply, you have a very serious problem for thirsty plants. In periods of rationing many could die. That's why we need to concentrate on establishing a basic landscape of plants that can survive drought. Now's a good time to begin.

Pitcher Irrigation

You can provide controlled irrigation by burying porous clay pots in strategic locations and periodically filling them with water by hand or a pipe network. Use several of these in a ring around the drip line of a tree; use two or three to water a shrub, or bury a central pot to provide water for a circle of vegetables, like beans or peas. Pitcher irrigation has been used in China for more than two thousand years. Brazilian research finds pitcher irrigation more efficient than drip.

CALIFORNIA NATIVE PLANTS

It's easy to fall in love with California's native plants, and in most zones autumn is the time to plant them. (In the mountains, high deserts, and other cold-winter areas, plant them in spring.)

El Niño and What It Means to Gardeners

El Niño is a global weather phenomenon caused by shifting patterns of sea surface temperatures in the Pacific Ocean. During an El Niño year, an enormous pool of warm water that normally resides in the western waters of the Pacific drifts toward South America. This movement weakens the prevailing east-west trade winds, heating the ocean surface and upsetting the world's normal weather patterns. Some geographical areas that are normally dry experience floods, while others accustomed to rains suffer from drought. In Southern California El Niño means strong winds, heavy rains, and storms resulting from what is called the "Pineapple Express" crossing the Pacific from Hawaii, instead of, as is normal, storms wheeling down from the Gulf of Alaska.

For gardeners El Niño means that their plants can be damaged by soil erosion on slopes and by flooding in low-lying areas. Plant roots can drown in waterlogged soils when their roots are deprived of oxygen. Wet soils also increase the incidence of water molds that kill plant roots. When an El Niño is predicted, take steps to protect plants from excess moisture. Make sure your garden has good surface drainage. Design the landscape so surface water flows from the highest parts of the property to an outlet such as the street or a drainage ditch. Check runoff from slopes, roofs, and patios to make sure these do not flood plants. If water stands in a particular area after rain, take action to improve the drainage. Remove obstructions stopping the flow of surface water or install a catch basin feeding into a drainpipe with an outlet at a lower elevation. If water stands in irrigation basins for several hours, remove some earth so the water can flow out.

Few other places in the world can rival the number and diversity of our native plants. Early explorers were quick to see their value and spread them around the world, but most settlers were so intent on enjoying the sunshine or making a living they were blind to the beauty of the landscape and desecrated much of it. The answer most newcomers gave to Southern California's dry Mediterranean climate was to declare the region a desert, import water, and introduce exotic plants. Native plants were condemned as difficult and bulldozed aside. California lilac *(Ceonothus)*, flannel bush *(Fremontodendron)*, Matilija poppy *(Romneya coulteri)*, and others were taken abroad. English gardeners treasured them, but here for many years it was up to the rare enthusiast to keep alive the appreciation of wild plants and try growing them in gardens. Most gardeners thought of California native plants as temperamental, nice in spring on a wild hillside, but quick to die if planted on flat ground or in irrigated soil. But now, almost a century after the building of the first Los Angeles Aqueduct, our seemingly endless water supplies are finally running dry and, faced with this conundrum, people are taking a second look at native plants. Perhaps they're not so difficult or demanding after all, and this perception might contain a grain of truth. For the last fifty to sixty years horticulturists have been quietly selecting and developing a host of named varieties that are easier to grow in gardens and more spectacular than many of the species from which they came. Gardeners who once scoffed at native plants are now seeing them with fresh eyes and tumbling to what should have been obvious. No one needs to teach California native plants how to survive in our dry climate and alkaline soil; they learned how eons ago. Maybe the best way to solve our water crisis and create a beautiful, fragrant, virtually carefree natural garden is simply to use the plant materials right under our noses—California's astounding array of native plants.

Experts now tell us that there's no better way to put in a landscape exclusively of native plants than to plant them straight into bare bulldozed ground, even if parts of it are flat. Native chaparral often grows on flat ground, not only on slopes, so why not in gardens too? But native plants abhor the various soil fungi brought in with soil mixes, organic soil amendments, and exotic plants. Planting on bulldozed ground avoids all the diseases and root rots that exist in soils where other plants have grown. When planting natives it's fine to apply gypsum in planting holes and it's fine to mulch the top of the ground after planting, but it's usually not wise to mix organic amendments into the native soil. (Some gardeners find that mixing a small amount of fresh, clean, organic soil amendment helps plants get established in fast-draining soils.) The system for planting is to water the entire area a day or two prior, dig planting holes, water the holes, and let the water drain out. Also, water the plants in the cans, and then plant them straight into the bare ground using soil amendment only when planting in something akin to pure sand. Water them again after planting. Though some species can be mixed in with garden plants in an irrigated landscape, many grow and survive better when planted in a landscape devoted exclusively to native plants. (For more pointers, see the box on page 372.) For a wide choice of natives and to avoid over-watered specimens already suffering from root rot, purchase your native plants from nurseries that specialize in them, like Tree of Life in San Juan Capistrano, or find them at such botanical gardens as the Santa Barbara Botanic Garden Theodore Payne Foundation in Sun Valley and Rancho Santa Ana Botanic Garden in Claremont. Also, in mixed gardens grow native plants on banks and in raised beds, concentrate on the best and easiest to cultivate, and learn their watering requirements.

Not all native plants are drought resistant. Some are native to streambeds and need constant moisture. Other native plants are so well adapted to our wet winters and dry summers that they can accept no summer water at all. Still others are more adaptable to garden conditions. They can withstand irrigation in summer if it's given to them but will survive without it if necessary. Many drought-resistant plants from other parts of the world mix well with California natives. Perry's *Trees and Shrubs for Dry California Landscapes* and *Landscape Shrubs for Western Regions* are excellent books on the subject. Also see the books mentioned on pages 440–445, as well as Bornstein, Fross, and O'Brien's up-to-date *California Native Plants for the Garden*, which recommends dozens of species and new cultivars for various situations along with plant requirements and excellent photos for identification.

✹ QUICK TIP

Pine Needles Are Precious. *When you rake fine-textured pine needles from a driveway, don't throw them away. Save them to mulch acid-loving plants, such as camellias, azaleas, and blueberries, or to cover informal, woodland, or vegetable garden paths.*

How to Divide and Plant Matilija Poppy

Matilija poppy (*Romneya coulteri*), one of the loveliest of California natives, has fragrant white flowers like crepe paper with large yellow centers that cover the plant all summer, complementing its handsome gray foliage. At any time of year you can, if you wish, purchase from native plant nurseries selected varieties, such as *R. coulteri x R. trichocaly* 'White Cloud', already growing in containers. But if you want to propagate a plant already growing in your own garden or a friend's, do the job sometime between now and January, while the plant is in its brief dormancy and just before it begins to grow again. There are two ways to propagate this plant. The first and easiest way is to dig up a whole clump; lift it into a bucket or basket to transport it. Prepare the soil as described below for root cuttings, and plant the clump at the same depth you originally found it. The second method is to take root cuttings. (This method is best if you want to start many of these plants.)

▸ For root cuttings, dig around the parent plant with a trowel; look for roots about pencil-thick in size with small but visible buds on them. (Small pieces work fine; take several cuttings to ensure success.)

▸ Unless you plan to plant the cuttings immediately, place them in a plastic bag filled with moist potting soil so they won't dry out. (Take them home this way if you're getting them from a friend.)

▸ If possible, plant in well-drained soil. Loosen it first with a spade, and then plant the roots by placing them horizontally and covering them with an inch of soil.

▸ If you must plant in hard clay soil, first spade it deeply, adding soil amendment. Then water the ground and let the area settle overnight. The next day spread a 3- to 4-inch-high layer of sand on top of the prepared area. (Use as much sand as you want; two or three bucketfuls are ample for a good start.) Plant the roots 2 inches down in the sand. The roots will grow right between the sand and the clay. (Never mix sand with clay—this makes clay even denser. In this case, you're stacking them to make a raised bed.)

▸ Keep the soil damp but not soggy until the cuttings sprout and you see growth begin; then water regularly until they're established. Summer water produces longer bloom.

▸ When the foliage dies back in late fall, cut down the plants to 4 to 6 inches. New growth soon springs again from the roots.

Among the hundreds of fine native plants that are well adapted to landscape use are California tree mallow (*Lavatera assurgentiflora*); Catalina cherry (*Prunus ilicifolia lyonii*); Cleveland sage (*Salvia clevelandii*); lemonade berry (*Rhus integrifolia*); monkeyflower (*Mimulus x hybridus*), with many lovely new hybrids available; St. Catherine's lace (*Eriogonum giganteum*); sugar bush (*Rhus ovata*); Torrey pine (*Pinus torreyana*); toyon (California holly; *Heteromeles arbutifolia*); and western redbud (*Cercis occidentalis*). Two outstanding native ground covers are trailing manzanita (*Arctostaphylos* 'Emerald Carpet'), which prefers shade inland, and evergreen currant (*Ribes viburnifolium*), a plant from Catalina Island that thrives

Special Tips for Planting California Native Plants

▸ When purchasing a native plant, gently slide it out of its container and check the roots. Don't choose a plant with a lot of top growth and too many roots in the can. (If it has been in a container too long, its roots will have become hard and taken on the shape of the can, and it won't readapt as well to the ground.)

▸ To avoid planting in bone-dry soil, water the area to be planted. To avoid compaction, wait a few days before planting.

▸ Prior to planting, check the drainage as described in the box on page 40 and eliminate low spots. When planting in poorly drained clay soil in an existing garden or when mixing natives with other drought-resistant plants, plant natives in raised beds and use sleeve drains on hillsides. (See page 435.) When planting in alkaline clay soil, apply gypsum, as described on page 21, and incorporate gypsum into the soil in the bottom of every planting hole.

▸ If gophers are a problem, line the planting holes with wire baskets made of ½- to 1-inch aviary wire.

▸ Dig a planting hole, fill it with water, and let the water drain out.

▸ Water the plant in the container prior to planting.

▸ Carefully remove the plant from the can and gently lower it into the hole. Native plants are fragile; take care not to break the crown or roots.

▸ Before filling the soil in around the plant, lay a stick across the hole and check how high you have placed the plant. Make sure the top of the root ball will end up 2 inches above the surrounding soil; this is especially important for native plants. Don't bury the crown in soil, or it will rot.

▸ Backfill the hole with native soil, gently pressing it down around the roots with your hands.

▸ Install a watering system using micro sprinklers or if planning to water with the hose, make a watering basin around each plant a little larger than the planting hole. (Break holes in basins before the winter rains so that water does not collect in them and cause root rot.)

▸ Mulch the ground with rocks and pebbles for desert plants. Mulch plants native to coastal, mountain, and inland valley zones with a 2- to 4-inch layer of mulch, such as shredded redwood or cedar bark. Keep a 4-inch-wide area surrounding the stem of each plant free from mulch.

▸ Water after planting to settle the plant into the soil. (Check after watering to make sure the top of the root ball is less than 1 inch above the surrounding ground.)

▸ Depending on your soil and climate zone, water newly planted specimens every other day for the first week, once a week for the first two months, and once a month until late spring or the onset of hot weather.

▸ Always check the soil with your finger before watering as suggested above. For the first two weeks after planting make sure the root ball of the plant is moist but not soggy. Thereafter, if the soil is dry, water, but if the soil is damp, don't water. Water during droughts and according to the needs of each individual plant.

▸ Once the plant is established, decrease irrigation. After one year, water native plants in winter when rains are inadequate. During hot weather, avoid watering those natives known to die of root rot when watered in summer. Pull them through heat waves by spritzing their foliage occasionally with a quick spray of water in the evening or early morning. Water other native plants in summer according to their specific requirements and needs.

in shade in all zones. Also don't overlook California lilac *(Ceanothus)*, which has many fine species and named varieties to choose from. Select plants for color, growth habit, and adaptability to your soil and climate.

Within your landscape of native plants, why not use native grasses to create a natural California meadow? Blue grama grass *(Bouteloua gracilis)* is a fine-textured, warm-season native bunchgrass with attractive one-sided blooms in spring that can give you the look of a meadow or of a rough lawn. It seldom needs irrigation and thrives in the high desert. It won't grow in shade, so plant it to the south of trees, but it withstands foot traffic and can take mowing. To achieve the tousled look of a mountain meadow, let it grow long. To use it as a lawn, mow it to 2 inches once a month in summer. Plant blue grama from seeds in spring or from plugs in early summer. Blue grama grass goes brown in winter; in coastal zones it keeps some green year-round. You can enliven the scene in late winter and early spring by planting native bulbs and wildflowers now around the edges.

Seeds of California native plants, including wildflowers, can also be planted this month. The seeds of many native plants are difficult to germinate without special treatment prior to planting. In some cases this means subjecting them to fire in an aluminum pie pan beneath a handful of burning pine needles. Methods for germinating seeds of native plants are given in Emery's *Seed Propagation of California Native Plants*. (Directions for planting wildflowers are given on page 354.)

PRUNING

Prevent Storm Damage. November, with its wind and rain, brings a natural cleanup, but unless you prepare for it, it can often cause damage. Open up spaces in dense trees. Allow the wind to pass through. A full tree with no gaps in it acts like a sail on a mast. A strong wind may capsize it, especially if the ground is wet. Remove dead and weak branches.

Make sure young trees are well staked. Tie them loosely, so they can move back and forth in the wind without being toppled. Trees need to flex in wind in order to develop strong trunks. When using wire for tying, run it through a section of old hose so it doesn't damage bark. Check all staked trees now to make sure no wires are restrictive. Once trees have become well rooted remove the stakes and wires, so bark doesn't grow over them.

Prune Acacias. Cut back top-heavy shrubs, such as acacia. Where necessary remove whole branches to allow wind to pass through. Head back young acacias to force branching and strengthen their trunks. With proper pruning, these fast-growing, brittle but beautiful shrubs and small trees, often listed as short-lived, can be kept going almost indefinitely.

Prune Cane Berry Plants. Prune selected cane berry plants, including blackberry, boysenberry, loganberry, and spring-bearing raspberry. Cut the old canes down to the ground, leaving the new ones that grew this year. On fall-bearing raspberry plants (which grow well only in the mountains) cut off the top of the cane that has borne fruit. Leave the bottom of the cane to fruit in spring.

Don't prune the canes of subtropical (low-chill) raspberries like 'Bababerry', 'Fallgold', 'Oregon 1030' (also called 'California'), and 'Rosanna'. These are the only kind of raspberries to grow in most Southern California climate zones, and all of them produce their best berries on new wood. Wait until December or January; then prune these by cutting them nearly to the ground. Dig up the suckers (sprouts coming up near the old plants) to make new rows (see page 405).

SHRUBS AND YOUNG TREES

Now through January is the best time to move shrubs and young trees that are growing in the wrong places. For evergreen shrubs and trees dig a deep trench around each one. Then cut through the earth under the root ball, saving as many of the roots as possible. (You may unavoidably have to slice through some.) Ball the roots in burlap or chicken wire before lifting them from the hole. Once the plant is in its new hole, remove the chicken wire; but if you have gophers it may help to leave it in place and let the roots grow through it. Burlap may be either removed or opened up and left in the hole to rot, as desired. After transplanting, stimulate root growth by soaking the ground with a product containing humic acid, diluted according to package directions.

Transplant deciduous plants after the leaves fall and the plant has gone completely dormant. Then dig up as large a root system as possible, knock off all soil, and replant as for bare-roots, by holding the plant so its soil line is even with the surrounding ground and sifting the soil in with a trowel. Prune the top, to balance it with the loss of roots.

GROUND COVERS

November is the traditional month for planting carpetlike ground covers. The term ground cover is often used to describe a wide range of vines,

shrubs, perennials, wildflowers, bulbs, and herbs used to cover flat or sloping ground, and these are planted at various times of year according to species. Here we're discussing only those low-lying creepy-crawly things generally sold in flats and used to replace lawns. Some can be walked on; others cannot. These true ground covers are among the most important plants in the landscape and the most difficult to choose.

Some nurseries carry a wide assortment of ground covers. Before making a final choice, consider the site, the conditions, and your requirements. See displays in botanical gardens, such as the Los Angeles Arboretum. Also study lists in the *Sunset Western Garden Book* and pictures in Mathias's *Flowering Plants in the Landscape* and Taylor's *Guide to Ground Covers*.

Colorful ice plants, gazanias, pelargoniums, trailing African daisy (*Osteospermum fruticosum*), cape weed (*Arctotheca calendula*), pork and beans (*Sedum x rubrotinctum*), and lippia are among many fine choices, of varying drought resistance, for full sun. Beware of red apple ice plant (*Aptenia cordifolis* 'Red Apple'); it needs a lot of water and frequent fertilizing to look good. It's fine for quickly covering and holding a bank but builds up thickly and needs replacement in about six years.

For shady spots, fine-textured needlepoint ivy (*Hedera helix* 'Needlepoint'), Indian mock strawberry (*Duchesnea indica*), carpet bugle (*Ajuga reptans*), and star jasmine (*Trachelospermum jasminoides*) are among possible choices. (These plants use moderate irrigation in shade, but all are water hogs if grown in sun.) For small spaces and between stepping-stones, blue star creeper (*Pratia peduculata*), common thrift (*Armeria maritima*), creeping thyme, Irish and Scotch moss (in coastal zones only), and—in moist shade—baby's tears (*Soleirolia soleirolii*) are possible choices. Sprenger asparagus

(*Asparagus densiflorus* 'Sprengeri') is drought resistant. It's sold in cans—not flats. It will hold the steepest bank but once it gets going birds spread the seeds, and it will pop up all over where you can't weed it out. Pride of London (*Crassula multicava*) is a better choice, easy to pull out where you don't want it, but easier to obtain from other gardeners than from nurseries. Once established, it makes an 8-inch-thick mat of round, fleshy leaves, blooms in winter with light pink flowers on 1-foot stems, needs little or no irrigation, and spreads itself by plantlets. Collect spent flower stems and toss the plantlets onto bare areas in spring. Sprinkle these areas occasionally to get the plants growing.

On large slopes in full sun it's always better to combine shallow-rooted ground covers, such as trailing gazania 'Sunrise Yellow', with taller, deeper-rooting plants, such as bougainvillea 'Crimson Jewel', Cape plumbago (*Plumbago auriculata* 'Royal Carpet'), and lantana 'Radiation'. A combination of these four plants can provide a permanent bank cover with stunning color year-round and drought resistance once established. (Gazania can be planted now; bougainvillea, plumbago, and lantana take off better when planted in spring. It's too late to put in tropicals and subtropicals now except in the mildest zones, and then only during warm years.)

BULBS

You don't have to wait any longer to put in anemones, daffodils (*Narcissus*), Dutch irises, grape hyacinths, and ranunculus. It's a fine time for planting these and all other spring-flowering bulbs you haven't yet planted, except tulips, hyacinths, and crocuses. Put the last three in brown paper bags and chill them in the refrigerator for six to eight weeks prior to planting time in late December or early January. Make sure they don't freeze, and mark the bags so you know what's in them. Species tulips (wild tulips) *Tulipa bakeri* 'Lilac Wonder', *T. clusiana* (lady tulip), *T. saxatilis*, and *T. sylvestris* do not need chilling. Plant them right away in pots or the ground. Choose spots up front in the border or next to paths; they aren't tall, but they are charming and will come back year after year.

Bulbs look best planted in natural drifts rather than rows. Prepare the soil, toss the bulbs on the ground, and plant them where they fall. Consult a bulb chart for proper planting depths. Put a little bone meal under every bulb you plant in the ground, and cover it with an inch or two of soil before adding the bulb. You can also plant bulbs in containers. Daffodils of all types are especially good candidates for container planting. (For instructions, see the box on page 376.)

What Is a Daffodil? If you're confused by the names "narcissus," "daffodil," and "jonquil," you're not alone. Even longtime gardeners muddle these terms, but the solution is quite easy. The words "narcissus" and "daffodil" have exactly the same meaning, but *Narcissus* is the botanical name for a whole genus of bulbs encompassing more than twenty-six species and innumerable cultivars. Daffodil is the common name for all of them. (Tazetta and Tazetta hybrids, however, are seldom called "daffodils" in actual practice. Gardeners and bulb catalogs alike usually refer to these only by the botanical name *Narcissus*, though without italics.) Jonquil is the name of one small group of narcissus that bear a cluster of little blooms on a single stem, bloom late, and are usually yellow and fragrant. Jonquils are very hardy, and they're more common in the East and Middle West than here.

How to Plant a Pot of Daffodils

This is simply a method for growing daffodils in containers so you can enjoy them on your patio or porch at their natural time for blooming. You're not forcing the bulbs, so you can keep them if you wish; they may flower again next year. (Each cultivar will bloom according to its built-in time schedule and your climate zone. The popular trumpet daffodil 'King Alfred' usually blooms here in February or March.)

▶ Buy the largest bulbs you can find. Leave double- and triple-nosed bulbs whole. They'll produce a flower from each point.

▶ Choose a container of appropriate size. (Five or six bulbs will fit in a 12-inch pot; more if you crown them.)

▶ Cover the drainage hole in the bottom of your pot with a piece of broken crockery or plastic fly screen.

▶ Place a layer of fast-draining potting soil in the bottom of the container. Add a handful or two of bone meal. Cover this with more soil.

▶ Add the bulbs. Jamming them in as close as possible won't impair their growth, but it's wiser to leave a little space around each one so they don't touch each other or the sides of the container. That way if one rots you won't lose them all.

▶ Cover the bulbs with potting soil. When you've finished, the top of the soil should be 2 inches lower than the edge of the pot and the tips of the bulbs should be just below or even with the surface of the soil.

▶ Water the pot, and add more potting soil, if necessary.

▶ Place the pot in a cool, shady place, near a hose bib for convenience. Cover it with an upside-down cardboard box to keep it dark.

▶ Water the pot daily. When rain falls, uncover the pot and let nature do your watering; recover it when rain ceases.

▶ Once the leaves are up 3 to 4 inches, remove the cover for good. Move the pot into bright light; put it in "skyshine" (under the open sky but not in full sun). Keep it there, or in cool semishade, until you see the first flower buds.

▶ Once buds appear, move the pot into full- or half-day sun. The flowers will face the sun, so put them where you can see their smiling faces. Once they open, they'll last longer in partial shade.

▶ After the flowers fade, clip them off. You can then either dump the bulbs out of the pot and discard them or plant them in the ground; leave the roots and bulbs all together as a clump and keep them damp. Sometimes the leaves will stay green for several months; don't cut them off until after they go brown.

Begin Forcing Tazetta Narcissus. Tazetta and Tazetta hybrid narcissus, including 'Cheerfulness', Chinese sacred lilies, 'Geranium', 'Grand Soleil d'Or', paper whites, and others, have bunches of tiny fragrant flowers on each stem. They can be planted outdoors here as early as September, and they bloom in fall and winter; some of these may be already in bloom now. You can also begin now to force, in pebbles and water, the Tazetta and Tazetta hybrid bulbs you've set aside for this purpose. By the method described in the box to the right, you can make them bloom in six weeks and schedule them to bloom just when you want them to do so. This method of forcing bulbs is also used for indoor bloom in cold-winter climates.

Gardeners in cold-winter climates also force many bulbs by another method: They subject the bulbs to a certain period of winter chill outdoors in buried pots. They then bring the bulbs indoors and place them in a sunny window to force bloom in the dead of winter, months ahead of the bulbs' natural schedule. Here, there's no point in forcing bulbs in this manner and its not even possible, so ignore the sections pertaining to this process that you find in most bulb books; they don't apply here. (All bulbs that have been forced, regardless of the method used, must be thrown out after the blooms fade. They'll never bloom again.)

✹ QUICK TIP

Plant Double for Twice the Show. *Plant a layer of daffodils 8 inches deep. Half-cover them with potting soil. Fit a second layer of bulbs into the spaces between the tips of the lower layer. Cover these with soil mix. The upper layer will bloom first, then the lower.*

✹ QUICK TIP

How to Make Small Holes for Small Bulbs. *When planting just a few small-size bulbs, such as ranunculus, anemones, sparaxis, and oxalis, dig individual holes with a melon scoop.*

How to Force Narcissus Bulbs in a Basket for Holiday Bloom

▸ Purchase plump premium bulbs of Chinese sacred lilies, 'Cragford', 'Geranium', 'Grand Soleil d'Or', or paper whites.

▸ Choose a suitable flat basket—one approximately 6 to 9 inches in diameter and 3 to 4 inches high. Leave it plain or spray it with quick-drying paint.

▸ Line the basket with a circle of heavy-gauge (4-millimeter) plastic sheeting cut to fit.

▸ Fill the basket halfway to the top with clean pebbles or gravel. Add six or eight bulbs, fitting them closely together. Fill in with more pebbles to hold them upright.

▸ Add water to the rim of the plastic. Add more every two or three days.

▸ Cover the basket with an upside-down cardboard box. Place it in a cool spot, such as the garage, for one and one-half weeks or until sprouts are up 3 to 4 inches.

▸ Uncover the basket and place it in a sunny window or in the sun on your patio or porch until the flowers open. Direct sun keeps the stems from growing too long and floppy, but if you put the basket outside bring it in at night for warmth. Turn it daily for even growth.

▸ Enjoy the fragrant flowers in the house during Christmas or Hanukkah, or make these baskets for gifts. If you plant six weeks before Christmas, a few flowers will open that day. Allow six and one-half weeks for fully open flowers.

▸ Discard the bulbs after flowers fade. Bulbs forced in water won't bloom again.

ANNUAL AND PERENNIAL FLOWERS

There's still time to plant spring flowers. November planting is not quite as good as October, but it's a thousand times better than waiting until spring, seeing everything in bloom, and regretting that you didn't plant in fall. First-time gardeners often fall in love with annual spring flowers when they see them blooming in April, then buy them and plant them at great expense. But instead of six months of bloom from December through May they get a month or two at the most, and decide they have purple thumbs. Not so; it's just their timing that's wrong. Remember this all-important **Rule of Thumb:** *For colorful spring flowerbeds, the time to plant is fall.*

Plant Cool-Season Annual Flowers.

Annuals and perennials used as annuals that can now be put in from pony packs and color packs include calendula, cineraria, columbine, coral bells, cyclamen, delphinium, dianthus, English daisy, evergreen candytuft, foxglove, flowering cabbage and flowering kale, hollyhock (for summer bloom), Iceland poppy, Johnny-jump-up, nemesia, pansy, paludosum daisy (*Chrysanthemum paludosum*), phlox, primroses (polyanthus, malacoides [fairy], obconica, and others), schizanthus, snapdragon, stock, sweet alyssum, sweet William, and viola. Get them into well-prepared ground and feed them often with a complete organic fertilizer recommended for flowering plants or your own concoction such as the all-purpose formula on page 77, or use liquid fertilizers such as a fish emulsion, in addition to bone meal and Sul-Po-Mag (0-0-22) in the soil. Nitrogen is less active in winter than in summer months, but liquid fertilizers like compost tea and alfalfa tea can often give growth a

How to Plant Ranunculus

Ranunculus provides longer-lasting color than any other spring-flowering bulb. Each large-size tuberous root will give as many as fifty to seventy-five blooms.

▶ Choose a good strain, such as Tecolote Giants. Plant in mid-November.

▶ Choose a spot in full sun where ranunculus hasn't grown for three or four years. (If sprinklers keep the bed soggy, presprout the tubers in flats of damp sand; as soon as they've grown some roots, plant them in the bed.)

▶ Cultivate the soil deeply, adding organic soil amendment, bone meal, and organic flower fertilizer according to package directions. Water the bed and let it settle overnight.

▶ Toss the tubers in drifts onto the bed. Rearrange them slightly so they're approximately 6 inches apart.

▶ Plant each tuber where it fell, making sure the points face down. Cover them with 1½ inches of soil in heavy ground or 2 inches in light, sandy soil.

▶ Soak the bed deeply. Except in dry, sandy soil or very dry weather, don't water again until green growth shows. Then, if rains are mere sprinkles, water often enough to keep the soil moist but not soggy. The tubers can rot if they're soaked prior to planting or if they're planted in soil that stays soggy wet. (See note above about presprouting.)

▶ Protect the sprouts from birds with wire or plastic garden netting until they're up 4 inches.

boost even when nights are cool. Don't let beds dry out now; unless rains are adequate, water well to get plants growing. Even planting now you'll have a gorgeous display beginning for sure in February—maybe sooner—that will peak in April and last until June.

Plant Nasturtiums and Wildflowers from Seeds.

If you regret you didn't plant from seeds earlier, you can still plant some types now. In fact, this is the best month to plant nasturtiums. Nasturtiums will grow and come back year after year if thrown, yes, simply tossed, onto a north-facing hillside—that is, they will if the hillside is just right, damp enough and earthy enough for them to take hold. But this fact shouldn't be taken to imply that this is the correct way to plant nasturtiums. Both wildflowers and nasturtiums do much better if you prepare the ground, dig deeply, add soil amendment (no fertilizer), cover the seeds according to package directions (rake wildflowers in lightly), and protect them from birds.

Wildflowers to plant from seeds now include baby blue eyes (*Nemophila menziesii*), California poppy, Chinese houses (*Collinsia heterophylla*), clarkia, larkspur (it blooms in June), linaria, Southwestern species of lupine (see the tips on page 380 for success), scarlet flax (*Linum grandiflorum* 'Rubrum'), sweet alyssum, and mixed packages of western and Southwestern wildflowers.

Plant wildflowers in full sun. Keep the seedbed damp by sprinkling it by hand every day, or twice a day if it's dry and windy. Be patient. At November's cooler temperatures it's going to take a little longer for the seed to germinate; don't let the bed dry out or all is lost. (See page 355 for more on growing wildflowers.)

Feed Flowers Planted Earlier.

If you've already planted flowerbeds with wildflowers and other cool-season annuals and perennials, they should be spreading out and growing now. A few may start to bloom. Protect them from snails and cutworms, but first look carefully in the middle of the day for bees. If none are visiting your cool-season flowers, it's safe to bait with Sluggo Plus for cutworms, snails, and slugs. (Sluggo Plus contains iron phosphate to control snails and slugs and Spinosad to control cutworms, earwigs, pill bugs, and sow bugs. But Spinosad is toxic to all types of wild and domestic bees, even though it bears the OMRI seal of approval awarded to organic products. See the organic control for earwigs on page 380.) Water when rains aren't adequate. Plants put into the ground when small build better roots in the ground. Iceland poppies, for example, bloom better and longer when planted early from tiny plants instead of later from more expensive 4-inch containers.

Don't forget that it's a race between you and the weather to get such winter-blooming plants as Iceland poppies, cyclamen, primroses, and pansies to bloom before Christmas; feed them for both growth and bloom. The trick with winter-blooming annuals is to fertilize them often, because nitrogen is less active in cool soil. You can use granulated organic flower fertilizer if you wish. Scatter it onto the soil and use a cultivator to work it into the top few inches of soil. Follow up with irrigation. But cool-season flowers respond best when fertilized every two weeks with a liquid product high in growth as well as bloom ingredients, such as, Fox Farm Grow Big (6-4-4). (This does not mean you need to dash out and find this exact product. Suggestions regarding specific fertilizers are given simply as examples of the type of

Tips for Success with Lupines

▸ Choose a western variety, such as arroyo lupine (*Lupinus succulentus*).

▸ Scarify the seed (see page 194). For a quick start also presprout the seed indoors, as for corn and beans (page 172).

▸ Prepare ground that's in full sun for planting wildflowers (see page 354).

▸ Plant the seeds 4 to 6 inches apart. Cover them with ¼ to ⅛ inch potting soil.

▸ Thin the plants to 6 inches apart when they're 2 to 3 inches tall. Bait for cutworms, and use BT against caterpillars.

product or formula to search for on the Internet or in your nursery or to concoct yourself out of ingredients you already have on hand.) Always dilute liquid fertilizers according to package directions. Liquid fertilizers are always the best method of feeding plants in containers.

Continue to feed cineraria with a high-nitrogen product for growth, such as fish emulsion, Bat Guano (10-3-1), or Fox Farm Grow Big (6-4-4), mentioned above. Don't fertilize wildflowers at all—they don't need it unless you've grown them for several years in a patch of poor soil and you notice yellow leaves and an obvious decline in vigor. In that case, only fertilize after they're up and growing with a light application of organic flower food. Liquid plant food is easiest to use since it can be applied with a sprayer, and Tiger Bloom (2-8-4) is an example of the sort of formula that would be best, since it's low nitrogen. Spraying the ground with humic acid can also help a sluggish stand of wildflowers take off and grow. In ordinary circumstances, fertilizer makes wildflowers grow too much at the expense of bloom. Most western wildflowers are more drought resistant than other garden flowers. They can often survive on natural rainfall, but keep an eye on them and water when rains aren't adequate to keep them growing.

Plant Flowering Cabbage and Flowering Kale for Winter Color. Flowering cabbage and flowering kale are two similar plants that are not only decorative but also edible. They can be cooked, though the result won't win a prize for taste. A better culinary use is as a colorful raw garnish under salad greens and with such edible flowers as violas and daylilies. Grow the plants in full sun as winter bedding plants, flowerbed edgings, unusual additions to hanging baskets, or ornamental touches in your vegetable garden. They do well in large containers and mix well with other flowers. Flowering kale and flowering cabbage are among the best plants for winter color in the cold low-lying valleys that regularly get winter frost. Frost, far from fazing them, improves them by making their colors more brilliant.

☀ QUICK TIP

Eliminate Earwigs Without Using Poisons. *To get rid of earwigs, loosely roll sheets of newspaper. Secure them with rubber bands and soak them in water until thoroughly wet. Before dark, place these traps around the strawberry patch and other places where earwigs congregate. Pick up the traps every morning. Earwigs will have found their way inside. Close up the ends and discard them in a tightly covered trash can, not the compost pile.*

Don't feed flowering kale or flowering cabbage for bloom; this stimulates bolting. Frequent applications of a light-nitrogen fertilizer, such as fish emulsion, produce the best results. Protect the plants from cabbage worms with BT.

Continue to Plant, Divide, and Deadhead Perennials. Several perennials continue to bloom throughout October. *Hypoestes aristata* 'Lavender Cloud' is at its best now. This plant makes a very pleasant-looking green shrub for most of the year and then bursts into its full glory in November, just when we're happy to have a splash of color in the garden and to use the long salvia-like sprays in flower arrangements. Look for plants now at specialty nurseries or ask friends for seedlings. This plant is amazingly drought resistant and trouble free, and it seeds itself around the garden. Cut back *Tagetes lemmonii* and other late bloomers, like tall rudbeckias, to good basal growth after flowers fade. You can deadhead and clean up Mexican sage (*Salvia leucantha*), but don't cut this one back too far—it may die during the winter rains; wait until spring. Lift and divide summer phlox (*Phlox paniculata*). This phlox does well inland and even thrives in full sun as long as the roots are mulched. The stalks may reach 5 or even 6 feet tall. Cut down any of these that may remain and divide the plants every few years, throwing away the centers and replanting the young shoots growing from the outside of the clump. Continue to deadhead bulbine; it blooms almost year-round along the coast. Cut off faded flowers from coreopsis and any wooden stalks sticking above the clump. Remove faded flowers from *Sedum spectabile*. Continue to watch ornamental grasses for new growth springing from the ground when rains begin. When you see it, cut off the faded foliage and blooms down to the new growth. (With evergreen types deadhead only. See page 327 for more information and cautions on cutting back ornamental grasses.)

Cut off dead bloom stalks down into the basal leaves of asters, Jerusalem sage (*Phlomis*), kangaroo paws (*Anigozanthus*), lavender, lion's tail (*Leonotis leonurus*), pincushion plants (*Scabiosa*), sea lavender (*Limonium perezii*), and Shasta daisies. Clean up ornamental grasses by removing fistfuls of dead leaves and unsightly flower stalks. Clean up parts that have died out of lamb's ears (*Stachys byzantina*) and Jerusalem sage (*Phlomis*). Mulch the bare ground. Cut back *Helichrysum* 'Limelight' and others to control their spreading growth. Make the cuts to an adjoining branch so that the plant does not look as though it has been pruned.

CHRYSANTHEMUMS

Cut back chrysanthemums (*Chrysanthemum x grandiflorum*) growing in the ground after bloom, leaving 6- to 8-inch stalks. New growth will spring from these stalks. In March take fresh cuttings from them, dig up and discard the old roots, and start over with the new plants.

After cutting the plants back, clean up the ground and discard dead leaves. Chrysanthemums are notorious disease carriers, so don't add their remains to the compost pile. When cutting back potted chrysanthemums after their blooms fade, never cut them back to short, bare stubs. Just take off the flowers and cut back the stalks lightly. They need their leaves to survive. When fresh growth begins, cut off the old leaves and stalks above the new growth.

ROSES

In most climate zones roses will continue to grow and to flower throughout November and December. In fact, if you've taken good care of your plants, November's blooms are often the best of the entire year. The lack of care roses need at this time of year makes the flowers all the more pleasing. You can, if you wish, continue to pick roses for bouquets, but by midmonth stop deadheading. Instead of cutting off faded flowers, allow rose hips to stay on the plant and simply pull off faded petals that don't fall off by themselves. Stop fertilizing roses, lighten up on watering, and after midmonth, water only when rains aren't adequate. Don't let the roots dry out completely, but a little calculated neglect now encourages them to slow down and prepare for winter. By withholding fertilizer, by not pruning, and by reducing irrigation you help them to get ready to drop their leaves and go dormant in late December and January.

CITRUS, AVOCADO, AND MACADAMIA TREES

Wrap the trunks of young citrus, avocado, and macadamia trees with an insulating material of some kind, such as wood pulp, corrugated paper, or gardener protective tree wrap, by mid-November, to protect them from frost damage. Thoroughly cover the trunk, from the soil line to the main scaffold branches. Tie or tape the material in place. Once the trees are two or three years old and have grown a good head of branches with a rooflike covering of leaves they usually don't need this protection.

Don't let the roots of young citrus, avocados, and macadamias—or mature trees either, for that matter—go dry in cold or frosty weather. Wilted leaves are more susceptible to frost damage.

CONTROL OF PEACH LEAF CURL

Peach leaf curl is an airborne fungal disease that impairs the leafing and fruiting of peach and nectarine trees, and eventually kills infected trees. This disease is so prevalent in Southern California that it's fair to say every unprotected peach or nectarine tree will eventually fall prey to it. The spores are spread by wind so it is everywhere in the air, but it spreads more rampantly during wet winters. Peach leaf curl thickens and stunts new shoots, and it curls, puckers, and thickens new leaves. It changes the color of freshly emerging growth from green to red or orange. Later the foliage turns pale green or yellow followed by a coat of gray or white powder, after which the leaves drop off the tree. Peach leaf curl makes trees bear sparse inedible fruit that's small and wrinkled, with raised areas and irregular lesions. Eventually affected trees are so weakened they die, and once a tree has this disease there's no cure. Luckily there is a time-honored solution. You can protect peach and nectarine trees, including dwarf trees growing in tubs, from peach leaf curl by applying dormant spray beginning now right after leaves fall. Apply an organic dormant spray, such as Bonide Organic Lime Sulfur Spray, in fall and winter. Apply the spray at least once in November after leaves fall, once in December, and again in January or early February just before buds swell. If it rains right after you spray, repeat the process in a day or two.

Before spraying, clean up the tree by removing loose leaves, clipping off mummified fruits, and raking up and destroying all debris. Then

How to Grow Strawberries

You can, if you wish, grow strawberries on flat ground, in a raised bed edged with wood, or on raised vegetable rows between furrows; you can water them individually by hand, with overhead sprinklers, or by flooding the furrows. If you want to plant and water in any of these ways, follow the instructions below only insofar as they pertain to your particulars. But the mound method watered by a drip system, as described here, produces berries most successfully and with the least work in the long run.

▸ Plant a prechilled, locally adapted variety between November 1 and 10. (If you chilled your own plants, get them in the ground no later than November 5; you'll have fruit in one and a half months.)

▸ Provide deeply spaded, rich, slightly acid, preferably sandy soil with a high proportion of organic matter.

▸ Construct mounds 6 to 8 inches high and 2½ to 3 feet wide, flat on top and with slightly sloping sides. Leave 18 inches between the mounds.

▸ Fertilize by mixing into the top 6 inches of soil a complete organic fertilizer recommended for vegetables, such as Dr. Earth Organic 5 Tomato, Vegetable & Herb Fertilizer (5-7-3) or mix your own, such as the formula on page 77. Fertilize again in spring and then once more in summer.

▸ Set the plants in alternate positions 12 inches apart, in two rows that are 13 to 14 inches apart on top of the mound.

▸ For each plant make a crevice with a trowel, fan out the roots, and close up the hole so that the middle of the crown is even with the soil line. (If you plant it too deeply the crown will rot, but if you plant it too shallowly the top roots will dry out.)

▸ Install two drip lines of a type like Drip-In that is designed for watering row crops, one drip line for each row of plants. Arrange the drip lines on top of the ground so that the crowns of the plants will be dry and the roots moist.

▸ Water lightly every day for a week, or until the plants are established. After that, water once a week when it doesn't rain.

▸ In mid-January cover the entire bed with clear plastic mulch. Carefully cut an X or a round hole 4 inches in diameter directly over each plant. Gently slip the plants up through the holes. Cut the plastic to fit the bed, and bury the bottom edges in soil to prevent it from blowing away.

▸ Harvest berries daily as they ripen. Cut runners off as they occur.

▸ Bait for sow bugs, slugs, and snails. Protect the plants from birds with netting.

▸ After fruiting stops, let runners grow, and remove the plastic to allow them to root in the ground. Then dig up the runners, bare their roots, and prechill them (as described on page 362). Replant them in the same bed for three years; then choose another spot.

put on protective clothing, a mask, gloves, and goggles before mixing the spray according to package directions. Go over the tree carefully to wet all parts of the bark with the spray, from the trunk to the branch crotches and twigs. In fall and winter beneficials are less active, so dormant spray does not damage the environment, but don't broadcast it on everything in sight. It is a good idea, however, to finish up by lightly spraying the ground under the tree, including the bottom of the trunk. Also you can mix the lime sulfur with horticultural oil so you are smothering at the same time any pests that may be overwintering in the crotches of the tree or in cracks in the bark. Even organic gardeners

Peach tree with fruit

can use dormant spray safely, and farmers use it without losing their organic status. While you are about it, also use dormant spray on all other varieties of deciduous fruit trees except apricot. Lime sulfur can burn the buds of apricot trees and damage leaves and flowers. (See page 57 for more about dormant spray.)

Despite the prevalence of peach leaf curl in Southern California and the efficacy of controlling it by spraying with lime sulfur, many organic gardeners no longer use dormant spray and they claim that their fruit trees and other traditional candidates for dormant spray, such as roses, no longer need such care. The reason is that organic soils contain a thriving community of beneficial organisms that protect the plants growing in them from diseases. There are also some organic sprays that are effective against plant diseases, including biofungicides and other products discussed on pages 58 and 59, and some organic gardeners may opt to use these. The same beneficial organisms isolated in biofungicides actually flourish in organic soils. Chemical pesticides and synthetic fertilizers kill all these organisms and produce dead lifeless soils, thus leaving plants unprotected from pests and diseases. That said, it takes a year or two for the full benefits of the organic method to take hold and flourish in the soil and even in the air that flows through an organic garden. Half-hearted methods don't work. It's not enough to take away the synthetic products, sprinkle a box or two of organic fertilizer around, and otherwise let plants starve. One really does need to mulch the ground, fertilize organically, water sufficiently, and build up the organic structure of the soil so that it in turn can feed the plants. So unless you are a devoted organic gardener who has gardened the organic way exclusively for a year or two, it would be better to protect your peach and nectarine trees and other deciduous fruit trees by spraying them now and twice more before spring with dormant spray according to package directions. However, never spray apricot trees with lime sulfur because it burns the bark, twigs, and buds of apricots.

LAWN CARE

Cool-Season Lawns. There's still time, if you didn't do the jobs last month, to plant cool-season lawns (page 359); to overseed Bermuda with annual ryegrass (don't wait any longer; it has a short growing season, described on page 357); to dethatch cool-season lawns that need it (page 360); and to get rid of crabgrass (page 357). Continue to feed all cool-season grasses regularly—once a month, every six weeks, or less frequently according to the product you buy. This is their best growing season. Mow cool-season lawns at the proper heights for each type of lawn. Mow tall fescue once a week with a rotary mower set at the highest setting of 1 1/2 to 3 inches and perennial ryegrass at 1 1/2 to 2 1/2 inches. (Bent grass and Kentucky bluegrasses are also cool-season lawns but not adapted here, though Kentucky bluegrass is still included in some mixes.)

Warm-Season Lawns. Warm-season lawns are beginning winter dormancy. Stop fertilizing and mowing them when their growth slows. Renovate kikuyu—cut it right down to the ground—if you didn't do this job last month.

Gopher Traps. Mankind's war with gophers is probably as ancient in these parts as the history of agriculture. Almost anywhere in Southern California where you grow a garden—unless it's protected by a natural barrier of underground rock—gophers will move in, push up disfiguring mounds of earth, and help themselves to the roots of your plants. For example, one local gardener who planted a new lawn woke up one morning to discover an army of gophers had invaded overnight and ruined the lawn. He tried various methods of attack, including flooding, poison bait, toxic gas, and metal traps; he even bought a cat. (His dog killed several gophers, too, but did more damage digging up the lawn than the gophers had done.) This gardener finally conquered the gophers when he discovered the Blackhole, a trap made by FBN Plastics in Tulare, California.

The Blackhole trap is smaller than box-type traps, and though it's slightly more expensive than they are it's easier to use. It's shaped like a tube and contains a lethal wire snare that kills the gopher instantly. You dig down and fit it into the gopher's run. Your victim comes charging along its tunnel, sees light ahead, and runs right into the trap; that's when his light goes out. The Blackhole trap is available at many local nurseries, which is lucky, because when a gopher attacks the best defense is a speedy one. One of my daughters phoned last Saturday to ask what to do about their first-ever gopher, who had popped up overnight. I told her about the Blackhole trap and warned her against the BlackBox trap; it sounds similar but didn't

---

◉ QUICK TIP

Send Gophers a Message. *When you've trapped a gopher, don't throw the body in the trash; stuff it back in the hole where you caught it. Other gophers will take the hint, leave your property posthaste, and never return—or not for a long time.*

How to Grow Globe Onions

▶ Choose a short-day variety, such as 'Granex', 'Grano', or 'Crystal Wax'; plant from seed, and put the seed in the ground between November 1 and November 10.

▶ Prepare a row of loose, well-drained (preferably sandy) soil with a high content of humus, in full sun.

▶ Add organic vegetable fertilizer according to package directions. Water the bed and let it settle overnight.

▶ Sprinkle the seeds thinly in a wide, shallow row.

▶ Cover the seeds with a ¼ inch of potting soil. Pat it down with the palm of your hand.

▶ Install a drip line down the row, such as Drip-In, that can be used for watering row crops. (This is the easiest way to water onions, but if you wish you can use any other method commonly used for watering vegetables.)

▶ Sprinkle the bed by hand, to make sure it stays damp, when rains aren't adequate. (Or, if possible, adjust the drip system to water daily until the seeds have germinated.)

▶ Once the seedlings are up, let the drip system kick in to keep the rows evenly moist throughout the growing season.

▶ Remove weeds when they're small, and continue to weed regularly. (Because onions have shallow roots, they don't compete well; weeds will stunt their growth.)

▶ Thin the seedlings in late December or early January. No need to throw out all the thinnings—transplant some to another row.

▶ Leave the biggest ones in the existing row, spaced 4 to 5 inches apart.

▶ Give onions frequent light applications of fish emulsion throughout their leafy green stage to maintain a steady rate of growth. Stop feeding them in early to mid-March. (Fertilizing onions with nitrogen after they begin to form a bulb makes them split.) The previously straight plants will suddenly grow fat. Start to pull and eat them in early May. When necks weaken and tops begin to fall over (usually before the end of May), turn off the drip system to let them cure. Dig up the remainder of the bulbs when the tops die.

▶ Place the onions in a shady, well-ventilated area until they're thoroughly dry. Then store them in a cool place. Mild onions don't keep as well as pungent types, but they will last several months if properly cured and stored. (One of the best ways to store onions and garlic is to braid and hang them as described on page 251.)

work for me. She bought the correct brand at a local farm supply; her husband set it immediately in broad daylight and a little haphazardly, he said. Forty-five minutes after setting the trap he phoned me and said, "I can't believe this. I already caught the gopher." This story proves my point, though it may never happen again. (See the Quick Tip on page 385 for a somewhat unpleasant but effective trick, which one of my neighbors learned from her gardener.)

VEGETABLE GARDENING

Continue to plant beets, carrots, kale, kohlrabi, lettuce, mesclun, mustard greens, radishes, spinach, and turnips from seeds to keep fresh crops coming along. If you're late in planting vegetables, there's still time to put in transplants of broccoli, Brussels sprouts, cabbage, cauliflower, celery, parsley, and Swiss chard, as well as seeds of fava beans, peas, globe onions, and parsley (see the box on page 361 for an easy way to make the seeds of parsley, celery, carrots, and parsnips come up in three days or less, a trick well worth doing in cool weather). It's best to plant earlier, but in most climate zones it's still warm enough in November to germinate seeds as long as the weather doesn't turn cold and wet. You'll just have a later harvest. Do plant as soon as possible, though. Among plants that are well adapted to November planting, artichokes, strawberries, and rhubarb can be put in bare-root—though I personally don't recommend rhubarb. (Hot summers inland rot the roots, and along the coast there's not enough winter chill to stimulate the growth of tender, pink stalks. The leaves of all rhubarb plants are highly poisonous, and I have a hunch that the stalks, when they're overly sour and green or brownish in color, contain too much oxalic acid for good health.) Potatoes can still be planted from seed potatoes and scallions from onion sets.

Also plant garlic now. Purchase large globes with good-sized sections in any market, or elephant garlic at the nursery or produce market. (It's a different species, and milder, but grown much the same way.) Break up the garlic cloves and plant them individually, with the points facing up, in fertile soil rich in humus. Plant them in full sun, 4 inches apart and 2 inches beneath the soil surface. Some gardeners have

How To Get Through Winter with a Bare Vegetable Patch or with Bulldozed Ground, Dogs, Kids, and No Landscaping

When a house is sold without landscaping and there's no money left for putting in a garden, one solution is to plant a cover crop, also called green manure. This system is also a great way to improve soil in a vegetable garden, instead of letting it lie fallow in winter in case you can't plant winter vegetables. Purchase seeds of a leguminous cover crop that can be planted in fall and will grow throughout winter, such as scarlet clover (*Trifolium incarnatum*). Rent a tiller to loosen the top layer of the ground—you may need a pick axe for some bits—then broadcast seeds according to directions, and sprinkle frequently to get plants established. Once the clover is up 4 inches, it can take some foot traffic. Water deeply each time the plants begin to wilt, letting rains do some of the watering. In spring, allow the clover to bloom and then rototill it under or in raised beds, dig the plants into the ground; wait two weeks before planting a garden. Cover crops hugely improve the fertility of soil.

told me that interplanting garlic with cabbage crops reduces problems with cabbage worms and aphids. However, test data, plus my own experience, makes me doubt the efficacy of this method. Heavy rains and cold weather usually have more to do with reducing the numbers of aphids and cabbage butterflies, whose larvae do the damage. I recommend BT against cabbage worms and Safer's Insecticidal Soap against aphids. (Both are harmless to humans.)

The Secret Lives of Strawberries and Onions. Strawberries and onions seem at first glance to be an unlikely pair to lump together for discussion, but they share certain characteristics. In order to grow an abundant harvest of large, luscious strawberries and premium globe onions, you have to understand some of their innate secrets.

Both are regional crops—that is, varieties of each are designed to be grown in certain geographical areas and not in others. Both have specific temperature requirements that, for best results, require their being planted during an identical and extremely short slice of time—sometime between November 1 and 10—though they require this schedule for somewhat different reasons.

Exhaustive tests by the University of California Agricultural Extension, paid for by strawberry growers, have proven that strawberries planted between November 1 and 10 get winter chill at the precise moment in their growing schedule to trigger fruit production rather than foliage. When planted at the wrong time they'll put out runners but won't produce much, if any, fruit. (Watch any professional strawberry growers near you as a good indication of when to plant.)

Either plant runners from your own garden that you've already prepared as prechilled, bare-root plants (as discussed on page 362) or plant from bare-roots purchased from nurseries now. (See the box on page 383 for planting instructions.) As a general rule, don't order strawberries, other than alpine varieties, from catalogs, because they usually don't carry varieties that are adapted to our climate. Strawberries are a highly regional crop—even more so than onions. Just a few hundred miles up the California coast entirely different strawberry varieties are grown, so be sure that you plant a locally adapted variety, such as 'Camarillo', 'Douglas', 'Sequoia', 'Tioga', or 'Tufts'.

Onions are photothermoperiodic—that is, they're sensitive to temperature and also to day length. An onion plant is stimulated to stop making leafy growth and to start making a bulb not so much by temperature as by the lengthening of days, as the sun moves north in spring and summer. Each variety will form a bulb only after it has received a certain number of hours of daylight each day for a certain number of days. However, varieties vary greatly in the number of hours of daylight they need. Accordingly, all onions are categorized into long-day (northern), intermediate-day (central), and short-day (southern) varieties.

Long-day varieties, grown in northern states and in Canada, need fourteen to fifteen hours of daylight to make a bulb. Northern European and Alaskan varieties need sixteen hours or more. No long-day varieties can possibly receive enough hours of daylight in Southern California to make a bulb. If you plant them your crop will always fail, and yet you can often find seeds of long-day onions on local seed racks, and almost all onion sets are of long-day types. These sets can be used only for growing scallions (green onions). Here, in order to get the best globe onions, we must plant seeds of short-day (southern) varieties in fall or, alternatively, plant intermediate varieties in late winter.

Also, once an onion has reached a certain critical size, which differs by variety, temperatures of between 40° and 50°F will make it go to seed prematurely, or bolt. The way to grow good bulb onions here and avoid bolting is to follow this **Rule of Thumb:** *Plant globe onions only from seeds, never from sets (small bulbs). Plant only such "short-day" (southern) varieties as 'Grano', 'Granex', and 'Crystal Wax'; put the seeds in the ground between the first and tenth* *of November or plant these varieties bare root in January).*

'Grano', 'Granex', 'Crystal Wax', and '1015Y Texas SuperSweet' are sweet, mild flavored, and juicy, like 'Vidalia' and 'Maui' onions. Eat them raw in sandwiches and salads. Nothing better. 'Crystal Wax', sometimes called 'Crystal Wax White Bermuda' or simply 'White Bermuda', and '1015Y Texas SuperSweet', a globe-shaped yellow onion that keeps two months, also make good pickling onions when closely planted. Neither 'Crystal Wax' nor 'Grano' keeps well; on this score 'Granex' is a little better. Seeds of intermediate day-length onions, including 'San Felipe' and 'Pronto S', will also produce a bulb if you plant them in February; they'll ripen in summer. Two other onion varieties can be planted from seeds in fall or from transplants in January: 'Superstar', an All-America Selections winner in 2001, is a large, white, daylength-neutral sweet onion that's easy to grow from seeds in most parts of the United States, but is not a long keeper. (Braiding and hanging sweet onions is the best way to keep them. After two or three months, clip off, bag, and refrigerate the few that are left. These onions are so good in sandwiches and salads they go fast.) 'Cippolina' is an Italian heirloom variety with a pungent taste. It makes a small, flat, golden bulb, useful for pickling or shishkabobs, that keeps well and looks lovely braided (see page 251 for how to braid onions and garlic).

Onion seeds sprout extremely easily; there's no problem involved. I've often planted onions on the same day I took off for a two- or three-week vacation, and left them with an automatic drip system as a baby-sitter; when I came home my onions were always up and growing. (See the box on page 386 for instructions.)

By all means plant a row of onions sets now—if you want them only for scallions. For best flavor pick scallions when they're young, and plant successive crops. If you leave them in the ground too long you may eventually get a large onion, but it will be green through the middle, and it will have a thick stalk on top that won't dry out properly, so your onions will rot. Some gardeners think the way to cure thick stalks is to knock the tops over in spring when the globes are full grown, but tests have shown this practice to have no influence whatsoever on the proper ripening of onions.

NOVEMBER CHECKLIST

PURCHASE/PLANT

{ } Continue to plant wildflowers, 379

{ } Plant California native plants, 368

{ } Now through January transplant shrubs and young trees that are growing in the wrong places, 374

{ } Plant ground covers, 374

{ } Plant anemones, all kinds of daffodils, Dutch irises, grape hyacinths, ranunculus, and all other spring-flowering bulbs except tulips, hyacinths, and crocuses, 375

{ } Plant daffodils in pots, 376

{ } Plant a basket of narcissus for holiday bloom, 377

{ } Finish filling flowerbeds with cool-season flowers for winter and spring bloom, 378

{ } Plant nasturtiums and continue to plant wildflowers from seeds, including lupines, 379

{ } Plant flowering kale and flowering cabbage, especially in interior zones, 378

{ } Plant cool-season lawns from seeds early this month, 385

{ } Overseed Bermuda with annual ryegrass if desired, 385

{ } Continue to plant winter vegetables, including garlic, 387

{ } Plant bare-root artichokes, 387

{ } Plant bare-root strawberries between November 1 and 10; use the runners you prechilled or purchase plants at a nursery, 388

{ } Also between November 1 and 10 plant globe onions from seeds of short-day varieties, 388

{ } Continue planting perennials, 381

TRIM, PRUNE, MOW, DIVIDE

{ } Prune pine trees and other conifers now through February, 267

{ } Divide and transplant agapanthus, 346

{ } Divide Matilija poppy, 345

{ } Open up spaces in dense trees to allow wind to pass through, 373

{ } Prune acacias, 373

{ } Prune cane berries other than low-chill raspberries, 373

{ } Cut back chrysanthemums after bloom; clean up the ground, 381

{ } Watch red fountain grass (*Pennisetum setaceum* 'Rubrum') for new growth, the sign to cut it back, 355

{ } Continue to divide and deadhead perennials, 381

FERTILIZE

{ } Fertilize cool-season bedding flowers; don't feed wildflowers, 379

{ } Continue to fertilize cineraria for growth, 380

{ } Don't feed roses this month, 382

{ } Continue to fertilize cool-season lawns; stop fertilizing warm-season lawns when their growth slows, 385

{ } Feed the basic landscape for a whole year by mulching with aged horse manure, 367

WATER

{ } Once rains arrive, stop watering succulents growing in the ground, 273

{ } Water all garden plants less frequently now as weather cools and rains begin, but if rains don't arrive, be alert to signs of stress and water as necessary, 368

{ } Install pitcher irrigation, 368

{ } Water bulbs, especially potted ones, 93, 397

{ } Water roses until midmonth, but only when rains aren't adequate, 382

{ } Don't let citrus go dry in cold or frosty weather, 382

{ } Water cool-season lawns when rains aren't adequate; stop watering warm-season lawns when they go brown, 411

CONTROL PESTS, DISEASE, AND WEEDS

{ } Bait flowerbeds, especially wildflowers, for cutworms and slugs and snails, 115

{ } Spray peach and nectarine trees against peach leaf curl after leaves fall, 382

{ } Trap gophers on lawns and elsewhere in the garden, 385

ALSO THIS MONTH

{ } Use pine needles as mulch, 370

{ } Stake young trees loosely so they can develop strong trunks, 373

{ } Prechill tulips, hyacinths, and crocuses, 375

{ } Begin forcing paper whites, Chinese sacred lilies, and other Tazetta and Tazetta hybrid narcissus in water and pebbles, 377

{ } Wrap the trunks of young citrus and avocado trees with insulating material to protect them from frost damage, 382

December

THE HOLIDAY MONTH

Camellia sasanqua
(Christmas Camellia)

If there's one thing we can say for sure about December weather in Southern California, it's that we can never be sure just what it's going to be. December is supposed to be a winter month, and sometimes it acts like one. Snow blankets the mountains and frost hits all zones. At other times there's a heat wave between Christmas and New Year's that reminds us of August—unless we go to the beach and stick a furtive toe in the icy sea. The weather forecaster is forever informing us that this is the coldest (or hottest) temperature ever recorded for the particular date. And we're inclined to chorus, "What unusual weather we're having!" as if that weren't the most usual thing in the world. So be alert this month: On the one hand protect tender plants from possible frost, but on the other hand continue watering if the weather's hot, dry, and windy. If you garden in an interior zone, don't be fooled by this month's sunny days. An ice-cold javelin may be hidden behind December's back, ready to strike at night.

If you're too busy to give the garden much attention this month, you're in luck. Most plants will roll along quite happily with only an occasional boost from you. Gardeners who prepared for winter in the fall, when time was easier to come by, can rejoice now because their gardens will cooperate in December by making fewer demands. Plant lovers overwhelmed by the holiday rush can let many jobs slide. But if you're an eager beaver or were an early shopper, you can get the jump on the New Year by tackling a few of January's chores, such as pruning deciduous fruit trees or planting bare-roots. Nurseries stock bare-root plants beginning this month.

How to Make Poinsettias Last Indoors Until March

▸ Purchase one to three premium plants—healthy specimens of such varieties as 'Eckespoint', 'Pixie', or 'Everlasting' (which holds onto its foliage longest).

▸ Line a large ornamental basket with several layers of plastic cut to fit.

▸ Pour in a layer of Styrofoam packing pellets, to hold the roots above water.

▸ Arrange the poinsettias in the basket on top of the Styrofoam pellets.

▸ Surround the poinsettias with four to six low-profile green houseplants, such as Chinese evergreen (Aglaonema modestum) or 'Dallas' or 'Kimberly Queen' ferns, to add beauty and provide the moist atmosphere that's highly beneficial to poinsettias.

▸ Place the entire arrangement out of drafts in bright light, such as 18 inches to 2 feet below an electric light source, but away from direct sunlight. This should provide the required temperatures; 70°F in the daytime and 60° to 65°F at night are ideal. Don't subject blooming poinsettias to extremes of temperature—80°F days and 50°F nights will make the leaves and bracts fall off. (So will drafts and over- or underwatering.)

▸ Water the plants when the surface of the soil feels dry to the touch; then water them enough to make excess water flow out the bottom of the container. Beginning in late December start feeding them occasionally with a weak, balanced fertilizer, such as deodorized fish emulsion.

PREPARING FOR FROST

In areas where frost is expected, move tropical and other frost-tender, container-grown plants under eaves, under spreading trees, or into shade houses. Don't forget to water them. Plants withstand cold weather much better when provided with adequate moisture. Some tropicals, including species often grown as houseplants and tubbed specimens of plumeria, can be brought indoors for the winter. Keep these in bright light or filtered sun, and let them go somewhat but not totally dry. Plumerias will probably go semidormant and drop their leaves but will come back when you put them outdoors again in spring. (See page 67 for more about frost protection.)

POINSETTIAS

Fifty years ago poinsettias (*Euphorbia pulcherrima*) were popular 10-foot tall, somewhat leggy, garden shrubs. If you had a white, south-facing wall—often the back of the garage—chances are you'd embellish it with a gangly row of poinsettias. Beginning just prior to Christmas every year, you could count on them for several months of stunning bright red blooms. Most folks started with just one nursery specimen and planted the rest of the row from cuttings taken when they cut back the spent bloom stalks down to a good bud on the first of May. New plants were easy to propagate; all you needed to do was stick large cuttings into the ground, pinch back their growth tips to encourage branching, and water them. All this changed when two rows of poinsettias flanking a pathway leading to a hotel ballroom failed to make a good display. The left-hand row bloomed spectacularly as usual for a holiday party and the right-hand row didn't bear a single bloom. The perplexed hotel manager called in UC agricultural scientists to solve the problem and they discovered that a night watchman walked down that path every night while holding a flashlight in his right hand. The light of the flashlight hitting the row of poinsettias on the right had been enough to break the hours of darkness into two parts and prevent the plants from blooming. Subsequent experiments showed that the poinsettia is a photoperiodic plant that needs fourteen hours of unbroken darkness nightly for six weeks in order to set buds and bloom. When Paul Ecke, Sr., a grower of poinsettias as cut flowers, read this news he immediately saw the commercial promise of poinsettias as potted plants. He quickly threw up range houses (temporary wooden structures covered with plastic) and began growing poinsettias in pots, and by managing the hours of light and darkness hitting the plants forced them to bloom early for the holidays. Outdoor varieties didn't do well in containers, so Ecke developed indoor varieties. Garden styles changed, the old outdoor varieties—'Hollywood' was the best known—died out or were difficult to find, and the new varieties didn't do well outdoors. But today the need for colorful, easy, drought-resistant outdoor plants is reviving the interest in the poinsettia as a landscape plant. 'St. Louis' is one variety that will grow in gardens, and even hardier plants may be coming onto the market soon. Give outdoor varieties full sun and don't allow garden lights or car lights to hit the plants at night during autumn months or they won't bloom that year. On the first of May, cut off each faded flower stem making the cut just above a strong bud close to the bottom of the stem. Fertilize them occasionally, and water deeply but infrequently.

If you've been subjecting a potted indoor variety of poinsettia to fourteen hours of darkness nightly since October, it should be in full bloom now. Stop fertilizing it for now, and bring it into the house to enjoy. For bloom that lasts several months, give it the light, food, and water as described in the accompanying box. Buy more potted poinsettias early this month if you want them to give as gifts or to decorate your home or entryway. The best plants are usually sold early. Wherever you purchase your plant, be selective. Choose a plant that hasn't already been abused. Exposure to extremes of temperature and over- or underwatering can occur before you get your plant, and these factors can make the green leaves fall off prematurely, a common fault of poinsettias. The colorful bracts should look healthy, not wilted, and the leaves should be green and firmly attached to the stalk. If several have fallen off, that's a bad sign. Also inspect the flowers, the tiny little buttons in the center of the colorful bracts. Make sure they're fresh looking, not brown or mildewed.

When you get your plant home, give it the location, light, and other conditions that will help it last, as described in the box on page 394. (One of the worst places to keep a poinsettia is on top of the TV.) If you leave the foil on the pot, don't allow the plant to suffer wet feet—tear holes in the foil so water doesn't collect in it. The best way to water is to put your plant in the kitchen sink, water it thoroughly, and let it drain before putting it back on display.

CYMBIDIUMS

Many cymbidiums start to flower in December, some as early as November. Most bloom between February and May, a few in May and June, and one or two year-round. Choose wisely and you can have these exotic orchids decorating your home, patio, and garden for six months or more. (As explained on page 319, avoid buying inferior plants.)

Protect cymbidiums' bloom spikes from snails. Stake the spikes to avoid breakage, but allow each spray to maintain its natural, arching form. Allow miniatures in hanging baskets to cascade naturally. Continue to feed the plants for bloom (as described on page 319) until buds open. Once they bloom stop feeding the plants, but keep them damp, though not soggy. For longer-lasting flowers move blooming plants into more shade and away from bees. (The flowers "blush" and fade after pollination.)

Once cymbidium spikes have set buds, you can force some into bloom for holiday decoration ahead of their natural schedule. Wait until the buds on the bloom spikes are full size and look fat and ready to open. Then take the plant into the house and place it in bright light. The warmth plus the longer day will open the buds quickly. Continue to enjoy the plant indoors or, for a longer-lasting display, place it outside again.

There's one drawback, however: Plants you force into bloom early won't perform as well next year. You'll get a few spikes but not as many. This is also a factor to consider when buying new varieties. Some may have been forced into bloom, and you won't get as many spikes the following year. Wait for the third year, and they'll be loaded.

SASANQUA CAMELLIAS AND EARLY-FLOWERING AZALEAS

Choose sasanqua camellias for winter color that will return year after year. They're in bloom now. *Camellia sasanqua* 'Yuletide' is one of the best. Bright red blossoms with yellow centers dot the handsome, small-leafed foliage from November into January. Although sasanqua flowers are usually smaller and not as long lasting as those of *C. japonica*, the plants bloom abundantly and can take more sun, and the flowers are usually immune to blossom blight.

Also look for early- and long-blooming varieties of azalea. A collection of them can provide color fall through spring in frost-free zones. Combine them with camellias on north-facing slopes and the north side of your home. Some varieties to look for include 'Alaska', 'Albert and Elizabeth' (note that it rarely survives in Zone 24), 'Avenir', 'California Peach', 'California Sunset' (inland only—it dies or does poorly in Zone 24), 'Carnival Time' (and other members of the Carnival series), 'Chimes', 'Eric Shame', 'Lucille K.', 'Nuccio's Happy Days', 'Red Wing' (sometimes called 'Red Bird'), 'Rosa Belton', and 'Vervaeneana Alba'.

ROSES

Don't fertilize or prune roses this month. Let the flowers stay on the bush, and water them less. These steps help roses harden off for winter. Perhaps your garden isn't properly zoned and you have heavy water users like roses growing next to drought-resistant plants such as bougainvilleas. Winter is a good time for moving roses to a better spot. Prepare the new beds now; dig up the roses and move them there next month. Despite the demands of holiday activities, some gardeners also find time this month to prepare the beds for January bare-root planting. To do so, spade the ground deeply and put in plenty of soil amendment. Don't be dismayed if you have clay soil. Roses thrive in it, but be sure to test the drainage, and if it's severely impaired dig in gypsum, install drains, or build raised beds for your roses.

Study your rose collection with the idea of weeding out poor performers. Why struggle along with a plant that's worn out or simply not right for your climate zone? In the interest of water conservation, it's far better to grow a handful of choice roses than a great many mediocre ones.

If you are going to plant a few roses next month, plan your color scheme now so decisions will be easier later. All too often roses are planted with a shotgun approach; no thought is given to color compatibility. Don't, for instance, put one of the new brilliant oranges next to a bluish red. The best-looking rose gardens are designed like a rainbow, with a progression of harmonious colors flowing from one side to the other. Clashing colors are well separated. For a bigger display, plant at least three roses of one variety together. It's easier to take care of roses when they are growing in a separate rose garden, but roses have far greater charm when grown as companions in mixed flowerbeds. Use climbing roses wherever possible to add vertical accents.

BULBS

Finish Planting Spring-Blooming Bulbs. If you bought bulbs this fall but didn't plant them when you should have, don't despair; you still have a little time to get them into pots or the ground. The **Rule of Thumb:** *Finish planting*

spring-flowering bulbs such as daffodils on or before Christmas Day. When planted later the flowers will be smaller and fewer. The exceptions are tulips and hyacinths (crocuses too, if you live in an interior zone). They need cold earth, so start planting them between Christmas and New Year's Day, unless there's a heat wave. If that occurs wait until early January; plant before the tenth.

Leave the bulbs in the refrigerator until you're ready to plant. If you choose to plant tulips in pots, keep the planted pots in a cool place and cover them with an upside-down cardboard box to cut out light and encourage the growth of good root systems. Water them often. When the foliage is 2 to 3 inches tall, remove the covering and bring the pots out into the sun. Try to keep the roots from heating up by shading the containers in cool foliage, or by double-potting. Water daily unless rains are adequate.

Tulips do well in half barrels and in the ground to the north of trees or houses. Study the shadow pattern annually, and plant them where the ground is cool and shady in winter and then sunny beginning in February or March. Or plant them in full or morning sun and shade the ground over them with a bulb cover, such as Johnny-jump-ups, paludosum daisies (*Chrysanthemum paludosum*), or violas. They respond well to a treatment of light liquid fertilizer, such as 1 tablespoon fish emulsion and 1 tablespoon Tiger Bloom (2-8-4) or other bloom formula per gallon of water. Apply once at planting time and again when the leaves show.

As mentioned previously, be sure to leave tulips and hyacinths in the refrigerator where they have been chilling for six weeks prior to planting, and don't take them out until you're ready to plant them. Once chilled, hyacinths grow well in the ground, planted 5 inches deep and 6 inches apart, or in shallow pots of fast-draining soil mix, planted just below or at the soil surface. Bury some bone meal under each bulb. (Keep the pots watered, cool, and darkened, as described above for tulips.) Or force them in pebbles and water or a special reusable "hyacinth glass," which keeps the roots immersed in water. Keep these forced ones cool and dark, under an upside-down cardboard box, until the tops are up 3 to 4 inches; then place them in a sunny window or outdoors in sun every day when the weather's warm (bring them in at night). Turn the ones on window ledges to make their stems grow straight.

Plant crocuses in either low pots or the ground. Because the flowers are low they often show up better in low-level pots. Nestle them among well-placed rocks and a few pebbles to add charm and keep the soil cool.

Lift Dahlias. When dahlias have gone totally dormant, in early December, dig up the tubers. First cut back the tops to 6 to 8 inches; then use a spade to slice down through the soil and loosen it in a circle 12 to 14 inches out from each plant. Finally, use a garden fork to carefully pry up the tuber, which you will find has now grown into a round clump of tubers, all attached to a central stem in the same way the spokes of a wheel are attached to the hub. Shake off the soil, cut the tops back to 2 inches, and lay the whole unseparated clump on newspaper in the sun to dry until evening. Continue the drying process for a day or two in a dry shady place, such as the floor of the garage. Then dust the clumps with bulb dust or sulfur and pack them, not touching each other, in perlite. Store them for the winter in a cool, dry area, in hanging baskets lined with newspaper or in boxes.

Divide the clumps in spring when growth begins and you can see the eyes (growth buds) beginning to form; cut each clump into individual sections. Each must have an eye. (Throw out the old center stalk.) Dust the cut portions in sulfur and allow them to callus off overnight. Plant each tuber separately. You may have extras to share with friends.

Prepare Amaryllis to Bloom. Amaryllis (*Hippeastrum*) bulbs are on sale at nurseries now; you can also purchase them from mail-order companies. Many are preplanted and already starting to grow. These are entertaining bulbs to grow for holiday color (they'll bloom for Christmas) and make excellent hostess gifts.

Place a preplanted amaryllis whose growth has begun in a sunny window and turn it daily so the stalk won't bend toward the light. Keep it well watered but not overly wet. If growth has not yet begun, water the plant and keep it cool and dark until growth begins; then move it into a warm, sunny location. A thick scape (stalk) will emerge from the bulb and shoot rapidly upward, often to 15 inches. Sometimes two will appear, each one bearing three or four spectacular blossoms. When the bloom begins to show color, move the plant to a cooler spot, where it will last longer.

After the flowers fade cut them off, but leave the tall scape in place until you can see that the juices have gone back down into the bulb. Then cut it off. This nourishes the bulb. Put the plant outside in semishade for the summer. Feed it occasionally and protect it from snails and slugs. In September lift it from the container and let the root ball dry out. Cut off the leaves when they die. Brush the dry root ball with bulb dust or sulfur, slip it back into the pot, allow it three months of complete dormancy, and then start the process over; this time it will bloom in spring. (Once an amaryllis

Long-Handled Scoops Simplify Measuring.
Many fertilizers require measuring by cups, half-cups, quarter-cups, and tablespoons. To make the job safer and easier, purchase a sturdy set of plastic measuring cups, a few plastic measuring spoons, and a bundle of sturdy green bamboo stakes. Use florist's wire or package wrapping tape to firmly bind the handle of each measuring cup and spoon to the end of a sturdy green bamboo stake.

Use two stakes tied together for 1-cup and larger-size scoops. Place these home-made long-handled measuring tools with the stick ends down inside an old umbrella stand or other heavy narrow container next to the potting bench. When mixing liquids, you'll find it much easier to measure the liquid fertilizer correctly and then to stir the mixture with the spoon end of the stick.

has been forced to bloom at Christmas you can't repeat the process.)

If you purchase a bare, unplanted amaryllis bulb now, choose one that has just begun to sprout but has not yet pushed up a flower scape. Plant it in rich, fast-draining soil mix in a small pot—just 4 inches wider than the bulb. Before putting the bulb in the pot, though, place a few tablespoons of bone meal in the soil in the bottom. Cover this with a little plain potting soil. Plant the bulb with its upper half above soil level. Water it and treat it as described above. Repot amaryllis bulbs annually into the next size of container.

WINTER COLOR

Permanent landscape plants that are colorful in winter enliven gardens and make good gifts. Choices include purple princess flower (*Tibouchina urvilleana*); silver-leafed princess flower (*T. heteromalla*), which is easier to grow; flame vine (*Pyrostegia venusta*); marmalade bush (*Streptosolen jamesonii*); Carolina jessamine (*Gelsemium sempervirens*, an attractive, evergreen, yellow-flowered vine though unfortunately poisonous not only to us but also to honeybees); variously hued New Zealand tea trees (*Leptospermum scoparium*); and strawberry tree (*Arbutus unedo*). The last two are among our finest slow-growing, drought-resistant plants that can be grown as shrubs and eventually become small trees. Both develop interestingly shaped trunks. Strawberry tree bears its flowers and colorful fruit now. (The fruit is edible but not flavorful.) There are striking dwarf forms that grow naturally into eye-catching shapes.

ANNUAL AND PERENNIAL FLOWERS

Care for Cool-Season Flowers. If you planted annual flowerbeds in September or October, by now the garden should be full of color. If not, remember that the trick is to get things into bloom before Christmas and they'll bloom all winter. Once cold nights begin, cold-season annual plants slow down and won't bloom until the weather warms up, in February or March. Of course, some plants are naturally programmed to bloom in late winter, spring, or early summer. We don't expect them to bloom ahead of time. But among the flowers you can expect to be colorful prior to Christmas in most zones are calendula, dianthus, flowering cabbage and flowering kale (ornamental members of the cole or cabbage family that are grown for their colorful foliage rather than flowers), Iceland poppy, linaria, nemesia, paludosum daisy, primroses of all kinds, pansy, schizanthus, dwarf stock, sweet alyssum, sweet pea, sweet William, viola, and wallflower (*Erysimum cheiri*). With the exception of linaria and sweet pea, feed these plants regularly to speed them into bloom, with a liquid fertilizer high in nitrogen and bloom ingredients such as Metanaturals Professional Organic Bloom Formula (1-5-5), Tiger Bloom (2-8-4), Earth Juice Bloom, Super Tea Organic (5-5-1), or liquid guano. As you can see by this, there is a wide range of such products at nurseries and over the Internet, but you may have to hunt and also read the labels. You could also make your own balanced liquid fertilizer by mixing 2 tablespoons fish emulsion, 2 tablespoons of fish bone meal, and 2 tablespoons of Sul-Po-Mag (0-0-22) in a 2-gallon watering can filled with water. Stir well before applying. Sul-Po-Mag (0-0-22) dissolves easily in water. Fish bone meal won't entirely dissolve, but some of it will.

Dwarf delphiniums ('Dwarf Blue Mirror') and dwarf foxgloves ('Foxy') bloom in fall or early winter shortly after planting. Cut off spikes that have bloomed now, and follow up with fertilizer. Delphiniums will bloom again in spring; dwarf foxglove 'Foxy' will also if it has sprouts that haven't yet flowered. (Tall varieties of delphiniums, foxgloves, and stock also bloom in spring.)

When planting for winter color in the ground or containers, choose pansies over dwarf snapdragons, which are prone to caterpillars and rust. Make a note to plant seeds of giant rust-resistant snapdragons next year in October.

Care for Biennials. Early December is your last chance for moving biennial plants that have sprouted from seeds and sprung up in the wrong spots. Biennials are plants that grow in the first year after planting and then bloom, set seed, and die in their second year of growth. If you transplant them after winter solstice, when the tilt of the earth's axis is at its farthest distance from the sun, sometime between December 20 and December 23, biennials interpret the move as a fresh start and won't bloom for another whole year. The sooner you move them the more strongly they get the message that they were planted in one year so they can flower in the next. It's better to do this job in October, so don't move any biennials unless you absolutely have to. Among biennials you might be growing are Canterbury bells (*Campanula medium*), tall varieties of foxglove (*Digitalis* 'Shirley' and others), hollyhock, sweet William (*Dianthus barbatus*), and Madeira geranium (*G. madierense*). It doesn't take long to transplant just one or two biennials, but first use a trowel or a small spade to dig up and prepare a planting hole by mixing in a little aged compost and a handful of organic all-purpose or flower fertilizer so it will be beneath and around the root of the plant you're moving. Then dig up the plant and settle it immediately into the new hole, pushing the roots down gently with your hands, never with your foot. Water thoroughly after transplanting and water it again the next day, then keep an eye on it for a week or two to make sure it doesn't dry out.

Deal with Frost. What if you planted early but nothing's in bloom? One possible reason is that you live in an interior zone and cold nights have held things back. If this is the case, don't worry: You'll just get flowers a little later. Some gardeners feel that frost is a natural kind of pinching, making their plants stronger and bushier in the long run and keeping things from growing too rank. Trial and error is the best way to find out which plants perform best in your climate zone, under local conditions, and with the care you give your plants.

In very cold low-lying gardens, like those in Zone 20, frosts kill some of the more tender bedding plants such as primroses, pansies, and cineraria. The best bets for winter color under such conditions are hardier plants like flowering cabbage and kale, tall calendulas, snapdragons, and bulbs, particularly paper whites and oxalis. Stock and many wildflowers will survive the cold winter and bloom in spring.

It's important even in coastal zones to protect tender annuals, especially florist's cineraria *(Senecio x hybridus)*, from frost. This plant can fool gardeners because it so obviously loves cold weather and grows best and fastest in it, but frost "melts" its leaves and turns them black or brown. It actually prefers night temperatures of 45° to 50°F with a daytime increase of no more than five or ten degrees. When growing cineraria in your garden, cover the beds with a tent of sheets or beach towels, supported on bamboo poles, on nights when frost is expected. Take off the covers first thing in the morning, before the sun hits the bed. (Cineraria is well worth this trouble.) Plants under a tree or overhang usually survive unharmed. Continue to feed cineraria for growth.

Florist's cinerarias *(Senecio x hybridus)* were developed in the nineteenth century for growing in greenhouses. One of their wild ancestors is a blue or purple cineraria from the Canary Islands called *S. cruentus* or *Pericallis cruentus*, which is easier to grow outdoors in coastal gardens if you can find it. Annie's Annuals and Perennials sells it as *Senecio stellata*, Giovanka's select. Botanical gardens sometimes sell the seeds and plants are occasionally sold. This wild type of cineraria has leaves 6 to 8 inches across and grows 2 to 3 feet tall, bearing 1- to 2-foot-wide clusters of blue or purple flowers often with a white or contrasting-colored band on the petals. The flowers self-seed readily but are not invasive. Just one small plant of *S. cruentus* purchased now at a botanical garden and put into the ground early this month could give you this species forever. Canary Island cineraria grows best on the north side of houses or in the shade of open trees and, if happy, will come back from seeds every year.

QUICK TIP

How to Attach a Vine to a Smooth Wall or Fence. *To make inexpensive invisible wall hangers for vines, glob dots of clear silicone sealant where needed. Stick the center of a short piece of twist tie into each glob. Allow it to dry overnight. Come back the next day and tie up the vine.*

Grow Plants in Adequate Light. Another factor inhibiting winter bloom is too much shade. New gardeners are sometimes unaware of how the movement of the sun in winter creates shade to the north of trees and buildings where it didn't exist in summer or fall. (See page 259 for an explanation of the movements of shade.) If you have this problem, wait until the sun comes back in spring; your flowers will then bloom. If you have plants such as malacoides (fairy) or polyanthus primroses that are full grown but just sitting there doing nothing, try feeding them with a liquid organic fertilizer high in bloom ingredients such as Fox Farm Tiger Bloom (2-8-4) or any other high-bloom formula once a week during December. This can stimulate bloom in areas that are too shady. Once flowers open, switch back to a fertilizer high in both bloom and growth ingredients.

In the future, use these shady areas to plant cyclamen, cineraria, bulbs, azaleas, and obconica primroses, which will bloom in darker shade than other primroses. Under north-facing overhangs clivia and camellias are good choices for winter bloom. If plants in containers aren't blooming, move them into more sun and continue to fertilize them with a product high in both nitrogen and bloom ingredients.

In Coastal Zones Plant Annual Flowers Even Now.
It's too late this year to plant annual flowers in most interior zones. But let's say you've just moved into a house in a mild or coastal zone and it has some bare beds that need filling, or you were too busy in fall to tackle the job. You don't have to wait until spring to plant winter and spring flowers. That's the joy of living here. Seeds that can be planted now include African daisy *(Dimorphotheca)*, ageratum, calendula, California poppy, clarkia, coreopsis, forget-me-not, gaillardia, godetia, hollyhock, larkspur, lavatera, nemophila, annual phlox *(Phlox drummondii)*, schizanthus, Shasta daisy, sweet alyssum, and mixed wildflowers. You'll just get later bloom, and some plants, such as larkspur, may not grow quite as large. Follow the planting directions beginning on pages 324 and 351. Plant early in the month, and be sure to plant in full sun. These seeds won't germinate in partial shade, especially now.

Sprinkle the bed faithfully every morning until the seeds come up and then water as necessary. For a faster effect, in full sun put in bedding plants of calendula, candytuft *(Iberis)*, columbine, coral bells, English daisy *(Bellis perennis)*, Iceland poppy, nemesia, pansy, polyanthus primrose, sweet alyssum, sweet William, viola, and wallflower. For semishade use cyclamen as well as malacoides or obconica primrose. Put these in a flowerbed now, and much of the bed should be in bloom before April.

Care for Perennials.
Many perennial plants are in total dormancy at this time of year, particularly in interior zones. If your garden is subject to heavy frost, cover the ground over tender plants with mulch. But gardeners who live in valleys or on mesa tops where frost hits also have the advantage of growing a wider range of those plants we so often think of as "eastern" here in California. Now is the time they can get the winter chill they need for best performance.

By month's end when blooms have faded on *Hypoestes aristata* 'Lavender Cloud', cut flower spikes down to 16 inches in height and shape the plant. Look around the garden for those that may have seeded themselves last fall and move them now or next spring into sun or partial shade.

The ubiquitous heliotrope *(Heliotropium arborescens)*, an old-fashioned plant beloved for its fragrance and purple or white flowers, needs protection from frost—grow it in pots if necessary. It blooms throughout winter in mild climates given adequate water and good drainage; soggy roots mean quick death. Well-grown specimens of heliotrope are knockouts next to pink roses or plants with silvery leaves, like curry plant *(Helichrysum italicum)*, but there's nothing worse than an unkempt heliotrope. When their flowers and leaves fade, the shriveled black or brown foliage ruins the appearance of the whole plant. So either deadhead and groom heliotrope assiduously or don't grow it. Pinching it back often will also keep it growing and blooming.

Brunfelsia pauciflora 'Macrantha', usually sold as 'Royal Purple', is an exception to all other plants that I can think of. It likes a double shot of nitrogen twice in winter during the coldest time of the year, treatment that would kill any other plant. Grow this spectacular subshrub in well-amended acid soil, in the ground if there are no competing tree roots, or in pots or hanging baskets. When treated right it literally drips with blossoms in June and it will bloom in more shade than almost any other plant, including clivia. The trick is to now drench the soil around the roots with a nitrogen fertilizer—fish emulsion is ideal—mixed, believe it or not, double-strength. Do the job again in January.

When other late bloomers like Japanese anemones, lion's tail *(Leonotis leonurus)*, common sneezeweed *(Helenium autumnale)*, and *Verbena rigida* stop blooming, cut back the bloom spikes down to basal foliage and remove dead and dying portions. Remove the old bloom spikes and dead growth from lamb's ears. It's best to cut baby's breath *(Gypsophila paniculata)* almost to the ground at the end of December to produce a compact plant with strong flowering stems next season. Deadhead and cut back *Knautia macedonica*, a scabiosa look-alike (often incorrectly labeled) that blooms later than scabiosa, has wine-colored flowers on taller stems, and has more character though it is rangier. Look for *Loropetalum chinense*, with fringelike ruby pink blossoms and burgundy or variegated foliage. Vibrantly colorful now in winter, it blooms heavily again in spring and lightly throughout the year, needs acid soil and good drainage—like an azalea—but with full sun along the coast, partial shade inland. These long-lived, easy-to-grow plants work well near entryways, and new, supposedly improved varieties are coming out often. Some varieties can grow tall; all are brittle—don't put

it where it can get hit by an edging machine. Also for winter color is *Cestrum* 'Newellii', though it blooms all year with red flowers followed by red berries. It's often still going strong now. Cut cestrums back after each wave of bloom to force fresh foliage and keep them shaped. (If burned by frost, they soon bounce back.) Though cestrums' fruit and sap are poisonous to humans, their tubular flowers attract hummingbirds. The pink variety *Cestrum elegans smithii* is particularly choice, good in a narrow bed against a wall and attractive near swimming pools.

PRUNING

A number of plants can be pruned this month, but don't prune such tender or tropical plants as bougainvillea, eugenia, hibiscus, lantana, natal plum, or philodendron. Pruning tropicals now will stimulate growth that could be nipped by frost.

Deciduous Fruit Trees. Once deciduous fruit trees have gone dormant and dropped their leaves, they can be pruned. You can do this job now or wait until next month. Every type of deciduous fruit tree needs different treatment. Personally, I study more than one reliable manual on pruning western trees before tackling this complicated and all-important job, because they all say things slightly differently and in various lengths on the various trees; what is omitted in one book may be covered in another. (The pruning of deciduous fruit trees is discussed in more detail beginning on page 42, and pruning in November on page 373.) Follow up your pruning with dormant spray. Dormant spray is best used more than once, so even if you don't prune this month it's wise

How to Make the Classic Southern California Succulent Wreath

▶ Gather about a hundred cuttings and little rooted plants of various succulents. Good candidates are panda plant *(Kalanchoe tomentosa)* and the many different species and cultivars of crassulas, echeverias, and sedum.

▶ Let the cuttings sit for a day or two to callus off so they'll root and not rot.

▶ Purchase two wire-form rings, green florists' wire, and fern pins from a crafts or florists' supply store. You'll also need clear vinyl fishing line.

▶ Line one ring with premoistened sphagnum moss (or a substitute, discussed on page 407). Fill this with potting soil mixed with 2 tablespoons of dry balanced organic fertilizer. Wad more sphagnum moss on top.

▶ Cover this ring with the other, (empty) one and wire the two together. Clip off excess moss on the outside to make it smooth.

▶ Make a hole with a chopstick, through the sphagnum moss, to the same depth as the length of the stem of a cutting, insert the cutting, and secure it with a fern pick. Vary the types of succulents, the textures, and the colors as you work, fitting them together closely.

▶ It takes three months for cuttings to anchor themselves, so tie nylon fishing twine to the frame and wind it around as you go to make cuttings more secure.

▶ Leave room for a bow at the bottom. Place a hook on the back of the wreath, and hang it.

▶ The finished wreath should look like a piece of Della Robbia pottery. (Rose-shaped echeverias, especially, provide this look.)

▶ After the holidays, hang the wreath in semi-shade where rains will provide adequate moisture during the winter and spring. During summer and fall squirt it with a hose occasionally, or soak it in water once a week. Recycle your wreath for several years by snipping off leggy cuttings in November or December and replacing them closer to the form, and by filling in with fresh cuttings. Feed it occasionally with a well-diluted fish emulsion. (The pros and cons of sphagnum moss and possible substitutes for it are discussed on page 407.)

to use dormant spray now (as described beginning on page 57) on all deciduous fruit trees and the many ornamental trees that drop their leaves in winter. Many organic gardeners no longer use dormant spray because trees growing in humus-filled soil that's totally free from pesticides and synthetic fertilizers are protected from diseases by natural organisms, but if you're new to organic gardening and not yet confident in the health of your trees, it would be wise to continue using dormant spray in winter. Use an organic product such as Bonide Organic Lime Sulfur Spray, except on apricot trees. For apricot trees, substitute fixed copper or Bordeaux mix; lime sulfur can burn the buds and bark of apricots.

Grapes. Prune grapes this month. There are three major pruning methods, depending on the type grown. Young plants of each type must be pruned differently from those that are mature. (The *Sunset Pruning Handbook* contains diagrams and a good basic explanation of this subject. Also see R. Sanford Martin's *How to Prune Fruit Trees*, which you can find at nurseries.) Save the trimmings to make ornamental wreaths and baskets. Start a wreath by wiring one bendy stem into a circle; then wind others around it. Add ribbons, dried flowers, and berries, and use the wreath in holiday decorations.

Low-Chill Raspberries. Before the arrival in 1978 of the low-chill red raspberry called 'Oregon 1030' (also called 'California'), Southern Californians couldn't grow real red raspberries like the ones that grow in cold-winter climates.

Now several additional varieties have been discovered or developed that will bear good crops here, including 'Bababerry', 'Fallgold', 'Rosanna', and 'San Diego'. These "subtropical" raspberries are now grown here commercially as well as in home gardens. They require different and much easier pruning than other types of cane barriers.

All low-chill raspberry varieties bear their berries just about year-round on new wood that they put out almost continually. The simple pruning method for all low-chill types of raspberry is to cut all the canes down to 3 to 4 inches, now or in January. New growth will spring from the ground. Dig up the suckers

How to Make a Miniature Western Ranch

- Buy two 1-gallon-size Tam junipers (*Juniperus Sabina* 'Tamariscifolia'), one gallon-size lavender starflower (*Grewia occidentalis*), and a flat of Irish moss (*Sagina subulata*). Purchase tiny toy cowboys, a fence, a bridge, horses, and wildlife at a cake-decorating store. You'll also need red plastic plates, an old (preferably brown) plastic wastebasket, a few small rocks, and a small bag of blue gravel available at aquarium supply stores.

- Make several holes in the bottom of a flat 18-inch plastic dish designed to fit under a large planting tub. (The Quick Tip on page 409 tells how. Pottery dishes are too heavy and too shallow, and it's impossible to drill holes in them.) Cover each hole with a piece of broken crockery.

- Cut the walls of a barn from the centers of the red plastic plates. Cut the roof out of the plastic wastebasket. Fix these together inside the barn with tear-proof package-wrapping tape.

- Fill the bottom of the dish with a 2- to 3-inch layer of potting soil. Shape the junipers into bonsai "cypress trees" and the lavender starflower into an "apple tree" by pruning the roots and clipping off excess foliage from the trunks and branches. Plant these in the dish, and surround them with rocks.

- Plant a "meadow" of Irish moss, cut to fit. Cut a winding streambed through it and fill this with the blue aquarium gravel. Add the barn, cowboys, fence, bridge, and animals.

- Water the plants and let the dish drain. Keep it in the house for one week if desired; thereafter keep it outdoors in sun or semishade. Water it regularly, feed it occasionally, and prune as necessary. In a year or two, take out the bonsai, reprune their roots, and replace them.

to form new rows of plants; if you let your existing rows get too wide, they'll become unmanageable.

Fertilize raspberries in spring when they start to grow, with an evenly balanced organic fertilizer, or in early spring mulch the ground down the sides of the rows with a generous layer of well-aged horse manure or other manure of your choice, and give them plenty of water. Spray them regularly with BT against caterpillars, who relish raspberry leaves. (If you didn't prune other cane berries, like blackberries, boysenberries, and loganberries last month, do it now, as directed on page 373.)

Native Plants. Native plants can be pruned any time during the winter growing season, with the exception of ceanothus, which is better pruned after bloom. Some gardeners prefer not to prune natives at all except to remove dead and diseased branches. Other gardeners prune to show the "good bones" of certain plants. A little judicious pruning can often uncover an artistic shape that's already there but hidden by foliage. Remove spent stems from Matilija poppy *(Romneya coulteri)* to encourage new growth and heavier spring flowering. Lemonade berry *(Rhus integrifolia)* and sugarbush *(R. ovata)* can be easily shaped into hedges, espaliers, or small trees.

Wisteria. If you didn't prune wisteria in summer, do it now. Study the buds first. Small, narrow buds are leaf buds; round, fatter buds, often found on short stubby growth called "spurs," are flower buds. Don't cut off the flower buds or flower-bearing spurs. Prune off long "streamers" or "twiners" (thin, young stems that grew rapidly this year). Carefully untangle them from older wood if necessary

A Freewheeling Way to "Bonsai" Nursery Plants

Cut off half the roots of a well-shaped 1-gallon-size Tam juniper removed from its container. Cut off unwanted branches, bare the trunk, and clip all foliage from under the branches, leaving the top foliage intact. Choose one strong root near the top of the root ball, and wind it tightly around the trunk just beneath the soil line. Plant the juniper in a Japanese bonsai pot. As the root you wound around the trunk grows, it will slow the growth of the plant.

and cut them back to two or three buds to stimulate the growth of more flower spurs. Retain twiners going in desired directions and tie them loosely in place. If an established wisteria never blooms, cut into the ground around the plant with a sharp spade to prune the roots. This may stimulate bloom, perhaps not next spring but the year following. (Next year prune and train wisteria throughout summer, as explained in detail on page 294.)

HOMEGROWN HOLIDAY DECORATIONS

Look around the garden to see what can be used to make the house look festive for the holidays. Some gardeners recycle tubbed pine trees, bringing them indoors year after year to do the annual stint as Christmas trees. Gardens can also proved sweet-smelling evergreen cuttings from pines, firs, cedars, and cypresses. Red berries from pyracantha and toyon and the leaves and berries of English holly are naturals, though not as long lasting as conifer foliage.

(Florist's supply stores carry products that can keep berries and foliage fresh longer.) Cuttings of succulents such as jade plant and echeverias last all month and mix well with ornaments. The most spectacular way to use succulents is for making topiary and wreaths (see instructions in the box on page 404).

Other possibilities to dye, paint, glitter, or leave plain are pinecones, strawflowers, bunches of dried herbs, thistles, agapanthus stalks, old twisted leaves of bird-of-paradise (great in arrangements when sprayed gold), and the decorative seedpods of plants including jacaranda, certain acacias, lotus, and eucalyptus (the heavy pods of flame eucalyptus [*Eucalyptus ficifolia*] are especially prized for their unique shape). For a last-minute touch, tape fresh red geraniums to packages; they last only a day. A tall dried stalk of century plant with the seedpods still in place can be held upright by rocks hidden in an earthenware tub. Festoon it with decorations for a southwestern-style Christmas tree.

Finding Substitutes for Sphagnum Moss and Peat Moss.

As recently as ten years ago most gardeners and growers, regardless of philosophy, used sphagnum moss (a live moss harvested from rainforests and northern hillsides) and peat moss (partially decomposed sphagnum moss or sedge mined from ancient peat bogs) without much thought for environmental consequences. But now that sphagnum moss and sheet moss, a similar species, are being harvested faster than they can regrow, using them has become a matter of individual conscience. Live sphagnum moss in rainy habitats absorbs carbon dioxide, gives off oxygen, and absorbs rainfall like a sponge and slowly releases it to plants, streams, and lakes. Though peat bogs are plentiful, it takes thousands of

years for a peat bog to grow. Existing peat bogs have many environmental benefits, while mining them releases CO_2. Instead of using peat moss, most gardeners and farmers now substitute coir (pronounced "koy-er"), or coconut fiber, which is plentiful and renewable. Coir liners for wire baskets drain well and last longer than sphagnum moss, and ground coir fiber is a clean substitute for peat moss in planting mediums, despite the fact that coir has a neutral pH; it's not acid like peat moss. It's more difficult to find a good substitute for sphagnum moss or sheet moss when lining wire forms for topiary, succulent wreaths, or ornamental baskets for indoor use. Thus instructions for many holiday crafts and gifts often call for the use of sphagnum moss or sheet moss. (If for any reason you wish to use moistened sphagnum moss for any purpose, be sure to wear rubber gloves when handling it, and do not let it come in contact with cuts or abrasions.)

Some substitutes for sphagnum moss include softened and preserved, spring-green reindeer moss (*Cladonia rangiferina*), a product of Norway, but reindeer moss, besides being expensive and in small bunches, is a staple food of caribou and also a human food in the far north. Reindeer moss regrows slowly if overgrazed or overharvested. "Super moss" is a different species of moss than sphagnum moss, more like mosses in our own gardens, which have been collected in small sheets, preserved, and treated to retain more green. Sheet moss is still another type of wild forest moss. Spanish moss, a bromeliad that hangs from trees in the Deep South and Caribbean forests, is sold either in its normal gray form or dyed green. Spanish moss is a safely renewable resource, good for lining ornamental baskets but not for lining wire forms, as is excelsior, a wood product sometimes dyed green and used for packing fruits. Several manufacturers make various types of artificial green moss sheeting. Green moss sheeting works well in a number of applications, but it's not biodegradable. Coir matting is too thick for making succulent wreaths but good for lining baskets. EarthWorks Gorilla Hair and similar products (shredded and matted cedar bark used as ornamental mulch), and palm fiber from home-grown Senegal date palm trees *(Phoenix reclinata)* and other palms work well for some applications but not for succulent wreaths. A sheet of woven green shade cloth, useful as a liner to keep soil mix from sifting out of the bottom of seed flats, may be the best substitute for sphagnum moss when lining a wire wreath form for succulent wreaths.

If instead of using sphagnum moss, you wish to line a wire wreath with green shade cloth or with artificial green moss sheeting from a florist's supply store, first lay the wire wreath on top of the shade cloth or artificial moss sheeting and, using the wreath as a pattern, cut two doughnut-shaped circles out of the cloth, making them large enough so they can be fitted into your wire forms. Push these liners down into the forms and wire them into place with florist's wire. Cut off the excess cloth and fill one lined ring with premoistened water-retentive potting soil, mounding it up so it will fill both forms, as described in the instructions on page 404. Once the forms are wired together with the potting soil in the middle, it's quite easy before inserting each plant to make a small hole with a paring knife through the shade cloth or artificial moss liner, and then use a chopstick to make a depression in the soil mix to hold the stem of the cutting. Woven shade cloth has a beneficial tendency to close up around the stems of the succulents as you push them through the holes into the potting soil inside the ring. (An optional step is to line the shade cloth

with a thin layer of "gorilla hair," before putting in the potting soil. In that case use a chopstick to push aside the threads, which helps hold the soil mix inside in the same way moss does. Cedar gorilla hair" rots quickly when kept damp, but by then the succulents will be well rooted. Soak the ring in diluted fish emulsion to provide enough nitrogen for the plants. Once rotted, gorilla hair will give back to the plants any nitrogen that it's absorbed in order to rot.)

GIFTS FOR AND FROM THE GARDEN

Nurseries and garden supply stores are great places to do Christmas shopping. Lines are usually short, parking easy, stocking stuffers abound, and children can find inexpensive gifts for grownups such as a rain gauge or a measuring cup. Some ideas: tools of all kinds; gadgets such as thermometers that record high and low temperatures (good even for non-gardeners); soil augers; tensiometers; heat cables for sprouting seeds; ornamental objects such as bronze faucets, birdbaths, and garden sculptures; houseplants; bare-root roses; fruit trees; soil-test kits; miniature greenhouses, and hummingbird feeders.

For a personal gift that doesn't need wrapping choose a sturdy basket for bringing in vegetables or flowers. Stuff it with a colorful apron, a pair of gloves, a trowel, a book or two, a few packs of seed, and a potted plant.

Make a Child's Fantasy Garden for Christmas or Hanukkah. A dish garden with a playful theme can spark the imagination of a child and create an interest in gardening at an early age. Make one yourself and give it to the child to play with. Better yet, give the ingredients with a promise to help make it. Older children can be given a construction kit with a set of instructions. (If you go this route stick to succulents, and give cuttings rather than plants. They're easier to deal with.)

Arrangements using houseplants and succulents can be kept indoors for as long as a year. For these, don't make a hole in the bottom of the container; put a layer of fine gravel on the bottom mixed with agricultural charcoal, to keep drainage water pure. Some possible themes: zoo, tropical jungle, Mickey Mouse garden, space stations among weirdly shaped succulents, forests of ferns and miniature cycads inhabited by dinosaurs, Indians stalking cowboys in a desert scene of rocks and succulents, or a western ranch (see the box on page 405) complete with trees and stream.

Make Homemade Gifts for Adults. Start early to pot such bedding plants as primroses, pansies, and miniature cyclamen in baskets and containers for holiday and hostess gifts. Line baskets with dry Spanish moss and then line the moss with plastic. For outdoor arrangements, make holes in the bottom of the plastic lining and fill it with potting soil and bedding plants in bud, fitting them closely together for the best effect. Keep the basket in sun and feed the plants to get them blooming before the holidays.

For indoor arrangements make no holes in the plastic; place a layer of gravel for drainage and agricultural charcoal to absorb impurities in the lined basket before adding soil mix. Then fill it with small houseplants, varying the colors and shapes. If gray-leafed ivy is available, drape it over the side. For a finishing touch, pop a red African violet in one corner. Keep indoor baskets in bright light but out of direct sun, and feed them with high-bloom fertilizer.

☀ QUICK TIP

How to Make Holes in the Bottom of a Plastic Container. *Steadily hold a plastic container upside down over a lit candle until a spot visibly softens; it will bubble up slightly and may change color. Then lay the container right-side up on a wooden board. Use a hammer and chisel to cut a square or triangular hole.*

Another idea is to make an outdoor entryway arrangement. Spray-paint a basket white, add chains for hanging, and fill it with poinsettias, kalanchoe, cyclamen, or an azalea. Or make dishes of succulents from your garden. In a terra-cotta pot combine driftwood with jade plant, gray-foliaged shore juniper (*Juniperus rigida conferta*) draped over the side, and pink cyclamen. You might also fill a footed Mexican pot with cacti and euphorbias plus a rock or two, and cover the surface of the soil with gravel. Or pot individual herbs, and present them in a wooden crate.

HERB GARDENING

Herbs have been cultivated, used, and treasured by men and women for thousands of years. Many are ornamental as well as useful. Even a few of them can add charm, history, and mystique to any garden. You can grow enough culinary herbs, such as marjoram, parsley, rosemary, sage, and thyme, in your garden for your Christmas turkey, or plan to plant a whole garden of herbs next spring.

You can now, if you wish, plant culinary herbs in individual pots and grow them indoors on a sunny kitchen windowsill, and then, in spring, plant them outdoors. Pot the 2-inch nursery size into 4-inch containers when you purchase them; then repot them into 6-inch containers as soon as their roots fill the smaller size. When you grow herbs indoors they grow fast at first and then slow down. You can keep them to size by pruning off leaves now and then for cooking. Too much fertilizer makes herbs overgrow and lose their savor, but when they're grown in containers they do need occasional light fertilizing because potting soils are low in nutrients.

In spring plant culinary herbs outdoors in the ground in your vegetable garden mixed in with any garden plants, in a special herb garden, or in a small space right outside your kitchen door. One organized and artful way to grow them in a small space is to lay an old ladder or wagon wheel on the ground and plant in the spaces. (When you clip leaves from an herb for cooking, choose which ones you take so that you're also controlling the plant's size and shape.) Another way to grow just a few herbs is to plant them in a strawberry pot or hanging basket. (For easy care, attach containers to a drip system.) Here are some basic facts about herbs:

- An herb is any plant used for medicine, fragrance, or flavoring. (In botany the word *herb* means any nonwoody plant. In cold-winter climates all these plants die down in winter, but many biennial and perennial herbs are evergreen when grown here.)
- *Not all herbs are edible. Some medicinal herbs, such as comfrey, pennyroyal, rue, and tansy, contain toxic chemicals. They must not be taken internally by anyone and especially not by pregnant women.*
- Fresh culinary herbs from your garden are not only tastier than the dried herbs you can

buy but safer. (Dried herbs purchased in markets are often imported and have frequently been sprayed with chemicals not allowed in the United States.)

- Herbs thrive in our mild climate and adapt to most soils, but they prefer good drainage, which you can provide by growing them in rock gardens or raised beds.
- Unless you grow your herbs in containers, as described above, don't fertilize them; it makes them less flavorful. (An exception is an herb like sage that's been in the ground for several years, has often given its leaves to you, and shows an obvious decline in vigor. You can pull it out, amend the soil, and replace it; or you can feed it lightly and mulch its roots to bring it back.)
- Some herbs, such as mint and watercress, need lots of water. Others, such as rosemary and society garlic, are drought-resistant plants; these two are grown as ornamentals more often than as culinary herbs.

VERMICOMPOSTING

Vermicomposting, or worm composting, is an efficient way to recycle kitchen scraps back into the ground instead of sending them down the garbage disposal or to the dump. In order to begin you will need a worm bin, bedding, water, worms, and food scraps. Some gardeners build a wooden bin similar to a raised bed but with a lid on top and air holes drilled in the sides. Wooden bins stay warmer in winter and cooler in summer, but you can also purchase a ready-made plastic bin especially made for vermicomposting. Commercially made worm bins of recycled plastic come in many sizes and shapes and are sold through catalogues, the Internet, and some recycle centers. Having chosen a design suitable for your needs and built or purchased the bin, install it in a shady place where the temperature remains between 55° and 77°F. Follow the directions that come with your worm bin. These differ depending on design and size, but basically they all include filling the bin with bedding materials—usually shredded paper—keeping the bedding moist, purchasing a supply of redworms or composting worms, and adding the correct amount of kitchen scraps to feed the worms without overheating the bin. A well-maintained worm bin can produce a steady supply of earthworm castings ideal for use in an organic garden. Once your original population of worms has begun to multiply you will also have plenty of worms for beginning new boxes or for spreading worms along with their castings to improve garden soil.

LAWN CARE

Cool-Season Lawns. Feed cool-season lawns every four to six weeks during the growing season with an organic fertilizer recommended for lawns. If the grass blades turn red-brown and brown dust gets on your shoes, it's rust. Don't spray the lawn with chemicals; just feed it. The rust will clear right up. Mow weekly and water when rains aren't adequate.

Warm-Season Lawns. Most warm-season lawns, such as Bermuda and zoysia, are dormant now and require little, if any, care. Once the grass has gone completely brown and stopped growing, you can turn off the irrigation water and stop mowing. The exception is Bermuda that's overseeded with winter ryegrass. Treat this like cool-season grasses, feeding it to keep it growing and mowing it to keep it looking nice. If we have warm weather, St. Augustine

may continue to grow; mow it if needed. Once the weather gets cold it won't need mowing.

VEGETABLE GARDENING

December is an exciting time in the vegetable garden because most winter crops are in full swing, and some are starting to produce. As crops are harvested, plant more. Among crops that can be planted this month are artichokes, asparagus 'UC-157', beets, broccoli, Brussels sprouts, cabbage, carrots, cauliflower, celery (see the box on page 412), kale, kohlrabi, head lettuce, leaf lettuce, mesclun, peas, potatoes, radishes, Swiss chard, and turnips.

Tie the leaves over the heads of cauliflower as soon as they begin to make a head in order to prevent the curds from turning green, and watch them carefully; once cauliflowers begin to expand, they grow rapidly to maturity. Purple cauliflower doesn't need this blanching (it tastes like broccoli). Some cauliflower is "self-blanching"—the leaves naturally cover the heads. Even so, tie the leaves together and you'll get a better product in the end. Occasionally gardeners have a problem with cauliflower "buttoning": A tiny little curd forms prematurely, the leaves stay small, and you never get a big head. This can result from buying stressed plants at a nursery or from temperatures below 40°F, insufficient nitrogen, too much salt in the soil, or letting the plants go dry.

Take off the bottom sprouts and bottom leaves from Brussels sprouts. Control aphids with insecticidal soap and beneficial insects. Cut broccoli as soon as it makes a head, and leave the stalk in the ground to produce side sprouts. (See page 76 for more about harvesting cole crops.) Pull beets, carrots, kohlrabi, and turnips while they're still young and tender.

Pick peas to keep them coming. Start harvesting the outside stalks of celery. Harvest outside lettuce leaves as needed or cut off the whole head. Harvest mesclun by cutting with scissors or by pulling up whole plants, as described on page 108). (Leave the stalk in the ground and feed and water it; it'll grow another head.) Control slugs on celery, lettuce, and mesclun.

Side-dress rows with organic fertilizer, according to the individual needs of vegetables, to keep them going. In general, if you're planting from seed, begin when the plants are 2 to 3 inches high to side-dress the rows with organic fertilizer every six weeks, or begin then to feed them once a week with liquid fertilizer such as diluted fish emulsion, compost tea, or manure tea. When you're growing vegetables from transplants, you should usually side-dress the rows with additional fertilizer six weeks after planting. Quick crops like radishes will need no additional fertilizer if you fertilized the soil, as you should have done, prior to planting. Give long-term crops, like broccoli and Brussels sprouts, additional fertilizer at intervals of six weeks throughout their growing season. Onions grow best with slightly more frequent and lighter doses of fertilizer. Because of this, liquid fertilizers work particularly well for them. Thin your onions by month's end and transplant the thinnings into another row. Don't neglect to weed them regularly. Onions have shallow roots and therefore they're more likely to be stunted by weeds than most other crops. If you plant them too closely they'll even stunt each other and you'll end up with pickling-size onions instead of nice big globes. Thin out onions so they are growing 4 to 5 inches apart, and plant the thinnings 4 to 5 inches from each other. (Short-day onion transplants are available in December or January by mail order and at some local nurseries.)

Grow Sweet, Crisp, Juicy Celery

When you bite into a stalk of celery grown this way, juice will squirt into your mouth and run down your face.

▸ Dig a trench 14 inches wide in rich, well-drained soil in full sun.

▸ Add manure and homemade compost or commercial organic soil amendment.

▸ Cultivate organic fertilizer into the top 6 inches and then water the trench. (The finished planting area should be 3 inches lower than the surrounding soil.)

▸ Plant celery transplants 6 inches apart down the center of the trench. Water them deeply.

▸ Water frequently throughout the growing season to keep the celery growing fast.

▸ Beginning six weeks after planting, feed the celery every two weeks with diluted fish emulsion.

▸ Control slugs; they can ruin celery.

▸ A month before harvest, blanch the stalks by wrapping them with a newspaper and tying firmly. Push earth around the bottoms of the stalks, and continue to water and feed them.

DECEMBER CHECKLIST

PURCHASE/PLANT

{ } Begin planting bare-root roses, trees, vines, berries, and vegetables, if you wish, 393

{ } Purchase poinsettias early in the month, 395

{ } Choose and plant sasanqua camellias and early- and long-blooming azaleas, 396

{ } Finish planting all spring-flowering bulbs, except tulips, hyacinths, and crocuses, on or before December 25, 397

{ } Plant tulips, hyacinths, and crocuses between Christmas and New Year's Day, 397

{ } Purchase permanent plants that are colorful in winter, to plant or use as gifts, 399

{ } Continue to plant cool-season flowers in coastal zones only, 399

{ } Purchase gifts from nurseries and garden supply stores, 408

{ } Plant a child's fantasy dish garden, or give the ingredients and a promise to help make it, 408

{ } Plant bedding plants in baskets and pots for holiday and hostess gifts. Also use indoor plants, succulents, herbs, and plants in bloom, 409

{ } Plant culinary herbs in pots for use in turkey stuffing, 409

{ } Continue to plant winter vegetables, 411

{ } Plant celery, 412

TRIM, PRUNE, MOW, DIVIDE

{ } Stop picking and deadheading roses; leave the hips on the bush, 396

{ } Cut off flower spikes that have bloomed from dwarf foxgloves and delphiniums, 400

{ } Start pruning deciduous fruit trees, if you have time, 403

{ } Don't prune tropicals, 403

{ } Prune grapes, 404

{ } Prune low-chill raspberries, 405

{ } Prune native plants, 406

{ } Prune wisteria by cutting off unwanted long twiners, and prune roots of vines that fail to bloom, 406

{ } Pick plant materials from the garden to use as holiday decorations, 406

{ } Mow cool-season lawns, including Bermuda that's overseeded with winter ryegrass, 411

{ } Don't mow warm-season lawns, except St. Augustine if it continues to grow, 411

FERTILIZE

{ } Stop fertilizing potted poinsettias; bring them into the house to enjoy, 395

{ } Continue fertilizing cymbidiums until flowers open, 396

{ } Don't fertilize roses, 396

{ } Feed cool-season flowers with a complete fertilizer for growth and bloom, 399

{ } Continue to feed cineraria for growth, 380

{ } Feed shade plants for bloom; give them adequate light, 401

{ } Feed cool-season lawns, but don't feed warm-season lawns except for Bermuda that's overseeded with winter ryegrass, 411

{ } Side-dress vegetable rows according to the individual needs of plants, 412

{ } Drench the ground under *Brunfelsia* 'Royal Purple' with fish emulsion mixed double-strength, 403

continued . . .

DECEMBER CHECKLIST

WATER

- { } Don't water succulents growing in the ground, *273*
- { } Continue to water if the weather's hot, dry, and windy; include California native plants now because this is their growing season, *178, 368*
- { } Keep cymbidiums damp but not soggy, *396*
- { } Remember to keep all bulbs, but especially potted ones, well watered, *397*
- { } Don't water roses, *396*
- { } Water cool-season lawns when rains aren't adequate, *411*
- { } Water St. Augustine grass if it continues to grow, *411*
- { } Turn off the irrigation systems of all other types of warm-season lawns once they have gone brown, *411*

CONTROL PESTS, DISEASE, AND WEEDS

- { } Spray peach and nectarine trees for peach leaf curl if you didn't do so in November, *382*
- { } Protect cymbidiums' bloom spikes from snails, *396*
- { } Use dormant spray on deciduous fruit trees and other woody plants that drop their leaves in winter, *403*
- { } Control rust on cool-season lawns by fertilizing and mowing them, *411*
- { } Control aphids with insecticidal soap and beneficial insects, *411*
- { } Control slugs on celery, lettuce, and mesclun, *115, 412*

ALSO THIS MONTH

- { } Prepare for frost in areas where it is expected by sheltering tropical plants growing in containers, *394*
- { } Force budded cymbidiums into bloom for the holidays, if desired, *396*
- { } Keep an eye on the growth of potted bulbs; remove covers when they reach the right height, *397*
- { } Prepare beds for planting bare-root roses next month, *396*
- { } Lift dahlias and store them for the winter, *398*
- { } Prepare amaryllis to bloom, *398*
- { } Protect tender annuals, especially cineraria, from frost, *400*
- { } Tie up permanent vines so they don't get knocked down by rain or wind, *401*
- { } Use the bendy stems of grapevines to make wreaths, *405*
- { } Make a holiday wreath from succulents, *404*
- { } Harvest winter vegetables as soon as they mature, *411*

References

Seed, Plant, and Garden-Supply Sources

Annie's Annuals and Perennials
801 Chesley Avenue
Richmond, CA 94801
888-266-4370
www.anniesannuals.com

Brent and Becky's Bulbs
7900 Daffodil Lane
Gloucester, VA 23061
877-661-2852
www.brentandbeckysbulbs.com

Burpee Seeds
W. Atlee Burpee & Co.
300 Park Avenue
Warminster, PA 18974
800-333-5808
www.burpee.com

The Cooks' Garden
PO Box C5030
Warminster, PA 18974
800-457-9703
www.cooksgarden.com

Entomo-Logic
21323 232nd Street, S.E.
Monroe, WA 98272
306-863-8547

Gardens Alive!
5100 Schenley Place
Lawrenceburg, IN 47025
513-354-1482
www.gardensalive.com

The Gourmet Gardener
12287 117th Drive
Live Oak, FL 32060
386-362-9098
www.gourmetgardener.com

Gurney's Seed and Nursery Company
PO Box 4178
Greendale, IN 47025
513-354-1491
www.gurneys.com

Heirloom Roses, Inc.
24062 NE Riverside Drive
St. Paul, OR 97137
503-538-1576
www.heirloomroses.com

Heritage Roses of Tanglewood Farms
16831 Mitchell Creek Drive
Fort Bragg, CA 95437
707-964-3748

High Country Gardens
2902 Rufina Street
Santa Fe, NM 87507
800-925-9387
www.highcountrygardens.com

Jackson and Perkins Co.
2518 South Pacific Highway
Medford, OR 97501
800-872-7673
www.jacksonandperkins.com

Johnny's Selected Seeds
955 Benton Avenue
Winslow, ME 04901
877-564-6697
www.johnnyseeds.com

Larner Seeds
PO Box 407
Bolinas, CA 94924
Shop & Demonstration Garden
235 Grove Road
Bolinas, CA 94924
415-868-9407
Fax 415-868-2592
www.larnerseeds.com

Le Jardin du Gourmet
PO Box 75
St. Johnsbury Center, VT 05863
802-748-1446
www.artisticgardens.com

Organica Seed Company
PO Box 611
Wilbraham, MA 01095
413-599-0264
www.organicaseed.com

Park Seed Company
1 Parkton Avenue
Greenwood, SC 29647
800-213-0076
www.parkseed.com

Peaceful Valley Farm & Garden Supply
PO Box 2209
Grass Valley, CA 95945
888-784-1722 or 530-272-4769
www.groworganic.com

Renee's Garden
6116 Highway 9
Felton, CA 95018
888-880-7228
www.reneesgarden.com

Seeds of Change
888-762-7333
www.seedsofchange.com

Stokes Seeds
PO Box 548
Buffalo, NY 14240
800-396-9238
www.stokeseeds.com

Territorial Seed Company
PO Box 158
Cottage Grove, OR 97424
541-942-9547
www.territorialseed.com

Theodore Payne Foundation
10459 Tuxford Street
Sun Valley, CA 91352
818-768-1802
www.theodorepayne.org

Thompson & Morgan Seedsmen, Inc.
220 Faraday Avenue
Jackson, NJ 08527
800-274-7333 or 732-363-2225
www.tmseeds.com

Tree of Life Nursery
PO Box 635
33201 Ortega Highway
San Juan Capistrano, CA 92673
949-728-0685
www.californianativeplants.com

Wahmhoff Farms Nursery
11121 M-40 Highway
Gobles, MI 49055
888-645-7337
www.mitrees.com

ROSE-PRO CALENDAR

MONTH	PLANTING	PRUNING	PEST AND DISEASE CONTROL
January	Plant bare-root roses. Transplant roses growing in the wrong places.	Prune shrub roses and everblooming climbers. Remove leaves and clean up the ground around the plants. Remove leaves of deciduous roses.	Dormant spray, if desired, with a mixture of Bonide Organic Lime Sulfur Spray and horticultural oil.
February	Finish planting bare-root roses purchased locally.	Begin disbudding if necessary. Take off excess buds inside the plant if necessary.	Wash off aphids with water. Release ladybugs on plants to control aphids.
March	Finish planting bare-root roses purchased from mail-order catalogs.	Begin or continue disbudding hybrid teas and grandifloras. Cut back blind shoots as soon as they appear.	Check for pests and fungal diseases. Spray with bio-fungicides, worm-castings tea, or Cornell Fungicide Formula if necessary.
April	Plant roses from nursery containers.	Pick blooms or deadhead spent flowers. Disbud hybrid teas and grandifloras. Remove blind shoots.	Apply earthworm castings to control pests. Release beneficials. Use BT against caterpillars or release trichogramma wasps.
May	Plant roses from nursery containers.	Pick or deadhead flowers. Disbud hybrid teas and grandifloras. Watch for blind shoots; remove if necessary.	Check for pests and fungal diseases. Spray with biofungicides, earthworm-castings tea, or Cornell Fungicide Formula if necessary. Release beneficials.
June	Plant roses from nursery containers.	Pick or deadhead flowers. Disbud hybrid teas and grandifloras.	Continue watching for pests and diseases. Use hand-picking and organic controls.

IRRIGATING	FERTILIZING	OTHER ACTIVITIES
Water new plants every other day for the first three weeks after planting.	Give all plants 2 tablespoons John and Bob's Organic Soil Optimizer, 2 cups Dr. Earth Organic Rose Fertilizer, and 2 cups of Biosol Mix.	Apply mulch. Attend public demonstrations of rose pruning.
Begin watering all plants with at least 1 inch of water a week when rains aren't adequate.	For plants that were put in last month, apply fertilizer as described above.	Watch for development of blind shoots.
Apply at least 2 inches of water once a week when rains aren't adequate.	Apply liquid or granulated humic acid according to package directions. When growth measures 4 to 6 inches, apply alfalfa tea or compost tea.	Add fresh mulch when necessary.
Apply approximately 1 1/2 inches of water twice a week.	Give each plant 2 cups Dr. Earth, 2 cups Biosol, and 2 tablespoons John and Bob's Organic Soil Optimizer (unless applied in January).	Attend rose shows.
Apply approximately 1 1/2 inches of water twice a week.	Apply 1 tablespoon fish emulsion per gallon of water for standard-size plants.	Rate your roses on performance. Plan to replace inferior plants next year.
Apply approximately 1 1/2 inches of water twice a week.	Apply 2 cups Dr. Earth or other organic rose food of your choice.	Attend rose shows.

MONTH	PLANTING	PRUNING	PEST AND DISEASE CONTROL
July	Begin thinking about next year's planting.	Pick or deadhead flowers. Disbud hybrid teas and grandifloras.	Continue watching for pests and diseases. Use organic controls. Try PROBIOTICS sprays if necessary.
August	Plant roses from nursery containers.	Give all roses a light summer pruning, removing as much as one-third of the growth if desired to encourage fall flowers.	Continue monitoring for pests and diseases and controlling with beneficials, earthworm castings, and other organic methods.
September	Plant roses from nursery containers.	Pick blooms or deadhead spent flowers.	Continue watching for pests and diseases. Use handpicking and organic controls.
October	Plant roses from nursery containers.	Pick blooms or deadhead spent flowers.	Continue watching for pests and diseases. Use handpicking and organic controls.
November	Tag any roses that you wish to replace next year.	Pick blooms if desired, but stop deadheading them. Pull off faded petals that fail to sift to the ground.	Rake up fallen rose leaves to cut down on disease problems next year.
December	Tag any roses that you plan to replace next year.	Pull off faded petals that fail to sift to the ground. Leave rose hips on the plant. Begin pruning after the winter solstice, if desired. Save thorny canes to use for keeping animals out of flowerbeds.	Rake up fallen rose leaves and debris to cut down on disease problems next year.

IRRIGATING	FERTILIZING	OTHER ACTIVITIES
Apply approximately 1 1/2 inches of water three times a week. (Inland, water more.)	Apply an optional feeding of compost tea, kelp, or humic acid, if desired.	Renew mulch, using homemade compost or bagged compost.
Apply approximately 1 1/2 inches of water three times a week.	Apply 2 tablespoons of John and Bob's Soil Optimizer and 2 cups Dr. Earth; scratch in lightly.	Enjoy books and magazines about roses.
Apply approximately 1 1/2 inches of water twice a week.	Fertilize with organic liquid fertilizer such as alfalfa tea, compost tea, soil soup, or other liquid of your choice.	Network to learn about improved varieties. Keep a notebook with names, colors, and special characteristics of fine varieties.
Apply approximately 1 1/2 inches of water twice a week.	Give each rose 2 cups of Dr. Earth or other organic rose food of your choice.	Attend rose shows. Rate your roses for disease resistance, pest resistance, ease of care, and abundance of bloom.
Water until midmonth if rains aren't adequate. After midmonth, withhold water.	Do not fertilize. Roses need to begin slowing down now in preparation for dormancy.	Study the rose garden for possible improvements.
Water roses less in order to promote dormancy.	Do not fertilize this month. Allow roses to go into dormancy.	Prepare beds for bare-root planting. Remove weeds.

Glossary

ACTUAL NITROGEN. The amount of pure nitrogen in a fertilizer. To determine the number of pounds of a specific fertilizer you must use in order to give a plant 1 pound of actual nitrogen, divide 100 by the first number on the package. (The concept of actual nitrogen applies more to synthetic fertilizers than to organic ones.)

AIR-LAYER. To propagate a plant by growing roots from an above-ground node of a branch or trunk. The node is wrapped with moist sphagnum moss or compost and kept damp (usually by covering it with plastic). The entire portion of the plant that includes the new roots can then be severed to create a new plant. (Compare *layer*.)

AMMONIC. Containing ammonia (NH_4), a primary source of nitrogen in such synthetic fertilizers as ammonium sulfate, which will acidify soils as well as fertilize them. Ammonium sulfate (21-0-0) is a cheap source of fast-acting nitrogen that dissolves quickly in water, but it can burn plants and destroy earthworms as well as the natural bioorganisms in soil that create free nitrogen and protect plants from diseases.

ANNUAL. A plant that completes its life within twelve months. An annual germinates, grows, blooms, sets seed, and dies all in one season. Warm-season annuals begin life in spring and die when the weather gets cold in fall. Cool-season annuals begin life in fall and die when the weather gets hot in summer. Some perennial plants, such as delphiniums and petunias, are grown mainly as annuals. Some perennials that are grown as annuals in other parts of the country, such as impatiens and geraniums (pelargoniums), are grown here as true perennials.

ANTHER. The pollen-bearing flower part. It consists of pollen sacs and is located on the end of the stamen, the male reproductive organ of flowers.

ANTITRANSPIRANTS. Products sprayed on leaves that leave a film in order to slow transpiration and thus prevent wilting. They can help plants survive heat, cold, dryness, salt sprays, and transplanting.

AREOLES. Spine cushions. They're found on all cacti but not on any other succulents. (Many other succulents, including the cactus-like euphorbias, have spines, but they do not have spine cushions.)

AXILLARY BUD. A bud that occurs in the leaf axil (the upper angle where the leaf joins the stem). Tomato suckers arise from axillary buds.

BALANCED FERTILIZER. A widely used but somewhat vague term for a fertilizer that contains all three major elements (nitrogen, phosphorus, and potassium) that plants need. (*See* complete fertilizer.)

BAREROOT. Describes a plant that has had all soil removed from its roots. Many deciduous plants are sold bareroot during the winter months.

BENEFICIALS. Insects, arachnids, nematodes, and other organisms that eat or parasitize pest insects and mites. Many, such as spiders, exist in our gardens; others can be purchased for release.

BENTONITE. An absorbent but impure clay, first discovered in 1889 in Fort Benton, Wyoming. It is rich in minerals, mainly montmorillonite, and is usually a product of ancient volcanic ash. Bentonite swells when exposed to moisture, thus giving it many commercial and agricultural applications.

BIENNIAL. A plant that requires two growing seasons to flower and then sets seed and dies. Bedding plants that are biennials are usually planted in fall; seeds of biennials are planted in summer to bloom the following year. Some biennials, such as the foxglove 'Foxy' and the sweet William 'Wee Willie', can be grown as annuals.

BIODEGRADABLE. Capable of decomposing by natural biological means.

BLOSSOM-END ROT. Black, sunken, leathery areas on the bottom of tomatoes (also on peppers, squash, and watermelons) caused by insufficient calcium. The insufficiency is caused by uneven moisture in the soil or by roots damaged from cultivation, salty soil, or extremely wet soil.

BOLT. To go to seed prematurely. Typical of vegetables, such as onions.

BOTRYTIS. A fungal disease characterized by fuzzy, wet filaments and the blackening and swelling of plant parts, especially flowers, leaves, and stems. Promoted by prolonged wet weather or frequent overhead irrigation.

BRACT. A leaflike organ between the flower and the leaves or one that is part of an inflorescence or that has taken on color to look just like a petal, as on poinsettias.

BRANCH COLLAR. The swollen area surrounding a tree branch where it meets a larger branch or the trunk.

BROAD-SPECTRUM PESTICIDE. An organic or poisonous chemical pesticide that kills a large number of various pests rather than being designed to control one specific pest. In general, specific pesticides, whether organic or chemical, are better because they protect beneficials. (*See* integrated pest management.)

BT. *Bacillus thuringiensis*, a bacterial disease that kills caterpillars and is sold under several trade names (including Attack, Dipel, and Thuricide) in liquid or powder form to be used as a spray or dust. Caterpillars that ingest treated leaves stop eating and die in about three days.

BUD UNION. The location on a grafted plant where the variety was grafted onto the rootstock. It may or may not be swollen. On older plants, it is often difficult to distinguish where the bud union is, but in some cases it's easily seen. On citrus, for example, there may be a change in the size of the trunk from smaller to larger or vice versa. On bare-root trees, the bud union is often no more than a slight bend in the trunk. On roses, the bud union is the knob, bump, or large swollen area from which the canes arise. (On old roses, bud unions can grow to enormous size, sometimes a foot or more long.)

BULB. A modified subterranean leaf bud; it has a basal plate above which are food-storing scales (rudimentary leaves) surrounding a bud from which comes a plant. Also used loosely to describe all plants that grow from thickened underground food-storage organs.

CALICHE. A highly alkaline type of soil found largely in desert areas. Its high lime content may be visible as white flecks throughout or as a white crust on top of the soil, or it may occur in a hard buried layer.

CALLUS. The dry crust of plant cells that forms over the open cut on a cutting. (To develop this crust is to "callus over.")

CANE. The woody stem of a rose or cane berry, such as raspberries and blackberries, or a somewhat flexible, jointed, and often hollow or pith-filled stem arising from the ground, as in bamboo, sugarcane, and cane begonias.

CHAPARRAL. A group of drought-resistant plant communities making up a habitat of dense brush and small trees native to the Mediterranean climate zones of California. Chaparral periodically burns and regenerates itself through fire.

CHELATE. Technically, an organic molecule that prevents iron, manganese, and zinc from becoming "locked up" (insoluble) in alkaline soil by binding itself to them. In this combined form they stay soluble, and thus plants can use them. Iron chelate, chelated iron, or a chelated or chelating formula are included in products that contain the trace elements iron, manganese, and zinc in a form plants can use.

CHILLING REQUIREMENT. The number of hours between 45° and 32°F that a plant needs to overcome dormancy in order to grow, flower, and fruit properly. (When the temperature drops lower than freezing, little action occurs within the tissues of the plant.) A plant with a low chilling requirement is one that needs few, if any, hours between 45° and 32°F in order to bloom and bear fruit.

CHIMNEY DRAIN. A narrow drain, dug with a spade, crowbar, or posthole digger, in the bottom of a planting hole on flat ground when the cause of poor drainage is a layer of hardpan that is thin enough to break through with hand tools. The hole is then filled with sand or ground bark to allow water to escape through the layer of hardpan down into a layer of soil that drains.

CHITIN. The substance from which the hard outer shell of arthropods, such as insects, spiders, and crustaceans, is made. (Crabshell contains chitin.)

CHITINASE. An enzyme that can break down chitin. (Earthworm castings contain the enzyme chitinase.)

CHLOROSIS. The condition of lacking chlorophyll (a green pigment in plant cells), often brought about by insufficient soluble iron in the soil. A chlorotic plant has yellow leaves and dark veins. Sometimes, especially in citrus, this is caused by waterlogged soil. Highly alkaline soil also can cause chlorosis by preventing plants from absorbing enough iron, zinc, and manganese for health.

CLAY. A fine-grained earth made up of tiny mineral particles less than 0.002 millimeter in size. When you grip a damp handful, it holds together. Pure clay is good for little besides making bricks or pottery, but clay soils contain humus and may also contain some admixture of sand or silt.

CLIMATE ZONE. A geographical area in which the yearly temperature range, length of seasons, average precipitation, humidity, amount of sunshine, and other factors combine to make certain plants grow better than others. The climate zones described and mapped in the *Sunset Western Garden Book* make up the zone system most widely used by western gardeners.

COIR. (Pronounced "koy-er.") The fibrous substance that fills the cavity between a coconut husk and the coconut shell. Coir is plentiful and has many commercial uses, including rope, bristly floor mats, and woven matting. In recent years coir has gained popularity in agriculture and gardening as a substitute for sphagnum moss for lining hanging baskets, as a substitute for peat moss in soil mixes, and for sandwiching the top and bottom of soil mixes on green roofs. Coir is clean, long-lasting, has a neutral pH, and has tiny air holes in it, which peat moss doesn't have.

COLE CROP. Any member of the cabbage family, including cauliflower, broccoli, and Brussels sprouts. All cole crops descended by means of spontaneous mutation and subsequent human selection from a common wild ancestor.

COMPLETE FERTILIZER. The correct term for describing a fertilizer containing all three major elements (nitrogen, phosphorus, and potassium) that plants need. The formulas—the relative amounts of the three—may vary widely, however. A complete fertilizer high in growth ingredients has a high first number, and a complete fertilizer high in bloom ingredients has a high second number or second and third numbers.

COMPOST. A soil amendment made by farmers and gardeners by piling up organic materials and keeping them damp until they rot.

COOL-SEASON FLOWER. An annual, biennial, or perennial flower that's native to a cool climate and that grows and flowers best at cool temperatures.

COOL-SEASON LAWN. A lawn variety that's best adapted to a cool climate and thus grows best and fastest during late fall, winter, and early spring.

COOL-SEASON VEGETABLE. A vegetable that originated in a cool climate and grows best at cool temperatures.

CORM. A thickened subterranean stem that is a solid piece of food-storage tissue and that produces a plant from buds on its top. Gladioli and freesias grow from corms.

COROLLA. The collective name for the petals of a flower. The collective name for the sepals is the calyx. The corolla and calyx combined make up the perianth. (For example, on a fuchsia the corolla is usually the downward facing "skirt" of the flower, and it may be of any color available on fuchsias; the sepals of a fuchsia flare back toward the stem and are always red, white, or pink.)

CRABGRASS. An annual weed (*Digitalia sanguinalis*) forming a thick clump of coarse grass that spreads out in a crab shape, turns red at the first frost, and dies out in winter.

CROP ROTATION. A system used by farmers and gardeners since ancient times to preserve the fertility of soil and minimize pest and disease problems. It consists of planting those crops (including flowers) that are subject to specific soilborne pests and diseases on a particular piece of ground no more than once every three years.

CROWN. The place at soil level where a plant's roots end and its trunk or stem (or group of stems) begins. Also used to denote the top of a tree's canopy of branches.

CROWN ROT. A general term describing any number of fungal diseases that can attack the crown of a plant. Usually they are the result of planting too low or allowing water or mud to collect around the plant's trunk or stem (or stems).

CULTIVAR. *See* variety.

CURD. The white head of a cauliflower or the individual sections of a head.

CUTTING. A section of a plant that's cut off for grafting or rooting.

CUTWORM. A large black, brown, or gray hairless and fleshy caterpillar that is the larva of one of several species of moth and curls into a C shape when disturbed. Often found underground or under fallen leaves when you dig or cultivate. Surface cutworms chew off stems at ground level overnight. Subterranean cutworms eat roots. Climbing cutworms destroy fresh shoots and young foliage.

DAMPING OFF. The disease that causes sudden death of seedlings when they are attacked by one or more of several destructive fungi.

DEADHEAD. To clip off faded flower heads before they can set seed.

DECIDUOUS. Describes plants that drop all their leaves once a year.

DECOLLATE SNAIL. A small carnivorous African snail introduced here to eat brown garden snails. (Their use is not legal in all counties. Check with the nearest University of California Cooperative Extension office for rules in your area.)

DECOMPOSED GRANITE. A grayish, creamy, or light brown granular and sometimes flaky soil composed of small particles of granite. It drains well and is high in potassium.

DEFENSIBLE SPACE. A clearing surrounding a house planted with fire-resistant landscape that can greatly help the house survive through wildfire.

DIATOMACEOUS EARTH. A powder made of a mined product that's filled with the sharp skeletons of tiny diatoms, one-celled algae. The silica in diatomaceous earth kills pests by piercing their bodies like broken glass.

DIVIDE. To break apart the roots or to separate the bulbs of a plant that has formed a clump in order to make new plants, to limit the plant's size, or to renew the plant.

DORMANT. Describes the "sleeping" state, when a plant isn't growing but remains alive.

DORMANT SPRAY. A pesticide and/or fungicide, such as oil or lime sulfur, used in winter on deciduous plants that have gone dormant and dropped their leaves. Dormant sprays are usually too concentrated for use on foliage; in most cases, they would burn the leaves. Some dormant sprays are chemical, and others are organic and bear the OMRI label of approval.

DRAIN. *See* chimney drain, French drain, sleeve drain, *and* sump.

DRAINAGE. The passage of water through soil and the soil characteristics that support such passage. When drainage is good, water passes rapidly downward through the soil. When drainage is poor, water puddles on the surface or is held for a long period within the soil, traveling downward very slowly, if at all. If the passage of water is seriously impeded, plant roots can die from oxygen deprivation. Drainage is usually fast in sandy and decomposed granite soils; in clay soils it is usually slow. Hardpan or buried rock can also seriously impede drainage.

DRIFT. A gracefully shaped area with rounded edges in a flowerbed, planted with one type or one color of plant. Drifts extend from the foreground to the middle ground or from the middle ground to the background as well as from side to side in the bed.

DRIP LINE. An imaginary line encircling a tree directly under the outermost tips of its branches. (Also often used loosely to describe the various tubes and hoses or tube-type emitters, either buried or above ground, that are used in drip irrigation.)

DRIP SYSTEM. A method of watering plants by which water at controlled low pressure is fed through a hose that in turn feeds small tubes leading to individual plants, where emitters release water to the root zone or mist it onto foliage. (In some cases, emitters are attached directly to the primary hose. *See* header.)

DROUGHT. A prolonged period of absent or inadequate rainfall—it can last several months, a season, or several years. "Summer drought" describes our customarily dry summers.

DROUGHT RESISTANT. Describes plants from dry regions of the world that have developed various means of enduring drought without dying. Drought-resistant plants require less irrigation than do others once they are established.

DROUGHT TOLERANT. A term often used to describe a plant that, once established, can survive on natural rainfall alone, with little, if any, irrigation.

EMITTERS. Various types of plastic gadgets that release measured quantities of water. They attach to microtubing and, in some cases, to headers by simple push-pull methods. Emitters are not all interchangeable; they have to be the right size for the tubing used.

EPIPHYTE. A plant that grows by attaching itself to another plant but doesn't sap nourishment from the host plant, as do parasites.

ESPALIER. To train a plant into a flat, formal shape on wires or against a wall or fence. Also describes the trained plant and sometimes the framework it grows on.

EYE. Describes the center of a flower that is a different color from the outer petals; the bud on a tuber; a cutting that has only one bud; or an undeveloped bud, which looks like a line, bump, depression, or other demarcation on the stem of a plant.

FARM ADVISORS. Agricultural scientists who are representatives of the agricultural and natural resources advisory system that's supported by the state, county, and federal governments through the University of California. Reach them at your local county's UC Cooperative Extension office.

FERTILIZER. Any material, either organic or inorganic, that's applied to soil or foliage to feed plants and aid their growth.

FIREBLIGHT. A bacterial disease (*Erwinia amylovora*) that causes blackening and dieback of leaves, twigs, branches, and fruit on apple trees, evergreen pear (*Pyrus kawakamii*), pyracantha, and other members of the rose family.

FORCE. To make a plant bloom months ahead of schedule by simulating natural conditions that make it bloom.

FRASS. The dust or pelletized excrement of insects, such as residues of boring left by bark beetles.

FRENCH DRAIN. A trench in which perforated pipe has been laid and then covered with a 3-foot layer of sand or gravel. It's used to drain excess water from flat or sloping ground. The top of the gravel in the completed French drain may be level with the surface of the ground or buried at any depth underground. If buried, the top of the gravel should be covered with plastic sheeting or landscape cloth prior to burying so that clay soil above the French drain can't drift down into it and clog the spaces in the gravel.

FULL SLIP. Characterizes a ripe cantaloupe; a crack forms around the stem end so the melon slips off the vine easily, without tearing.

FURROW. A groove or trench made in garden soil for the purpose of planting, carrying irrigation water between rows, or controlling erosion.

FYNBOS. A group of drought-resistant plant communities making up a habitat of dense brush and small trees native to Mediterranean climate zones in South Africa. Fynbos periodically burns and regenerates itself through fire.

GENUS. A group of plants of one or several species that are related structurally and belong to the same family but differ from other genera within the family. Designated by the capitalized first word in a botanical name, which is followed by the uncapitalized species name. For example, in *Aquilegia desertorum*, the botanical name for Arizona columbine, *Aquilegia* is the genus name given to all columbines and *desertorum* is the name of this specific species.

GLOCHID. A short, barbed, almost invisible, and hairlike spine. Glochia grow from the areoles of some but not all cacti.

GRAFT. To propagate a plant by inserting a section of one plant into another.

GREEN MANURE. A plant or plants, in most cases a legume grown on a plot of land for one growing season (usually over winter) for the purpose of being plowed, tilled, spaded, or otherwise worked into the ground to improve soil fertility.

GYPSUM. Calcium sulfate ($CaSO_4.2H_2O$), a natural rock product used as a soil amendment to loosen clay soils and make them drain better when the cause of poor drainage is a high level of exchangeable sodium (alkali) rather than texture or compaction. Somewhat soluble in water, gypsum supplies soluble calcium to replace excess exchangeable sodium (alkali). Also used to reclaim sodic (salty) soils. Mined gypsum is the natural granular form of calcium sulfate preferred by organic gardeners. Soluble gypsum, or gypsite, has been chemically treated to make it soluble, and its use can contribute to increased leaching of alkaline salts from gardens and agricultural lands.

HARDEN OFF. A plant's process of gradually becoming accustomed to colder weather in fall. This includes slowing down or stopping top growth so that the foliage will be hardy. (Young leaves are most likely to suffer frost damage.) Gardeners help plants harden off by reducing water and fertilizer in fall. Also refers to the gradual exposure of young seedlings to outdoor temperatures and sunlight after they've been grown in a greenhouse, indoors, or under lights.

HARDPAN. A layer of hard, compacted soil of any type that's cemented together by minerals and almost impenetrable by roots or water. Often buried beneath a layer of good soil.

HARDSCAPE. Any feature in a garden that's made of a construction material, including pools, decks, hot tubs, patios, steps, walks, walls, gazebos, pergolas, and planter boxes. Most gardens include some hardscape; some have more hardscape than landscape (areas of ground with plants growing in them).

HARDY. Describes a plant that can take various degrees of frost and freezing temperatures without dying. (Does not mean a strong or easy-to-grow plant.)

HEAD BACK. To cut back the growing end of a branch or young tree in order to stimulate branching farther back on the branch or trunk, thus redirecting growth.

HEADER. A hose that carries water from the water source to microtubing and emitters in a drip system. Headers aren't all interchangeable; they and the various parts that are used to connect sections must be of the right size to fit together.

HEATHLANDS. A group of drought-resistant plant communities making up a habitat of dense brush and small trees native to the Mediterranean climate zones of Australia. Heathlands periodically burn and regenerate themselves through fire.

HEEL IN. A way to keep bare-root plants from drying out when you can't plant them right away: laying the plants in the shade with their roots in a trench, covering the roots with soil, and keeping them damp.

HELIX SNAIL. *Helix aspersa*, our common brown garden snail.

HERB. Any plant used for medicine, fragrance, or flavoring. (Not all herbs are edible.) In botany, indicates any nonwoody plant that dies down in winter.

HERBACEOUS BORDER. A traditional flower border planted entirely with nonwoody plants.

HUMIC ACID. A dark-brown, concentrated form of humus, this form of organic plant matter was discovered in the 1960s to have highly beneficial agricultural applications. It is possible to extract humic acid from humus, but a more usual source is leonardite ore, a type of lignite containing over 85 percent humic acid and less than 7 percent fulvic acid. (See *leonardite*.) Humic acid can be purchased in liquid or solid form and is an ingredient in some fertilizers. Among a host of other benefits, humic acid increases water retention and the nutrient-holding capacity of soils, prevents fertilizers from leaching out of the root zone, promotes growth of microorganisms, stimulates root growth (especially their length), increases the total nitrogen in soils, promotes the conversion of nutrients into forms available to plants, and improves the structure of soils.

HUMUS. The organic portion of soil, made up of largely decomposed animal and vegetable matter and usually light or dark brown in color. Homemade or bagged compost, leaf mold, peat moss, and manure are organic soil amendments that eventually become humus in soils, but they're not the same as humus.

HYBRID. The offspring of a cross, by intention or chance, between two plants that are more or less unalike. Some hybrids are sterile. Seeds from a hybrid plant don't produce plants like the parent.

INSECTICIDAL SOAPS. A group of biodegradable fatty acids that are sold as environmentally safe sprays (such as Safer soap). They kill pests, especially soft-bodied pests such as aphids, on contact by clogging their pores.

INTEGRATED PEST MANAGEMENT (IPM). A system of balancing pest populations with populations of beneficial insects, so that few, if any, chemical sprays need to be used. When sprays are used, specific sprays for the individual pest are chosen rather than broad-spectrum sprays that kill many beneficials. (Although agreeing in principle with the concept of IPM, organic gardeners go one step further by eschewing all use of pesticides, and using natural and organic systems for controlling pests and diseases without exception.)

JUNE DROP. Describes the dropping of many immature fruits, usually in early June but sometimes at other times. It is nature's way of thinning fruit on trees that set more fruit than they can ripen.

LATERALS. Side branches.

LAYER. To propagate a plant by bending a living branch to the ground and burying a portion of it in soil while it's still attached to the parent plant, allowing the branch to root, and then cutting off and removing the rooted portion. (Prior to burying the branch portion, a slanting cut is made halfway through it; it's then brushed with rooting compound and held open by a sliver of wood or a pebble. Once buried, it's usually pegged down on both sides or weighted down by a brick.)

LEGGY. Describes a plant that tends to grow too tall, with long, bare stalks.

LEGUME. Any member of the Leguminosae, a family made up of plants having a pod shaped like a pea pod.

LEONARDITE. A soft ore, found in North Dakota, Utah, and New Mexico, that is similar to lignite but contains at least 85 percent humic acid and less than 7 percent fulvic acid; a low-grade brown coal made of terrestrial plant matter that is an outcropping of lignite and usually found close to the surface. Leonardite is named for Dr. Dave Leonard of the University of North Dakota, who discovered it in 1919. It is used in oil drilling, in iron foundries, and as a detergent or decontaminant of soils or bodies of water. Since the 1960s, leonardite has been used as a major source of humic acid. (*See* humic acid.)

LIGNITE. A low-grade form of coal found in surface deposits worldwide. Lignite has industrial uses but usually contains too much water for use as fuel.

LOAM. Technically, a soil type that is a combination of clay, sand, and silt. Loam soils vary greatly and are often described by such terms as *clay loam* or *sandy loam* depending on the percentages of their components. Also used popularly to describe any soil that's full of humus and is rich, crumbly, productive, and dark in color (as in "good garden loam").

LOW CHILL. Describes a plant that needs few hours between 45° and 32°F in order to bloom and bear fruit.

MANURE. Animal excrement of horses, cows, chickens, rabbits, or pigs, used for fertilizer and soil improvement. Bat and seabird droppings are concentrated, beneficial manures, usually referred to by the Spanish word *guano*, which means "bird dung" or "excrement." Some guanos can burn plants if not properly applied. (Cat, dog, pig, and human manures carry diseases and must never be used.)

MANURE TEA. A liquid fertilizer made by putting a shovelful of manure into a bucket of water and allowing it to stand overnight.

MAQUIS. A group of drought-resistant plant communities making up a habitat of dense brush and small trees native to the Mediterranean climate zones in southern Europe. Maquis periodically burns and regenerates itself through fire.

MATTORAL. A group of drought-resistant plant communities making up a habitat of dense brush and small trees native to the Mediterranean climate zones in Chile. Mattoral periodically burns and regenerates itself through fire.

MEDITERRANEAN BIOME. Refers to various unique, drought-resistant plant communities all over the world that are native to Mediterranean climates and that share a mix of certain characteristics that help them withstand a dry-summer climate, such as fragile but far-reaching roots, fragrant oils, thick or waxy leaves, gray and hairy foliage, summer deciduous leaves, long-lived seeds, and the tendency to burn and regenerate themselves through fire.

MICROCLIMATE. Small area within a climate zone where a plant will or won't grow because of factors of climate particular to that spot.

MICROTUBING. Quarter-inch plastic tubing used in drip systems to carry water to emitters. Because most microtubing is the same size, it is interchangeable.

MILDEW. Various fungal diseases (brown, powdery, and downy mildews) that grow on the surface of plant leaves and stems. They discolor and distort plant parts, sap plant energy, and can cause leaf drop.

MONOCARPIC. Describes a plant that blooms only once and then dies.

MULCH. A layer of loose organic matter applied to the surface of the soil to keep the ground cool, preserve moisture, stop the surface from cracking, cut down on weeds, and improve bacterial action. Also describes black, clear, or red plastic, agricultural fabrics, rocks, pebbles, and newspapers used in the same way.

MUSHROOM COMPOST. Humus in which mushrooms have been grown; an inexpensive organic amendment made largely of manure mixed with hay, straw, or the like that can be bought bagged or in bulk, sometimes directly from growers. It may have a high salt content.

NATIVE PLANT (OR "NATIVE"). A plant that, in its original form, grows wild in a certain geographic region such as California. Many native plants have been improved by selection and hybridization.

NATIVE SOIL. Soil dug from a planting hole that's like the surrounding ground.

NATURALIZE. To multiply and come back year after year under normal garden conditions; also to escape gardens and go wild, mixing in with and sometimes choking out native plants; examples of naturalizing plants include mustard, nasturtium, oxalis, pampas grass, statice, and valerian. Additionally, describes placing plants in natural-looking, less artificial settings in gardens—mounting an epiphyte on a tree branch, for example.

NEMATODE. A microscopic, occasionally parasitic worm that lives in soil. Root knot nematodes enter the roots of plants, causing swollen galls called root knots. The plant may become yellow and stunted, and its fruit may be small. Beneficial nematodes kill various soil pests and plant pests that touch the ground. They enter the pests' bodies, kill them with a bacteria, and then devour them. Some beneficial nematodes kill harmful ones by wrapping themselves around their victims and squeezing them to death.

NITROGEN. The chemical element, known by the symbol N, that is a colorless gas forming almost four-fifths of the atmosphere and that is part of all living things. It's absorbed by plant tissues in the form of a soluble salt (nitrate or ammonium), makes them grow, and contributes especially to top and green growth. The first number in the trio on a fertilizer package indicates the percentage of nitrogen in the product.

NODE. The place on a plant from which leaves and axillary buds sprout.

OMRI (ORGANIC MATERIALS REVIEW INSTITUTE). A national nonprofit organization that decides which products are to be used for organic production and processing. Products that are OMRI listed are certified as organic and permitted to bear the institute's seal of approval. In most cases, the system is beneficial; however, in some cases, a product may be listed as organic because it is derived from a natural source but may nonetheless harm the environment. An example is the product Spinosad, containing a fermented form of the soil bacteria *Saccharopolyspora spinosa*, a organism originally found under the floorboards of an abandoned rum factory in the Caribbean. Despite its natural origin and OMRI label of approval, Spinosad is lethal to wild and domestic bees.

ORGANIC. In chemistry, describes any chemical compound that contains carbon. When applied to farming and gardening, *organic* means products grown without chemical pesticides and with only animal or vegetable fertilizers, such as manure, bone meal, blood meal, or compost, and also with only naturally mined forms of minerals, as opposed to water-soluble salts.

PEA STAKE. A plant stake, cut from shrubbery, with a straight piece to stick into the ground and many twigs to support plants as they grow.

PEAT MOSS. Naturally occurring, usually acid, partially decomposed sphagnum moss and sedge that has been mined for centuries for use as fuel from peat bogs that are hundreds of thousands of years old. Peat moss is also used in agriculture and gardening as an acid soil amendment and an ingredient in soil mixes. Peat moss sheds moisture when dry, but once moistened is water-retentive. It is long lasting and usually acid. Peat moss is an nonrenewable resource and is currently being replaced in agriculture and gardening by coir.

PERENNIAL. Technically, any nonwoody plant that lives for more than two years and produces flowers and seeds for more than one year from the same roots. Some perennials are evergreen; others die down in winter. Some plants often classed as perennials will eventually make woody stems when grown in Southern California. Some plants with fleshy roots, such as agapanthus and day lilies, are technically perennials but are often classed with bulbs. Many perennials, including violas, pansies, and petunias, are customarily grown only as annuals.

PETAL BLIGHT. A fungal or bacterial disease that afflicts flowers. It can ruin camellia and azalea blossoms by browning, discoloring, and rotting them.

PH. A symbol that indicates degree of acidity or alkalinity—of soil, for example—and is measured on a scale numbered from 0 to 14 (7.0 is neutral). As the numbers decrease in value from 7.0, the soil is increasingly acid; as they rise above 7.0, the soil is increasingly alkaline.

PHOSPHORUS. A nonmetallic chemical element that's known by the symbol P and is one of the three main ingredients in fertilizers. It contributes to root and flower growth and the overall health of plants. The second number in the trio on a fertilizer package indicates the percentage of phosphorus in the product.

PHOTOPERIODIC. Responding to the length of daylight hours by the onset of a physical change, such as flowering. For example, chrysanthemums, which naturally bloom in fall, can be made to bloom at any time of year by artificially controlling the number of hours of daylight they undergo.

PHOTOSYNTHESIS. The method by which the chlorophyll in plants, when acted on by sunlight or appropriate artificial light, changes carbon dioxide and water (H_2O) into carbohydrates that feed the plant.

PINCH BACK. To prune off growing tips in order to make a plant bushier.

PISTIL. The female organ of a flower, made up of the stigma, style, and ovary.

POLLEN. A yellow dust usually produced inside the pollen sacs that make up the anther on top of the stamen of a flower; pollen grains (in seed plants, they are called microspores) contain the male sex cells of seed plants.

POLLINATION. The transfer of pollen from the anthers (the male part of flowers) to the stigma (the female part). If bees, other insects, or the wind carry pollen from flower to flower on the same plant, the plants are self-pollinating. If plants need another plant, called a pollinator, to supply pollen in order for them to bear fruit, they are cross-pollinating.

PONY PACK. A small, oblong, undivided nursery container customarily holding six small transplants.

POTASH. Potassium carbonate obtained from wood ashes, or potassium from any salt; expressed as K_2O and used in fertilizers. A common name for potassium.

POTASSIUM. A chemical element that occurs abundantly in nature and is one of the three basic ingredients of fertilizers, known by the chemical symbol K. It contributes to flowering and overall plant health. The third number in the trio on a package of fertilizer indicates the percentage of potassium in the product.

POT ON. To successively repot a plant into a container that's just one size larger whenever its roots fill the old pot.

PREEMERGENT HERBICIDE. A weed killer that kills germinating seeds or inhibits their growth.

Most preemergent herbicides are chemical, but corn gluten meal is an organic preemergent herbicide.

PRIMARY WILT. A stage when a plant barely begins to wilt from water stress; signaled by a dull, lackluster look and the tips of the leaves turning down slightly. A lawn with primary wilt won't spring back when stepped on.

PSEUDOBULB. An aboveground bulblike thickened stem on certain orchids, such as cymbidiums, that stores food for the plant.

PUP. A common name for the offshoots of some plants, including bromeliads and staghorn ferns, which produce sideshoots that can be separated from the parent plant to make new plants.

RHIZOBIA. A group of beneficial soil bacteria, each of which has a symbiotic relationship with a particular species of legume. Rhizobia help legumes take nitrogen directly from the air for nourishment. Studies by land-grant university agricultural scientists have proved that rhizobia have functions in soil biology that extend far beyond their benefits to legumes. Rhizobias of many types work with roots to help all plants access nutrients in soil. Since this discovery, live rhizobias have been incorporated as an ingredient in many organic fertilizers, thus enhancing health and growth of plants.

RHIZOME. A thickened stem that grows horizontally underground or on the surface of the ground, such as in bearded irises or calla lilies.

ROOTBOUND. Describes a plant whose roots so fill a container that they've taken on its shape. The roots become thickly concentrated around the outside of the root ball, often wound around and around themselves.

RUST. A fungal disease that attacks many plants, including snapdragons, hollyhocks, roses, and lawn grass. Yellow spots show through on the upper side of leaves where rusty pustules of brown powder occur on the underside.

SAND. A loose, gritty earth made up of tiny particles of rock. Grip a damp handful and it won't hold together. In its pure form sand contains little or no nutriment, but sandy soils usually contain a mixture of sand and humus and may also contain various small percentages of clay or silt.

SANTA ANA. A dry wind, sometimes of gale force, that blows from the interior to the sea. High pressure over the Great Basin causes the westerly flow of air, which is heated and dried by compression as it flows over and down mountains and through canyons.

SCARIFY. To carefully nick or sand through the outer covering of seeds with hard seed coats, allowing them to germinate more easily.

SEPAL. One section of the calyx of a flower. (The calyx is the outer covering that encloses and protects the flower while it is developing inside the bud.) After the flower opens, the calyx usually splits into individual sepals, though with some flowers, such as primroses, it stays in one piece. Sepals are usually green and may be small, hairy, and insignificant, but in some flowers, including fuchsias, the sepals may be colorful and look somewhat like petals, though they are not. (*See* corolla.)

SHADE CLOTH. A landscape fabric, usually made of plastic, that's used mainly for covering trellises, shade houses, and other structures; it creates an appropriate environment for shade plants, which are grown under it. Shade cloth is usually black or green, and it's available in weaves that provide shade of varying degrees, including 25 percent, 50 percent, and 75 percent.

SHEAR. To clip plants on the outside, like a hedge, with hedge shears or an electric hedge clipper. Shearing results in dense outer foliage that shades out inner foliage, leaving bare branches in the center of the plant, a condition that doesn't harm hedges but may harm other plants.

SHELTER-IN-PLACE. A term used to describe a community of fire-resistant homes in which each home is surrounded by defensible space (*see separate definition*) and from which people do not have to evacuate when wildfires threaten.

SIDE-DRESS. To apply dry fertilizer, as a booster, on the ground on one or both sides of a vegetable row, and then water it into the soil. When black plastic mulch is in use, side-dressing is applied by pouring liquid fertilizer through holes made in the plastic, or foliar-feeding is substituted.

SILK. Sticky fibers that spill out of the tops of the ears of corn and are the female flower of the corn plant. Each fiber leads to one kernel of corn and must receive one grain of pollen in order to make that kernel grow. (*See* tassel.)

SLEEVE DRAIN. A pipe, often covered by gravel, that drains water from the bottom of a planting hole beneath the roots of a plant on a slope and releases it farther down the slope. It is constructed either by drilling a hole with water or machinery through hard soil from a lower point on the hill, or by digging a trench that is later refilled.

SLOW-RELEASE FERTILIZER. A fertilizer that's coated with a plastic or otherwise constituted in such a way that small, measured amounts of plant food are released over a period of time. Most organic fertilizers release nutrients slowly, but slow-release fertilizers are chemical fertilizers, not organic ones. Slow-release fertilizers cause less runoff than fast-acting synthetic fertilizers, but they also kill natural organisms in the soil.

SOIL AMENDMENT. Anything added to soil to improve its texture, structure, or pH. Some soil amendments are organic and break down to make humus. Others, including soil sulfur, lime, and gypsum, are inorganic. Organic gardeners use natural forms of minerals mined from the ground. They avoid using forms of these minerals that have been treated with chemicals to change their composition; sometimes this treatment makes them faster acting, but it can also make them detrimental to soil or the environment. For example, organic gardeners prefer mined rock gypsum over soluble gypsum, which has been chemically treated.

SOIL SULFUR. A type of sulfur (a pale yellow, nonmetallic chemical element whose chemical symbol is S) that can be purchased in small or large bags at any nursery. It's used to acidify soil for acid-loving plants and to correct soils that have a high pH. The usual method of application is to sprinkle the recommended quantity on the ground and water it in.

SOIL TEST. A chemical way to determine the pH of soils and soil mixes. More sophisticated soil tests determine some of the basic nutrients in soil.

SPECIALTY PLANTS. Plants that require special know-how or attention; frequently plant societies are devoted to their culture.

SPECIES. One kind of plant, or a group of plants, with a high number of similar characteristics that usually can interbreed only with each other. Designated by the uncapitalized second word in a botanical name. Also describes a plant in the form (or close to the form) in which it was originally found in the wild, as in "*Rosa banksiae* is a species rose."

SPHAGNUM MOSS. A live moss, growing naturally in northern rain forests and on open ground in cool, rainy climates. Sphagnum moss and other mosses, such as sheet moss from Oregon and reindeer moss from Norway (a major food of caribou), are being harvested for use in agriculture, gardening, and the floral trade and do not regrow fast enough to keep up with demand. In some circumstances, coir can be substituted for sphagnum moss. Artificial mosses are another substitute.

SPIKE. A long, flowering stalk with flowers usually attached directly to it.

SPORT. An entire plant that differs from the typical form of the plant, or a shoot of a plant that differs from the rest of the plant when it first occurs. Sports come about either from spontaneous mutation or from segregation. Many climbing roses, for example, have occurred as sports that began as one atypical shoot on a rosebush. All cole crops, such as Brussels sprouts, cauliflower, and cabbages, came from a series of sports that occurred over many centuries. They're all descendants of one ancestor, a wild plant that man segregated and grew as a crop.

SPREADER-STICKER. *See* surfactant.

STAMEN. The male part of a flower consisting of the filament (stalk) and anther or anthers.

STIGMA. The upper part of the pistil (the female part of the plant), which is sticky when receptive and which receives the male pollen during pollination.

STOLON. A stem (in some cases called a runner) that grows aboveground or underground and that sprouts roots at the nodes, thus forming new plants. Bermuda, kikuyu, and zoysia are stoloniferous grasses; the runners of strawberries, too, are stolons, as are the long shoots of currants and gooseberries, which, unable to support their weight, arch to the ground and sprout roots.

SUBSOIL. A layer of any kind of soil lying beneath a layer of topsoil.

SUCCULENT. Any plant that stores water in leaves or stems that are thickened for the purpose. Aloes, cacti, crassulas, and most euphorbias are examples of succulents.

SUCKER. On a rose, a cane that arises below the bud union and thus comes from the rootstock rather than the variety grafted onto it. On other plants, any usually unwanted, upright, fast-growing growth from roots, trunk, crown, or main branches. On tomatoes, a sprout from an axillary bud. (*See also* water sprout.)

SUMP. An inefficient drainage system consisting of a small, deep hole dug in the center of the bottom of a planting hole and then filled with sand or ground bark, supposedly to drain off excess water. Not recommended; it soon fills with water and does more harm than good. (*See* chimney drain *and* sleeve drain.)

SURFACTANT. A chemical product used to break down the surface tension of water. Some, often called wetting agents, are used to help water penetrate soil. Others, often called spreader-stickers, are mixed into sprays to make them more effective. Sprays containing surfactants cover leaves in a smooth film rather than in droplets. Powdered Mohave yucca (*Yucca schidigera*) is a natural surfactant included as an ingredient in many organic products and fertilizers and is also available as a liquid. Quillaja is natural surfactant derived from the soapbark tree (*Quillaja saponaria*) native to Chile.

TASSEL. The male flower of the corn plant that emerges from the tops of silks and bears pollen. (Some hybrid corn varieties sport a few distorted bisexual tassels or ears; they do no harm.)

TENSIOMETER. An instrument that measures soil moisture. It's made up of a handle, a probe to push down into the ground, and a dial that registers the moisture content of the soil below the surface.

TERMINAL BUD. The bud at the tip of a branch or stem.

THATCH. In lawns, a layer of partially decomposed leaves, stems, and roots that forms between the earth and the grass blades.

THERMOPHOTOPERIODIC. Describes a plant, such as an onion or a petunia, whose flowering and growth habit depend on the length of days combined with the temperature.

TOPIARY. The art of training plants into formalized and stylized shapes, such as circles, triangles, animals, or birds. Also describes the shaped plants themselves.

TOPSOIL. Any type of soil, whether based on sand, decomposed granite, loam, or clay, that's rich in humus and makes up the top layer of soil, where plant roots live. In arid regions, it can take centuries for nature to create a few inches of natural topsoil. Commercial topsoil is often manmade by mixing decomposed granite, sand, or river-bottom silt with organic amendments.

TRANSPIRATION. The giving off of moisture from plant leaves into the air.

TUBER. A thickened stem, usually shorter, thicker, and rounder than a rhizome, that serves as a food-storage chamber and from which a plant grows. It grows totally or partially underground. A potato is a tuber.

TUBEROUS ROOT. A thickened root that grows underground and has growth buds on top, in the old stem portion from which the plant springs. Dahlias and sweet potatoes grow from tuberous roots.

VARIETY. In taxonomy (the science of naming plants), the rank subordinate to subspecies (a name with varying meanings, usually a geographical difference) and above forma (a fifth name given to a plant by botanists to list a minor difference). However, in actual practice the variety is generally a third italicized name that's tacked onto the usual binomial (genus and species) to indicate a particular and distinct form of a species that's found in nature. For example, in the name *Pinus mugo mugo*, the second *mugo* means a particular wild type of mugo pine that's different from others. All varieties first occur in nature (usually by spontaneous generation or mutation). Horticultural varieties (those that first occur under cultivation or that occurred first in nature but then persist only under cultivation by artificial means, such as propagation by cuttings) are more correctly called cultivars. The names of cultivars are written in plain type and enclosed in single quotes, and they follow the italicized names, however many there may be. For example, in the name *Juniperus chinensis procumbens* 'Nana', the first name is the genus, the second name is the species, the third name is the natural variety, and the fourth name is the manmade cultivar. Nevertheless, in common parlance, most gardeners and many garden writers, including this one, often use the word *variety* loosely when referring to any plant to which a name has been given by its commercial producer or hybridizer— for example, in speaking of named zinnias or roses as varieties, although they are actually more properly called cultivars. *Mandevilla splendens* "Alice du Pont," for example, is a particular cultivar of mandevilla.

VEGAN AGRICULTURE AND GARDENING. Vegan farmers and gardeners fertilize their crops with vegetable sources or with manures from animals from known sources, such as their own cows, chicken, and rabbits, not from factory farms. They do not use bone meal or blood meal from factory farms.

VOLUNTEER. A cultivated plant that comes up in a garden of its own accord, and often in the wrong place, from a seed deposited by the wind, a bird, or some other wild or domestic creature.

WARM-SEASON FLOWER. An annual, biennial, or perennial flowering plant that's native to a warm climate and thus grows fastest and flowers best during the warmest part of the year.

WARM-SEASON LAWN. A lawn variety that's best adapted to a warm tropical or subtropical climate and thus grows best and fastest during our warm late-spring, summer, and early-fall months. Some examples include St. Augustine, Bermuda, and zoysia.

WARM-SEASON VEGETABLE. A vegetable that originated in a warm climate and thus grows best in warm temperatures.

WATER SPROUT. A long, whippy sucker that sprouts, usually in summer, from the tops of branches or from the trunks of trees and shoots up rapidly.

WETTING AGENT. *See* surfactant.

Bibliography

Ayensu, Edward S., et al. *Underexploited Tropical Plants with Promising Economic Value.* Washington, DC: National Academy of Sciences, 1976.

Baldwin, Debra Lee. *Designing with Succulents.* Portland, OR: Timber Press, 2007.

Ball, Vic, ed. *Ball Red Book.* 14th ed. Reston, VA: Reston, 1985.

Barash, Cathy Wilkinson. *Edible Flowers: From Garden to Palate.* Golden, CO: Fulcrum, 1995.

Bartel, Janice R., and Sage Culpeper Belt. *A Guide to Botanical Resources of Southern California.* Los Angeles: Natural History Museum of Los Angeles County, 1977.

Beley, Jim, ed., and Ortho staff. *All about Azaleas, Camellias & Rhododendrons.* San Ramon, CA: Ortho Books, 1985.

Blackmore, Stephen, and Elizabeth Tootill, eds. *The Facts on File Dictionary of Botany.* Aylesbury, UK: Market House Books/ New York: Facts on File, 1984.

Bornstein, Carol, David Fross, and Bart O'Brien. *California Native Plants for the Garden.* Los Olivos, CA: Cachuma Press, 2005.

Blomberry, Alec, and Tony Rodd. *Palms: An Informative, Practical Guide to Palms of the World: Their Cultivation, Care and Landscape Use.* London: Angus and Robertson, 1984.

Brenzel, Kathleen Norris, ed. *Sunset Western Landscaping.* Menlo Park, CA: Sunset Books, 2007.

Bryan, John. *Manual of Bulbs.* Portland, OR: Timber Press, 1996.

Capon, Brian. *Botany for Gardeners: An Introduction and Guide.* Portland, OR: Timber Press, 1990.

Carson, Rachel L. *Silent Spring.* Boston: Houghton Mifflin, 1962.

Chamberlin, Susan. *Hedges, Screens and Espaliers.* Tucson, AZ: HP Books, 1983.

Chatto, Beth. *The Dry Garden*. Sagaponack, NY: Sagapress, 1996.

Clausen, Ruth Rogers, and Nicolas H. Ekstrom. *Perennials for American Gardens*. New York: Random House, 1989.

Clebsch, Betsy. *A Book of Salvias*. Portland, OR: Timber Press, 1997.

Connelly, Kevin. *The Gardener's Guide to California Wildflowers*. Sun Valley, CA: Theodore Payne Foundation, 1991.

Courtright, Gordon. *Trees and Shrubs for Temperate Climates*. 3rd ed. Portland, OR: Timber Press, 1988.

———. *Tropicals*. Portland, OR: Timber Press, 1988.

Cox, Jeff. *Perennial All Stars: The 150 Best Perennials for Great Looking, Trouble-Free Gardens*. Emmaus, PA: Rodale Press, 1998.

Creasy, Rosalind. *The Complete Book of Edible Landscaping*. San Francisco: Sierra Club Books, 1982.

Deans, Esther. *Esther Deans' Gardening Book: Growing without Digging*. Sydney, Australia: Harper and Row, 1978.

DiSabato-Aust, Tracy. *The Well-Tended Perennial Garden: Planting & Pruning Techniques*. Portland, OR: Timber Press, 1998.

DK Publishing, Inc *Smart Garden Regional Guide: Southwest*. London: DK Publishing, Inc, 2004.

Doutt, Richard L. *Cape Bulbs*. Portland, OR: Timber Press, 1994.

Emery, Dara. *Seed Propagation of Native California Plants*. Santa Barbara: Santa Barbara Botanic Garden, 1988.

Everett, Thomas H. *The New York Botanical Garden Illustrated Encyclopedia for Horticulture*. 10 vols. New York: Garland, 1981.

Farrell, Kenneth R., and staff. *Agricultural Publications Catalog, University of California Division of Agriculture and Natural Resources*. Special Publication 3020. Oakland: 1989.

Feathers, David, and Milton Brown, eds. *The Camellia: Its History, Culture, Genetics, and a Look into Its Future Development*. Columbia, SC: R. L. Bryan, 1978.

Fell, Derek. *Annuals: How to Select, Grow and Enjoy*. Tucson, AZ: HP Books, 1981.

———. *Vegetables: How to Select, Grow and Enjoy*. Tucson, AZ: HP Brooks, 1982.

Graf, Alfred Byrd. *Exotica Pictorial Cyclopedia of Exotic Plants from Tropical and Near-Tropic Regions*. East Rutherford, NJ: Roehrs, 1976.

Greenlee, John. *The Encyclopedia of Ornamental Grasses: How to Grow and Use over 250 Beautiful and Versatile Plants*. Emmaus, PA: Rodale Press, 1992.

Harper, Pamela, and Frederick McGourty. *Perennials: How to Select, Grow and Enjoy*. Tucson, AZ: HP Books, 1985.

Harrington, Geri. *Grow Your Own Chinese Vegetables*. Pownal, VT: Garden Way, 1984.

Hogue, Charles L. *Insects of the Los Angeles Basin*. Los Angeles: Natural History Museum of Los Angeles County, 1993.

Holmes, Roger, ed. *Taylor's Guide to Ornamental Grasses*. New York: Houghton Mifflin, 1997.

Howard, Sir Albert. *An Agricultural Testament*. Oxford: Oxford University Press, 1943.

Hoyt, Roland Stewart. *Checklists for the Ornamental Plants of Subtropical Regions: A Handbook for Ready Reference*. Los Angeles: Livingston Press, 1938.

Hunter, Beatrice Trum. *Gardening without Poisons*. Boston: Houghton Mifflin, 1964.

Jekyll, Gertrude. *The Illustrated Gertrude Jekyll*. With an introduction by Richard Bisgrove. Boston: Little, Brown, 1988.

Jekyll, Gertrude, and Edward Mawley. *Roses*. Revised ed., Stuart Graham Thomas. Salem, NH: Ayer, 1983.

Johnson, Eric, and Scott Millard. *How to Grow Wildflowers*. Tucson, AZ: Ironwood Press, 1997.

Johnson, Huey D., and Ronald B. Robie. *Plants for California Landscapes: A Catalog of Drought Tolerant Plants*. Bulletin 209. Sacramento, CA: Department of Water Resources, 1979.

Jones, David L. *Palms Throughout the World*. Washington, DC: Smithsonian Institution Press, 1995.

Labadie, Emile L. *Native Plants for Use in the California Landscape*. Oakland, CA: Sierra City Press, 1978.

Lane, Clive. *Cottage Garden Annuals: Grown from Seed for Summer-Long Color*. Newton Abbot, UK: David & Charles, 1997.

Lanza, Patricia. *Lasagna Gardening: A New Layering System for Bountiful Gardens: No Digging, No Tilling, No Weeding, No Kidding!* Emmaus, PA: Rodale Books, 1999.

Lathrop, Norma Jean. *Herbs: How to Select, Grow and Enjoy*. Tucson, AZ: HP Books, 1981.

Latymer, Hugo. *The Mediterranean Gardner*. New York: Barrons, in association with the Royal Botanic Gardens, Kew, 1990.

Lenz, Lee, W. *Native Plants for California Gardens*. Claremont, CA: Rancho Santa Ana Botanic Garden, 1977.

Lenz, Lee W., and John Dourley. *California Native Trees and Shrubs for Garden and Environmental Use in Southern California and Adjacent Areas*. Claremont, CA: Rancho Santa Ana Botanic Garden, 1981.

Levick, Melba, and Helaine Kaplan Prentice. *The Gardens of Southern California*. San Francisco: Chronicle Books, 1990.

Lindsay, Lowell, and Diana Lindsay. *The Anza-Borrego Desert Regions*. Berkeley, CA: Wilderness Press, 1985.

Loewer, Peter. *Step-by-Step Ornamental Grasses*. Des Moines: Better Homes & Gardens Books, 1995.

Lowenfels, Jeff, Wayne Lewis, and Elaine Ingham. *Teaming with Microbes: A Gardener's Guide to the Soil Food Web*. Portland, OR: Timber Press, 2006.

MacCaskey, Michael. *Lawns and Ground Covers: How to Select, Grow and Enjoy*. Tucson, AZ: HP Books, 1982.

Mac's Field Guides, The Mountaineers Books. *Mac's Field Guide of Good Garden Bugs of California*. Seattle: Mountaineers Books, 2000.

Malek, Edith M. *Simply Clematis: Clematis Made Simple*. Irvine, CA: American Clematis Society, 2004.

Martin, R. Sanford. *How to Prune Fruit Trees*. 10th ed. Van Nuys, CA: Press of Document Engineering, 1978.

———. *How to Prune Western Shrubs*. Culver City, CA: Murray & Gee, 1947.

Mathias, Mildred, ed. *Flowering Plants in the Landscape*. Berkeley: University of California Press, 1982.

Mielke, Judy. *Native Plants for Southwestern Landscapes*. Austin: University of Texas Press, 1993.

Milne, Lorus, and Margery Milne. *The Audubon Society Field Guide to North American Insects and Spiders*. New York: Alfred A. Knopf, 1980.

Munz, Philip A. *California Desert Wildflowers*. Berkeley: University of California Press, 1962.

———. *A Flora of Southern California*. Berkeley: University of California Press, 1974.

———. *Shore Wildflowers of California, Oregon, and Washington*. Berkeley: University of California Press, 1964.

Nottle, Trevor. *Gardens of the Sun*. Portland, OR: Timber Press, 1996.

Padilla, Victoria. *Southern California Gardens*. Santa Barbara, CA: Allen A. Knoll, 1994.

Patent, Dorothy Hinshaw, and Diane E. Bilderback. *Garden Secrets: A Guide to Understanding How Your Garden Grows and How You Can Help It Grow Even Better*. Emmaus, PA: Rodale Press, 1982.

Paul, Anthony, and Yvonne Rees. *The Water Garden*. New York: Viking Press, 1986.

Perry, Robert C. *Landscape Plants for Western Regions: An Illustrated Guide to Plants for Water Conservation*. Claremont, CA: Land Design, 1992.

———. *Trees and Shrubs for Dry California Landscapes: Plants for Water Conservation*. San Dimas, CA: Land Design, 1981.

Peterson, Tru, ed. *The New A to Z on Fuchsias.* San Francisco: National Fuchsia Society, 1981.

Picart, François. *Escargots from Your Garden to Your Table: How to Control, Raise and Process the Common Garden Snail.* Santa Rosa, CA: F. Picart Snails, 1978.

Pollan, Michael. *The Omnivore's Dilemma.* New York: Penguin, 2006.

Quiros, Alice, and Barbara Young. *The World of Cactus and Succulents and Other Water Thrifty Plants.* San Francisco: Ortho Books, 1977.

Ray, Richard, and Michael MacCaskey. *Roses: How to Select, Grow and Enjoy.* Tucson, AZ: HP Books, 1980.

Redfield, Margaret. *The Southern California Month-by-Month Flower Gardening Book.* Los Angeles: J. P. Tarcher, 1976.

Reilly, Ann. *Park's Success with Seeds.* Greenwood, SC: Geo. Park Seed, 1978.

Relf, Diane, Judy Schwab, Elissa Steeves, and Virginia Nathan, eds. *The Virginia Master Gardener Handbook.* Petersburg, Virginia Cooperative Extension Service, 1987.

Robinson, William. *The English Flower Garden.* Rev. ed., Graham Stuart Thomas. New York: Amaryllis Press, 1984.

Rodale, J. I., ed. *How to Grow Vegetables and Fruits by the Organic Method.* Emmaus, PA: Rodale Press, 1976.

Scheider, Alfred E. *Park's Success with Bulbs.* Greenwood, SC: Geo. Park Seed, 1981.

Schmidt, Marjorie. *Growing California Native Plants.* Berkeley: University of California Press, 1980.

Scott, George Harmon. *Bulbs: How to Select, Grow and Enjoy.* Tucson, AZ: HP Books, 1982.

Sedesko, Jerry. *The Butterfly Garden.* New York: Villard Books, 1991.

Sinnes, A. Cort, and Ortho staff. *All about Fertilizers, Soils and Water.* San Francisco: Ortho Books, 1980.

Smaus, Robert. *52 Weeks in the California Garden.* Los Angeles: Los Angeles Times Syndicate, 1996.

————. *Los Angeles Times California Gardening: A Practical Guide to Growing Flowers, Trees, Vegetables and Fruits.* New York: Harry N. Abrams, 1983.

————. *The Los Angeles Times Planning and Planting the Garden.* New York: Harry N. Abrams, 1983.

Smith, Ken. *Western Home Landscaping.* Tucson, AZ: HP Books, 1978.

Smith, Michael D., ed. *The Ortho Problem Solver.* 4th ed. San Ramon, CA: Ortho, 1994.

Spellenberg, Richard. *The Audubon Society Field Guide to North American Wildflowers, Western Region.* New York: Alfred A. Knopf, 1979.

Starcher, Allison Mia. *Good Bugs for Your Garden.* Chapel Hill, NC: Algonquin Books of Chapel Hill, 1995.

Stout, Ruth. *How to Have A Green Thumb Without an Aching Back: A New Method of Mulch Gardening.* New York: Exposition Press, 1955.

Streatfield, David C. *California Gardens: Creating a New Eden.* New York: Abbeville Press, 1994.

Sunset Books and Sunset Magazine. *Garden Pools, Fountains & Waterfalls.* Menlo Park, CA: Lane, 1974.

———. *Lawns: How to Plant and Care for a Healthy Carpet of Green.* Menlo Park, CA: Sunset Books, 1997.

———. *Sunset Introduction to Basic Gardening.* Menlo Park, CA: Sunset Books, 1981.

———. *Sunset Pruning Handbook.* Menlo Park, CA: Sunset Books, 1975.

———. *Sunset Waterwise Gardening: Beautiful Gardens with Less Water.* Menlo Park, CA: Sunset Books, 1989.

———. *Sunset Western Garden Book: Completely Revised and Updated.* Menlo Park, CA: Sunset Books, 2007.

———. *Sunset Western Garden Problem Solver.* Menlo Park, CA: Sunset Books, 1998.

Tanner, Ogden. *Living Fences: A Gardener's Guide to Hedges, Vines, and Espaliers.* New York: Houghton Mifflin, 1995.

Taylor, Norman. *Taylor's Guide to Annuals.* Rev. ed., Gordon P. DeWolf, Jr. Boston: Houghton Mifflin, 1986.

Taylor, Norman. *Taylor's Guide to Ground Covers.* Rev. ed., Nan Sinton and David C. Michener. Boston: Houghton Mifflin, 2002.

Tekulsky, Mathew. *The Butterfly Garden.* Boston: Harvard Common Press, 1985.

Uber, William C. *Water Gardening Basics.* Upland, CA: Dragonflyer Press, 1988.

Walheim, Lance, and Robert L. Stebbins. *Western Fruit, Berries and Nuts: How to Select, Grow and Enjoy.* Tucson, AZ: HP Books, 1981.

Wasowski, Sally, and Andy Wasowski. *Native Landscaping from El Paso to Los Angeles.* New York: McGraw-Hill, 2000.

Waters, George, and Norah Harlow, eds. *The Pacific Horticulture Book of Western Gardening.* Boston: David R. Godine, in association with the Pacific Horticultural Foundation, 1990.

White, Hazel. *Water Gardens: Simple Projects, Contemporary Designs.* Chronicle Books, 1998.

Wright, John I. *Plant Propagation for the Amateur Gardener.* Poole, UK: Blanford Books, 1983.

Wyman, Donald. *Wyman's Gardening Encyclopedia.* 2nd ed. New York: Macmillan, 1986.

Yepsen, Roger B., Jr. *The Encyclopedia of Natural Insects and Disease Control.* Emmaus, PA: Rodale Press, 1984.

Yronwode, Catherine. *The California Gardener's Book of Lists.* Dallas: Taylor, 1998.

Index

446